THE CHINA DIARY OF GEORGE H. W. BUSH

THE CHINA DIARY
of George H.W. Bush

﷽

THE MAKING OF A
GLOBAL PRESIDENT

Edited by

Jeffrey A. Engel

PRINCETON UNIVERSITY PRESS   PRINCETON AND OXFORD

Diary and preface copyright © 2008 by George H. W. Bush
All other material copyright © 2008 Jeffrey A. Engel

Requests for permission to reproduce material from this work should
be sent to Permissions, Princeton University Press

Published by Princeton University Press, 41 William Street, Princeton, New Jersey 08540

In the United Kingdom: Princeton University Press, 6 Oxford Street, Woodstock,
Oxfordshire OX20 1TW

Library of Congress Cataloging-in-Publication Data

The China diary of George H. W. Bush : the making of a global president / edited
by Jeffrey A. Engel.
    p. cm.
  Includes bibliographical references and index.
  ISBN 978-0-691-13006-4 (hardcover : alk. paper)
   1. Bush, George, 1924–   —Diaries. 2. Diplomats—United States—Diaries.
3. United States—Foreign relations—China. 4. China—Foreign relations—United States.
5. United States—Foreign relations—1974–1977. 6. Presidents—United States—Diaries.
I. Engel, Jeffrey A.
E882.A3   2008
973.928092—dc22   2007047900

British Library Cataloging-in-Publication Data is available

This book has been composed in Sabon and Bernhard Modern by Princeton Editorial
Associates, Inc., Scottsdale, Arizona

Printed on acid-free paper. ∞

press.princeton.edu

Printed in the United States of America

10 9 8 7 6 5 4 3 2 1

Dedicated to the students of the Bush School,
for whom public service is indeed a noble calling

🀫🀫🀫🀫🀫🀫🀫🀫🀫🀫🀫🀫🀫🀫🀫🀫

Think about this. We have the Soviet Union to the north
and the west, India to the south, and Japan to the east. If all
our enemies were to unite, attacking us from the north, south,
east, and west, what do you think we should do? . . . Think
again. Beyond Japan is the United States. Didn't our ancestors
counsel negotiating with faraway countries while fighting
with those that are near?
—Mao Zedong, *August 1969*

Not only we but all the people of the world will have to
make our very best effort if we are going to match the
enormous ability, drive, and discipline of the Chinese
people. . . . Otherwise, we will one day be confronted with
the most formidable enemy that has ever existed in
the history of the world.
—Richard Nixon, *February 1972*

It is my hope that I will be able to meet the next generation of China's leaders—whomever they may prove to be. Yet everyone tells me that that is impossible.
—George H. W. Bush, *October 1974*

CONTENTS

CONTENTS

Nearly thirty-five years ago I made a decision that not only profoundly changed my life, but would forever change my view of the world, particularly of the land then called "The Sleeping Giant."

Richard Nixon had just left office, forced out by Watergate, and I finally was able to leave my job as chairman of the Republican National Committee. Never in our lives, before or since, have Barbara and I craved change more. We wanted out of Washington and as far away as possible from the ugliness of Watergate. We also wanted both a new adventure and a new challenge.

President Ford kindly asked me to choose between two of the most plum assignments he had the power to offer: an ambassadorship to either London or Paris. I shocked President Ford, and certainly my family, when instead I asked if I could go to China. (The look I got was reminiscent of 1948, when I broke the news to friends and family that I had turned down a job on Wall Street and that Barbara and I were moving to West Texas.)

The United States had only recently ended its quarter-century-long silence with the People's Republic of China. Only two years before, President Nixon had been the first American leader to speak directly with his Chinese counterpart, Mao Zedong, since Franklin Roosevelt. China was then, both figuratively and literally, very far away. To most Americans—to most of the world—it was an unknown entity. It was a country clearly on the move, but still restrained by the strict bounds of communism.

My reasoning was actually quite simple: It was obvious then that Asia would rise in importance on the world scene. And it was inevitable that China would eventually become a power broker, not only in the Pacific but in the world. China was, quite simply, the place to be.

Because we still did not have formal diplomatic relations with Beijing, I would not actually be an ambassador. Instead, I would simply be head of the United States Liaison Office. This minor point of protocol did not matter. Barbara and I set off for what would be one of the greatest adventures of our lives.

From the minute we landed, we knew life would be different for us. The first night, when we took our dog Fred for a walk, we got confused and sometimes even scared stares. As it turns out, dogs were scarce in China, and some people had never seen such a creature. I can only imagine what our Chinese neighbors must have thought to see such a strange sight, two Americans walking a dog.

You have to understand that Beijing then was not the modern-day, bustling city it is today. (Barbara likes to say that over the years, through our many visits to China, we've seen the country go from black and white to Technicolor.) And the Chinese were not in the 1970s the global power they are today. They were, instead, a proud people with a proud heritage and powerful aspirations. But they lacked a certain confidence in their dealings with foreigners, especially Western diplomats. It was hard to get to know my Chinese counterparts. Some told me not to bother. "The Chinese don't want to talk to Americans," I heard time and again. I didn't believe them. Barbara and I determined that we would make the most of our time in Beijing by making as many friends and contacts as possible.

We bicycled around the town. We went shopping and called upon our neighbors. We kept walking Fred all around our neighborhood. We invited friends and family to come visit from America. We even learned some Chinese, studying four or five times a week. All with the intent of putting an open face on the United States for the average Chinese citizen.

Sometimes I was frustrated when I was not allowed to see the top Chinese leaders. What I didn't realize then was that the friends I was making would one day be leading China at the same time I happened to be leading the United States. In particular the friendship I began then with Deng Xiaoping was very valuable during my presidency, especially during the Tiananmen Square protests. I took some hits for not being tougher on the Chinese, but my long history with Deng and the other leaders made it possible for us to work through the crises without derailing Sino-American relations, which would have been a disaster. I was a big believer then, and still am, that personal diplomacy can be very useful and productive.

Which brings me to the China Diary. When Professor Jeffrey Engel first approached me about publishing the diary, I really had no hesitations. I had not looked at it in years and did not recall what it said. My one fear was that perhaps I had dwelled a little too much on the great hot dog bun crisis of 1975, instead of more substantive issues. But I readily put all such misgivings aside and gave Professor Engel complete editorial control. Although the musings of a young diplomat from thirty-five years ago are barely a footnote in the history of these two great nations, I did hope that maybe some of my and Barbara's personal observations might give readers insight into what life was like then in China, and how it has changed.

When I finally did reread the diary, I was amused by some of my frustrations with then–Secretary of State Henry Kissinger, a man whom I greatly respect and consider a friend, and from whom I learned a great deal. It made me realize how much my views have changed since those days, and just how much my experience in China changed me.

In August 2008 I will return to China for the twenty-second time since leaving office in 1993, this time to attend the Summer Olympics as the honorary captain of the American team. It will be one of the great thrills of my life: to help represent my country, which I love so much, in a country that over time I have grown to admire and respect. And yes, I love the Chinese people. One of my dreams for our world is that these two powerful giants will continue working toward a full partnership and friendship that will help bring peace and prosperity to people everywhere.

George H. W. Bush
October 2007

Bush's China Diary—
What You Are About to Read

This is the diary George H. W. Bush kept while in China from October 1974 until December 1975. These are his own words, dictated from the small American outpost in the heart of massive Beijing. As head of the United States Liaison Office (USLO), Bush was Washington's chief representative in China, a crucial job that was not easily defined. The United States and the People's Republic of China did not establish formal diplomatic relations until 1979. Washington instead placed its official Chinese embassy in the Republic of China (Taiwan) after 1949, refusing to recognize the legitimacy of the Communist regime which came to power on the mainland after China's bloody civil war. Neither was Mao Zedong's Communist government eager to treat with an American government it repeatedly chastised as the leader of reactionary forces worldwide. In the chilly Cold War that followed, the two countries exchanged little trade, hardly any cultural contacts, and scant few formal talks. Instead they exchanged bullets and blood during the Korean War, and came close to doing more of the same during the frequent crises of the 1950s and 1960s.

Bush landed in China soon after the first tentative thaw in the two countries' otherwise frosty relationship. In 1971 President Richard Nixon announced his intention to go to China. His national security adviser and trusted aide Henry Kissinger had only recently returned from secret meetings on Chinese soil. These encounters quite literally changed the globe's geopolitical map. Both the Americans and the Chinese hoped that improved relations might help each counter the Soviet Union's growing influence around the world. Each government established a diplomatic office in the other's capital in the months that followed, in order to facilitate closer relations and to manage their growing set of business and cultural ties. David Bruce opened the USLO in Beijing in 1973. Bush served as its second head. He was Washington's ambassador to the People's Republic of China in all aspects save his formal title.

This diary recounts Bush's experience in his own words, and it is thus extraordinarily valuable for understanding both this complex man and this confusing time. Many books have been written detailing the Sino-American rapprochement. Few historians have studied the less earth-shattering, but arguably no less important, day-to-day workings of Sino-American diplomatic, cultural, and commercial relations as they evolved in fits and starts in the years between Nixon's 1972 visit and the 1979 reestablishment of full relations. Bush's diary paints an intimate portrait of two great societies in transition: China in the first days of its transformation from the isolation of the Cultural Revolution to its full integration into the international community and global economy, the United States beset by the quandaries and malaise of the early 1970s. Nixon's visit to China produced headlines around the world. Bush's journey did not. But whereas Nixon left China having charted a path to better ties between the two nations, the diplomats, business-people, educators, and tourists who subsequently trod that path truly made the relationship grow and prosper.

Bush's China Diary shows the future president in a new light, and indeed the intimate portrait it paints is without easy parallel in the annals of presidential history. Presidential memoirs abound, detailing their authors' experiences in office after the fact. Only a handful of future presidents kept detailed private journals in the years before they moved into the Oval Office. An even smaller number took time to enunciate their views on global affairs before their time in office, beyond campaign stump speeches. Those future presidents who did write frequently on international relations before their election—Theodore Roosevelt, Woodrow Wilson, and a post-1960 Richard Nixon leap to mind—generally did so for a public audience. Bush wrote for himself alone. He never intended his diary to be read by others. He certainly never imagined it would someday be published. The pages that follow reveal his private views on American politics, Sino-American relations, the Vietnam War, Watergate, and a host of other events and issues. They offer an unvarnished look at a man of great ambition at a crossroads in his life and career—a man hoping to do more in life, yet struggling to determine exactly what he should hold dear in his future pursuits.

This China Diary is fascinating, but to a historian it is hardly a perfect text. Bush never wrote the diary in a traditional sense. He dictated it into a tape recorder, typically at day's end, most often in the privacy of his changing room. These tapes were transcribed only years later by assistants. He sometimes made his journal entries nightly for weeks on end. If particularly busy, he would record the events of a whole week in a single sitting. Sometimes, especially while traveling, he failed to make an entry for weeks on end. As the diary was intended for his use alone, he felt no compulsion to make entries beyond a desire to record his unfolding Asian adventure.

The original tapes have been lost. All we have left are those transcriptions. Thus the pages that follow must be understood as Bush's words interpreted by assistants. The syntax of the "original" typed document, which remains available for review at the George Bush Presidential Library, is at times garbled. Authors of memoirs or letters have the benefit of editing their words to achieve precision. Bush spoke his memories, and he had no time (and even less inclination) for subsequent revisions. Moreover, even Bush's most fervent supporters concede that verbal elegance is not his strongest suit. The diary "sounds" like Bush, for good or for ill. When reading his diary one can easily hear him in the mind's ear, because in fact these are his words. Yet they were routinely recorded, often in fatigue, and then interpreted well after the fact by an assistant with the best of intentions but no independent guidance.

These facts about Bush's diary presented methodological challenges in preparing it for publication. For the reasons enunciated above, some sentences run on, meander, or, quite simply, make little sense. I have tried to edit these sentences whenever necessary in order to create a readable text, yet without altering the tone and the cadence of a voice well known to most readers. Sometimes this meant starting a new paragraph where I believed Bush was turning to a new idea or train of thought, rather than where the transcriber had chosen to make a break. Very infrequently this meant excising extra words, adding conjunctions between sentences, or changing punctuation. I performed such grammatical surgery with the lightest hand possible, changing the text only on those rare occasions when it appeared absolutely necessary to enable the reader to comprehend fully Bush's meaning. As noted previously, the full text of the transcription—the nearest thing we have to an original—is available to researchers at the Bush Library.

Other issues posed greater methodological problems. Of greatest significance was the fact that some names of persons and places were unintelligible. No amount of forensic work could resurrect them. Bush does not speak Chinese, and neither did his transcribers. Given these circumstances some names, and Chinese names in particular, have been quite literally lost in translation despite the best efforts of native Chinese speakers employed in this detective work. Other names in the "original" diary were unintentionally misspelled by the original transcribers or lacked sufficient information for a full identification. Bush wrote for himself, after all. Thus, to give one example, he was perfectly content to record his happy meeting with a young couple, the "Smiths," from Texas. Identifying these two from among all the Smiths in Texas proved impossible. Indeed their name might have been Smythe or Smithe; each would have sounded the same to the transcriber. Yet, in my opinion at least, no such failure to identify a person or place should detract from a reader's ability to understand the larger themes with which Bush grappled in these pages.

Such small negatives aside, Bush's diary sheds tremendous light on his Beijing experience, especially when illuminated by the annotations I offer. These footnotes, designed to explain the context of Bush's experience, draw upon secondary works by historians; memoirs of participants and witnesses to these events; contemporary press accounts; documents from the National Archives of the United States and the National Archives of the United Kingdom; documents from the Bush Presidential Library; and a series of interviews with President and Mrs. Bush and some of their closest associates from these years. Many of the diplomatic records cited in this context were made available to researchers only in January 2007, and thus many are being published here for the first time. To minimize clutter, documentation for this information appears in endnotes grouped at the back of the book. Where a footnote is associated with an endnote providing such documentation, the number of the footnote, both in the text (^{5}) and at the start of the note itself (5), has been set in italics. The specific endnote can be quickly located by reference to the running head on each page of the endnotes section; it identifies the text pages with which the endnotes on that page are associated. A bibliographic essay describing the most helpful secondary works is also included as part of the endmatter.

To further enhance the readability of Bush's diary, I have converted Chinese spellings from the older Wade-Giles form used in the diary's initial transcription to the Hanyu Pinyin style adopted by Beijing in 1979. When quoting from other contemporary documents, however, and especially from the diplomatic documents used to illuminate various passages, I have retained the original spellings in deference to the documents' authors.

This book could not have been written without President Bush's endorsement, though in order to minimize his influence over its historical interpretations his contact with the workings of this project was purposely kept to a bare minimum. He cleared away the legal barriers to its publication; he and Mrs. Bush sat for numerous interviews; and his office helped facilitate interviews with some of his associates. At no time, however, has he or anyone in his office requested the right to review or to alter my interpretation of these events as described in the pages that follow. Issues of editing and transcription aside, the words that follow in the diary text are Bush's alone, and those in the introduction and notes are mine alone. I take no responsibility or credit for his; he bears no blame for mine.

Bush's China experience—what he terms in his preface "one of the greatest adventures of our lives"—dramatically changed his life. It rejuvenated him after the tribulations of Watergate; it inspired his passion for foreign affairs; and it set him on his course for the White House. To emphasize the ways in which his time at the USLO influenced Bush, an interpretive essay follows the diary text. It describes Bush's diplomatic legacy and the ways in which his China Diary illuminates the diplomatic principles he came to hold while in Beijing.

China mattered to Bush. He came to believe, during his presidency and after, that Sino-American relations held the key to a peaceful and prosperous twenty-first century. This is one of the diary's crucial stories, because the George H. W. Bush who landed in Beijing in the fall of 1974 was hardly the international statesman he later proved himself to be. On the contrary, he was a relative neophyte in the world of high-level diplomacy, wholly unaccustomed to the nuances of American diplomacy as practiced overseas. By 1989 he was considered something of a foreign policy expert, and his reputation in this field has only improved with age. As readers will surely see, Bush's time in China played a central role in his diplomatic education.

Jeffrey A. Engel

ACKNOWLEDGMENTS

Many deserve thanks for helping bring this project to light. Dean Richard Chilcoat, Sam Kirkpatrick, and Arnie Vedlitz generously coordinated the financial support provided by the George Bush School of Government and Public Service, including the Ed and Evelyn Kruse Faculty Fellowship, which provided me with the historian's most valued commodity: time. Having the opportunity to meet Mr. and Mrs. Kruse as a consequence of their generosity has proved a true pleasure. Joe Dillard's exceptional staff expertly facilitated the Bush School's financial support, even at a distance. Michael Desch and the Bush School's Scowcroft Institute of International Affairs provided research assistance for the final footnote push, and Mike proved ever generous with his own sage counsel. My thanks also go to the dedicated librarians and research staff of the National Archives in College Park, the British National Archives in Kew, and the Bush Presidential Library in College Station, whose work quite literally makes the writing of history possible. Warren Finch, Robert Holzweiss, and Mary Finch in particular deserve hearty thanks, although with the book in print I now owe Bob service on his softball team. Yale University's International Security Studies provided a much-beloved office and valuable resources during a visiting semester when the bulk of this book was written. Ted Bromund, Ann Carter-Drier, John Gaddis, Paul Kennedy, Mihn Luong, and Monica Ward each deserves deep thanks. As always, the Mine Hill Road Development Fund generously smoothed the rough edges whenever needed.

Charles Hermann deserves particular praise and acknowledgment. As program director of the Bush School's international affairs section, he generously facilitated a timely and much-appreciated teaching leave to allow me to work on this book. Indeed it was

Chuck who first casually suggested that "there is a diary over at the library you ought to take a look at." He opened numerous doors, provided wise advice in response to all my queries, and helped guide me through some of the political minefields a study such as this inevitably confronts. He is a most valued and insufficiently heralded leader for our program, and this book would not exist without him.

Bush School students helped research this project, including a memorable capstone group comprising Lillian Gaa, Jasper Mason, Jennifer Simar, Katie Kaufman, Mark Sones, Michael Swanzy, Mike Hannesschlager, Reid McCoy, and Rusty Rodriguez. Jessica Hart copyedited the final draft with speed and efficiency. This book is dedicated to these students and to their peers, past and future. My colleagues at the Bush School gave meaning—and contributed more than a few laughs—to each day's work, while Rose Williams and Janeen Wood went above and beyond to keep our offices functioning with a smile. Their dedication is inspiring.

Several members of President Bush's staff provided invaluable assistance, including Tom Frechette, Claire Pickart, and Michele Whalen. Terry Lacey's efforts were most appreciated as well.

And then there is the incomparable Jean Becker, whose knowledge of Bush's history is unprecedented, and whose enthusiasm for enabling historians to write that history—in their own words and drawing their own conclusions—is second to none. With a million tasks on her daily agenda, she still found time to answer my queries, always ending with the reminder that further questions were welcome. She is undoubtedly one of the kindest souls with whom I have ever worked.

One of the great pleasures of this project was the opportunity it afforded to interview several of its principal subjects, including President George H. W. Bush, Barbara Bush, James Baker, James Lilley, Nicholas Platt, and Brent Scowcroft. Ronald Kaufmann helped track down the elusive "ghosts" that haunt the pages of the diary. President Bush took time out from his retirement—the most peripatetic on record, I'd venture—to compose this book's invaluable preface. That each so generously gave of his or her time and recollections speaks volumes about their collective commitment to history and to the scholars who write it.

Needless to say, it is George Bush's own words that fill the diary pages that follow, and his support for bringing these pages to the public has never wavered. Yet never once did he interfere with the scholarly process. He understands the way academics work, and he appreciates that history must be written without after-the-fact influence from the men and women who made it. I only wish his views on this matter were more widely held.

Princeton University Press did a marvelous job with this book, and special thanks must go to Brigitta van Rheinberg and Clara Platter, who presided over this project with grace and enthusiasm from the beginning. They are the kinds of editors who make one want to do more. My thanks as well to the anonymous reviewers engaged by the press, whose perceptive comments improved the manuscript immeasurably, and to Sydelle Kramer, who handled the business side of the project. Princeton Editorial Associates performed a truly marvelous job of producing the book.

This foray into what is, for me, a new period of history would not have been possible without the generous aid of friends and colleagues. Richard Immerman, Mark Lawrence, Jason Parker, Andrew Preston, and Tom Zeiler each offered line-by-line edits of my interpretive essay, a feat far beyond the normal bounds of friendship. Andy Scobell did the same for the entire diary, and Ren Mu (and family) helped identify those depicted in the book's photographs. Their comments undoubtedly saved me from numerous mistakes. The good Dr. Preston deserves praise as the world's most trusted sounding-board, while Mark helped piece together the more complicated aspects of Bush's personal diplomacy during a memorable jaunt down the New Jersey Turnpike. Tom McCormick offered his usual wise counsel, while Jason Castillo, Chen Jian, Christopher Layne, Brian Linn, Larry Napper, Adam Seipp, Jeremi Suri, David Vaught, and Susan the breadmaker each offered invaluable comments. Further sound advice came from attendees at a roundtable on personal diplomacy sponsored by the Society for Historians of American Foreign Relations and from participants in a forum organized jointly by the Bush School and the Shanghai Institute for International Affairs.

Jennifer Turner performed a modern miracle in helping our son Marshall thrive. Hope played her part as well. Friends and relatives who think they deserve mention here should reread what I wrote in my first book, as what I wrote there still stands.

The last to be mentioned are always the most important, but prudence typically dictates that they receive the fewest words. I was Marshall's age when Bush served in China. Experience with my own toddler makes me appreciate all the more the trials my parents endured during the mid-1970s. Yet Marshall's embrace of life's passions inspired me (when not, on his command, flipping pancakes or edging the lawn for the thirty-second time that week) to add that one last footnote or to perform that one additional edit— to give the book real meaning—even when all I desired was a ra-ra of my own. The desire to make Katie proud served as all the additional inspiration I could ever need. Everything I wrote in the last book still holds true, even if her sense of propriety demands I keep these acknowledgments from becoming more personal still. But she knows there is so much more to it than that.

CAST OF PRIMARY CHARACTERS

Richard Akwei

Chargé d'affaires of the Ghanaian Embassy in Beijing during Bush's tenure at the United States Liaison Office. Akwei also became one of the Bushes' most frequent tennis partners.

David K. E. Bruce

One of the most esteemed and honored diplomats in American history. Bruce is the only American envoy to have served as ambassador to the United Kingdom, France, and West Germany. He opened the United States Liaison Office in Beijing in 1973, and he was posted to NATO as Washington's ambassador once President Gerald Ford selected Bush for the China post.

John Burns

Noted journalist later awarded the Pulitzer Prize. Burns reported for Toronto's *Globe and Mail* from China between 1971 and 1975, before leaving Beijing to begin a long career at the *New York Times*. He was a frequent companion to Bush during the period of the China Diary.

Barbara Bush

Wife of George H. W. Bush. Barbara Bush accompanied her husband to China in October 1974, although she returned to the United States more frequently than he during their stay at the United States Liaison Office.

George H. W. Bush

Forty-first president of the United States and author of the China Diary. During the period 1974–75, Bush was head of the United States Liaison Office in Beijing, People's Republic of China.

Deng Xiaoping

General secretary of the Chinese Communist Party from 1956 to 1966, chairman of the Central Military Commission from 1981 to 1989, and one of the most influential leaders in modern Chinese history. Deng had only recently returned from political exile when Bush arrived in Beijing. He ushered in the wave of economic liberalization that followed Mao's death. It was Deng with whom Bush attempted to communicate during and immediately following the Tiananmen Square protests of 1989.

Stephen Fitzgerald

Australian ambassador to China during Bush's tenure and one of Bush's frequent social companions. Fitzgerald was a noted sinologist before entering his country's diplomatic service.

Gerald Ford

Thirty-eighth president of the United States, who assumed office upon Richard Nixon's resignation in 1974. It was Ford who offered Bush the ambassadorship to either London or Paris, and who consented when Bush declared (much to Ford's surprise) that he would rather be stationed in Beijing. Ford subsequently named Bush head of the Central Intelligence Agency in 1975.

Bryce Harland

New Zealand's ambassador to China during Bush's time in Beijing. Harland also became a frequent companion (and sometimes confidant) of Bush during their frequent meetings on Beijing's social circuit.

John Holdridge

Noted Chinese linguist and diplomat. Holdridge served as deputy chief of mission for the United States Liaison Office in Beijing from its opening in 1973 until his appointment as U.S. ambassador to Singapore in 1975, subsequently serving as assistant secretary for East Asian and Pacific affairs in 1981 and as ambassador to Indonesia in 1982.

Huang Hua

Noted Chinese diplomat. Huang served as Beijing's first ambassador to Canada and then the United Nations. He returned to China in 1976 to serve as his country's foreign minister.

Huang Zhen

A veteran of the Long March and head of the Chinese Liaison Office in Washington during Bush's tenure in China. Huang was in this sense Bush's direct counterpart in the United States, having served in that role since Bruce's posting to China in 1973.

Henry Kissinger

National security adviser and secretary of state to Presidents Nixon and Ford. Kissinger held these two posts during Bush's tenure in China. He retained only his State Department position following the 1975 shake-up of Ford's national security team that saw Bush selected as head of the Central Intelligence Agency.

James Lilley

United States Liaison Office employee in 1974, who worked undercover for the Central Intelligence Agency (a fact the Chinese already knew). Lilley returned to Washington after an American journalist blew his cover, and his subsequent employment by the State Department culminated in 1989 with his appointment as ambassador to Beijing.

Winston Lord

Henry Kissinger's principal assistant while the latter was national security adviser, before moving with Kissinger to the State Department, where he headed the Policy Planning Staff. He subsequently served as ambassador to China from 1985 to 1989.

Neil Mallon

Longtime family friend and mentor to George H. W. Bush. Mallon visited the Bushes in Beijing in the spring of 1975.

Mao Zedong
Chinese Communist leader and later leader of the People's Republic of China from 1949 until his death in 1976.

Brunson McKinley
One of Bush's principal USLO advisers in 1974, McKinley left Beijing in 1975 for another Foreign Service post, eventually serving as Washington's ambassador to Haiti and as the State Department's humanitarian coordinator for Bosnia following the Cold War.

Richard Nixon
Thirty-seventh president of the United States, frequent mentor to Bush, and primary player in the Sino-American rapprochement of the early 1970s. His resignation in 1974 started the chain of events that culminated in Bush's appointment to the United States Liaison Office.

Qiao Guanhua
Vice minister of foreign affairs when Bush arrived in Beijing in 1974, Qiao was soon elevated to foreign minister, a position he held until 1976.

S. Dillon Ripley
Secretary of the Smithsonian Institution from 1964 to 1984. Ripley visited Bush at the United States Liaison Office and was a frequent correspondent throughout Bush's time in China.

Brent Scowcroft
Deputy national security adviser to Henry Kissinger in 1974 when Bush was named to the United States Liaison Office. Scowcroft later served both Presidents Ford and George H. W. Bush as national security adviser. His friendship with Bush blossomed during these early years, and he served as a key communications channel for Bush's messages to Ford.

Norodom Sihanouk
Cambodian leader, exiled to China by the time Bush arrived in Beijing. The two never met during the time of Bush's China Diary,

although Sihanouk's presence in the city made Cambodian affairs an omnipresent issue for the United States Liaison Office.

Wensheng "Nancy" Tang

English-language interpreter for Mao Zedong on foreign affairs during the mid-1970s. The American-born Tang was also a frequent Chinese attendee at meetings with Bush and on the diplomatic community's social circuit.

Wang Hairong

Head of the Protocol Department of the Ministry of Foreign Affairs during Kissinger's and Nixon's initial visits to China, and by the time of Bush's arrival vice minister of foreign affairs in charge of protocol. Wang was also a grandniece of Mao's, a fact that gave her particular political power until his death.

Sir Edward Youde

British ambassador to China during Bush's time in Beijing, and one of his closest confidants and mentors during those months.

Zhou Enlai

Premier of the People's Republic of China from 1949 until his death in 1976, and one of the most influential of all Chinese Communist leaders. Zhou served as foreign minister from 1949 to 1958, though he retained great influence over foreign affairs throughout his life. He suffered from cancer throughout much of Bush's time in Beijing, making his appearances rare but particularly valued by the Americans.

"Everybody in the United States Wants to Go to China"

October 21 to November 1, 1974

*I*n *late October 1974, George H. W. Bush flew to China. He left behind Washington and Watergate, seeking in what he termed this "important assignment" a means of rejuvenation after years spent amid political scandal. He got no further than Alaska, however, before Watergate reared its ugly head. Investigators tracked him down by phone during a scheduled layover to pose further questions about his role in President Richard Nixon's political machinations. The brief incident set the tone for Bush's first weeks in China, where he threw himself into his new environment as though eager to occupy his mind to the point of exhaustion, leaving little time or mental space to ponder all he had left behind. Jet lag only added to this state of exhaustion. It was during these initial weeks in Beijing that Bush met his staff and the prominent members of Beijing's diplomatic community, including Ambassadors Bryce Harland, Stephen Fitzgerald, and Sir Edward Youde, of New Zealand, Australia, and the United Kingdom, respectively. These diplomats would become his closest confidants and in many ways his tutors in understanding his Chinese hosts. He also met the Oxford-educated Richard Akwei, a Ghanaian diplomat who would become his most frequent tennis partner over the ensuing months.*

Bush also made the rounds on the Chinese side. Determined to "meet the next generation of China's leaders—whomever they may prove to be," he pushed for State Department permission to attend national day celebrations at the various embassies and consulates scattered throughout Beijing. Ambassador David Bruce, Bush's predecessor as head of the United States Liaison Office, had been strictly denied this privilege by the State Department. Officially, Washington objected to American attendance at such events as a matter of protocol. Bush—as only an American representative in Beijing, not officially an ambassador—would be shunted to the side of any formal ceremony, in which official delegates from even the smallest countries would be recognized before him. It would be unseemly for the United States to be treated in such a way, argued deputies to Secretary of State Henry Kissinger. Yet their real objection to American attendance lay in their desire to control nearly every interaction between American officials and their Chinese counterparts. These receptions would provide opportunities to mingle among the city's diplomatic community, Bush argued, as well as a chance to get to know the men and women who ran Beijing's government in an informal setting. But these were exactly the sort of unscripted conversations and meetings the professional diplomats at the State Department wanted Bush to avoid at all cost.

Though his diary is modest on this point, recently declassified documents, highlighted in the notes to this chapter, reveal that Bush did not so much ask for permission to make this symbolically important change as make the decision unilaterally. Determined to meet China's leading players despite Foggy Bottom's objections, he plunged into Beijing's diplomatic community with gusto. He thus spent his first weeks in Beijing working to exhaustion, exploring the city, and meeting every important Chinese official and foreign diplomat he could. This first section of the diary includes descriptions of Bush's first meetings in China with Qiao Guanhua, who would in a few weeks be named China's foreign minister, and with Deng Xiaoping, China's future leader, then embroiled in a power struggle that would determine the country's leadership and indeed its very course. He also encountered for the first time the sort of official Chinese reluctance that would come to infuriate him. In the end, his first weeks in China provided exactly what he sought: opportunity, adventure, and a job far from Washington.

This is the beginning of the Peking Diary.[1]

[Monday,] October 21, 1974.   Japan Air Lines. Flight that went to Osaka, [and] Shanghai, [from] Tokyo. Just completed three days at the Tokyo Embassy with Jim and Marie Hodgson.[2] Extremely hospitable and generous in every way. A delightful, down-to-earth guy—plucked out of one year back at Lockheed to be a business-presence ambassador along the lines of the highly successful Bob Ingersoll.[3] I think he will do well.

My emotions are mixed about this. I read the *Japan Times.* I begin already to wish I had more details on American politics, the elections. You read the tired AP [Associated Press] replay, some of the same stories we saw in the states before we left.

When we got to Anchorage there was a message for me to call Leon Jaworski.[4] After countless details and fumbling around by Washington [telephone] operators, Ben Venisti and James Neal came

---

[1]Bush began the diary on October 21, 1974, recounting in his first entry the events of the previous week. This would be a common practice. While Bush most often began his entries with the date of the recording, he often recorded the events that had transpired since his previous entry. This first diary entry was made while en route to Shanghai, Bush's first stop in China.

[2]James Hodgson, U.S. ambassador to Japan from 1974 to 1977, had served as secretary of labor between 1970 and 1973. An advocate within the Nixon administration for stricter standards for workplace safety—an interest he had developed while in the aircraft industry—Hodgson later lectured and wrote extensively on the topic of Japanese-American business relations.

[3]Robert Ingersoll, deputy secretary of state during Bush's time in Beijing, U.S. ambassador to Japan in 1972, and subsequently assistant secretary of state for East Asian and Pacific affairs.

[4]Jaworski headed the special prosecutor's office for the investigation into Watergate that ultimately led to Richard Nixon's resignation. The investigation remained under way as Bush traveled to his post in Beijing.

on the telephone.[5] They explained that Jaworski had placed the call
but had gone home. I expect that this was true though I am not totally confident. They were asking me about a conversation on tape
in April 1973. They had not heard the tape but they saw a transcript.[6] In it, Richard Moore apparently told President Nixon that
I had been approached by Mardian to raise $30,000 for the Wa-
tergate defendants, and that Moore told the President that I refused
to do this and had urged the whole thing to come out.[7] They were
asking me my recollection. I told them that I had absolutely no recollection of this; that I was confident I had not talked to Mardian
about this; that I hadn't seen him since I had become national
chairman.[8] Indeed I hadn't seen him since perhaps a year before
that and then only in passing. All in all I thought they were on the
wrong track. They told me that Moore had not been cooperative.
This, when I said they ought to get Moore in and ask him about
the conversation. I told them I would look at my notes and try to

[5]Richard Ben Venisti, chief of the Watergate Task Force of the Watergate special prosecutor's office, subsequently worked on several high-profile issues in
Washington, including serving on the National Commission on Terrorist Attacks
upon the United States (more commonly referred to as the 9/11 Commission).
James Neal was lead trial counsel for the Watergate hearings.

[6]Nixon's private recordings of personal conversations became central to the
Watergate investigation and to his ultimate downfall.

[7]Richard Moore was a speechwriter and presidential aide in the Nixon White
House. Robert Mardian was political coordinator of the Committee to Re-Elect
the President. Mardian was convicted for his role in the Watergate cover-up, a ruling that was later overturned on appeal—the only such reversal of any Watergate
conviction.

Bush formally responded to Jaworski's inquiry during his first week in China,
though he did not record the event in this diary. On October 22, he confirmed his
side of these events in a letter to Jaworski that read, in part, "I have now checked
and I am absolutely certain that I never had any such conversation with Mardian.
Indeed, I do not believe I ever saw Mardian or talked to him at any time in 1973
or 1974 for that matter."

[8]As described in the interpretive essay that follows the diary text, Bush served
as chairman of the Republican National Committee (RNC) from 1973 to 1974,
immediately preceding his posting to Beijing, and following service as United
States ambassador to the United Nations from 1971 to 1973.

recall any conversation. I did remember some vague reference by Anna Chennault to "another project" where Anna came to me try-ing to build her Republican credentials.[9] And I put two and two together and figured this might have had something to do with rais-ing money for defendants. But I don't recall that it was in April. And I had not in any way tied it in with Dick Moore.

The incident itself is not important except that here I was leav-ing the United States, last point of land, and a call out of the ugly past wondering about something having to do with Watergate, cover-up, and all those matters that I want to leave behind.

In going to China I am asking myself, "Am I running away from something?" "Am I leaving what with inflation, incivility in the press and Watergate and all the ugliness?" "Am I taking the easy way out?" The answer I think is "no," because of the intrigue and fascination that is China. I think it is an important assignment; it is what I want to do; it is what I told the President [Gerald Ford] I want to do; and all in all, in spite of the great warnings of isola-tion, I think it is right—at least for now.

General Notes. People at the State Department seem scared to death about our China policy. Kissinger keeps the cards so close to his chest that able officers in EA [State Department Bureau of East Asian Affairs] seem unwilling to take any kinds of initiative. This troubles me a little bit because I worry that our policy is "plateaued out," and that if we don't do something the policy will come un-

[9]Anna Chennault, spouse of the famed World War II aviator Claire Chennault, chaired the National Republican Heritage Council during Bush's time in Beijing and was active in national party circles, including service as a committeewoman for the Washington, D.C., Republican Party. Ever eager to influence the course of Sino-American relations, Chennault criticized Washington's failure to secure Tai-wan's United Nations seat in 1973, implicitly criticizing Bush in the process. Fol-lowing the Tiananmen crisis a generation later, she met with various Chinese of-ficials while conveying what she termed a "message to Beijing's leaders from President Bush" calling for the reestablishment of positive diplomatic relations. Public scrutiny forced Bush to deny that he had ever asked her to deliver such a message, however, and the incident led to Chennault's ultimate refusal to back Bush's reelection bid in 1992.

der the microscopic scrutiny the CIA [Central Intelligence Agency] has come under, [and] that the Middle East policy has come under.[10] And indeed the American people are going to be looking for forward motion. And it is my hope that I will be able to meet the next generation of China's leaders—whomever they may prove to be. Yet everyone tells me that that is impossible. I have the feeling that David Bruce felt it was best to have a small mission, keep a very low profile, do [a] little reporting, and to feel his way along on this new relationship.[11] He was revered—properly so—and respected. But my hyper-adrenaline, political instincts tell me that the fun of this job is going to be to try to do more, make more contacts. Although everyone all along the line says that you will be frustrated; won't be able to make contacts; won't be able to meet people; they will never come see you, etc. etc. I fear this may be true, but the fun will be trying.

[10]Bush left China in 1975 when Ford offered him the directorship of the CIA. The agency endured tremendous political pressure and public scrutiny during this period as previously secret operations—especially in Latin America and Southeast Asia—came to light through leaks and investigative reporting. Congressional involvement came to a head following investigations by a Senate committee headed by Idaho's Frank Church, which led to significant reforms of the agency and limitations on its operations.

[11]David K. E. Bruce preceded Bush as head of the U.S. Liaison Office (USLO) in Beijing. A long-serving American diplomat with a well-deserved reputation for managing sensitive international relationships, the aristocratic Bruce served every Cold War president from Truman to Ford and honed his skills as ambassador to the three vital European capitals of London, Paris, and Bonn. He remains the only American diplomat so honored. More comfortable (and ultimately more able) as an implementer of policies than as a Washington policymaker in his own right, he was Nixon's initial appointee to China, arriving in March 1973. Bruce had been heading the American delegation to the Paris peace talks, intended to end the Vietnam War. Nixon and Kissinger toyed with the idea of sending either Nelson Rockefeller or Alexander Haig to Beijing, but in April 1971 the President ultimately concluded that Bruce was simply "the best qualified man." Bush's name came up during this 1971 discussion of possible candidates to open the USLO, but Kissinger quickly dismissed the idea by brusquely telling the president, "Absolutely not, he [Bush] is too soft and not sophisticated enough."

I understand that we are walking into a situation where morale is a little low. Time will tell you this as well. I am looking forward to Jennifer Fitzgerald coming over to be my secretary.[12] I think there is a lot to be said to having a buffer between the State Department and the ambassador. It worked at the UN and I am satisfied it can work here.

Before I left, briefings at Commerce, Agriculture and Defense all resulted in requests for a presence from their department there. Military attaché which would include three or four people. Agricultural attaché and commerce attaché. EA seems opposed to this. My own judgment right now is that maybe we ought to have an agricultural man, but again I will have a better judgment on this when I get there.[13] Eighty or ninety percent of our commerce is agriculture. Our trade is going to fall dramatically off this year from a high of close to a billion dollars to around $500 million. This is going to be viewed by the American people as going backwards in trade, and I think we need some work to see that we keep it up.

The question of newsmen in China concerns me. I can see where they [the State Department] don't want every controversial Lyndon-type negativist rushing around, criticizing. But I also can see that responsible reporting perhaps by the news agencies, AP [Associated Press] and UPI [United Press International], might be the best possible thing right now. China should not be on the front burner. But if the policy is going to move forward, nor should it be on the back burner, in terms of awareness in the U.S. The Kissinger trip can help on this enormously.[14]

[12]Fitzgerald would continue as Bush's private secretary during his CIA years and would serve as deputy chief of protocol for the State Department during his presidency.

[13]Bush eventually rejected the Agriculture Department's initial choice of an attaché in Beijing, Harold Champeau, possibly because of his links to the CIA. See Bush's entry and my footnote for June 5, 1975.

[14]Kissinger was next scheduled to visit China in the fall of 1974, though the dates for his visit remained in flux until after Bush's arrival. Kissinger eventually

Random Recollections. Everybody in the United States wants to go to China.[15] Everyone wants a visa. The professors don't know a hell of a lot more about what's going to happen in China than the politicians or the military. Going-away reception at Huang Hua's;

---

landed in Beijing during the last week of November, traveling directly from Ford's summit meeting in Vladivostok with the Soviet Union's Leonid Brezhnev. Bush described Kissinger's China visit in his late November entries.

[15]Not everyone in Kissinger's State Department shared Bush's enthusiasm for such trips. As USLO head, Bush had the power (based on prior informal agreements with the Chinese) to offer personal invitations to Americans. These visitors would subsequently be granted the sorts of business and tourist visas typically difficult to pry out of inflexible Chinese officials, who, in the early 1970s, were still eager to limit foreign access to their society. Such invitations from Bush were therefore prized. Indeed, in a 2005 interview Bush recalled that "the president of Coca-Cola" was "dying to do business in China, [but] he could not get a visa to come talk to the Chinese about selling cola in China. But he's a friend of mine, or even if he wasn't, if I invited him they had a rule that they would get a visa . . . and be able to come. So we had the Coca-Cola [chairman], we had the Pepsi-Cola [chairman], we had Dillon Ripley from the Smithsonian, we had all these people that were dying to get a musk ox or sell a Coke."

State Department officials in Washington recognized at once that Bush's natural enthusiasm as a host, and his desire in 1974 to further develop his political war chest through distribution of such valued invitations, might limit their own ability to control high-level access to China. There would be a risk of international incidents when Americans without diplomatic experience (or, put less gently, without a desire to curtail their opinions on Sino-American relations) came into contact with ranking Chinese policymakers. Weeks before Bush's departure for Beijing, in fact, the State Department's Arthur Hummel cautioned Kissinger that "Bush has already started arrangements to request visas on 'a personal basis' for two Congressmen and their wives to visit Peking this winter. . . . [W]e have so far strictly followed a policy of not promoting any Congressional visits (except those officially arranged); Bush is creating a problem for himself, and for us, that will involve which Congressmen to support in the future." No record exists of Kissinger's response, or of his instructions to Bush on the matter, which (if there were any) were most likely delivered orally before the latter's departure. As Hummel concluded, "Bush has grasped very well the low key nature of his job. . . . However, on this issue he appears determined to retain his 'personal' flexibility." Tension between Bush's desire to host friends and political contacts in Beijing, and the State Department's desire to control access to China during this tense period in Sino-American relations, would be a continual theme throughout Bush's tenure in Beijing, and thus a constant refrain of the diary.

a dinner at Huang Zhen's; the UN dinner; our lunch for Huang Zhen; Stewart's Supreme Court dinner to which Huang Zhen was invited—all were very good.[16] Huang Zhen was rather expansive, suggesting that we could have visas for those people who were "friends of Ambassador Bush." He started suggesting that many, many people could come to China on this basis, all of which I hope proves to be true. It would seem to me that if we had interesting people perhaps we could use this as a way to have more contact with our Chinese friends. Nick Platt, who was let out of China because of hitting a person on a bicycle, and his wife Sheila came to see us in Tokyo at the embassy.[17] They are stationed there. They indi-

[16]One of the most seasoned diplomats of the People's Republic of China (PRC), Huang Hua became China's first ambassador to Canada in 1971. Three months later he moved to New York as Beijing's first official ambassador to the United Nations. In 1976 Huang rose to the position of foreign minister, a position in which he remained until November 1982. He survived the Cultural Revolution as ambassador to Egypt—after all other Chinese ambassadors were recalled, many never to return abroad again—because Zhou Enlai believed "we have to have at least one pawn abroad." A favorite of Zhou's, Huang also had the honor of introducing Kissinger to Beijing's Forbidden City during the latter's initial secret visit to China in 1971.

A veteran of the Long March, General Huang Zhen headed China's liaison office in Washington from 1972 to 1977, and he was in a sense Bush's direct counterpart in the United States. Arguably his nation's most distinguished overseas diplomat, he had previously been ambassador to Hungary, Indonesia, and France. While stationed in Paris prior to his move to the United States, Huang served as a crucial conduit for information during Nixon and Kissinger's first tentative overtures to Beijing. When Nixon and Kissinger first decided on David Bruce as the first USLO head in Beijing in 1973, Chinese officials warmed to the idea that the Americans were sending their most eminent ambassador, and, in their view, they responded in kind.

Potter Stewart served as an associate justice of the United States Supreme Court from 1958 until 1981. (His seat was later filled by Sandra Day O'Connor, the court's first female justice.) He and his wife Mary Ann were particularly close to the Bushes; the families had been neighbors on the same Washington, D.C., street since the late 1960s.

[17]Nicholas Platt was a career foreign service officer and China expert who helped open the USLO in 1973 under Ambassador Bruce. He was later posted as Washington's ambassador to Zambia, the Philippines, and Pakistan. Platt helped

cated that there was a lot to be done in terms of the happiness of the American families, the boredom aspect. They felt that the ambassador should be more active, should push for more contact, should not be quite so subservient or take a lot of stuff off the Chinese.[18]

We were wondering what shape Fred will be in when we arrive in China.[19] He has been in Japanese quarantine for three days and there seemed to be some confusion at the Japanese airport as to whether he was on the plane. But we are assured that he is safely in the bowels of this JAL [Japan Airlines] DC-8.[20] Though I couldn't

---

brief Bush during his stopover in Japan, and he later recalled being the first to suggest that Bush travel Beijing by bicycle as a way to meet Chinese citizens. A memo he wrote during the USLO's early days advocating bicycles as the best means of negotiating Beijing's streets—and of encountering daily life while doing so—can be found in Priscilla Roberts's edition of David Bruce's diary while in China, Roberts, pp. 97–98: "The best way for a foreigner to move around and see things is on two wheels, which carry him fast enough to avoid collecting a crowd, and slow enough to observe life and chat with other bikers, all of whom wobble along at roughly the same pace." Tragically, Platt was forced to leave China when a car he was driving accidentally struck and killed a young Chinese cyclist.

[18]Bush's use of the term "ambassador" here is worth considering. Clearly this was how he interpreted his new role. Yet, as mentioned in the introduction, he was not technically Washington's ambassador to China, as the two countries had yet to establish formal diplomatic relations (a process not completed until 1979). Bush was instead head of the United States Liaison Office in Beijing. He still carried the title of ambassador from his days at the United Nations, of course, but the larger point is that—in Bush's own mind, and in the minds of the American diplomats who worked with him—he was for all practical purposes their ambassador on the spot. There was therefore an inherent tension in Bush's position in Beijing: he was the representative of the world's most powerful nation, yet technically he ranked below the official representative of even the smallest state that enjoyed formal relations with the PRC. As we shall see throughout the text, however, both the Chinese and the Americans conveniently exploited both sides of this tension when doing so suited their own purposes.

[19]According to the Bushes' youngest child, Dorothy, C. Fred, the Bush family cocker spaniel, arrived in China with his own important baggage: seventeen cases of American dog food.

[20]Japan and the PRC had only recently agreed to implement direct air service, officially signing the accord in April 1974. Japanese officials had wanted to es-

hear him barking at Osaka. The weather in Tokyo is humid and fairly warm. A reasonably heavy gray flannel suit was too much. We had a delightful visit on Sunday down at Kamakura with John Roderick of the AP who showed me fascinating pictures that he had taken in Tiananmen with Zhou Enlai, Chairman Mao, Huang Hua and others.[21] Roderick was from Maine. A decent man whom I had met years before with Joy down at the Kennebunk River Club though I did not recall it.[22] He is fascinated with China and wants to go there as the AP man. He is sensitive to the problems and I do not think would cause difficulties for the United States or China in his reporting. Because of the great sensitivity in China it is important to have seasoned journalists when the door is opened. I would hate to spend all my time trying to explain that adverse stories could not be controlled by us. Miss Hollingsworth, a British reporter, told us some experience she had had of being called in to explain some of her writings.[23] This concept is alien to our country.

---

tablish such links years before, but they had always bowed to American pressure to keep Beijing as isolated economically as it was politically. Once Nixon opened informal relations with the Chinese—and after Beijing purchased its first American-built jet airliners months later—there remained little reason for such containment measures.

[21]Associated Press special correspondent John Roderick reported for the news service for thirty-nine years, mainly from Asia. Zhou Enlai and Mao Zedong were, of course, the premier and chairman of the Chinese Communist Party, respectively. Zhou impressed leaders throughout the world, including those who gave praise grudgingly. Kissinger would describe him as "one of the two or three most impressive men I have ever met," while United Nations Secretary General Dag Hammarskjold thought Zhou possessed "the most superior brain I have so far met in the field of foreign policy." By the time Bush arrived in China, Zhou was already stricken with the cancer that would take his life in 1976. A list of biographies of both men is included in the bibliographic essay.

Kamakura is a distant seaside Tokyo suburb.

[22]Joy Dow managed the club during this period.

[23]A veteran British war correspondent who began reporting during the German invasion of Poland in 1939, Clare Hollingsworth worked for London's *Daily Telegraph* and the *International Herald Tribune*, focusing on the Middle East before moving to Asia to cover the Vietnam War during the 1960s. In 1972 she opened the *Daily Telegraph*'s first bureau in Beijing since 1949. She became a particular

Note. I read in the Japan papers some comment about the threats to the freedom of U.S. journalists and I thought to myself, "My God, what are they talking about," compared to what happens in terms of reporting in China.

Note. I will try to make this diary factual without going into too much of the sensitive policy nature of things. I will make comments on people, places, recollections, hopefully a little color. It will be fun to look back to see how initial impressions check out, whether the initial enthusiasm I feel about this assignment becomes jaded, gives way to a jaded cynicism as a result of contact.

In a selfish sense I do not see this as a political dead end. Many political friends tell me, "out of sight, out of mind." But I think in this assignment there is an enormous opportunity of building credentials in foreign policy, credentials that not many Republican politicians will have. Kissinger has mentioned to me twice, "This must be for two years, George," "You will do some substantive business, but there will be a lot of time when you will be bored stiff." I thought of Henry and I am sure his role in having Nelson Rockefeller get the VP situation, but I will say that he was extremely generous in telling Qiao Guanhua that I was close to the President.[24]

---

favorite of Ambassador Bruce during his time in China, though Bush would find her less entertaining and less helpful. See Bush's entry and my footnote for May 4, 1975.

[24]Standard-bearer of the Republican Party's liberal wing during the 1960s and New York's governor beginning in 1968, Nelson Rockefeller became vice president in December 1974. As RNC head, Bush was considered his chief rival for the position, the two men representing competing visions for the party's future. As described in the concluding essay, Bush actively lobbied President Ford for the nomination. When the president chose Rockefeller, China became Bush's consolation prize. It was perhaps natural for Bush to have believed that Kissinger played a role in Rockefeller's selection, as Rockefeller had long been one of Kissinger's most generous patrons, dating to the latter's days as a promising though relatively obscure Harvard professor. While Kissinger undoubtedly approved of Rockefeller's selection, little evidence exists suggesting that his opinion was either decisive or particularly influential. Histories of the Ford administration are described in the bibliographic essay.

Bush flew from Tokyo to Shanghai, spending several days there. His next entries were made following his arrival in Beijing.

The "picture" of the Great Wall and the other.[25] We sat up for forty minutes talking to Mr. Lo who spoke pretty darn good English. He looked 20. He was 37. He is a member of the Shanghai greeting committee of some sort. We sat there making small talk. I asked him the age of the airfield and he was a little vague on that. It looked like an old World War II air base. A lot of Russian planes around—large and small. No other airlines sitting inside except our JAL DC-8. We flew to Peking on a very clear day. When we arrived it was cold. Greeted by their acting protocol chief, Mr. Zhu Qiusheng, and the head of their American section, Mr. Lin Ping.[26]

Qiao Guanhua, China's vice minister of foreign affairs when Bush first arrived in Beijing, became foreign minister less than a month later. A trusted Zhou protégé, like his mentor Qiao had studied and lived abroad before the Cultural Revolution, earning a doctorate in philosophy while in Germany. Having participated in the difficult diplomatic negotiations that eventually produced an armistice in Korea in 1953, Qiao later headed the arguably far trickier negotiations with the Soviet Union in 1969, which were designed to settle tensions following the outbreak of hostilities along their mutual border. Bruce had found Qiao to be as engaging as Bush would, referring to him in his diary as "my favorite" and as "an extraordinarily companionable, sophisticated, gifted man." He was purged from power in 1976, largely because of his loose connection to the discredited "Gang of Four."

[25]"Picture" is italicized in the original transcript. As this notation may suggest a vocal intonation familiar to his transcriber, I have decided to retain it. The "other" is Bush himself.

[26]Zhu Qiusheng was deputy director (and acting director) of the Protocol Office of the Ministry of Foreign Affairs. He was later China's consul general in Houston when Bush was president. Lin Ping, who had previously served as China's ambassador to Australia, directed the Americas and Oceanic Division of the Foreign Ministry, and thus was a principal contact for both Bruce and Bush. Bruce chafed at having to participate in meetings with someone he considered beneath his diplomatic station. Having "visualized an ongoing dialogue with Zhou Enlai," American diplomat Don Anderson later recorded, Bruce "lost interest early on . . . [in] being called in by. . . . about the equivalent of an assistant secretary, and at that time not a very pleasant fellow." Bush also found Lin exasperating at times,

John Holdridge, Brunson McKinley and a bunch of the officers from the mission, the New Zealand and Australian ambassadors were out there.[27] We were escorted up to the reception room set up there in rather a formal air exchanging pleasantries with Mr. Lin, and then Holdridge suggested that it was time to push on. I gave them a brief press statement to a gaggle of about six press journalists and off we went on a very windy day.[28] The wind was really howling. It reminded me very much of West Texas and also of a trip to Kuwait, a combination of Kuwait and Midland. The Kuwait-Midland axis. There were very few cars. I was struck by that. Lots of bicycles. Everybody plain and drably dressed. We swung into the mission: nice, clean, great-looking U.S. seal, two PLA [People's Liberation Army] guards at the gate, and into the residence which is tastefully done. More on that later. Staff was impressive. I toured through, met everybody, unpacked, failing to

---

noting near the conclusion of the diary—following a weeklong trip to China's Northeast for which Lin had been Bush's primary host—that he "saw Lin Ping at the Peru reception—almost as if our trip had not taken place." See Bush's entry for July 29, 1975.

[27]John Holdridge served as deputy chief of mission for the USLO from its opening in 1973 until his appointment as U.S. ambassador to Singapore in 1975. He subsequently served as assistant secretary for East Asian and Pacific affairs in 1981 and as ambassador to Indonesia in 1982. A well-regarded Chinese linguist and West Point graduate who first visited Beijing in 1937, he had been Kissinger's senior assistant for Asian affairs on the National Security Council staff. He traveled with Kissinger during his first visit to China in 1971 and then advised Nixon during his own historic first visit a year later. His memoirs, *Crossing the Divide: An Insider's Account of the Normalization of U.S.-Chinese Relations,* are particularly insightful on the personal interactions of Sino-American rapprochement.

Brunson McKinley's career as a foreign service officer included time in Vietnam, London, Beijing, and Berlin, and he would later become U.S. ambassador to Haiti (1983–86), before serving as the State Department's humanitarian coordinator for Bosnia. He subsequently headed the International Organization for Migration in Geneva.

[28]Bush told reporters gathered to record his arrival in Beijing that "there will be a continuation of the quest for normalization, and I know this from talking to President Ford."

14

have packed much of the stuff we need. The clothes were there and the air freight was there. C. Fred arrived looking dirty and tired, and damned confused. All in all we are in good shape on the pleasant things of life. The staff had completely changed out. Mr. Bruce had raved about his first man but now we have a new man, Mr. Sun Jiangang, Mr. Zhang Bolong, Yan Zuqi, the first waiter.[29] There is a second waiter and two female cleaners. There was a couple of extras in there. The guy making the vodka and tonic filled it half with vodka, a little less than half of tonic and some ice. Fred was confused and delighted to see all the kids. First thing, I have told Bar to get a ping-pong table and a couple of bicycles. We then went to John Holdridge's for dinner at his apartment. The school is in the lobby of the apartment.[30] John is knowledgeable in Chinese, and Martha was also extremely helpful.[31]

We went to bed early. They put a board under my bed, making it properly hard but we were confused. The wind was whistling outside and yet the heat inside was enormous. I went around and turned off all the heaters. Bar got snoring again just like West Texas. I turned on the Sears dehumidifier and she did OK. She'll have that place singing in a day or two. It needs pictures, it needs some warmth, it needs some tabletop items, but other than that we have inherited a lot in the Bruce style. It's great. All's well. End first night. No substance. Lots of new sights and sounds and smells. Don't drink the water. The soap is good. The eggs are little. Shortwave

[29]Members of Bush's house staff, and a prime example of the Anglicization of proper names that occurred when Bush, a non–Chinese speaker, dictated his diary for later transcription by other non–Chinese speakers. A picture of the USLO's Chinese and American staff is included in the photograph section.

[30]In 1974 Patricia Holdridge, John and Martha Holdridge's daughter, taught the four American children of USLO personnel in their apartment, as these American children were unable, for political and logistical reasons, to enroll in any of the local schools. See Bush's entry for November 12, 1974.

[31]Trained in Asian studies at Cornell University, Martha Holdridge informally hosted China's initial skeleton staff for the PRC's Liaison Office in Washington during the spring of 1973, in return for which the Chinese rewarded her with the first official visa issued to an American from their office.

15

makes a lot of whistling sounds—sounds just like 30 years ago. Lots to do. Lots to learn.

[Tuesday,] October 22[, 1974]. Took Fred for a run about 6 o'clock in the morning. Guards looked a little startled. Ran down one side of USLO and then another. A lot of people were bicycling, going to work. Many stared expressionless. The old-timers smiled and looked very friendly at Fred, and me even. Whereas the younger ones remained somewhat inscrutable and though they showed an interest they did not show any emotion at all.

Had a long conversation with Bryce Harland, the attractive young ambassador from New Zealand.[32] We reviewed the contacts he has with Chinese officials. In fact he gets a lot out of the diplomatic corps. He made a couple of interesting comments to me. He felt the United States was making a mistake if only Dr. Kissinger talked to the Chinese. "No one is immortal." He probed on Kissinger's forthcoming visit, seeming to know when the visit would take place. He showed me through his house, the new tennis court he has built with a slick surface, designed also to be flooded and used for ice skating in the winter. A great idea. Rest of the day reading cables, doing some mail, getting acquainted for a staff meeting in the morning. Lunch at home with Bar, trying to get some understanding with the new staff. The English-speaking mâitre-d' Bruce was so high on was gone. Replaced by a very pleasant but sloppy man who speaks French and wants to please. He seems very nice. The number two man, a younger man, speaks English but really only says a few words. Weather, clear. Fall kind of day. A little brisk without an overcoat but pleasant. Harland of New Zealand appears to me a very active, outgoing, youngish ambassador born about 1931. He has got a lot of ideas.[33]

---

[32]New Zealand's first ambassador to China, Harland served in Beijing from 1973 to 1975, before reprising the experience as his country's first ambassador to Vietnam. He was subsequently posted to New York as New Zealand's United Nations representative and to London as his country's high commissioner.

[33]Harland would become one of Bush's closest colleagues in Beijing, but, at least

16

Observation at the end of this first day. The amount of information not available. Great speculation because Chairman Mao met with Denmark's Prime Minister and there is all kinds of speculation as to where Mao is.[34] The Danes were not at liberty to say, being sworn to secrecy. Some think that Mao was out in the country to see how the group in Peking will do. Others feel that he is home because of his advanced years. But the point is people don't know. They speculate about it, they talk about it. Here we are in a country of 800 million people and it is a well-kept secret. At least from our ears. Amazing, absolutely amazing.

[Wednesday,] October 23[, 1974]. A spectacularly beautiful day. The sky is a bright blue. Fred and I went for a run after I did those abominable exercises at about six in the morning down past [the embassies of] Kuwait, Greece, Chad and then back past our mission and down to the International Club and back once again. People stared at Fred the same as yesterday. Some smiling, most showing interest but going on. Morning spent at our regular 8:45 staff meeting. I am not adjusted to sleeping very well. Woke up early. When dawn breaks it happens all of a sudden it seems to me. Called on the French ambassador, Mr. Manac'h.[35] He does not

---

according to British sources, he was not among Bush's confidants. Bush preferred to share sensitive information with London's ambassador, Sir Edward Youde (introduced in Bush's entry for October 25, 1974). Youde frequently passed such information—as Bush would have expected—back to London under the heading "UK Eyes Only" in order to ensure Bush's confidentiality. "It is also clear that he [Bush] is very selective about what he says to whom," Youde reported in December 1974. "As you would expect the New Zealanders are not among his confidants: Bryce Harland complained . . . that all he got out of Bush was 'blanket and flannel.'"

[34]Poul Hartling was prime minister of Denmark from 1973 to 1975. Mao was frequently in ill health throughout the 1970s and as a consequence did not spend much time in Beijing. Discussion of his health and his whereabouts—in essence, speculation on the real center of power within China's government—was a perennial pastime among Beijing's diplomatic corps.

[35]Previously director of Asian affairs for France's Foreign Ministry—and with a solid reputation in Washington despite his public sympathies for North Vietnam —Étienne Manac'h arrived in Beijing in 1969. He subsequently authored *Mémoires*

speak Chinese. He has been here four years. Very pleasant. Told me that De Gaulle had talked to Nixon in February of '69 and then had told him, Manac'h, to tell Zhou Enlai that the United States wants contact with the PRC [People's Republic of China].[36] He agrees that there will be a coalition leadership from the bottom not from the charismatic top. He told how when Pompidou was coming he asked to meet the party people as well as the city people.[37] They said "Why?" He told them that he had been in Communist countries before and he knew very well how important the party people were. He [Manac'h] had just come back from a week in North Korea. A private, non-official visit. His house was beautiful, full of artifacts. He has a new wife after some 30 years.

It is amazing to watch their reactions when the Chinese see the American flag on the car. Many of them point at it or look at each other and seem to be commenting on it. I am not sure if this is true with other missions as well. But for years we were criticized and now they see the stars and stripes flowing from time to time all around Peking. Our Chinese bikes are back today. I say back. They had to get licenses.

October 23. Lunch with the Lilleys.[38] Bright, Chinese-speaking officer and his young kid. On Wednesday afternoons the office is

---

d'Extrême Asie (1977), detailing his time in China, including his interactions with Bruce and Bush.

[36] Charles de Gaulle, leader of the Free French forces during World War II, served as president of France from 1958 to 1969.

[37] Georges Jean Raymond Pompidou was president of France from 1969 to 1974.

[38] James Lilley, one of Washington's most renowned China experts, moved from the CIA to the State Department following his time in China, after his cover was blown by a published newspaper report. Born in China in 1928 (his father worked for Standard Oil in the country), Lilley subsequently held the unique distinction of serving as ambassador to both the Republic of China (Taiwan) and the PRC. For Lilley's experience in his own words, see James Lilley and Jeffrey Lilley, *China Hands: Nine Decades of Adventure, Espionage, and Diplomacy in Asia* (New York: Public Affairs, 2004), especially pp. 192–96 for his recollections of service during Bush's time at the USLO.

closed—Wednesday and Saturday afternoons. Lilley was off to do some Boys' Club work. There is something nice about having his son around here. It prompted me to hurry up and get a ping-pong table and hurry up and get a basketball hoop up—both of which we are in the process of accomplishing.

Played tennis in the afternoon with Akwei of Ghana, a member of the Italian mission and some other guy.[39] Courts are small in the sense there is little room on the side and in the back. The wiring around the court is good. The surface is bland, white concrete. They should have mixed some color in with it. It is hard as a rock and really not too attractive. And the ball was very hard to see. Akwei, warm nice guy. I asked him if it would be possible to put some topping on these courts and he indicated that it might be difficult as far as the Chinese went. They might not want it done. They might feel it was presumptuous of us. If it should be done, they should do it. I told him of the great surface at the White House court and other courts but he didn't think they would be too receptive. I have in mind that we ought to have a good court and a pool for our people even if we had to have it in a separate place. I don't care about it here, but I just think if other missions have it, by God we ought to have it too. I am hoping that by having some of these little athletic facilities around the house, some of the kids will come here.

Four of the help in the back ran away when they saw Fred. Bar called him over and had him do his tricks and they were soon out watching him and laughing. Initially they were scared. Rode over with Brunson McKinley to make our first call on the Chinese, Mr. Zhu, Acting Chief of Protocol, that took Ambassador Han's place.[40] He is a very pleasant individual. He had two others with

[39]Educated at Oxford, Richard Akwei was chargé d'affaires of the Ghanaian embassy in Washington during the early 1960s. He served as his country's permanent representative to the United Nations before arriving in Beijing and later chaired the United Nations International Civil Service Commission.

[40]Though he conducted the meeting himself in English, Zhu Chuanxian was

him. We exchanged initial pleasantries. I told him his "ears should be burning" because Dr. Kissinger spoke so highly of the kind of work they were doing in protocol here. He mentioned Qiao Guanhua, [and I responded] that I wanted to have an exchange of views about politics, having been in the political arena, with him or any others; that I would prefer frank, informal discussions if possible; that Qiao Guanhua ought not to feel that he should have a formal kind of reception for me of any kind; [and] that I would much prefer a very small meeting where we could talk more frankly. I knew Qiao had many banquets and felt he didn't need yet another one. I told him that he was very nice and he told me to make requests. And yes we could travel. Yes he would be glad to receive our requests for anything we wanted. I told him not only would we do that, but on the other hand if there is any place where he should be critical of us he should call me and tell me. That I wanted a frank relationship. We want to comply. We think we have done well, but if we are doing anything at all that is causing them concern we want them to tell us and to tell us frankly.

What I was attempting to do was to establish a frank relationship and to try to move out of the normal diplomatic, stiff-armed, stilted deal. It may be difficult. It may be impossible but I want to keep pushing for it. The only tack that I have got that can be helpful is this approach of having been in politics. I used it again with Mr. Zhu and said that if they wanted to talk about the American political scene I would be prepared to do it from the unique vantage point of having run one of our parties. It will be interesting to see if they are willing to do this at all.

On the way back from the visit Brunson and I went into a sports store. Tremendously crowded street. Many, many bicycles. We bought a couple of sweatshirts, some ping-pong rackets and ordered a ping-pong table for the next day. People clustered around. I must say that people are the same the world over. Basically friendly

---

joined at this meeting by those Bush termed "protocol department functionaries Tang Longpin and Cheng Haogeng."

if you are friendly with them. After an initial wondering, they couldn't have been more friendly as we went along and bought the goods. Brunson spoke to them in good Chinese, and all in all it was a happy little experience seeing all those people looking at the basketballs, sweatshirts and soccer balls. The store was stocked with dark blue, dark maroon sweatshirts, some colored socks, white athletic socks, a good range of balls (soccer, basketball), other little round rubber balls, ping-pong stuff—not an overly stocked store, not bulging at the seams like an American sports store, but not a bad selection either. The man was most anxious to show us his championship ping-pong table which was too much money for us—$250—but I did buy one for about $125. The sweatshirts were cheap, the ping-pong rackets not bad. I saw the Great Hall of the People and other buildings for the first time from the car. I must say you get a very different feeling when you see all of those things than when you just drive around the USLO Office.

We had dinner at a Mongolian place with the Holdridges on the 23rd. One cooks his own dinner on a common potbelly stove in the middle of the room. The food was spicy. Chinese wine was served. And all in all it was delightful.

Thursday still [October 24, 1974].   A very interesting visit with Fitzgerald, the Australian ambassador.[41] He is young—30 some odd—35ish. Was in the foreign service. Early on became opposed to Australia's foreign policy and felt that future lay with China and the PRC. He took a PhD and majored in the language and then when Whitlam came in, he was sent to Peking.[42] He is aggressive, attractive and very interesting. He is concerned on two major points: the relationship of the Soviet Union and India. He felt that

---

[41]With a doctorate in Chinese studies, Stephen Fitzgerald was appointed Australia's first ambassador to the PRC in January 1973, just weeks after formal relations between the two countries commenced.

[42]Australia's prime minister from 1972 to 1975, Edward Gough Whitlam simultaneously served as foreign minister during his first year in office. It was Whitlam who withdrew the final Australian troops from Vietnam.

India is very uptight. And he felt that China was very uptight about India. And with India's growing nuclear capability and China's, the PRC might miscalculate along the border.[43] The second point where he thought he could be useful to us as was some kind of contact with Sihanouk but mainly with Sihanouk's Foreign Minister.[44] He was less concerned about Sihanouk himself than he was about the total settlement in Cambodia. Fitzgerald ventured that they have good relations with Sihanouk and his foreign minister, and he might be able to help if we wanted them to.

Speculation on Kissinger's trip. Fitzgerald is extremely interested. I hedged and told him that nothing was definite. These things have a way of changing. He pressed very hard on this. It seems to be the number one topic in the diplomatic corps in China. Fitzgerald indicated that the PRC had told him they would be willing to sell them [Australia] substantial amounts of oil in the future.[45]

Notes on Peking. At a quarter of six in the morning you can hear

[43]The Sino-Indian border remained one of the world's geopolitical hotspots in the mid-1970s, having erupted in violence in 1962. The conflict helped reorder the region's strategic makeup, bringing New Delhi closer to the Western fold and striking a severe blow to Prime Minister Jawaharlal Nehru's foreign policy of neutrality within the Cold War.

[44]Norodom Sihanouk ruled Cambodia under a variety of titles from 1941 until he was deposed by Lon Nol in 1970 during a trip to Moscow. He eventually found sanctuary in China, whose leaders had long been his sponsor, and he remained in Beijing throughout Bush's tenure there. His ouster contributed to Cambodia's subsequent decline into chaos, which included military involvement by the United States and North Vietnam, and the ultimate rise to power of Pol Pot and his Khmer Rouge. Indeed Sihanouk's constant political maneuverings, which intersected both Cold War power politics and the growing humanitarian crisis of his homeland, would present Washington, and Bush in particular, with the thorniest of political problems over the months to come. He would be a constant topic in Bush's diary. Histories of the American involvement in Cambodia's traumas during the 1970s are described in the bibliographic essay.

[45]Ambassador Bruce left China convinced that the country would soon come to dominate world oil markets. "If they pursue their current policies they are going to be rich long before anyone expected them to be," he told the Senate Foreign Relations Committee upon his return from Beijing.

voices from PLA units shouting commands, almost cheers. Other than that, there is a silence. Things get gray here. The water is very hard. Fred the dog has adjusted a little bit by now. He looks kind of gray. Bar has given him two baths but he still looks gray. So do our shirts. Water softeners don't work.

It is hard in a house when no one speaks English. The food is varied and excellent. We are asking the interpreter to speak to Mr. Yen in the house and have him write down what he serves at each meal. We will then know what these dishes are when we have them translated.

Thursday night I went to bed at 8:30 simply dead tired. I hadn't done that much, though I am doing my exercises and running in the morning between 6 and 7. It must just be an adjustment to schedule. Total fatigue struck me and I was asleep by quarter of nine I am sure.

I saw a big black crow on the run this morning. The first bird I have seen. He called out and sounded kind of weird. I wonder about Fred. He stopped to sniff what a couple of donkeys left on the street. He was most enthusiastic about this. We never see a dog on our runs.[46]

Friday, the 25th [October 25, 1974], two visits.[47] One with Teddy Youde, the British ambassador.[48] This is his fourth trip to China. He is an extremely interesting man. Terribly well informed. Knows the cast of characters. Lives in splendor, something far more than we live in, but something less, he informed me, than what they used

[46]Ownership of dogs and cats as pets was effectively banned by Chinese authorities during the still-ongoing Cultural Revolution, as a symbol of middle-class values.

[47]Bush's diary entry for October 25 appeared in the original transcript preceding that for October 22. This appears to have been a filing error, and not the order of Bush's original dictation. For the sake of continuity it has been returned to chronological order.

[48]Sir Edward Youde later received greater fame as Hong Kong's governor during the final negotiations over the colony's return to formal Chinese control.

to live in. He told me about the burning of their chancellery during the Cultural Revolution though he wasn't here.[49] It was a terrifying experience for which the Chinese subsequently made clear they were not responsible. In other words they disapproved of its happening. We sat outdoors in a very relaxed way on the lawn. I think we will have good relations with him. The other visit was with Deputy Director Zhou De, Deputy Director of the MFA [Ministry of Foreign Affairs], the information department.[50] During that meeting we talked about his role with cultural exhibitions etc. and I made a pitch for expanding contact with U.S. journalists coming here.[51] I did not get into the question of the AP being stationed here, but I did get into the question of more U.S. journalists in the spirit of the Shanghai Communiqué.[52] At these meetings with the

[49]The British consulate was burned by zealots of the Cultural Revolution in August 1967 during a period of particular violence and national upheaval. Inspired by Mao's declaration that "everyone should be prepared to take up bayonets," revolutionary elements additionally focused on the Ministry of Foreign Affairs and its old-guard leader, Chen Yi, urging instead the appointment of more militant "red revolutionary fighters." Foreign diplomatic missions came under assault as well, a phase highlighted by the destruction of London's chancery at the hands of an angry mob. In this sense, both foreigners and Chinese associated with the outside world, and with China's inglorious past association with Western diplomacy and imperialism, were simultaneously targeted for attack. As the final entries to his diary would show, Bush was particularly moved and influenced by Anthony Grey's *Hostage in Peking*, which describes in detail the sacking of the British Consulate (pp. 121–32) See chapter 8 and the bibliographic essay for a discussion of recent works on the Cultural Revolution.

[50]For an additional discussion of China's foreign policy bureaucracy, see the source provided in the endnotes.

[51]Zhou was receptive to Bush's overture, though he noted that his small staff imposed a structural limit on the size of any foreign journalistic presence. According to the American version of the meeting delivered to Washington, Zhou admitted that "the information department is seriously overworked" and that "the department's offices are [often] completely empty with all of their people on the road escorting groups of journalists." Clearly, unbridled access to the Chinese countryside for foreign reporters was not yet in the cards.

[52]A genuine turning point in Sino-American relations, the Shanghai Communiqué was signed by Nixon and Zhou Enlai on February 28, 1972, at the end of the president's weeklong visit to China. It stressed mutual coexistence and the search for a peaceful resolution to the Taiwan controversy; signaled a start to ex-

Chinese officials John Holdridge, Don Anderson and Brunson all attend.[53] There is a certain stock formality to them. Sitting in the room with cigarettes and tea in front of you, antimacassars too prominently displayed. Prompt arrival, the friendly wave at the steps and all in all rather politely and nicely done. I had lunch with the McKinley family. Another spectacular lunch. We have yet to have the same course of any kind served except for the rice. Tonight we had the Linguists and the Philadelphia Council for International Visitors, a group of Main Liners.[54] The reception is 6 to 7 at the residence. I hope they don't drink up too much of our whiskey.

---

panded trade and communications between the two nations; and, perhaps most important, pledged each country to work against any country that would "seek hegemony in the Asia-Pacific region." This was a none-too-subtle reference to the Soviet Union, and thus the communiqué offered at once a visible new start to Sino-American relations and also a public success for Nixon and Kissinger's policy of geopolitical triangulation as a means of thwarting Soviet advances. Mao subsequently quipped to Kissinger that, having established "friendship," the two nations were now pledged to "work together to commonly deal with the bastard [the Soviet Union]." Historian Nancy Bernkopf Tucker noted that, after Nixon went to China and signed the communiqué, informally at least, "the United States had more communists on its side than did the Soviet Union," though she has recently argued that Kissinger's private discussions with the Chinese severely undermined Washington's public commitment to Taiwan.

[53]Don Anderson's foreign service career as a China specialist and interpreter included not only service in Beijing under Bruce and Bush but also time as the American interpreter for the informal talks between the PRC and the United States held in Warsaw during the late 1960s and early 1970s. He was the point man for the secret discussions between Chinese and American officials that were held in Paris before Kissinger's first historic trip to China. He became head of the USLO's political section in 1974 upon Nicholas Platt's departure. He was subsequently appointed Washington's consul general in Hong Kong.

[54]The "linguists" to whom Bush refers were scholars visiting China through the Committee on Scholarly Communication, dedicated to promoting Sino-American cultural and educational ties as a subgroup of the American Council on Learned Societies. Though Bush does not mention it in his diary, their impending October visit sparked a minor incident for the USLO when, during the first week of October, Chinese officials summarily rescinded a visa for one member who had been with the Office of Strategic Services (the OSS, a wartime precursor to the CIA) during World War II, including service in China. The matter was eventually cleared up, and the group proceeded with their visit unimpeded. Yet, as Robert

Another beautiful day in Peking. Absolutely perfect weather.

Sunday[, October 27, 1974]. The wind is blowing, the sky is clear. But dust is everywhere. Gray dust in the post reports, is all around and everyone jokes about it and laughs about it. Fred is looking even grayer. But I am feeling better. Less tired. Impressed with much around me. And yet wondering, wondering about the policies and where we ought to be a year from now.

Off to church: the Protestant service. The Bible Institute. There is a Catholic service at the Cathedral. Church service at the Bible Institute was unbelievable. Beat up old house. Four old Chinese including the minister who in this instance was Presbyterian. Two others who I understand were ministers. One a Methodist, and one an Anglican. The rest of the congregation consisted of the Austrian ambassador and his family, another from the Dutch embassy, several Africans including Mrs. Akwei and her kid.[55] All in all a congregation of about fourteen people. It was a most moving service. The hymns were the old familiar ones. Sung off an English song sheet with the Chinese voices singing the same hymns in Chinese.

Ingersoll warned the USLO, from Washington's perspective Chinese interference in such a high-level cultural exchange designed to promote normalization "will inevitably spark speculation among the press and other observers" that relations were headed for a rocky course. Though allowed to proceed with their trip, the group was subsequently confronted by Chinese customs inspectors, who claimed to have found currency from the Republic of China in their bags—a claim the linguists fully rejected, believing the money had been planted in order to embarrass them.

The International Visitors Council, based in Philadelphia, is a citizen diplomacy group, funded in part by the State Department, that is tasked with "promot[ing] mutual understanding among nations and prevent[ing] wars by bringing people 'face to face' and creating a dialogue." This was their first trip to mainland China.

Philadelphia's Main Line area, so named for its development of one of the nation's first commuter rail lines, has historically been home to some of the city's most prominent families.

[55]Austria and China first established official diplomatic relations in May 1971, and Franz Helmut Leitner served as his country's second ambassador to Beijing from 1973 to 1974.

The service was conducted entirely in Chinese including communion. It was moving.[56]

Sunday, October 27, 1974. On Saturday we climbed up the Western Hills with John and Martha Holdridge. A beautiful but tiring climb. There was a sign at the gate saying, "Do Not Pick the Red Leaves" and yet all through the climb we saw soldiers and kids carrying red leaves. Bright red fall colors. The path and the walk were a bit grubby. There was a lot of dust around. A lot of popsicle wrappers and paper wrappers. Sitting around the various way stations there was garbage left and I was unimpressed by the cleanliness of the place. It reminded me of some of the spots in New York. I would have thought that the discipline extended to this kind of thing. There are propaganda speakers throughout the whole park. They were not on at first. When they came on, four kids in gray Mao coats in front of us looked at each other and one of them put his hands up into his ears as if to fend off the announcements. You see boys and girls glancing at each other but no hand holding. No he-ing and she-ing, and you wonder in this beautiful setting.

On Saturday we made a call on the DSB [Diplomatic Services Bureau].[57] They are the group that provide the servants and the facilities. A Mr. Xu is in charge.[58] A jovial older man who must get jillions of requests. I point out to him that we needed some recreational facilities though I was not pressing for this.[59] I told him the

---

[56]"The service was held in Chinese," Barbara Bush later recalled, "but we all had our own Bibles and could for the most part follow the service."

[57]As the official clearinghouse for staff employed by foreign diplomats, the DSB collected a set fee for services provided to embassies and consulates, a fraction of which went to the employee. As Bruce noted in his own diary, the idea of a Maoist bureaucracy skimming off the top of its employees' wages was "a tantalizing mystery it is preferable not to fathom."

[58]Xu Huang was the director of the DSB. He later became the Chinese ambassador to Laos.

[59]Xu was not entirely encouraging of this request, noting that "the Liaison Office has very little room for expansion." Bush in time would argue to Kissinger that expansion of the USLO's physical layout would, if nothing else, prove a tan-

cooperation had been good. I told him we were satisfied with our people. Though none of them spoke English they were all trying very, very hard. And in our opinion were doing a good job. I think he interpreted this as a request for somebody who did speak English. I reassured him that that was not the case.

We went by the tennis courts.[60] Here they were rolling some kind of red powdered stuff into a really good-looking two-court indoor building. I talked through Brunson and John Holdridge to the man in charge of tennis. He is an old-timer. He seems friendly and I am looking forward to getting on the courts. They ought to be all right for a while but it would be an ideal place for some of those Arlington "Y"-type courts. The outdoor courts are absolutely useless. The surface that they put on them fell apart in less than a year. Great potholes in it. Again little technology but a desire to please the international community in a fantastic setup with basketball, pool, ping-pong, cheap meals, barbershop (thirty cents a haircut). All in all, an excellent facility.

The calls on Chinese officials are all very formal. I have been to the information agency where I made a pitch for more journalists to come into the country. I feel strongly that in terms of our policy we must have manifestations of forward progress. The journalist area is a good one. They will never discuss these things. They simply take note of your comments. It is strictly a one-way street in terms of getting any response.

On the climb to the Western Hills it is exactly the same as everywhere else. People stare are you. Gather around the car. Look at you. Once in a while smile. No hostility but tremendous curiosity. Our driver, Mr. Guo, is amazing. It looks to me like we are going

---

gible sign of positive Sino-American relations, even if agreement on matters of trade or geopolitics proved trickier to achieve.

[60]Bush refers here to the International Club, a facility operated by the DSB for the benefit of Beijing's international community. The hub of the diplomatic community's social life, it would prove one of Bush's most frequent destinations during his time in China—not least because it offered the most easily accessible tennis courts.

to crash into bicycles, donkey carts, overloaded buses, trailer-type setups, or get lost in a dust storm, but sure enough Mr. Guo manages. Yesterday a bicyclist almost ran in front of us and Mr. Guo held up his finger and disciplined the young bike rider with a rather serious reprimand. The kid looked somewhat chastened but continued boldly across the great breadth of highway and was soon blended into a jillion other cyclists, a bunch of buses and a few donkey-pulled carts.

Saturday night we attended a dance. The Spanish embassy. I had no tuxedo but it didn't matter. The Africans just as they do in the UN—some of them—showed up tuxedo-less and I felt right at home. The Spanish ambassador is a kind of a swinger. He had a most attractive French-speaking house guest with him and all in all it was a gala evening. Lots of Frank Sinatra music and relaxed. The diplomatic community seems starved for this kind of entertainment. The Spanish did it well. The food was Western: sliced ham, sliced beef, and lots of typical-type buffet-style things.

Sunday morning I am reading the Xinhua news agency (Red News —this is put out by the government propaganda pieces). The Blue News is more objective.[61] Foreign service reports. It is culled news from foreign agencies and press. Xinhua has got the propaganda tone. All through the Xinhua News you read anti-American stuff. The Koreans giving a big dinner to celebrate the Red Volunteers going into Korea. A big long propaganda piece against the "oil monopolists" in the United States. A lot of anti-Soviet stuff. And all in all it is the party line. This contrasts with the Blue News which is a rather straight presentation of the wire service and byline pieces

---

[61]China's news services clearly left an impression on Bush. When queried on the utility of public rhetoric (and of Ronald Reagan's use of the term "evil empire" to describe the Soviet Union) while vice president, Bush told one reporter that, while in China, "every day he heard the 'red news and the blue news,' the former filled with bombast, the latter with fact. When he asked about the contrast, the Chinese referred to 'empty cannons of rhetoric.' There's a parallel, he suggested. 'I don't think rhetoric has any influence on what states do. They act out of self-interest.'"

from international newspapers. None of it critical to China but one gets a good feel from it as one does of the problems we are up against from the Xinhua News.

October 24.[62] "All school-age children in the mountainside Yan Zhen people's commune in East China's Fujian province are attending school. Before the Cultural Revolution only half of them attended." Great accomplishments in education. And yet we are not allowed to go into Peking University without some kind of special permit. One of our people was invited in by a student there but he wasn't able to go in—just walking in the gates of a great open university.

I am already struck by the contrast in China. The beauty in many ways. The courteous friendliness of the individuals with whom you do talk. The desire to please in many ways. And then that is contrasted with the basic closed society aspect of things. Lack of freedom. Discipline of people. Sending them off to communes. Little criticism. No freedom to criticize. There is a certain gray drabness amongst the people that makes one wonder how they could possibly be happy. Makes one wonder if there is real happiness there. And the incessant propaganda on radio and television and papers. The attack and criticism of Lin Biao and Confucius continues, and in reams of propaganda it goes on and on throughout this whole country every day.[63] Grilled into the people from top to bottom.

---

[62]Bush refers here to the date of the news article, not to the date of the diary entry. The image of him reading the piece while dictating his entry for the evening should remain with the reader, because it further suggests that Bush's journal was no spontaneous affair, but instead frequently the product of forethought. At the least, he often had the presence of mind to bring articles or news snippets that had caught his attention with him when making his diary entries—reminders perhaps of the issues he most wanted to discuss and record for later consideration.

[63]His fate and history still shrouded in controversy, Lin Biao became China's defense minister in 1959, and by 1969 he was Mao's designated successor. In September 1971, after allegedly plotting a coup, he perished in a plane crash while en route to the Soviet Union. The circumstances surrounding these events remain unclear. It is particularly uncertain what role Lin might have played in any growing opposition to the zealotry of the Cultural Revolution. What is clear is that op-

Incessant propaganda. It is cooled in terms of being anti–U.S. running dog, but the "imperialist" theme is still prominent and all of this makes me wonder what should our overall policy really be. What is right? Where do we go from here? How much movement can we make? And what is in our national interest? I was struck by a visitor from the linguistic exchange program who gave me this enormous pitch that we must normalize relations. We must get on with solving the Taiwan question. We must recognize that [the] Taiwan problem needs to be solved instantly. I asked him why and he said we must because we want to have more exchanges with your students and we want to know more about their language and we want to have their people come so we can exchange ideas. All of this is fine but there was a certain unreality to the pitch. Lack of recognition that in a quest to discover more about language he was prepared to forget any global political problems. Simply do things their way on Taiwan or anything else apparently. He did recognize in the conversation that they were putting on a show for him in a sense but he was so overawed with this getting his toe in the door of language that he was making this sincere pitch to totally move forward in terms of solution of the Taiwan problem.

Note. So much discussion of the people's army, people's revolution, people's thwarted aggression and imperialists. When I think of what really motivates the average citizen in the United States it is difficult to recognize that we are the imperialists and that we are the aggressors. My mind flashed back to the hot rhetoric at the United Nations. It's funny. I have been out of that for two years. And now I am back in it much more so than ever.

Note. North Koreans: "The U.S. imperialists must accept our just proposal on the conclusion of a peace agreement and must with-

---

position was indeed afoot—and that it was subsequently harshly repressed by the authorities. Lin himself became a public scapegoat for all of the regime's failings.

Confucius, the famed Chinese philosopher of the fifth century B.C.E., came under attack during the Cultural Revolution as well, his works repudiated in a campaign that mixed criticism of them with condemnation of Lin Biao, termed Pi-Lin Pi-Kong ("Criticize Lin [Biao], Criticize Confucius").

draw the U.S. imperialist aggressor troops occupying South Korea under the signboard of the United Nations forces." On and on it goes in Xinhua. Reporting from Cambodia: "Cambodian people in liberated areas overcome natural calamity" and then go on to blow up the fantastic accomplishments these people are allegedly making. In Xinhua "soaring profits in giant U.S. oil companies—Ecuador readjusts its prices posed by the U.S. monopolists." A discussion of a news story: "Canada opposed U.S. continental energy policy" showing that Nassikas and our oil monopolists Jamieson of Exxon and others were trying to ram a program down Canada's throat that Canada did not want.[64] A long explanation of how "many U.S. Western European banks go bankrupt or incur losses," and then talking of Lloyd's Bank and the Franklin Bank. Some attacks on Russia by the Albanians but of course we are thrown in. Then talk of China's own accomplishments.

[Monday,] October 28, 1974.   This is Veterans Day, a holiday in the United States and one here at USLO. We did have the signing of the archaeological exhibition in the Foreign Ministry, a major deal with ribboned copies, two of us sitting at the signing table as though we were signing a massive treaty.[65] The Deputy Foreign

[64]John Nassikas chaired the Federal Power Commission from 1969 to 1975. Canadian-born John Kenneth Jamieson was the chairman and chief executive officer of Exxon Corporation from 1969 to 1975.

[65]Supported by a grant from IBM, the "Exhibition of Archaeological Finds of the People's Republic of China" offered the first major exhibit of Chinese art and artifacts outside the country since World War II. Previously displayed in Paris, London, and Toronto, the exhibit received its first American showing in late 1974 in the National Gallery of Art in Washington, D.C. Kansas City and San Francisco subsequently hosted it before its return to China. It was at the time the largest single exhibit to have been housed in the National Gallery, its 385 objects viewed by over 680,000 visitors. More than 800,000 viewed the exhibit in San Francisco over an eight-week period. Longtime foreign policy pundit Joseph Alsop, no fan of Beijing, offered a lengthy artistic and political critique in the *Washington Post*. "Even in times of direst trouble," Alsop posited, "the Chinese have never ceased to be richly creative." As later entries demonstrate, Bush became increasingly uncomfortable with stipulations the Chinese imposed on the exhibit, including restrictions on media access.

Minister was present, a Mr. Yu Zhan.[66] He and Nancy Tang and several others were present.[67] Nancy did a good deal of the talking in the discussion that followed the actual signing. The Deputy Foreign Minister was in charge of Soviet Affairs and as he later told us had an interest in India. This was the first shot any of us had at talking to him. He was fairly responsive. He came down very hard on the Russians, including some rather unpleasant references to Brezhnev being dumb, etc.[68] On the whole though he couldn't have been more cordial and courteous to us. I tried to point out that nothing in the Kissinger trip to Moscow or India would in any way be detrimental to the interest of China nor would any of our foreign policy be designed to be detrimental to China. There is an interesting cable detail on this meeting.[69]

All in all it was a fairly encouraging meeting in that we visited for close to an hour in discussion with them. John Holdridge, Don Anderson and Brunson McKinley attended. Brunson very ably taking care in advance of the actual mechanics of signing. Don Anderson had worked very hard on the project. They made a great deal about it and they made some laughing references to the age of the thing, dating from Peking Man up till more recent times. The concern they felt about the Soviets came through over and over

[66]Yu Zhan had also previously negotiated with Soviet officials over their military installations along the countries' disputed border.

[67]The Brooklyn-born Wensheng "Nancy" Tang served as one of Mao's primary translators for most high-level discussions held with American officials, including those with Nixon. Her father had been working in New York as editor of a Communist newspaper, the *Overseas Chinese Daily,* at the time of her birth, a fact Kissinger could not easily ignore during his first trip to Beijing in 1971. She could become president of the United States, he informed Tang—something his own foreign birth precluded. Either's appeal to voters, of course, was another matter.

[68]Leonid Ilyich Brezhnev led the Soviet Union, in various official capacities, from 1964 until his death in 1982. Sino-Soviet divisions constituted one of the crucial geopolitical issues of the age, and they catalyzed Nixon's and Kissinger's overtures to Beijing as a means of countering Soviet strength. The literature on this topic is covered in detail in the bibliographic essay.

[69]Also present were Wang Yanqui, introduced to Bush as the director of the State Administrative Bureau of Museum and Archaeological Finds Data.

again in this meeting.[70] I am pressing to find things that are interesting, to extend the conversation, to urge that we have conversations about easy matters and difficult matters, but I get very little response. I asked one question: namely, whether they felt India was moving away from the Soviet Union or something of that nature.[71] And after the meeting Nancy told me, "You ask many questions. Next time we will get a chance to ask them." That was the only one I had asked but we did have a good frank exchange and I would hope that we can do more of that kind of thing.

In the afternoon I played tennis with John Burns of the Toronto paper and Urin Olifinish, a Finnish correspondent.[72] Not bad at all. We played on the New Zealand court. The courts looked slippery but the ball stayed in play pretty nicely. It slowed down very good. The only thing that is really bad is the visibility and of course the courts are very hard. Fall Peking weather persists. When the sun was up it was warm. But the minute it got low in the sky it became very cold, much colder than it looked just standing around there on the court. Back to USLO where some pouch mail had arrived. Mail that was supposed to have left about the same time we left the

[70]Vice Minister Yu later cautioned Bush, in words he immediately passed to Washington, "'The Soviets are not as honest or as frank as you' (my Chinese advisers tell me the word . . . might better be translated as 'naive'). 'If the Soviets seek détente it is sure to be at our expense and at yours as well.'"

[71]Vice Minister Yu noted that increasing influence in India "is the Russian policy, and has been ever since the days of the Czars. . . . [Yet] the warmth which the Indians feel for the Soviets has been on the decline recently." In his view, "it is therefore an opportune time for Dr. Kissinger to visit India."

[72]John Burns wrote for Toronto's *Globe and Mail* in China from 1971 to 1975, before leaving Beijing for a position with the *New York Times*. He returned to Beijing as the paper's bureau chief in 1985 and went on to win two Pulitzer Prizes. Chinese officials accused him of espionage the following year and expelled him from the country.

It is unclear who "Urin Olifinish" refers to, but the most likely candidate is Göran Leijonhufvud, a Swedish reporter for the Finnish daily newspaper *Helsingin Sanomat*, who reported from China throughout the 1970s. Leijonhufvud wrote an influential study of Mao in 1975, and then in 1990 published *Going against the Tide: On Dissent and Big-Character Posters in China* (London: Curzon Press, 1990).

States. Tons of stuff to sort through. I miss the order, having all the files in one place, but I guess we can get used to that. Bicycled to tennis and back and now about to bicycle to Brunson McKinley's for a movie. Not many blocks away. I am told that before too long it will be too cold to bicycle at all. It will be too bad. The fatigue has totally worn off now in that I am on full China schedule. It took a lot longer than I would have thought and I don't know how Kissinger and those real travelers shooing hither and yon do it without getting tired. I don't know quite how President Nixon and the others moved around Peking without being tired on their trip. The Chinese at the meeting today were like the others I have talked to about Nixon: giving him credit for the things he did and butting out of Watergate without commenting on the adversity of it.[73] A good day.

[Tuesday,] October 29[, 1974].   A cable came back from the State Department approving the plan to attend national days.[74]

[73]Chinese leaders consistently told Bush, and other American diplomats, that they did not consider Watergate important (and, implicitly, that they did not believe it warranted Nixon's removal from power). During a meeting during this last week of October 1974, for example, Nancy Tang told Bush that "we are not repeat not interested in Watergate, we never were, and we have specifically told you so."

[74]Because China and the United States did not enjoy official diplomatic relations during this period—a formality given the USLO's presence in Beijing, though an important one where issues of protocol were concerned—officials in Washington initially did not allow Bruce to attend the festivities various embassies hosted on their respective days of national celebration (such as July 4 for the Americans or July 14 for the French). As John Holdridge quipped, on an official pecking order in Beijing, at least when protocol was rigidly enforced, "we ranked just below the PLO [Palestine Liberation Organization] contingent." Bruce, as well versed in protocol and high-society norms as any American official, took his official status to heart and used his office's lack of formal diplomatic status as a rationale for keeping the low profile he considered best for this embryonic American presence in China.

From his first moments in China, on the other hand, Bush lobbied hard to have this ruling overturned, believing that a higher profile might help improve Sino-American relations. He also anticipated that his appearance at national celebrations would not only prove a warm gesture to each host country but also provide unparalleled opportunities to mingle with Chinese diplomats who, for reasons of

This may get some press attention but it will increase the mission contacts and increase the contacts with Chinese that the USLO has. It will probably be noted in the press as a change in policy or certainly as a change in style but our mission officers were unanimous

---

protocol, might not otherwise be willing or able to meet a representative without official ambassadorial status. As he explained to Congressman (and House Minority Leader) John Rhodes in a private letter from late November 1974, his "frustrations stem from a wholesale lack of information and the difficulty of engaging the Chinese in day-to-day substantive talks." Bush later recounted that, while not ideal, his visits to these national day celebrations could prove useful. "You'd get to see what they called a responsible person who was going to be the top guy representing China at the Hungarian National Day or whatever it was, and you'd get to say a few words with him, and sidle up to him."

While Bush later claimed to have "lobbied" and "consulted" with the State Department over this issue, the documentary record reveals he was much more unilateral in his decisionmaking. In Beijing less than forty-eight hours, Bush cabled the State Department that "after full discussion with a unanimously concurring top USLO staff, I have decided we should attend National Day diplomatic functions here." Doing so would increase the opportunity to meet diplomats from third-world countries in particular, he argued, and "there seems no longer to be any compelling reason not to do this, except the damage to our collective livers." He knew the decision went against precedent, but "I wanted to advise the department of my decision." Though Bush recorded in his diary approval from the State Department for his plan, the documentary record again suggests a more complicated dynamic. Whatever Foggy Bottom's initial response, Kissinger subsequently disagreed with Bush's plan to attend national day celebrations—and in fact most other diplomatic events. He cabled Bush in early November: "In light of your unique status in Peking, I believe you should not ask to attend any diplomatic functions. Instead, you should adhere to the procedure followed by David Bruce until I have a chance to discuss it with you." It appears Bush simply ignored this request, and indeed no record exists of the two men discussing the matter during the secretary's late November trip to Beijing. Bush and the USLO contingent continued to attend such celebrations as though Bush were in fact a recognized ambassador. Indeed, on November 11 he reminded Kissinger that "the facts are that we have about as much access to Chinese officials as any other non-socialist country and in some cases more. Our high level delegations have been given first rate treatment and access, and our cultural exchanges, with few exceptions, have proceeded very smoothly." In sum, Bush believed these personal contacts mattered, especially in an era when visible signs of progress in Sino-American relations were sometimes lacking. Believing that the perception of status and progress mattered as much as actual status and progress themselves, he simply determined

in thinking this was a good idea. And apparently the Department approves. Good first step.

I called on Tian Ping, the Deputy Director of the Consular Department.[75] Had lunch at home with some of the staff and that afternoon called on ambassador Ogawa, Japanese ambassador.[76] He is a friend of Taro Nakagowa.[77] Indeed he gave me a letter from Taro saying he was sorry to miss us. At five o'clock a good, rather wide-winging session with Qiao Guanhua reviewing principally the oil matters. The first day of rain in Peking. Fred got his third bath. Nancy Tang did the interpreting.[78] She is considered very, very good. Mao's niece, Wang Hairong, Vice Minister, was there.[79] She is very quiet and almost shy. Mr. Lin, Mr. Zhu and others with their eyes followed the conversation, smiled, nodded, entered in, but she sat very silently but obviously in a position of importance. Minister Zhu talked about giving us a dinner and he said that he and Miss Wang would host this dinner.

As we walked out of the meeting Mr. Zhu, head of protocol, said that the Minister [Qiao Guanhua] would like to have the dinner for

---

to act as though he and his mission belonged, regardless of Kissinger's and the State Department's concerns.

[75]The subject of the meeting was a contentious one: legal claims to property by Americans of Chinese heritage or their descendants who had left the country before 1949.

[76]Heishiro Ogawa left his position as president of Japan's Foreign Policy Training Institute to serve as his country's ambassador to China from 1972, when the two nations established formal diplomatic ties, until 1977. Before Ogawa's arrival, Japanese interests in China were represented by Kinkazu Saionji, who signed informal agreements between the two countries as Tokyo's "private ambassador."

[77]All efforts to identify "Taro Nakagowa" have proven fruitless, and as of 2007 Bush himself had no recollection of this person.

[78]Tang presumably performed translating duties for the meeting with Qiao Guanhua, not for C. Fred's bath.

[79]Wang Hairong, though frequently identified as Mao's niece, was in fact his mother's great grandniece. The head of Beijing's Protocol Department during Kissinger's and Nixon's initial visits to China, by the time Bush arrived she had been promoted to vice minister of foreign affairs. Bush would track her influence within China's government closely. See, for example, his entry of August 16, 1975.

us this coming Friday. I had impressed on him that I recognize how busy he was, that there was no need to do anything for us, that whatever was done I could most understand if he elected to do it down the road. He made a personal inquiry and told me that he had heard that my mother was upset that I was coming to China. I told him, "just the opposite." I told him she felt there was much more respectability to my being head of the Liaison Office in Peking as compared to being Chairman of the Party. He made some reference about Chairman Bush and I made the point that there was quite a difference being chairman of the Republican National Committee. I let my voice trail off. They all got the message and laughed like mad. He was very courteous and full of humor. Don Anderson told Qiao that I had started my Chinese lessons that day. At the end of the meeting I looked very serious and said I have one very serious personal favor to ask the Vice Minister. They all looked rather alarmed. I said, "When you meet my wife would you please tell her to stop laughing at me when I take my Chinese lesson." He told me this was a matter of great importance and that he would take care of it, laughing all the while.

I have been concerned by several ambassadors suggesting that our relations have deteriorated, and I made a point of telling Qiao that two ambassadors had raised this question with me. I also told him I wouldn't be here if I felt that the relations were going backwards and he told me that several people sometime ago had asked him about that but not recently. Qiao is the freest-swinging person that people deal with and all diplomats look forward to visiting with him. They feel they get more out of it. He pressed me very hard on the oil situation.[80] I must say that one doesn't have the chance to keep as fully informed as one should on questions of this nature.

[80]Bush made his business career, and his personal fortune, in the oil industry. Starting first in the oil fields of Midland and Odessa, Texas, he eventually moved his operations off shore, establishing in the mid-1950s the Zapata Off-Shore Company, based in Houston.

I did feel up to commenting on the domestic side of things however by frankly telling him that in response to his question that domestic measures had not worked in either increasing supply or in curtailing demand, but that after the elections progress would be made.[81] I sometimes think the Chinese don't realize the effect of our elections on congressional activity or inactivity. Why should they?

There is a little flu around in Peking. The rains settle the dust but there is still a kind of dust in the air. Smog. It gets colder after the rain. A wet, penetrating cold but no wind, thank heavens.

Wednesday, October 30[, 1974]. Today was marked by my meeting with Minister of Trade, Mr. Li Qiang.[82] It was a routine visit except we spent a great deal of time talking about the offshore oil business. He told me that they had bought one drilling rig from Japan capable of drilling in 20 meters of water. I then went back to the office and was shown a document showing purchases of many deep-water rigs. I can't believe that China has purchased this many rigs right now but certainly they are alleged to have tremendous potential. I tried to drag Mr. Li Qiang out to get him to be willing to discuss things in the future. He pointed out the answer "when necessary." I told him it would be good if he and some of his associates went to look at some of the offshore drilling business in the United States. He smiled but didn't respond. He asked some questions about my experience in offshore. It was like pulling teeth trying to get them to respond. I can understand their being wary about "imperialist domination" over their resources or imperialist ownership, but here was a minister reluctant to really have

---

[81]During this meeting Bush also expressed surprise that developing nations, in Africa in particular, had not pressured the oil-producing nations to reduce costs, lest their development suffer. He "wondered if the third world might not eventually split into the third and fourth worlds since there were such great differences in their interests."

[82]Li Qiang had been China's vice minister of foreign trade since 1952, during which time he had simultaneously served as a counselor in Beijing's embassy in Moscow from 1952 to 1955. He was minister of foreign trade from 1973 to 1981.

a good frank dialogue at all. I must confess it is very, very frustrating. I will keep trying.[83]

Wednesday afternoon Bar and I cycled down to a shopping area several blocks from the railroad station. We were the only foreigners around and we were stared at constantly. At one point we were followed by a rather pleasant-looking, Chinese-looking woman who literally "shadowed" us. We would turn around in a store and there she would be. We followed on down the block, I would look quickly around and there she was. What the hell she was doing I don't know. I bought a red drum and some bicycle covers without speaking one word of English. Through hand signals we made our will known. And the people were very pleasant—all being able to write down in Arabic numbers the price when we inquired about an item. Weather a little cooler and windy but very pleasant for bicycling. A little flu took a 24-hour spin through USLO. John Holdridge and Brunson McKinley were both down but snapped back quickly. The inspectors are coming soon and there is considerable consternation about that.[84] I have a little concern that we are not let known about the change in dates on the announcement of the Secretary's [Kissinger's] trip. I sent a telegram to ask about it. It will be interesting to see what the reaction is.

The Department acted favorably on my move to have USLO people attend national day receptions in order to increase our contacts with both the Chinese and the representatives of the diplomatic corps. Algeria will be the first of what I am sure will be a long and seemingly endless series of national days. Dinner alone. Early

[83]"Li was cordial and relaxed," Bush cabled Washington, "but generally unsubstantive in remarks."

[84]Bush's post was scheduled for a routine review by a team headed by Ambassador Edward G. Clark, a career foreign service officer who had served as Washington's representative in Mali and Senegal. The inspectors offered two major recommendations: that the USLO undertake "specific measures to improve our knowledge of the Chinese economy" and also investigate the impact of American investment in Taiwan, which "may appear to the PRC as incompatible with normalization."

to bed, troubled by the VOA report that President Nixon is in critical condition.[85] I remember my last two phone calls with him, the only two I had since he left the White House. I felt I was talking to a man who wanted to die. Here we are in China largely because of him, and the whole damn thing is sorry.[86]

[Thursday,] October 31[, 1974].   Listened eagerly to the VOA [Voice of America] at seven to find out how President Nixon was getting along. Yesterday the communicators told me that they had heard that he was critical. We got some evening report that confirmed this. Our communicators in Peking also listened to the round-by-round broadcast on the Ali-Foreman fight, hearing it very clearly.[87] Even though we get broadcasts and good cable service it is funny how fast one gets out of touch. I find myself avidly reading the wireless file on questions from press conferences. I read them much more closely here than I did at home. I even sat and listened to a twenty-minute speech by [the] Secretary of State given in India. In calling on Zhou Qiuye, Vice President of Chinese Peoples' Institute of Foreign Travel, I made the point that if the reg-

[85]Nixon suffered physically in the months after his resignation, and he underwent a surgical procedure in late October 1974 to treat a blood clot in his leg. Complications from the surgery demanded a two-week hospital stay, during which time he lost a reported fifteen pounds, while suffering from the depression that plagued him throughout his life.

[86]It is unclear here if the "we" to which Bush refers is the United States or his family. Clearly Bush would not personally have been in China had it not been for Nixon and, arguably, for the president's having precipitated the Watergate crisis, which demanded the reshuffling of roles that ultimately saw Bush accept the USLO post. Given the positive tone of the entry, the former interpretation appears more likely. While almost invariably loyal—arguably to a fault—Bush was not always so positive in his consideration of Nixon. His diary entry recounting Nixon's resignation in 1974 pondered: "One couldn't help but look at the family and the whole thing and think of his accomplishments and then think of the shame and wonder what kind of man is this really. No morality—kicking his friends in all those tapes—all of them. Gratuitous abuse. Caring for no one and yet doing so much."

[87]Muhammad Ali regained his heavyweight title in an eight-round decision in this, the famed "Rumble in the Jungle" held in Zaire.

ular organizations are bypassed and the far-outs get a disproportionate amount of travel to China, this will adversely affect the overall policy.[88] Mr. Zhou, a delightful, pleasant man who believes in "frankness," indicated that this did not come under the heading of his business. It will be interesting to see whether some other official raises the question with me. I feel strongly about this in terms of our overall policy.

Note. Our Double Happiness [ping-pong] table, solid as the rock of Gibraltar, is now located in the dining room. I had said to put it crosswise but Mr. Ye and Mr. Zhang felt it should be put lengthwise so that you could get way back and knock the hell out of it I guess.[89]

Called on Peter Kasanda, the Zambian Chargé.[90] The Africans are extremely pleased when one shows attention. He is a friend of Vernon Mwanga, the Foreign Minister of Zambia, and Mwanga had told him on the phone that we would be coming.[91] He seemed shocked that I had come to call on him. I am convinced that one way to learn more about China is through the Africans and their royalty, when their chiefs come here, and then they have a very close-knit society amongst themselves. He told me there is a good Sudanese here because of my relationship with Khalid.[92] I want to especially look him up. We have also decided that our first attendance at a national day observance will be Algeria. This will be getting some notoriety. The Kuwait chargé, Al Yagout, was the first caller at the residence.

---

[88]Zhou was in fact the vice president of the Chinese People's Institute of Foreign Affairs. He later served as ambassador to Australia and Yugoslavia. Bush refers here to Beijing's invitation to "friendship" groups from abroad, some of whose political leanings were far from Bush's own. See, for example, his entry for July 15, 1975.

[89]Ye and Zhang were two additional members of the USLO's house staff.

[90]Kasanda later served as Zambia's official representative to the United Nations.

[91]See Bush's entry and my footnote for March 10, 1975.

[92]Dr. Mansour Khalid was Sudan's foreign minister from 1971 to 1975 and again from 1977 to 1979. He was also a frequent participant in United Nations affairs, having worked sporadically for the organization since the late 1950s.

42

Weather got cold—clear skies. Halloween Party for USLO children.

[Friday,] **November 1[, 1974].**   Day was crystal clear and beautiful. Getting colder though. I called on the Pakistani ambassador, Mr. Mumtaz Ali Alvie.[93] Had a nice visit with him about recognizing Pakistan's special role with the Chinese.[94] He had traded places with our friend Agha Shahi.[95] Ambassador Alvie: somewhat formal, rotund, pleasant, seemed pleased that I had come around to call on him so early. He asked if I was going to go to national day receptions. I told him "yes." He commented that that was good, that no one saw Ambassador Bruce much, and that he felt this had worked against the United States, that we had not gone. I told him that each person should do his own ways, that Bruce was one of our most respected ambassadors and that perhaps he needed the contacts less than I. The subject was dropped.

The house is coming along. Getting settled though we lack pictures and tabletop things. The inspectors are coming in tonight and the post is in an uproar. Not being foreign service, I am perhaps less concerned or sensitive than I should be on these matters. I met Ambassador Clark and one of his associates in Washington and reviewed their mission a little bit.[96] This afternoon I called on Mr. Zhou Qiuye, the head of the Friendship Association. I had made the point with Mr. Zhou—who handles a lot of delegations—

[93]Alvie was also a ranking member of Pakistan's Foreign Ministry, having been director general of the ministry and ambassador to the Netherlands, Czechoslovakia, and Poland.

[94]Pakistani-Chinese relations had warmed throughout the 1960s, especially following the Sino-Indian border war of 1962. Beijing had supplied arms and ammunition to the Pakistanis during the 1971 Indo-Pakistani war. Moreover, Pakistan was in some sense the initial doorway to the wider world for the Beijing regime, before and during the Cultural Revolution, as it was Pakistan that provided the first direct airline service between the PRC and a non-Communist nation.

[95]Shahi was Pakistan's permanent representative to the United Nations during Bush's tenure in New York.

[96]Edward G. Clark, head of the State Department's inspection team.

yesterday that the Chinese ought not to rely too heavily on friendship groups in the United States. It hurt the policy. Mr. Zhou apparently was awaiting my initiative on this, and Brunson and I both
agreed that he anticipated my raising it. I didn't raise it directly but
I did ask about his jurisdiction and through using the example of
the Japanese I asked if the Japanese friendship groups were com-
patible with the Japanese government. He said not always. I then
inquired if it wouldn't hurt their relations with Japan if they dealt
exclusively with the friendship groups. He said that that is true but
that they didn't plan to deal exclusively with friendship groups or
any other one group. He got the message I am sure.[97]

We went to our first national day reception. It happened to be
the Algerian. The Holdridges and ourselves walked in together and
the Algerian ambassador looked like he was going to fall over in a
dead faint when he saw us arrive. The affair was very formal. After the guests had come in, the Chinese guests and the Algerian host
took overstuffed chairs at one end of the room. The ambassadorial
corps kind of formed in the room, milling around eating lavish hors
d'oeuvres. At the other end of the room were table after table at
which the Chinese guests gathered around and ate and ate and ate.
The only people that visit with the Chinese officials are the foreign
minister and other Algerians. And this was interrupted only by long
interpreted speeches that went on too long and bored the hell out
of everybody. There was a great deal of comment by other ambassadors about our being there. I met many ambassadors there including the Soviet, Polish, Romanian, several Africans. The Europeans all sought me out and told me they thought the change in policy
was a very good one.[98]

[97]Though Zhou refused to engage the issue directly during this meeting, the
USLO reported home that "a full report will probably be made" to higher-ups.
"Just to be sure, Mr. Bush intends to make similar remarks in his call on the Chinese People's Association for Friendship with Foreign Countries November 1."
[98]The national day celebrations did not always prove a useful venue for encountering high-ranking Chinese officials. Typically, Bush later recounted, "you'd
have about 50 Chinese guys who came in and ate the whole time standing there—

I then came home, formed in a big group and about 14 strong from the US Mission went off to one of the guest houses where Qiao Guanhua gave us a beautiful banquet. We sat in overstuffed chairs in the reception room to start with where we had a chance to discuss some things with substance. He raised the question of oil and we discussed that.[99] He thinks I am a bigger oil expert than I am. We also discussed Kissinger's trip. World Food Conference in which he didn't seem to have too many disagreements. We both felt that they should expand supply. And he expressed his concern about Tanaka and Japan, making the point that the Right and Left are equally as bad, referring to Sukarno and the communist revisionist left.[100] The atmospherics were great. He opened his tunic at the end of the meal and leaned back. Instead of giving a standing toast, he made the point of giving a sitting toast and I made the point of trying to leave fairly early to try to keep the atmosphere informal. I had the distinct feeling that Huang Zhen might have told him about the way we threw the oysters in the middle of the table in Washington because they had a lovely mixing pot of all

---

peasants and cab drivers or whatever the hell else they were, and only a few people that were with the foreign office."

[99]Kissinger, ever capable of finding a geopolitical silver lining even in the midst of a broad financial downturn, found Qiao's repeated discussion of oil to be particularly revealing. "Their public backing on the oil weapon notwithstanding," he responded in a private telegram to Bush, "the Chinese are clearly concerned about the implications for them of an economic unraveling of the US, Europe, and Japan, and the concomitant rise in relative Soviet power. . . . If Qiao raises these issues again, you should make clear that I will be prepared to go into them in depth during my forthcoming visit."

[100]Kakuei Tanaka, prime minister of Japan from 1972 to 1974, numbered among his achievements in office the establishment of formal diplomatic relations between his country and China in 1972. The leftist (and periodically Communist) Sukarno ruled Indonesia from its independence in 1945 until his deposal in 1965; during this time he made positive relations with Beijing and equitable treatment of Indonesia's ethnic Chinese minority a priority. The anti-Communist backlash that occurred following his violent removal from power manifested itself in anti-Chinese sentiments, resulting in wholesale attacks on ethnic Chinese and the ransacking of the Chinese embassy.

kinds of Chinese delicacies and flavors where people get up and hold their meat or fish or chicken in this common kettle of water, cooking all the ingredients and turning in the end into a wonderful soup. The dish had a way of relaxing people and getting them together in an informal way. There was plenty of wine, plenty of mao-tai, and plenty of frank conversation.[101] I made the point for example that we got attacked an awful lot at these international conferences when we really went there to help. I liked the tone of the meeting. Qiao's wife was charming.[102] She told Bar she had been to the States five times—UN. She had almost a western-style hairdo and was very very pretty. Qiao kidded Bar, telling her not to laugh at me during my Chinese lessons. And once he referred to her as Barbara during his toast. I thanked him as effusively as I could at the end of the meeting and he told me we would want to have a nice banquet for you anyway, but I wanted to especially repay you for your hospitality to me at your mother's home, referring to the time when he and Huang Hua came out to mother's in Greenwich that informal Sunday.[103] It is wonderful how he remembers. The entrance to the guest house when we drove in was a real contrast to some of the rest of Peking. Beautiful, well kept, plenty of greenery. It was apparently the old Austria-Hungary legation where we had the dinner.

The next day Holdridge, Anderson, Brunson and I went to call on Deng Xiaoping.[104] He was a very short man. We went to the

[101]Maotai, a high-alcohol Chinese liquor distilled from sorghum, was an omnipresent feature of diplomatic functions in Beijing and one of Bush's frequent libations during his tenure at the USLO.

[102]Zhang Hanzhi was deputy head of the Asian Department of the Ministry of Foreign Affairs and deputy representative to the United Nations.

[103]Bush frequently hosted diplomats at his mother's Connecticut home during his time as U.N. ambassador, finding it more relaxed than his official residence at the Waldorf-Astoria. He also made good use of his uncle's part-ownership of the New York Mets baseball team to secure prime tickets for further evenings of relaxed personal diplomacy.

[104]One of the most influential figures in modern Chinese history, Deng Xiaoping rose in postrevolutionary China to the positions of vice premier by 1954 and

Great Hall of the People and met in a room where Zhou Enlai apparently meets a lot of the people. As we walked in we were ushered over in the middle of the room for a picture. Holdridge and I were flanking the very short Deng. We then moved on into the reception room where we had a long good discussion with the Vice Premier. It lasted about an hour and a half. He gave us a lot of interesting agricultural statistics. We talked about world politics and a need for continued relationship. I gave him my thesis that there must be visible manifestations of progress for our China policy so it will avoid some of the hyper-microscopic analyses that we are getting on other policies in the States.[105] He touched briefly on Taiwan but I let it go by until our late November meeting. Deng seemed very much in control, clicking off minute agricultural population statistics, concerned about India, thought we hadn't done enough

---

general secretary of the Central Committee of the Chinese Communist Party by 1956. He was ousted from the PRC's ruling hierarchy during the Cultural Revolution. He returned to power and resumed his post as vice premier by 1973, only to be ousted yet again in April 1976. It would take Mao's death later that year to bring him back to power for good, and he subsequently initiated China's rapid modernization program, including a cautious embrace of Western tactics and nascent capitalism. Included in this push was the instigation of full diplomatic relations with the United States on January 1, 1979. His reforms led to difficulties throughout the 1980s, as conservative forces battled with more reform-minded groups for control of the country's future, culminating in the student protests of 1989 and the subsequent crackdown on dissent in Beijing and other Chinese cities. It was Deng who ultimately authorized PLA soldiers to use deadly force in removing the student protesters, and it was also he who, along with Bush and National Security Adviser Brent Scowcroft, helped orchestrate the survival of Sino-American relations in the aftermath of the crisis. When asked in 2005 if his personal relationship with Deng helped ease the crisis of 1989, Bush answered, "Had I not met the man, I think I would have been less convinced that we should keep relations with them going after Tiananmen Square."

[105]"Teng raised question of the state of U.S.-China relations," Bush cabled Washington, "and I elaborated on American political factors that argued strongly for some concrete signs of progress in our relationship as a result of the Secretary's forthcoming visit." From Deng's perspective, the Americans reported, "The essential thing is that both sides desire to move forward . . . but if conditions are not right, we are prepared to go slowly and wait."

at the time of the India-Pakistan war. I was too polite to ask them what they had done. Nancy Tang did the interpreting. Qiao Guanhua sitting to the left of Deng and Wang Hairong down from there. She is a very quiet little girl and it is believed she is put into this high position so she can be around all functions by Chairman Mao. She lacks the outgoing appeal of either Nancy Tang or Mrs. Qiao Guanhua. As we left, Deng left the door open for future visits though he indicated I would be seeing "others."[106]

[106]In addition to the official USLO telegrams covering this and other meetings during his first weeks in China, Bush also composed a lengthy message to Kissinger detailing his first impressions and outlining his strategy for the future, which included meeting as many Chinese officials as possible and traveling as widely as Chinese officials would allow. His letter, and Kissinger's response, highlight the tension between the two men that remained to be played out. Kissinger expressed concern at one aspect of Bush's discussions with the Chinese: his repeated suggestion that the American people would support improved Sino-American relations so long as progress continued to be apparent. "For tactical reasons related to forthcoming normalization discussions," Kissinger advised, "we don't want them to think that we don't have domestic problems or that we don't risk criticism if we give away too much on Taiwan. Also in fact we do face potential difficulties at home on this." Regarding the complexities of triangular diplomacy, he was less supportive, indeed hardly encouraging. "We should not be overly reassuring to the Chinese about our Soviet relationship," Kissinger wrote. "This requires very fine tuning and you will generally want to stay off this subject."

"Public Posture versus Private Understanding"

November 2 to November 21, 1974

*I*t *took Bush nearly a full month to complete his formal calls on Beijing's diplomatic corps and China's leadership. He remained optimistic that his personal style might yet win favor with the policymakers he met, though the initial enthusiasm of his arrival had clearly begun to fade. He worried incessantly about the state of Sino-American relations during these weeks, especially given Henry Kissinger's impending visit at the close of November. Kissinger would arrive directly from a Soviet-American summit in Vladivostok. Bush's time during November was consumed not only with preparations for the secretary's arrival but also with fending off queries from his diplomatic colleagues, who were eager to discern what the visit might entail. They were forever taking the pulse of Sino-American relations, Bush lamented in his diary—but then again so was he. "Many people here think our policy has deteriorated with China," Bush related to his diary. "I don't think so. . . . How far we move ahead will depend on events in the next few months, but to say that the policy is deteriorated or gone backwards is simply not accurate, and yet it seems to be becoming the sophisticated thing to say."*

As the diary and the cables he sent back to Washington clearly show, it was during this period that Bush became firmly convinced that some positive sign was needed to demonstrate progress, to show the world that the two powers were indeed on the right path to solving their problems and normalizing their relations. Just what that positive step might be, without yielding too much to Beijing, he did not yet know. The cables are most revealing for the understanding they offer of Bush's political approach to diplomacy and of his penchant for synchronizing rhetoric and policy.

Bush also entertained several visiting delegations from the United States during these weeks, as well as a routine State Department inspection team. He experienced firsthand the frequent civilian critique of the slow pace of Sino-American relations, which he so deeply feared. Many found fault with Washington's policies, though he had little patience for their complaints. "One should stand up for his country and make damn sure the Chinese understand the workings of the country," he told his journal. "But groups persist in feeling that they can solve all the diplomatic problems if only they are left out of the clutches of the U.S. Government."

Bush's November was a period of work touched by the first frustrations with his difficult assignment. Most vexing was the disconnect he perceived between official public Chinese criticisms of American policy—which he subsequently termed "cannons of rhetoric" in a nod to the phrase his Chinese hosts frequently employed—and the more conciliatory tone he repeatedly heard when speaking privately with Chinese officials. This disconnect simply made little sense to Bush, who feared the impact of such harsh Chinese language on American public opinion, and in turn on Washington's freedom of action in the diplomatic arena. "They [Chinese policymakers] don't realize that this eventually will not help our policy at all. They must feel that they must make brownie points with the Third World and we will understand. But if Americans focused on what they were saying they wouldn't understand, unless they were in on all the policy decisions. They ought to knock it off but they don't seem to want to." This disparity between rhetoric and policy, which Bush disdained in favor of a more open style of diplomacy, would befuddle him throughout his entire time in Beijing.

[**Saturday, November 2, 1974.**]   Had lunch at home for the inspectors who are visiting at the residence.[1] Excellent, multicourse meal. Followed by a walking tour of the spectacular Forbidden City. Blanche Anderson took us first to the top of the Peking Hotel where one gets a vast sweeping view of the Forbidden City roofs giving an idea of the magnitude of the thing. The weather was delightfully warm. That evening we went to a dinner dance given by Akwei of Ghana. He apparently has been the leader in the diplomatic community for injecting a little sociability into the diplomatic community via dancing. He has a hi-fi set rigged up, a table overflowing with Western food, a young son whose eyes sparkled and who did a little dancing himself and seemed like one of our kids when asked to run the tape recorder or something. A charming, vivacious wife, and a lot of friends. The party was a going-away party for the Austrian ambassador who keeps bitching to Barbara about how bad things are here and for Makonnen of Ethiopia who is going back to a very uncertain fate.[2] I asked him about another Makonnen who was my colleague at the UN and then Prime Minister.[3] He indicated that he was in serious trouble. Holdridge fears that this Makonnen may meet the same fate.

Sunday, November [3, 1974].   Went to the church service again. Total in parish was 20 (maximum). We came back and then on a beautiful, warm sunny day went to the Great Wall in two trucks.

[1]See Bush's entry for October 30, 1974.

[2]Dr. Franz Helmut Leitner, previously his nation's representative in Japan and Canada, was Austria's ambassador to China. His complaints left an impression on Bush, who returned to them in the diary in his March 21, 1975, entry. Makonnen Kebret was Ethiopia's first ambassador to China and served from 1971 to 1974.

[3]Endalkachew Makonnen, the last imperial prime minister appointed by Ethiopian emperor Haile Selassie, served in that post from February until July 1974. He had previously been Ethiopia's ambassador to the United Kingdom and his country's representative to the United Nations during Bush's own tenure in New York. Makonnen lost his life in November of that year following a military coup that removed Selassie from power.

A hazardous ride, unbelievable. Going around blind curves. Honking like mad. Pushing pony carts and various forms of decrepit-looking vehicles off to the side. We climbed to the top of the left-hand side of the wall. A real workout, tough on the legs, but exhilarating when one gets through. We had been told that it might be windy and very very viciously cold but it was neither. We must have hit a lucky day. It is hard to describe the spectacle of the wall. I can just hear a whole bunch of coolies sitting around and the foreman coming and saying to them, "Men, we got a new project. We are going to build a wall, yep—2,000 miles. OK, lets hear it for the engineers. Let's get going on the job." What a fantastic undertaking. We then drove down and had a picnic near one of the tombs. All by ourselves in a courtyard. The sun was out. I sat in my shirtsleeves and we ate a delicious picnic. A kind of a sweet and sour fish. Excellent fried chicken. Lots of hard boiled eggs. The inevitable tasty soup. The only thing we forgot was ice so the beer was warm, but we had worked hard enough walking up to the top so that we devoured about six bottles of it. It's a heavy beer and I find it makes me sleepy but it's awful good. We then went to the Dingling Tomb and looked around there.[4] Plenty of exercise climbing up and down. When we got home at about 5 o'clock I totally collapsed. Took a hot bath and fell asleep till 8, almost as though drugged. We got up and had a dinner consisting of a vodka martini and caviar—great dinner. Caviar—they have a big shipment of caviar into the Friendship Store.[5] It is very good caviar and it is cheap—something like 3 ounces for one yuan. We bought several pounds of the stuff and froze it. I understand it is OK if you defrost it once. There is time to do some reading here but not as much as

---

[4]The Dingling Tomb is one of the thirteen royal tombs of the emperors of the Ming Dynasty. These royal tombs, often called the Ming Tombs, remain among Beijing's most popular tourist attractions.

[5]State-owned, China's Friendship Stores offered imported goods and luxury items to foreign diplomats and visitors as well as privileged Chinese officials and selected Chinese citizens with access to foreign currencies.

I thought there would be. I think I have finished most of the important Chinese calls now and Monday we will concentrate more on the diplomatic community.

Friday, November [1], we went to the Algerian reception. The first time Americans had attended a diplomatic reception here. It was the talk of the town. The Algerian ambassador looked like he was going to collapse. And at the Akwei party this was the subject. Called on the Romanian ambassador. Took my language lessons. Called on the Egyptian ambassador.[6] Then had a fascinating visit with Zhu Muzhi, Director of the New China News Agency [the Xinhua News Agency or NCNA].[7] In my discussion with the head of the New China News Agency he mentioned the fact that he had visited with Wes Gallagher in New York.[8] I asked him where Wes Gallagher's proposal stood to get wire service people in China. He completely stonewalled me. It is amazing how you can ask a question and get no response whatsoever—just move on to some other topic—even something as obvious as talking about the weather. I also tried to make a point about getting some good entertainer like Bob Hope into China so he can present a favorable side of China for the United States mass market.[9] This point was not clear to the head of the NCNA either, because he started talking about "Well, we've had acrobats and others travel to the United States, etc." They simply do not understand what I was talking about when I talked about a Hope special, something like the one he did in Russia where he went and did a program with the humor self-deprecating but not against the existing regime and something

[6]Egypt's ambassador, Salah El-Abd, who had previously served in India, retired at the conclusion of his tour in Beijing in 1976.

[7]Zhu directed the Xinhua News Agency from 1972 to 1977.

[8]Wesley Gallagher joined the AP News Service in 1937, rising to become its president and general manager before his retirement in 1976.

[9]Bob Hope, longtime American comedian and entertainer, whose inoffensive humor made him a favorite of American presidents and a frequent White House entertainer, died in 2003 at the age of 100.

that would be widely reviewed in the United States.[10] He did come back and thank me for the suggestions and hoped I would make other suggestions etc., but I gathered that we were just not on the same wavelength.

Note. I am impressed how everybody in China is on time for appointments. Our driver will circle the block so that he will pull up at exactly the appointed hour. When we went into the NCNA office, we were a few minutes late. We went upstairs and there was this horrible smell emerging from one of the latrines. It reminded me of my stop in the latrine at the Great Wall. They have a different standard on this than we do, although in the residence the baths and plumbing are excellent in my view. Water is hot, bathtubs are big.

I enjoyed my visit with the Egyptian ambassador in his tremendous house filled partially with furnishings from the King Farouk era.[11] He told me that some of the treasures were prized possessions of King Farouk. He [the ambassador] had been in Peking for six years. Expressed a really believable friendship for the United States and all in all I think we have a good contact here. The same is true for the Romanian. He speaks absolutely no English but because of Romania's special position I think they will prove to be good friends.[12] He is relatively young, active, told me he had been

[10]"We had a very successful trip to Russia," Hope deadpanned upon his return to the United States following his 1962 trip. "We made it back." Hope later recounted his travels in *I Owe Russia $1200*.

[11]Farouk I of Egypt was the country's penultimate royal leader. Overthrown in 1952, he died in exile in 1965.

[12]Romania and the People's Republic of China enjoyed a special relationship of sorts during this period, as leaders in Bucharest (especially Romanian president Nicolae Ceaușescu) sought closer ties with Beijing as a way to balance their frequently tense relationship with Moscow. Within the Soviet bloc only Romania and Albania retained party-to-party relations with the Chinese Communists following the Sino-Soviet split of the early 1960s, while only Romania, Albania, and Bulgaria refused to endorse the Kremlin's crackdown on the 1968 Czechoslovakian protests. Economic and political ties between China and Romania were accordingly strengthened in the 1970s, especially as Beijing curried favor with any Communist state willing to stand with it against Moscow's hegemonic aspirations. Trade between

sick, but all in all an attractive fellow. Some of the Eastern Europeans have a marvelous sense of humor. I can't quite get over yet
their serving cognac in the morning meeting. They did have a little
caviar with it. So who's to complain!

Note. I have been trying to have all the USLO families to luncheon. I think it's a good deal. We get to know them. One commented
to me that she had never seen the upstairs at USLO. It is private, it
is our residence, but in the final analysis it is government property
and I think it is well that they understand how we live here.

Note. Fred looks grayer, blacker now. He'll need a bath. We got
our first mail of any size. A great letter from Dorothy.[13] And one
from Herbie Walker.[14] God, news from home means a lot here. Inspectors are here. All during Ambassador Ed Clark's very good
presentation to our whole staff in the residence living room Fred
was eating on a half-destroyed rubber hamburger. I put him outside but he kept scratching to get in during the meeting to the
joy of a few USLOers in the back row. I am going to try to make
my way through the diplomatic corps in calls, although some who
are bitching about Peking really should not get a lot of attention. I
want to deal with those who can help us learn more. One of our
men had an incident at the Tombs yesterday. He was stopped by a

Beijing and Bucharest increased sevenfold during the 1970s, leading, as Bush
noted, to a privileged place for the Romanian ambassador in China during this
period. It is a telling statement of Bush's ingrained belief that he could win favor
through friendship that he offhandedly suggested the Romanian would prove a
"good friend"—in other words, a useful source of information and political aid—
on account of his special relationship with the Chinese. As he said in a later paragraph, "I want to deal with those who can help us learn more." And he believed
that, through friendship, he would.

[13]Dorothy Bush, born August 18, 1959, was the youngest child of George and
Barbara Bush. Her memoirs, *My Father, My President,* include a lengthy discussion of her own visit to China.

[14]George Herbert Walker Jr., one of Bush's three maternal uncles, was a co-
founder of and minority shareholder in the New York Mets organization and a
Wall Street investment banker who helped finance Bush's early investments in the
Texas oil business.

PLA man as he drove with his front wheels just past the line that says "no foreigners pass here." He had not intended to violate any laws. He was flagged down by a PLAer. He stopped "just over the line." A two-and-a-half-hour hassle followed when finally other officers arrived and he was permitted to leave after a thorough interrogation. Here he sits in the middle of a field being berated by PLAers. Not a happy arrangement. But it shows you the other side of the friendship, banquets and great decency. There is this other regimented, inflexible, unreasonable side. No question about it. Another example. I asked for a map for my office. Mo Morin gave one to one of the Chinese to put on a frame.[15] The carpenter came back and berated Morin saying that Taiwan was a different color from the rest of China and therefore the map was bad, etc.[16] This process went on for quite a while and Mo could do nothing but take it.

Tuesday, November 5[, 1974]. Election Day. I think back to the whole political climate during the last two years—my many predictions on *Today Show, CBS Morning News, Face the Nation, Issues and Answers, Meet the Press,* etc. about how we would do in the elections. Here it all is. I kept saying that Watergate will not have an effect but now the pardon and of course the economic situation seems to be the big issues.[17] I worry about my close friends. I wonder how we'll do. Soon we'll know.[18] I had a good visit with

[15]Emile F. Morin, the USLO's general services officer, was responsible for maintenance of the facilities and staff operations.

[16]Arguably the most sensitive political issue within the Sino-American relationship, Taiwan was to officials in Beijing wholly part of China; to paint it a separate color on a map, therefore, was to make a significant political statement regarding the island nation's sovereignty and autonomy.

[17]On September 8, 1974, President Ford pardoned Nixon for any crimes associated with Watergate.

[18]Angered by Watergate and the continuing conflict in Vietnam, and fearful of further unemployment and inflation, voters dealt the GOP a serious blow in 1974. In the House of Representatives, Democrats gained forty-nine seats, while in the Senate their gain was four.

the Sudanese Ambassador, Al Zainulabidin.[19] I couldn't help but raise the point that I had been in Khartoum and stayed with Curt Moore, the man who was killed.[20] We talked about the PLO [Palestine Liberation Organization]. I could see great discomfort on the part of the ambassador, but he shouldn't have misinterpreted the remark because there I was calling on him. I still feel we can get good information from some of these African ambassadors by getting out to see them. Lunch at John and Martha Holdridge's, a beautiful spread with endless Chinese dishes tastefully served. Henry Brandon and his attractive wife, journalists, are here.[21] I had my fourth or fifth Chinese language lesson and it is extremely difficult but oddly enough some of the sounds are beginning to click.

Beginning to get a few comments in on the forthcoming visit of the Secretary of State. I expect this place will be turned upside down. I got a nice letter from him in response to a letter I had written him inviting Nancy Kissinger to stay with us should she want to.[22] Several meetings with the inspectors. Ed Clark is a thorough, decent guy. Having had an embassy, he understands I am sure some of the problems. It is difficult to define what our function is here. How much leeway we think we should have. How much initiative we should take, etc. I am beginning to formulate some ideas on this.

[19]Dr. Abdelwahab Zainulabidin, who had been medically confined to his embassy during much of Bruce's tenure in Beijing.

[20]George Curtis Moore served as interim chargé d'affaires for the U.S. embassy in Sudan from 1972 until his abduction and subsequent execution by members of the Black September Organization (BSO) in March 1973. The terrorists took hostage a group that included Moore, U.S. ambassador to Sudan Cleo Noel, and Guy Eid, chargé d'affaires of the Belgian mission to Sudan. The BSO intended to use the hostages as bargaining chips to gain the release of Sirhan Sirhan, the Palestinian assassin of Robert Kennedy, as well as other prisoners held in Germany, Israel, and Jordan. The White House's refusal to negotiate with the terrorists sparked an acrimonious internal debate with the State Department, where some foreign service officers believed that the principled stance against such negotiations would place their lives in jeopardy in the event they were captured.

[21]Oscar Henry Brandon, chief American correspondent for the *Sunday Times* of London. His wife, Mabel, later became First Lady Nancy Reagan's social secretary.

[22]Nancy Kissinger, Henry Kissinger's second wife.

I know we should reach out more than we have reached out in the past, but clearly any of these decisions will be made by the secretary and, given the overall perspective he has, it is best that the really important ones be handled on that end. I feel relaxed about this and I think the whole thing is going to work. Weather—gray, sun breaking through, not cold, plenty of mail, lots of dictation. Days are full and go quickly. All those books I brought over here will remain unread, at least a lot of them will. End of November 5.

[Wednesday,] November 6[, 1974].   An anxious day on account of the elections. With the predictions becoming very clear after a phone call from Fred Zeder (interrupted) and a phone call from Dean Burch with Peter Roussel and Jennifer on the line.[23] Very clear. Heard every word both ways. Wiley Mayne went down along with others on the Judiciary.[24] Sandman, Maraziti, Dennis, Froehlich.[25] Wiley meaning something to me as a friend. It is so hard to assess things, to get the flavor, to keep in touch from this far out. The day was an interesting one with a discussion with Mr. Wang, head of CCPIT [China Council on the Promotion of International

[23]Fred Monroe Zeder II was director of the Office of Territorial Affairs in the U.S. Department of the Interior. Zeder was also a family friend, having been Prescott Bush's (George H. W.'s brother) roommate at the University of Michigan. He would eventually visit Bush in Beijing (after some initial complications over his visa) in the fall of 1975.

Dean Burch was counselor to the president for political affairs from February to December 1974. Burch later served as chief of staff in Bush's 1980 vice presidential campaign.

Peter Roussel, White House staff assistant to President Ford, had been Bush's press secretary during his tenure in Congress and his time at the United Nations. Roussel subsequently served in the Reagan White House as deputy press secretary. "Jennifer" is Jennifer Fitzgerald, Bush's secretary. See my footnote to Bush's entry for October 21, 1974.

[24]Wiley Mayne represented Iowa in the House of Representatives from 1967 to 1974.

[25]Charles Sandman represented New Jersey in the House from 1967 to 1974. Joseph Maraziti of New Jersey served a single term, from 1973 to 1974, as did Harold Froehlich of Wisconsin. David Dennis represented Indiana in the House from 1969 to 1974.

Trade], the trade man. Then a courtesy call with Ambassador Gódor of Hungary.[26] A very sad fellow. Politician from Hungary sent here not as a reward obviously. Discouraged. Disgruntled. No access, no travel. Declining trade. The only bright spot was the fact that he had a very pretty American-speaking interpreter.

The language lessons are taking on more dimension and I am gradually making some headway, but heavens it's tough. Wednesday afternoon off—after lunch with our security guards—we are trying to have everyone in the mission to lunch—we played a little tennis.[27] Still warm enough. And then went on the national day circuit. Going to Ambassador Tolstikov's USSR's national day in their palatial mission.[28] A total jam of cars. Mr. Guo our driver has ter-

[26]Ferenc Gódor represented Hungary in Beijing from 1970 to 1976. Budapest and Beijing maintained a frosty relationship during the 1970s. Chinese leaders had recoiled at Moscow's intervention in the 1968 Czechoslovakian uprising, fearing in particular the Kremlin's justification that it might intervene in a neighboring state to save a Communist revolution gone awry. Mao's government subsequently shunned those Soviet bloc governments, such as Hungary's, that supported Moscow's hard line. Indeed, although formal diplomatic ties remained, the Chinese and Hungarian Communist parties held no official meetings between 1970 and 1979. Much like the members of the Soviet delegation, Hungarian diplomats stationed in Beijing found their service more like life in a hostile state than a posting to a nominal ally.

[27]Unlike most American embassies, the USLO was not protected by United States Marines. A Marine contingent had been included when the office formally opened under Ambassador Bruce, but Chinese officials objected to this quartering of foreign troops in their capital, citing the history of injustices perpetrated by foreign troops on their soil, the Marines' penchant for exercising in formation (and in matching clothing, if not official uniforms), and their rambunctious bar, which had become a hotspot for the city's expatriate community. "This is another example of zenophobia [sic] and sensitivity over the 'Century of Humiliation,'" Bruce recorded in his diary. His USLO staff generally believed that such protests signaled Beijing's interest in keeping Sino-American relations on edge. In the event, the Marines were expelled in 1974, before Bush's arrival, and replaced by civilian security guards employed by the State Department.

[28]Moscow's embassy in Beijing was closed during the Cultural Revolution as a further sign of Sino-Soviet tension. Moscow initially chose Vladimir Stepakov to reopen its embassy in 1970, but ill health demanded his replacement by Vasily Sergeevich Tolstikov, formerly the Communist Party head in Leningrad.

rific eyes. He reminds me of Earl Bue in the Texas Commerce Garage. He can spot people coming miles away. There are all kinds of Russians around trying to get the cars out of this congested parking lot. I wandered around, spoke to Mr. Zhou and Mr. Li, the head of the Friendship Association. But the rest of it was seeking out other ambassadors from Africa, Eastern Europe and of course European. These things are deadly but I'm glad we are doing it. Stopped by yet another going-away party for Ambassador Makonnen to a fate unknown in Ethiopia. Sad hors d'oeuvres at the International Club. That kind of sameness to it all that makes me determined to do things differently when we do them. We showed our first movie, *Laura,* with the two Canadian journalists, Walker and Burns.[29] And the wives of Peter Kasanda and Bryce Harland and their kids. I asked Mrs. Kasanda if her kids like dogs. She said, "Oh, yes, she has a nice doggie," at which Fred came down the stairs and the girl burst into horrendous screams.

[Thursday,] November 7[, 1974].   Called on Zhuang Zedong who is the head of the physical culture and sports commission, a very famous ping-pong champion in China.[30] The minute I walked in I could tell I was in the presence of an athlete. He still had a bounce in his step, looked reasonably trim. We talked about different ping-pong grips and the visit was marred only by his giving me a long lecture about the reason for sports was to keep strong because of the million troops on the Northern border etc.[31] I like

[29]Most likely the 1944 film *Laura,* winner of the 1945 Academy Award for best cinematography.

[30]Zhuang Zedong was the men's singles world table tennis champion in 1961, 1963, and 1965. He also played an important role in 1971's famed "ping-pong diplomacy"—which signaled renewed possibilities for improved Sino-American relations—when, at the world championship games, he warmly greeted an American player who had mistakenly boarded the Chinese team's bus. "Take it easy," he told the Chinese team's official leader. "As the head of the delegation you may have concerns, but I am just a player. It doesn't matter."

[31]Sino-Soviet difficulties made this border among the tensest in the world, with both sides massing troops in the frequently barren Siberian wilderness. These troops

the man. I told him I was very interested in ping-pong. Like all athletes he warmed up to the subject. Told me how with attack shots when you are way back you use the upper part of your arm, when you are fairly close to the table you use the lower part of your arm and when you are in right next to the net you use the wrist. We talked a little bit about exchanges and then just visited on sports in general. Always with a slight political propaganda overtone.

The French Ambassador Manac'h who is leaving came to see me. He is a very seasoned diplomat. He spoke mostly in English, occasionally in French and I began to understand more. I should practice my French more. I know I could master it or at least understand everything he said. His thing is Sihanouk these days and thinks we are wrong on that. Language lessons once a day, five days a week. They are becoming more interesting. I am beginning to catch a little bit on tone. I am beginning to have a feel for it. I like it and Mrs. Tang is terrific. After lunch called on the Yemeni ambassador.[32] Reaching out to the smaller countries. Here was a guy who doesn't get around too much I guess. Very interested and I think appreciative of the fact that the head of the U.S mission came to see him. In any event he was very pleasant and I am glad I did it.

Good news. A memo has appeared saying there is a masseur. Only one yuan for a treatment of 30 minutes to an hour. The Jiaqing Lu House. I also ran into the wife of the ambassador from Denmark, Mrs. Paludan.[33] She has been to the man, and says he is

---

engaged in open (if fortunately limited) combat in March and August 1969. Chinese officials expected a Soviet attack at different times during the Cultural Revolution, and Bush's visit to the underground tunnels they constructed in Beijing (as well as other cities), in preparation for such an assault, are detailed below.

[32]It is unclear from the text if Bush called on the Arab Republic of Yemen's ambassador (Abdo Othman Mohamed) or the representative of the Democratic Republic of Yemen (Ali Saleh Moaward).

[33]J.A.W. Paludan, Danish ambassador to China and North Vietnam from 1972 to 1975, also served in East Africa and Iceland. Ann Paludan, a British diplomat before her marriage, published three works of Chinese history and art history following her time in Beijing.

great. My neck suddenly went out so everything is falling in line together. I visited with C. J. Wang and wife.[34] Dr. C. J. Wang is an
American businessman doing a lot of business. He impressed on me
the need for American businessmen to be patient. Several times his
clients packed up and were about to go to the airport. Wang talked
them into staying and sure enough they closed the deal. He has
done business with the Siresiree, Westinghouse Air Brake Company (ABCO), and several others. Dinner with the Andersons,
Paludans and several others etc. and a very attractive German
couple at a Mongolian restaurant where you throw all the ingredients into a sauce. Flop it out onto an open grill in the middle of the
room. Throw a raw egg on it, mix it all up and eat it. Fantastic. Ate
too much. End of November 7. Still not having heard from the elections. Feeling far away but very much at home. I asked what we
could do about Christmas for our Chinese people in the Mission.
Would they take a present. The answer is "no."

[Friday,] November 8[, 1974].   The first really cold day. The
wind wasn't up too much. But the cold really penetrated. I spent
an hour with Janus Paludan, the Danish Ambassador, in his brand-
new Danish embassy done by Danish architects. It is most attractive and compared most favorably to the standard of Soviet style
of some of the others. Many of the embassies were built when Russia was in its total glory here and they reflect the solid kind of a
look, which is not unattractive, but not as attractive as the Danish.
We went to a luncheon (a going-away) for the Austrian ambassador.[35] A disgruntled kind of man but very pleasant. Lunch was at
the New Zealanders' and it was highlighted by the toast. The Aus-

[34]A Shanghai native, Dr. Chao-Jen Wang left his position as director of the Pentagon's Office of Advanced Engineering in 1972 to pursue trade opportunities in
China through the International Corporation of America. He eventually rose to
become president of the company and was named to President Clinton's Export
Council in December 1994. His repeated appearances in Bush's diary throughout
1975 highlight the omnipresent desire for native Chinese contact among American corporations seeking entrée into this new market.
[35]Leitner was succeeded in early 1975 by Eduard Tschoep.

trian, a rather formal but friendly man, tried to describe his relationship with New Zealand. He talked about screwing his way through the earth to New Zealand. This brought out a tremendous guffaw from Richard Akwei, the diplomatic corps swinger apparently, and everybody else was in hysterics too. I am glad to know there is a ribald sense of humor in the diplomatic corps. It was too much and Bar could only think of Johnny Bush and what he would have done with that Austrian-accented toast with the man talking about screwing his way to New Zealand.[36]

In the afternoon visited with businessman Martin Klingenberg, a young man who just on his own set up contacts with the Chinese.[37] He is doing a fair amount of business for Baker Oil Tool and other companies here. The way he got the original contact was simply to call somebody he knew in Canada that he had read had contact with China. He went up and met him and the man liked him. Martin stayed with him and the next thing he knew he had been introduced to Huang Hua and the next thing he knew he had a visa to China. He's parlayed this into a pretty good business and now he has started on the same track to Cuba. One night out of the clear blue sky he gets a call from Canada from the Cubans there saying that they want him to come to Cuba to talk about trade. He is a young man from Oklahoma. He seems nice. And I was rather amazed. Had my first rubdown in China at the Jiaqing Lu Bath House. Not too clean, but not bad. Walked past a bunch of women fixing their toenails with a machine. And also standing up combing their hair. I wondered if I was in the right place. I was greeted at the door by a man who assured me that I was [in the right place] from the very outset though, and I walked back. He unlocked a private door and there proceeded 45 minutes of jujitsu. He is more of

[36]John Bush was George H. W. Bush's brother.
[37]Klingenberg headed the China Trade Association of Washington and attended the fall 1972 Canton Trade Fair, the second such fair in which American businesses participated. "I wasn't born on a China Clipper," he told one American reporter at the Fair, "yet we're the oldest organization for the promotion of Chinese trade." Others made this claim as well.

an osteopath than a rubber. But he was very good and the price for 45 minutes was 60 cents. I had neck and back problems, both of which are still there but both are better I think.

University presidents arrive today, but I am sure we will not see them until the end of the visit. So many groups come to China and think that if they see USLO they won't get to see the real China and that the Chinese would resent our government presence. So many also come here and apologize for their country and point out how China does things much better. I have compared notes with others and I think this is the wrong technique. One should stand up for his country and make damn sure the Chinese understand the workings of the country. But groups persist in feeling that they can solve all the diplomatic problems if only they are left out of the clutches of the U.S. Government. It is a rather fascinating, naive view. I am not sure the university presidents will have this, but I am anxious to see what their thoughts are. Jay Rockefeller and Granville Sawyer are supposedly in the group.[38]

Inspectors have been here. Ed Clark is a first-class fellow. There seems to be some lack of communication with PRCM [the People's Republic of China Mission in Washington] and the State Department but nothing too serious right now. China unloaded on us at the World Food Conference in spite of my tactful suggestions to both Qiao and Deng that this not happen. They don't realize that this eventually will not help our policy at all. They must feel that they must make brownie points with the Third World and we will understand. But if Americans focused on what they were saying they wouldn't understand, unless they were in on all the policy decisions. They ought to knock it off but they don't seem to want to.

Many people here think our policy has deteriorated with China. I don't think so. I am reading sophisticated stories out of Hong

[38]John David Rockefeller IV served as president of West Virginia Wesleyan College from 1973 to 1976, before serving as his state's governor (1977–85) and then senator (1985 to the present). Granville Sawyer served as president of Texas Southern University from 1968 to 1979.

Kong both by Greenway and Kingsbury Smith saying this.[39] But there was an overanticipation at the beginning and there are no signs of deterioration. How far we move ahead will depend on events in the next few months, but to say that the policy is deteriorated or gone backwards is simply not accurate, and yet it seems to be becoming the sophisticated thing to say. Trade is up, exchanges are back on track. True, the attacks on the U.S. are up, but permission to travel etc. for USLO is in good shape. And I am reasonably relaxed, though not totally so, about where things stand.[40] End of November 8.

[39]Journalist Hugh David Scott Greenway wrote foreign affairs pieces for the *Washington Post* from 1972 to 1978, including dispatches from Southeast Asia and Hong Kong. Howard Kingsbury Smith's journalistic career included stints as a leading reporter for CBS News and later as coanchor of the *ABC Evening News*. He was widely perceived as a particularly close ally (and sometime mouthpiece) of the Nixon White House. His access to Nixon was seriously curtailed, however, when in 1974 he joined the growing chorus of commentators calling for the president's resignation.

[40]This issue of press perception creating a difficult reality for Sino-American relations would trouble and intrigue the politically attuned Bush throughout his time in Beijing, far more than it concerned the geopolitically focused Kissinger. "I am increasingly concerned over the growing number of articles which are appearing in the press indicating that US-PRC relations are deteriorating," Bush advised Kissinger in a cable dated Nov. 11. "I can see no advantage to us in letting this impression of disillusionment go too far. The Chinese are not going to change their spots. . . . I also doubt that a Chinese sense of U.S. displeasure in these areas is likely to have any positive influence regarding the larger issues between our two governments. I suggest, therefore, that we consider an on-the-record interview or a clearly identifiable backgrounder in which we set the record straight." Kissinger immediately replied that "I have read your report on US-PRC relations and must say I do not share your concern about the articles that may have appeared indicating that US-PRC relations are deteriorating. You and I know this is not true, as do the Chinese; any effort either publicly or on background to set the record straight would probably be misread in Peking as excessive concern on our part, with possible consequences for my visit later this month. Therefore I strongly believe we should keep our cool and avoid any public or private display of concern." Of course, Kissinger was not wholly uninterested in domestic opinion as a force within international relations, if he could in turn use such domestic pressures (or fear thereof) for leverage with his fellow diplomats. "For tactical reasons," he wrote Bush in early November, "we don't want them to think that we don't have

November 9, [1974,] Saturday. Teddy Youde, the very knowledgeable British ambassador, came to call. Visited with inspectors.
Lunch with the staff. I am trying to have all the staff and most of
their families to lunch early in our tour here. We are almost through
it now, including all the security guards, code clerks. It is one big,
fairly close-knit group out here. Afternoon tennis in cold weather
pounding my back and neck. Playing with Akwei, a good Pakistani,
and an Indian. In the afternoon I read for two hours, something I
never did at home. There seems to be time for this but not as much
as I thought there would be. Dinner with the Kuwaiti Chargé
Qasim and his wife. Like so many they are very interested in the
United States. She spends two or three months there a year. Her
children, Arabs from Kuwait, go to Pakistani school and also go to
Chinese school in China. They speak Chinese fluently.

Sunday[, November 10, 1974]. All day in Tianjin with the
McKinleys. We did some shopping. The prices are amazing. $15,000
for a large yellow vase. The prices looked to me like they are put
way high. And the old looks very little different from the new. We
bought a few odds and ends, little kits, a bead-holding thing, but
mainly we looked around. We were the objects of curiosity. Large
crowds crowding in around the car. One woman as I opened the
door, had her nose stuck up against the glass. Didn't even notice
that I was there. She was so engrossed in looking into the car. Nancy
McKinley sitting there. The kids were friendly once you smiled at
them. But they just swarmed us. They swarmed so much that the
storekeepers would keep them out of the store while we were in
there. What a land of contrast. Driving down and back you see the
most unbelievable kinds of overloaded carts, overloaded bicycles,
no tractors, people out working with hoes, rake, leaf sweepers. The

---

domestic problems or that we don't risk criticism if we give away too much on
Taiwan. . . . You will recall that the purpose of my dinner talk with Chiao was to
put Chinese on notice to our problems and try to get some elbow room on Taiwan formulations."

baby horse running along free behind two horses or donkeys in harness. A hundred men by the side of the road loading by hand dirt onto one-wheeled, hand-pulled carts. Hazardous drive back from Tianjin in the evening. No lights of any kind. I once saw two lights coming at us and I thought I was coming near some town. But it was a truck coming our way. Cars turn the lights off as they approach each other. And it is really hazardous. Dark-clad figures are darting in and out of everything. There seems little for the people to do in a city like Tianjin. You wander around the streets looking into stores that have very little merchandise in them. The guide from the China Travel met us. A Mr. Liu took us to a first-class restaurant. We were hustled in typical style upstairs to the isolated room. The food was absolutely fantastic. Many many courses. Four of us ate with wine and the driver and the China travel guy for 37 yuan.

[Monday,] November 11[, 1974]. In looking over the international issue of *Newsweek* I noticed that we still have the same press problem. Speculating on the President Ford's trip to Vladivostok in *Newsweek,* there is a mischievous piece about the Vladivostok meeting upsetting the Chinese.[41] "No doubt the issue was raised privately when George Bush, the new head of the U.S. Liaison Office in Peking, saw Deputy Premier Teng Hsiao Ping [Deng Xiaoping] late last week. And American officials admit that even Henry Kissinger will receive less than an enthusiastic welcome when he arrives in Peking later this year. Says one Chinese, Premier Chou [Zhou Enlai] will certainly interrogate Kissinger closely during his forthcoming visit." The fact of the matter [is], Deng did not raise

[41]Ford met with Soviet leader Leonid Brezhnev in Vladivostok in late November, and their summit produced a communiqué on the Strategic Arms Limitation Treaty. Bush most likely refers to the critique of one unnamed "adviser to the Republican Congressional leadership," who argued that Ford was "bound to run into hostile demonstrations in Japan. He'll appear to be endorsing a repressive regime in South Korea. And by going to Vladivostok, he'll offend the Chinese who look upon that area as Russian only by virtue of aggression."

the matter. Our inquiries through other ambassadors show that the Vladivostok issue is not demonstratively sensitive.[42] Kissinger might not even see Zhou for substantive talks and all in all, the story is not accurate.[43]

Observations. Some groups want to come to China and don't want to see anybody at USLO, thinking this will compromise their ability to get the true facts on China from their host groups. One friendship or guardian group, leftist in the U.S., simply told Nancy McKinley, "You're from USLO. We don't want to have anything to do with you." Another incident. This leftist group at the Hong Kong border sat observing Ambassador Bruce taking pictures and then finally in a gesture of defiance sang "The Workers Internationale."[44] They looked like idiots but I guess because they are so disdained in the United States they felt here above all they could show their solidarity and put Bruce and others on the defensive.

One wonders how happy the families are. Yes, they are being fed. But what do they do? The workers along the Tianjin Highway look healthy. There is some running and playing and laughter. Plans are beginning for the Secretary's visit. It will be announced today. This place is beginning to stir. Diplomats have all been speculating on it for a long long time. And indeed I feel it has been leaked. Snow Sunday in Tianjin. And snow in Peking. A little on the ground but melting fast early Monday morning. There are not many laughs

[42] "The Chinese supposedly raised objections" to the Australian ambassador, Bush had reported to Washington the previous week. "While we have no clue what the Chinese may be thinking privately, at least they have chosen not to raise the matter directly with us."

[43] Press speculation continued to link the next tenuous steps in developing Sino-American relations with Ford's diplomatic overtures to Moscow. This public discussion of triangulation was not entirely unwelcome to Kissinger, who had long hoped to balance one Communist power against the other. See for example the way in which the *New York Times* first reported the dates of Kissinger's next trip to China: "The latest trip was clearly intended, in part, to assure the Chinese that Mr. Ford would not be acting against their best interests during his two-day visit with Mr. Brezhnev in Vladivostok."

[44] Bush refers to the "Internationale," the anthem of international socialism penned in 1870 by Eugène Pottier.

around here.[45] It is amazing how fast one gets out of touch with the details of the domestic scene in the United States. Sunday Mr. Liu, our travel agency guide, would not eat with us. He goes off and eats with Guo, the driver, in another room, leaving the McKinleys and Bushes in banquet-like splendor by ourselves.

The food is clearly the matrix between present and past. The restaurant in Tianjin was built as a restaurant well over 50 years ago. The proprietor obviously takes great pride in the food. It was fantastic. Painstakingly prepared obviously. And thoughtfully presented. The food doesn't seem to know any ideology nor have the ideologists insisted on changing the eating patterns.

Cabbages, cabbages everywhere. Getting ready to bring them in for storage. They are in the streets, in piles for markets, they are on trucks and bicycles—they are hanging stuffed out of grates in windows. A man walking along the street with cabbage stuffed out of one pocket and a big fish sticking out of the other. What would this society do in terms of conventional warfare? The roads are all bottlenecked. I expect all the oxcarts and people on bikes would be shoved to the side and then it would be OK for fast movement of men and equipment.

Observation. China is going to have to determine how much to attack us and how much not to. I have subtly made the point with Deng and Qiao—not so subtly as a matter of fact. But then at the World Food Conference there they go, "Colonialism, imperialism, superpowers—main cause of the world food [crisis] is long-term plunder by these."[46] In talking to the leadership I get the feeling

[45]The original transcription included quotation marks around this sentence.

[46]Bush may be referring here to comments made in March 1974 (or to later comments like them) by Xu Lichang, observer of the People's Republic of China to the Third Special Session of the Population Commission of the United Nations. "The fundamental reason why there are poverty and 'population' problems in some developing countries is the hegemonism, aggression and plunder perpetrated by imperialism, colonialism and neo-colonialism, especially the two superpowers." Despite such heated rhetoric, China (and the Soviet Union) declined to attend follow-up sessions of the United Nations–sponsored food conference held during the last weeks of 1974.

they feel the third [world] countries must increase their supplies. We told them we would be willing to help them on that but then there is the attack, exploitation, etc. Population in China seems to have a problem here. They talk about growth in certain areas. Publicly they take pride that their ability to handle increased population is because they have increased their agricultural output, but privately they do a pretty good job on population although the figure given me by Deng is 2 percent which isn't fantastic at all—given the big numbers we are dealing with.[47]

Dilemma. Public posture versus private understanding versus private position. Enormous complexity here, and something that eventually can get our policy in trouble or carry it a long, long way.

[Tuesday, November 12, 1974.][48] Continued the calls. We talked about overseas schools. Right now there are four kids projected for next year too.[49] It is hard to know. We can't get too high visibility with cooperative schools between other English-speaking nations because the Chinese would not want this. We can't use the International Club because they don't want to encourage this commencement of a separate educational institution. School is now held in John Holdridge's lobby to his apartment, taught by Holdridge's daughter and another kid who is an assistant.[50] The Norwegian ambassador had a little school built into his embassy complex. They have a teacher there for just two children. It is one of the prob-

---

[47]Bush comfortably discussed with Deng the use of widespread and arguably radical birth control methods to limit China's ever-growing population. "I mentioned new discoveries in birth control technology such as injections which bring about temporary sterility which in the future may provide the answer to birth control administration in rural areas," the USLO's report of Bush's initial conversation with Deng read. The Chinese leader replied, "We are not opposed to such new developments, and are working to develop new birth control methods ourselves." But the real problem, for China and India alike, Deng concluded, was not controlling population growth so much as ensuring sufficient grain production.

[48]The original text reads "November 11," but from the diplomatic record it appears this entry refers to the events of November 12.

[49]Bush refers here to the children of USLO staff and foreign service officers.

[50]Patricia Holdridge taught these courses.

lems we have got to solve. We have a teacher coming in for next year. It is the wife of one of our new people and perhaps she can handle it. Ambassador Pauls, German ambassador here—first ambassador to Israel, formerly in Washington, received me at his beautifully decorated mission.[51] Germany is fourth in trade, having been replaced by us. Japan, Hong Kong, U.S., Germany. Pauls' wife is unhappy here. Quite social. There is no question that it is a real adjustment. Pauls is one of their best diplomats. And he is interesting to talk to. The language lesson. I am intrigued with the tones but I am not making much headway. Lunch with the Danish, Anne and Janus Paludan, in their beautiful embassy. And then went to call on the Norwegian Ravne who was the deputy at the UN.[52] I am amazed at the UN contacts. First Peking duck dinner at the Sick Duck.[53] Guo took us to the Big Duck. We were received regally until we told them that we were Americans. Then they raced after Guo across the street in the cold, winter air, brought him back in. A couple of phone calls followed and we found we were at the wrong place. Holdridges were having a farewell dinner for the inspectors at the Sick Duck and it was beautifully served. Most attractive.

Big Question. How do you get balance between the critical stories that are coming out in Hong Kong, super critical, about the U.S. Mission not having access, etc. (there seems to be a large number of them right now) and the fact that we do want to see progress out of the Kissinger visit which was announced at 1 o'clock on the twelfth. And thus want the Chinese to know that we are not overly happy with things. Interesting dilemma.[54]

[51]Rolf Pauls was the Federal Republic of Germany's ambassador in Beijing from 1973 to 1976; he had been ambassador to the United States between 1969 and 1973.

[52]Per Ravne, Norwegian ambassador to China, North Korea, and North Vietnam from 1971 to 1975, had twice before worked in New York as part of his country's delegation to the United Nations.

[53]The Sick Duck was a restaurant named not for the quality of its food but for its location near a large Beijing hospital.

[54]See note for Bush's November 14, 1974 entry.

Tuesday, November 12. A call on the Swiss Ambassador, Natural.[55] At the last ambassadorial residence in downtown Peking. A delightful Chinese-style house, formerly owned by Mr. Shoemaker of the United States. It is filled with Chinese art objects and has a charm that is great. Language lessons—complexity of it all intrigues me. I can mimic Mrs. Tang's tones but I am not moving very fast. A visit with Peruvian ambassador in his apartment, used as an embassy.[56] Mr. Valdez seems pretty far to the left. Good English and a nice cordial man. The objectivity seems to have vanished however. Reception we had for two Chinese groups—the photosynthesis study and the pharmacological theory study group —both of the Chinese medical association, both heading for the United States. We are trying to have them come before they go and hopefully get them when they come back. It increases our contacts with the Chinese. And we may pick up tidbits from time to time. After that Barbara and I attended a banquet that the U.S. linguists were giving for their hosts, having completed their tour of China. It was at the Hunan Restaurant. Very nice. Many toasts etc. The linguists genuinely feel that the Chinese are doing a good job on language reform. Highly complex when you consider the numbers of dialects and the enormity of the population.

I continue to wonder about how big this USLO ought to be. Should we have an agricultural person here? I don't at this point feel that we need a military attaché, as at other embassies, because of Chinese sensitivity.[57]

[55]Albert-Louis Natural served Switzerland in Beijing from April 1972 until June 1975.

[56]Eduardo Valdez, Peru's ambassador to China from 1972 to 1974, was followed before Bush's own departure by Cesar Espejo-Romero, who served in Beijing until 1977.

[57]Ever concerned about the appearance of progress in Sino-American relations, Bush the next day suggested to Kissinger that perhaps the USLO delegation should be enlarged immediately following the secretary's impending visit, as announcement of even a relatively minor expansion at the conclusion of such high-level talks would be a "small but visible step" demonstrating continuing progress within the Sino-American relationship.

[Wednesday,] November 13, [1974]. The inspectors left. Called on ambassador of Netherlands, Vixseboxse.[58] Lunch with peppery, pushy, interesting Bryce Harland of New Zealand. He presses enormously for information. He is useful in telling us things. He is vitally interested in his work here in China. Young, enthusiastic, and terribly interested. Called on Vice Chairman Ding Guoyu of the Peking Revolutionary Committee.[59] He has the responsibilities of mayor plus the responsibilities for schools, embassies and many other things. He was very forthcoming. I was impressed with him. He looks confident, willing to discuss politics to a degree. And problems like pollution, traffic, subways, mass transit, etc. I want to see him again. And he indicated that would be OK with him. A quick bike ride. Muscles aching. Glad to get the exercise. And then a good meeting where we invited the university presidents. An hour before their hosts—the Chinese hosts—came, we had a good discussion with them. They are a most prestigious group and they seemed to enjoy it. I got John Holdridge to run down some of the policy matters. Don Anderson the same. All in all they assured me afterwards it was worth their while. They seem more realistic than the linguists. They were somewhat amazed at the lack of facilities in the physics labs. They wonder where we go from here. One wondered whether we couldn't have a quid pro quo. They [the Chinese] want things from us and we should only give them those things provided we get something in return. I used the example of the UN where we started off cautiously in our consultations and eventually we learned more from them. Good day. I am a little tired hustling from appointment to appointment but it wouldn't be forever. Got some mail and that sure makes a difference. End of November 13.

[58]Though a China and East Asia specialist, Jan Vixseboxse's long diplomatic career also included stints at the United Nations and, after his tour in Beijing, as ambassador to Italy between 1976 and 1981.

[59]Ding's committee oversaw the city's municipal development, and he and Bush primarily discussed those two omnipresent factors of modern life in Beijing: traffic and pollution. As vice chairman of Beijing's Revolutionary Committee, Ding was essentially Beijing's vice mayor.

Thursday, November 14[, 1974]. Called on Spanish and Yugoslavian ambassadors. Language lessons. Quiet lunch for a change. Interesting visit with the President of Kellogg, Mr. Latin.[60] They are building a petrochemical plant. Met a young couple, the Smiths, she from Rosenberg, Texas. They are about to head out for Southwest China. Fascinating mission. Living way out alone. If I were young I would like to be doing just that. Note the possibility exists that maybe one of our kids can go to Peking University to their international school. They would live there five days a week and get to come home on weekends. Neil or Marv might want to try it though I don't know if it would be right for them.[61] Farewell to Ambassador Leitner of Austria at his residence. Retiring, sad, glad to be leaving China, wondering what he did. What [do] all these people do in terms of real substance? But the diplomatic corps seems lively and pleasant. Qiao Guanhua was there. I thanked him for the banquet and told him I would like to have him over but it might be better to do it after the Kissinger trip. Went off to the banquet for the university presidents. An impressive group of eleven with nine of them presidents. Roger Heyns in charge.[62] Mr. Zhou Peiyuan is the Vice Chairman of the People's Institute for Foreign Affairs, a very distinguished gentleman who had been to the States

---

[60]M. W. Kellogg was an engineering firm specializing in petroleum drilling and production, based in Houston during this period. It later became part of Kellogg Brown & Root. In 1973 the firm signed a series of major contracts with Beijing, totaling more than $200 million (at the time the largest package of Chinese contracts awarded to an American firm), to construct eight fertilizer-processing plants in China. Though overruns and inflation nearly doubled the final cost of the plants, eroding profits, company officials in 1976 agreed to stand by the original terms of their deal with Beijing, hoping the decision would generate goodwill and follow-on deals. Chinese engineers who arrived in the United States for training at Kellogg's facilities in Texas and Oklahoma the following year were warmly greeted, though they were also advised, "No Mao suits in public."

[61]Neil and Marvin Bush, George H. W. Bush's third and fourth sons, respectively.

[62]Roger W. Heyns was chancellor of the University of California at Berkeley from 1965 to 1971.

years ago.[63] Gentleman is the proper word. We had a beautiful banquet at the Cheng Tu Restaurant.

Note. What can we do to make the Kissinger trip a success, to show progress, to show that things are moving ahead?[64]

Note. The policy matters are tightly held [by Kissinger]. I am wondering if it is good for our country to have as much individual diplomacy. Isn't the President best served if the important matters are handled by more than one person? End of November 14.

I have a lot of appointments, but not that many, and yet I am getting a little tired.

[Friday,] November 15[, 1974].   Now I can understand what people were trying to tell me about the weather. A light snow came down. But what was most noticeable was the icy cold. I called on the Minister of Public Health, Liu Xiangping, in a beautiful Chinese building near the lake, the north side of Peking.[65] It was ice cold. She greeted us wearing a big heavy overcoat. She took it off. Why, I don't know. The room was ice cold. I wolfed down about three cups of tea and that helped. She is an interesting lady, a member of the Central Committee. She gave me a good deal of the Party line at the outset and it was sticky going, but then we talked a little politics and talked about how the health ministry works both through the bureaucracy and through the party and it was very interesting. She warmed up considerably. I spent the morning talking

[63]Zhou Peiyuan was also a distinguished scientist and professor at Beijing University.

[64]Bush had only recently received Kissinger's reply to his concerns over press coverage of Sino-American progress (or lack thereof). See my footnote to the entry for November 8, 1974. "I strongly believe we should keep our cool," Kissinger advised. Bush responded in kind, writing Kissinger the following day, "We will give no interviews on or off the record. Unfounded speculation still persists on policy deterioration but USLO will stay calm and cool. I did not want to overstate the case, but felt you should be aware, as PRC officials are, of this speculative climate."

[65]"This was a pro-forma call," Bush reminded the State Department, "since USLO has minimal business with the Health Ministry." Bush did add that Liu was "solidly built mannish in appearance owing to short-cropped hair and strong features," though "her frequent laughter did not seem at all forced or nervous."

to Ambassador Tolstikov of the Soviet Union. Most interesting fellow but he is kind of isolated, living in this massive white marbled palace. There is no thaw there between the Soviet Union and China or if there is he damn sure hasn't been clued in on it. Language lessons continued. I do better alone. Hope Bar will get transferred out of the class. She wants to but I must say I am a little self-conscious.

Lunch with Governor and Mrs. Shapp of Pennsylvania.[66] He was here on a private visit. I gave him some old *Herald Tribunes* and I noticed that wonderful streak that we politicians have. He devoured it eagerly as we were talking. All about the elections and stuff. He and Bar went shopping. Visited with Gene Theroux and Sandy Randt of the NCUSCT [National Council for United States–China Trade] talking about trade with China.[67] They are finding it

[66]Milton J. Shapp, Democratic governor of Pennsylvania from 1971 to 1979.

[67]An international lawyer, Gene Theroux first visited China in July 1972 as a member of the entourage of U.S. Representative T. Hale Boggs of Louisiana, the House Majority Leader, and (then) Representative Gerald Ford of Michigan. Theroux was later placed in charge of his firm's first offices in Beijing and Shanghai. The congressional junket sparked a minor diplomatic firestorm when Ford and Boggs told reporters that Zhou Enlai desired a "continuing" American presence in East Asia, particularly as a means of precluding further Soviet influence. Both Moscow and Beijing vigorously disavowed such statements.

As Bush had earlier remarked, "everybody in the United States wants to go to China," and House members complained bitterly in 1972 when Nixon's White House arranged for the Senate leadership to visit Beijing but offered no such junkets for those from the lower chamber. It was "most unfortunate," Ford said, "that in such a major diplomatic effort a coequal branch of Congress was not included." House Speaker Carl Albert—who subsequently visited China during Bush's tenure at the USLO—reminded the White House that "cooperation is a two-way street," threatening "appropriate action" as retribution should the White House not be more vigorous in their pursuit of House invitations. Nixon's White House rebutted that any such invitations were China's to offer, not the president's. Beijing proffered just such an invitation to Boggs and Ford by the end of March. Boggs subsequently perished in an airplane crash in Alaska that November.

Clark T. "Sandy" Randt's experience in China included work at the Canton Trade Fair and as commercial attaché at the American Embassy in Beijing during the 1980s. He became Washington's ambassador to China in 2001.

The National Council for United States–China Trade, "a private organization based upon corporate memberships," was established in 1973 and subsequently sponsored trade delegations between the two countries.

difficult to get the Chinese to send a group to the United States as they agreed to do. They really feel it would help China sell more but it hasn't taken place.

Note. The pace here is much more than I thought it would be. I think after our calls it will calm down. The diplomatic calls are taking a lot of time and so have the protocol calls. Today Qiao Guanhua was named Foreign Minister. Very good as far as I personally am concerned and I think as far as the U.S. Government is concerned.[68] He is articulate, communicative, frank and all in all a good man. We are going to have a large turnover soon and this whole mission's character will be recast in six to eight months. It will be very interesting. End of November 15.

Saturday the sixteenth [November 16, 1974]. It is almost like school. Wednesday afternoon off, Saturday afternoons off. I look forward to them. Saturday the catch-up day. One call: the Egyptian ambassador came to call on me. Return call. It was rather deadly though. Everyone I call on feels he must come call on me. I received him in the den of the residence. Coffee and tea. It really is rather pleasant. Talk swung over to the Middle East, to Kissinger's visit, to the relations between China and the United States. Everyone is debating that. Most get the embassy gossip that the relations have deteriorated. There is a standard question in the diplomatic circles.[69]

---

[68]Contemporary analyses of Qiao's appointment as Chinese foreign minister include varied interpretations of whether the appointment signaled Zhou Enlai's continued control of foreign affairs or that Zhou—who was undergoing intensive treatments for the cancer that would take his life months later—had lost his de facto control over Chinese foreign policy. At the least, owing to his expertise in Western European and American affairs, the appointment of Qiao, head of the first PRC delegation to the United Nations, suggested a renewed Chinese commitment to strengthening relations with the West.

[69]Questions concerning the future of Sino-American relations dominated Washington political circles as well, as many in the United States continued to argue that, despite the diplomatic successes of Nixon and Kissinger, the honeymoon period in relations with Beijing was clearly at an end. As the influential columnist William Safire wrote during the same week as this diary entry from Bush, "The

Are the Chinese mad because Ford is meeting Brezhnev in Vladivostok?[70] Vladivostok with its history of antagonism between
China and Russia. The Soviet ambassador had told me that Russia
had changed the names of all its cities. He had assured me that the
Chinese were probably sore about Vladivostok but allowed that
"no Chinese had told me that." The Egyptian raised a question. I
asked him if anyone had told him they were sore—any Chinese official had told him the Chinese were upset—and he said "no." He
had heard it in the diplomatic community. This is true for almost
every ambassador I have talked to. There is a story out now by Wallach of Hearst papers saying that Kissinger had told him that
Kissinger presumably had checked this out with Huang Zhen as to
the meeting place.[71] I wouldn't be surprised.[72]

In the afternoon took a long trip past the Forbidden City, near
the drum tower on bicycles, a long, flat, cool but pleasant bike ride.
You see more color in Peking when you've been here a while. You
look for it. Child's scarf. A flower. Whatever. The walls along the
streets are gray and everything remains gray but there is color. The
contrasts are enormous. There will be a waft of marvelous odors
from cooking and then a few yards further some horrendous stench

---

Chinese-Soviet split was our once-in-a-lifetime opportunity, and we made the most
of it; we are hurrying now to get the most leverage before the opening really begins
to close."

[70]Bush reported the previous week that, in all the meetings USLO officials (himself included) had held with the Chinese, "there is no hint . . . [that] the Chinese
are unhappy about the Vladivostok site."

[71]John Wallach, an award-winning foreign correspondent, was credited with
breaking major parts of the Iran-Contra scandal. Kissinger spoke at Wallach's funeral in 2002.

[72]Wary of a Soviet-American rapprochement, Chinese officials ultimately down-
played the Vladivostok summit in their own media reports—though, significantly,
they did report it. The Xinhua news bulletin for the summit's final day made only
the briefest mention of its occurrence, listing the event sixteenth out of twenty-
two international news items for the day. Nor did it mention the important nuclear agreement reached between Ford and Brezhnev. Kissinger flew directly from
Vladivostok to Beijing the next day, his visit publicized by a front-page photograph in the *People's Daily* of his greeting from Zhou.

from garbage or sewage. In the stores some of the packaging of Chinese goods is rather pretty—bright reds, simple, clean-looking labels. But they call their things outrageous names, or names that would be outrageous for the American market. White Elephant is a great name. Double Happiness for ping-pong equipment. Fu Kung for a hammer . . . might not be too inappropriate come to think of it. Cycling back I stopped at the International Club—tennis courts are still not open. Drying, drying, drying they keep telling me. Oh, for one of those great surfaces. I stopped in the barbershop—twenty-minute shoulder, head and neck massage and a shampoo and a haircut, all 60 cents U.S.

Saturday night a party at the Ruges.[73] Mostly reporters, press corps. Attractive, young. I was the only ambassador there. Governor Shapp came and John Burns of Canada was very nice to him. I told Burns he might get a story out of him because Shapp says weird things, like when it was his turn to toast at a dinner given in his honor, he got up and said he didn't see why Nixon should be respected. Nixon had been a big buddy of Chiang Kai-shek, and Nixon had not after all done much. I was shocked at this, knowing the Chinese revered Nixon and have really never quite understood driving him from office. Shapp is a mixture at times of a kind of an open, gregarious and almost with a kind of shy quality and other times making outrageous statements like telling the Governors Conference that he felt we might not even have free elections in 1976. Funny rich little guy. Young marrieds in this group at the party were very attractive. There were two students there. One German. One Canadian. From the Chinese schools. The Canadian was returning thoroughly disillusioned, highly critical of the Chinese. The German also saw a lot of bad things and he had already advised his government that students should return for a couple of months every year. Otherwise they come home hating China. On

---

[73]The reference is to Gerd and Lois Ruge. An expert on Communist states, Gerd Ruge was Beijing correspondent for Germany's *Die Welt,* having previously worked throughout Indochina and in Moscow.

the other hand he had nice things to say about living conditions. Adding, "I was in the Army so it's not bad for me."

[Sunday, November 17, 1974]. Sunday, our little church service. Head count—two African ladies, one African man, three Canadians, two Bushes, four Chinese in the audience, and one preacher. They sing the most wonderful hymns. "Nearer My God to Thee," "Holy, Holy, Holy." All the old favorites. It is a nice touch. Did some shopping after church. Mr. and Mrs. Augustine Marusi, he is chairman of Borden Company, came for lunch.[74] Delightful, outgoing people. The Chinese wanted to buy powdered milk from him but they also discussed selling it under their own label. No mention of Borden Company. He had been to the Canton Fair and was back up for just a couple of days. I had my first cold so I turned down going to dinner with them. Lots of telegrams coming in for the Kissinger party (about 46 people). Press, security, communications, schedule, room requirements, banquets and return banquets. Slept for an hour in the afternoon. Quiet dinner at home.

How are the kids? Things are so different.

Cold today though the sky was clear. The wind was up. Bites right through you. Jeff Lilley gave Fred a great big bone and Fred's personality has changed.[75] Anyone that gets within twenty yards of him gets a growl. Lilley and son came for ping-pong Saturday afternoon on the Double Happiness table. Two real nice people.

Observation. It is annoying beyond belief to read the attacks in the Red News on the United States. China feels it must attack the United States—imperialist, exploiter of small nations, etc. I see Qiao Guanhua. I just have this inner feeling that these Chinese leaders do not subscribe to that view in its entirety. Perhaps I am wrong. But I have heard them talk enough to know they don't believe that. How does one balance that with their desire for frank-

[74]Augustine "Gus" Marusi, chairman and chief executive of Borden, Inc., for eleven years, helped steer the dairy company out of financial trouble in the early 1970s.
[75]Jeff Lilley was the son of the USLO's James Lilley.

80

ness in dealing, their desire for openness, their desire to "keep their word" etc. Also would China understand it if we struck back in these areas, diplomatic fora, against China. We don't do it and I am not convinced we should. Certainly in every instance. But I am wondering how they would feel if we attacked their closed system, no freedom of press, without taking away from their many accomplishments, the total lack of individual freedom. There is no point in debating whether China has made progress or not. They have. Good progress in many ways. But one of them has not been human rights or individual freedoms. The children are taken away to communes, property rights are almost totally restricted, and the state is the master, and criticism is very restricted unless orchestrated from the bottom. One has a closed society. They are much more delicate about it. There is a certain deceptive gentleness, culture, and kindness that sets them apart from the Soviets. But it is hard to tell the real . . . [sentence trails off].

Saw Elie Boustany of Lebanon at his apartment at San Li Tun.[76] Some of these countries have essentially one-person embassies. Boustany has one assistant. They have little contact with the Chinese. He is a delightful person. Friendly to the United States, spent some time all around the world. Nice conversationalist but really without too spectacular an insight on China. Mexican ambassador, that afternoon.[77] A very young, dynamic, attractive, good English-speaking individual, is different. They have a staff of about nine and he loves to travel. He is enthused over China. He has his children and wife in school. He sees the shortcomings but he also is an advocate of the good things. Governor Milton Shapp gave a going-away banquet. He had Mr. Zhou of the University of Peking Foreign Affairs Institute, the same man who was the honored guest at

[76]Elie Joseph Boustany served as a Lebanese diplomat throughout Europe before becoming ambassador to Mali and Senegal (1966–67), Gambia and Guinea (1967–72), and then China, beginning in 1972.

[77]Mexico and China established formal diplomatic relations in February 1972, and the 33-year-old Eugenio Anguiano Roch, trained as an economist, served as Mexico City's ambassador in Beijing until 1975.

the university presidents. He is a delightful man, speaks English, lived in Los Angeles for four years. His wife came in a red brocade jacket. He is very precise, advocating the system under Chairman Mao. I asked him about Professor Fairbank of Harvard.[78] He indicated, as have many other Chinese officials, that Fairbank is not considered too objective. He talked about Edgar Snow and how he was most revered.[79] How some of his ashes were buried on the campus at the university. How he stood next to Mao in the People's Square on one October first.[80] The banquet in terms of food was the biggest we have attended. The courses went on and on and on. I am sure Milton Shapp said, "Just give me the best one, whatever it is." He also produced a bottle of champagne which was politely received and indeed consumed fairly widely.

[78]John K. Fairbank, considered the founder of modern Chinese studies in the United States, spent a career at Harvard that saw the publication of more than two dozen books and edited collections on Chinese history, shaping a generation of China scholars. In 1966 he served as president of the American Historical Association. "Technological progress, which we once so admired, now has us by the throat," he told the group during his presidential address, and Sino-American relations were thus the key to the future in an age of rapid change. "If China were not the most distinctive and separate of the great historical cultures, if the Chinese language were not so different and difficult, if our China studies were not so set apart by these circumstances, our China problem would not be so great. But the fact is that China *is* a uniquely large and compact section of mankind, with a specially self-contained and long-continued tradition of centrality and superiority, too big and too different to be assimilated into our automobile-TV, individual-voter, individual-consumer culture. China is too weak to conquer the world but too large to be digested by it. China's eventual place in the world and especially America's relationship to China therefore bulk large on the agenda for human survival."

[79]American Edgar Snow taught journalism in Beijing during the 1930s. He used the opportunity to visit Mao and the Chinese Communist headquarters in Shaanxi province in 1936, and the product of that trip, *Red Star over China* (New York: Random House, 1938), chronicled for the West the movement's purpose and goals. Blacklisted during the McCarthy years, he subsequently moved to Switzerland, and in 1960 he was the first American journalist admitted to China after the 1949 revolution. Half of Snow's ashes are buried in Beijing on the grounds of Peking University.

[80]Bush refers to the anniversary of the official founding of the People's Republic on October 1, 1949, and to Tiananmen Square.

In a computer printout on our trade with China we have a very favorable balance, over 10 to 1.[81] And this worries us. They do not seem eager or in a hurry to take the steps that would help their trade—sending delegations to the U.S., special packaging seminars etc. They buy from us what they need and I think they are buying things that they might well get better from others, simply because they don't want to increase the balance nor get a dependency on us. The long protocol lists on the Kissinger trip arrived. I am on the protocol list. Up on the top after Secretary and Mrs. Kissinger. We are debating why this is. Last year the Chief of the USLO was not on the list. John Holdridge raises the point that he wonders if they are including him out on some of this. I hope not. And I would certainly think not.

Tuesday[, November 19, 1974]. A nice return visit from Ambassador Ferenc Gódor of Hungary. Bringing with him a young English-speaking interpreter. An unlikely-looking couple. He has that kind of earthy East European humor that I like. Interested in Kissinger's visit, interested in a Cambodia solution, interested in Taiwan. Almost a replay when I went to see the Italian ambassador, a man who has been here too long. Was the first Italian ambassador. Feels he has been here long enough. Language seemed interesting today. Our Mr. Sun put on a great lunch for the Romanian Ambassador and his interpreter. I am continually amazed at the man's artistic talent and pride in his work. He is first class and though I am [not] a connoisseur of Romanian food, I could tell from watching the ambassador [he] thought it was great. Gus Marusi of Borden stopped in again. I took my stock portfolio and took a recent copy of the *Herald Tribune* and even that was up a little bit. Went home early feeling pretty good. Brunson walked over and

---

[81]By 1985 the balance of United States–China trade had reversed, with Americans importing $6 million of goods more than they sold to the Chinese. The imbalance has only grown since then, and in 2007, according to the Foreign Trade Division of the U.S. Census Bureau, the American trade deficit with China totaled more than $237 billion.

said there is an immediate from Kissinger saying Bar could ride home with him. We had been turned down on this in a very gracious, nice way by Scowcroft.[82] In this environment it is funny how little things matter. I am getting into some reading now. Weather warm and beautiful. In contrast to some of the icy cold days we have had. I am concerned about our level of trade. Whether it will continue. Saw a report from the Japanese that the Chinese told them they want to cut back on their trade with us. They won't buy agricultural products anymore from us. That they were offended by what we said at the Rome Food Conference about China buying up grain etc. I don't believe they will follow this road but if they do it would really knock our trade figures in the hat because agriculture takes care of about 80 percent of it. More planning for Kissinger visit. End of day. Evening off. I am glad.[83]

[Wednesday,] November 20[, 1974]. Highlight of it was a lovely dinner given by Ambassador Salah El-Abd of Egypt. Both the Egyptian and the Lebanese are very melancholy about peace in the Middle East, this being at a time when there are rumors of increased fighting. Here they are in China but the Middle East predominates all their thinking, understandably. Interesting talk with the Sri Lanka[n] ambassador.[84] He has been here four and a half years. He said, "I am considered pro-Communist and pro-Socialist but I am convinced that the Chinese system will have to change.

[82]Brent Scowcroft—whose friendship with Bush later became especially close during his service as Bush's national security adviser—was deputy assistant for national security affairs when Bush first arrived in China. The next year saw his promotion to national security adviser.

[83]During this period Bush directed several lengthy USLO analyses of the up-to-the-moment state of Sino-American relations in preparation for Kissinger's visit, including one specifically on trade issues and one titled "China's Internal Scene on the Eve of Your Visit." His staff concluded: "It seems to us that the direction of Chinese policy remains very much in the hands of the same establishment which first decided to permit the opening of the present US-PRC relationship, even if the active cast of characters within this establishment has changed somewhat."

[84]The ambassador was R.L.A.I. Karannagoda.

It can't keep the people happy the way it is." He talked about more need for freedom. He did say that during the Cultural Revolution there was a lot more openness on matters like sex "by the kids." One of the officers in their mission was stopped, hauled out of the car and made to read quotations from Chairman Mao. Concluded our lunches for all of the staff. Bicycled in a tremendous headwind downtown and did some shopping. I am impressed with the amount of consumer goods around. The counters are relatively well stocked. Prices for everyday items pretty good. Prices in the craft shop very high. But when it comes to things like face creams, candies, chinaware, and even fairly colorful shirts for women, the shelves are bulging. Photographical equipment appears to be one luxury the people are encouraged to enjoy.

Back to the bathhouse for a return visit. It is funny how the Chinese lessons just in a ten-day period make me at least understand a little bit about what he is saying. Very little I might add. Language is a barrier. We were supposed to be out at the United Arab Republic of Egypt at 7:30 and we end up at the United Arab Republic of Yemen. An enormous communications gap existed.

[Thursday,] November 21[, 1974]. Today we were turned down by the Chinese for our U.S. Information Agency billboard outside the USLO. Most embassies have these billboards and people along the streets stop and look at them. Stare at them. We were told that our situation was different and that it was inappropriate for us to establish a bulletin board. It's the feeling here that they simply don't want us to show a lot about the U.S. to their public. They have not even recognized that a man has landed on the moon. Or at least their population is unaware of that. Too bad.[85]

---

[85]Though it was hardly unexpected, State Department officials found this Chinese rejection particularly frustrating. It was true that China's mission in Washington did not possess a bulletin board outside its compound; the official reason for rejecting the USLO's request for such a board had been on the basis of "reciprocity." But as Robert Ingersoll reminded Bush and his office, that ruling "disregards the very great advantage that PRCLO has over USLO in informational

Yemen ambassador came to call. Middle East, Middle East, Middle East. Little progress in language—numbers. Chest cold for the first time. And everybody tells me this is normal. There is tons of bronchial infection here. "Don't worry. It will last all winter" etc. It is accepted due to the dust and the dryness and wind and cold in Peking. Czech ambassador received me in his two-hectare compound—lonely man, discouraged, not pleasant—his wife sick with a heart attack. I really feel he has given up. The Eastern Europeans really enjoy a kind of isolation here that is not their lot in other parts of the world. The ambassador is a very pleasant man, seemed anxious to talk but appeared critical of the Chinese and their strange ways. Dinner with Teddy Youde. A very pleasant relaxed dinner with two top people from his office and Sven Hirdman from Sweden.[86] It was a nice early evening. Youde gave some credibility to the Sri Lanka[n] ambassador's remarks and feels he is a bright and astute observer.

Increasing speculation on when there is going to be the next People's Congress.[87] Speculation goes on and on everywhere. No-

---

and public relations matters." More important, the ruling reinforced yet again the uphill battle the Americans would have to wage if they were ever to offer their propaganda messages directly to the Chinese populace. "Except for intermittent reception of VOA broadcasts, the US has virtually no access to the Chinese public," Ingersoll concluded. Indeed, "In living memory, NCNA has never published any 'good news' about social or economic developments in the US."

[86]Hirdman later served as Sweden's ambassador to Moscow.

[87]The National People's Congress was the governmental body formally responsible for voting on major political decisions in China, including amendments to the constitution, election of the state's leadership, and social and economic policymaking. In reality it was merely a legislative rubber stamp for the party's decisions, and accordingly it was convened only erratically. Indeed Chinese officials preferred to publicly announce a People's Congress only after its conclusion. Speculation over its commencement was always a frequent topic of conversation for visiting diplomats and China watchers. The Fourth National People's Congress, to which Bush here refers, was eventually held on January 13–17, 1975. It was the first such meeting since 1964. Some 2,800 delegates gathered to ratify the changes in policy and personnel decided by the party's Central Committee the week before, most prominently that of Deng's appointment as one of twelve new vice premiers.

body seems to know. People watch the Hall of the People to see if there are cars lined up and lights burning at night.[88] And then speculation goes wild when there is a flicker of life. There is a lot of wonder as to what the NPC [National People's Congress] will produce. Will we know more about the leadership? Will it signal a change in direction on policy? Further speculation as to whether Qiao Guanhua's appointment to foreign minister has anything to do with the Kissinger visit. In my judgment it probably did. It will be interesting to see, as I think will happen, that Kissinger spends a good deal of time with Qiao Guanhua. There is one speculative story by John Burns that this will be difficult because Kissinger's relationship with Qiao is sticky since Kissinger said he couldn't remember his name. That's not true. I have seen them together. The press speculation on this field is just as weird as on Watergate but it's not quite as mean.

[88]Constructed at the western edge of Tiananmen Square in 1958–59, the cavernous Great Hall of the People is used primarily for ceremonial activities of the Chinese government, including the National People's Congress. Bush would, later in his career, give several speeches there.

"We Must Not Capitulate on Matters This Fundamental"

November 22, 1974, to January 15, 1975

Secretary of State Henry Kissinger visited China during the last week of November 1974, in a meeting designed to show Beijing, and the world, how much Washington valued positive Sino-American relations. He flew to Beijing directly from the Soviet-American summit in Vladivostok, leaving President Ford to return to Washington but taking Ford's new chief of staff, Donald Rumsfeld, with him.

Kissinger's visit dominated Bush's holiday season between Thanksgiving and Christmas. Though the secretary's formal agenda held little of substance—intended more for symbolism than to achieve real breakthroughs on such thorny issues as formalizing the Sino-American relationship or the sensitive issue of Taiwan—preparations for the meetings nevertheless occupied the USLO for weeks. It was a time for Bush to evaluate what he considered important in Sino-American relations. As the diary and the cables he composed at the time reveal, Bush feared the growing public perception that the relationship between the two countries was deteriorating. Without visible signs of progress, Bush worried, this perception might force an unwanted reality on American policymakers. He warned Kissinger and Scowcroft as much in letters highlighted in the footnotes below, and he hoped—in vain—for some public display that relations were indeed on the right course.

What he received instead was classic Kissinger—by turns brilliant yet equally frustrating, unconcerned with public perceptions of progress yet convinced that he, Deng Xiaoping, and Zhou Enlai could jointly navigate the rocky diplomatic shoals. These eyewitness accounts of Kissinger at work in China are among the China Diary's most valuable sections. They also demonstrate that, despite their previous friction, Kissinger recognized that Bush had a political future. His probing for information on Bush's political plans is particularly noteworthy.

Of equal interest are Bush's continued musings on the disconnect he perceived between China's rhetorical assaults on the United States, designed to curry favor within the developing world, and the private assurances he and other American policymakers repeatedly received from Chinese leaders of their desire for strong Sino-American relations. These public assaults came to a head, ironically, not in Beijing but in Washington. Chinese officials initially banned certain journalists from attending the press preview of their highly anticipated archaeological exhibit. Bush found this partisan attack particularly galling, as it came on American soil. "We blew a great opportunity to stand up for freedom of the press," he wrote in his journal. Fearful of invoking Beijing's wrath, American officials canceled the press preview altogether rather than stand up for the ostracized journalists. Bush decried this approach: "We must not capitulate on matters this fundamental in the United States." It would not be the last time he returned to the theme of American versus Chinese principles and to the issue of Beijing's public hostility versus its private overtures for peaceful relations.

This long month between Thanksgiving and New Year's also saw Bush travel to Hawaii for a State Department conference, his wife's departure for a Christmas celebration at home, and his mother's arrival in Beijing to spend Christmas with her son. Struck by the differences he already perceived between life in "drab" China and that amid the "lights" of Tokyo and Hawaii, by the year's close Bush would be preparing for his own first visit back to the United States in January. Before his departure, however, he hosted Foreign Minister Qiao Guanhua at his USLO residence. The dinner must be considered not only a high point of his tenure in Beijing but also a signature moment in his quest to personalize Sino-American relations. Bush would never achieve the kind of intimacy he sought with Chinese leaders, but this dinner would be as close as he would ever get to the kind of working relationship he so desperately longed to cultivate with Beijing's top policy-makers.

[Friday,] November 22, [1974].   Made a call on the Laotian ambassador.[1] Interesting pro-American who is in a very tough situation, being as now they have a coalition government.[2] Delegations friendly to the Pathet Lao come by to see him and all is quite cordial but the strain must be enormous. We had rumors that the Chinese were sending aid to Laos through North Vietnam but he was not able to help me confirm or deny this. Very nice call on Ambassador C. J. Small of Canada.[3] Bright, attractive, pleasant individual. National day reception by Boustany of Lebanon. Same deadly format. Chinese guests and hosts sitting alone and isolated. Bored stiff. At the front of the room. Chinese guests milling around the food tables. And others standing around bitching about the whole setup. By the time it was over my cold was killing me. But we went on to the black tie dinner given by the German ambassador. I left at about 10:30 as a guest of honor. Well ahead of the 11 departing time. I don't think Mrs. Pauls liked it. Rolf certainly understood.

[1]Phagna Lien Pravongiengkam, who later met with Bush throughout the summer of 1975 to discuss his posting to Washington. See, for example, Bush's entry and my footnote for June 13, 1975.

[2]The Laotian coalition government, a product of the 1973 Vientiane Treaty, ceded control of Laos to the Communist Pathet Lao in 1975.

[3]Born in China to missionary parents, Small became Ottawa's ambassador to Beijing in October 1973, having previously served as Canada's high commissioner to Pakistan and ambassador to Afghanistan. Small authorized American use of his embassy's secure communications network during the USLO's initial months in Beijing.

Racked by a cold. It is too bad that at diplomatic dinners like this no Chinese are present.

Saturday, November 23[, 1974]. Met with newly named protocol chief, Zhu Chuanxian. Reviewed plans for the Kissinger trip. All arrangements sound fine. Meeting with our staff in the residence to review the plans. And the rest of the time I plan to stay in bed due to this wretched cold. Weather is perceptibly warm today and clear. Just the kind of day one should be off bicycling. It is hard to tell from the protocol arrangements exactly whom Kissinger will see. Qiao Guanhua is going to host one banquet. And they mentioned holding Wednesday open for a dinner with Deng Xiaoping. But I am wondering if he will see either Mao or Zhou Enlai.[4] Rest of Saturday spent reading in bed trying to get rid of a miserable chest and head cold.

Sunday[, November 24, 1974]. The church service at 9:30. The place is desolate. Congregation still small. But it is easy to follow the familiar hymns. No sermon. Three bible readings. Communion. Lord's Prayer; the Apostles' Creed; and that's about it. Wandered around after Church and did a little shopping. Walked over to the International Club for a good Chinese lunch. It is a nice

[4]Secretary of State Henry Kissinger did not in fact receive an audience with Mao during this particular visit, though the secretary of state very much desired one—an outcome that led to press speculation that Beijing was snubbing Kissinger and Washington's diplomatic overtures. Moreover, owing to Zhou's declining health, Kissinger was permitted only a thirty-minute informal session in the latter's hospital room. Such meetings were considered important symbols of Washington's ongoing relationship with Beijing, especially as Kissinger was visiting China primarily to demonstrate his continued commitment to Sino-American relations. This nonspecific agenda led to much speculation, even by the USLO, as to the goal of the trip. "Quite apart from such bilateral matters such as Taiwan (and as you know we are uncertain as to whether they will actually press for rapid progress on Taiwan at this time)," Bush advised Kissinger immediately before the secretary's arrival, "we believe that what they really want most from your visit is prestige—recognition on the U.S. part that China's word counts in world affairs, and that the U.S. side finds it necessary to consult with China on major international issues in the same way that it consults with the Soviet Union."

place, arranged so people can drop in there. They need a good kind of "cruise director." He could really get the place humming with events, and contests and tournaments and dances. But dancing is prohibited. And a bar is unthinkable.[5] That's really what the place needs. Although you can get beer there and can buy liquor. Tennis courts opened. A man courteously calling me, [since] I had been by there a time or two. I thought they had notified every embassy but when I saw the manager he said, "We know you are interested in tennis so we called you to say the courts were open." I couldn't play due to my health, but Akwei played and told me that the courts are still too soft and they will be all torn up again.

In the evening we had a bunch of ambassadors over and showed the "Hustler"—fine old movie.[6] A very relaxed way to entertain. Right in the living room. Six or so ambassadors. Popcorn. Relaxed and informal. The kind of thing I like to do. Mr. Wang, the man who replaced Mr. Ye, hustled up the drinks and hors d'oeuvres, etc. Mr. Ye spoke no English and was replaced. It was a sad farewell for me anyway because I thought he did a good job and I felt sorry I had ever mentioned to the DSB just in passing that he didn't speak English. But now Mr. Wang is there. Bright, young, very accommodating.

I am determined to go out in the park some morning. I keep hearing these cheers and shouts from the park long before it is light. It could be the shadow boxing. It could be calisthenics. In the morning about seven when I am listening to the VOA you see single lines of school girls running by in step, jogging, running in opposite di-

---

[5] The USLO's Marine Corps guards had a bar of their own, built by Navy Seabees, during Ambassador Bruce's time, and the site had become a major after-hours meeting place for Beijing's international community. Chinese officials demanded its closure early in 1974, however, when reports mounted of patrons of this "Red-Ass Saloon" having a bit too much fun on their way home from the USLO compound after closing time. Bruce described his negotiations with local officials over the Marine presence, and their saloon, in great detail throughout his own diary.

[6] *The Hustler* (1961) featured Paul Newman's classic portrayal of pool shark "Fast Eddie" Felson.

rections from the school. Kids all look quite healthy. A French AFP [Agence France-Presse] correspondent told me that during the Cultural Revolution he witnessed ten-, eleven-, and twelve-year-old kids running after old people in the streets, beating them with whips and sticks, yelling at them, calling them "revisionists" and "old reactionaries." Cultural Revolution tales are almost unbelievable when you see the order now but I guess it could happen again if that was dictated from above.[7]

Monday, the 25th [November 25, 1974]. The Secretary of State arrives. The whole day looking forward to it. Out to the airport. Holdridge and I ushered off to the side room with the Foreign Minister. Plane arrived right on time. Melee at the airport as the Secretary came off. The security people came off first. Too much. They should have gotten off the back door and walked around the front. Nancy Tang commented on the security people. "So many," she said. It was noticeable, particularly here in China for some reason.[8] The Secretary and his wife said hello to us, greeted the ambassadorial corps, and then were whisked off to the guest house. I had been out that morning to inspect the beautiful guest house. Guest House 18, the one where President Nixon stayed,

[7]The Cultural Revolution, the social and political turmoil that roiled China for a decade beginning in the mid-1960s, became in time an omnipresent factor in Chinese life, and the constant beat of drums and screaming of slogans affected even the air. "Noise in fact was the hallmark of the revolution," one British diplomat later recalled, "and before long earplugs became standard embassy issue." Sweden's ambassador similarly recalled that "many of us are kept awake until the early morning hours by the monotonous beating of drums and clashing of gongs by groups marching or riding past our building on the back of trucks. The tom-tom of the Africans strikes me in retrospect as full of harmony compared with this noise."

[8]Bush recalled this incident when preparing for President Ford's 1975 visit to China. Nancy Tang "rather pointedly" commented that "the number of security personnel was excessive," he wrote Scowcroft. "China does pride itself on the safety of foreign friends here in this country . . . [and therefore] perhaps a way can be found to have the security people be not quite so conspicuous as the Secretary de-planes."

was assigned to us.⁹ Barbara and I had a beautiful suite there. There is grass there, flowing stream or lake with beautiful bridges, beautifully landscaped. The overstuffed chairs are the same in the guest house but everything is thoughtfully done. All kinds of little cosmetic and bathroom aids scattered around. And everything that one wants for his own personal comfort is there—bathrobes, slippers, etc.

The banquet at the Great Hall was a tremendous success. The Hall fantastic in its elegance.¹⁰ Built in a hurry. The banquet was considered one of the very best our staff has seen. Kissinger gave an excellent toast, talking about the determination and continued relationships etc. etc. More than perfunctory, and the next day his comments were carried in the *People's Daily*. The first such comments of a Western leader, according to John Holdridge.¹¹

November 26, [1974,] Tuesday. We had sightseeing at nine with the full party to the Forbidden City. Press of TV and coverage, cold on the feet and my cold got worse. The lights and the cameras and the crowd made sightseeing almost impossible but it was good to have all that attention. Kissinger is good at this kind of thing. He enjoys it. Nancy looks sick, ailing, tired.¹² But was a pretty good sport about it. I wonder whether she likes this kind of "on

⁹The Diaoyutai guest houses and compound have hosted many of China's highest-ranking visitors, not only President Richard Nixon but also North Korea's Kim Il Sung, Nikita Khrushchev, and Che Guevara. According to historian Margaret Macmillan, Villa 18 can today be rented for $50,000 a night.

¹⁰Original transcription reads "The Hall fantastic in its eloquence."

¹¹Calling the recommencement of Sino-American relations "one of the most significant initiatives of American foreign policy," Kissinger pledged in this toast that "the beginning of the process of normalization of relations with the People's Republic of China, and its continuation in the years since then, has not been a matter of expediency but a fixed principle of American foreign policy." He vowed that under the new President "we would continue to follow the goal of normalization of relations with the PRC."

¹²Recently married to the secretary of state, Nancy Kissinger's frequent travels in his official party drew attention, and some degree of sympathy, from policymakers and pundits alike. Longtime Washington columnist Art Buchwald, in his usual style, imagined a conversation between the oblivious secretary and his in-

stage." I noticed last night she and the Secretary at the Guest House told the press not to take pictures of the two children who are along for the trip. Official party counts for about 30 some odd. And it is quite a sight.

In the morning we had the first large-scale meeting at the Great Hall of the People with Deng Xiaoping and others. General review was undertaken and schedule was decided on for the following. I will not report on the details of the meetings as that is classified.[13] I came home for lunch and we went to the International Club to save the staff, who are killing themselves over the Tuesday night reception.[14] Mr. Sun the cook had gone out and bought six shark skins for $150 U.S. Check that [cost?]. Plus swallows' spit, for bird's nest delicacies, etc.[15] The house was polished and looking beautifully clean. The flowers arranged and great pride in the work by Mr. Wang, Number One. In the afternoon we had a meeting at the guest house. There is a great hustling around.

People on his staff are scared to death of Kissinger. It is unbelievable. Too much so. There is too much entourage feeling. Too much kind of turmoil. Is he coming? Is he coming? Is he late? Is he late? Nobody is willing to bite the bullet and speak up. Amazing—mixed feeling. Great respect for the man and his accomplishments

---

creasingly fatigued wife in late November 1974. "When we got married you never mentioned anything about the fact that your job would involve travel," he sarcastically imagined her complaining. One British diplomat in the Washington embassy dryly noted of her upcoming travel plans that "Buchwald speculated a couple of days ago that Nancy was getting tired of stratospheric tourism. If he's right, the Chinese really will send her up the wall."

[13]Holdridge reports that, with Mao unavailable and Zhou unwell, Deng was physically uncomfortable in his new role, not an unreasonable anxiety given his previous firsthand experience of life as a political outcast. "When Kissinger met with Deng and his colleagues . . . Deng glanced to his left or right after every statement, as if to reassure himself that he had said the right things." Bush was primarily a quiet witness to these discussions.

[14]Bush hosted this reception for Chinese officials and Kissinger's entourage at the USLO.

[15]Bush describes here bird's nest soup, a delicacy made by dissolving the nests of cave swifts, made by the males of the species with liberal use of their saliva.

and yet concern about some of the trappings and some of the ways of handling people. Everyone with him talks about how difficult it is and yet he can be extremely charming. Pressures on him are immense, and the accomplishments immense, so one forgives the eccentric things. But there is a certain graciousness that is lacking. No question about it. The morning and yesterday: ungracious. The afternoon after the meeting: gracious. At the reception very good. I introduced him to Mr. Sun and Mr. Wang, Mrs. Tang, and in all of these cases he seemed very pleased. So is the press. He does a first-class job with them. We invited the local press for the first time. Many of them commented on it and all of them enjoyed meeting him and getting a chance to visit. This was an important part and he does this exceptionally well. After the reception we went to a musical performance. All revolutionary of course. Good voices. Pianist could have played anywhere. The dancers were fine. It was the first time I saw a woman's shape on the young dancers. The costumes were bright. And as we are starved for entertainment the heavy revolutionary themes didn't even seem too much.[16] The crowd consisted of on the one side a lot of the PLA types that apparently were let in to see the performance. On the other there is a representative off-the-street crowd. They didn't clap very much. But I watched their faces and they seemed enthralled by the performance. They also spent a good deal of time staring at Kissinger and all of us who were lined up in protocol order. A classic: the picture of the Monday night banquet. It looked like a high school picture. The head table, so to speak, was off visiting with the Deputy Premier. We all walked out. There was all USLO, all press, all the traveling party lined up for the big picture. It was a real yak!

---

[16]Chinese performances during this period, particularly the opera, were by nature political, offering revolutionary themes. Nixon's party had witnessed one such performance during their 1972 visit (*The Red Detachment of Women: Tale of the Liberation and Reunification of Hainan Island*), and White House adviser H. R. Haldeman recorded in his diary the "rather odd sight to see the P[resident] clapping at the end for this kind of thing, which would have been horrifying at home, but it all seems to fit together somehow, here."

There are so many things to note and see but the Kissinger visit is a good thing. It is getting things lined up. We'll begin to understand policy. Kissinger has made a couple of needles about excessive reporting and the fact that "George doesn't think I am spending enough time on China," he says to the Deputy Prime Minister.[17] But I think I can convince him that we have been right in the fact that some think our policy is declining and that we need to do certain things to demonstrate that it is not. In any event it has livened things up and it is right and good and so far it is going pretty well.

I attend, sitting next to the Secretary, meetings in the morning at the Great Hall and in the afternoon at the guest house, meetings with Deng Xiaoping. Notes of these meetings are in a separate file. Kissinger is brilliant in these talks. Tremendous sweep of history and a tremendous sweep of the world situation. He is at his best. It is a great contrast to the irritating manner he has of handling people. His staff is scared to death of him. The procession is almost "regal." People quake: "He's coming. He's coming." And don't dare tell him when he's keeping them waiting. In the Wednesday morning meeting, "I want my staff. I want them all in this room. I want them right here now. Where are they?" All kinds of yelling of that nature goes on. I guess it is the way he keeps from getting ulcers at the pace he is working at. I came home and had lunch with Bar at the International Club. It is a nice place to be able to drop in for a quick bite. In the morning we went sightseeing at the museum. A great sweeping entourage. Tons of cameras. Difficulty at seeing a darn thing. I am sure the Chinese were thoroughly confused

[17]The rate of Bush's personal reports back to the State Department declined precipitously after Kissinger's visit. In the days leading up to the secretary's Beijing stop—during which time he was, of course, primarily preparing for Ford's Vladivostok summit with the Soviets—Bush's USLO had sent long reports home to Foggy Bottom with titles such as "China's Internal Scene on the Eve of Your Visit," "US-PRC Trade Relations," and "What the Chinese Want from Your Visit." While Bush's USLO staff kept up their own reporting standards in the months to follow, his personal reports declined after Kissinger's visit from an average of one a day in October and early November 1974 to less than one a week in September and October 1975.

by it all. That evening, the 26th, we had a reception at the residence. Mr. Wang and Mr. Sun did a first-class job. The great care and attention they put into the hors d'oeuvres etc. The ranking Chinese guest was Wang Hairong. Ambassador Huang Zhen from Washington was there. He and his wife were very friendly. The Foreign Minister [Qiao Guanhua] and the ambassador are very warm to Barbara and me. Distinctly so. One feels it very easily. After the reception we raced madly to a musical show—our first. One guy had a lute or a guitar of some sort, playing "Home on the Range" and the rest of it local revolutionary music.[18] Ballet dancers with the big red flag carried across the stage. Sopranos singing the glory of the chairman, how the people won the fight at Tiger Mountain, etc.[19] An interesting evening. Not the kind that our taste would like to do every night, but well worth seeing. The pianist was excellent. One of the leading pianists in China I think. I sat next to the Foreign Minister's wife. Couldn't have been more pleasant.

Wednesday, November 27[, 1974]. More meetings. Morning at the guest house—just Lord, Bush, Kissinger and a secretary for the first hour and a half.[20] Then the whole team. Break for lunch

---

[18]Chinese officials frequently offered traditional American music at their banquets for visitors from Washington, selecting tunes designed to make travelers feel right at home. For Nixon's final banquet in Beijing, for example, the band played "Billy Boy" and "She'll Be Coming 'Round the Mountain."

[19]Bush refers to *Taking Tiger Mountain (by Strategy)*, an opera based on the 1957 novel by Qu Bo titled *Tracks in the Snowy Forest*. The play epitomized the widespread movement throughout China before and after the Cultural Revolution to bring revolutionary ideas to the masses through theater.

[20]Winston Lord served as Kissinger's principal assistant while the latter was national security adviser, before moving with Kissinger to the State Department, where he headed the Policy Planning Staff. He was subsequently named ambassador to China from 1985 to 1989. Lord was given remarkable latitude by Kissinger to meet and negotiate with his Chinese counterparts—a relaxation of the secretary's usual controlling style necessitated by his long absences from Washington during these years, in particular for his episodes of Middle East shuttle diplomacy. The omnipresent Lord was also frequently a foil whom Kissinger could use to defuse tense discussions or avoid sensitive topics. During one meeting with Huang

at the guest house. Then back to a meeting at the Great Hall of the People with John Holdridge attending. The Secretary does not follow through clearly on whom he wants where and how it's done. And thus people are always up in the air as to what he really desires. He is a man of great contrasts. He can be pleasant and flattering and warm. And then he can do nasty little things. He is not gracious with people. There is no real kind of courtesy to the little waiters standing around or anything of that nature. I keep coming back to the word "regal." Mobs of security people. Mobs of traveling entourage. All aides quaking in their boots. We came late to the dinner given by the Deputy Premier Deng at a Manchurian restaurant. Excellent dinner. I sat between the ambassador and Qiao Guanhua. Great relaxed evening. They must have [put] something stimulating in the food. I couldn't sleep all night.

Thursday, November 28[, 1974]. More wrap-up talks in the afternoon. In the morning I stayed in the office and worked. The Kissinger party did some sightseeing and the Secretary received the German ambassador before coming to our house for lunch.[21] We invited Henry and Nancy and the two children and Don Rumsfeld.[22] On a three-hour notice Mr. Sun whipped up a very nice

Zhen in late August 1974, for example, the Chinese representative asked whether "they will announce the new Vice President tomorrow." The decision would come down to Bush or Rockefeller, he suggested. It would be neither, Kissinger deadpanned. "It will be Win Lord." To this Lord could only reply, "I'm not sure I'm old enough to qualify."

[21]Kissinger and Ambassador Pauls knew each other well from the latter's time as Germany's ambassador to the United States.

[22]Rumsfeld, who accompanied Kissinger on his trip to China, was then two months into a fourteen-month term as President Ford's chief of staff. He subsequently served as secretary of defense under Ford and reprised the role under George W. Bush. He had accompanied Ford to Vladivostok, and his inclusion with the Kissinger party was decided only on November 18. "Within a few seconds I saw the many advantages to having Ambassador Rumsfeld go to Peking," Winston Lord confided to Kissinger. "His exposure to and support for the Chinese connection in coming months should prove helpful in various quarters. The only people who might be unhappy about this addition to the traveling party would be

luncheon. Great detail and wonderfully thoughtful. Very much like his reception only this was very small and private.

After that lunch I had a very good private talk with Kissinger. We covered a list of agenda items. Generally he seemed pleased with the way things were working out. He agreed that I should come back [to Washington] for consultations. I told him I would like to come back at the end of January and he approved that. He did not seem to me well focused to the fact that trade with China was going to be less this year than we expected and that it was going to fall off next year. Both matters will affect the continuing speculation that our policy is deteriorating. They will add to the fuel, although you can point to the trade decline and say that agriculture makes up about 80 percent of the trade. They have had good crops and thus don't need as much of our agricultural goods. Secondly, they have a big balance of payments problem with us. Thirdly, they don't want to be over-embraced by the United States in trade. And they are even buying things such as off-shore drilling equipment from others where we have the best technology.[23]

---

other possible Vice Presidential candidates residing abroad!" The latter was a none-too-veiled reference to Bush.

Lord erred in his suggestion that no one would be unhappy with Rumsfeld's inclusion. With economic difficulties mounting, and with the energy crisis in full swing, many critics believed the new presidential chief of staff needed to be in Washington with the president. Rowland Evans and Robert Novak asked in their influential column, "Why Is Donald Rumsfeld in China?" Their answer: only to salve his ambitions for higher office.

Bush and Rumsfeld shared something besides vice presidential aspirations in 1974. Writing to Bush in early November 1974, Rumsfeld admitted, "I've been borrowing your car (the Gremlin) these past few days. We borrowed Jack Marsh's the first couple of weeks and after that became embarrassing, I decided to impose on you since you were in China." Further correspondence between the two men is sadly silent on Bush's reaction, or the fate of the car. Bush had purchased the purple Gremlin while he was head of the Republican National Committee. He chose to drive himself to local functions, rather than take the chauffeured limousines of his predecessors, in an effort to reduce the Republican Party's stigma of elitism.

[23]Perhaps perceiving that Kissinger did not share his views on the importance of trade as a bilateral issue, Bush cabled Scowcroft a detailed analysis of the current state of trade issues between the two countries on the eve of the secretary's

Kissinger was anxious to know my plans. He asked how long I planned to stay. This is the second reference he made to it. I had in my mind that he was probing to see what my political plans were. I told him I had no political plans, that I thought the ticket for '76 was locked in with the appointment of Rockefeller, which I do, and that I had no plans at all. Kissinger made some reference to my running for President in 1980. I told him I couldn't see that far ahead but I was very much interested in doing a good job here—learning the substance of our foreign policy and getting an overall view of it. He pointed out that this was a good place to do it because of the kinds of reviews the Chinese get from him and also because from time to time there are substantive items here.[24] I made clear to him that I was not expecting high profile, I knew the limitations of this post and that it didn't bother me. I really think he is still curious as

---

arrival the previous week. The economic merits of further trade were rather obvious, though complex, Bush concluded, but the opportunity such deals provided to show "progress" could not be discounted. "We should be mindful of the symbolic as well as potential trade value of an agreement on future trade mission and possible exhibitions," Bush wrote. "Unlike scholarly and cultural exchanges, there has been almost no forward movement in this area. An agreement during the secretary's visit on such trade issues would be tangible evidence of further progress in the US-China relationship." Given that this letter found its way to the State Department's Policy Planning Staff, there is little to suggest that Bush expected Scowcroft to keep its contents secret.

[24]The extent of the "reviews" Kissinger gave to the Chinese has only recently come to light. Hoping to maintain Beijing's trust, Kissinger passed to the Chinese top-secret American intelligence reports detailing, among other things, Soviet military and nuclear capabilities. "I don't tell this out of abstract altruism," he told Zhou Enlai during one November 1973 discussion, but rather "because I believe it is in our interest to prevent such an attack" on China by the Soviets. Kissinger had already passed to Chinese officials copies of several top-secret Soviet-American agreements detailing their joint methods for preventing accidental nuclear war, and he further promised to provide Beijing with any and all details of agreements produced by the delicate Strategic Arms Limitation Talks (SALT) even then ongoing between Moscow and Washington. "Incidentally," he reminded Huang Hua in late 1971, "just so everyone knows exactly what we do, we tell you about our conversations with the Soviets; we do not tell the Soviets about our conversations with you. In fact, we don't tell even our own colleagues that I see you."

to why I am here, when, as he knows, I could have gone to Paris or London. That afternoon we met with Deng Xiaoping for our wrap-up meeting. And then went to the return banquet. We retired then.

The mood was somewhat subdued. The press jumped on this as strain—making it "strained." People were simply exhausted. We went back after the banquet and negotiated the communiqué at a very small meeting with Qiao Guanhua.[25] Broad-ranged guy. More so in my opinion then Deng Xiaoping, although Deng speaks with authority and obviously has the political strength that Qiao Guanhua doesn't have. I got to bed late that night, very tired, plagued by a horrible cold.

The next day we took off in two Tridents for Suzhou.[26] A delightful warm "gentle" day as Qiao Guanhua called it. We went through a park, an embroidery factory. The streets had been cleaned to a tee. Lynn Pascoe had been down to Suzhou the week before with the university presidents and then returned with us.[27] There was a big difference. Then there were people bicycling, bustling about, typical. Whatever litter was normal was on the street then. Yesterday the streets were clear. As we went by we looked down al-

---

[25]The four-sentence communiqué, notable for its brevity, was in fact the first Sino-American communiqué following such a high-level visit that did not include mention of the "progress" made in shoring up the bilateral relationship. It read: "Dr. Henry A. Kissinger, Secretary of State and Assistant to the President for National Security Affairs, visited the People's Republic of China from Nov. 25 through Nov. 29, 1974. The U.S. and Chinese sides held frank, wide-ranging, and mutually-beneficial talks. They reaffirmed their unchanging commitment to the principles of the Shanghai Communiqué. The two governments agreed that President Gerald R. Ford would visit the People's Republic of China in 1975."

[26]Suzhou is located in eastern China's Jiangsu Province. Since 1949 it has been home to numerous textile and machinery manufacturers. The Trident was a British-produced jet airliner, so named for the shape of its tail assembly, housing three Rolls-Royce engines.

[27]A career foreign service officer, Lynn Pascoe later served as director of the State Department's Office of Soviet Affairs at the end of the Reagan administration, before returning to Beijing as chargé d'affaires of the American embassy during the first Bush administration.

leys, and way down the middle of the streets and alleys we saw barricades with people jammed up against them. Whereas on the street there was just a normal amount of traffic in terms of people. No cars. No vehicles and the bicycles you could count on one hand. It was eerie but considerate. At the park they had children playing, representative groups. Small tiny children and a group of boys playing with a ball. And a group of girls. Obviously structured. But nice. Some of our journalists were super critical and I was very pleased that they had indeed turned these kids out. At least we got a good look at them and others got a chance to see these attractive Chinese children.[28]

I wish we weren't always so cynical. Of course they arranged it. But why not? The embroidery factory would drive me blind. The detail that goes into those tapestries is just simply unbelievable. We had a good chance to visit informally with the whole traveling party, Qiao Guanhua, Wang Hairong, Nancy Tang, Zhu of the protocol office, Lin Ping, and others. We went to a charming guest house. The attendant at the guest house called [it] the Hotel of Suzhou. Beautifully arranged. And then to a fantastically large banquet. We stuffed ourselves. Finished off the afternoon of sightseeing. Another park. Another embroidery factory.

Flew on a 25-minute flight to Shanghai and there we had yet another banquet given by the Shanghai municipal committee. The municipal committee of Suzhou joined the provincial committee in hosting that banquet in Shanghai. The banquet was excellent. Sparrows in whole, candied, and barbequed sparrows being the piece-de-resistance. Actually they were pretty good. I just wish I didn't know they were sparrows. Barbara boarded the plane with the

---

[28]Kissinger would rather have spent the time negotiating with the Chinese, and, as Holdridge later explained, "I somehow doubt that the chance to see Suzhou's scenery compensated Kissinger for not seeing Mao, but for the rest of us, including the Chinese who accompanied us, it was a grand excursion. Few, if any, of our Chinese hosts had ever visited Suzhou, a city world-famous for its gardens, which evidently had escaped the depredations of the Red Guards."

Kissinger group and headed off for the first Christmas we will be apart in 30 years.[29] I asked if there was extra room on the plane. Scowcroft first wired there was none. Then Kissinger invited her. Then the day of the departure they told me there was a little flap in the States about Kissinger's kids and wife and that the press was insisting that they pay. And Karen Jenkins thought it would be better if I paid. So I, a little sore about it, wrote out a check for sixteen hundred dollars to the U.S. Air Force and said, "Now you tell them I paid in advance," for approximately the first class trip which she said they were being charged at to go one way from Peking to Washington. Ironically Bar had gotten round trip flight Peking–New York–Peking—$967. What a massive financial whipping. She could have stayed here four days longer and then done that. C'est la guerre! Anyway she will have an interesting trip back.

Saturday, November 30[, 1974]. The German ambassador came to get debriefed and so did the New Zealand ambassador. Bryce Harland of New Zealand pushes very hard for information. It is almost like a press conference. I finally told him that I liked my job; that I wanted to keep it; and I simply wasn't at liberty to give him the information he wanted on the discussions of normalization and on Taiwan. He said, "Well if I don't get it, I'll just have to write it from sources that aren't good." Thus using the old press trick on it. [After] my last two years this comment stuck out like a sore thumb and I must confess I didn't appreciate it, though I like Harland. I cycled over and saw Teddy Youde, the British ambassador, where we had a very grand talk—very very different in the way he seeks the information. So was Pauls. They are curious as hell.[30]

[29]"Although this was planned for months," Barbara Bush recalled in her memoirs, "I was heartsick." But "we both missed our children, and George could not leave the post so soon after arriving."

[30]British diplomats proved particularly interested in verifying rumors that Kissinger had passed to the Chinese top-secret American intelligence information concerning Soviet nuclear deployments. As mentioned in the footnote to Bush's November 28 entry, Kissinger had in fact done this very thing. On January 8, 1975, for example, one British diplomat stationed in Peking cabled home that "the

The conclusions I have put in the file but generally speaking the visit went along pretty well. The press and some of the diplomatic corps were looking for a dramatic breakthrough. The Ford trip is a dramatic announcement but in my view the press overall will play the visit like "Ford trip salvaged what otherwise would have been a negative visit."[31] At some point our relationship, whether the Taiwan problem has been solved or not, should get to the point where Kissinger can come here, have frank discussions, and there not be this over-expectation. But that is not where it stands now. My concern is that the decline in trade next year will increase speculation that the relationship is deteriorating. The pressure will mount on the president for his visit. I personally believe the president can come and go without solving the Taiwan issue, but I am

---

story persists that the United States are notifying China about Soviet military activity on the other side of the border." A Danish colleague had said as much, he reported, and the rumor swirled throughout Hong Kong's intelligence community. The Foreign Office in London proved skeptical of this claim, primarily because officials there could not believe that Kissinger would be so bold (especially when it was unclear whether the Americans had provided the same data even to their British counterparts), and also because the story's very sensitivity made it unlikely that it would be so easily and quickly leaked. "We are still puzzled by the stories that the Americans are notifying China about Soviet military activity," concluded the Foreign Office's Far Eastern desk. "We are not disposed to believe them but we are left with the question why the Chinese should want it to be thought the Americans tip them off if in fact they don't." By the end of that spring, after extensive further investigations, London's strategists had erroneously concluded that the story of Kissinger passing such sensitive information to the Chinese was simply too incredible to be believed. Unable to verify his initial contention, the Beijing embassy's M. H. Morgan sheepishly conceded, "I must abandon this hare; I am sorry to have wasted Library's time."

The rumor did not die there, however. In December 1974, Oscar Armstrong, head of the State Department's China desk, directly denied to a British counterpart in Washington that his government was passing military information to Beijing. The USLO did eventually concede to one of Youde's diplomats in Beijing that Washington had passed along to the Chinese warnings of potential Soviet attack, but these were hardly as sensitive (or as unknown to the Chinese) as Kissinger's additional offerings to them.

[31]Kissinger announced that President Ford would visit Beijing "in the latter half" of 1975.

105

sure this will be in doubt as far as others go. And of course maybe the issue will be resolved by then. I am convinced the policy is solid at this point. They need us, actually more than we need them in my judgment. This is the consensus of the diplomatic community incidentally. I publicly expressed lack of concern about the Soviets. In my judgment this is not true.

I played tennis with the Canadian ambassador [Small], an Indian and an Italian. Hard to see but we are lucky to have that surface. Indoor facility. I just hope it holds up through the winter. I am not sure it will. In any event we had a good match and I realize how much I need exercise. Playing again tomorrow. Had lunch at the house all alone. Very good small lunch. I told Brunson I wanted an omelet and a soup. Of course when I get here there is omelet, there is soup, there is a fish dish. In any event it was first-class, the whole thing. Dinner I just had him leave me soup and some flavored hard-boiled eggs. The day was clear and fairly warm. Unusual one would say, when it was predicted it was going to be so icy. I was sent an inhalant mask, like a gas mask, for cycling. If it weren't quite so prominent looking, I'd use it. I still might. It's first-class. Goggles too. Mail situation is erratic. We got a massive group of things that were sent around the first of November. And yet last week ended up with a lot of mail that came in much much later. It is nutty.

Observation on the Kissinger visit. Kissinger is an extremely complicated guy. He is ungracious, he yells at his staff, he is intolerable in terms of human feelings. Dictatorial. "Get people here." "Have those people here." "Where are they?" "Why do I need these papers?" "Where are my papers?" And yet all those petty little unpleasant characteristics fade away when you hear him discussing the world situation. He comes alive in public. Walk up the steps and the salute rings out from the PLA guard. He literally is so alive within, you can see it on the outside very clearly. He is like a politician with the roar of a crowd on election eve or the athlete running out at the 50-yard line just before the kickoff. The public turns him on. I remember going up to the Hill with him just before I came to China. So we could get our one chance to chat. He was so concerned about the traffic and the officers but when we climbed out of the car he again came alive, smiling and waving to the crowd. I am convinced some of this is what keeps him going. He bitches about the press and yet he always sidles over to them and talks to them. The press came to our reception, local press invited for the first time. This will help us. Nevertheless Kissinger was not enthralled with the idea. But once he got there he spent a good deal of time with them. And you could see him coming out of the Great Hall of the People sidling over to the press or them to him and he entertained them and chatted with them and joked with them. He does a first-class job on that whole press operation.

He is very openly critical of the bureaucracy at the State Department.[32] Clearly he is not an administrator. He is so concerned about security leaks that information we should have is not forthcoming. And yet he tells me he wants me to have it. I am sure he really does. I am also sure he gets people aside—"I don't want anybody to know about this—nobody. Do you understand?" And then of course we are cut off. There is a communications breakdown here that is fairly serious but I think we can resolve it when I go

---

[32]Kissinger—and Nixon as well—famously had little but contempt for State Department bureaucrats. The president considered them too liberal, too careerist to take necessary risks, and too fascinated with the intricacies of protocol to be capable of real forward action. "If the Department of State has had a new idea in the last 25 years," Nixon declared during his first year in office, "it is not known to me." Kissinger shared many of these views, but he was equally—and with some justification—consumed by fear of the department's penchant for leaks to the press. Together the two men reinforced in each other a desire to manage foreign policy with as little formal influence as possible from the department's large bureaucracy and its pool of area experts. "Our basic attitude was the hell with the State Department," Kissinger said, "let them screw around with the little ones." Margaret Macmillan notes that Kissinger's tenure at the State Department prompted a wry joke among its career policymakers about why working for the mercurial Henry the K was like being a mushroom: "because you're kept in the dark all the time, because you get a lot of s**t dumped on you, and, in the end, you get canned." Kissinger was of course not without his proponents. As one of Nixon's speechwriters later concluded, "The care and feeding of Henry was one of the greatest burdens of his [Nixon's] presidency, but he was worth it."

back for consultations if not before. I am wondering how long Kissinger will stay. He made one comment to me about that subject. Saying "this will be somebody else's problem." It was a subject that looks like it will be taken up fairly soon. I wondered exactly what he's planning. I remember the big argument I had with Kissinger [at] the time of the China vote.[33] And yet at lunch he graciously turned to Barbara and said that "George is the finest ambassador we've had up there anytime since I've been in government." Very pleasant. Unsolicited and I might add totally unexpected. At other times he can be so preoccupied that he doesn't even know one is around. I must say he was very good about including me in on all the talks. Going to all of them and without there being any doubt about that apparently. The visit was a big plus for us. It set the direction. It shows us where we stand. I think there will be a period of calm now that the visit is over.

November 30, Saturday. End of reading mail, going over much that has stacked up. Reading. Tired. Early to bed. It is funny. In Suzhou the cold and coughing stopped. Some of it has got to be something in the air around this place. Dust or whatever it is. Generally feel good. Even though I am looking forward to going to Honolulu I wish it weren't going to be for quite so long.[34] On the visit to Suzhou posters criticizing [unintelligible] which had been there a week before had been totally removed from the streets. Only one, talking about learning from Daqing oil fields, remained.[35]

[33]Bush refers here to the 1971 United Nations vote on the PRC's admission to the body, a topic discussed at length in the interpretive essay following the diary text. The two men engaged in a heated argument several weeks later, as tensions over the matter bubbled over. Bush never fully forgave Kissinger for scheduling a trip to China to coincide with a critical vote at the U.N. on the issue, as news of the secretary's visit to Beijing undercut Bush's uphill efforts to rally votes for Taiwan. "That just essentially signed the death warrant for Taiwan" in the U.N., Bush later concluded.

[34]Bush would visit Hawaii for a State Department conference in early December. See his entries beginning December 4, 1974.

[35]The Daqing oil fields in northeastern China were developed during the Great Leap Forward of 1958–60 and provided a significant boost to the development of

Sunday, December 1[, 1974]. A very quiet relaxed day. Played tennis. Nice lunch at Emile Morin's. Plenty of time to read and rest. It was rainy and cold. I went to the little church service. Congregation slightly larger. Went down to the big department store. Did some Christmas shopping in the afternoon. I am amazed at how many things there really are in these stores if you look. I wanted towel bathclothes. And sure enough they had a wide array. Got caught up in correspondence. Did little else.

[Monday,] December 2[, 1974]. We had celebrated Thanksgiving Day here. It was a quiet one for me. Lunch at home alone. Getting all caught up on letters and correspondence. A big pouch came in. Gray outside. I have got to get some exercise. Nothing to report at all. A few cables. Speculation on the Kissinger trip cropping up as predicted. International Club closed. No tennis. Painting going on in the house. Massive production just to paint two guest rooms upstairs and one guest room downstairs. Amazing. My lunch was good. Fishbones turned to jelly. Cooked celery—bright green with a lot of sauce on it. And a soup. This guy really produces meals. Mr. Wang has spruced things up. He and Mr. Jin wear very clean jackets. Quite a difference from Mr. Ye. End of a quiet December 2 with Mrs. Boehm for a reception to present us with a panda at 5:30 and dinner at Blackburns at 6:30.[36] The McKinleys are getting ready to leave.

Lucille Zaelit went off this afternoon.[37] Yesterday the brunch at the Morins included two kinds of sausages, pancakes—a marvelous

---

heavy industry. Bush visited this area in the summer of 1975, a trip discussed later in the diary. In 1977 PRC oil production was estimated by the U.S. Department of Energy to be approximately 1.8 million barrels per day. More than half of this output was contributed by the Daqing fields.

[36]Helen Boehm was co-founder of E. M. Boehm Inc., long a producer of presidential gifts, including porcelain swans presented by President Nixon to his hosts during his own visit to China in 1972. Robert Blackburn was chief administrative officer of the USLO.

[37]Lucille Zaelit, a member of the USLO staff, had previously served under Ambassador Bruce.

western breakfast which I ravaged. It is funny how you appreciate things like this. I even noticed the wallpaper in his bathroom he had put up. The Blackburn Thanksgiving dinner was very American, very good, very warm. Mrs. Boehm came by and presented a porcelain panda. She was absolutely ecstatic over the porcelain work being done in a Chinese factory. She said there were 120 million pieces turned out of this factory as opposed to 20 million by Lenox in the United States, a very large producer. The craftsmen were excellent. She said they were extremely interested in some of the craft used on her porcelain work. Mrs. Boehm is typical of many who come to China. Gushingly ecstatic. Warm, treated regally, given presents, wined and dined and all in all on cloud nine.

Beginning of December 3, [1974,] Tuesday morning. Many calls. Belgian—I am calling on him. Lunch. Australian, New Zealander, Japanese and Spanish calling back. Australian, a very young, attractive ambassador who because of his affiliation with the Labor Government knows China well. A little less hard sell than Bryce Harland, who I also like. I went to call on the Belgian who I was told by John Holdridge had hurt feelings because I had not been to see him. He is an attractive guy, pro-West, had an interesting chat. Had a four-way lunch, apparently a regular thing here. Australia, New Zealand, Japan, and the United States. This one was at the Australian's.

I then called on the head of the CAAC [Civil Aviation Administration of China], Mr. Ma, and talked about aviation and the possibility of buying planes.[38] He kept coming back to the fact that they might be interested in more planes.[39] But he talked about how

---

[38]Established in 1949, the CAAC regulated Chinese civilian flights. In 1974 its director was Ma Jen-hui.

[39]Forced to fly a mix of aging preindependence and Soviet planes throughout its first decades, the CAAC purchased its first Western aircraft of the Cold War— six British-built Viscount turboprops—in 1961. The first of the planes was delivered two years later. China would not purchase Western aircraft again until the 1970s, this time jet-powered British Tridents. Boeing made its first headway in the Chinese market following Nixon's historic visit, and by the 1990s one in six Boeing planes flew for a Chinese airline. "His [Ma Jen-Hui's] great interest was

they were unsatisfied with the guidance system on the Boeings. He is an older man, very attractive and seemed to enjoy the chat. I talked about the Dallas / Ft. Worth Airport. He showed some interest in this although he was a little confused as to where Dallas was and I guess why I was even bringing it up. That was the first time I was ever stopped by a bayoneted guard. That was when we were going into the CAAC. The guard stopped us. Guo explained we were coming to visit. But he had to make some phone calls to get us in. Rushed back for a return call by the Spanish ambassador.

All very interested in Kissinger's trip. Australians and New Zealanders both asking who originated the invitation and the speculation abounds that relationships are not going too well. I do all I can to lay that to rest. I can do it with conviction because I happen to think they are going pretty well. They need us more than we need them, and we certainly profit by the relationship. As long as that is in existence, the relationship will be pretty good. Farewell tennis game at six. It is so awfully hard to see the tennis balls. They stay bright red. I am determined to push to get those courts resurfaced one way or another with good stuff. Fred knows I am leaving. Bill Lucas will be staying at the house.[40]

Monday the fourth [December 4, 1974].[41] Brunson McKinley and Lucille are gone. There is going to be a massive turnover at the USLO soon. It will take on an entirely new personality. We are going to miss some of these people's expertise but I am sure others will be coming along just as enthusiastic.

Bush would depart on December 4th for a twelve-day trip, including stops in Tokyo and Hawaii. The following entries all appear to have been recorded upon his return to Beijing.

---

in large wide-bodied types," Holdridge reported to Washington of this meeting, "and he specifically mentioned the Boeing 747sp."

[40]Bush later nominated William Lucas to head the Civil Rights Division of his Justice Department. The nomination proved controversial, and his name was withdrawn from consideration.

[41]December 4, 1974, was in fact a Wednesday.

December 4.   Off to Tokyo and then Honolulu.[42] At the airport
all the things that looked so strange a month and a half ago don't
look strange at all. The PLA uniforms, the people with their children, the old-fashioned train along the outside of the airfield, chug-
chugging away as if we were back in the '30s in the United States.
The airport was bitterly cold. But even that seemed normal. As I
headed east I wondered how many Americans would put up with
the inconvenience of a cold airport with such lousy facilities. Peking
looked very gray down below. Mud walls. Gray plains extending
as far as the eye can see. Creeks are frozen over. Even the canal is
showing ice along both banks. Mr. Wang and Mr. Sun the cook
gave me a warm farewell. I asked Mr. Sun if there was anything I
could bring from the States and through Mr. Wang I got a list—
small paring knives, knife for peeling potatoes, nutmeg, and little
cones to go on the end of those bags for decorating pastries. An interesting assortment. Sun is a true artist. It seems to be a quiet time
as far as diplomatic activity goes. Not many cables. Perhaps a good
time to be gone for a week or so.

Spent the night with Jim and Marie Hodgson in Tokyo. Amazed
even after six weeks at the differences. Tokyo bustling—lights,
stores, stocked shelves, prosperous Western-dressed people, automobiles everywhere. After just six weeks in Peking one is much
more aware of the standards he has taken for granted all his life.
Visited at the U.S. Embassy with Burma Ambassador Osborn, ROC
Ambassador Unger, Korean Ambassador Sneider.[43] Lunch with the
Hodgsons.

---

[42]Bush traveled to the East Asian Chief of Mission Conference, convened by
the State Department for its ambassadors in the region, which was held December 6–8, 1974, in Honolulu.

[43]David Osborn, formerly deputy chief of mission in Tokyo and consul general
in Hong Kong, was ambassador to Burma between 1974 and 1978. Leonard Unger
served as ambassador to the Republic of China from 1974 to 1978, having previously held that post in Laos and Thailand. Richard L. Sneider was ambassador
to South Korea from 1974 to 1978, having previously been deputy assistant secretary of state for East Asian affairs. During his time at the State Department, his

Then at 4:00, helicoptered to the U.S. air base where we met up
with other ambassadors—Bill Sullivan from the Philippines, Charlie Whitehouse from Laos, Graham Martin from Vietnam, Dean
from Cambodia, Cross from Hong Kong—flying on a big KC-137.[44]
No windows but extremely comfortable. General Gallagher gave
us all a couple of drinks at his new residence at the air base and off
we flew, against the dateline but with the clock. Arriving at seven
o'clock on the morning of the day we left. On the plane there were
seven of us in the second compartment. We drew for the four
bunks. Hodgson and I each got an ace. So I was comfortably en-
sconced in a comfortable, very long bed. We went to the base PX
in Japan and again the day-to-day stocking of shelves caught my
attention. Shaving cream, a few food stuffs, clothes, row upon row
of things. You would never look twice on it in the States—but now
catching my eye. The Air Force does things well—as do all of the
military. It is a good idea to have a conference of this nature. Chief
of Missions Conference to meet the people whose cables you see
everyday. Just from preliminary talks it is clear to me how separate
and apart China is from the main stream of things in terms of communication, in terms of understanding what's going on, contacts
with leaders etc.

Arrived Honolulu after a long, long night. Went to the PX—bought
a trunk and loaded it up with miscellaneous goods for Peking—

---

phone was tapped by Nixon's White House, under Kissinger's coordination, when
Sneider and twelve other officials were suspected of leaking information to the
press.

[44]William Sullivan served as ambassador to Laos (1964–69), the Philippines
(1973–77), and Iran (1977–79). Charles Whitehouse was ambassador to Laos
(1973–75) before serving in the same capacity in Thailand (1975–78). Graham
Martin was ambassador to Thailand (1963–67), Italy (1969–73), and finally Vietnam (1973–75). John Dean served as ambassador to the Khmer Republic in 1974,
before transferring the following year to Denmark; he subsequently served as ambassador to Lebanon, Thailand, and India. Charles Cross was consul general in
Hong Kong and ambassador to Singapore; he recorded his recollections in *Born
a Foreigner: A Memoir of the American Presence in Asia* (Lanham, Md.: Roman
and Littlefield, 1999).

hopefully to put on the Mansfield airplane.[45] Mansfield coming through with a rather large contingent on a 737 heading for Peking, some say to see Sihanouk. I bought some small pots and pans for our upstairs dining room. Shelves at the PX glitter in comparison to the Peking stores. Water softener. Some items for Mr. Sun. Nutmeg, cake decorating kit, knives, potato peeler were his four requests.

I lost weight. I have never eaten more in my life and on one scale I appear to have lost 10 pounds. Must be the absence of bread and butter. Although when protocol calls I nibble away on ever-present peanuts and candy-covered nuts. And little candies that are always appearing at every embassy I visit and certainly at our own house where Mr. Wang whips out all these little delicacies. A day of total rest. A hamburger. Evening visit with most of the ambassadors.

Gone for twelve days to Honolulu for the Chief of Missions Conference. And for the Kapa'a War Game Exercises.[46] I will not make notes on each except to say that I was tremendously impressed with the military and their contribution. They have the facts. They talked less than U.S. State Department types and they were concise. On our team Mickey Weisner, a four-star admiral; Walt Gallagher, three-star Air Force general in Tokyo; Dick Stillwell, a four-star general commanding in Korea; John Elder, three-star Air Force general, Glue Wilson, three-star Marine general—all had a good grasp of their subjects. Marshall Green, a little garrulous, conducted our team.[47] He tended to dominate the exercise too much. I was im-

[45]Mike Mansfield was the Democratic senator from Montana for twenty-four years, including fifteen as majority leader. Known for his expertise and influence in foreign affairs, he was appointed ambassador to Japan in 1977, serving in Tokyo until 1988.

[46]During this period these maritime exercises typically featured some five thousand marines and a nuclear aircraft carrier group. Joining the Americans in that year's exercise were Australian and Canadian forces.

[47]Green, ambassador to Australia, had previously served that same role in Indonesia. From 1969 to 1973 he was assistant secretary of state for East Asian–Pacific affairs, and thus it fell to him and Holdridge to shore up support among Washington's nervous allies following Nixon's historic visit to China in 1972.

pressed with Len Unger, with Bill Sullivan of the Philippines, Chuck Cross, a knowledgeable guy. I think he is a little concerned about his own standing. Perhaps that results from his having that run-in with Agnew although overall my reaction was a plus.[48] Habib, who does a good job of running the meetings—he stimulates discussions, he gets things moving, and I have seen him stand up to Kissinger.[49] There is a general feeling among the State Department people that they are uninformed. Green put it well when he talked about "secrecy but not secretiveness." The EA Missions Conference was excellent including the relaxed session on the North Shore at Mrs. Alexander's house. I remember less of the substance than I do just general impressions of people. Generally favorable although some seemed too bureaucratic and too bogged down in appearances and old shibboleths. Played a lot of tennis with Admiral Gyler—sink attack.[50] Charming wife, pleasant and great competitor. 60 years old—he looks forty. Pleasant family reunion with the Athertons, the Spauldings.[51] Spent the last two days out of that Sheraton Waikiki madhouse and in the 4999 Kahala apartment—

[48]Vice President Spiro Agnew had personally intervened with the State Department in late 1971 in order to secure Cross's transfer home from his ambassadorship in Singapore. Cross contends that Agnew did so because Cross had warned against a second visit by Agnew in under a year, given that the vice president's golf outing would occur immediately after Singapore's prime minister had publicly accused the CIA of backing a local newspaper critical of his regime. As Cross explained, he did not think the prime minister's remarks should be even tacitly rewarded by the honor of yet another vice presidential visit, but Agnew "had taken my earlier opposition to his visit personally, fearing that President Nixon would question his [Agnew's] ability to deal with even minor international issues." Of course, Cross's career in government far outlasted that of Agnew, who resigned in disgrace in late 1973.

[49]Philip Habib served as ambassador to Korea from 1971 to 1973 and assistant secretary of state for East Asian and Pacific affairs from 1974 to 1976.

[50]Noel A. M. Gyler was commander of the U.S. Pacific Command. "Sink attack" refers to his tennis style.

[51]Alfred L. Atherton Jr., assistant secretary of state for Near Eastern and South Asian affairs in 1974, subsequently became American ambassador to Egypt and then director general of the Foreign Service.

just lovely. Flew out with CINCPAC [commander in chief, Pacific Command] and back with CINCPAC.

At the EA Mission Conference Dean Brown and Ernie Calentino both mentioned to me Barbara's trip back on the Kissinger plane— how they hoped to get me a refund, etc.[52] There is some need to clarify this kind of policy although it is a minor matter.

Again sponged off of Jim Hodgson at the Embassy. He and Maria put Jennifer Fitzgerald and me up for the afternoon. Hodgson is really a first-rate fellow. Broad-gauged business experience, cabinet experience, low-key, a man of moderation but I think great intelligence. Checked out the bathhouse again at the Okura.[53] Totally relaxing. Someday I will write a book on massages I have had, ranging all the way from Bobby Moore and Harry Carmen at the UN to the steambaths of Egypt and Tokyo. I must confess the Tokyo treatment is the best. Walking on the back, total use of knees, combination of knees and oil, the back becoming a giant slope does wonders for the sacroiliac, and a little something for the morale too. Massage parlors in the U.S. have ruined the image of real massage. It is a crying shame. Flew back to Peking on Iran Airlines. Jennifer and I alone in first class. Four or five others in the whole rest of the 707 and a crew of about 8 or ten. The food was fantastic. The plane was a little late. Service was excellent. And we arrived very tired but well fed on the finest Iranian caviar. I would like to try that airline again—going home maybe. It was cold when we got back.

Monday[, December 16, 1974]. I had more mail than I have ever seen. I really haven't digested it yet. Our things arrived. Mr. Sun seemed pleased at the knives I brought him. Perhaps it is egotism but I really think the staff was genuinely glad to see me in the house. I certainly felt that way about Mr. Wang and Mr. Sun, Mr. Jin and the girls. Mansfield has come and gone.[54] Great specula-

---

[52]L. Dean Brown was deputy undersecretary of state for management.

[53]The Hotel Okura was located near the American embassy in Tokyo.

[54]In Bush's absence, John Holdridge hosted Senator Mansfield's visit to China.

tion as to whether he was going to see Sihanouk again. He did see Zhou Enlai, he did see Deng Xiaoping, he did see Qiao Guanhua. Sam Jaffe of ABC leaked to Romensky of AFP that Mansfield had detected a concern about the slowness of development of normalization.[55] Mansfield apparently has denied this. I would like to see him before he leaves to get debriefed on what he has done but I don't know I will with mother here and his not being overly enthusiastic about that. He told me he would not see Sihanouk unless Sihanouk approached him and then unless Qiao Guanhua approved. They put him up in a guest house next door to Sihanouk's palace—Sihanouk's downtown place—but whether he saw him or not I simply don't know. Mansfield is a thoroughly decent man.

Policy. The archaeological exhibit, the agreement for which I signed when I first came from the U.S., went to the U.S. It is beautifully presented apparently in the gallery in Washington but we blew a great opportunity to stand up for freedom of the press. The Chinese insisted that Israel, South Africa, South Korea journalists and one other not be permitted to go to the pre-press preview.[56] So instead of standing up and insisting on it some deal was cut between the gallery, the State Department, and the Chinese under which the Chinese had their way. We must not capitulate on mat-

---

Mansfield was also granted the high and unusual honor of a session with Zhou Enlai, who was then undergoing treatment for the cancer that would eventually take his life.

[55]Jaffe in fact wrote for the *Chicago Daily News* at the time. This was not the last time Bush and Jaffe would find their paths crossing in the matter of media leaks. In 1976 Jaffe reported seeing newsman Walter Cronkite's name on a list of journalists who had worked for the CIA, and, in denying the charge, Cronkite demanded that Bush, who was then director of the CIA, release a full list of journalists who had performed such clandestine work. Bush refused. Ironically, Jaffe later admitted having secretly worked for the Federal Bureau of Investigation while publicly working as a journalist. Indeed, recently declassified records reveal that Jaffe passed along notes from his conversations with high-ranking Chinese officials—deemed too sensitive to publish—to the USLO for Washington's use.

[56]See Bush's initial discussion of the exhibit in the entry for October 28, 1974, and my accompanying footnote.

ters this fundamental in the United States. It will contribute to the deterioration of our policy in my view. Editorial comment is already lousy not just from liberals but from others. And both right wing and left wing in the United States can join together and denounce the Chinese for this kind of behavior. We should have forcefully explained to them what they were doing, raised the level of our explanation and then insisted. I hope the matter will not come up again in Kansas City.[57] China is very vulnerable on human right excesses just as the Soviet Union was. Some day sure as can be the Congress will turn its attention to these aspects of the Chinese policy. We must therefore not permit them to flaunt their way in the United States. The policy is important because of the balance. But this euphoric analysis of this society as an open society, as a free society, a soft or gentle society, is simply wrong.

While I was gone PRC was really blasting us about the UN vote which we won and the Cambodian vote which we won. The UN vote—they were claiming we lied when we stated that most of our troops were not under the UN command. Factually we are absolutely correct. But they were very bitter.[58] They are walking a very fine tightrope when they criticize and berate us before the Third World in the hope that we will understand their empty cannons of rhetoric. It is a very tricky business. I can't help but feel that we might do a better job with presenting these points to the Chinese leadership but the access is the problem.

On Monday tired but less than when I first arrived, nice lunch with Jennifer, Bob Blackburn and Bill Lucas to whom Fred has sold out since Lucas was feeding him his burgers and rice. Fred is now back on PD [dog food] and to show his disdain he spent the night on Lucas' bed instead of mine. This didn't break my heart but it seemed a little faithless after all we have done for old Fred. Right

[57]The exhibit was scheduled to open in Kansas City following its Washington showing.

[58]This minor dispute arose over the official status of American forces serving in South Korea. Bush subsequently asked the State Department to verify the USLO's position.

now, early Tuesday morning, he is back on my pillow looking gray but my heart is a little brighter since he seems to be veering back toward me. During the time I was gone apparently the staff let him in on the real cold days into the office. They really do like him and that is good.

Great talks with Bar on the phone. The kids all doing fine. It is as if each one of these five kids, recognizing that the family was undergoing a different experience, are pulling together much more. There are no longer those juvenile battles and each one comes through strong, vibrant, full of humor and different, full of life and we are awfully lucky. It is right that Bar be there but boy do I miss her.

Listening to the VOA Tuesday morning hearing about Watergate. It seems so far away. So irrelevant. So rehashed. Perhaps it's just my own experience but it is such a pain. Elliot Richardson is going to replace Moynihan.[59] I cabled Pat [Moynihan] asking him to come by for a few days. I hope he will do it. It will liven things up here considerably. I am in the mixed doubles and men's doubles, round robin, at the tennis club. They have got it so fouled up and drawn up in such a peculiar fashion—a tiny example of how a little bit of help would make the thing flow smoothly. They have got all kinds of crazy scheduling of times, inconveniencing the hell out of people. I have researched out the lake hole situation a little and am starting my offensive on that.[60] Chinese lessons started again. I really enjoy the challenge of it. I know I won't speak it but after

---

[59]Elliot Richardson became ambassador to the United Kingdom before returning to Washington to serve as Ford's commerce secretary. Richardson had served as attorney general under Nixon; in that post he refused to fire Watergate special prosecutor Archibald Cox. Richardson subsequently resigned, as did his deputy. He also served as secretary of health, education, and welfare from 1970 to 1973, secretary of defense from January to May 1973, and secretary of commerce from 1976 to 1977. Daniel Patrick Moynihan, whose long career included four terms as U.S. senator from New York, was then serving as Washington's ambassador to India, though he would soon take up Bush's former post as ambassador to the United Nations. Moynihan indeed visited Bush in January 1975.

[60]Bush most likely refers here to holes in the tennis court surface.

a two-week layoff the tones came back. Mrs. Tang smiled upon me although I must confess she is always very tolerant. And all in all I am glad to be back.

Tuesday, the 17th [December 17, 1974]. Whipping back on to the new time change. Concerned about the mail. A lot of our mail is opened when it goes international. Indeed it has been checked through some very sophisticated methods that international mail is read rather regularly. Several of my letters arrived opened—the Zeder one and Buck Byers. In checking around I find this is not unusual. I write the mail that I send international knowing that it will be checked. Mother arrives tomorrow.[61] I have that kind of high school excitement—first vacation feeling. Weather still cold, but very clear. Great for bicycling. I hope it holds out for her. Mr. Wang hustling around the house. Three guest bedrooms have been painted and they are pale yellow. Much different and better than the flat waterpaint. Apparently they started using some kind of a plastic paint. I am inviting Qiao Guanhua and his wife for dinner next week. Interesting to see if they come. He is very busy and on this new schedule he looks worse than Kissinger. Clare Hollingsworth from the *Times* (check—maybe it's the *Guardian*) came to call.[62] Very interesting person. Agrees readily to the ground rules of deep background, etc. She was griping that Kissinger and Mansfield wouldn't give her the time of day. Mansfield's secretary, Sybil Sahagian, and Dr. Carey, the party doctor, came for lunch. In the first round of the round robin tennis tournament Small and I won. Then Carey and I hit with the Chinese. I rode over on my bike. Cold and clear. It felt pretty good. I came home to find a big practice going on for our Snoopy Christmas play.[63] Peking is full of rumors about the People's Congress.

---

[61]George H. W. Bush was the second of the five children of Dorothy Walker Bush (1901–1992).

[62]As noted in chapter 1, Hollingsworth in fact worked for the *Daily Telegraph* of London.

[63]In 1974 the USLO children performed a *Peanuts*-themed Christmas play.

[Wednesday,] December 18[, 1974]. Mother arrived on a beautiful day. Gave her a nice 20 minutes or so to shape up and then we took a long bicycle ride down past the Great Hall of the People. You should have seen the people stare at old momma on the bicycle. They would stand by and watch her. It reminded me of the old joke—about the railroad train crossing at the time zone—it left at five minutes of and arrived 100 miles later at 3 minutes of. The crowd stood around to watch that mother take off. At each traffic light a little group would stand around, nudge each other, look at each other, the kids were openly incredulous, but she cycled majestically off at each stop, doing beautifully in her PLA hat, teenage-looking ski outfit and did just great. There wasn't much wind but it was a good test and she passed with flying colors. I took her by the friendship store and the tennis place where they were extremely friendly. Aunt Marge cut her finger to the bone on the airplane.[64] She had a Japanese doctor sew it up in Tokyo and then ended up on the morning of the 19th with a very swollen hand. We have got to get her to a doctor. Early evening, first dinner at home, went well.

The more I think about our handling of the art critic thing the worse I think we handled it. We must not permit China, particularly in the United States, to dictate terms to us in an area as sensitive as freedom of the press. I had a long talk with the Sri Lanka[n] ambassador about the balance between the rhetoric aimed at us for getting support from the Third World purposes and that same rhetoric having a tendency to erode away the policy in our country. I have a feeling people think we are suckers putting up with this.

[Thursday,] December 19[, 1974]. The big game is trying to figure out whether what they say in public is what they mean or not. Example. Mobutu is here.[65] He is praised—the toasts of the din-

---

[64]Margaret Bush Clement, Bush's aunt, sister of his father Prescott Bush Sr., traveled to China with Mrs. Bush.

[65]Mobutu Sese Seko was president of Zaire (later Democratic Republic of Congo). Having seized power in 1965, Mobutu established a one-party state under his dictatorial rule, though he enjoyed tacit support from Western countries

ners hit the superpowers. Mobutu enters in by saying "For Africa the peril is white rather than yellow." Mobutu I am sure will have a different view when he talks to the United States. But I am increasingly upset at the public blasts at the United States. The other day on Korea they used the word "lie" to describe our claim that most UN troops were not under the UN flag. I am absolutely convinced that American public opinion will turn against this at some point and a relationship which is very important to China will be damaged. Maybe China's rhetoric is more important to them than the relationship, but I don't really think so. After they lost both Korea and Cambodian votes, they almost had to come out with strong blasts, but their decision has to be how strong should the blasts be. Most people in this town feel that this relationship is the most important one they have got. But they have a funny way of showing it. At least as far as I am concerned.[66]

---

who viewed the Congo as a bulwark against communism in Africa. His regime collapsed at the end of the Cold War, and he was overthrown in 1996.

[66]Bush was even blunter in his depiction of the problem during a lengthy telegram to Kissinger the next day: "There is little doubt that PRC officials are using the press to convey dissatisfaction concerning pace of normalization of US-PRC relations." In his view, the "Chinese are saying that while basis of our relationship remains sound and, on the whole, relations have developed in accordance with Shanghai Communiqué, they expected more from US as a result of the US declaration on Taiwan contained in the communiqué." In his view, "Chinese [public] statements appear to be taking on aspect of orchestrated campaign . . . [which] seems typically Chinese—conveying displeasure indirectly while expressing patience and seeming unconcern in face to face discussions wit[h] American officials."

Bush was not the only American policymaker concerned with Chinese impressions. Following Kissinger's orders, on December 24 Philip Habib conveyed a personal note to the PRC's liaison office in Washington which remarked on the Chinese press reports expressing concern for the pace of Sino-American rapprochement. The note reminded Beijing that "the appearance of pressures complicates the process of ensuring public support for what needs to be done." Lest the rebuke sting too much—and a rebuke it surely was—the Americans further noted that "we offer these comments in a spirit of candor and a constructive effort to proceed with normalization which we remain firmly determined to pursue."

Importantly, this was not the only message delivered to the de facto Chinese ambassador, though it was the only message relayed to Bush and the USLO.

I had a talk with the Lebanese ambassador today. He finds it hard to know what China's position is on the Middle East. Do they favor the step-by-step approach as proposed by Kissinger or the Geneva approach as proposed by the Russians.[67] They oppose Geneva but they don't favor the step-by-step approach he tells me. Very useful.

Note. The panda bear cake made in the panda mold I picked up in Sears is unbelievable. Two colors inside the eyes. Expression on the face. Detailed fluffy-looking covering where the fur should be. Chocolate and white over a white cake. A classic. I went out to thank Mr. Sun. He seemed very pleased with himself and the work of his chef. Ironically they had it down that the number 2 chef had made the cake. I think this was rather as much a fallback in case the cake failed. When it became clear it was a great success there was plenty of credit for all. End of December 19.[68]

A great relaxed dinner at Steve and Gay Fitzgerald's, Ambassador of Australia. The Harlands of New Zealand, Boustany from Lebanon, Argentinean Ambassador, Rolf Pauls without his ailing wife, and a few others. It was good relaxed evening with singing of Christmas carols and other songs at the dinner table and then after. It was a wonderful spirit. Steve is an aggressive, energetic sinologist. Sang the Chinese national anthem in Chinese. But most of these were ambassadors who enjoy it here or certainly want to put the best light on it instead of being critical. Mother and Aunt Marge were impressed with the youth, vigor and spirit of the evening. It was great. Tennis tournament got massively fouled up but I made

---

Kissinger also passed word to Beijing, through Habib, that he had authorized the French to serve as a conduit for expressing American plans for Cambodia to Sihanouk. Both for the sake of appearances and out of a clear desire to keep the delicate matter as much under his personal control as possible, Kissinger did not involve Bush in these discussions.

[67]Bush refers here to the Geneva Conference, begun in late December 1973, which offered an opportunity for face-to-face negotiations between Israeli and Arab diplomats.

[68]Despite this observation, the entry continues.

some inroads with the officials by taking over at their request the Gene Scott tennis book and the magazines.[69] I got talking about different surfaces and I now have their interest started.

Turned down in our request to see the Minister of Fuels. "Not convenient."

[Friday,] December 20[, 1974]. Frantic tennis. A good way to meet people from various missions and I think we should reach out and participate in this manner as much as possible. As you see the long line of kids with the Red banners flying, chanting in unison (they come by our house every morning early), you can't help but stop and wonder at the discipline and order of this society. We are torn now as to what we should be doing in terms of how they are viewing our relationship. The big game in town is whether the U.S. relationship is deteriorated or not. The New Zealand ambassador and others are writing think pieces; the press is speculating on it; the diplomatic community is talking about it all the time. Overall I continue to feel that China needs this relationship, they want the relationship, [but] they are walking kind of a tight-rope because of their public attacks on us do appear to have escalated and because of confrontations like the archaeological exhibit re: the press. Which inevitably will deteriorate the support of this policy in the United States.

Quiet evening at home after a nice Clement-Bush lunch. In a way the U.S. is in a peculiar position here. Many of the embassies spend most of their time analyzing our relations with Peking, Peking's relations with Russia, and Russia's relations with Peking. Once they get by their rather minimal bilateral requirements this is the only game in town. And indeed it is much of the game as it relates to us because we don't have that much day-to-day bilateral business. In fact we have less than I think would be useful. We have made some

[69]Eugene L. Scott founded *Tennis Week* magazine in 1974 and wrote more than twenty books on the subject before his death in 2006. Bush most likely refers here to his 1973 publication, *Tennis: Game of Motion* (New York: Crown, 1973).

requests for commune, street committee and caves on the 20th.[70]
We'll see what happens. I also will make some requests for travel
early next week.

[Saturday,] December 21[, 1974].   Tennis. John Small and I won
the men's doubles. Actually a pretty good game. Rosanne Harland
and I are in the finals to be played Sunday for the mixed doubles.
She plays way back, doesn't understand the game at all. Barbara is
much better and steadier than any I have seen out here. It is amazing how much effort they put into tennis. Linesmen, referees sitting
up in the chair, another guy at the net calling very seriously ins and
outs. It really makes it fun. And it is a good mixer. Evening at the
Mongolian restaurant with the four Youdes, the Belgian and Mexican ambassadors, Bob Blackburn and Bill Lucas. That cooking
around the Mongolian stove is a great leveler. The food is good.
Many hors d'oeuvres—first course to start with and then fixing your
own lamb in the soy-based sauce, raw eggs, garlic, greens mixed in.
A good fun evening. I like the Chinese hours: arrive promptly at 7
and out of there by 9. In the sack early. Weather still cold and clear.

[Sunday,] December 22[, 1974].   Lost in the mixed doubles in
a desperate finals. They sure did the tennis up great. Loudspeaker
playing the Chinese martial music. Specific seats arranged for the
bigwigs including the head of the DSB and certain of the ambassadors. Linesmen; referee; announcements. Marvelous arrangements
for a sad little tournament. They take such pride in the way they
did it. There was a big crowd of the diplomatic community and although we bit the dust it may be worthwhile to be out there competing. We went to the Summer Palace for an enchanting lunch. Just
four at a courtyard restaurant. All by ourselves, excellent food. And
then a walk near the frozen lake with people skating. Beautiful
sights. We must go back more and more. Guo drove us through a

---

[70]Bush here refers to a request made to the Diplomatic Services Bureau for an
official visit to these sites.

teeming part of the city back to San Li Tun and the USLO. The USLO kids party was fine. Lots of different faces. Colors from around the world. Snoopy brought Christmas to Peking. Al Reilly and company worked very hard on the play. Christmas lights. I asked Mr. Wang whether they wouldn't like to take home some of the surplus sandwiches. I phrased it as carefully and tactfully as I could knowing the answer would probably be "no." He said, "Thank you very much." We went upstairs and there were all the sandwiches in plastic bags in the icebox. The panda cake Mr. Sun made for Al Reilly was just great. The house looks increasingly dirty. The rugs simply cannot stay clean. And now with candy wrappers, peppermint sticks, sandwiches all mixed in with Coke and beer, it's a real mess. I closed all the doors. Went to bed last night and walked out without even peeking to see what it looks like in the day.

[Monday,] December 23, 1974. The visit to the Street Revolutionary Committee—57,000 people, 18,000 homes, 8 different kinds of factories.[71] We went into three homes in a little courtyard —barren and cold. Clean as a whistle. Dirt in the courtyards. No grass. Nice little trees that probably look beautiful in the summer. Modest houses. One with man and wife, man recovering from cancer, retired, wife working. Their three children off in some other place we didn't see. We didn't see a bathroom the whole time. Must be one communal head for each courtyard. Went to one of the highrises. The apartments were a little better. This one had one of the leaders. The hard sell was on, the revolutionary line: "before the Revolution things were bad and how Chairman Mao made it possible and they are healthy." One woman with three generations [of family in her home] and who apparently was on display for John Small of Canada as well. It is hard to tell how many layers of authority really exist and how happy the arrangement is. The children do look healthy there. We did see the little clinic where they can get

---

[71]Precursor to the Chinese Street Welfare Committee, the Street Revolutionary Committee was the Communist Party's effort to "construct a community-based urban welfare system."

free or very cheap medical care. The women at the clinic did say we used to do this for free and now we are paid. But you see the old women making flowers reporting after their housework is finished. And in a rather dreary cold room. And one can't see how this contributes to enormous . . . [sentence trails off]. You respect the discipline. You respect the order. You respect the progress but you question the lack of gaiety, the lack of creature comforts, the lack of freedom to do something different. Really cold at the Street Committee. Biting wind. Remarkable how things change. In the afternoon the wind dies and it wasn't cold at all. I thanked Mr. Ren, our new translator, for a good job of interpretation. Instead of saying thank you he said, "Much to be improved." This self-criticism is fine but there is a certain lack of graciousness. Mr. Wang on the other hand handles it with a great deal more finesse.

Ambassador Anand of Thailand, an old friend, came to see me.[72] He was here on a trade and political mission to see Qiao Guanhua that afternoon. They are talking relations.

Bryce Harland of New Zealand told me Anand would probably not come by. Anand was interested in the Martinique communiqué, whether there was a shift in the French position, away from their abstention position at the UN.[73] In other words, Ford and Giscard

[72]Anand Punyarachun served as Thai ambassador to the United Nations from 1967 to 1976 and concurrently as ambassador to the United States from 1972 to 1976. He was twice appointed prime minister during the early 1990s following periods of political instability within his country. Ethnically Chinese, Punyarachun led Thai efforts to reinvigorate trade with Beijing, which had been thwarted by a Cold War ban on trade that was enforced nearly as vigorously as Washington's.

[73]President Ford and President Valéry Giscard d'Estaing of France met in Martinique for talks on December 14–15, 1974. The meeting offered the two leaders, each recently elevated to his position, an opportunity to bridge the gaps in Franco-American relations that had opened in previous years while enhancing their own claims to leadership. As might be expected given the times, oil and the ongoing tension in the Middle East dominated the agenda. Tense talks ultimately produced a joint pledge according to which Washington would support Paris's initiative for a general conference of oil-producing and -consuming nations, while the French agreed to increased development of alternative fuel sources, at Ford's urging. As Kissinger made clear during a news conference following the close of the talks, no

d'Estaing came out for negotiation between the parties and he thought this was a shift in the French position. Word came in that Qiao Guanhua has accepted our dinner invitation for December 27 and will let us know who else will be with him and his wife. Ah for the difference in customs.

Dinner on the twenty-third at the Sick Duck. Course after course of duck including the webbing and the feet, the brain served handsomely.

[Tuesday,] December 24, 1974. Christmas Eve in Peking. The British carolers under John Boyd practiced and practiced and then the big day and they circulated around to about six or eight embassies.[74] They came to the USLO at 6:00. Excellent, marvelous-looking group of people, all ages: kids, old people, four-part harmony. Terrific.

Martha Holdridge had run into men from a "friendship group" from the United States. These groups are often far left, Maoist types. This one was mixed. The leader, Mr. Star, Museum Director from Milwaukee, seemed fine. Some of his compatriots were wild. One started telling me there was no freedom of the press in the United States and started saying that China was right, castigating Israel and the Middle East. I started to argue, made the point that there was, made the point that there was much more freedom of the press in the States than here, and then realized, "My heavens, it's Christmas Eve. What am I arguing with this nut for?"

We went to the little Christmas Eve service—all in Chinese. Glorious Christmas hymns, first-class. Strange feeling—missing one's own family but feeling close.

---

similar common ground had been found on the Middle East, yet the *New York Times* thought enough of the accord to call it the "Martinique Compromise," while Leonard Silk wrote in the same paper that the "agreement is remarkable not only for its general spirit of 'solidarity' but also for the comprehensiveness and careful linkage among its various elements."

[74]Sir John Boyd, first secretary of the British embassy in Beijing from 1973 to 1975, later served as London's ambassador to China before retiring from the Foreign Office in order to become master of Cambridge University's Churchill College.

Christmas Day [Wednesday, December 25, 1974]. I inspected the tunnels.[75] Deng Xiaoping and Zhou had brought [them] up when Kissinger was here. "Has Ambassador Bush seen the caves?" I requested it and we went to a clothing store downtown. We were met at the curb by PLA and street committee people. Into the clothing store. Pushed the button, trap door slid majestically back and down we went into a long honeycomb of tunnels and big meeting rooms. Girls on display there from the stores practicing what looked like dancing. Show biz but nevertheless giving a feel for what they were doing. Lecture in the committee room as to Mao's doctrine about dig caves deep, about store millet, rifles, do not practice hegemonism. The caves looked pretty primitive; they are supposed to be 25 feet deep. These were under stores in the area— 70 percent of the digging done by women. I asked if tunnel digging

[75]Beneath Beijing lay a honeycomb of tunnels. Emblematic of Mao's fear of the Kremlin—and of the worsening Sino-Soviet division that made Washington's triangular diplomacy possible in the first place—the tunnels had been built as a defense against Soviet attack. Beijing's leadership expected a Soviet assault, most likely nuclear, at numerous points throughout the 1960s. Beginning in 1964–65 Mao ordered critical industries moved inland, away both from the vulnerable coast and from possible routes of Soviet invasion from the northwest. The cost of creating this "Third Front" considerably diminished funds otherwise available for industrial development. Toward the end of the decade he ordered construction of a vast underground world capable of supporting the Chinese government and its people in the event of a protracted siege by Soviet forces. Previously, of course, the Americans had posed the greatest danger, though Mao approached the problem of war with the United States far more clinically. During the 1958 crisis over Jinmen (Quemoy) and Mazu (Matsu), for example, Mao seemed unafraid of nuclear war. "Russia will drop its atomic bombs on America and America will drop its atomic bombs on the Soviet Union," he told increasingly terrified Soviet diplomats, and "you may both be wiped out." In the end, China would persevere because "we will have four hundred million [people] left over." He later confided to Soviet Foreign Minister Andrei Gromyko his plan to lure the invading Americans into China's hinterland—just as the Soviets had done to the Nazis years before— where Chinese guerilla assaults and Soviet nuclear strikes against the American occupiers (on Chinese soil!) would decimate the imperialist forces. By the close of the next decade, however, Moscow had clearly replaced Washington as Mao's primary concern, and the fear of an impending attack gripped Chinese leaders throughout the years before and during the Cultural Revolution.

was going on right now. They said, "yes." I don't quite bring my-self to see it in action. It didn't seem to be that kind of activity go-ing on. There was no sign of a sophisticated filter system. There were drains on all tunnels themselves in the rooms on the bottom. There were air ducts. There was a machine room but again rather primitive. There were bathrooms down there. There were no signs of beds though there was a lot of room. They have no problem with drainage they say. Tunnels stay cool in the summer. Temperature is very comfortable on a summer day.[76]

We had our first Western meal at the house. Turkey, cranberry sauce, tons of vegetables. Mr. Sun doing a first-class job. Peking dust for dessert.

Played tennis with the Chinese pros and some doubles with John Burns and the Italian No. 2. Called home. Couldn't hear the kids except to get the feeling that they had been broken out of the sack at 7:45 a.m. their time. All was well at home. Neil having racked up good marks. Jeb made Phi Beta Kappa officially. Marvin's star-ring in basketball. All these little mundane things are of tremen-dous importance here in China. It was funny to see Peking bustling here on Christmas Day. Worlds apart in some ways and yet most of them wished us a happy holiday, etc.

Mother and I went bicycling on Christmas Day. Icy cold but no wind. My hands had gloves on but got really frozen at the ends. We stopped in the British Embassy to wish Ted Youde a Merry Christ-mas. Cycled around and saw all the embassies near the U.S. Walked over to the Lilleys at the end of the day for a whiskey sour. Marvelous family.

[76]Bush criticized the Chinese project in a later telegram to Kissinger, though, as was so often the case, he found something else on the visit more noteworthy. "When you were here Teng suggested I go see the 'caves," Bush recorded in a mid-January cable home. "I went and saw a rather unsophisticated network of tunnels under a shopping street—impressive in the amount of hours it must have taken to build them, but clearly more for morale than for real defense against heavy bomb-ing. I was not half as impressed with the caves as I was with seeing 3 year old kids in [a] revolutionary street committee singing about their 'industrial hands' and the glory of the PLA. What a delivery system for the party line they have."

Qiao Guanhua coming for dinner on the 27th. Enormous activity in our house on the 25th. I went down into the kitchen at the end of the day thinking Wang and company were gone, but there was Wang and Zhong and Sun sitting in the pantry all with their fingers in one big bowl pulling away and shredding shark skin. Mr. Wang said they wanted it to be excellent and it would take two hours extra work. Mother offered Wang Christmas presents in the morning all wrapped saying that in our country it is a custom to give presents to those we like. Mr. Wang respectfully and politely turned it down. Mrs. Tang had indicated that they might take the presents if they were small but certainly they would not be resented if they were offered. Our USLO kids played hockey down at the Russian embassy. Being whipped by the Russian kids. There are hockey games every Sunday for the Russian kids versus an international team. Sports really are marvelous for getting across political lines. It is hard to equate the decency, kindness, humor, gentility of the people of China with some of the rhetoric aimed against the United States. I think back to our own recent experience. World War II. We sought no territory. We were trying to defeat a common enemy. We came to help and yet we are bitterly attacked and lumped in with those who tried to colonize and pillage. We are the imperialist.

[Thursday, December 26, 1974].   Off to the Great Wall on the 26th. Ming Tombs. Cold day but a beautiful sun-drenched picnic inside one of the tombs. The air is exhilarating out at the Wall. Crisp and clear. Cold but not unbearable. There was no wind that day. In a way China is a very backward country. I have never seen so many mule-drawn wagons, overloaded with hay, bamboo, all kinds of primitive-looking carts. I don't know what would happen if they ran into some kind of war situation. They would obviously have to clear the streets. Just a few miles past Peking it is very very primitive.

I went to the Nepal national day. The Nepalese ambassador was genuinely pleased to see me there. I had a good visit with many of different ambassadors. It was a typical kind of an evening with the Chinese officials with the Nepalese ambassador off at one end sitting, and the others milling around. Madame Zhang, Qiao Guanhua's wife, was by herself at the doors so I had a good chat with her.[77] Qiao was up at the front end with the Nepalese. Hordes of Chinese eating like mad at the little table, and the ambassadorial corps milling around. It was not a very pleasant way to mix but one can cruise through the room in a hurry saying hello and getting to know one's fellow diplomats. On the way to the Wall I picked up a hacking cough. It seemed like it came from breathing in dust. That night it blossomed into a full-scale case of the flu.

[Friday,] December 27[, 1974]. In bed. Fever about 100.5. Tons of great fresh orange juice. Decision having to be made as to whether to cancel the dinner for Qiao Guanhua. I decided to go ahead with it in spite of feeling rotten. Six Chinese, three Bushes counting Aunt Marge, and the Holdridges will be there. Mr. Sun has gone through the darndest orgy of preparations you have ever seen. The menu is something to behold. And the concern has got to be unsurpassed. I did a little reading but most of the time I just slept—tired and aching.

Out of the sack. Fever dropped at four-thirty miraculously. Then fantastic dinner prepared by Mr. Sun. Pigeon eggs; swallow nest soup; crisp duck; shark skin (yang gou style?); stuffed mushroom; grilled chicken; mushroom and fresh bamboo shoots; steamed pancakes; rice, sugar and white fungus; and a lot of maotai. It was a great evening. Qiao Guanhua was in good form—relaxed. His wife Zhang did a lot of interpreting. In addition, we had Mr. Zhu from the Protocol office and his assistant Mr. Tang, both very warm, friendly kinds of guys. And two from the American and Oceanic Department, Mr. Ding Yuanhong and Zhou Qihua who was supposed to serve as interpreter. The dinner went well. We had a lot of

[77]Zhang Hanzhi, an accomplished English linguist who had previously worked for the foreign ministry at the United Nations, became Qiao's second wife in 1974. She and her husband both suffered in the 1976 purge of the "Gang of Four" for their alleged close relationship with Jiang Qing, Mao's fourth wife.

good, warm discussion with Qiao Guanhua. Qiao telling me at the end that Rumsfeld had told him we ought to stay in very close contact. I told him I would like to do more of that and all he had to do was say when. I didn't want to impose on him but I was available. We talked about the Middle East; the Japanese situation. I told him I was going to Pakistan which he thought was good.[78] Madame Zhang brought up the point that Moynihan had applied to come to China, which seemed strange in light of the fact that he had held a press conference in India recently saying that he didn't understand why so many people were going to China when it was a dictatorship. We talked at length about whether the relationship had deteriorated between the United States and the PRC. Qiao insisting it had not. They arrived at seven and left around ten. Sat around after dinner in the living room chatting. Discussing these affairs of state. It was the most interesting evening I have had since I have been in China by far.[79] The Holdridges joined us. John Holdridge was excellent, speaking Chinese and entering in on substantive points.[80]

[78]Bush had recently agreed to visit Pakistan on his way home to the United States in early January—a brief trip, discussed below, that would have longer-term consequences for his health.

[79]Qiao's appearance at the USLO for such a personal event drew notice throughout Beijing's diplomatic community. For Bush, Qiao was primarily repaying a family debt to Bush's mother, who had once hosted the Chinese in her own home. For the British embassy, however, the evening suggested far more. "There is a further indication that they [the Chinese] are fairly relaxed about their relations with the US in that Ch'iao Kuan-hua [Qiao Guanhua] went to George Bush's for a family dinner this week," Ambassador Youde reported home. "The ostensible reason was that George Bush's mother is here on a visit and the Bush family entertained Ch'iao Kuan-hua at their home in Connecticut when Ch'iao Kuan-hua was in New York. I understand that there was not much political discussion but the fact that Ch'iao accepted an invitation of this kind is to me a sign that the MFA at least are reasonably content with their relations with the Americans."

[80]Bush reported at length on the evening to Washington, including Qiao's remark that American use of force to quell the unrest in the Middle East—should the crisis come to that—would only provide "a great opportunity to USSR to move in and strengthen its position."

[Saturday,] December 28[, 1974].   All day in bed. Good opportunity to get caught up on writing letters. Finished the *Centennial* by Michener.[81] Almost finished *Thunder out of China* by Teddy White.[82] Time to reflect. Their coverage of the news. The Blue News with its supposedly "straight" coverage—yet they are quoting us voluminously from the *Guardian* and other weird American publications that no one ever heard of, thus giving credibility to the line.[83] Red News—blatant propaganda. Softened in its overtones against the United States, certainly from the olden days, but nevertheless they are openly critical. China is playing a delicate game. They want to be able to criticize us to make gains for their Third World position and yet they need this relationship. It seems like they are walking a tightrope. They went too far in the archaeological exhibit but I don't think they realized it. Insisting that the Israeli, ROK, South African and Taiwan journalists not attend. They can push these things too far. They are sensitive to British criticism. Qiao Guanhua mentioning Jenkins's speeches.[84] They are sensitive

---

[81]James Michener, *Centennial* (New York: Random House, 1974).

[82]Originally published in 1946 by White and Annalee Jacoby, both Time-Life correspondents, *Thunder Out of China* offered a firsthand account of the country's tumultuous experience during World War II, detailing in particular the rise of the Communists under Mao.

[83]The *Manchester Guardian,* published in England, was generally considered to lean toward the political left, though over time its editorial views came increasingly to be seen as within the mainstream.

[84]Bush refers here to Alfred le Sesne Jenkins, deputy chief of mission in Beijing under Ambassador Bruce, who had only recently retired from the State Department, and who frequently commented on Sino-American affairs in the press during these years. His November 1974 trip to Taiwan, where he was treated by the government more as a dignitary than as a recent retiree, received significant press coverage when Jenkins favorably compared the Republic of China's government to that in power on the mainland. Jenkins's writings—though rooted in his professional experience and in convictions about the nature of the Beijing regime that ran similar to Bush's—still struck Bush as a transgression of an unwritten code of conduct for foreign service officers, according to which they should not, upon leaving government service, make matters more difficult for colleagues left behind. Jenkins was free to criticize Beijing as a private citizen, Bush realized, but doing so this soon after leaving Beijing was hardly helpful. Curiously, however, Bush was

to affronts—their being concerned about the opening of the consulates and putting an ambassador into Taiwan. But they think nothing of slamming us hard in public. I say they think nothing of it. I am sure they balance it out and decide they have to do this to maintain their revolutionary credentials and to clearly establish themselves as the leader of the Third World. It is rather awesome to think what would happen if China and Russia ever got back together closely again.

From this vantage point that seems unlikely, at least in the foreseeable future. The graciousness is there. Qiao's comments to mother last night: one of the reasons he was anxious to come was that he had enjoyed his visit to Connecticut, he had seen our family and it meant a great deal to him—what he saw in our family life.[85] They

---

not above going outside the USLO to voice his complaints: He complained bitterly about Jenkins's writings, and about having to explain them to the irate Chinese, to Ambassador Youde as Christmas approached. As Youde later cabled London, "in a talk which I had with George Bush at the end of last week he told me in confidence one piece of news which I had not seen referred to elsewhere. This was that the Chinese had taken the recent articles by Al Jenkins, formerly of the US Liaison Office, very much amiss. Chiao Kuan-hua [Qiao Guanhua] complained to Kissinger about them. Bush himself thought that Jenkins should have maintained a decent reticence about China at least for some time after his retirement. Writing generally was one thing but commenting publicly on the country he had just left was not helpful to the US position." (Nevertheless, Bush's willingness to confide in Youde speaks volumes about the intimate nature of Anglo-American relations and his own growing friendship with Youde.)

Given Bush's reference to the *Guardian* early in this entry, it is possible—though extremely unlikely given the evidence—that Bush was in fact referring to Peter Jenkins, a columnist for the *Manchester Guardian*. Jenkins commented on foreign affairs and Sino-American relations in particular, though his barbs were more typically aimed at Kissinger than at Beijing's leaders. Of the Ford-Brezhnev summit, for example, Jenkins wrote: "The continuity of American foreign policy personified in Dr. Kissinger today points in the direction of a new adversary: change."

[85]Kissinger might have held his foreign policy close to the vest, but Bush was not above reminding him of his own considerable political power base and of the depths of his personal networks, which had been fostered by his personal style of diplomacy. "The Foreign Minister mentioned that only twice in the U.S. had he been outside of NY City," Bush reported home to Kissinger of the evening, "once on a trip to New Jersey, and the other time to my mother's house in 1972. He

are attentive to details. The foreign minister knew I had won a prize in the tennis tournament and on a more substantive basis that Moynihan had applied for a visa. I have the feeling that what we do is very accurately reported to them.

Mr. Wang was offered Christmas presents by mother. He turned them down. And it seemed to me he bent over backwards so as not to hurt her feelings. He made clear that he understood the spirit in which she had offered the presents. Enormous pride in their work, in personal attention. Wang particularly. And yet they don't kill themselves in terms of housework, in keeping this place shining etc. Wang does and Sun takes enormous pride in his cooking, but the others I don't think are going to knock themselves out over the cleaning detail. Perhaps it is the domestic servitude, being a domestic servant is not a calling in keeping with the equality of the masses, etc. I wonder how these campaigns like the campaign for Confucius and Lin really settled with the average worker. A Belgian renegade, who fled to the North Koreans and Chinese during Korea and came to China and has lived here for twenty years, reported great disenchantment in the factories with the indoctrination and propaganda and low standard of living etc. He claims it is widespread. Yet control is such that you might not know about all this.

Most of Sunday spent recovering from cold. In the house. Did have dinner at the Cheng Du Restaurant with Ambassador and Mrs. Vixseboxse of Holland. They had both been here in Peking in 1948 or 9 and in south China before that. Cheng Du Restaurant used to be the home of a former head of the Republic. Courtyard after courtyard. Very good Sichuan food.[86]

---

made some very touching and flattering comments about the family atmosphere at my mother's house stating this had made a real impression on him."

[86]Bush's friendship with Vixseboxse would pay dividends in early January, when he received immediate word from the ambassador of inflammatory comments about the United States that Qiao Guanhua had made at a banquet for the visiting foreign minister from the Netherlands. It would appear from later diary entries and cables that such words influenced Bush's impression of Sino-American relations, coming as they did immediately before his first trip home.

Monday, 30th [December 30, 1974]. Left for Shanghai with mother and Aunt Marge. Plane took off around 10 o'clock. A Boeing 707. Every seat taken except two in tourist. One between mother and me thank heavens. Easy one-and-a-half-hour flight. Met by the travel service people—a Mr. Liu and a Miss Song along with the responsible person Mr. Ling. They pointed out that we would have two cars out of courtesy—one a Red flag into which I was ceremoniously piled with the responsible person Mr. Ling. The ladies coming along behind into Shanghai. We stayed at the Jin Jiang, a beautiful old hotel.[87] I had a beautiful living room with several brightly colored overstuffed chairs and the ever-present antimacassars there. It had a large bedroom with two beds and a very nice bath. Mother and Aunt Marge each from the first day we were in the hotel—either dining or anywhere else [sic]. We never saw anyone on our floor. The hotel has a beautiful entrance. Sweeping. You could picture carriages or cars whipping up to the entrance years ago. Food excellent. They asked if we would like the meals pre-

---

Qiao stated of both the United States and the USSR that, "with honey on lips and murder in heart, they prate about 'détente,' but actually both are stepping up their arms race and preparing for war. In [these] circumstances, the people of all countries, including European countries, must get fully prepared against a war being launched by either superpower." As Bush reminded the State Department (undoubtedly with Holdridge's assistance), "Reference to 'honey on lips and murder in heart" is old Chinese expression . . . which more literally could be read 'honey dripping from one's tongue and daggers concealed in one's heart.' Any way you read it," Bush concluded, "it is pretty offensive." The USLO noted that at least the United States was not attacked more than the Soviets—it was typically the other way round for the generally anti-Soviet Chinese—but Vixseboxse privately assured Bush that "in private discussions Chinese were much tougher on the Soviets than on us." Still, what worried Bush most of all, as usual, was the public perception. "This is not the image they are conveying publicly," he concluded in his cable to Washington about the matter. He advised that "the department may wish to find an appropriate occasion to draw this to the attention of PRC officials in Washington." Vixseboxse later confirmed to Bush that "Ten Hsiao-Ping had made it very plain in talk with Vanderstoel [the visiting Dutch foreign minister] that the Chinese looked upon the Soviets as China's main enemy."

[87]Opened in 1929, the posh Jin Jiang Hotel hosted the formal signing of the 1972 Shanghai Communiqué.

pared and then ordered them and provided them European plan. Seven yuan per person per day ($3.50 for 3 days—not bad). The food at lunch and supper was excellent. In the afternoon we did some sightseeing. Looking over bustling Shanghai from the rooftop of another hotel and then heading to the Children's Palace, the large emporium looking like a school where kids come after school to practice various arts. They had painting classes, model building, Morse code, dancing, all kinds of athletics. We were greeted by two boys and two girls, both of whom had very good English. They said "My name is . . ." and then gave the name. That proved to be the extent of their English. We went to the inevitable cup of tea in the reception room and two of the kids gave little propaganda speeches about how they were fulfilling to the best of their ability the tasks set out for them by Chairman Mao, etc. The propaganda was ever present. The dances, the songs, the puppet show all propaganda, all soldiers "Liberating Tiger Mountain," and their people with bayonets and their red flags prancing across the stage just like the show we saw with Kissinger and like the one we saw later that night. At the end the responsible person asked that we extend our friendship to the American people. There was a little wrestling and fighting in the corridors. The head man came across a couple of wrestling young kids. He very politely and firmly picked them up. They jumped back against the wall, embarrassed that they had been caught wrestling.

Back to the hotel for dinner after a day that was much more than we expected. Eight degrees centigrade as we got off the plane. I collapsed and for forty minutes was out like a light with my cold. I had a bourbon with hot water and then proceeded to the cultural performance that was almost a direct repeat of the Kissinger show. To give you an idea, the titles of some of the acts were "Truck Drivers Meet Chairman Mao"; "Buckets Displayed by Commune Member Showing Soil from the Commune"; "Famous Battles 1,000 Years Ago"; "The Hon versus the Chew" or "Song of Tractor Drivers"; "I Contribute My Bit to the Exploration of Oil"; "Baritone Solo to Be Loaded with Friendship to Carry Abroad by Sailors in China-Made Ships," "The Compatriots in Beloved Taiwan Are Our

138

Kith and Kin (Beloved Brothers)"—done by eight cellos. Next a lady singer, "I Contribute My Bit in Production of Grains and Cottons to the Motherland." Next one—"Red Star Will Show Me How to Fight," and "I Present Presents to Chairman Mao." Next a soprano voice, "So Much to Praise in Mao's Favor." Next one, "The Red Sunshine Had Lighted Up the Platform around the Steel Furnace," a violin number. Another one—"Long Live Chairman Mao, Long Live the CCP."

[Tuesday,] December 31[, 1974]. Spent the morning in Shanghai at the industrial complex. Shanghai Industrial Exhibition. It is a good way to see the number of industries they have in Shanghai. My overall impression is that I am less impressed with their technological skills. Indeed in automobiles and compressors and generators they are way way behind the United States. But more pride—and the distance they have come in a relatively short period of time. The director of the exhibition showed us through and there were a lot of bright, proud girl guides pointing out various features of the exhibit. They have come a long way baby![88]

It is difficult to ascertain through questions exactly how much is being done in each of the various fields. In oil exploration I notice the catamaran drilling ship. It looked like an exact replica of the first one ever built and that was our *Nola* vessel.[89] A lot of groups going through. A lot of Eastern Europeans, Australians, mostly of the so-called friendship variety. A lot of the things in which they take the most pride, computer-driven machines etc., appear to me almost noncompetitive with U.S.-made products of this nature. Their trucks made me think of the Laturno plant years ago, only without as good finishing and welds and that kind of thing.[90] The

---

[88]A catchphrase of the early 1970s, "You've come a long way, baby" was the slogan at the center of a popular (and effective) ad campaign for Virginia Slims cigarettes beginning in 1968.

[89]The ocean drilling ship *Nola I* was developed and operated by Bush's Zapata Offshore Company.

[90]The reference is most likely to the Laturno Steel Company, located in Odessa, Texas (sister city to Midland, where Bush began his years in the oil business).

textiles of course are beautiful and I assume quite competitive. I get the feeling that there is an increase in photography in China and also in the sale of Chinese watches and televisions although there are not two TVs in every courtyard as yet. Much more color in Shanghai. Women are much more feminine. Perhaps because it's not as cold. Mr. Liu, the travel translator, came in and explained that on our arrangements for Wusong, there were two options. The 7:30 p.m. train to Wusong was not available, so we could go at 5:40 p.m. tonight, spend the night at Wusong, but it would rush us this afternoon, or leave at 7:30 a.m. the next morning. We took option two. Yesterday he presented me with two options for sightseeing in Shanghai. Mr. Liu is a two-option man. Both of them usually acceptable.

This was Bush's last diary entry of 1974. Indeed he made only one more entry for January 1975, leaving for a trip home to the United States immediately following this entry. He took the time before departing to compose a lengthy cable to Kissinger, transcribed below, detailing his thoughts at this point in his China stay. "I continue to agree with many diplomats here who feel that our relationship is the most important game in town for the PRC," he wrote, though he acknowledged that his own desire for a more intimate relationship full of progress did not necessarily match Kissinger's.

January 15, 1975—Moynihans depart.[91]
I am thinking about the basic conservatism of the regime in China. Our academicians don't understand it, but because of Rus-

---

[91]The text of the diary here reads "(rest of segment on tape not recorded)." Moynihan and his wife visited the Bushes in Beijing during January, and Moynihan was additionally received by Qiao Guanhua. Bush accompanied his friend from New York, who was returning to the United States after a stint as ambassador to India. Though the initial small talk during the meeting involved such topics as Moynihan's colleague (and China expert) John Fairbank, the bulk of the discussion centered on the Sino-Indian relationship.

Not everyone in the State Department warmed to the idea of Bush and Moynihan, two politicians with a penchant for speaking freely, together and unchaper-

sia, China worries about the left, they worry about the Communist parties in Europe, they worry about the Communist party in Japan. I think they are convinced we don't seek hegemony, we don't seek territory, and thus they are caught on the horns of a dilemma. They want a strong US; they want a strong Japan close to the US; they want a moderating presence of the US in the subcontinent or certainly a relationship that would give us some leverage there in order to moderate. They obviously want US troops in Europe for a strong NATO and publicly they are not able to be out front for these goals. There is a certain decency and culture about the Chinese. It has enormous appeal. How they could have been exploited for so many years is hard to understand. And how they could have conducted their own internal affairs for so many years, without any regard to what the people felt, clearly makes one understand today though why we get the incessive propaganda, incessive references to the masses.[92]

---

oned in meetings with China's top officials. In response to Ambassador Bill Sullivan's request in late February 1975 to visit China, the department's Oscar Armstrong (who headed the China desk at Foggy Bottom) gently advised Sullivan to await a more propitious moment by noting that "Pat Moynihan made his arrangement" for a visa not through the State Department, but rather "through some special channel, if he used any channel at all except for George Bush." More to the point, Armstrong also hand-wrote at the bottom of the letter, "Strictly fyi, the 7th floor was decidedly less than thrilled by some aspects of that visit."

Bush's penchant for entertaining clearly disturbed State Department officials. The day after Armstrong's memo to Sullivan, Philip Habib wrote his own warning to Kissinger of the potential difficulties ahead if Bush's open-door policy were not curtailed. "Before he went to Peking," Habib reminded Kissinger, "we alerted Bush to the problem he might have in handling requests for all friends for personal visits to Peking. . . . We believe we should accede to Bush's request [for Senator William Roth of Delaware to visit as his personal guest], while writing to him to point out again that he may be creating potential problems for himself, conceivably including his relations with the Chinese, if he issues many such invitations."

[92]Bush most likely means "incessant" here. As noted above, he was not alone in disliking the Beijing government's repeated rhetorical attacks against the United States, and the reader will recall the late December private protest lodged with the Chinese liaison office in Washington by the State Department's Philip Habib.

Upon departing from Beijing in mid-January, Bush paused to provide Kissinger with "a few comments," summing up his experience in China to date and also his plans for his future there. He also took the time to send a separate copy to Ford through his private communications channel with Brent Scowcroft, described in the interpretive essay. As the diary is quiet during this period of departure and travel, this cable offers a useful glimpse into Bush's thinking as he prepared to return home. Unlike other letters he sent Ford through the State Department's telegraph system, which he often wrote out in traditional sentences, his message carries the more clipped style of a traditional telegram.[93]

[Text of Bush's cable to Kissinger, January 15, 1975.] Generally relations continue along about the same as when you were here. Press speculation, mainly out of Hong Kong, continues that our relationship is worsening—not so.

The diplomatic corps spends endless hours speculating on our relationship with the PRC. Some diplomatic observers feel there has been a shift and that the PRC is growing increasingly restless at the lack of progress on Taiwan.

Ambassador Youde of UK, whom I respect, has tried unsuccessfully to run down these many rumors and has concluded for now that they are just that—rumors. He agrees with me that at this moment there is not an increasing pressure to get the Taiwan question solved. [. . .]

Though they had no way of gauging if the démarche had any impact on Beijing's policies, by the end of January American officials were increasingly pleased with what appeared to be a general toning-down of Chinese rhetoric. Perhaps, Richard Solomon, Kissinger's chief China expert, told him, this was a sign that Zhou Enlai was firmly back in power, as the "'old Chou' approach to dealing with the U.S. [respectfully, if cautiously] may be reasserting itself . . . through an] apparent drying up of the stimulated campaign of press sniping which we say begin at about the time of our November trip to Peking." Since the end of the year, he noted, "there has been sufficiently noticeable a shift in the tone of PRC public and semi-public statements on the U.S. and Sino-American relations that even CIA analysts (who do not know about the Habib-Han conversation) had commented on it."

[93]The source for this information is provided in the endnotes.

[M]y own personal view is that the PRC is running a risk in criticizing us as much as they do. So far American public opinion has not focused in on all the attacks on us. When it does so focus we can expect some grief on the hill.

One basic problem is that the press wants to see visible signs of progress and there just aren't that many areas where we can keep saying "look at all that progress." Trade and exchanges are rocking along ok.

USLO hasn't expanded the "scope of its functions," but the PRC has not hit your recent bid on that one.[94] For even one more person we would need more space. I feel we could use more people productively, but certainly we are not short-handed. The one main reason in favor of expansion would be to demonstrate forward movement in the relationship. In terms of day-to-day operations or treatment in Peking we don't miss full embassy status. We attend diplomatic receptions without having [to] meet the Prime Minister of Malta at the airport. We see as much if not more of high Chinese officials as any other mission here.

On the Taiwan issue, the domestic political scene convinces me that that question cannot be solved without compromise on the part of the PRC.

The President will have to be making some tough decisions in the domestic field. These will understandably antagonize his conservative "convention-going" support. This issue should not be solved in a manner adding to his political worries. There is no pressure here in Peking at this juncture that would cause me, at least, to recommend that the President solve the Taiwan question on the PRC terms.

Naturally, I would like to see the Taiwan question out of the way and our relations normalized; but the President must not be postured as having "sold out" Taiwan.

In my view US public opinion is conditioned to accept embassy status here and something less for Taiwan, but it has not yet focused

[94]Bush refers here to Kissinger's suggestion, made during his Beijing visit the previous November, that the USLO expand its functions and physical size.

on the details. The people Ford needs at the GOP convention would accept downgrading Taiwan to less than embassy status but would not accept sell-out.

I continue to agree with many diplomats here who feel that our relationship is the most important game in town for the PRC. Even without embassy status this USLO is the most important office here as far as the PRC goes.

I set these views out not that I sense disagreement with them in the Department rather because I feel the question will increasingly be asked "can the President go to China in 1975 without solving the Taiwan question?" I think thought should be given to how best to get an answer in the affirmative spread throughout the press so as to avoid getting the issue built up in the minds of the public.

Regarding my own job here: I like it. I am trying to show the Chinese that Americans are not aloof. Going to the receptions of the small third world countries help[s]. We see Chinese there and the word spreads. Bicycling in Peking helps. Having the Chinese in our residence helps. The trade minister comes today for lunch. Living informally helps. Hitting with the Chinese tennis players helps.

I continue to be amazed at how our activities are reported to high Chinese officials—they know what we do. I am not sure they yet know what I'm trying to convey but I am hopeful on this point.

"Much of the World
Depends on the United States"
February 6 to March 9, 1975

*B*ush *left China on January 16, 1975, for his first trip home since arriving at the USLO. He traveled via Pakistan, as a guest of Prime Minister and President Zulfikar Ali Bhutto. Bush experienced more on this trip than he bargained for, contracting a stomach ailment so debilitating that it required a stay of nearly a week in a Washington, D.C., hospital upon his return to the United States. His diary entries for the first months of 1975—which thankfully are not fully detailed on this particular experience—include repeated references to his long recovery.*

This section of the diary begins with Bush's recollections of his Washington trip, in particular his consultations at the State Department with Kissinger and his staff. Yet again, the secretary of state draws most of Bush's attention, his brilliance once more set against a leadership style Bush found "amazingly insensitive" and likely to "tyrannize" his subordinates. Kissinger again warned Bush against placing any faith in personalizing the Sino-American relationship by building closer ties to individual Chinese leaders. Yet with ample time to reflect during his long trip back to Beijing, Bush ultimately came to a different conclusion. It "seems to me however that he is overlooking the trust factor," Bush told his journal, "and the factor of style." As Bush's diary and the cables detailed in the footnotes demonstrate, Kissinger's staff certainly took to heart his advice against seeking stronger Sino-American ties through im-

CHAPTER FOUR

proved personal contacts in their ongoing campaign against Bush's prolific invitations to family and friends for a China visit.

The spring of 1975 saw Bush fully engaged in the day-to-day maintenance of the USLO and of Sino-American relations, as his own staff came down from the manic high of Kissinger's visit the previous November. Bush longed as before for greater contacts with high-level Chinese officials, but his frustrations in this area did not keep him from maintaining those very sorts of contacts with the remainder of Beijing's diplomatic community. His growing friendship with Soviet ambassador Vasily Tolstikov is particularly informative in this regard, especially their friendly competition over which of their two countries was more maligned by China's ongoing rhetorical damnations.

What Bush considered China's incessant rhetorical attacks, when set against the background of his own recent visit to the United States, prompted him to consider at length the state of American society and diplomacy during the last stages of Vietnam and the aftermath of Watergate. These passages are among the China Diary's most revealing, in particular Bush's impassioned call for Americans to "be what we are." He wanted his country to stand up for its principles in the face of such frequent attacks from critics at home and abroad, and he longed for Washington to maintain its international commitments even in the wake of ongoing difficulties over Vietnam. "Much of the world depends on the United States," he wrote on George Washington's birthday. "So much depends on our own self-confidence in our ability to cope. If we project this confusion and failure and discouragement it will show up all around the world. People wonder anyway when they see commitments un-kept."

These pronouncements would become more impassioned still in the weeks and months to come—and in the diary's next chapter—as Saigon fell to Communist forces in April. This period of Bush's time in China was thus one both of transition and of settling in to the day-to-day running of his mission. It was a period during which

146

Bush saw more of China, and also thought more about Washington's role in the world, than he had to date. If Bush ever wanted the time to think and to live far beyond the glare of Washington's political spotlight, it was during these weeks that he got his wish.

Bush renewed his diary entries upon returning to China in the second week of February 1975—though departing from his prior habit of beginning most entries with the date—by recounting the previous week's events.

I left Washington on Thursday, February 6, 1975, after seeing Henry Kissinger that afternoon along with Win Lord and Phil Habib.[1] Kissinger was hectic as usual, ordered people in and out of the rooms. He seems to tyrannize his staff; he's disorganized; he shouts for paper; he yells "Lord, go get it"; then he leans back, pushes a button, "Where's Lord, get him back in here." Amazingly insensitive to people. Habib stands up to him. An aide comes rushing in with the paper, Kissinger drills a hole through him with his eyes, "Where was the paper." He seems to put no faith in individual relationships, telling me "it doesn't matter if they like you or not," referring to the Chinese. It seems to me however that he is overlooking the trust factor and the factor of style. I do think it is important. He is marvelous with the public, can turn on the charm unlike anyone I've ever seen, loves the public adulation, but takes it very well.

---

[1] As was his practice, Winston Lord wrote Henry Kissinger a detailed series of reminders for his scheduled meeting with Bush. Included among more mundane points, such as a reminder about Bush's illness since his Pakistan trip, Lord noted that "Bush's first few months in Peking seem to have made him more than ever conscious of our domestic political considerations which may limit our own room for maneuver on the Taiwan issue."

More intriguing is Lord's assessment of Bush's activities since arriving in Beijing. As noted throughout this diary, many in Foggy Bottom found Bush's desire to personalize Sino-American relations troubling at best. "Bush has energetic plans to try to meet as many significant Chinese as he possibly can, especially political leaders," Lord wrote. "We doubt that he will have any breakthrough in this regard but you may wish to outline your concept of his *proper* role in the policy area."

I was supposed to see him at 5:30 on Wednesday, waited until 6:30 with Habib and Lord sitting there. Eagleburger came out and took Habib and Lord in, apologized to me, and asked if I could be back at 2:30 on Thursday.[2] I explained that I was going to China at 9:30 p.m., but yes I could. As a matter of fact the way it worked out was better for me. But they did know it for some time that I was leaving then. It seems a small point but everyone tells me that it's typical. I worry that one can't get the most out of people by tyrannizing them. Discipline certainly, but he has these people scared to death of their own shadows. The press will begin to play on it more in an effort to bring him down. It would be bad if he left at this point but I think the President must be careful about continued statements of support thus creating an aura of indispensability. He still holds all the cards on China right up close to this breast. He is more sensitive about China than any other subject I do believe.

Thursday night I was feeling weak.[3] I flew as far as Chicago. Spent the night at Chicago. Went on to Honolulu to the Athertons' apartment for 24 hours. Friday two p.m. Honolulu time to two p.m. Saturday. Wonderful respite and it made the adjustment easier on the Peking end. Saturday the long flight to Tokyo where Jim Hodgson was out to chat with me during the hour and a half layover between Northwest and Tokyo run into Peking. Arrived Peking at midnight on Sunday Peking time—the one-hour day change.

Bar and Mr. Guo were out to greet me at the airport. It was cold but not as bitter as I had feared. The next day and all that week were perfect. My only business February 10 was Ambassador Ed-

[2]Lawrence Sidney Eagleburger, Kissinger's executive assistant from 1975 to 1977, was a career foreign service officer who ultimately became secretary of state in December 1991, having first assumed that position in an acting capacity when James Baker took command of Bush's reelection bid. Eagleburger also accompanied National Security Adviser Brent Scowcroft on his then-secret mission to China, undertaken to soothe Sino-American tensions in the immediate aftermath of the 1989 Tiananmen crackdown.

[3]Asked about the illness years later, Bush stated simply, "It was a good thing to forget."

uardo Valdez of Peru came to call. He is a proud Marxist though differentiating between that and communism apparently. We did not talk about that. He came to tell me he was leaving for Peru.[4] The rest of the week was spent resting up.

Chinese Lunar New Year started a great three-day holiday, February 11, 12 and 13 (Tuesday through Thursday).[5] There was a marvelous family festival. The streets were quiet but families were out walking; mother, father and children, grandparents. During these festivals families get together and visit. There is some gift exchanging though not too much of an outward manifestation of this. The weather was perfect. The parks were full. Bar and I bicycled downtown. A few stores were open such as the markets. The markets were arranged with the fruits and vegetables all making beautiful designs. Grubby market but fantastic presentation of the foods.

I keep getting reminded how much a part of the Chinese culture food is. Mr. Sun was glad to see me back, I think, as was Mr. Wang. The food again perfection in our house as far as we are concerned. The tangy beef in a dark brown sauce cooked with oranges has got to be the greatest. Played tennis with Akwei on both Wednesday and Thursday—still very weak. But again the friendship of the few Chinese that I know comes through. Mr. Wang at the tennis club gave me a warm welcome. Bar is taking Chinese shadow boxing Fridays and Wednesdays but I can't do it because it comes early in the morning and I just don't want to break this limited routine that we have here in the office.

Bryce Harland of New Zealand came for lunch on Wednesday. He speculates ceaselessly about what is happening in China and how the United States' relations with China are. Most agree that nothing bad has happened to us out of the Nationalist People's Congress which was held in total secrecy. Amazing that several thousand people could be in and out of town and none of the diplomatic community really know it. After the Congress there is great

---

[4]Valdez would be replaced by Cesar Espejo-Romero.
[5]1975 was the Year of the Rabbit.

analysis going on as to whether the Shanghai gang were down-graded or whether the youth have been set back.[6] Deng Xiaoping and Zhang Chunqiao both emerge in strengthened positions as does Zhou Enlai.[7] The big fascination is what is happening with Chairman Mao who did not attend.[8] There is a lot of discussion about this all the time. Thursday night we went to the Russian Embassy where Tolstikov showed a movie of the defense of Stalingrad. Not too bad although the acoustics were impossible. The translation was almost unintelligible. I bought two beautiful old mandarin coats for Johnny and Ray Siller, thanking them for Alfalfa.[9] One hundred dollars apiece. The most fantastic stitching work you have ever seen.

The week got increasingly warmer. The days almost light-sweater temperature at midday. The dust has not started blowing, as I am told it will all spring.

[6]Bush refers here to the hard-liners, with Shanghai origins, within Beijing's government who had been primarily responsible for fomenting the Cultural Revolution.

[7]Zhang Chunqiao, originally a journalist from Shanghai, was at the time vice premier of China. He was later purged and tried as one of the infamous Gang of Four. MacFarquhar and Schoenhals argue that he was instrumental in launching the "first salvos" of the Cultural Revolution, when he had been one of Shanghai's chief propagandists.

Zhou in fact significantly reduced his role in Chinese affairs after the Party Congress, acting on Mao's suggestion that "your health is no good . . . you must relax and take treatment. Leave the State Council to Xiaoping."

[8]Mao in fact had departed Beijing in July 1974 for warmer climes, hoping that more humid air would help his health. He would not return to the capital until mid-April 1975.

[9]The "Johnny" here is Johnny Carson, whose head writer for *The Tonight Show with Johnny Carson* was Ray Siller. The latter also worked as a speechwriter—and, perhaps more important, a political joke writer—for Bush and other leading GOP politicians. He is credited, for example, for one of the most publicized one-liners of Bush's 1988 Presidential campaign: "The extent of Michael Dukakis's experience in foreign affairs was that one morning he had breakfast at the International House of Pancakes." Bush was the Alfalfa Club's 1975 nominee for president, an honor afforded every year (election year or not) to a prominent politician or government official at the club's annual dinner, where the strictly enforced ban on reporters affords speakers a bit more freedom in their choice of words. President Gerald Ford was the club's official guest of honor in 1975, and Demo-

I returned from the States worried about the mood on the Hill and in the White House. There is a pessimism and a down quality that is not befitting our country. The Hill worries to some degree about the seniority system but really our people there worry about "having no answer" and seeing criticism of the President.[10] The State Department worries about whether they will be able to keep commitments. I am wondering what other governments will say if they see us make commitments and then have the Congress undo them. There has got to be close cooperation or something to guarantee that we can keep our commitments. The mood was gloomy at State over Vietnam and Cambodia and there seems to be no will by the Congress to fulfill commitments already made.[11] Time will tell. All of that in some way affects our work here in China.

---

cratic Senator Hubert Humphrey its incoming president, though Supreme Court Justice Potter Stewart gave Bush's official nomination speech.

[10]The ninety-fourth Congress, elected in the wake of Watergate, brought not only a political windfall for the Democratic Party but also a flood of new legislators, thus complicating Capital Hill's long-cherished seniority system for assigning committee work, committee chairs, and, with them, political power. Historian Douglas Brinkley has recently argued that, despite ongoing concerns about poverty, Vietnam, inflation, and the like, the Democratic gains in 1974 were really about one thing: "The public wanted government at all levels sanitized from Nixon contamination."

[11]Congress in fact intervened throughout the early 1970s, primarily during Bush's tenure as head of the Republican National Committee, to limit the American commitment to Vietnam. Watergate undoubtedly stayed President Richard Nixon's political hand in beating back these congressional efforts, aimed at curtailing the executive's foreign policy prerogatives. The most limiting congressional directives were issued in the late spring and early summer of 1973. In May the House, in a decision that cut across party lines, voted to cut off funds for further bombings of Cambodia. Several months later it directed that no funds were to be provided to Hanoi as part of a peace settlement until the North Vietnamese gave a full accounting of U.S. soldiers missing in action. By June, with the war still languishing and Nixon's credibility in shambles, most legislators agreed with Republican Congressman Norris Cotton of New Hampshire that "as far as I'm concerned, I want the hell out" of Indochina. Congress consequently demanded an immediate cessation of military operations in (and over) the region. Nixon's bitter veto was subsequently upheld by further House votes, but, as Kissinger remarked, "It would be idle to say that the authority of the executive has not been impaired."

When I was home Scotty Reston wrote a piece saying that while Bush is cycled around Peking they [American diplomats] had less contact with the Chinese.[12] I called him and told him this was not true. For indeed we are having more contact according to the USLO

Yet the most wide-ranging Congressional legislation concerning the war in Vietnam was still to come. In November 1973, Congress passed the War Powers Act, requiring the president to inform Congress within forty-eight hours of deploying American military force abroad, and demanding withdrawal of those forces within sixty days in the absence of direct congressional approval.

The year 1974 proved no better for the South Vietnamese, nor for the White House's ongoing efforts to stave off the regime's inevitable collapse. Nixon pleaded for additional funds for the withering government, which, despite having the world's fourth-largest air force, proved unable to fully defend itself. His resignation in August left Ford to oversee the bitter end. In September Congress approved a bitterly disputed aid package of $700 million for South Vietnam, though the amount was far less than the administration had desired—and arguably came far too late. The once-vaunted South Vietnamese air force in particular suffered for lack of funds, having trained to fight and to coordinate logistics with ever-present American support. It was forced to curtail air operations by 50 percent. Yet old habits, the product of years of training to fight with American methods, died hard: by one count, the South Vietnamese military expended an astounding average of fifty-six tons of ammunition and arms for every single ton deployed by their adversaries. Indeed, while South Vietnamese leaders bitterly complained of a lack of funds and matériel, accusing Congress of failing to meet its obligations, Washington's nonpartisan General Accounting Office reported that the South was unable to account for over $200 million of equipment, including 143 small warships. By war's end, despite frequent partisan charges that Congress had sabotaged the South Vietnamese regime by cutting off essential funding, the Saigon government still had over $15 million in unallocated Congressional funds awaiting use.

By the end of 1975, all of South Vietnam would be in Communist hands, after events described from Bush's perspective later in the diary. Explanations of the South's quick fall are as numerous as scholarly works on the Vietnam War itself. To some, Congress's actions approached treason, or at least, to use Kissinger's words, "pulling the plug" on South Vietnam and on a generation of American commitments; their impact, he believed, "on the United States in the world would be very serious indeed." In the opinion of others, of course, Congress had taken steps that were not only responsible but in fact required by the Constitution. As the reader will soon see, Bush himself fell primarily in the former camp, concerned as he was not only with the Vietnamese people but also with American credibility in the wake of Saigon's fall.

[12]James "Scotty" Reston was Washington bureau chief and later executive editor of the *New York Times* and one of the country's leading journalists during

people than Mr. Bruce had. Not near as much as we'd like. I mentioned to Huang Zhen in Washington that I would like very much to meet some of the political leaders as he was meeting them in Washington. He indicated that if I took that up with the Foreign Office that would be possible. Very interesting. I don't believe it will happen but I certainly think it is worth a try. It seems to me that one thing we could do here is to have more contact with the future leaders of China. We do have as much as other embassies but not as much as I would like. Gabon embassy has moved in across the street. When I see the makeshift arrangements they have to go through, I am thankful for the organized way in which the United States approaches things with our DSO Admin people etc.[13] The poor guy sitting up there with three kids, three or four other black associates—carpets rolled up and nothing much happening. During one of our holiday walks Bar and I had Fred with us and the parents had their children out to watch him, at first terrified and then friendly. My stomach is recovering.

Friday, February 14[, 1975]. First day following the celebration of the Year of the Rabbit. Mainly catch-up. Luncheon—many Chinese dishes for the new arrivals. The [unintelligible] and Salzers with children—both in communications. A visit with the British journalist, Peter Griffiths, a new Reuters man in town.[14] All want to know about Taiwan. All want to know if President Ford can come here without solving the Taiwan question. All want to know whether our relationship is going to hell. I try to be candid with them to the degree of saying I am not at liberty to talk about Tai-

---

much of the Cold War. "There is," he wrote in the article Bush references, "very little reliable information out of Peking. The new U.S. Ambassador, George Bush, bikes around the capital but sees even less of top Chinese officials than his predecessor, David Bruce. The diplomatic corps in that city is largely isolated, ill-informed, and left to the mercy of rumor and speculation."

[13]The Department of State's General Services Office helped manage American installations abroad.

[14]Griffiths had recently reported that "with moderates in ascendancy over radicals" following the National People's Congress, "steady but not dramatic improvement in foreign relations [is] expected."

wan so let's talk about subjects we can. They wanted to know about the cancellation of the grain contract with Cook which will guarantee a much lower amount of sales from the U.S. to China in '75.[15] I told him I did not feel this was political, but rather dictated by economic circumstances, balance of payments, large Chinese crop, overall balance 9-1 in favor of U.S.[16] They continue to buy Canadian and Australian wheat but they have long-term governmental commitments here, where commitments with us are to private companies and they are not long-term. Time shot by—feeling a little better although weak at the end of the day at 5:30, which is certainly not long hours. Beginning to hear more of Mao's cam-

[15]Chinese officials canceled orders for 600,000 tons of American wheat, contracted through Cook Industries, in late January 1975. The canceled contracts represented more than two-thirds of the American wheat scheduled for export to the People's Republic during the year. Though rumors persisted that the wheat in some of the shipments had been diseased, and no official reason for the move was ever offered, the most likely explanation was simple economics: the price of wheat on world markets had dropped to less than $4 a bushel by early 1975, whereas the Chinese had contracted for the commodity from Cook the previous year, when the price had been more than $5 a bushel. The sudden cancellations nevertheless took commodity traders by surprise, and the price of wheat plunged. Coming as it did on the heels of a Soviet cancellation of orders for American wheat, the Chinese move prompted the American government to virtually eliminate all barriers to sales to Communist states.

[16]Bush's emphasis on the economic motivation for Beijing's cancellation echoed the State Department's own internal conclusion. Writing to Kissinger in early February 1974, the State Department's Richard Solomon noted, "Despite Chinese balance of payments problems, which have led Peking to cancel major grain contracts with American and other foreign suppliers, PRC trade officials have taken pains to make settlements which will be quite acceptable to the American merchants (in essence, paying the firm the difference between the contracted price and the current market price)." British observers, who kept keen watch over Sino-American economic interactions for any clue about the broader state of Beijing's relations with Washington, concurred in this assessment. In early February 1975 the British embassy in Peking cabled home as follows: "In our view the cancellation of the American contract is primarily because of Chinese balance of payments worries and there is no sign yet that they are making this up by purchases from other countries. In all probability they will go pretty slow on grain purchases this year following their reasonable 1974 harvest and will then assess the situation again at the end of 1975."

paign on the dictatorship of the proletariat, a line that is being interpreted by some as Mao getting back because of his unhappiness with the outcome of the People's Congress—a strange world.[17]

Off to the opera tonight, "Azalea Mountain"—in the Hunan border area. All about a party member, Ke Xiang, a female who is captured by the enemy, rescued by the peasant self-defense force, then becomes the party representative to the force, teaching them about Mao's work etc. The old landlords strike back, but Ke sees through the vicious plot of the enemy. The party triumphs and the peasants triumph. The viper is defeated, the self-defense force joins with the main forces, they do away with the viper, the self-defense forces merge into the worker peasant revolutionary army and they go off to meet Mao. A nice light evening! The opera was full. The diplomats sat in the front of the hall, with a few of the Chinese dignitaries—the head of the DSB and a few others. Wide representation of ambassadors there. The opera was purely propaganda but the people pointed out to me that the rolling of the eyes, the posturing, the posing, the singing with the voice going in and out, was all a carryover from the old opera. The opera was too much, as it talked about the comrades and the party representative coming and teaching the workers and the peasants how to do their thing. The party representative was the great hero and all the peasants seemed too docile for a while but then they took her leadership and straightened things out. Granny Tu is captured and her son, in trying to save Granny Tu, didn't listen to the party representative and fell into a trap. There is no lightness in the opera. Some of the movement, the ballet, the gymnastics were fantastic, the staging was highly professional with rain scenes and marvelous staging effects, but the message was heavy all the time.

---

[17]The *People's Daily* carried an editorial in its February 9 edition that urged readers to "Study Well the Theory of the Dictatorship of the Proletariat." The USLO interpreted this new line, which was said to emanate directly from Mao, as proof that the central government was "going to make a major effort to enforce law and order," as some cadres remained too violent and active for Beijing's liking, even as the Cultural Revolution entered its last days.

Saturday, February 15[, 1975]. Another clear and beautiful day. The weekend, George Washington's birthday, celebrated only by USLO, was a good one. Saturday we went shopping downtown, played tennis—the three Chinese and I (the three young ones, very competitive). It is funny how sports bridge the political gap. Somalia showed a highly propagandistic movie about the OAU [Organization for African Unity], many references to imperialism. One gets immune to those around here and certainly at the UN. Went to lunch with the Ambassador of Ghana and Akwei; a very nice but tremendously heavy luncheon of great Ghanaian and African food. Corn meal—many dishes etc.

[Sunday, February 16, 1975]. On Sunday we went to church— a little church service with about 10 people in the audience plus three or four Chinese. Communion service every day. They seem genuinely glad to see us back. It is good that we are permitted this worship here. At tennis mixed doubles the Canadian ambassador [Small] and his secretary played Bar and me. It was good exercise. Had lunch with John Burns, Canadian journalist. John is going to go off to the *New York Times*. He has been here three or four years —very able and perhaps the best and fairest journalist in town. He feels three years is plenty. Four is too many. His wife is back studying in Canada. A most peculiar relationship. He is a most attractive 30-year-old who I would think would be going places in his business. That afternoon a haircut and a massage. One yuan ten, the equivalent of 55 cents. The barbers take great professional pride and they are pretty darn good.

That evening on the VTR I showed the "13 Days in October— the Missile Crisis."[18] It was shown from ABC. It's funny when you're

---

[18]The VTR was the video tape recorder, forerunner of the video cassette recorder (VCR). The movie Bush viewed was *The Missiles of October* (1974), a made-for-television version of Robert Kennedy's retelling of the Cuban missile crisis, *Thirteen Days*. Kennedy's inside account helped set the historical record of the crisis for the ensuing generation, although recent scholarship—and the availability of tape recordings of President John F. Kennedy's deliberations with his

abroad, you're much more sensitive to criticism of your own country. That play had the military Max Taylor and George Anderson as the real heavies, the Kennedys of course came off very well indeed—soul searching but strong, determined to be fair.[19] [Nikita] Khrushchev as a matter of fact came off pretty good in it; in his restraint when he himself was up against trigger-happy militarists in his own government. To me it was very obvious that they made Bobbie and Jack Kennedy look so tremendously heroic and everyone else kind of psychopaths off on the side, except for Adlai Stevenson who didn't want to really do anything in the movie.[20] But they had him as the conscience of the whole world. I wonder whether it's my own political bias that makes these propaganda touches so obvious. It's more subtle than the Somalian movie but nevertheless propaganda in a sense.

Weather continued good through the weekend. The 17th was George Washington's birthday. I went downtown and did some shopping. Amazing theater shop down there has amazing antiques all mixed in with a bunch of junk but nevertheless there are some marvelous old copper things, bronzes, some porcelains and one just wishes he had limitless resources in order to purchase things. They had dresses on display for the Chinese to look at, various models, all rather pristine, frocked-looking dresses with numbers on them. The Chinese were allowed to look at the dresses and then they could

---

advisers—has made our understanding of these crucial days more nuanced while continuing to show Kennedy as an impressive crisis manager.

[19]General Maxwell Taylor chaired the Joint Chiefs of Staff during the Cuban missile crisis. Taylor was a favorite of President Kennedy's thanks to his persona as an intellectual soldier—and his public criticism of President Dwight Eisenhower's New Look military program, which was predicated on nuclear weaponry in contrast to the "flexible response" Kennedy favored. Admiral George Anderson was chief of naval operations.

[20]Adlai Stevenson, the former Democratic senator from Illinois who was twice defeated by Dwight Eisenhower for the presidency, was United States ambassador to the United Nations during the crisis. His presentation of photographic evidence of Soviet missiles in Cuba helped turn the tide of international opinion against the Kremlin's plans.

record which they thought was best. It looks like they are going to have some summer fashions here in Peking. They were not striking, they showed the figure a little bit, and they were rather prim and pristine but nevertheless different colors and rather attractive. It will be interesting to see whether they really blossom out in these dresses come summer.[21] I then cycled over to the tailor shop where Ambassador Bruce had bought some suits. I picked out some excellent fabric. Prices very reasonable. The best fabric in the store was $15 or 30 yuan per yard. It was excellent stuff. A suit out of that will cost $65 tailor-made to my specification. I bought two suits and a white coat. I left them a hundred yuan ($50) and the man said, "You can pay the rest when we finish." I am going to take down a model—one of my own jackets—and they will tailor the suit exactly that way, as to pleats and everything else. Sounds like a marvelous arrangement.

I was impressed as I cycled along about the cleanliness of the streets. The street cleaners go by whirling up dust all the time but when they leave it, there are very few sticks, no wrappers, no papers laying around for the most part. Peking is kept clean in terms of human litter.

People universally stare of course everywhere one goes. I am wearing my PLA army hat, my Marlborough Country wool jacket, sometimes my Chinese overcoat. The diplomats look askance at this informality or at least some do. But on the other hand I get the feeling that the Chinese like the feeling that the U.S. ambassador is not some stuffy guy above everyone else. In fact I am quite confident of this though not absolutely positive. We prefer not to use

---

[21]As Bush cabled the State Department on the matter, "USLO suspects the prime topic of conversation in the alleys of Peking these days is not the outcome of the National People's Congress or who controls the People's Liberation Army, but the new dress styles being shown in a major Peking clothing store." Surely the "foreigners in Peking are all cheering on the masses to add a bit of color to Peking's streets," and, as Bush was quick to point out, the "simple dress" on display "actually uses less material than the now standard long-sleeve shirt and pants combination." Who knows, Bush concluded, "next year, miniskirts"?

our car when we go to the International Club three blocks away but I notice our African neighbors all driving in Mercedeses with the flags flying. I like to see the American flag flying here in China both on the flag pole and on the car going around town. But I think it is a little inconsiderate to the driver to have him come all the way in, wait three hours to take us home three blocks.

The staff is doing very well. Mr. Wang continuing to be the supervisor, a marvelous fellow. I showed him the moon landing, he and Sun and Chen the other day on the VTR. They were absolutely amazed. They stayed glued to their chairs throughout the whole performance. I asked Mr. Wang if the staff would all like to bring their children to watch cartoons if we ever got them and they said they certainly would like to do that. He is the politest guy and the best fellow. On Monday, George Washington's birthday, I had the Kuwait chargé Al Yagout and his wife Madria. She is going back to Kuwait to have a baby. And then had the Boustanys, the Lebanese ambassador and his wife, for lunch. Mr. Sun put on a beautiful Chinese lunch, a very relaxed informal way to entertain. The round table set downstairs in the bright, cheery living room. They seemed to enjoy it.

After lunch I worked at the desk both morning and afternoon, then went to the Yugoslavian film which was a Richard Burton story of how Tito and his troops broke through the German wall during World War II.[22] The Nazis came out real bad and we were sitting next to Gerd Ruge, the German correspondent. The British as a matter of fact did not do too well either. They just sat around and didn't bring aid to Tito and Tito said, "Well we won't owe anybody anything after this is over, since you haven't brought us the planes." I tried to see Teddy Youde, the British ambassador, to see how he took all that. I am sure he takes it in stride just as we do when we are referred to as imperialists all the time. My health is getting better but oddly enough another cold is coming on. People

[22]The film was *Sutjeska*, released in 1973 on the thirtieth anniversary of the battle for the village of the title.

159

get sick a lot in Peking. The weather is not that bad but there is something that causes a lot of flu, a lot of common colds, a lot of dragging down. I don't think it is diet because when I am well here I feel really well. I am beginning to put back on some weight and I believe the amoeba is officially dead.

This week I am starting on a new offensive to have more of the Chinese back. I am going down my protocol call list with the Minister of Sports, the Minister of Information, etc. and am going to invite them back. In addition, I am supposed to call on Qiao Guanhua. We must find ways to increase our contacts with the Chinese. It is a really frustrating part of this job that we cannot see more of them informally, socially etc. But I believe they will come. And I am determined to make more of an effort in this. The diplomatic calls are going very well. The main thing is to get more of the Chinese contact.

Sidelight. The Voice of America is good but I have never heard of so much news that I would rather have replaced by some real domestic news from home. You just don't get the depth or the feel of the news out here, either from the wireless file or from the Voice of America. Hard as they try and valuable as both services are. I am amazed when I went back to the States at the malaise, the tearing down of institutions, the discouragement there and none of this one can really pick up from news broadcasts this far away. I have more confidence in our country than the mood that was prevailing back home would have one believe one should have. But nevertheless I assume that it is because of the way the Congress started and of course the tremendous problems of inflation and recession at the same time, particularly with high unemployment.

It is a tough situation we are in but I am confident that this country can and will prevail. We just must not lose sight of our own perspective and of our own *raison d'être* as a nation. So much of the world depends on the United States. So much depends on our own self-confidence in our ability to cope. If we project this confusion and failure and discouragement it will show up all around the world. People wonder anyway when they see commitments un-kept. I think of Cambodia, and I think of Vietnam, and I think of what that means to the Chinese government and others as they see us unable to fulfill commitments made. I happen to be concerned about Cambodia and Vietnam and think the American people don't care about them anymore. But that isn't the point. The point is that if we make a commitment we ought to keep it. We must deal straight forward so we can have trust. I hope that the Chinese continue to trust the United States. It is important to our relationship that they believe what we say and that we deal truthfully and openly and honestly with them. In spite of the fact that they in history did not always deal direct, much of their dealings have traditionally been through nuances and in great subtleties. I don't think we must adopt the same method in dealing with them. We must be Americans. We must be what we are. We must be sure they understand what we are. And that we not be devious or be indirect in dealing with them. I think they would appreciate it if we are more frank. End of George Washington's birthday, Monday, February 17, 1975.

Tuesday, February 18[, 1975]. Relaxed day at the office. Some friction in the office between Jennifer and other girls. They seem to be against political people in the system, and she feels they are too much for regulations and unhelpful, gossipy, etc. I hate these kinds of problems. I talked to Blackburn about it and asked him to try to resolve it. Spent some of the day talking to Don Anderson about the Hong Kong situation.[23] Hong Kong has their noses, many of

---

[23]Bush refers here to the American consulate in Hong Kong, which throughout the Cold War was among the most important American sites—often referred to as a "listening post"—for gathering information on the PRC. Before the opening to China and the creation of the USLO in Beijing, a posting to Hong Kong was among the most coveted for an American China expert. "It was," James Lilley later wrote, "as the long distance telephone ad used to say, 'the next best thing to being there.'" Ambassador Charles Cross, who served in Hong Kong both before and after the establishment of the USLO, noted that "the Consulate General in Hong Kong had been the main American China watching post for twenty-five years. [But] its function had not qualitatively changed with the creation of the

them, pressed up against into the PRC and there seems to be some competition between Hong Kong and the USLO. There shouldn't be. Both are necessary. Both perform necessary functions. I am amazed at how much analysis goes on on so much limited data. The earthquake in Liaoning two weeks ago was reported by the Chinese at 7.3 on the Richter Scale. The ambassador from Canada told me that they reported this because if it had been 7.5 they would have had to call in the Red Cross by international law. They are also predicting an earthquake for Peking.

The Chinese pride themselves on their ability to predict earthquakes by reading water silt levels in wells and all kinds of mysterious techniques. It will be interesting to see if this develops. At the New Zealand embassy there was a reception for C. H. Moyle.[24] [I met] the Minister of Agriculture of China, a very jovial guy. I introduced myself and two times he asked who I was and what I was doing. I also told him I would like to come see him and [he] readily agreed to that. I was surprised, not because of me but because of the USLO, that he was as unclear of my role here as he seemed to be, particularly with agriculture being such a big deal. The agriculture sales have fallen off. They canceled out a tremendous contract with Cook, both corn and grain sales will be way down, reducing our trade rate almost in half. It is not political.

Had a great men's doubles game. I have learned how to keep score in Chinese and how to talk about playing tennis—Da Wangqiu.

United States Liaison Office in Beijing the year before." While the USLO was limited in size and oftentimes preoccupied by matters of protocol, "the Hong Kong consulate's greatest advantage was its staff of experienced Chinese, who provided institutional memory and canny insights for the regular reports sent in by its trained American officials." Cross concluded that, "except for occasional flashes of professional irritation over the interpretation of events—and some scorekeeping by both posts on successful guesses—the two posts worked well together."

[24]Moyle was a member of Parliament and minister of agriculture and fisheries until 1977, when he was forced to resign following accusations of homosexual activities. He returned to politics in 1981, winning election once more to Parliament and subsequently regaining his former post as head of New Zealand's agriculture ministry from 1984 to 1990.

In fact I made my first phone call to Mr. Wang to ask him to play tennis. Men's doubles with the young Chinese is really the best form of competitive sport here by far. The kids love it. They are great competitors. Always polite but clearly they like to win. In spite of the dictate prevalent here that the game is the thing. Mother called from the States and I heard her just as clearly as if she were next door. End of February 18.

February 19, [1975,] Wednesday.   Rather relaxed. The Greek ambassador came for a call. A sweeping review of the Cyprus situation making the point that the United States is not beloved in Greece right now. We had a far-flung discussion about the U.S. presence in Southeast Asia and other places. It's kind of [a] "what have you done for us lately" approach. The Greek ambassador couldn't have been less interested in our keeping commitments in Southeast Asia or Cambodia but he was deeply interested in our keeping what he feels are commitments for balance in Cyprus. In the afternoon Ambassador Alvie of Pakistan came here. The Paks have a special relationship with the Chinese but at this particular visit I didn't feel that he was far better informed than anyone else around here. The wind and the dust are blowing mightily now—not quite as cold but reminding me of West Texas.

Thursday, the 20th [February 20, 1975].   The ambassador of Gabon, a neighbor, simply returned a call. The Africans here feel somewhat more isolated than the rest I think. They have reasonable contact but little things which are very important to them, such as being able to use the U.S. commissary in Tokyo, seem to be major disappointments here. Many of the ambassadors seem concerned about their lack of contact. In talking to Ambassador Salomies of Finland that afternoon he pointed this out.[25] He made the point that he was impressed with the quality of the diplomatic corps here. He had served in Bern and in Bonn. Although Bonn was

[25]Martti Salomies served as Finnish ambassador to China between 1974 and 1976.

terribly active, Bern was more a place where many of the Europeans go for their last assignment—civilized, cultured but not too much activity. He felt that this was the toughest post in the foreign service in one way and yet one of the most interesting. Discussed air routes and said that the Finns had negotiated an air route or are in the process of negotiating with the Chinese. But there was some doubt that the Soviets would let them fly over Soviet territory and thus nothing would come of it. So many of the airplanes come in here—Air Iran, Pakistan, Ethiopia, etc. with practically no load on them at all. It is amazing to see how they can operate economically. In fact they can't. They probably are looking to a more open future.

Fascinating visit with the Vice Foreign Minister, Wang Hairong, who is thought to be the niece of Chairman Mao.[26] Indeed she has

[26]Bush composed a lengthy cable detailing this meeting, which began with his assurance that he had not violated Kissinger's order that he not discuss the possibility of a presidential visit to China. He did, however, broach with Wang the possibility of a visit to the United States by Chinese leaders—who at this time were adamant that they would not visit Washington until the two nations had established formal diplomatic relations (or at least until Taiwan's embassy was expelled from the city). To date Chinese officials had visited only New York, and they had done so officially only in order to attend meetings at the United Nations. Any other visit would be "unthinkable," Wang told Bush, and would be like "going through the side door or the back door." Bush countered that certain foreign leaders had met with American officials in cities other than New York or Washington, and that the American people would care little which city Chinese officials visited, being more impressed that they had visited the United States in the first place. Wang angrily retorted that for the Chinese this was a matter of principle.

Returning to a frequent theme, the state of progress in Sino-American relations, Bush expressed his concern to Wang that "the probable decline in PRC grain purchases would lead to renewed speculation on the state of our relations despite that [sic] fact that both our sides knew the real facts of the matter." As Bush reported, "Wang was quite forceful in reiterating Chinese view that relations are moving forward on the basis of the Shanghai Communiqué and are not a function of the level of grain sales."

More ironically, given the dispute that was even then brewing over this visit, Bush noted that, "as if to emphasize her point that relations are continuing to develop normally, Wang informed me that the performing arts delegation to the United States will be headed by Hao Liang, a famous Peking opera star and recently elected member of the Standing Committee of the National People's Con-

had interviews with Mao. We had a far-ranging discussion. She has been a shy little rabbit in many of the meetings, never opening her mouth, but she was in command of this one, along with Nancy Tang and two others from the foreign ministry. She received us in place of the Foreign Minister who was off greeting the [unintelligible] leaders. She apologized for him and then we had a far-ranging discussion. She seemed to be relaxed, smiling, some jokes, reiterating Chairman Mao's line on self-reliance as far as agricultural goods go and Mao's line about students being able to criticize teachers, etc. It was an hour and fifteen minutes interview—far-ranging. I told her what I had been up to in the States. They seemed to feel Mansfield's report was "objective."[27] Indeed in the

---

gress." As described below, this trip in time caused considerable consternation in both capitals, as politics ran roughshod over art in the choice of songs performed.

[27]Upon his return to Washington, Senator Mike Mansfield delivered to President Ford a thirty-page report outlining his views on Sino-American relations. Among its major recommendations was normalization of the countries' diplomatic relationship, since failure to do so "puts us at odds with most of the rest of the world (which has already recognized Peking) and, most seriously, tends to freeze the potentiality of our diplomacy for contributing to the stabilization of peace, particularly in the Western Pacific and Asia." Details of the report were later widely published, with Mansfield's and Ford's approval. Bush's review of the report is detailed below.

British policymakers were unimpressed with Mansfield's report. "Mansfield's views on the internal situation in China are superficial and occasionally contradictory," one British diplomat concluded. "He makes some astonishing statements. For example, after remarking (on p. 1 of his report) that 'periodic political shake-ups are an essential feature of Mao's thesis. They are regarded as a necessity in order to cleanse the system of ever recurring "elitist" tendencies' he states quite baldly (on page 4) that: 'Charity to one another is an integral part of the new China.' It does not seem to have occurred to him that charity towards their victims has not been characteristic of the many campaigns in support of the current orthodoxy which have been mounted since 1949." More important than this mild condemnation, the British embassy in Washington viewed any such public comments, even from as distinguished a senator as Mansfield, as unlikely to alter Washington's predominant view of Sino-American relations and the likelihood of formal recognition in the near future. Mansfield's calls for immediate recognition of Beijing would fall on deaf ears, they concluded. "There is no present evidence that the pleas for change will produce any movement either in Congress or

papers they have been commending the report.[28] Though it is better to have contacts with the Foreign Minister level, I was very pleased with this visit. Some here feel that the report will be sure to go to Chairman Mao because of her special relationship.

Good visit with the Ambassador of Finland and then that afternoon Ambassador Tolstikov and wife and chargé Brezhnev and wife plus one interpreter came to our residence to see a screening of the TV tape on Stalingrad.[29] It was a very relaxed visit.[30] Tol-

---

within the Administration. For well-known reasons, U.S. policy on this issue is likely to remain static in the immediate future, i.e. at least until the Presidential election of 1976. After that, who knows? But even a Democratic President will not find it easy to go all the way publicly with Senator Mansfield, however much he may share his views in private."

[28]Bush cabled Scowcroft and the White House directly with his own assessment of the Mansfield report, including the summary that "Senator Mansfield clearly came away from China with a very optimistic impression of how China stands economically, politically and [in] the field of foreign affairs. Our own assessment of the situation would not be quite so optimistic." Yet again he pressed Washington to recognize that failure to produce public evidence of "progress" in the Sino-American relationship would come to be viewed (even if this were only a perception rather than the reality) as a sign of stagnation and perhaps even deterioration of the relationship. "A greater sense of momentum in US-PRC normalization would be desirable," he posited, and he urged that "a means be worked out for senior Chinese officials to visit to the US to engage in substantive discussions." Zhou Enlai had thus far refused to allow his foreign minister to visit Washington unless it was for a ceremony marking the normalization of relations between the two countries. While Bush believed this obstinate stance—itself a tacit attack on Washington's formal relationship with Taiwan—might be overcome through creative thinking, he worried most about the public perception the Chinese refusal caused. "The world has the impression that it is the US which has done all the traveling in order to talk to the Chinese. This is an undesirable impression, and indeed the facts are such as not to accord with the principle of equality and mutual benefit." Bush would return to this theme in a cable home on February 21, again offering Foggy Bottom his suggestions for maneuvering more Chinese officials to the United States.

[29]Yuri Brezhnev, son of Soviet leader Leonid Brezhnev, was a trade specialist with the Ministry of Foreign Affairs.

[30]Bush's cable summarizing this meeting detailed Soviet reluctance to discuss the Sino-Soviet border dispute, and contrasted it with the willingness of the Chinese to forever lay out in great detail their view of Moscow's historic faults in the region.

stikov very outgoing—feeling the U.S. came out ahead in the National People's Congress. Tolstikov sits up there in splendid isolation but because of his treatment here by the Chinese he seems to be much more outgoing to Westerners than others. We are developing a good relationship at least in terms of frankness. We exchanged war tales. He is telling me how he met a crew, a man on the Finnish-Russian border who had his soldiers walk across a minefield in order to find the mines. He is jovial, friendly, possessed of a good sense of humor. The wives seemed very pleased as Barbara showed them our house. The movie, put together by the British, clips of old German and Russian footage, was very good. It was about 30 minutes. Day ended with dinner at Jim and Sally Lilley's since they are preparing to leave. They had with them a sister from Andover and a brother-in-law and sister of Sally's. They will be missed here—outgoing, very knowledgeable on China, a lot of quality. We had arranged for Mr. Guo to take us since the wind was blowing and it was colder than hell but I canceled that and we rode pleasantly over for the six blocks on the bikes. Clear stars and wind down. A rather good way to work off a meal.

[**Friday, February 21, 1975**].   Friday we had a big day. We invited Mr. Xu Huang, the head of the Domestic Service Bureau [Diplomatic Services Bureau], over to the USLO for lunch. He came accompanied by two interpreters, one very attractive lady and two functionaries. Xu Huang has a very difficult job. All ambassadors and embassy types who need apartments, maids, servants, [or] have complaints over anything talk to him. He also is in charge of the International Club. He is a very interesting fellow and seemed to enjoy the lavish eight-course meal that Mr. Sun put on for him. We also had a chance to show him on our new VTR machine Nixon's trip. This machine is great for entertainment and demonstrations to the Chinese. Our problem is the films we've got are not particularly good.

That afternoon Ruggiero of Italy called on me—very pleasant guy who'd been at the UN.[31] Ruggiero is married to an American

[31]Renato Ruggiero later served as Italy's foreign minister.

wife of Hungarian extraction. She has an American child. They want to put him in the American school. I think we can work it out. Peter Stroh, Detroit brewing company, a friend of Tom Devine's, came by with two other guys and we talked business.[32] They had been out to see the breweries and they were most impressed not with the mechanization but with the beer itself. They are living in a belts-and-shaft age—old breweries that would be well pre–World War II. Their packaging is terrible. The Japanese on the other hand have the most modern packaging and brewing facilities in the world. But China goes about it in the same old way with excess labor and nevertheless their beer is considered very very good. We enjoy it. It seems lower in carbonation. It's more like a draft beer here and it's excellent. That evening we had dinner with Ambassador Vixseboxse of the Netherlands. Some of the diplomatic evenings are so kind of formal and boring. You sit around afterward and religiously have to wait until 11 o'clock. I wish we could get away from that here. The dinner was good—European style. They had the same help in their house for twenty years. But it just went on and on.

I had an excellent visit with Wang Hairong, Chairman Mao's niece, the day before. Saturday my amoeba after-effects came back and right in the middle of my meeting with the Bulgarian ambassador. I was seized. I rather diplomatically explained to him to wait, flipped on the VTR machine so he could see Nixon's coming to China three years ago almost to the day, and whipped into the downstairs men's room, returned weak. Stayed flattened out most of the day but in the afternoon got up and bicycled to the Friendship Store and around. There is so much to see and look at here.

Carpets are real interesting. They are very expensive. We looked at one old one for 3,500 yuan (about $1,700–1,800) at the Friendship Store. Prices are going up rapidly right in front of our eyes.

---

[32]Peter Stroh was at the time president of the Stroh Brewery Company. Thomas Devine, a longtime Bush family friend, was also an initial financial backer of the Zapata Offshore Oil Company during the late 1950s.

The exchange rate when I came here was 1.85 yuan to the dollar. Yesterday it was 1.74. Prices in the Friendship Store are going up fast although the staples like food remain pretty much the same. Leather pants for example have almost doubled since looking at the prices and so have some of the porcelains gone up tremendously fast. It is very hard to get any real figures on the Chinese economy.

Deng Xiaoping greeted the new leaders of Mozambique and keeps escalating the thesis abroad now that the two superpowers will be at war, that the superpowers are in chaos, that the world needs revolution. Here is a sample of his writings:

> At present the international situation is excellent. The people of the world are striving forward in this situation characterized by great disorder under heaven. Countries want independence, nations want liberation, the people want revolution. This historical torrent is surging forward irresistibly. The two superpowers which are contending for world hegemony are condemned and opposed ever more strongly by the people of the world, particularly the countries and the people of the Third World, and are having a very tough time in an attempt to extricate themselves from their crises at home and abroad. They are intensifying their contention for world hegemony and stepping up their expansion abroad. Every day they are talking about peace but actually preparing for war. The danger of a new world war is increasing and the people of all countries must get prepared against this. But looking into the world's future we are full of confidence the people of the world are forging ahead and the factors for revolution are increasing. Whether war gives rise to revolution or revolution prevents war, in either case the future of the world will be bright.

This thesis continues all the time. They always keep talking about the dictatorship of the proletariat. There is some feeling that that is Chairman Mao's push, as opposed to the line of other leaders, but nevertheless there is constant talk about the two superpowers seeking hegemony. When we have meetings with them these subjects never come up unless we raise them, but there is constant reference to this ideological struggle and they are obviously doing it to get Third World attention and to be champions of the Third World as opposed to the superpowers. I must say it gets somewhat annoying, however, at times when we know and they know that they want the United States to remain strong.

[Saturday, February 22, 1975]. Saturday was a pleasant day. The Bulgarian ambassador came to call and right in the middle of our conversation I had a slight return to my amoeba problem. Excusing myself rapidly with no embarrassment whatsoever. It's funny how if this had happened to me several years ago I probably would have been blushing and embarrassed and in great agony. But I simply flicked on the VTR set and showed Nixon coming to China and said, "please excuse me." He seemed to be fully understanding as do experienced people from around this part of the world. I took it easy in the afternoon sleeping. I had been feeling very good and suddenly this thing seemed to catch up with me again. My health is good here, the weather is clear—beginning to warm a little now, although there has been an awful lot of dust running around in the air.

Sunday, a very relaxed day. Church which we wouldn't miss—9:30—and then browsing around the shops at Liulichang, its beautiful porcelain, beautiful paintings and beautiful jade and other historical items. We also went to the carpet shops—carpets in Peking and Tianjin are very good. They are expensive, nothing cheap about them. I am amazed at some of the differences in prices. We bought a little hand-warmer at the Theater Shop the other day for around $4 and saw the same one for around $15 today. The rate of exchange is changing. There doesn't seem to be any particular similarity between these prices. The Friendship Store is more expensive than the other stores. We saw these basketware materials of little animals made out of straw or reed or whatever they are. They are almost twice as much at the Friendship Store as at the little theater shop downtown. This afternoon we stopped by for lunch at the International Club. We had juice, noodles, sweet and sour pork, for two and the price was 2 kuai 80 or about $1.60 for two. Not bad at all. Language goes slow. Mrs. Tang is the world's politest woman. She has written out all the expressions for tennis. I want to say to Mr. Wang, "You have a good forehand." She is very polite always. In putting it down she put, "You win" and telling me how to say that and then she put "he loses" because it would be impolite I guess to point out "you lose."

Personal contacts with the Chinese are marvelous. They are always courteous. They are very friendly. Extremely polite. In reading in history you see even when they visit people they've put in jail they are that way, or during some of the wars, they have this extreme politeness. But they are certainly tough and strong. They always emphasis principle. "These are our principles." "These are principled."

Dinner with the Lilleys on Sunday at the Cheng Du Restaurant. It used to be an old home of the First Republic of China, many courtyards running from one end to the other. Now rather bleak, clean as it can be, with little off the courtyards, many private dining rooms. Food is excellent. We had dinner for twelve for 137 yuan which included a hot shao shing wine and beer, juice plus many courses. The "standard" was 10 yuan per person. The rest was for the extras. No tipping of course. You don't tip for anything in China. The food was marvelous. Different hot Sichuan-style dishes —fish, chicken, Sichuan noodles, glutinous rice with sesame seeds and on and on. Many many different dishes. Party was a going-away party for Jim Lilley. He had some of his family with him.[33]

The line goes on in the papers about the dictatorship of the proletariat. The diplomatic corps is trying like mad to figure out what

---

[33] "As we prepared to board the train" to leave Beijing, Lilley reported in his memoirs, "Anderson handed me a letter from Ambassador Bush. . . . On the outside of the envelope were typed the words 'do not open till the train has left Peking.' . . . In a letter addressed to Sally as much as it was to me, Ambassador Bush expressed his appreciation for my work and my willingness to take on any assignment. . . . 'As you leave Peking tuck away into your heart of hearts the fact that you three have done well. You've made friends. You've given much to your country in a tough assignment. Bar and I will miss you very much.'"

the thrust is on this new campaign. You hear much more about it than you do about the anti-Lin or anti-Confucius campaigns since the National People's Congress.

Monday, February 24[, 1975]. The amoeba threatened again, leaving me awfully weak in the morning. I went to the office though and made a call on the ambassador of Turkey. Each ambassador in talking to the United States is interested in discussing not China but his own problems, so today we talked about the Greece-Cyprus deal. I hate to see us cross-threaded with an ally like Turkey. After that I went for a fitting at Hong Du Tailors where I am having two vests, two suits and a sports coat made. The prices as I mentioned earlier are very reasonable. The people are so interested and helpful. They study everything and go over the fittings very carefully. They had already cut out one of the suits and I had a chance to try it on, carefully fitting and discussing things. They have some beautiful cashmere material in and also a nice wool for a sports coat. I may end up with a whole new wardrobe here after I see how the first ones work out because it's extremely reasonable. Lunch quietly at home with the great Mr. Wang, his enormous courtesy, his laugh, his politeness, his thoughtfulness, his crisp white jacket and his wonderful smile. He told us that he took his child to the movies but that the child became scared in the dark after a period of time. He loves his family [and] talks about them quite a bit. Afternoon was rather relaxed. Caught up on a tremendous amount of reading of cables. Our Xerox machine is out and one wonders whatever went on in offices before the Xerox.

Ambassador Small of Canada came to call and then at 5 o'clock we attended a national day reception for Nepal. These receptions are a little deadly but you do have a chance to move around the room and see all the ambassadors. The Cuban ambassador shook hands today. As a matter of fact we shook once before but he seemed very uncomfortable. At the beauty shop after some small talk, Bar asked his wife where she was from. She said, "Cuba." She asked Bar where she was from. Bar said, "The United States," and she quickly turned away, and would have left the shop if her hair hadn't been wringing wet.

The North Korean Dean of the Diplomatic Corps did shake hands. Most do seem glad to see us at these receptions. Pakistan was happy, for today it sounds like they are getting their arms embargo lifted.[34] Most people, even the Russians and others, are very friendly to us here. The diplomatic community is fairly concise, closely knit and reasonably friendly. Home that night for writing letters.

Pick up dinner, trying to cut down on some of the exotic foods until the tummy gets in shape. Early to bed. I sleep very well here in China, cold at night but for some reason I find as well here as I have anyplace else. Lots of birds, sparrows, are appearing now in our vines outside of the house. They are the same kind of sparrows that we see in the States and also the same kind that we ate in Shanghai! The facilities in our USLO house are good. The bathtubs are tremendous, shower that I had them put into our room pretty good, water is hot most of the time, toilets in all the bathrooms appropriately named Victory. That will go with the pliers. I think the wallpaper in the hall makes the house look much cheerier now. We still need a bunch more pictures and color around but it is coming along well. Downstairs living room with the bright Chinese yellow that Mrs. Bruce put in is very stylish and bright.[35] A lot of

---

[34]Lyndon Johnson's administration had embargoed arms sales to both Pakistan and India in 1965 in an effort to defuse tensions in the volatile region. The 1971 Indo-Pakistani war strained this policy to the breaking point, as Nixon's White House tacitly allowed Western arms shipments to Pakistan, and even allowed Pakistan International Airways to shuttle arms from China aboard a leased Boeing 707, despite a strict prohibition on the practice in the initial lease agreement. It was better to arm the Pakistanis, even through subterfuge, Kissinger and Nixon reasoned, than to allow the Soviets to gain a further foothold in the region by virtue of their longstanding support for India. "If the Russians get away with facing down the Chinese," Kissinger warned the president, "and if the Indians get away with licking the Pakistanis . . . we may be looking down the gun barrel" of a global conflict.

[35]Evangeline Bruce worked throughout her time in Beijing to revamp and redecorate the USLO's formal accommodations, working throughout with May de

bright cushions around with Thai silk. My little office-den is much brighter now with pictures of astronauts etc. on the wall. I meet the ambassadors there rather than [in] the office which is still a little chilly looking. We are looking around for rugs, none of which seem cheap, all of which seem pretty nice however.

[Tuesday,] February 25[, 1975].   Quiet day. Lunch at home. Interview with George Witwer, Lilley's brother-in-law from Indiana.[36] General Indiana with pictures. Four-thirty: courtesy call on Ambassador Klibi of Tunisia.[37] Six to seven, Kuwait national day reception. Driving along the street it is so interesting here. One gets the feeling among other things of strong family ties. One of the misconceptions I had before coming here was that family was no longer important. Yet on the holidays and on any day one gets the strong feeling of family. Grown girls looking after their grandparents. Grown parents looking after their mothers. Children together with parents. The Chun Jie holiday was the best for this—seeing all the families with several generations together.[38] Respect for family. Talking about family. Talking about visiting family. All very important.

Ambassador Klibi, when he first came here, called on the Dean of the Diplomatic Corps, the Ambassador of Nepal, who had been here for 10 years. The Nepalese ambassador said, "I have been here for ten years and I think I know less about the Chinese than when I came." There is this feeling that we are close to the forest but somehow are not seeing the trees. And yet the other side of it is that you do get much more flavor for China being here. You don't know exactly what's going on in the government. They are secretive. The

---

Montaudouin, described by historian Priscilla Roberts as "the State Department's premier interior decorator."

[36]Witwer also worked for the CIA earlier in his career, sharing a Washington apartment with Lilley during their initial training. He eventually returned to his Indiana home and entered the newspaper business.

[37]Chadli Klibi would later serve as general secretary of the Arab League from 1979 to 1990.

[38]The Chinese lunar new year festival.

preparations for the National People's Congress were done in total secrecy. They are not outgoing. You can't go into their homes and yet you get a general impression of China that you can't get from outside. You see kids slugging it out in the streets, playing, fighting, just as you do in the States. You see little girls doing that funny jump rope game with kind of elastic-looking jump ropes in parallel, low to the ground where their feet weave almost like weaving in a loom. You see young teenagers kind of hanging together smoking. Men smoke a lot. You get used to people spitting on the street although I am told that they are working against this. The grayness is beginning to give way a little bit as warm weather approaches. The padding doesn't look quite as great on the clothes, both women's and men's. I am anxious to see summer and spring here. Interesting lunch today. Chicken, a great soup and one of the ingredients was chicken blood. Fresh blood of chicken made into a jelly, almost like a bean curd which was then cut into squares and served. Barbara told me what it was after we finished. I must say it tasted delicious, but I am glad she didn't let me know ahead of time what I was eating.

New discovery to go with the orange juice that is served absolutely everywhere in China. A lemon juice. I have got to find out where we get it. Pretty good. Marvelous letter from Marvin, saying things are great. Bar sat and cried as she read it. The kid has had a tough go until the last couple of years when he has really done a first-rate job. He was admitted to the University of Texas, still waiting to hear from North Carolina and Colorado.[39] Basketball going great. His great sentence was, "Johnny Bush is coming down to see a basketball game. You can't help but love a guy that would do a thing like that." I miss the children a lot every day and yet they seem to be holding together. They seem to be getting strength from each other. They spell out their love for their parents. We are very lucky.

[39]Marvin Bush initially enrolled at the University of Texas but eventually graduated from the University of Virginia.

I am finding a little more time to study China's history, read about Chairman Mao. There are great inconsistencies in Mao, what he says now and what he used to believe. Nothing too fundamental but time and again one can find them. But come to think of it who shouldn't "change his mind." Off to Tianjin tomorrow to the carpet fair.[40]

[Wednesday,] February 26[, 1975]. Visit to Tianjin. Left in the car with Mr. Guo and Jennifer, Bar, Bob Blackburn going to Tianjin. A beautiful drive, a much better drive than we had in the fall. The weather was clear but cold. Much going on in the fields, beginning to see some traces of green there. I am continually impressed by the primitive nature of some of the transport—women, children and men all mixed in with these uniwheel barrows with the wheel in the middle of the barrow—a design I am told is more efficient than ours but they really look weird and they are going off endlessly across the fields with great loads.

One time we came to a place where they were cutting down trees on the road. The maneuver was being handled in such a way as to cause a massive traffic block both ways. One major problem appeared to be a horse whose cart was weighted down so tremendously with these great heavy logs that the horse's back legs had buckled. Two lead horses were prancing around, jumping high on their hind legs and this immediately got a massive consultation going. We all jumped out and tried to lift the lumber to rid the load off the horse, public-service types in Shanghai in front of us were out consulting, many passers-by were consulting, trucks and buses were honking, way out in the middle of nowhere. Finally the horse moved off the road and traffic crept through the block.

---

[40]Tianjin (Tientsin in the original diary) held a renowned carpet fair, which attracted international visitors and buyers (including Bush), from February 25 to March 5, 1975. This first Chinese attempt at a carpet fair was not the success that trade officials would have hoped for: the USLO representative on site estimated that only 150 foreign buyers were in attendance, among them a total of twenty Americans, including spouses and dependents.

The kids all look so healthy as we go along and the people look well fed. You just don't see malnourishment in Tianjin for example. You see a lot of people. They crowd around your car unbelievably in no time at all. There are staring mobs touching the car, right up against it. A couple of young kids recognized us as American and so stated. Before you could even get out of the car there would be 40 or 50 people gathered around. Polite but staring with eyeballs almost popping out of the head. Kids grabbing their friends and pointing. Parents grabbing their kids and pointing. It caused great concern. Went to the Canton Carpet Factory No. 1 and I was delighted we did it. We saw the masterful craftsmen at work. The endless personal labor that goes into one of these Tianjin carpets is amazing. I am dying to have one. The prices are pretty high. Around $1,800 kuai I believe for a 9 × 12. We also went to the Carpet Fair where we saw carpets displayed from all over China—Tianjin, Peking, Shanghai and northeast China—Dairen as well. We bought a couple of oriental-type Chinese carpets which turn out to have been made in Peking but they were out of stock.

We discussed the trade with the United States and Mr. Zhu from Tianjin, and Mr. Xu from Peking reviewed carpet trade. They pointed out that many older Americans knew the value [of] Chinese carpets but since trade had been cut off for so long the younger people in the United States didn't know. They did not discuss most favored nations. They did talk about price differential between what they pay in Peking and what the carpets are actually sold for in the United States. I told them that we wanted to encourage trade between China and the United States in carpets.

I had a very good lunch at a good Tianjin restaurant—four or five dishes but the price was little higher than those we have been paying in Peking, 37 kuai (roughly $20 for four) although it was an excellent lunch. Ride service for the day cost 10 kuai (a little more than $5) and the car for the day in Shanghai cost 18 kuai (roughly $10 or $11). Not bad. All along the Tianjin road you see endless lines of carts with one horse or donkey with a little tiny one running in front. Or with two or three horses with a little tiny one in front. The little one is always alone either tethered with the others or just sitting there.

The thing that is impressive in the Tianjin [to] Peking run is the number of livestock going by: a whole bunch of chickens on the back of the guy's bike, or pigs. Today seemed to be a pig day. They were tethered on the back of these wheelbarrows, or tricycle-operated bike-type machines. Many of the carts looked overloaded with hemp. Here is a pig tied on the back of a bicycle—two big baskets underneath him with the pigs stretched out. It looks like he's been sedated across the back of the bike. Still some ice in the ditches along the side of the highway. When the horse manure or donkey manure hits the streets it's only a few minutes before somebody coming along behind them scoops it up, puts it into a basket and hauls it off probably for their own plots in communes or for the fields themselves. The streets are unusually clean in the cities and outside. Very little litter, very little trash. These things are great successes of this society. I am continually amazed by these carts. As soon as people pile on the back of them, they immediately fall asleep. It seems to me that that is part of the ingredient of riding the Chinese cart—no matter what the load is and how many animals, what condition, how much honking, how much traffic, they promptly fall asleep on the back of the truck, feet sticking out oblivious to the world, in padded coats in cold weather or warm.

A sight between these two cities is these separate adobe brown-colored-looking villages that look like they haven't changed in a couple of thousand years. Baked brick and then smoothed over by a brown mud on the outside. Set back from the street. People working away at them. One dusk there was a whole group of neighbors up putting on a straw thatched roof on one house. It looked like a big communal project—all helping out. Groups of older [and] wrinkled Chinese men sitting around playing some kind of Chinese checker game. On the way down we saw a rifle practice by PLA units and in the distance an airfield with tails of jet airplanes far away. We seldom see airplanes in the air. We did see one old biplane that looked like one of the old Beechcraft biplanes flying around.

At our house in Washington we hear the roar of the jets all the time but in China you never hear a plane except at the airport itself. Then seldom see one flying overhead. At one point they were widening the street, tearing up trees. When we came down in the morning there were many trees around the surface and when we came back at night they were cut up, hauled away on carts and all that was left was groups of people in each hole digging out the stumps and making remarkable progress at that. Amazing at how people are mobilized to do these chores. They really seem to be working. The chips are flying and progress was visible.

[Thursday,] February 27[, 1975]. Ambassador Boustany of Lebanon came over—very disturbed about the earthquakes. There was an earthquake up at Liaoning and it is hard to find out what the damage was, what really happened. It is the darndest society in terms of information. All kinds of rumors; very little fact. Now there are predictions of earthquakes in Peking. The diplomatic community is abuzz with rumors. The Chinese have methods of prediction. They tell the masses, as Mr. Lin Ping told me on the 28th, "the masses" help in this. Masses watch to see the snakes leaving their lairs, rats leaving the buildings, the levels of water in the well, and report all that data. Our scientists say that Peking does not have a good prediction service—our seismologists. But the rumors are rife. Boustany was telling me that the Chinese Army, PLA, was making arrangements to evacuate the wounded, giving instructions to people about leaving the buildings and pitching tents etc. The diplomatic corps now has something to discuss since the National People's Congress has finished. Richard Akwei of Ghana, a very European ex-UN, came to see me about helping an American friend of his do business with China at the Canton Fair. Had a good lunch with Ferenc Gódor, the Hungarian ambassador; Sri Lanka, Turkey, USLO and Hungary with a stylish Hungarian interpreter. A very nice thing for him to do. It worked out really well.

Friday, February 28[, 1975]. Lot of office work. Language lesson. Some progress. Fitting at Hong Du Tailors. They are most apologetic since things weren't going to be ready for thirty minutes. Go back Tuesday. Lunch with Lin Ping, American and Oceanic Department from the Foreign Ministry. Former ambassador in Chile. Considered not particularly friendly to the U.S. but very relaxed lunch. One of Mr. Sun's nine-course specials—fungus and all. Lin Ping informed us that Rhodes and the Speaker were coming here at the end of March—something we had confirmed by telegram the minute we walked back into the office.[41] These luncheons are very helpful.[42] No sooner had we shown them out of the door at 3:15 than we had to get ready to go to the Peru going-away reception for Ambassador Valdez at 4 o'clock. Got back to find that we had been invited to the Great Hall of the People diplomatic reception by the Prime Minister of the Congo. Am going to have to turn that down due to policy but they were nice to ask.[43] A full day—Peter Stroh, the brewery man from Detroit, and others are coming for drinks at 6 o'clock and a big dinner at 7:00. I'll be ready for that sack tonight. The Stroh dinner was excellent. We had a smoked duck as opposed to the more greasy Peking duck, but served with the pancakes and the plum sauce and light scallions. It was the Qin Yang restaurant. Duck was smoked but then served with pancakes and stuff Peking style. Very good.

General comments. I am concerned about some of the business types that come here. They seem to be the pushy middleman kind of approach. I hope they play it straight and honest and open with the Chinese. There are some hard-sell artists that reminded me of some of the brokers that poured into Midland when money was

[41]Republican Congressman and House Minority Leader John Rhodes of Arizona and Speaker of the House Carl Albert, Democrat of Oklahoma, jointly visited China, arriving at the end of March 1975. Bush describes their visit, and misadventures, in greater detail later in the diary.

[42]Bush in fact pressed Lin for "more frequent exchanges on a wider range of international issues," for example tensions in South Asia. "Lin responded very positively," Bush told Washington.

[43]The USLO, not being a formal embassy, was by prior agreement with the Chinese unable to accept invitations to functions at the Great Hall of the People that did not originate with the Chinese government.

flowing around pretty freely in the '50s. I worry about the lack of sensitivity towards the Chinese and some of these traders. The "fast buck" approach. The Chinese are so difficult about letting in people to talk business. El Paso [Natural Gas Corporation] wants to work a tremendous deal for liquefied natural gas, but they show no interest in inviting them at all. I can understand that because there may be some politics involved but it is one that really needs maturing and I guess more confidence.

The carpets we saw in Tianjin that we could buy $1,500 retail, we could get in the States for $5,000 I am told. We are determined to get one made.

Miscellaneous note. Visitor from Philadelphia. Mrs. Grace, former daughter-in-law of the late Eugene Grace, friend of dad's, recommended by a Washington lady, came for lunch with Bar.[44] She was with one of these friendship groups. She said they are very strange people. Keeping in mind that many of them are Maoists and real revolutionary people, I said to her, "Why, are they Maoists?" She said, "Oh no, that's not the problem. That wouldn't be bad at all." I said, "Well I don't like people tearing down our country." She said, "Well they have southern accents, [so] I just don't feel close to them." Marvelous look at Philadelphia!

Style of diplomacy. I get the feeling that some of our top China-watching people in Washington feel the style of diplomatic representation here is unimportant. I disagree with that. I think the Chinese know a great deal about what we do here. I think they can get an impression from the way the USLO people conduct themselves. And if we do nothing else perhaps we can convey the fact that people from the U.S. are not imperialists, not dominating imperialists, not superior, not super formal and super rich. With the market the way it is, the last is not hard to demonstrate.

Saturday[, March 1, 1975]. Relaxed. Staff meeting always in the morning. Few cables. Tennis at 2 with Finocchi and the Chinese.

---

[44]Eugene Grace was chairman of Bethlehem Steel Corporation, in its day one of the country's largest steel producers.

Dinner at 7:00 with Ambassador Karannagoda of Sri Lanka. I love these Saturdays. Time to read, write and think and travel around outside.

Sunday, March 2[, 1975].   A very relaxed and wonderful kind of day. Sack out, doing a fair amount of reading in the morning. Go to church and after that went to a marvelous kind of country-type store although it was in the city. Up clean but old, old streets and we bought some roughly glazed earthenware pots—great, big standing kinds of barrel-type seats that sell for around 40 to 80 kuai for the new ones, and many hundred kuai for the old ones. The pottery selling—one for 8 kuai with rabbits and birds on it, the other for 9.6, the equivalent of $5. We also bought some glazed bean pots. They are beautiful things. They are very new, roughly glazed—most attractive in their kind of humble primitive style. We went to the rug store, stood and stared and stared. Following that I cycled over to the International Club. It puts on great food. We had this marvelous Sichuan, which is hot, kind of beef, nice chicken and shredded chicken noodle and a great big bottle of beer. It's a relaxed way to do it. Bar and I get very close as we do these kinds of things together.

It is kind of sad at the International Club to see the Africans around here, the young ones. They have difficulty fitting in and they drift around, drinking too much beer, not doing well. That afternoon I came back to play tennis with the Chinese but since the courts were taken I played ping-pong with the young Chinese pro. Then he and Te showed me how a real match goes, the Chinese having dusted me off easily.[45] Then we played men's doubles— some guy from Malaysia sitting around here. Then I went off and played four sets of tennis with the three Chinese. We cut around. Zhou De, named "little stone," is the worst. He is too wild, but he occasionally makes a good shot. Wang and De are good. We had

---

[45]Bush recognized his ping-pong failings in comparison to the Chinese, yet Lilley noted, "I didn't play with him [Bush], because he was too good for me . . . my son could beat him, though."

marvelous tennis. Then went home and had about 20 diplomats, DCMs mostly, in to see a movie, "Citizen Kane."[46] We all wear old clothes. It is one of the best things we can do for entertainment and for representation.

Monday[, March 3, 1975]. We got caught up reading cables, and pouch came in.[47] Bar and I went to the Fur Fair. I don't believe their Chinese furs are going to be too competitive in the American market. There are beautifully soft designed lamb's rugs which feel silken to the touch. Must be priced here in China at around $3,000 kuai, more than $1,500. Their furs are nice: mink, sable, fox etc. but their styling is not too great and with the duty and the MFN.[48] I am not too optimistic about their being able to sell more. A Mr. Ren showed us around the Fair—the Number 1 person. He was very polite. He seemed interested in talking to us about expanding the trade. He spoke good English, had a good interpreter and all in all it was a good visit to the Fur Fair.

Quiet lunch at home. Reading in the afternoon. And then a big dinner given by the Yugoslavian ambassador with many ambassadors, most of whom are getting ready to go on a diplomatic trip. They have two diplomatic trips a year to interesting places in China, all of them paid for by the Chinese government. I am not included on these trips for understandable reasons.[49] The room was abuzz with the trip. I sat on the right of Mrs. Drulovic, the Yugoslavian hostess. I was disturbed with the diplomatic conversation. Every-

---

[46]The DCMs were the deputy chiefs of mission, typically the seconds-in-command at their respective embassies; most were career diplomats. *Citizen Kane* marked the 1941 directorial debut of Orson Welles.

[47]Bush refers here to a diplomatic pouch, one in which diplomatic documents are transported and that is by general agreement exempt from inspection by the host government.

[48]Bush refers to most favored nation trading status, an American designation designed to ensure that imports from one trading partner enjoy the same import duty status as all others.

[49]Because the USLO was not a formal embassy, its staff were not eligible to join such trips.

one out here is so down on our policy in Cambodia and Southeast Asia in general. The news is covered with U.S. losing and U.S. dissident opinion at home about Cambodia and Vietnam. We are just besieged by it. Even our allies talk about how wrong our policy is. I certainly don't think Lon Nol is too hot but on the other hand I do think that people misunderstand the U.S. position. We are not trying to prop up Lon Nol at all. And most people should know this, but they are super critical of the U.S. on both Vietnam and Cambodia and it gets a little tiresome to have to listen. I now sit majestically without getting into too much argument as everybody asks "What's happening?" and "Don't you think it would be better if you would withdraw?" and "Did you see the corruption about how your rice is being hoarded, converted into dollars, and being put into Swiss banks?" and on and on it goes. Last night I did ask them that if Cambodia changed would the standards that some people in the U.S. are demanding—such as totally free elections, totally free journalistic ability to come and go, total freedom to criticize one's own government—would these standards be met? There was deathly silence from the Yugoslav. He goes back to the fact that, "It is very much like your revolution." He is a very good guy, good values, and convinced that there is a great parallel between these revolutions out here and the U.S. revolution.

I am not making too much headway in getting the Chinese officials on whom I called back to the house. Two have accepted "in principle" leaving the time open. We have had two and now I am going back to try. If one gets frustrated by these attempts to get more contact with the Chinese, by refusing to ask or giving up, it will not be productive. I recognize that they are holding everybody at arm's length, maybe us less than some right now, but it is still worth, in my opinion, continuing to try to get to increase our contacts. It is not easy but it is worth the try.

Personal note. Telegram from T. Devine, coming in from London on Air France tomorrow. We are very excited about this. Marvin, Neil, [and] George will have a great time hitting with the Chinese in both ping-pong and tennis. The philosophy of the Chinese government is not competition itself, the friendship developed from those sports is what counts, not the victory.[50] I believe this somewhat though I am a little bit more like Bear Bryant—frankly the Chinese guys I am playing tennis with are a lot like Bear Bryant.[51] They are stoic in that they don't show their emotion and they don't get mad. They don't get sore when they lose but I am absolutely convinced from playing that they like to win. In fact Mr. Wang turned to me as he and I were taking on Te and Stone and said "6-1" and I conceded that we ought to make it "6-love." Beginning to feel that the informal style, riding on the bike, the informal dress, the openness with the diplomats and the Chinese may pay off. At first I wondered, but Mr. Lo at the store said, "You are getting to be a legend in your dress." He wasn't ridiculing me I don't think. In fact I am not sure he was not. And they all talk about our riding our bikes, Barbara and me. One mission man from Italy told me, "I can't imagine my ambassador riding a bike." And I am convinced the Chinese like it. They are not themselves as open and outgoing but they are warm and friendly, and I remain convinced that we should convince them, even though the limited contacts we have, that Americans are not stuffy, rich and formal. End of March 3.

[Tuesday,] **March 4, 1975.** The diplomatic tour is under way so most of the diplomats have gone on the jaunt. The U.S. does not get to go on these because of our diplomatic status. We had lunch with the Romanian Ambassador, Gavrilescu—Holdridge, Anderson and I, Gavrilescu and his interpreter.[52] Gavrilescu has a good entry with the Chinese, and we indeed had a good discussion about the Yao

[50]Officially the Chinese Communist Party's sports slogan was "Friendship first; competition second."

[51]Paul William "Bear" Bryant was the legendary football coach at Texas A&M University before (as he put it) "returning to mama" in order to coach at Alabama, his alma mater.

[52]Nicolae Gavrilescu served as Romania's ambassador to China from 1971 to 1978, and he was subsequently ambassador to the United States from 1984 to 1987.

Wenyuan document.[53] This is a major document. Yao, a former Shanghai-identified guy, has come out with a large article talking about discipline, talking about restricting the difference between the wage scales from the top to the bottom, and all in all there is a great deal of flurry in the diplomatic community about interpreting this.

That evening we had dinner—Holdridge, Horowitz and I—at Tolstikov's, given at the Russian Embassy for me.[54] The Russian Embassy is a massive compound—40 acres—their own school, their own services, completely furnished—and there they sit in almost splendid isolation. Tolstikov was very jovial. Plenty of Russian vodka and caviar, many toasts and a lot of good conversation. Tolstikov is much more pessimistic about China's economy. He discussed the fact that they really don't have much of a per capita income.[55] I told them if their oil [is] developed, and indeed they plowed some of that into mechanization of agriculture, they could increase their gross national product. But he keeps painting the picture of a rapidly increasing population, agriculture which is admittedly increasing but not as fast proportionately as population—so he draws a graph with his hands showing this gap ever widening and smiling noticeably all the time.

He didn't really have anything good to say about the Chinese at all. The feeling is bitter. He is hit all the time by these toasts at the

[53]Yao Wenyuan, a leading political actor throughout the Cultural Revolution, was later discredited as a member of the Gang of Four following Mao's death and Deng's return to power. The document in question was "On the Social Basis of the Lin Piao Anti-Party Clique," published in *Red Flag,* the Party's monthly journal, on March 1, 1975. Along with Zhang Chunqiao's "On Exercising All-Round Dictatorship over the Bourgeoisie," it argued vigorously against "revisionism" and "empiricism," as represented by reformers like Deng. The writers eventually lost this argument—and their grip on power—and thus the articles represent a last gasp of the Cultural Revolution's hard-liners.

[54]Herbert Horowitz served as chief of the commercial and economic section of the USLO until 1975, when he returned to Washington as director of the Office of Research for East Asian Affairs. He went on to serve as ambassador to Gambia during Ronald Reagan's second term.

[55]In 1975 China's real gross domestic product per capita was $688.79 in 2006 dollars.

Great Hall of the People, insults not just from the Chinese, but also from the other visiting dignitaries. I point out to him that the U.S. comes in for its share of criticism, but his theory is that it's much less than they themselves get.

Wednesday, March 5[, 1975]. T. Devine arrived. We had a very relaxed day with him. Hit a few tennis balls, showed him around, and all in all got caught up with him and visited. Dinner at the International Club—still the cheapest place in town. Food pretty good. Lunch at the Bush place.

Thursday, the 6th [March 6, 1975]. Devines still here. The big thing was we took a delegation of about 40 from the U.S. for our first subway ride. The subway is clean. It doesn't appear to have near the use as in the U.S. Indeed there is 22 or 25 kilometers of tracks compared to 270 miles of tracks in New York alone. I will say that the cars and platforms and all are beautiful and clean. No tickets taken yet but they will be in the future. The outside appearances are great. There are two tracks only and it doesn't have all the hustle and bustle of the New York subway train. The train is open now. Foreigners of course cannot go without permission. They are building a peripheral subway system around Peking that should be finished in 1978. I asked Mr. Li, the leading person, when it would be finished.[56] He said " '78" and it would be automated with computers and would have no people in the cabs. I sure think they're in for trouble on that. The English system, the one we were on, is not as fully automated. I was glad they say the switches are totally automated but we did see a man out turning one of the switches.

That day Bar looked like she was coming down with jaundice. She was pale and brownish-yellow. The British had a case of jaundice and we had a case at our embassy of hepatitis. Mr. Li and I were very worried about her but she went home to bed and stayed flat all day and recovered. This place is the darndest place for trav-

[56]Li Peng was chairman of the Power Supply Bureau for Beijing from 1966 to 1976.

eling bugs. They sweep through buildings—they are usually bronchial or have to do with dust in the air. She has had two cases of this flu but gets over them in twenty-four hours. We had a luncheon on Wednesday for Bob Malott, chairman of Fruit Machinery.[57] Also Bob McLelland, the vice president, Walter Chan and his wife Juni.[58] Malott thinks the machinery group is a very good one.

Thursday afternoon we had a reception—Bob and Libby Malott came and also Steve Allen.[59] Jayne [Meadows, Allen's wife] was sick a lot. Steve seemed like a pretty good guy. He rode his bike around. In fact the next day he brought us a nice book delivered from Jayne. He was here with Jayne who was born here in China. They had come in rather circuitously.[60] They tried and tried to get to China. They finally came in as interested in the rug business because Jayne has a decorating shop of some sort in Santa Barbara or Los Angeles. They did have some attractive people with them; Pollacks and Fishers and some others.[61] And so we had a reception at the USLO. I enjoy bringing U.S. citizens to the USLO, as they drop in.

[57]Robert Malott began work at the Food Machinery and Chemical Corporation (now FMC Corporation) in 1952 and stayed until his retirement in 1991.

[58]According to Bush, Chan worked for a Hong Kong bank and had been "instrumental" in securing Malott's contacts with Chinese officials.

[59]A television personality and former host of *The Tonight Show*, Steve Allen recorded his impressions from his first three trips to China in his book *Explaining China*. "I feel," he wrote in the introduction, "that a simply written study, addressed not to specialists but to laymen, can take at least a bit of the mystery out of the still mysterious East."

[60]Though Allen and Bush had met in the United States, where Bush had extended an invitation to visit the USLO, Allen made clear in his book that—unlike so many others from Bush's wide circle of friends and political allies—the ambassador had had nothing to do with arranging his visit. "In case the reader has had the pleasure of meeting Mr. Bush during his years of service to the Republican Party," he wrote, "or later as head of the CIA or presidential hopeful, I am sure he would appreciate my mentioning that it is not possible for him or his successors to be of the slightest help in your visit to China. He was not in a position to do anything of the sort, even during his tenure as liaison officer."

[61]The reference is to Helen Pollack, whom Allen describes as "an interior decorator from Los Angeles," and Jerry and Louise Fisher, "an executive of an industrial rug company" and "a teacher."

We've had all the rug dealers in town this week, interviewed them and I am now very interested in getting a rug purchased or maybe more so we can have it for the various generations. The rug dealers tell me these rugs, particularly the 90-count 5/8-inch pile, are as good as any rugs made in the world today, if not better than the others. The only problem is that some of the designs are not competitive for the U.S. market. We have had Mr. Hakimian, Mr. Rustaff and Mr. Mu Gee all on separate visits, all respectable and good rug men from the United States. Iran's costs are going up and therefore Iran is not going to be as competitive. India is the main competition but China does a different kind of work and in some ways I am told much better.

Thursday night. Receptions usually last from 5:30 to 6:30 because the Peking restaurants don't like you to come any time after 7:00. It is one of the beautiful things about this. You go to a restaurant at 7 and you are always out well before 9. We took the Devines and the Peritos to the Kang Le Restaurant where we had this marvelous 8-course dinner—total price for the six of us, including a lot of hot wine and beer, was 63 kuai, 93 mao, equivalent of $35.[62] Excellent dinner. Their specialty is emerald soup. Good sharks fin dish. Delicious food in every way.

That afternoon the Devines and I went out to the Summer Palace and it is certainly a beautiful thing to behold. Spring was coming. Chinese do not like to have their pictures taken. I worried that Tom might swing that photoscopic lens a little too much but there were no complications and we did get a few good shots for the Devines' scrapbook. End of March 6.

There are great inconsistencies in all the Chinese philosophy. Chairman Mao wrote a lot of articles encouraging students to speak up against the teachers and to encourage debate and criticism, the whole Cultural Revolution thesis. But then you keep getting reports

[62]Robert Perito spent thirty years in the foreign service before retiring to join the Clinton administration as deputy director of the Justice Department's International Criminal Investigative Training Assistance Program.

that the Chairman is adamant against certain kinds of art, certain kinds of books. Interesting contrast.

Friday, March 7[, 1975]. Quiet lunch at home. Worked in the afternoon and then a last dinner with the Devines at the Kao Rou Wang Restaurant—that's a Mongolian place where you all cook your own food on a massive grill. Steve Allen came along with a Lily Wen.[63] She is a little wild. She'd been here before to see her mother, pushed to get her visa extended. She's a little frantic, talked about the revolution, etc. Steve seemed a little calmer. Indeed their delegation seemed to have fallen apart at this time and they were mumbling about others on the delegation. Jayne regrettably was still sick.[64]

Saturday, March 8[, 1975]. Hit by the bug again in the morning, and thus stayed at the house. I just have rather violent flareups from time to time, one of which occurred out at the airport that I will not put on this tape. Unbelievable! Saturday afternoon and Sunday delightful. Saturday afternoon hit both tennis and pingpong. Totally relaxed. Early dinner.

Sunday[, March 9, 1975]. Church, shopping at the Theater Shop, bought a rug at the Friendship Store, lunch at the International Club. Ate some hot food that sent me for a loop again. Rested most of the afternoon and that night showed the move "Bananas."[65] Had a bunch of diplomats. Most of the ambassadors are gone on the diplomatic tour to the South, but it's fun to do this in-

---

[63]A longtime friend of Allen's, Lily Wen was the daughter of an officer in the Nationalist army who was killed during the civil war; she married the scientist Wen Kwan Sun and moved to California. With Jayne Meadows she was a co-owner of the East-West Carpet Company, under whose auspices the group was able to secure visas for entry to China, ostensibly to visit the Tianjin Carpet Fair.

[64]Her respiratory troubles eventually necessitated a trip to the hospital for Jayne Meadows; there the couple were pleased to discover that her chest X-ray cost only $0.30 and her medicines $1.30. They did question the hospital's decision to perform the X-ray with her clothes still on.

[65]*Bananas* was a 1971 Woody Allen film in which the protagonist, played by the director himself, becomes a Central American revolutionary leader.

formal thing. We also had some people from Houston. Pat O'Leary of Kellogg Company and a man named Dobi of Kellogg.[66] Also Mr. and Mrs. Costello of Peking, she an Argentinean, both going to be stationed here a year—now in the hotel hoping to get an apartment.[67] Time will tell on that. John Burns is writing a cover piece for *People* on life-style in Peking. It will be interesting to see how it works out. The house is looking prettier now. Barbara got the two panels from mandarin coats back. They are framed à la Chinese scroll and they look very handsome with their beautiful lasting gold threads.

Debate is still raging on among the diplomats about Chairman Mao. Last night three reporters were all talking about whether there was really something wrong with the Chairman, this time for keeps. John Burns of Canada told me that [unintelligible] and [unintelligible] both felt that the Chairman was out of it now since he hadn't received the last two visitors; the last one being the head of the Congo, Mr. Lopis. I have been reading a fair amount of books: *Centennial, Dogs of War,* a mystery story, and now *Before the Fall* by Safire.[68] On the Chinese side I have read Pearl Buck's *Good Earth,* I read the story of Empress Xi, *The Dowager Empress,* Barnett's book *After Mao,* Teddy White's book *Thunder Out of China.*[69]

---

[66] As mentioned in my footnote to the November 14, 1974, entry, the reference is to Kellogg Brown & Root, a Houston-based engineering firm.

[67] Robert Costello would be Kellogg's on-site project manager.

[68] Set primarily in Colorado, James A. Michener's *Centennial* was published in 1974 in honor of the upcoming U.S. bicentennial, and it was one of the bestselling books of the year. Frederick Forsyth's *Dogs of War* was also published in 1974. In *Before the Fall,* published by Doubleday in 1975, William Safire, one of Nixon's primary speechwriters (and later a prominent columnist for the *New York Times*), presented "an inside view of the pre-Watergate White House."

[69] Pearl Buck's *The Good Earth,* first published in 1931, helped imprint on a generation of Americans a vision of China and its trials at the hands of foreign powers. The book garnered for its author the Pulitzer Prize. Several books on Empress Ci Xi include the phrase "Dowager Empress" in the title. Given its publication date, and Bush's penchant for favoring recent publications, the reference is most likely to Marina Warner's *The Dragon Empress: The Life and Times of Tzu-Hsi, Empress Dowager of China, 1835–1908,* published in 1972. A. Doak Barnett,

I am reading a book by Han Suyin.[70] I am also reading a collection of articles by David Milton.[71] I am trying to mix one book on China with some fiction or current book at home. Weight still down to about 177, which is rather comfortable. In fact I feel almost euphoric in my happiness and health. Then I get stricken by this damn bug. I am adjusted to the time situation where I can control my own time. There is a luxury in being able to do a certain amount of reading that I haven't had at any time in the last twenty-five years.[72]

Note on the diplomatic corps. Many of the diplomats in Peking are politicians. At a dinner the other night [ambassadors from] Sri Lanka and Hungary were commenting that they thought diplomats should have political experience. It turns out both of them were politicians. I'd say the diplomatic corps is almost equally divided on that point. End of March 9.

---

born in China to missionary parents, published *China after Mao* in 1967 while teaching at Columbia University, before continuing his career at the Brookings Institution and the Johns Hopkins School of Advanced International Studies. As mentioned in chapter 3, *Thunder Out of China* was the journalistic account of wartime China written by Theodore White and Annalee Jacoby, first published in 1946.

[70]The book was *The Morning Deluge: Mao Tsetung and the Chinese Revolution, 1893–1954* (Boston: Little, Brown, 1972).

[71]Bush most likely refers to *People's China: Social Experimentation, Politics, Entry onto the World Scene 1966 through 1972* (New York: Vintage Books, 1974). Milton's better-known *The Wind Will Not Subside: Years in Revolutionary China, 1964–1969* (New York: Pantheon Books), was not published until 1976.

[72]Bush frequently noted his newfound appreciation for free time in letters home. Only three weeks after arriving in China, he told James Allison, a reporter and acquaintance from Midland, that "the pace is different, the telephone never rings, but as I said above there's plenty to do." He returned to this theme frequently in the months to come, in letters more than in his own diary. "The telephone is strangely silent. What a change," he wrote to one correspondent in November 1974, telling Congressman John Rhodes that "the change of pace is enormous. My phone doesn't ring—after many years of incessant ringing, it's rather weird." Six months later he struck the same chord in a personal note to Deputy Secretary of Defense William Clements. "I have plenty of time to think out here," Bush wrote. "There is plenty to do, but I find that for the first time in my adult life I can control my own time pretty well."

George and Barbara Bush bicycled throughout Beijing's busy streets.
(Photo courtesy George H. W. Bush Presidential Library.)

The Bushes during one of their frequent opportunities to see China as tourists. (Photo courtesy George H. W. Bush Presidential Library.)

This image, taken by Barbara Bush, demonstrates the ubiquity of Beijing's bicycle culture during the mid-1970s. (Photo courtesy George H. W. Bush Presidential Library.)

Bush and Qiao Guanhua, China's foreign minister during much of Bush's tenure in Beijing, at a USLO function. (Photo courtesy George H. W. Bush Presidential Library.)

Bush admired Richard Nixon, considering the president a mentor, and worked hard first for his reelection and then as Nixon's hand-picked chairman of the Republican National Committee. This personal affection for Nixon made the traumas of Watergate all the more difficult for Bush to bear. (Photo courtesy George H. W. Bush Presidential Library.)

As Bush noted in his China Diary, Polaroid photographs proved a perfect way to conduct some "personal diplomacy" with Chinese people he met on the street. (Photo courtesy George H. W. Bush Presidential Library.)

George and Barbara Bush spent much of their available time in China visiting the country's historic sites, though their formal clothing suggests that this particular visit to a Beijing monument was more than mere sightseeing. (Photo courtesy George H. W. Bush Presidential Library.)

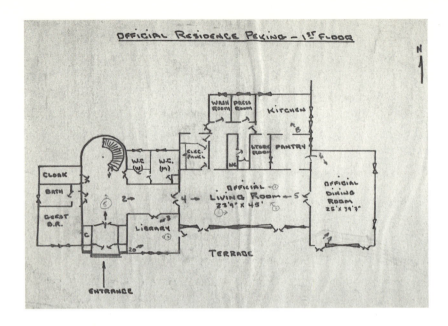

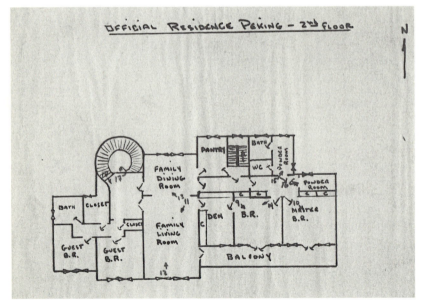

Schematic diagrams of the USLO compound, including Bush's official residence. (Photo courtesy George H. W. Bush Presidential Library.)

Bush with his USLO staff in early 1975, including Chinese employees of the Diplomatic Services Bureau assigned to the USLO. (Photo courtesy George H. W. Bush Presidential Library.)

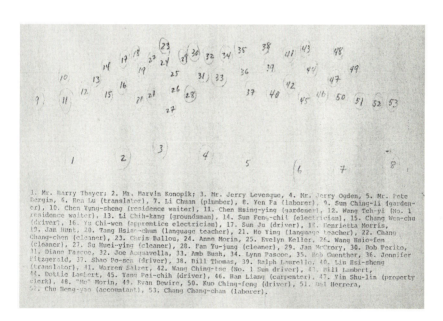

1. Mr. Harry Thayer; 2. Mr. Marvin Konopik; 3. Mr. Jerry Levesque, 4. Mr. Jerry Ogden, 5. Mr. Pete Bergin, 6. Rea Lu (translator), 7. Li Chuan (plumber), 8. Yen Fa (laborer), 9. Sun Ching-li (gardener), 10. Chen Yung-sheng (residence waiter), 11. Chen Hsing-ying (gardener), 12. Wang Teh-yi (No. 1 residence waiter), 13. Li Chih-kang (groundsman), 14. Sun Feng-chih (electrician), 15. Chang Wen-chu (driver), 16. Yu Chi-wen (apprentice electrician), 17. Sun Ju (driver), 18. Henrietta Morris, 19. Jan Hunt, 20. Tang Hsiao-chun (language teacher), 21. Ho Ying (language teacher), 22. Chang Chang-chen (cleaner), 23. Chris Ballou, 24. Anne Morin, 25. Evelyn Keller, 26. Wang Hsio-fen (cleaner), 27. Su Huei-ying (cleaner), 28. Fan Yu-jung (cleaner), 29. Jan McCrory, 30. Bob Perito, 31. Diane Pascoe, 32. Joe Acquavella, 33. Amb Bush, 34. Lynn Pascoe, 35. Bob Guenther, 36. Jennifer Fitzgerald, 37. Shao Po-sen (driver), 38. Bill Thomas, 39. Ralph Laurello, 40. Liu Hsi-sheng (translator), 41. Warren Salzer, 42. Wang Ching-tao (No. 1 Sun driver), 43. Bill Lambert, 44. Dottie Lambert, 45. Yang Pei-chih (driver), 46. Han Liang (carpenter), 47. Yin Shu-lin (property clerk), 48. "Mo" Morin, 49. Evan Dewire, 50. Kuo Ching-feng (driver), 51. Hal Herrera, 52. Chu Hong-yao (accountant), 53. Chang Chang-chan (laborer).

Chart identifying individuals in the photo of Bush with his USLO staff. (Photo courtesy George H. W. Bush Presidential Library.)

Bush with his American USLO staff. (Photo courtesy George H. W. Bush
Presidential Library.)

Chart identifying individuals in staff photo. (Photo courtesy George H. W. Bush
Presidential Library.)

Fresh from graduate school, George W. Bush spent a month in Beijing with his father during the summer of 1975. (Photo courtesy George H. W. Bush Presidential Library.)

A striking image of the youth the Bushes witnessed throughout their time in China, this photo was most likely taken by Barbara Bush. (Photo courtesy George H. W. Bush Presidential Library.)

Bush, Henry Kissinger, and Chinese foreign minister Qiao Guanhua during Kissinger's December 1974 visit to Beijing. From left, pictured are Nancy Kissinger, Yu Huiyong (Chinese minister of culture), Kissinger, Qiao Guanhua, Bush, and Huang Zhen (head of the Chinese Liaison Office in Washington). (Photo courtesy George H. W. Bush Presidential Library.)

Bush at a USLO function with Yao Yilin, vice minister of foreign trade. Yao later became vice premier. (Photo courtesy George H. W. Bush Presidential Library.)

Tennis, including games at the International Club pictured here, provided Bush with not only relaxation and exercise but also yet another opportunity to practice his brand of personal diplomacy. (Photo courtesy George H. W. Bush Presidential Library.)

When in Beijing, Barbara Bush oversaw the daily household work of the USLO staff provided by the Chinese government's Diplomatic Services Bureau. (Photo courtesy George H. W. Bush Presidential Library.)

Bush flying his Tianjin kite at the USLO compound. (Photo courtesy George H. W. Bush Presidential Library.)

George Bush during one of his frequent trips to China's Great Wall. (Photo courtesy George H. W. Bush Presidential Library.)

George and Barbara Bush before the Tiananmen Square entrance to Beijing's Forbidden City. (Photo courtesy George H. W. Bush Presidential Library.)

C. Fred, the Bush's much-beloved companion in Beijing. (Photo courtesy George H. W. Bush Presidential Library.)

The Bush family Christmas card for 1975. (Photo courtesy George H. W. Bush Presidential Library.)

During his December 1975 trip to China, Gerald Ford (*seated fourth from left, between Kissinger and Bush*) conducted bilateral talks with a Chinese delegation headed by Deng Xiaoping. Bush is seated to the president's left, Henry Kissinger on his right, and Brent Scowcroft to Kissinger's right. Hosting Ford's visit was one of Bush's last official acts as head of the USLO. (Photo courtesy Gerald Ford Presidential Library.)

CIA director designate George H. W. Bush and Gerald Ford meet in the Oval Office on December 17, 1975. (Photo courtesy Gerald Ford Presidential Library.)

CHAPTER FIVE

"When It Is a Matter of Principle
It Really Means Do It Their Way"

March 10 to April 15, 1975

*T*he spring of 1975 will not go down in history as a high point for *American foreign relations. In Southeast Asia especially, the consequences of a generation of failed diplomacy came to a head, as Cambodia crumbled into chaos and South Vietnam fell to Communism. These events pushed Washington's global policy to the fore of Bush's thinking. He began to reconsider the tropes and truisms that had dominated his country's foreign policy throughout the Cold War, in particular the reality of the domino theory. The notion that Communist states would of their very nature expand into neighboring countries had been widely disputed among America's foreign policy elite by the mid-1970s, but the events of these months made Bush reconsider.*

"The domino theory is alive and well," he wrote in his journal— though it was not the knee-jerk tumbling of nations predicted by many Cold War hawks of earlier decades. On the contrary, Bush's domino theory, as expressed in this chapter and the next, was more subtle and sophisticated—and quite revealing of the way he believed international relations functioned. For Bush, the real danger of nations falling to Communism was the effect their loss as allies might have on American credibility, and in turn on the way other nations then embroiled in the Cold War fight might hedge their bets, deciding to mend relations with Moscow and Beijing on the chance that Washington's word was no longer to be fully valued.

"As Cambodia weakens," he wrote, "[and] as North Vietnam makes gains, many of our allies are compelled to move toward the PRC." This fear of Washington's crumbling credibility connected directly to his continuing anguish over Beijing's harsh anti-American rhetoric, discussed yet again in these entries. If Washington did not stand up for its principles, if it did not rebuke such public attacks in the political arena while rebuffing Communist assaults against its allies, Bush lamented, then its position of leadership within the international community would ultimately be questioned, and the free world would truly be put at risk.

Bush's frustrations with Washington's foreign policy combined with his ongoing disappointment with China's leaders—who still largely refused to meet him halfway in his plan to improve personal contacts as a means of fostering better relations—to prompt him for the first time in his diary to consider directly his future after the presidential election of 1976. As the notes to this text suggest, Bush had considered his political future almost from the moment he arrived in Beijing. Friends and political allies frequently wanted to learn of his plans, as had Henry Kissinger during his own visit to China the previous November. But until this point, Bush had seemed, at least in the reflections he offered his diary, content with his political lot despite his evident ambition. By late March 1975, however, after half a year at the USLO, his frustrations began to bubble over, leading to a belief that "I should be planning a private life starting in '76," and also to withering attacks on China's leadership. "The Chinese can be tough," he recorded during these weeks. "They talk about principle. Their principles. And when it is a matter of principle it really means do it their way." Later he remarked, "They are polite, they are strong, but they always talk about principle. And when they don't want to give an answer they just obfuscate and sit there. It's the most frustrating thing in the world."

These frustrations mounted in the early spring of 1975, though the weeks were not without their highlights. Bush hosted Speaker of the House Carl Albert and House Minority Leader John Rhodes,

*and his reaction to Albert's unconventional style of diplomacy—
and its potential effect on their Chinese hosts—is particularly
noteworthy. So too is Bush's critique of his own State Department,
first for his nagging fear that the USLO was not the department's
first priority, despite China's importance, and second because of its
now-overt campaign against his frequent visitors and guests. The
early spring of 1975 would prove daunting for Bush. He still clearly
enjoyed his work and life in Beijing, but the strains of his job—
especially when coupled with the difficulties facing American diplomacy in general—were beginning to show.*

[Monday,] March 10[, 1975].   Primarily in the office. Did attend from six-to-seven the Zambian reception for Vernon Mwanga,
an old UN friend.[1] The reception at the Zambian embassy was still
rather deadly. Chinese on one side, black women on one side, white
women on one side, white ambassadors on one side, black women
on another side and then Qiao Guanhua and Mwanga and the
DCM [deputy chief of mission] for Zambia and couple of Chinese
in still another grouping. It seems almost impossible to break through
this pattern of segregation that emerges. The diplomats were back
from the diplomatic trip. They had a marvelous time, and though
they lived in some rustic surroundings—outhouses, bowls to wash
in carried in from outside—they enjoyed it immensely. We do not
participate in these diplomatic trips.[2] Language lesson went well.
Beginning to talk about studying and Mrs. Tang, ever patient, asked
certain questions.

The Dillon Ripleys and the Paul Austins arrived from Canton.[3]
Ripley had had his 16-millimeter film impounded at the border. He

[1]Vernon Mwanga, foreign minister for Zambia, later served as Zambian minister of information.

[2]As mentioned previously, because it lacked official embassy status, the USLO,
by custom and agreement with the Chinese, did not participate in such "official"
activities for visiting diplomats.

[3]S. Dillon Ripley directed the Smithsonian Institution from 1964 to 1984 and
was a frequent correspondent of Bush's. He traveled to China accompanied by
his wife, Mary. J. Paul Austin, who was accompanied by his wife, Jeanne, was a

carried it with him, but it was all sealed up. He was not permitted to utilize his 16-millimeter camera. We are requesting through protocol to see if he can get an exemption. Apparently 16-millimeter cameras are associated with commercial movies and therefore not permitted. We had not encountered this rule before.

Tuesday, March 11[, 1975].   We started a new policy of getting political briefings. We discussed today the so-called "Shanghai clique." There is a broad theory amongst ROC and USSR that the PRC is divided into major groups: the Shanghai clique, which is the radicals, against the others. We do not hold to this. A good background briefing on all of this with Don Anderson, Lynn Pascoe and John Holdridge. We are trying to arrange some receptions for the Ripleys. It is very difficult. We invite Chinese to come and they accept "in principle" but don't accept for the day you invite them. You ask dignitaries to come to a reception and there is no reply. We have asked a group of leading academics to come for Wednesday to meet Dillon Ripley and Paul Austin and here it is Tuesday noon and have not heard from any of them. It was the same way in trying to make arrangements in New York that time to get the Chinese to come to our home. They are very different than the U.S. on that.

The Xinhua [News Agency] had a scathing attack on March 10 on U.S. women being downtrodden and the decadence of the capitalist system. I get tired of reading all of this propaganda and being surrounded with it, and I sometimes think that we should react to these things but it is ever thus. China insists on hammering away at the decadence of our society and labeling us as imperialists, etc. I would think that if you want better relations you would lower one's voice on that kind of thing, but it doesn't work that way. Sophisticated China watchers say, "Don't worry, it's less than it used to be." And I am sure there is some validity to this.

---

member of the Smithsonian's board of regents and chairman of the board of the Coca-Cola Company.

On March 10 it was a terribly cold storm that charged down from the North. We worried what it would be; but here it is on the 11th warm and clear. Good day for the Wall. Dillon, Austins and Bar went, taking C. Fred to run at the Ming Tombs. Bar had a picnic out at the Wall in the Tombs and I had a quiet lunch at home. That night we had a going-away reception for the Chinese Solid Physics Investigation Group and three from the Chinese Performing Arts Delegation.[4] These receptions are very sticky. I did show

[4]The performing arts troupe eventually canceled their trip to the United States at the eleventh hour, over a dispute that reveals much about the nature of Sino-American relations at the time. They were scheduled to perform in five American cities, opening their tour in Los Angeles on April 3 and closing in Washington on April 26. During routine preparatory work for the visit, however, American officials decided that one song on the Chinese program, "People of Taiwan, Our Brothers," contained lyrics liable to disrupt Washington's sensitive relations with Taiwan. The image of Chinese singers declaring "We are determined to liberate Taiwan" from a Washington stage did not appeal to the State Department, which during the third week of March formally asked the Chinese for a different selection. There was some precedent for this request, as Chinese officials had altered the program for the Philadelphia Symphony's historic visit in 1973. (See my footnote to the entry for March 29, 1975.)

Beijing refused Washington's request to remove the potentially offensive song, however, and ultimately canceled the visit entirely. As Bush's counterpart in Washington, Huang Zhen, told the State Department's Winston Lord and Philip Habib on March 23, "The song 'People of Taiwan, Our Brothers' expresses the profound sentiment of the Chinese people who are longing for their Taiwan compatriots. In the Shanghai Communiqué the USG [United States Government] agreed that there is but one China and Taiwan is a part of China. If the US side is not retreating from the Shanghai Communiqué, there is no reason for it to object to the inclusion of such a song in the supplementary program." Habib responded that Washington's discussion of the controversial song had not been a "threat," but rather "a request such as the Chinese had made in a previous instance. It was our hope that the request would be accepted in that spirit."

This minor event epitomizes Sino-American difficulties in the post-honeymoon period of the administration of President Gerald Ford. American officials feared offending Beijing at every turn, and their Chinese counterparts took nearly every possible opportunity to stand firm on "principles" when it suited their geopolitical needs. The two sides could not solve their intractable problems, first and foremost among them Taiwan. So they instead battled—quibbled, really—over symbolic representations of their real differences. "We think it would be a major mistake to back down on this issue now," Lord and Habib advised Secretary of

some flashes of pictures of Washington on the VTR which seemed to interest them but it is very hard to engage in conversation. One of the Chinese physicists had studied at Cal Tech and another one at another west coast institution.[5] One spoke excellent English. Dillon [and] Paul milled around and added considerably to the group. That evening with the Harlands, the Balouks from Tunisia and Rolf Pauls and Mrs. Paludan we had dinner at the Kang Le, a very pleasant Chinese evening.

Next day. [Wednesday,] March 12[, 1975]. Bar went to the Summer Palace. I had another one of those ghastly attacks, felt lousy

---

State Henry Kissinger on March 24: losing face in Beijing by seeking compromise would do far more damage, they reasoned, than playing the song ever could.

From his post in Beijing Bush worried more about potential Chinese cries of American "censorship" than about any political fallout from the song itself. This reaction is not surprising, given his continuing concern with the public face of the relationship. Indeed he likened this case to the earlier dispute over the archaeological exhibit. "We must avoid charges of State Department censorship which inevitably will arise among certain elements of the press in coverage of the cancellation," he cautioned. "The issue on the cancellation of the press review for the archeological exhibit was 'freedom of the press.' Standing firm meant standing up for freedom of the press. On this question, the issue is different; and the PRC, if clever, can be against 'censorship' in the U.S. and pick up support on that question." There is no record in the Lord files at the State Department that he or his colleagues ever incorporated Bush's concern—which was in reality a fear of domestic political reprisal stemming from Washington's stand—into their own more geopolitical arguments to Kissinger, who was traveling at the time.

The *Washington Post* used the occasion of the Chinese cancellation to question the entire premise of such "cultural exchanges," noting that "With friendly states whose values we share, the whole idea of official cultural exchanges is redundant. It is only with adversary states whose values we do not share that these exchanges come to pass. On balance, we think, it is well to have exchanges with these states. But it is silly to think there is a way to conduct them in the context of an essentially adversary relationship without [such] recurring snags as the sequence that ended in the cancelled Chinese tour."

[5]One of the scientists to whom Bush refers was most likely Zhou Peiyuan, who headed numerous Chinese scientific missions abroad, including a month-long visit of physicists to the United States beginning in September 1975. With degrees from the University of Chicago and the California Institute of Technology, Zhou had been a research fellow at Caltech and at Princeton's Institute for Advanced Study during the 1930s.

but limped on out for lunch with them at the Summer Palace. Dillon is fun to go there with. He spotted some birds, pointed out some of the paintings along the long archway, the lesser panda and other Chinese animals.[6] He saw two birds that he had never seen, one of which was indigenous to Spain and the United States oddly enough, and a duck that sounds like "smoo."[7] He is a delightful guy and so is Paul Austin, both of them are broad gauged, appreciative and wonderful. Sometimes the wives are not quite as sympathetic and understanding. Some people come to China and they don't seem to understand that we have different things here, that we must be very careful with our help, we must be very careful about overburdening the household staff and making excessive demands on USLO. Both Paul Austin and Ripley understand this well.[8]

We had a reception for distinguished scientists and academicians to meet Ripley and Austin. We tried something new. We went from five to six-thirty instead of five to six or six to six-thirty. And we had Dillon give a few comments about what the Smithsonian Institution does. We didn't press it but it worked very well. I asked one question of a ranking member, a Professor Wong who had signed the archaeological things.[9] We had this very small discus-

---

[6]Ripley had spent his academic career as an ornithologist and had headed Yale's Peabody Museum of Natural History before assuming his Smithsonian post.

[7]The reference is most likely to the smew, *Mergellus albellus,* found in northern Europe and Asia.

[8]Bush had earlier imposed on Ripley for help in outfitting the USLO in a particularly "American" fashion. "We are sitting in a lovely Residence but with no pictures on the wall," Bush wrote after two weeks in Beijing. "I am wondering if you know of any cheap, but tasteful, prints or pictures that could be rolled up in a tube and sent to us here. I would, of course, be glad to pay for them and I would trust your judgment completely. Perhaps the Smithsonian has a series of early American prints (copies) that we could frame out here and scatter around a few little rooms in the Liaison Office and in the Residence?" No record exists as to whether Ripley fulfilled this request.

[9]In the coming weeks an extension would be sought for China's now-famous archaeological exhibit, on tour in the United States (and the subject of some controversy, as Bush has already described), thus necessitating further negotiations and agreements that would have to be signed by the USLO. Bush in fact hesitated to support asking Beijing for the extension, not because he disliked Chinese art or wanted to limit its availability in the United States but rather because he feared

sion out of that question and then broke up the meeting; but we were all ecstatic that we seemed to get much more out of this reception than others. I am determined to find new ways. Indeed Paul Austin has been talking with me about what we can do to have an old-fashioned Fourth of July national day this year, and he is talking about helping us with some of the ingredients.[10]

That night, the 12th, I rested and others went to the International Club. It was then that Fred made his break after Bar took him for a walk. Instead of running into the USLO as he does, he charged off into the Gabon Embassy across the street, past the PLA guard, in through the outer hall, into a tremendous living room filled with formally clad Africans all the way through the living room back into the dining room—Bar in hot pursuit. Fred heard music and excitement and just wanted to check in. Bar was humiliated, but the Africans were laughing like mad and very pleasant about it.

Thursday a.m. [March 13, 1975]. We went to the Marco Polo Romanian Friendship Commune while the ladies went to the Forbidden City with Martha Holdridge.[11] The Commune was most

---

making a request and thus putting the Chinese in the position of granting or rejecting yet another American favor. His response and his recognition of a growing power dynamic within the Sino-American relationship is indicative of his growing frustrations with Beijing's policymakers. "We are setting ourselves up for yet another cave-in," he warned the State Department later in March, "and are simply going through the motions of making the request to satisfy the museum [San Francisco's Asian Art Museum] while further eroding our negotiating position with the MFA [Ministry of Foreign Affairs] Furthermore, in their eyes the Chinese feel they have been very generous . . . and our continued pressure for further extension may begin to negate some of the goodwill generated by the successful exhibition."

[10]Bush would later call in Washington's aid in this plan. On June 17, 1975, he wrote the State Department: "There is not a hotdog roll to be found in China. Is there any way you could ship us 700 hotdog rolls for guaranteed delivery prior to July 4? We also need 100 large bags of potato chips in same shipment." This was the "great hotdog bun crisis of 1975" to which he alludes in his preface to this book.

[11]In the early 1960s, in an effort to build stronger ties with Romania—just as Romanian leaders struggled to edge their country out of Moscow's orbit in favor of a nonaligned brand of Communism—Chinese leaders named one of their state farms the Marco Polo Bridge Sino-Romanian Friendship People's Commune.

interesting, and notes kept on that separately. We had lunch (six of us) with the British Ambassador Youde, a delightful guy and well informed on China. That afternoon Bar took them to the Temple of Heaven when I worked.[12] We had drinks at the USLO for Ambassadors Ogawa, Akwei, and Hiriart of Chile. And then off to the Qin Yang restaurant where the specialty is a marvelous duck served not in pancakes this time but in very light, hollowed-out rolls with plum sauce and onions. Delightful. The whole day was a good one. Bar is knocking herself out for these guests and I do hope they appreciate it. She is marvelous at showing people around and all of that.[13]

On the substantive front there is much more debate about Yao Wenyuan and what is going on here in China.[14] Some, including the Russians, see much more turmoil in the situation than we now think exists. I continue to get depressed by the news on VOA and in the Red and Blue News out of Cambodia.[15] It is enormously difficult to have a strong foreign policy when it is being hacked away at in the Congress. I get a depressed feeling about Cambodia and, to a lesser degree but nevertheless a firm one, about Vietnam. I worry about what the Chinese will think. They are so set on principles and here we are apparently unwilling to fulfill our principles.

---

[12]The Temple of Heaven is a complex of Taoist buildings in Beijing. Construction began in 1420 and continued for several decades thereafter. It is the largest of Beijing's four major Taoist temples.

[13]Barbara Bush later noted that her enthusiasm for taking guests to these sights did wane over time. "Well, if we had at least a guest a week and probably more because they usually didn't stay a week, I went every single time. . . . I went every single time there, every single time to the Great Wall, every single time to the Ming Tombs. We'd go to the Great Wall, we'd then stop at the Ming Tombs on the way back, I'd take my cocker spaniel in the car and he'd run in the Ming Tombs. And that was great. Occasionally we'd go and there would be a whole herd of something there that would be a little nerve racking. But, I probably went, you know, maybe 52 times."

[14]See Bush's entry, and my footnote, for March 4, 1975.

[15]On March 13 the House Foreign Affairs Committee voted against increasing aid to Cambodia. Three days earlier, North Vietnam had invaded South Vietnam, driving south and routing South Vietnamese forces.

They appear to have principle. We appear not to. It boils down that way. I am very concerned about it, not for the lasting effect, because they know of our basic strengths and where we will firmly draw the line, but we do look impotent and we look like we are a loser on this one. Sihanouk makes it more complicated by being in Peking and talking all the time and making claims. His future at best appears uncertain to me.

Frustrations. We have requested the zoo tour for Ripley as head of the National Zoo in Washington and have no reply at all in the last three days. And we requested two or three business people for Paul Austin to see and we have had no reply at all. You ask Chinese to the house and they accept "in principle," setting a date at their own convenience. It is unbelievable.

Nice thing this week. Vernon Mwanga, the Foreign Minister of Zambia, and an old friend of mine from the UN, came to call; a most unusual step in the protocol field, given the big-shot nature of foreign ministers generally. He was relaxed, down to earth, gave us some interesting information about his visit with Zhou Enlai and all in all couldn't have been nicer. I cabled asking that someone at home acknowledge this and thank him for it. That was on Tuesday March 11.

Here we are Friday, March 14[, 1975]. Ripleys and Bar are off to the Forbidden City again. We are going to have a quiet lunch at home.

Just a quick run-through of the events from March 14 on. The Iranian Ambassador, speaking only French, came to see me. My French comes back fairly well in practice and I long since have gotten over the embarrassment of trying in French. I can see a silent chortle or so but the other side of it is that he feels the same way about his English, though it's better than my French. In Chinese I still feel a certain frustration. When I just sit and chat with Mrs. Tang I lose my embarrassment factor and I can do it, but my problem is practice, practice, practice. I don't practice enough. I don't take the time for the practice. But I love the Chinese lessons and I hate it when I have to miss them. Mrs. Tang has enormous dignity and a kind of serenity and I wish I could find out what is really in her heart. Our whole Chinese staff is that way. Mr. Liu, the marvelous fellow who has a reputation for being able to do anything or find his way through any bureaucratic maze—he is unbelievable. Mr. Sun has been most helpful also. Mr. Ren, the little interpreter, seems really good. He went to the rug factory with us and the communes and he is patient and very good. That evening, Friday the 14th, we went to the reception for the prime minister of Guyana, Burnham, [a] departure from the normal state return banquet function.[16] They asked me and I went because it was a reception and not official. Deng Xiaoping was there and worked his way rather uncomfortably through the crowd as did the model peasant Zhang Chunqiao, a vice premier also. He normally has a towel wrapped around his head but he sure looked like a peasant. His hand feeling less peasant-like however. The Guyanan Prime Minister had a booming kind of Channel 13 voice and was most gregarious and outgoing. The Vice Premier did not seem too comfortable but everybody at the diplomatic reception appreciated his doing this. It will be interesting to see whether the Chinese are [as] interested in this approach as the Guyanans were.

The reception lasted from 6 to 7:30. Chinese always appear right on the dot and leave right on the dot, you can set your watch by the arrival and set your watch by the departure. Mr. Guo, my driver, is the same way. He will circle the block a time or two in order to arrive punctually and if we are late departing he will speed it up a little. Sidelight—we almost got wiped out the other day when a PLA jeep driver with his head way up in the sky crossed the center line and almost hit Guo. Guo had to veer to the right. Fortunately there were no bicyclists in the right. This is a very heavily traveled place between downtown Peking and our house. Almost a wipeout. Scared the hell out of the Ripleys or the Austins, whichever were with us. After the Guyana reception we went to a beautiful

[16]Forbes Burnham was Guyana's prime minister from 1966 to 1980.

Japanese dinner with the Ogawas. Mrs. Ogawa has a charming grasp of flowers and delicacy and it was quite a contrast to a Chinese meal. The food was excellent but it was served with this great dignity and delicacy.

Saturday, the 15th [March 15, 1975]. I had to work. Bar went off sightseeing with the guests. Paul Austin and I took a walk to the Friendship Store, Austin not having heard from the three Chinese we requested he see on business. But Friday the 14th we went to the zoo. Dillon Ripley was disappointed in the zoo, and he also thought the zoo was well below standards of any other international zoo. He asked about the musk ox.[17] There were supposed to be two of them and there was only one there. We had requested to see three zoo people. None were available. I mentioned to Mr. Liu I thought it was a little unusual because when the Chinese zoo people had come they had been given the run of Washington, and I thought it was a little peculiar that we had never heard from them. Saturday noon I get a note from Mr. Liu saying that all three zoo people were out of Peking. We are speculating that the main reason for the failure to go to the zoo was either the condition of the zoo or possibly the dead musk ox. Probably the latter.

In any event, on Saturday, Paul Austin did get to call on a person who is interested in boilers. Coca-Cola has a boiler company. I had a nice lunch at the residence on the 15th, just as on the 14th, with the guests concluding that Mr. Sun was just as good a cook as any other in Peking. That afternoon we went to the Peking Carpet factory, saw their amazing carpet work, handmade. Now I am torn as to whether to get a Peking model or a Tianjin model for the family. I am determined to buy a carpet, have our chop woven into it, and keep them; hand them down from generation to generation—

[17]President Richard Nixon presented the Chinese with two musk oxen (Milton and Mathilda), raised in Washington's National Zoo, during his 1972 trip to China; he received two giant pandas for the zoo in return. The National Zoo is part of the Smithsonian Institution, hence Dillon Ripley's particular interest in the fate of the oxen.

"Don't [you] remember your old, old grandfather when he used to be over in Peking back in 1975."[18] Finished off the last night of the big visit with dinner at the Sick Duck, named because it is near the hospital. We had marvelous Peking duck. We started off at home with some marvelous Chinese caviar, excellent, and some Chinese vodka, excellent. I don't know the exact trade name but it is very, very good.

[Sunday, March 16, 1975]. Sunday morning off to church. Ripleys and Austins busily packing and getting ready. Guests flock to the Friendship Store for one last item. The Ripleys and the Austins are supposed to have been intrigued with the Street of the Antiquities, Liulichang. There is so much for guests to see. I hope they have enjoyed their stay. Week coming up is quiet and I am ready for a rest. I have received cabled instructions from the State Department about looking after my stomach. Tonight we will show "Carnal Knowledge."[19] Bar doesn't want a big one. Last week we showed "Bananas" and it was funny as hell, but fortunately there were no South American ambassadors there. "Carnal Knowledge" they say is depressing, and I am not sure that is what we need out here.

Pouch—we are missing mail all the time, and it is hard to explain to people in the States what this means. I remember in the Navy wondering where is our mail, where is our mail, but it is the same kind of feeling. But here we are thirty years later. You think it could be done better. But it simply reminds me of our isolation here. As far as creature comforts go we are really not isolated. There are some things we can't have and might say at a given moment that I wish I had, but in terms of things we need, we have them. I have just got my clothes back from Hong Du Tailors. Beautifully done. Take down a model. They copy it and you have one fitting of one suit and then one coat and then one pants and then all come back without alteration. I also bought some brocade and had two vests made. The prices are very reasonable. The suits are around $60,

---

[18]By "chop," originally a signature or identifying mark carved by furniture or cabinet makers to identify their work, Bush here means a family crest.

[19]Directed by Mike Nichols, *Carnal Knowledge* premiered in 1971.

with material being the biggest part of the cost. I have ordered a cashmere overcoat which will cost perhaps $100. But it is just lovely. And the tailoring seems to be excellent.

Middle of March 16. Dictated. Saw the Ripleys and the Austins off at the airport at noon. Now have new passes so we can go through the customs and head on out. We ended up with a good noodle, beer, shrimp luncheon—$6—the Austins and the Ripleys. I believe they had a good time. We discovered the following day that the musk ox, Milton, had died. We were officially notified by the Chinese. The mystery is solved. The Chinese did not want us to go to the zoo; Ripley was not received; Mr. Liu said the three Chinese we requested to see were out of town. But they didn't attend the reception either, and at the zoo they knew exactly when we got there because we were clocked in. The Canadian correspondent John Burns looked for us and they said, "Oh yes, they have come through." On Monday, March 17, just in passing Don Anderson was notified that Milton the musk ox had died. They even gave the name of the disease. He had had mange before he arrived in China.[20] And the Chinese said, "and perhaps you already knew he was dead since some Americans had been at the zoo." The Foreign Office knowing very well that it was me, and probably Dillon Ripley and Austin, that attended the zoo.

Tennis in the afternoon and ping-pong. Taking ping-pong lessons. Great interest in all of that. Mr. Liu tells me that Newcombe and three other men and one other woman player from Australia will be here on April 10.[21] The Australian ambassador still vague on this. They will play at the International Club or in the workers stadium. They sure operate in very mysterious ways.

"Carnal Knowledge"—we showed it and fortunately only Lois Ruge and John Burns were there. Pretty raunchy for diplomatic entertainment.

[20]Mange is a skin or ear condition caused by mites, which occurs primarily in domesticated animals.

[21]John Newcombe, an Australian tennis star, was the winner of five career grand slam events.

Monday, the 17th [March 17, 1975].   Lunch with Foreign Minister Rajaratnam of Singapore at Harland's New Zealand Embassy along with the UK, Canada, Malaysia and Australian ambassadors and four others in the Singapore party. Singapore is in an interesting position. They will not establish diplomatic relations before Indonesia but they are moving in China's direction.[22]

As Cambodia weakens, as North Vietnam makes gains, many of our allies are compelled to move toward the PRC. The domino theory is alive and well, whether some in our country want to recognize it or not. Three pouches came in on March 17. We have had hell with these pouches. Some mail was dated February 5, some as late as March 5. We have a small post and a tough area and yet we seem to be on the tail end of things. We get the worn-out films, it is hard to keep maintenance on old stuff around here, and I get the feeling that because it is a small outfit, this wheel seems to get less grease. I have got to do something about this. Ambassador Klibi of Tunisia came to call. The conversation was entirely in French. I am glad Mr. Humphrey, the French teacher, wasn't around.

4:30 p.m.—the California agriculture education group of about 20 led by Dean Brown—impressive farmers, all hard-working; all have the appearance of being hard-working, successful people, who have done it themselves in the fields.[23] They were an excellent group and appreciative of the briefing we gave at the USLO. So different than some of the blasé friendship types. At night a St. Patrick's Day party at the Lamberts. A touch of Eire right here in Peking. . . .

[Three lines have been redacted by George H. W. Bush.] I feel embattled here on Cambodia and Vietnam. Our case is right but even our allies seem kind of embarrassed about our position. I am continually amazed on the political side, on the Chinese news side, the FBI's tape, and others about the amount of criticism that goes

[22]Singapore ultimately established formal diplomatic ties with China in 1990, after Indonesia did so in 1989.

[23]Brown was co-founder of the California Agricultural Education Foundation, designed to develop leadership skills among the state's agriculturalists.

on—big character posters and this whole thing of criticize, criticize.[24] It is a fundamental part of this China.

[Tuesday, March 18, 1975].   Today in front of USLO on March 18 the whole school down the street was out for drilling—marching to command etc., getting ready, I guess, for the May 1 big day.[25] We keep getting various reports of struggles in provinces around China. There are fewer here apparently. When people are caught, they are publicly humiliated etc., led around with signs around their necks. I have still seen no crime first-hand. I did see a couple of Chinese who looked like they were getting pretty crocked at a reception but good god that can happen any place. They have some marvelous expressions to describe things. "Capitalist roader." And they always talk about the Spirit of Dazhai where the model peasant is from.[26] They now have a new campaign which seems to replace the anti-Lin, anti-Confucius campaign. It has to do with the dictatorship of the proletariat and it is repeated over and over again all across this tremendous land. Spring is here. It is warm. You can bicycle with no topcoat. Simply beautiful. Trees are beginning to come out. The dust has not been great so far. I hope it doesn't descend on us.

We are now having a political meeting every Tuesday to discuss some current events with my own staff briefing me. Today was on the PLA and the history of the army. To some degree its relationship with the center. The last week we talked about the Shanghai group, the right and left influences. Fitzgerald of Australia came for a courtesy call, then a quiet lunch with Mr. Wang sick. He came in

[24]Big-character posters, quite literally handmade posters proclaiming a political ideal in letters large enough to be easily read by a crowd, formed an integral part of the Cultural Revolution. They were employed by political activists, in particular students, for denunciation of enemies or exhortations to the political cause of the day.

[25]May Day, traditionally celebrating workers and the international labor movement, was a national holiday in most Communist countries, typically marked in the Soviet bloc by massive parades of military might.

[26]Bush refers to the model commune of Dazhai. During the Cultural Revolution the slogan "In Agriculture, Learn from Dazhai" was ubiquitous. (My thanks to Andrew Scobell for explaining this reference.)

politely and said he had to go to the hospital. He looked awful. I hope there is nothing wrong with him. Afternoon getting caught up—digesting the mail from the three pouches. Our children are doing great. The letters from all of them are mature, sensitive—they are doing well in their work, no drugs, no dope, no crime, no troubles. We should knock on wood. I think it would be awful to be way over here and have family problems where you'd want to be home helping out.

On the Fitzgerald call: it is others watching us, other countries studying the relationship between the United States and China. This is still the name of the biggest game in town. Tonight, dinner at 8 with the Groothaerts of Belgium—very European, but she is rather critical of serving Chinese food in one's home for example.[27] They were the ones who complained about their cook. The Chinese took the cook away to satisfy them but never, never replaced the cook for a long, long time to teach a lesson. It is extremely important in China how you treat people. The idea of being willing to do a little work oneself, to carry bags, to bicycle, to get with it and with the people in that sense, though you'll never be able to mingle with them. This, in my view, is important. Style to some degree is important in my view. When Holdridge and company went out to the technical university he told them Ambassador Bush would like to come by. The leader of the university said, "Fine, just have him bicycle out." Rather humorous reference, but it showed how word travels in this city. Nancy Tang mentioned, "You're having many guests." Why would she, a rather high official, know this?[28] Qiao Guanhua, the Foreign Minister, mentions, "I hear you won a prize in tennis." Xu Huang, head of the DSB, mentioned, "I under-

[27]Jacques Groothaert served in Belgium's foreign service for nearly forty years and was ambassador to Mexico before moving to Beijing in 1972. Accompanied by his wife, Madelyn, he served in China until 1976.

[28]Bush seems not to have considered this as evidence that the State Department might be right to fear the impact of his frequent guests on his diplomatic position with the Chinese. It is curious that he did not pass Nancy Tang's comment on to Foggy Bottom.

stand you gave some books to our people on tennis." The zoo logs us in. Barbara spots the same guy watching twice when she's at the Ming Tombs. In a way it is comforting. In a way it is rather eerie. End almost, March 18.

Steve Fitzgerald, a very aggressive, young ambassador from Australia came to see me. Fitzgerald digs very hard and gets good information.[29] Went over and played tennis with Mr. Wang on March 18. Just hitting. It is great fun. It's funny how one's legs give out on him. You always think of that happening when your little baseball players talked about it, but now it's true. Actually I am not hitting the ball too bad. On March 19 a very relaxed day—getting my health back, catching up on the pouches. The pouches are a terrible thing here. Three of them arrived at once. Mail arrived on about the 18th of March with mail postmarked February 5 through March 5. I get the feeling sometimes that there is no urgency about this post. It is isolated. It is tough. It is separated. And yet we always seem to be on the tail end of things. Send the old projectors up from Hong Kong; send the mail via Hong Kong. I would like to do something about it. It does demoralize morale for families here and I would like to get the bureaucracy moving on the thing.

[Wednesday,] March 19[, 1975]. Ambassador Ogawa and his wife of Japan had the Ford movie—his visit to Japan.[30] It was a beautifully done film. Tremendous photography—used the zoom lens. Tastefully edited. Japanese-accented voice speaking very good English. It was very thoughtful of Mrs. Ogawa to do that. Their daughter Cassy, admitted to Johns Hopkins that very day and won [a prize] the day before in Japan for her use of English. The Japa-

---

[29]More occurred at this meeting than Bush recorded in his journal. Of particular note, Fitzgerald told Bush that his sources had confirmed that Taiwan's government was actively trying to procure a nuclear weapon, presumably because they no longer had faith that Washington would provide sufficient security. Bush passed this news on to Washington with little comment.

[30]President Ford had visited Japan during November 1974. It was his first trip abroad as president and immediately preceded his summit with Soviet leader Leonid Brezhnev at Vladivostok.

nese are marvelous. They are all over the place. They are polite, able and they do a first-class job.

Thursday, March 20[, 1975]. Ambassador Natural of Switzerland called. He is living in a downtown old house owned by John Shoemaker, filled with beautiful relics that can't be taken out of China. They are all American owned, but the Swiss are building a new embassy to their own design, and he is negotiating currently— trying to get those relics and pottery etc. to be put into the embassy. Quiet lunch with Bar. These lunches are very nice, this one very light in preparation for dinner. Got briefed by Frank Scotten on Vietnam and Cambodia—discouraging sounding.[31] I was amazed at his report. It looks like both countries have had it. And yet I am wondering whether the President was not permitted to get too far out on requesting aid if the situation is like it is. He [Scotten] told me that it had deteriorated recently in Vietnam something awful. That night for dinner Mr. Zhuang Zedong came who is the Minister of Sports. Just made a minister at the last People's Congress. Along with Guo Lei who is the head of the International Affairs Division, a very jovial, large man; Sun Lan, division head; and Liu Qiu, an interpreter. Jennifer, John Holdridge, Don Anderson and Lynn Pascoe joined us. Zhuang has been made Minister. He is a former ping-pong champion. He is well known through all of China, a real celebrity you might say. The waiters and cooks were excited that he was coming and Sun put on an excellent dinner. We talked international affairs. I am told that Zhuang had been disciplined during the Cultural Revolution but here he is now as a young man, in his 30s, as a minister. Still athletic, big, but put on a little weight and smokes an awful lot. We discussed the concept of sports and friendship. Really I have concluded that friendship means sports-

[31]Scotten worked as an East Asian affairs officer for the United States Information Agency (USIA), the umbrella network responsible for overseeing all American information programs, including the Voice of America. He had recently worked in Vietnam, helping to organize information and propaganda efforts for South Vietnamese forces.

manship. He gave us an example of a championship match with the score 20-19. He thought his ball hit the net; the Japanese player thought the ball hit the net; [but] the referee didn't see it. The referee awarded the ball to the Japanese who promptly served the next one on purpose into the net, reciprocating friendship. Friendship sounds to me what mother drove into us as sportsmanship.[32] There is no question that the Chinese like to win.

The campaign is on. Dictatorship of the proletariat and eliminating bourgeois tendencies. It is gradually replacing the anti-Lin, anti-Confucius campaign. There is a lot of drilling now out on the streets. The other day there were a lot of commands shouted out when I was talking to Steve Fitzgerald. I jumped up, spun around, and there was the whole middle school from down the road being drilled and disciplined out on military drill. In the last few days we have seen many such schools including the very little ones marching by in cadence. Perhaps getting ready for a big parade on May first.

Word that Bemis and Bryans have their visas.[33] Am [a]waiting Jake Hamon's arrival on the guest front.[34] I get some feeling that the highest level in the State Department thinks I may be having

[32]Such admonitions from his mother later guided Bush's own views of personal diplomacy. When asked to describe the approach he took to his first diplomatic posting at the United Nations, especially given his lack of formal diplomatic experience, Bush recalled that he merely fell back on his mother's advice: "Be kind. Don't be a big shot. Listen, don't talk. Reach out to people. [It] doesn't have anything to do with diplomacy; it has to do with life. Treat people with respect and recognize in diplomatic terms that the sovereignty of Burundi is as important to them as our sovereignty is [to us]. Slightly different scale, I might add. But nevertheless this is just a value thing. This isn't any great diplomatic study from the Fletcher School or something. This is just the way you react to things."

[33]Gerry Bemis was a longtime correspondent of Bush's, their relationship dating back to family vacations in Kennebunkport, Maine. D. Tennant Bryan, accompanied by his wife, Mary, was editor and publisher of the *Richmond Times-Dispatch* and chairman of the board of Media General, Inc., a communications conglomerate.

[34]Jake Hamon made his career in the Oklahoma and Texas oil fields. He and his wife, Nancy, were longtime benefactors of the arts in Dallas, as well as the Dallas Public Library.

too many guests but I think it is important. I think it is in keeping with what we are trying to do. It finds ways for us to do things with the diplomats and the Chinese and all in all I will continue to do this. I am constantly amazed at some of the things in the States but it is very hard to figure them out here.[35] Elliot Richardson [made some] out-of-character statements about his being the next Secretary of State or running for President. They just don't sound right. Maybe he sees this as the only avenue from which to seek high political office, but it must have Kissinger climbing a wall.

Weather improving beautifully now. Warm, just right for bicycles, and dust storms, reminiscent of Midland, are here but not nearly as bad as some of those that we have seen in West Texas.

Ambassador of Poland on March 20. A very savvy guy. Stricken with encephalitis when swimming. He said it went in through the ears, something I didn't understand, but he got this terrible disease that caused him to be paralyzed from the waist down, caused him to lose his balance. There are also other cases of bad diseases here. Within the last two weeks an Australian embassy member got

[35]That day Bush had in fact written William Gleysteen, at that time deputy assistant secretary of state for Far Eastern affairs, with a lengthy and heated objection to the department's oversight over his choice and number of guests. He was not above either falling back on his record of high-level political service or making a none-too-veiled political threat at the letter's close: "I served in the Congress for four years and served as Chairman of our party for two years. Thus many of my closest personal friends happen to be members of the House and Senate—not professional friends, close personal friends. When I left Washington at one of several going away parties I naturally said to these people 'come see us' and I meant it. Frankly, I think it would be very useful to have them do just that. I cannot conceive of any member of Congress that I invited doing anything that would embarrass our policy but I can see how some might understand it a little better. . . . In the future, I will simply advise members of the House and Senate that I am not free to invite them without their first getting approval of the Secretary of State. However, I would strongly urge that this be carefully thought out back there. I do understand Congress pretty well, and I do not believe this would be understood very well on the Hill. . . . In short if it is a firm decision I will abide by it, but I want to be clearly on the record as disagreeing with it. I will do my best to see that it causes no problems but if pressed I will simply tell the truth and say that I am not free to invite members of Congress without prior State Department approval."

meningitis. He was delirious. They had to have shifts holding him down in the hospital. But miraculously he is going to live. The disease is endemic to China for March, April and May, and the Chinese according to Ambassador Fitzgerald are good at treating it. We don't have a doctor here. The State Department is sending Dr. Watson out. Things like routine medical care, although we have a chest full of medicine over here, are not good. Schools and doctors are not part of the hardships but part of some of the things that we take for granted in our life, not only in the U.S. but at most posts. Same with good entertainment and that kind of thing.

I mix my reading between Chinese—books on China—and light reading. Am now reading Bill Safire's story of the downfall of the Nixon people.[36] It is discouraging and I have mixed emotions as I read it. I noted a picture of the helicopter with the Kennedy children by the house Bill Clements had bought in McLean. This was a clipping Jane had sent me from the Washington paper. I wondered whether the reporters were swarming around in those days to see who was paying for the helicopter ride.

Giving a little thought now to possibly running for governor of Texas.[37] I have time to think these out. The plan might be to go home after the elections in '76, settle down in Houston in a rather flexible business thing, shoot for the governorship in '78, though it might be extremely difficult to win. Should I win it, it would be an

---

[36]The reference, as in chapter 4, is to William Safire's *Before the Fall* (1975).

[37]Two days earlier, Bush had voiced his ongoing political ruminations in a letter to Pete Roussel, a long-time political associate and frequent sounding board, who was working for Donald Rumsfeld at the White House at the time. The letter reveals that, to Bush, all short-term considerations were seen within the context of one overriding goal: a presidential bid. "For your info only. If the Texas Gov thing in '78 makes any sense at all I'd maybe take a look at it hard—Go back to Houston after the '76 elections, win or lose for Republicans, involve myself in academia and business, move around the state plenty and try one last gasp for '78 keeping in mind that I wouldn't do it unless there was a possibility of taking a shot at something bigger in '80—not necessarily on the latter, but having it way off dimly in the future. Just a reminiscence—not a hard thought, certainly not a plan at this point. As you know well a GOP Gov in our state is tough."

excellent position again for national politics, and should I lose, it would be a nice way to get statewide politics out of my system once and for all. I hate to undertake yet another losing campaign, and I am a little out of touch with what it all means down there, but I can get a little quiet work done on the situation.[38] Tower will be up that year which complicates things.[39] New politics doesn't seem to have affected Bentsen who is going to run for both Senate and President as Lyndon Johnson did, unlike Barry Goldwater's approach.[40]

Someone told Bar that many people in the diplomatic corps here use dope. I find that hard to believe in this country. Intriguing but not provable as far as I am concerned, I have heard nothing about that.

[38]Bush expressed a similar lack of certainty regarding his desire to run for office once more in a letter composed two weeks earlier to Clements—who would become Texas governor in his own right in 1979–83 and 1987–91. Writing during the first week of March, Bush confided, "I loved our talk at the house. I have plenty of time to think out here. There is plenty to do, but I find that for the first time in my adult life I can control my own time pretty well. I have been thinking some about the future. The advice you gave me is very good indeed. I do not have elective politics completely out of my system, but I am deeply interested in foreign affairs and in the security of our country." Seven months in Beijing had brought little clarity to Bush's thinking, though he did express enthusiasm for remaining a while longer in Beijing. Writing Clements that October, he admitted, "As to Bentsen's vulnerability in Texas, certainly you and Rita and the Connollys would be good judges. My problem is that at this point I just don't have the burning desire to give up this kind of work and spend another year of my life campaigning across our tremendous state. I don't think being in Peking for a year has hurt me politically, but it has put me out of touch (temporarily, I hope) with the main issues. I had a little talk with the President about my future when I saw him in Texas. You and I didn't have a chance to visit about that. All in all, I think it is best that I remain here for now, that I work hard and try to do a decent job, and that I forgo the Senate race. I can't see very clearly into the future, but this doesn't worry me at all."

[39]John Tower was the Republican senator from Texas, having first been elected to replace Lyndon Johnson in 1961.

[40]Lloyd Bentsen was a four-term Democratic senator from Texas and vice presidential nominee in 1988. Bentsen had been Bush's competitor in 1970 for Texas's senate seat. He later served as secretary of the treasury during the Clinton administration. Barry Goldwater was a long-serving Arizona senator and the Republican candidate for president in 1964.

215

Fred may be prejudiced along racial lines. He seems to jump on the Chinese. Actually he comes in friendship but at times it is hard to tell that, particularly [to] a guy with a mop or a broom outside. He is good with Mr. Wang and Guo, [and] likes him enormously. Bar took Fred downtown, went into the store yesterday, came out and there were a hundred people surrounding the car staring at the Guo-driven Chrysler. Really staring at Fred. I told her not to do that anymore. It put Guo in a funny position. Fred can go to the Ming Tombs and run around out there, but I don't want to have the image of chauffeur-driven dog kind of thing.

[Friday,] March 21[, 1975]. The Austrian ambassador and his wife, a Mr. [Eduard] Tschoep, came to call. Our first his-and-hers diplomatic call. Very formal but very friendly and relaxed and pleasant and smiling. He told me that Leitner, his predecessor, was telling everyone at home that he wished that he had stayed longer. That was not the same Leitner that was bitching here at the end in China at all. A call on Al-Atrash, Ambassador of Syria: Middle East, Middle East, Middle East. These Middle East ambassadors, whenever they talk to the U.S. wherever they are, I am convinced, want to talk about that one situation. Al-Atrash emphasized people-to-people friendship in the United States, how Arabs like the United States etc. but was critical of our policy. I in turn told him that the guerrilla-type activities are counterproductive in the United States. Frank Scotten, USIA, came for lunch. He is helping us with our VTR tapes. I had written Paley three months ago.[41] Paley apparently passed it on to the president of CBS News who in turn asked their Washington office to contact someone who in turn talked to the fourth guy in Oscar Armstrong's office who in turn talked to USIS.[42] I have heard nothing from Paley but the matter is floundering around at

[41] William S. Paley was founder of the CBS radio and television network.

[42] Oscar Armstrong, a career foreign service officer and Asian specialist, was born in China to missionary parents. He served in the American consulate in Beijing from 1947 to 1949, departing after the Communist takeover. He subsequently served as head of public affairs for the State Department's East Asian Bureau dur-

some low level in the bureaucracy. I am now going back to Paley direct. I have never seen such a monstrous bureaucracy and sometimes I can understand Kissinger's indignation at it. The guy in Oscar Armstrong's office never even told me he had heard from CBS. The only way we are going to get it done is to get it back on the high level.

Ambassador Bulak of Turkey came to call.[43] Then we went down —Harry, Liu, Jennifer and I did—to look for a birthday present for Bar in the China Store.[44] Liu is marvelous, great English and most helpful. Dinner that night at the Canadian Embassy with the sports minister and Spain's ambassador to Japan, former OECD [Organisation for Economic Co-operation and Development] colleague of John Small's. The Chinese were lecturing the sports minister on throwing Taiwan out of the Olympic games in Canada. Something the sports minister impressed on them was that neither his organization, the Canadian sports federation nor the government was in a position to do anything.[45] China harped away on it. He is also trying to get Canada to come to their international meeting of sports federation. He thinks they will do it in '76 if Taiwan doesn't come. The Chinese are rigid on their principles. We are having a hassle about what songs will be sung by the traveling troop in the United States. Liberation of Taiwan by force.[46]

Saturday, [March 22, 1975], dusty day. Put on our skiing goggles and masks and bicycled to downtown, stopping at Hong Du Tailors, getting a laugh out of the entire crowd in our "Man from Mars" outfit. There was the beautiful cashmere overcoat ready to

---

ing the mid-1960s and during Bush's tenure in Beijing was head of PRC and Mongolian affairs for that bureau.

[43]Adnan Bulak, who began his service in Beijing in 1974, would later serve as Turkey's ambassador to France.

[44]Probably Harry Thayer, a Yale graduate and recent arrival at the USLO, who later served as Washington's ambassador to Singapore and as director of the American Institute in Taiwan.

[45]Montreal hosted the 1976 summer Olympics. Host nations do not determine the list of participating nations.

[46]See Bush's entry, and my footnote, for March 10, 1975.

be fitted. The people are so pleasant. The workmanship excellent. Cycled to the theater shop, then by the international post office and then back. It is a lot of work riding against the dust storm, but great exercise. Played tennis in the afternoon, hitting with Mr. Wang. Almost through Bill Safire's book. He captured the Kissinger problem very well and does a good job on Nixon, the enormous arrogance, the pressures that I only began to see when I first got into the National Committee job are well handled. Early dinner Saturday night.

Sunday [March 23, 1975].   The church service. We don't know quite how to handle the money gift to Lily Wen's father.[47] I am putting the money in a little at a time, having been advised that it would not be appropriate to give a large sum of money. John Small and I were talking and we don't know whether the money goes to the church or is turned over to the state or what. It is hard to tell. Telephoned home. Talked to Doro and Mum.[48] Very clear connection. It is exactly 9:30 at night Peking and 9:30 morning Florida time.

Note. The Chinese can be tough. They talk about principle. Their principles. And when it is a matter of principle it really means do it their way. How do we get them to understand what our principles are, particularly as you see the demise of Cambodia and Vietnam? This is a different period. All the news, red news and blue news, radio etc., talks about Cambodia and Vietnam. Cambodia, less Vietnam, but still both of them—imperialists. We are hit less than the Russians but we are hit. They talk about the decay of the West and the decay of our society. Things like the security of diplomats is excellent. You ride around totally unfettered and I think back to my host country ambassadorship at the UN when all the rapes, robberies and shootings, dynamitings, protests, and one has to give good credit for security. But what is the price? It is nice to

[47]As noted in chapter 4, Lily Wen's father was a Nationalist officer, killed fighting the Communists during the civil war.
[48]Bush refers to his daughter, Dorothy.

be able to go and have a picnic at the Ming Tombs or wander around downtown Peking and not worry about your security at all. There is robbery and petty thievery but we have not been exposed to it in any way, nor have I ever heard of an example of it in the diplomatic community. A French mission girl was attacked the other day by a guy with a sickle. Hit her over the head, jumped into the Mali embassy and in a minute troops surrounded the place and they hauled him off. The French called him a "fou" meaning he was out of his mind. They hauled him out. Three or six years ago this happened and the guy was shot and the government person who was attacked was so informed. We don't know what happened to this "fou."[49] The PLA guards are beginning to smile and almost recognize Fred's existence as he chases balls, runs after the kite etc.

Sunday, March 23. A beautiful picnic at the Ming Tombs following church. Bob Blackburn gave it with all kinds of soup and fancy things. Beautiful hillsides, totally isolated. Spring in the air. It was perfection, surrounded by the great beauty itself. There was

[49]Bush may have misspoken when he first referred to this incident as having occurred "the other day," or, equally likely, this story may have grown in the retelling from the original incident. It was a well-worn cautionary tale. Steve Allen notes in his memoir that the Bushes and the Allens discussed the matter over a lunch at the USLO several months later. However, Allen dates the story to 1965. The earlier date correlates, at least more closely, with Bush's later statement that the incident occurred "three or six years ago." John Holdridge tells a remarkably similar story in his own memoirs, yet with important differences. A butcher shop employee "took the bill-hook used to pull the carcasses, went storming outside the Friendship Store and in a rage struck down the first foreigner he encountered. This happened to be the wife of a French diplomat, who was pushing her little boy in a stroller just outside the store. Fortunately, while she suffered a jagged cut over the ear, she was not seriously injured; her attacker then rushed across the street into the Iraqi embassy compound from which he was later dragged by the omnipresent PLA guards. We heard that he was later shot." For our purposes, the specific details of this story would seem less important than what they tell us about how the American (and international) community in Beijing communicated with each other about the dangers, and the safeties, of their temporary home. In each retelling, though details varied, the message was the same. The perpetrator was summarily dealt with, and peace was restored with an iron fist.

a Chinese family cooking on a little gas burner when we came in and having their own picnic. But we went off in the back of the main entrance and had the entire hillside to ourselves except for one couple that wandered out, obviously having enjoyed the quietude of the hills where we arrived. After the doubles game went to see the Nigeria v. Peking women's basketball match. They packed the stadium for a lousy, mediocre basketball game. Unbelievable. Girls marched out—Chinese in the red suits, Nigerian in the green. Holding each other's hand[s] on high. Then when one girl would foul another, there would be a great display of "friendship." They overdid the friendship aspect of it and underdid the basketball aspect. We left after the first twenty minutes. I just can't imagine 10 or 15 thousand people, and the place was packed, sitting watching that kind of a performance. They seemed to love it. The sports minister was there and the place for the guests was regal. We had gone in the wrong entrance and were ushered into that place over my protest pointing to a seat. The guide said "you and your spouses can sit anyplace." We finally acquiesced. Then a rather serious functionary appeared and said, "You will have to leave. You will have to sit in your own seats." I said, "Look we want to sit in the other seats." Instead of seeming apologetic about it, he was rather imperious. The first time I have seen this kind of behavior towards us. Not unfriendly but slightly arrogant and a little bit demanding. The African girls had that marvelous walk and strut but the Chinese girls were much more athletic looking, trim and tall and much better passing and handling the basketball. China was leading at half. End March 23.

Just read in the wireless file where the CIA insisted the Post Office read mail going to "Mainland China" till '73. Here we worry about our mail being read and the same thing was true for our country. As you read the home news things take on a different meaning when you are in a country like this. I see where the doctors are on strike or have just ended their strike in New York. What a concept.

[Monday,] March 24[, 1975].   Got a call from Rex Ellis, ABC Hong Kong, who calls in regularly—very clear.[50] Roussel has been calling me for two days at the White House and they could never hear, but Hong Kong is very clear. He told me that they had heard there that Cambodia had contacted us saying they would permit U.S. citizens to leave Cambodia without getting shelled. I told him nothing to it. Lots of diplomatic rumors. The red news and the blue news full of Cambodia and Vietnam all the time. Diplomats look at you with a kind of "we feel sorry for you" kind of concept. Really sad—the demise of those two countries. Sihanouk sounding more and more frantic.

Monday, the 24th. Lunch at the residence with Ambassadors Ogawa and Fitzgerald, and Holdridge. Normally Harland would be there but he is in New Zealand. These little regional lunches are informal and very nice. Wang and Sun continue to do a very good job on them. The Hamons arrived that afternoon and we had a little light dinner at the International Club. Jake and Nancy seem to be enjoying everything very much.

Tuesday, March 25[, 1975].   Lunch. Hamons went sightseeing with Bar. I had lunch with them. At five o'clock the French Ambassador and Mrs. Arnaud came on a courtesy call and on business, discussing Cambodia and Sihanouk. Six to seven, the Greek Independence Day reception next door. Tons of diplomats crammed in there. Chinese representation pretty good—minister of education, couple of vice ministers. Dinner at Kang Le with the Hamons. News consists of further deterioration in Cambodia and Vietnam. Kissinger's trip to the Middle East aborted and it worries me about our foreign policy, this effort to destroy Kissinger—criticizing him enormously at home, and the feud between him and the Congress concerns me. Newspaper reports make it sound at this juncture like

---

[50]Ellis later reported from Saigon for ABC, witnessing the final American helicopter flights off the roof of the U.S. embassy.

he is going to leave and be succeeded by Elliot Richardson. At home I would have some insight into this. Here we simply do not.

Spring is here. Walked through the park on Tuesday the 25th and watched them do the shadowboxing. Watched the kids assemble. Fighting and struggling and dancing and teacher blowing a whistle. Men with their legs stuck up in the trees stretching their muscles for their shadow boxing. Going through these weird and wonderful motions, oblivious to people around them. Of course they're staring at the Hamons and even more than we are staring at them in action. One man standing under an arch singing in a glorious tenor voice oblivious to our coming or going. The juggling of house guests' schedules is very complicated from out here. End March 25.

[Wednesday,] March 26[, 1975]. The head of the Consular Group from PRC and three others came for lunch. A man asked why do we make people who want a visa come to Peking. It is very expensive for them to come all the way across China. We replied that maybe the answer would be to have consulates in other places. Also once they get a visa they are free to travel all over, unlike China. The last one was my offering and it was fairly weak. The point, however, is well taken. I am not sure we try to do enough to help reunite families and help on the consular work. It is very complicated and I just can't get over how unresponsive the Chinese are to these requests. Perfectly normal requests. There seems to be a great caution or a great reserve or a great isolation from things foreign in responses.

The tennis courts are being fixed now. I have furnished them all kinds of information and yet they never discuss it. After I get it and talk about it in the beginning, they never will discuss it. I think they want to be totally self-sufficient. I saw Mr. Wang and about 30 people out sifting lime through screens. Apparently that will now be mixed with red clayish stuff and the courts will be resurfaced hopefully to make them better. But they simply will not ask for help and really don't want advice, although they are very polite about receiving the information. Magnificent dinner at the Qin Yang restaurant with the Hamons, the Steigers and the Tawliks of Egypt.[51] Too much food though—on and on and on came the food. I believe Mr. Sun puts on the best kind of dinner for my stomach. Less pepper, more bland, but still delightful and subtle fragrances. Stamp collecting is my new thing. You can get the history of post-liberation China from the stamps. They are beautiful and tremendously interesting looking. Jake Hamon at 72 is a great sport. He will do anything. Great stamina. Goes to the Wall, to the Ming Tombs yesterday with Bar. Always game to walk. After dinner he and Fred and I took a good long walk. He is just as sharp as he can be. I'd like to be that way at 72.

I don't know why they use the term Chinese Fire Drill. The Chinese seem to be pretty organized. You see them unloading trucks, etc., and there's pretty darn good organization. There seems to be an under-utilization of labor in places. Lots of people leaning on the hose in the field, standing around during the work gangs, but still the work gets done. They rebuilt the Norwegian embassy in a week by just putting hundreds of bodies to work on it after the fire. I noticed them unloading a truck in front of our house this morning. Pretty good, pretty good. Pretty well organized. Much marching around now by students, drilling, trumpets, bands. I am wondering if there is going to be a great big parade one of these days —something China hasn't had in a long time.

Tennis last night. Akwei and I losing to Te and Wang in one set. They both played well, serving better than I've ever seen them, and you talk about really happy to win. They deserved to win and they clearly were pleased, though they were very polite about their victory. Reading Shirley MacLaine's book.[52] The naiveté and the emo-

[51]William and Janet Steiger had befriended the Bushes when William represented Wisconsin in Congress. Janet Steiger later became the first woman to head the Federal Trade Commission.

[52]MacLaine's 1973 travels in China spawned *You Can Get There from Here* (New York: Norton, 1975), a narrative of her journey and impressions, as well as a documentary film, *The Other Half of the Sky,* directed by MacLaine and Claudia Weill, which was nominated for an Academy Award as best documentary.

tional kind of acceptance of things (her salute, fist held on high and wink to Chairman Mao), her kind of acceptance of everything Chinese as well organized and perfect, except not for her, leaves me feeling a little strange about her work. End of March 26. I am almost through Safire's book.

Note. Two great Chinese expressions. First, Xiu Shou Pang Guan. That equals "standing on sidelines with hand in sleeves." As campaigns come and go people do this, watching to see what develops. A great expression. They also write about the "rust-proof screw" (clean screw) as a thing to be emulated.

[Thursday, March 27, 1975].   Called on Ambassador Naimbaye Lassiman of Chad. Spoke French on the call. The Africans need more attention. They sit in an embassy with little communication and yet occasionally, because of China's interest in the Third World, they do get excellent contacts. We need to do more, more, more in making these people feel at home, and on demonstrating that we are not "imperialists." It is an effort, it is hard to communicate, it is hard to get phone calls returned, hard to keep up with when they are in and out of town; but each contact in my view is worth making and even if it is not productive they are nice and warm and friendly people. Lunch with the Ogdens and Henrietta Morris (and the Hamons), welcoming them to the USLO.[53] Bar had the 24-hour flu. She has had it two or three times and it is prevalent right now, as is encephalitis this time of year, and meningitis. Both much more serious than what she had. She staged a great recovery and we had a big dinner at the Peking Duck.

Walking in the park is fun before breakfast. You see the tai chi chuan. You see the other form of Chinese boxing which is more

[53]Jerome Ogden, a career foreign service officer, subsequently served as consul general in Guangzhou and Shanghai. He later told one reporter that, during his entire three-year stint in Beijing during the 1970s, he processed a total of three visas from Chinese citizens to visit the United States. Henrietta Morris had recently arrived at the USLO to work in the administrative pool.

vigorous. You see people with their legs in trees. You see one on one pressing muscles going slowly through tai chi chuan but it is two people. You hear people singing. Today we heard a tenor and a baritone in harmony in a little pagoda on top of the one hill in the park. The other day a baritone singing under the arches in the middle of the park. You see families. You see he-ing and she-ing in the park which surprised me, not aggressive petting but sitting close against each other. And quite clearly in love. You see a lot of old people visiting there. You see propaganda all around. This morning school was being lectured. Everyone had a book with Mao on the cover and a teacher had them all sitting in a very disciplined way, giving them a lecture with other teachers standing around. The park is beginning to be beautiful. There is no grass but it is beautiful. The trees and the buds and the hedges. Propaganda billboards.

Sihanouk, Sihanouk, Sihanouk. News still full of Cambodia and Vietnam, decline in U.S. position.[54] Red and blue news carrying the break-off of the trips and the defeats for the Americans in all these areas. Obviously China wants us strong and wants us involved in many places and yet publicly they must be on us as imperialists. A dilemma. Studied the most highly classified cables from the time USLO opened. Interesting how history seems to be repeating itself as far as Southeast Asia goes. Feeling better each day. Bar decided to go back for Marvin's graduation.[55] I am very, very happy about this. He's done a good job that boy.

Peking Duck dinner. Ambassadors from Tunisia, Burma, Pakistan, Serge Romensky of Agence France-Presse and Pilgrim of Guinea. A very good duck dinner at the best duck restaurant. Beer, chou chang

[54]On March 25, 1975, Hue fell after a three-day siege. South Vietnamese troops retreated en masse. Da Nang had fallen by March 30; 100,000 South Vietnamese soldiers surrendered. On March 31 the North's Ho Chi Minh Campaign—the final push toward Saigon—began.
[55]Marvin Bush graduated in 1975 from the Woodberry Forest School, a small all-male boarding school.

wine, thirteen people, price tag 186 kuai, 186 yuan which is about $105–6. The Hamons are great house guests. End March 27.

[Friday, March 28, 1975]. The 28th was the Hamons' wedding anniversary. We celebrated it at the International Club that night. That morning Jake and I went down and bought some Cuban cigars. They cost 1.60 kuai which is about 90 cents, which is about 4 or 5 times cheaper than a comparable cigar, the Churchill variety, I was told, in Paris or in other markets. I played a little tennis and the rest of the day was mostly around the office.

Saturday the 29th [March 29, 1975]. The Hamons left. We ended the visit with seeing the cultural relics in a special showing. It was the other half of the Washington Museum at the Forbidden City. Beautifully done. Walks in the parks with the Hamons were fun.

The Hamons left on Air France on the 29th and I went out before them to meet John Rhodes and Carl Albert. Mary Albert got off looking stoned, but it turned out she had nothing to drink, was just unstable. Albert has not conducted himself well here. He was particularly bad on Monday the 31st in a meeting with Qiao Guanhua.[56] Talking and not letting the translator work. All in all I was amazed. He is such a nice guy and very pleasant in person, but he was very terribly ineffective and I was horribly embarrassed by it all. The Hamons were great house guests and seemed to appreciate everything. They are very, very rich and yet both of them are down to earth, thoughtful to Guo and thoughtful to Wang, Sun and all the rest. In fact they gave tiny little presents to all the help and fortunately the help accepted them. Mr. Wang looking a little apprehensive, but all in all the Hamons handled it with great taste and tact.

The Congressmen appeared, and on Good Friday evening we went to Good Friday service. There were only about ten people in our whole little church. On Sunday the 30th it was a different story. The Church was packed. The Catholic Church had two hundred. Our church was overflowing, largely because of an African chris-

[56]Sources documenting this visit are provided in the endnotes.

226

tening that went on with two little babies, the church mainly filled with Africans. The Rhodes, Poseys and Dr. Carey joined us for Easter service which was very nice. Then they all went off to the Great Wall and Bar and I cycled down with John Burns to the Great Square for some picture taking. The dust was really bad. We used our goggles and it made a hell of a difference. The people stare at us like mad with the goggles and masks on, but it was necessary. Some places the wind almost made the bike stand on end, you almost felt you were going to be blown over. The weather was warmish. I had a good tennis game in the afternoon playing with old Mr. Chi who suited up for the first time. I played with Finocchi of Italy who doesn't know the doubles game at all. Mr. Chi couldn't hit the ball but knew the game well. Always in proper position, careful, thoughtful, marvelous old fellow. Wang and De beat Finocchi and me 6-love. Finocchi and I beat Wang and Chi in two straight sets.

On Easter Sunday evening we went to the Sick Duck where Wang Hairong and Nancy Tang gave the Congressmen a very good verbal exercise. The Chinese are wed on this subject of principle. They canceled out the cultural performance because of refusing to give way on the song about Taiwan liberation. The Philadelphia orchestra came here, yielding totally with what they thought would be a proper program.[57] But when we asked them to change the song

---

[57]The Philadelphia Orchestra, arguably the nation's finest, toured China September 10–23, 1973, under the direction of Eugene Ormandy. As this was the first such trip to mainland China for an American orchestra, the group's leaders, with support from the State Department and the USLO, worked with Chinese officials to ensure that their playlist carried no unintended political themes that might have repercussions. Indeed the full program had been decided upon before the orchestra departed American shores. But Chinese officials insisted upon a last-minute addition for the final performance of Beethoven's Sixth Symphony, apparently owing to the personal intervention of Jiang Qing. John Holdridge contends that Zhou Enlai subsequently took the opportunity to initiate a campaign against Jiang. The *People's Daily* included an editorial a fortnight after the concert denouncing such music, claiming that it "watered down the revolutionary enthusiasm of the masses." Such cryptic charges and power struggles were part and parcel of the Cultural Revolution, but the important lesson from the USLO's perspective was that, for PRC officials, even music was political.

on liberation of Taiwan which hadn't even been submitted in the first place as part of the program, they balked and cited principle. They are amazing. They are polite, they are strong, but they always talk about principle. And when they don't want to give an answer they just obfuscate and sit there. It's the most frustrating thing in the world.

[Monday, March 31, 1975]. On Monday the 31st, a big part of the day was the meeting [with] Qiao Guanhua, with Rhodes and Albert—Albert interrupting the interpreter, not letting Qiao Guanhua finish. He almost threw up his hands but he is too polite for that. The meeting lasted for two hours and ten minutes during which Qiao Guanhua indicated that they were not in favor of going back to Geneva on the Middle East and the step-by-step approach. They want to see us withdraw but they don't want to see us withdraw as far as troops go. They want us to fulfill our commitment fully but they are also realistic.

It was a great exercise for Albert and Rhodes to see firsthand some of the frustrations that we experience here. Quiet lunch on the 31st here at the house downstairs with just Bar and I eating these delightful foods. My weight is beginning to creep up. I feel a lot better. Weather is good. Called on the ambassador of Somalia on Monday the 31st, trying to get these African calls going. The Africans are of good value here. We have got to do more with them.

Quiet dinner on the 31st at the house. Relaxed, early evenings. These are marvelous fun events—almost euphoric in the happiness. Great letters from the kids. I don't know what we'd ever do if the kids weren't happy when we are way out here. I miss them. And I miss Don, and Jane Kenny, and Tom Lias, and Pete and Rose and Mary Lou, and Aleene, and all the people who have just given so much of their lives to me over the years.[58] Great loyalties mean an

[58]These individuals all served on Bush's staffs in Washington and New York. Don Rhodes first joined Bush's 1964 congressional campaign as a volunteer and later became a close friend and associate. It was Rhodes, for example, who helped arrange travel for Bush's friends and family on their visits to China. Jane

awful lot. Now I am troubled by the news at home and the seeming weakness of the President—the challenge. It looks to me like, without predicting who will win, I should be planning a private life starting in '76. In fact, it has an enormous appeal in a lot of ways. Though I expect having been in the public arena, going back to private will be somewhat complicated. Oh well, I don't fear the future. I look forward to it. Marvin wrote me that death worried him. I sent him an article from the paper about a column Bill Buckley wrote about the courage of Charles Luckey in death, a guy who couldn't take his own life because of his great faith.[59] Also I wrote him about some men who had died and had been brought back to life, all of whom were almost euphoric in their comments on how great death really was. I don't fear it now. In fact, I can't say that I welcome it, because I want desperately to live longer and do something and to accomplish things, and to see my kids grown and happy, but I must say that scary teenage feeling is no longer around me. End of March 31.

The congressmen are staying in the guest house next door to Hong Du Tailors. Apparently it was a former Austrian Embassy,

---

Kenny later served as special assistant to Bush in his vice presidential office. Thomas L. Lias was special assistant to Bush when he was ambassador to the United Nations and served as his executive assistant when Bush was chairman of the Republican National Committee (RNC). He went on to be deputy director of Bush's 1980 presidential campaign. Peter Roussel was press officer for Bush when he served in Congress, and he was later press secretary for Bush's U.N. office and then at the RNC. Roussel went on to serve as deputy press secretary in the Reagan administration. Rose Zamaria, Mary Lou Schwarzmann, and Aleene Smith were all members of the staff in Bush's congressional office.

[59]The original text reads "Luckheed." The article, "Death of a Christian," was written by William F. Buckley, founder of the conservative journal *National Reiew*. It concerns Charles Pinckney Luckey, minister of a Congregational church in Connecticut, who was stricken with Creutzfeldt-Jakob disease, a rare brain disorder. There is no cure for the disease, and virtually all who contract it die within a year. Pastor Luckey, upon learning of the destructive personality and behavioral changes that often result from the ravages of the disease, considered taking his own life to spare his friends and family "the horrible beast within himself." He ultimately decided against suicide, believing such an act would violate his faith.

very high ceilings, overstuffed chairs, very convenient. The Foreign Minister met them in the Foreign Ministry Guest House which is right diagonally across from the Peking Hotel but behind big walls. I have driven by there a million times on my bike and never realized it was there. I am always amazed about being on time in China. You're never late. We orbit around, circling, waiting to make sure we are on time.

The difference between Rhodes and Albert at the meeting [with] Qiao Guanhua was amazing. Rhodes was first class. Nice, respectful but forceful, soliciting answers. Albert was platitudinous, interrupted, vague, kept looking at his notes and just didn't seem to have a grasp of foreign affairs at all. Every time Qiao Guanhua started to reply, Albert would interrupt. Right in the middle of one reply Albert started out on how bright Wang Hairong and Nancy Tang were, hauled into his pocket, handed out his pen, and said "Give them all a pen, Charlie," handing her a little red pen. He made one statement saying we all agree there is but one Taiwan. They all laughed and then corrected it. Then he kept calling the Shanghai Communiqué the Chinese Communiqué. Qiao Guanhua referred to the relations as generally good but "some frictions occur." Then he talked about the performing arts troop, indicated they didn't want to make a big deal of it. I handed Rhodes a note saying is there any way you can get Carl to let Qiao finish.

March 31. Also called on Mr. Darman of Somalia—Middle East, Middle East, Middle East.

[Tuesday,] April 1[, 1975]. Hoarding CODELs [congressional delegations] met with Deng Xiaoping, [and the] foreign minister [Qiao Guanhua]. Nancy Tang was there. Albert did a little better but he still interrupted a lot and just simply doesn't understand interpretation. It was not a disaster but it was pretty bad. We had a message saying the President wanted him and Rhodes back for a Joint Session of Congress on April 10. Albert raised hell saying that he had pledged his best friend in Oklahoma that he would give a speech that night. It later turns out the speech was going to be in

Washington and after we sent a telegram saying he couldn't be there, he then relented. His view was to let Burton and Tip O'Neill get this through the Congress.[60] I feel sorry for Albert. It has been a disappointment to me to see that he is not a big man. His wife is sad, tries hard—not drinking—but very difficult.

Afternoon spent in the office. We were concerned about the press conference and whether they would want to go too much into the policy statements of the Congress but they didn't. The Speaker and Rhodes handled it very well indeed. We had a large reception for the Chinese, friends, the press, American business people, UOP [Universal Oil Products] and others in Peking.[61] Sun knocked himself out. In a reception like this waiters and food are sometimes brought in from the Peking Hotel and the International Club. This time the Peking Hotel. Everyone seemed to enjoy it.

Dinner at the International Club, for just John Rhodes, Bushes, Holdridges, Alberts and Gleysteens.[62] Nine for dinner with beer and a bottle of wine—1,907 yuan which is about $10 and I thought the food was darn good. Mr. Fay and Mr. Lo came over to chat, both of them very Western, both of them very pleased to meet our CODELs, had read about them in the paper. Apparently there has been some coverage of this visit. They are being treated pretty well indeed which is somewhat reassuring given the flap we had on the art troop going to the States. Guest house that they are staying in used to be the Indian Embassy. High ceilings, very pleasant. The Foreign Ministry Guest House was the Austria-Hungary Embassy—great big beautiful thing. It must have been some life in Peking in those days. I mentioned to Nancy Tang that I would like

[60]Phillip Burton, a Democrat, represented his California district in Congress for ten terms beginning in 1963. Thomas "Tip" O'Neill, a titan of American politics, would become speaker of the House in 1977.

[61]Universal Oil Products Company (now UOP LLC), a company that researches and licenses petroleum refining technologies, signed its first contracts with China in 1975.

[62]William Gleysteen, a career foreign service officer specializing in East Asia, was subsequently appointed ambassador to South Korea in 1978.

to see Zhang Chunqiao, No. 2 Vice Premier. She said it might be possible but it might take a while, which means that I won't see him, indicating the idea that everybody would have to. I am going to request it anyway through protocol and see what happens. End of April 1.

[Wednesday,] April 2[, 1975]. Last day of Rhodes and Albert visit here. They went off to a commune in the countryside; a very good one, two hours drive out and back, [and] were a little tired when they returned. I received a Mrs. Ellison from the *Cleveland Plain Dealer* who was on a forty-man tour sponsored by one of the Friendship groups. Showed our Apollo 8 movie to the Chinese staff. It had a Chinese language track on it. They loved it. Took my language lesson. Quiet lunch. Received the Director General of the Bureau of Asian and Pacific Affairs from Ottawa, Mr. R. L. Rogers, and Mr. Small, for a discussion of errors in Southeast Asia. Went to the carpet showroom in the Animal By-Products Corporation. Amazed at the lack of marketing. The guy couldn't have cared less. "We can't sell this to you." "That one is not for sale." No selling techniques that are used in the United States. It was almost like you had to pull teeth to buy anything or to place orders. They have a long, long way to go in marketing to the West. Because of the balance of payments they want to sell more now but can't do it.[63]

Six-thirty, the whole CODEL group met with Zhu De, 90 years old.[64] Nancy Tang interpreted. Here was one of Mao's earliest

[63]China's share of world export volume had dropped significantly from the 1950s to the 1970s, standing at 0.81 percent between 1970 and 1976. Aid from the Soviets had wholly disappeared as a result of the two countries' titanic split, and, with the Cultural Revolution now entering its final throes, China's economy was hardly booming. The impact of the foreign investment that would follow the Sino-American rapprochement had yet to be fully felt. In 1973, for example, Chinese trade totaled $4.89 billion in exports and $4.975 billion in imports. The economic liberalization now associated with Deng Xiaoping's leadership did not fully begin until after Mao's death.

[64]In 1975 Zhu was chairman of the National People's Congress standing committee. Born in Sichuan in 1886, he served in the army of the Kuomintang, the Nationalist Party, but secretly joined the Communist Party in 1922. He became a

comrades at arms. He seemed fairly sharp but very, very old and tired easily. We were with him for a few minutes. The speaker did pretty darn well. We had a return banquet at the Cheng Du Restaurant, far too much to eat and by the time it was over everybody was ready to shut 'er down and move on.[65] A visit of two or three days is plenty. The Speaker talked to Nancy Tang all the time. He got better about his interpretation and translation etc., but he rather rudely wouldn't let people finish. He didn't realize it was rude and he argued, discussing Taiwan in great detail and our defense treaty and many things. Gleysteen was nervously going right up the wall. Frankly I don't think those things hurt too much because the Chinese must understand our system and this is a good way for them to learn about it.[66]

Gleysteen raised the question with me about guests coming here and I was a little indignant. Cabinet people and congressmen are giving him a fit. I think we are too damn goosy on the program and they have too little confidence in me in the sense that they seem scared that everybody is going to blow it. It is the result of Kissinger's strong arm on everything to do with China. I told him these congressmen and Cabinet people are my guests. I understand about the

---

leading military figure during the civil war, rising to become commander-in-chief of the People's Liberation Army, and was later named vice chairman of the Chinese Communist Party (CCP). He was in fact only 88 in 1975.

[65]The original transcription reads "shutter down." Resident Bush School experts in West Texas linguistics suggest that Bush is here employing the local vernacular of "shut her down," which may be transcribed as "shut 'er down," meaning to close down or cease operations, typically for the night.

[66]Philip Habib later briefed Kissinger on Albert's tone and behavior, noting that "the talk with Chiao [Qiao Guanhua] was badly marred by the Speaker's repeated interruptions before Chiao could finish his statements let alone have them translated. With Teng, the performance was much better. On several occasions the lubricants served at dinner prompted blunt comments from the speaker. He told Vice Foreign Minister Wang Hai-jung [Wang Hairong], for example, that he was tired of China's 'holier than thou attitude,' and he went on to make a number of ungarnished [sic] comments about 'just wars and unjust wars,' which were probably healthy for the Chinese to hear. . . . The net effect may have been to lessen the stature of the delegation in Chinese eyes."

Cabinet people and clearly that might take on significance beyond what would be intended by a private visit, but on the Congress I said, "I'll abide by your decision but I think it is a big mistake to have a policy where congressmen can't come unless the secretary of state approves it. These are my friends. They are close personal friends, someone like Rog Morton, and I just want you to know that I disagree with the policy."[67] I also had a feeling we are not being informed on policy. There was much happening on Cambodia that involved Peking and we should have known about it. I think that the State Department makes a big mistake on not keeping ambassadors informed. End of April 2.

[Thursday,] April 3[, 1975]. Youde came around to see whether the Chinese during the Congressional talks had expressed great concern about the fall of Southeast Asia, Cambodia, etc., and also to find out about the art troop, how that was going to work out, whether they would recriminate. The Chinese did blast us in the NCNA but it wasn't too much at all. I told Youde that Cambodia and Vietnam were not mentioned. One wonders exactly how the Chinese feel about the rapid fall down there and about Cambodia particularly given their commitment to Sihanouk and the question mark about his future. I do worry about the rapid disintegration of our policy in the Middle East. We shouldn't be expected to bring it peace, or to bring peace to that area alone, but people do expect that of us. Portugal is falling apart.[68] The Cyprus and Greece situ-

---

[67]Rogers Morton served as secretary of the interior from 1971 to 1975. Morton would visit Bush later that spring.

[68]Almost a year before this diary entry, on April 25, 1974, the Movimento das Forças Armadas (Armed Forces Movement), made up of elements of the Portuguese army, overthrew Portuguese dictator Marcello Caetano. Portugal had become a member of NATO in 1949, so this issue was of great concern to the United States. General António de Spínola was the most prominent leader of the coup, which was prompted by anger within the armed forces over Portugal's costly wars to maintain its colonial possessions in Africa. General Spínola and his more moderate followers advocated a gradual decolonization, with the former African colonies remaining in a confederation with Portugal. Almost immediately after the

ation still is difficult.[69] Pressure on troops to come out of NATO, which is not an imminent thing, but NATO itself is under great pressure.

And then you shift over to Southeast Asia and you see the Cambodia-Vietnamese situations and you have a rather vivid unraveling, that causes us a lot of heartburn.[70] Everybody kind of looks at me more in sorrow than in anger about Vietnam. And I bite back a little bit, about our commitments, need to guarantee some kind of self-determination, and wondering when the free elections will come after these people are overthrown. It is amazing how certain ambassadors couldn't care less about those kinds of things. They want peace and harmony and maybe they have got a point.

Quiet lunch, then a Canadian showing of a wolf movie and a travel movie at the International Club. The International Club has a big theater. You stand around and drink juice and beer and then go in to see it. Actually it is a very nice facility. They are poor marketers though. They could have entertainment. They could have a little bar setup. They could put this thing on a money-making basis, but instead they subsidize it at a very low cost. A nice thing— the operation runs rather haltingly but in a friendly fashion. We are lucky to have it.

Dinner at the Greek Embassy. The European approach to diplomacy is much like the UN. Dinner at 8, not leave until 11, rather

---

coup, battles erupted between Spinola's moderate forces and leftist elements of the military. Spinola was driven from power by the more revolutionary elements, including, much to the dismay of Portugal's NATO allies, a powerful Portuguese Communist Party. However, the Portuguese people ultimately voted for centrist candidates to craft their constitution and gave the left wing comparatively few votes. After months of social and political chaos, moderate forces prevailed, and Portugal enjoyed its first parliamentary elections in April 1976.

[69]Bush here refers to the ongoing conflict between Greece and Turkey, both members of NATO, over the island of Cyprus.

[70]On April 1, 1975, Lon Nol, prime minister of Cambodia, fled the country in the wake of the Khmer Rouge takeover. All American embassy personnel were evacuated from Cambodia on April 12. On March 9 North Vietnam began its final offensive into the South. By April 30 the North had taken Saigon.

formal settings, serving Western food in all the embassies, none of which is as good as our Chinese food but nonetheless you do have a little bit of Greece or Belgium or France here in China. It is a nice change. The evenings somehow seem boring here to me, where they didn't at the UN so much. That kind of evening seems boring.

We are in the midst of a major staff turnover at USLO. It will be nice to have our own new staff, my own new imprint on things for better or for worse. As people get ready to leave they become hardened, particularly after a couple of years, to the inconveniences and to the frustrations of this life. John Holdridge reflects a very hardline approach now and I think it is an accumulation of frustration as well as a very realistic look.[71] Lucian Pye just wrote an article that calls for a realistic appraisal, and I firmly believe that when we stand up for our principles, the Chinese understand.[72] So many China lovers in the United States want to do it exactly their way. There is a double standard on their China policy. The Russians get the kind of criticism that the Chinese avoid, and I am sure it drives the Russians right up the wall because the discipline, and the closeness of this society, and the unpredictable ways of doing things, and the stiff-arming approaches is bad, if not worse, here than anything like this in the Soviet Union now or in the past. Compared with

[71]"Martha and I left China with some regret, but also a certain amount of combat fatigue," Holdridge later concluded. "We were simply tired of hearing too many 'bu fang bien's' ('It's not convenient') and 'bu qing chu's' ('It's not clear'), the standard responses from Chinese officials to requests (such as for permission to travel) and to difficult questions."

[72]Pye, a China specialist who spent his career at the Massachusetts Institute of Technology, was author of numerous books on contemporary Chinese affairs. In the 1975 article to which Bush refers, he argued that American policy toward China had heretofore been based on idealism, from the "romanticizing of the Nationalists . . . to the vision of the Chinese Communists as mere 'peasant reformers,'" and that a dose of realism was needed to put America's China policy back on track. In a vein clearly in line with Bush's own thinking as expressed in these diary pages, Pye criticized the disparity between the negative rhetoric that Chinese leaders aimed at the United States and America's continued restraint. Washington policymakers, he argued, needed "to accept the truth that good relations cannot be built by sweeping disagreements under the carpet."

other embassies we get as much done as they do, have as much access as they do, but compared with what the Chinese do in the United States, we get nothing and nothing comparable in terms of contacts etc.

The State Department is worrying about my house guests— congressmen and cabinet people. They are uptight, uptight. It is this clutched-in policy, in the whole experience, to one's chest that worries me. Secretiveness instead of secrecy as Marshall Green called it.[73]

Flew the Tianjin kite the other day.[74] Great silk kites. Crowds gather outside the wall. Kids look in until they are shooed away by the guard. Kite gets as good a crowd as C. Fred, and that's saying something! Got a new bicycle from the Marines to use. $40. A big sturdy black thing. I waxed it up and it looks pretty good, ready for the kids.

Health. The doctor situation here—you get mixed reviews. Some think they do a great job, but the Polish Ambassador had a very serious infection and they couldn't figure out what it was. The German was wasting away, almost died, until we got him to a Tokyo hospital. Jerry Ogden had his Chinese wife go down and get some herbs to fix his gut and sure enough it worked. You worry if anything real serious would come up but you can get to Tokyo in four or five hours—we could—to the hospital there. We do not have a doctor here although there is a regional man that is supposed to come in. People get a lot of colds and flu out here. You can go from feeling really awful to feeling almost euphorically well. Great highs and lows. I don't know whether it is the climate or the society. There is a lot of dust in the air and it is dry. I turn on one of those water vaporizers a lot. Your nose gets dried out and there is a lot of coughing. Of course the Chinese are great spitters and coughers

---

[73]Marshall Green, a foreign service officer, was at the time Washington's ambassador to the South Pacific island nation of Nauru. He had previously served as ambassador to Indonesia (1965–69) and assistant secretary of state for East Asian and Pacific affairs (1973–75).

[74]This was a Chinese kite shaped like a bird. Bush is pictured with his Tianjin kite in the photograph section of this book.

right on the street, [with] Deng Xiaoping making liberal use of the spittoon in our meeting. People appear healthy but there is a fair amount of absenteeism due to colds and flu and things of that nature. It hasn't rained here in weeks. Dust gets up in the air a lot and into the house. It is like West Texas, only so far it hasn't been quite as bad as some of the dust storms there. Our goggles and face masks get a laugh out of the crowd as we cycle along. End of April 3.

[Friday,] April 4[, 1975]. I went to the Animal By-Products Import and Export Company to negotiate for carpets. It is unbelievable. Bar and I were there with Mr. Liu who had had the most venerable and respected chop maker in Peking make us chops—beautiful artwork. We wanted to have them sewed into some rugs. We sat down opposite a formidable array of Chinese including the responsible person, the designer, the man who handles the Tianjin carpet factory in Peking and several others. They all drank tea. They discussed the weather and finally we got down to business. We order five 9 × 6 rugs and one 10 × 14. Our chop to be woven in. The design changed. We agreed on the colors. It was a wonderful negotiation. Light, respectful, not too difficult. The price a little over 8,000 yuan for five rugs. A 9 × 6 rug at the Friendship Store cost between 1,200 and 1,900 yuan so I think we made a pretty good deal. They will be ready—one in October-November, the other five in January-February. They did not want any money down. There will be a contract. Traditional design. They asked that we not advertise the price. I think he gave us a pretty good price.

Went to Hungarian national day from 11 to 12. A massive array. Chinese off on one side with Ambassador Ferenc [Gódor]. Much discussion of rumor going around that I had contacted Sihanouk. It was all over the place. Rumors fly through this diplomatic community.[75] Four o'clock Mr. Horie, former head of the

---

[75] According to Henry Kissinger's memoir, *Years of Renewal,* on orders from the State Department Bush had attempted to obtain a face-to-face meeting with Sihanouk but had been rebuffed by the Cambodian leader. When informed that Beijing's diplomatic community was pressing Bush for details, Kissinger person-

Bank of Tokyo, came to call.[76] Discussed the international economic situation. A most attractive fellow who had been here with a high-level Japanese delegation.

April 4. Had some diplomatic types over to see "The Great Northfield Minnesota Raid."[77] The film cratered and it was all very embarrassing. The film was all worn out. We get in on the tail end of things here—films, etc. End of April 4.

[Saturday,] April 5[, 1975].   Relaxed weekend. Tennis—Akwei and I beat Te and Wang three straight. Very easy. It's funny. Sometimes these guys are tough and sometimes not so much. Got a message from the White House and had to send a courier on down to give a message from the President to Carl Albert. Rode bikes way downtown and got back very, very tired. Spring has come. It is fun to browse through the shops. There is absolutely no effort to see anything at all. No marketing. You have to dig and look, and tons of people. Oversupply of people. The law of diminishing returns must have set in. At the airlines counter there are 20 to do the job of 3. Counters at the stores—there are always people standing there. Some must be training but some must be just a surplus of people. We are wearing our goggles downtown. People stare more but they are sure great for the weather, keeping the dust out. Watch science shorts on our cassette TV and hit the sack early. End of April 5.

[Sunday,] April 6[, 1975].   Had all the ex-staff over. Got a good clear phone call from the States including word from Marvin that he got into the University of Texas and had chosen that by "process of elimination." Chinese are status conscious. Discussing the car, Mr. Guo was afraid we might be getting a station wagon when we get a new car. He wants a Cadillac. He told Mr. Liu to tell me he

---

ally advised, "When your diplomatic friends talk to you about these things you might smile mysteriously and not comment."

[76]Shigeo Horie was chairman of the board and president of the Bank of Japan, at that time the largest commercial bank in Japan.

[77]The reference is to a 1972 film chronicling a bank robbery by the Jesse James and Cole Younger gangs.

thought that was the only car fitting for my position. The protocol is as stringent and strict here as in any place I know about. Took a ping-pong lesson, got royally beaten by Ho's assistant; a young kid, who put friendship first and toyed along with me. Lunch at the International Club. Prices cheap, food good. Sundays it's always full over there. Africans and a hodgepodge of nationalities. Some are rude to the management. Some of the students, particularly Africans, sit over there and drink too much beer, and I think it causes the Chinese some heartburn.

In the afternoon we went to the funeral of Dong Biwu, the only survivor, other than Mao, and founder of the Communist Party.[78] He was 90 years old. It was most impressive. It was in the Forbidden City, in the Workers' Palace end of it. Vast space, literally tens of thousands of people lined up with white carnations, four abreast, waiting to file through. Diplomatic community was led through open parks inside the walls of the Forbidden City up to this most impressive spot inside what had once been a palace I am sure. Ranking dignitaries of his government on the right, family standing near the urn and a large picture on the left. They shook hands with all the diplomatic community and then I am told did the same with all the masses. Black crepe around, floral wreaths, funeral music, perhaps the most impressive and symbolic thing we have done since we have been in China. It was amazingly tasteful and dignified and you wonder whether a man's family thinks there is a god.[79]

It was a warm day. I wondered as I shook hands with the widow whether her mind wastes back to the Korean War or some other hostility, or whether she thought back longer to times when Americans had helped the Chinese enormously. A young girl in the line was crying, obviously a niece or grandchild. There must have been fifteen members of the family there. Holdridge, Bar, and I walked

[78]Dong was considered one of the "five elders," the oldest group of Chinese Communists who had helped found the CCP. In 1948 he was made the head of the North China People's Government, one of the first large areas controlled by the party. Dong became vice chairman of the PRC in 1959.
[79]Sources documenting this event are provided in the endnotes.

across the courtyards representing the United States. I am very, very glad that we went. It is the first one of these that Holdridge has been to also.

In the afternoon Bar and I bicycled downtown. I was wearing blue checked pants and a red tee shirt, and the crowds stared and stared. That was all that I needed. It is warm now. It is fun just to go into plain stores. A glass store or a basket store or a hardware store. They are all the same. Not attractive for marketing, but probing around in the cases and pointing and talking with the little Chinese—you really get the atmosphere of Peking. Ken Jamieson and Ethel arrived on Iran Air.[80] Easy to get through customs. Both very pleasant. End of April 6.

Monday, April 7[, 1975]. Determined to increase our contacts with Africans. Today I called on Shibura Albert of Burundi and Langue-Tsobgny of Cameroon. Both conducted in French, both seemed pleased that I called. We have got to find ways to do more with them. And hope that we get a lead or two. Called on Tolstikov at the Soviet Union. Talked for an hour out in his mausoleum. He loves to chat. Always has great theories on China. Feels that their relationship and ours is about the same. Says that Sihanouk showed him and others a letter from me. No comment from me of course. Lunch at home with the Jamiesons, then shopping downtown. Tons of dust. Some of the bicycles looked like they were going backwards. Sand in the air. Most miserable day [we] have had since we have been in China in terms of weather. A busy day though. Plenty of action. Enjoyable. Dinner at the Minzu Restaurant with the Jamiesons, Bushes, Pascoes and Holdridges. One of the Mongolian pot deals.

[Tuesday,] April 8[, 1975]. Lots of wondering about the death of Chiang Kai-shek.[81] Nobody expects that this will facilitate the

---

[80]As noted in chapter 1, the Canadian-born John Kenneth Jamieson was chairman and chief executive officer of Exxon Corporation from 1969 to 1975.

[81]Chiang Kai-shek was president of the Republic of China (Taiwan) from 1950 to his death in 1975. The man who rose to power over mainland China only to lose it, Chiang at first worked closely with the Soviet Union, then opposed it; was

solution of our problems inasmuch as Chiang Kai-shek has not been running things over there anyway. But there is something significant of the fact that Dong Biwu and Chiang Kai-shek died at roughly the same time. Old old men. Then I think of Zhu De and Chairman Mao and even Zhou Enlai and I wonder what the line-up is going to look like a year from now. Jack Service is coming in to see Holdridge, and I will meet with him this afternoon.[82]

Went to the opening of the Belgium exhibit. Technical, pretty fair display, nothing like the U.S. companies would do however. I'll be interested to see if China sells anything through this exhibit. It is quite nicely done, with a gathering in the big exhibit hall—Moscow-Russian built years ago—where the ambassador and the minister of trade from Belgium plus a representative of the ministry from China spoke. Then we went through the fair. Long lunch at the Romanians. These Eastern Europeans, though flexible and though needing the U.S. to counterbalance the Soviets, are tough when it comes to the solutions of problems in Southeast Asia. They will not go for free elections or any of the things that we consider fundamental. Hot tennis game to work off the lunch.

Dinner at the house. News agency people canceled because of the death of Dong Biwu. Andersons, Bushes, Horowitz, and Jamiesons. Mrs. Jamieson was not attractive at dinner. Too bad. Arguing with the State Department people. Why do you all pay attention to Shirley MacLaine etc. when Shirley's book had just come

---

once allied with the CCP, then fought a bitter civil war against it; then joined with the CCP to fight the Japanese invasion of China; then resumed fighting the CCP until his ultimate defeat in 1949.

[82]John "Jack" Service grew up in China, the child of missionary parents, and subsequently joined the foreign service. Stationed in China during World War II, Service was dismissed from the State Department amid charges that he had been sympathetic to the Communist cause after 1949. The main piece of evidence used against him was that he had correctly predicted the Communist victory before 1949. He successfully sued to regain his job and was reinstated in 1957. He eventually left the State Department in favor of an academic career and became curator of the Center for Chinese Studies at the University of California at Berkeley.

out.[83] It was widely reviewed in the U.S. and of course was the main subject in China. What Mrs. Jamieson doesn't know is that Shirley has disproportionate influence in the United States. People read about her, she gets wide publicity. I am very worried about the whole American policy in Southeast Asia and am awaiting anxiously to see what the president has to say about it. There may not be a domino theory but clearly as the United States has reneged on commitments and pulled back, and is unwilling to support recommendations of the president, the free countries, the Asian countries and others in Southeast Asia are concerned. A good speech by Lee Kuan Yew of Singapore on April 7 spells it out very well.[84] These countries cannot depend on the U.S. any longer and thus they have to look toward Russia or more likely China. There could be a conflict between China and North Vietnam over all this.[85] Of course there is a domino theory, but it should not be called that because now it is a code word and all those who opposed it are rationalizing and thinking of other explanations.[86]

[Wednesday,] April 9[, 1975]. Visit from East German Ambassador, Wittik. He is an interesting guy, justifying East Germany's position, talking mainly about land redistribution and how they formed cooperatives. Wittik's father worked in the German underground, spent time in a concentration camp prison. Wittik told me that he himself deserted from the German Army during the war.

[83]Of her experience in China MacLaine said, "In China I saw an entire nation, once degraded, corrupt, demoralized, and exploited, that was changing its very nature. . . . I realized that if what we call human nature can be changed, then absolutely anything is possible. And from that moment, my life changed."

[84]Lee Kuan Yew was Singapore's first prime minister after it obtained independence. He held the office from 1959 to 1990. Under his rule Singapore emerged from the developing world to become one of Asia's economic powers.

[85]In 1979 Chinese and Vietnamese military forces clashed along their mutual border following Beijing's response to Hanoi's occupation of Cambodia.

[86]A list of historical treatments of the domino theory may be found in the bibliographic essay.

Very pleasant, very anxious to present their side of the FRG-GDR dispute.[87] Lunch with the Jamiesons. The worst day in terms of weather that we have had in Peking. Tremendously high West Texas–type wind storm. Dust all over the place. We went to the Hungarian movie show at the International Club. Two travelogs and one ghastly propaganda piece glorifying the Soviet Union. Two excellent travelogs with no voice, done to classical music. Great sights. On the way back, we walked and it was unbelievable—the dust. Dinner at the Big Duck with the Arnauds, Smitters of Canada, and Ballous, Bushes and Jamiesons.[88] Note: the people who work at USLO residence are really warm and friendly. The girls have warmed up appreciably. Mr. Wang is doing a great job and Chu—who has had a bad back—is a good young guy. He showed me a smelly plaster that the Chinese put on back injuries. I think I will have to try some when my back gives me grief.

Jerry Ogden had diarrhea problems and he got his wife to go to one of the herb doctors and it cured him instantly. Herb Horowitz had a broken tooth. They wanted to put a great big shiny aluminum cap on it. Herb resisted same. We may get another musk ox to replace Milton. I think it would be good.[89] It is funny how little tiny things like this matter here. The cultural artistic troop was canceled going from China to the United States, because of a Taiwan song. Now it seems to me to get a musk ox would be helpful. We'll ana-

[87]The reference is to the Federal Republic of Germany (commonly known as West Germany) and the German Democratic Republic (East Germany).

[88]Ballou was James Lilley's replacement in charge of "special communications," meaning he was assigned to the USLO through the CIA. We know this because, as with Lilley, Kissinger told the Chinese of his presence and his peculiar status, to ensure that his work would not inadvertently disrupt the steady progress of Sino-American relations. Indeed, in late March 1975, Lord—acting on Kissinger's instructions while the latter was out of town—informed Huang Zhen that, "as with his predecessor, Mr. Ballou is being assigned to USLO to maintain a special communications channel. He is not authorized to go out in Peking to do intelligence work."

[89]"Milty is dead," Bush advised the State Department, "but a young and virile bullwinkle could do a lot of good relations (diplomatic relations, that is)."

lyze it to death before the ox appears, I am sure. Albert and Rhodes are back in the states. On the VOA I heard them talking about Taiwan taking time, Chinese being the main subject—they are interested, very little comment on Vietnam. They did a good job and it was in keeping with the high-level talks we had here. As soon as Albert and Rhodes left, the diplomats were abuzz with what the talks were about etc. I am sure a jillion cables were fired after each one of them asked me how the talks went. End of April 9.

President Marcos and Prime Minister Lee both are talking about reassessment of U.S. role in Southeast Asia.[90] Both see PRC and the Soviet Union on the increase and the U.S. on the decrease. Both continue to feel probably that the U.S. is important but both feel that the non-communist countries will probably hang loose and certainly will not depend on the U.S. The domino theory is a valid one. I am wondering what I would have recommended if I had been in a position of major authority as far as funds for Cambodia and Vietnam. First, I don't know all the facts but from here it appears to be a losing cause. I think we are going to have to take a real hard look at Southeast Asia. The president presumably will be discussing this tomorrow night.[91] Certainly we have got to reassure Japan and in every way possible. I don't quite see what is going to take the pressure off Thailand, Malaysia, Indonesia, Singapore, Philippines as times goes by. A lot depends on Vietnam. A lot depends on the relationship between North Vietnam and China—not always a happy one. If North Vietnam has its hands full in taking care of its own problems in Vietnam, maybe it won't be fooling around so

[90]Ferdinand Marcos was president of the Philippines.

[91]President Ford's speech before a joint session of Congress on April 10 would include a request for $722 million in aid for South Vietnam in its fight against the North. "Fundamental decency requires that we do everything in our power to ease the misery and the pain of the monumental human crisis which has befallen the people of Vietnam," Ford declared. "Millions have fled in the face of the Communist onslaught and are now homeless and are now destitute. I hereby pledge in the name of the American people that the United States will make a maximum humanitarian effort to help care for and feed these helpless victims." Saigon would fall to North Vietnamese forces less than three weeks later, on April 28.

much in Laos and Thailand. Laos appears to me to have some real problems.

[Thursday,] April 10[, 1975].   Discovery that through stamps in China you can really get a great feel for the entire society. "Workers: valiant struggles against . . . ," "to liberate so and so," "support of Albania," "return of the glorious fighters from Korea," "support of the people of Vietnam in their quest for freedom." Stamp book spells out the entire philosophy and entire pride in art of this society. Relaxed free day. Another match in tennis with Wang and Te for relaxation. Welcoming Levesques, a party at the Morans, lunch at home.[92] More Cambodian work in the office. Reading the news, the continuing feeling that Vietnam and Cambodia are totally falling apart, desperately feeling the need for a realignment, re-statement of foreign policy. The President coming on tomorrow and that will be interesting to see what he has to say on that. Somewhere between isolation and over-involvement lies a reasonable end, but then, at the same time I am saying this, you hear Thailand talking, about [how] Thailand has just lost 17 people fighting in the North against communist insurgence. The domino theory?

Mr. Wang presented Barbara with all the menus that we have eaten since October. They really work in wonderful ways. He is the most polite fellow. Always available, always willing to try. End of April 10.

[Friday,] April 11[, 1975].   Jerry Levesque, Bob Blackburn's replacement, is around. Had a meeting with him. We will soon be re-shaping the whole staff. The night of the 11th we had a group for buffet and movies. The buffet was a combination of Chinese food and American food. Went quickly. One wine. Very informal. Showed "Night at the Opera."[93] Had a good mix. Italian correspondent, Prince Sagali, Mrs. Katapodis of Greece, the Czechoslovakian am-

[92]Jerry Levesque and his family had recently arrived in Beijing for his work at the USLO.

[93]The reference is most likely to *A Night at the Opera* (1935), starring the Marx Brothers.

bassador, the Australians, the Egyptians, the French, the Yugoslavs, Sudan and Somalia—all ambassadors, all seemed to enjoy the evening. It was an early evening.

Sihanouk. We continue to have fascinating indirect contact. Sihanouk is a man who without divulging any secrets is obviously trying to carve out a niche for himself. We worry about where he fits in, if at all. He is walking a tightrope. He probably wants to be [a] friend to the United States, or at least keep Cambodia nationalistic, but on the other hand he had no purchase with the Khmer Rouge. At times he talks like he does but I am beginning to conclude that at this point he has very little. The question is how much support does Sihanouk have when and if he gets back to Cambodia—support that is free and independent of the Khmer Rouge. He is not a communist. Cambodians are not communists, they are religious people, the Buddhists all currently want a nationalistic, relatively free Cambodia. But as the Khmer Rouge is within four or five miles of Phnom Penh they lose influence.

We listened to the President's speech and I wonder how it will be received. He called for $722 million of aid and here I sit with the distinct feeling, having talked to Carl Albert and Rhodes, that he won't get any military aid for Vietnam. We are going through a very difficult time for U.S. foreign policy. We talk strong, the President's voice was firm, made all the right sounds, and yet people, I am sure, are wondering what in the world we can really do, what can we deliver? The American people do not see us threatened at all by Southeast Asia—our security, or our well-being. And you add to this the enormous financial problems at home and it makes declarations of actions almost impossible. Time will tell but my prediction is that the Congress will not approve the military aid. In the meantime in a separate file I am keeping the "contact with Sihanouk" story and it should be woven in here.[94]

---

[94]This file has proved impossible to locate. Sihanouk would continue to dominate much of Bush's time in Beijing, as revealed in later footnotes that rely on available diplomatic records.

Saturday, April 12[, 1975]. We had the Cameroon children, the Ambassador from Gabon, wife of the Ambassador from Burundi all over to see the movie "Big Horn."[95] We invited the USLO children too. It was a good showing. We threw the Frisbee around, played horseshoes, played the game with the things that hook onto your hand outside (plastic ones), then went in and had Cokes and the movie. Lunch at the Club with Chris Ballou, a new officer here, a very attractive fellow, born in China. Jerry Ogden and his Chinese wife are here—attractive. We are putting together a whole new crew. I hate to see some of the others go, but again change is good. People should not be here more than two years—I am convinced of that.

We had a health care and schistosomiasis study group come here, led by Dr. Jung of George Washington University.[96] They came for a quick reception [and] seemed to be pleased to be on U.S. soil, so to speak, [and to] have a drink of whiskey. They were an attractive group, mainly doctors, very serious about their work. Some of the doctors in the health care group would come at their own expense. The schistosomiasis group was one of the exchanges, and Jay Taylor accompanied them.[97] The Chinese hosts for one group came. That was five to six-thirty, and then at nine we went to a dance at the Cameroon Embassy where I was bearded by Agence France-

---

[95]*Big Horn* was a Canadian-produced short film that debuted in 1970.

[96]Schistosomiasis is a parasitic disease contracted from contaminated fresh water. Though it is unheard of in the United States, hundreds of millions of people are infected with it yearly around the world; it is typically contracted by swimming in infected waters. This research group's trip took an unexpected turn several weeks later, when its deputy director, Stanford University's Dr. Paul Basch, suffered a heart attack, thus giving these traveling doctors a closer view of China's medical system than they had expected.

[97]A career foreign service officer and China specialist, Jay Taylor returned to China, after it was accorded full diplomatic recognition, as political counselor of the American embassy in Beijing. After leaving the foreign service he authored *The Dragon and the Wild Goose* (Westport, Conn.: Greenwood Press, 1991), a study of the Sino-Indian relationship, and *The Generalissimo's Son: Chiang Ching-kuo and the Revolutions in China and Taiwan* (Cambridge, Mass.: Harvard University Press, 2000).

Presse, Reuters, and the Italian news agency asking about the Sihanouk comment. Sihanouk made a statement saying that he had told us to get out of Phnom Penh etc. etc. I'll put this in the file. I gave it a "no comment." We got home very late. I think the Africans were pleased we were there. It is impossible for me dancing.[98] The big highlight was a Canadian girl doing the twist or something. She was fantastic. More action that we had seen around here since that girl that used to work in finance of the RNC who got fired by Odell.[99] End of April 12. Winds came up—"dafong." Tremendous wind and dust in the air. It was really a lousy night's sleep.

Sunday, April 13[, 1975]. Went to our church service. Henrietta Morris joins us. We pick her up at the Peking Hotel and then shoot up to the service. A relaxed day. Friendship Store. Shopping around. Interview with John Burns that he is doing for *People* magazine—on his way out of China soon, to work for the *New York Times*. A ping-pong lesson by a Chinese kid who put friendship first, who isn't as good as Ho, but a very nice fellow.

Consular case of —— who was here with a British tour group headed by Dr. Brown.[100] —— freaked out; threatened to kill Mao; threatened to blow up the Forbidden City; threatened the life of Dr. Brown and also the life of our consular officer; struck a Chinese in the hotel room; locked himself in; said he needed the seventh key; [and] cast a spell on Jerry Ogden, the consular officer, by holding his hand in the air and calling him Satan. The China Travel Service would at first not negotiate with the United States Liaison Office,

---

[98]African embassies in Beijing developed a reputation for hosting dance parties with music far more upbeat than that to which most foreign service officers might have learned to dance at cotillion or in prep school. "Having been trained only in ballroom-style dancing," Holdridge later recalled, "I found that I had to learn very quickly the kind of free rock-and-roll style favored by our hosts. (My adaptation was something akin to jogging in place to the beat!)"

[99]Robert Odell chaired the RNC's finance committee while Bush was party chairman.

[100]I have chosen to withhold this individual's name from publication in order to preserve the privacy of the medical history.

the Brits were leaving early Monday morning for Moscow, and they threatened to tell the Moscow airline people if —— tried to go along. The British tour director, though he behaved well, was trying to get his trip on its way and shake leave of this guy. Great calling back and forth. Good State Department support. They sedated the man late, late Sunday night and kept him in custody Monday in a hospital, and delivered him to the airport, sedated him again, and we sent a marshal, trained security guy, with him to Tokyo where he was delivered to the boy's father who got out of bed in the middle of the night in Utah and started arranging to go to Tokyo. Good consular work and good support by Department and Embassy-Tokyo. Kept us up at night.

Main topic of conversation is still Sihanouk and the Sihanouk-distorted story of what we tried to do.

Monday, April 14[, 1975]. The ambassador Cesar Romero of Peru and his beautiful German-speaking wife, whom we had met in Zambia, paid a courtesy call.[101] They should be a good addition to the diplomatic community. Going-away luncheon—very special and Chinese, at our house for Bob Blackburn. Going-away reception for Ambassador Stachowiak of Poland. 5:00 p.m. A great big affair, less deadly because we were outdoors and the Polish Gardens diametrically across from us looked beautiful. They have this tremendous embassy with apartments, massive swimming pool, [and] good tennis court. Our place looks minuscule in comparison. Showed the movie "40 Carats" that night with the Gerd Ruges.[102] Getting ready to go on the trip to Hong Kong and Canton. People are still wearing their padded clothes. I am told that on some mysterious signal from somewhere everyone changes to summer garb. Took a long walk Sunday after trying unsuccessfully to fly a couple of my Tianjin kites. Everyone stared at Fred. We had to tell [them] that he was a dog, "xiaogo." Some didn't know what he was. Some

[101]Espejo-Romero served in Beijing until 1977.

[102]Set in Greece and New York (and centered on a May-December romance similar to that in the 1967 classic *The Graduate*), *40 Carats* was released in 1973.

of the kids did. High school kids kind of barking at him as he went along. Little kids kind of ran alongside him. Others scared to death, jumped out of the way. Old people seemed to smile a lot. Some old cancer victims from the hospital next door were sitting outside near the park with their pajamas and bathrobes on, smiled warmly as we went by. Kids were following along behind us. Spring was in the air and it is very pleasant. We walked past the park, past the big, multistory apartment buildings that are up past the British Embassy and all around the block. Saw the soldiers lining up for their diplomatic guard duty, being lectured by some officer. They went on past and watched lots of action in the park. Then walked along the streets where the cyclists stared like mad at Fred. Cycling we are using our goggles a lot with the dust in the air. They help.

Note: My heart aches for the people in Cambodia who have battled for what they thought was right down there. It is going to be a lot of misery. Sihanouk's position is not clear but he doesn't appear to have too much flexibility from the Khmer Rouge. Watson Wise called.[103] He used to be so pushy at the U.N. and then at the National Committee, always asking some special favor, mainly wanting to be appointed ambassador. He wrote saying he was here representing an important furniture company. It turns out to be some small outfit. I told him he could not get a visa. He wrote back saying he figured out some way to get in and he now found out about the house guest visit visas. I told him we can't do it. He called today and asked if he could stay with Holdridge whom he has never met or heard of. I heard him on the phone when the line was dead saying, "Who was that fellow I saw yesterday—was it Cross?" and then when I got on the phone he said, "My good friend Chuck Cross told me to give you a call on this." Life goes on just the same.

---

[103]A fellow Yale graduate who had also made his money in Texas oil—though a full generation before Bush's own move to the oilfields—Wise had been appointed a delegate to the United Nations General Assembly in 1958 by Dwight Eisenhower, and he later served as a special counselor to NATO.

[Tuesday,] April 15[, 1975].   Lunch at the New Zealand Embassy. Morning in the office with the briefings by our political people for me, this one on Sino-U.S. relations, tracing the troubled history since liberation until now. Very interesting. Call from the Ambassador of Mauritius and dinner at Egyptian Embassy. The Ambassador from Mauritius is based in Pakistan but he is also accredited to Peking. Very nice guy—friend of Byroade's.[104] Interested in being sure the U.S. keeps its position in the Indian Ocean, thinks we need to do a better PR job showing the number of ship days, how many Russian ships there are there compared to ours.[105] He seems very friendly to the United States. Dinner at French [embassy]. Topic was the subject of Vietnam and Cambodia. Paludan, the Danish Ambassador, and the French tut-tutting. I always get the feeling at these talks that there are other sides, [besides the] position is clearly that all the violations and corruption and the lack of elections by South Vietnam is disgusting. And nothing comparable for the North. It does seem we are betting on the wrong people in some places.

[104]Henry Byroade had been an army officer in the China-Burma-India theater during World War II before transferring to the State Department. He later served as Washington's ambassador to Egypt, Pakistan, South Africa, Afghanistan, Burma, and the Philippines.
[105]"Ship days" refers to the days at sea and on station spent by a naval vessel in a particular area.

CHAPTER SIX

"We Do Have Principles and It Is Time We Stood Up for Them"

April 16 to June 2, 1975

*S*aigon's fall and Cambodia's descent into chaos sent shock waves throughout Washington's policymaking elite—even those members stationed abroad—and forced Bush to reassess fundamentally the limits of American power and America's international role. The lessons he drew from this period clearly left their mark. The key lesson was one to which he returned repeatedly in the diary: the importance of American credibility to American power. For Bush, true credibility meant not only that Washington should uphold its commitments and respect its allies, but also that American power should not be squandered where it was not required. Far removed from the human tragedy in Southeast Asia—and equally so from Washington's politicking—Bush came to view Saigon's fall less as a calamity or the end of an era than as the catalyst for a broader geopolitical reorientation. From Beijing he witnessed a steady stream of Asian leaders arriving to establish diplomatic relations with Mao's regime, moves he interpreted as Washington's allies scrambling to protect their own interests in the wake of the American defeat. "I have complete conviction that there is such a thing as a domino theory," he wrote, as he perceived "Thailand and the Philippines and others rushing towards new alignment." Vietnam had indeed been a terrible loss—one that would echo within international relations far longer than the sound of the final American helicopters departing Saigon.

As he witnessed Beijing's diplomatic corps—the representatives of geopolitical allies and adversaries alike—virtually celebrate Washington's defeat, he searched as well for some means of measuring his country's losses and weighing its future interests. Defeat sharpens the senses more than victory, imparting lessons that are far longer lasting than success. For Bush the lessons of Vietnam were at once clear on a theoretical level yet difficult to apply in practical terms. Indeed, in some of the China Diary's most revealing passages, Bush asked himself at April's end, and then again in early May, what he would do if put in sole charge of American foreign policy at this critical juncture.

His lengthy answers offer a snapshot of his broader sense of the international system. Bush's preferred strategy was multilateral, putting faith in the United Nations. Yet it was also concerned with the vital yet intangible value of credibility; he "would use the UN more and multilateral aid, but I would do it only with the insistence of credit." He would "redraw the lines" of America's commitment in the world, demonstrating that Washington had few hegemonic aspirations while simultaneously ensuring that "we are not committed in wars we shouldn't be involved in, where we'd have no support from the American people." He would continue to work with the Soviets and to cultivate détente with Moscow and Beijing. But in the final analysis "we have got to be realistic" and not so determined to push an American agenda based more on optimism than hard assessment. In short "we have to have our eyes open" to the realities of the world—including the world as seen through non-American eyes. Bush was hardly advocating a complete withdrawal from the world. Quite the contrary, his experience in Beijing had deepened his conviction that Washington had a central role to play within the international system. "The American people must understand," he wrote, "that as soon as America doesn't stand for something in the world, there is going to be a tremendous erosion of freedom." Washington needed a broad reassessment based on hard thinking and hard data. "But if somebody said to me today what would you declare" to be Washing-

ton's vital interest and broad strategy, he ultimately conceded, "I'd be damned if I know how I'd define it."

The daily business of American diplomacy continued even amidst these unfolding tragedies. The weeks following the close of the Vietnam War found Bush in Canton (today Guangzhou) to visit the city's famed trade fair, one of the first sanctioned international marketplaces for foreign buyers and businesses eager to deal with the Communist regime. Bush headed the USLO's delegation to the fair, though he found the event disappointing and the American businesspeople he met there lacking. "I am not impressed with the quality of the businessmen for the most part that come to the fair," he confided to his journal, terming them "promoters" interested more in a fast buck than in building long-term relationships with the Chinese. He took the opportunity of this visit to China's south to cross the border into nearby Hong Kong for a short personal holiday. And, amid the tennis and the dinners, he announced to friends his intention to seek the presidency.

Though these passages of the diary find Bush musing over his future—and especially his future political plans—they are hardly definitive on this point. We see in these pages a George Bush more interested in pondering his fate, and that of his nation's diplomacy, than in reaching any decisive conclusions. The searing events of the previous few weeks were clearly leaving a mark on Bush, who increasingly came to appreciate the complexities of his country's diplomacy while simultaneously viewing with frustration the rigid political limits on what was diplomatically possible. He questioned Beijing's true diplomatic motives, especially after the Chinese proved unhelpful in resolving the Mayagüez crisis in Cambodia (in which Bush played an ancillary though important secret role). Was the principal intent of Mao's government simply to meet China's immediate needs? Or was the Foreign Ministry perhaps playing some more elaborate game designed primarily to gauge the limits of Washington's flexibility? With the Chinese, Bush came to realize, everything was a test. "We do have principles and it is time we stood up for them without being contentious. Everybody in our *mission knows what I am talking about when I say that China talks about their principles, and when they want to turn something down, they can turn it down on principle. But they do not accord others the same courtesy when it comes to understanding their principles." Clearly Bush's frustration was rising throughout the spring of 1975. As it became clearer with each passing week that his initial plan of improving Sino-American relations by winning friends and increasing personal contacts with the Chinese would prove fruitless without Chinese consent, the lure of a return to domestic politics became that much stronger. "I am continually amazed at how hard it is to get close to the Chinese," he finally conceded. "You are held at arm's length. They are just determined [not] to let us, or any foreigner in that regard, get too close. It is impossible to pick up the phone, ask somebody over, and have a meaningful discussion about Southeast Asia or Russia or someplace like that. It just can't be done." At the end of the day, he concluded, "For polite people they act in very strange and tough ways."*

Wednesday the 16th [April 16, 1975]. Leave for Canton. The plane is a two-hour-and-thirty-minute flight, non-stop, Boeing 707, leaving at 9:00 a.m., getting in around 11:30 a.m. I noticed out at the airport again that people recognized me and I am amazed at that. There is no way that they should know, but some way they do. And you hear them discussing and pointing "Busher! Busher!" which is my Chinese name. The airport has a new board, and people stare at it, which flips the destinations, arrival times, etc. It is made by the Japanese and is the subject of tremendous interest. It would go unnoticed in other airports except for people bitching that their flights were not on it. They had us in first class. The flight was full in the back.

Mr. Lee of the China Travel Service met us at Canton Airport, escorted us all around Canton in the afternoon. He asked about the cancellation of the cultural performance for Washington. Asked whether there was a chance they would go in the future, etc. I told him that there was principle on both sides. We understood their principle; but our principle was that you ought not to politicize cultural performances. Indeed when we had been asked to make certain changes in the program for the Philadelphia Orchestra when they came to China, we did. And we thought it was only right that China make it in ours. I am absolutely convinced on these kinds of incidents that we need to make our position known to the Chinese in a friendly and frank fashion. We do have principles and it is time we stood up for them without being contentious. Everybody in our mission knows what I am talking about when I say that China talks about their principles, and when they want to turn something down, they can turn it down on principle. But they do not accord others the same courtesy when it comes to understanding their principles.

Bar and I were immediately struck by the difference in Canton—tropical, humid almost like the Gulf Coast, very, very different. The water is soft compared to Peking's rock-hard water. There are more pedicabs. There are as many bicycles, I guess, but they didn't seem as noticeable. The streets are more narrow than the wide streets in Peking. The costumes are more varied, but maybe it's because it's warm weather. In Peking it's been cold and there's been great similarity. The food was similar. The Cantonese of course, most of them, speak Canton dialect, but Mandarin does seem to get by. Stayed in the hotel right across from the fairgrounds.

Went to the fair, looked around. On the first floor of the fair there are exhibits of Chinese goods and then upstairs there are more exhibits and consultation rooms. You always sit down and have tea and consult when you buy something. The American contingent at the fair so far is quite small. China is still way back in the background as far as really pressing their sales to the United States. They just don't go about it correctly. Indeed many of the people they get to the fair are promoters. I am convinced they could attract much higher-quality people to the fair if they really went about it working hard. Lunch with Horowitz and Bill Rope, both of whom share a suite down here to help advise American business people.[1] Gene

---

[1] As mentioned previously, Herbert Horowitz headed the commercial and economic section of the USLO until 1975. William Rope also worked in the USLO's economic section, and he later became principal deputy assistant secretary in the

Theroux from the National Council for U.S.-China Trade, a very decent fellow, was there.[2] Had dinner with him, Horowitz, Rope and Schweitzers, a couple with Manufacturers Hanover out of Hong Kong, and Mrs. Ploudman whose husband used to be a professor at Berkeley.

It is warm and tiring. We slept under mosquito nettings in the bed. The bed was like a centerfold, went right into a big crevice. I didn't sleep at all. Just this trip re-emphasizes what I felt when I went to Shanghai and Tianjin and those trips—and that is that you must get out of Peking to begin to get the feeling for all of China.[3] It is oh so different here.

On the train there is music in the background—propaganda all around.[4] Trip from Canton to the border—one continual agricultural operation, terraced fields, every inch of ground used. In fact I wonder whether some of this isn't for the benefit of people coming in, although it is certainly farming for real. Lot of water buffalo, lot of geese, lot of ducks, some very, very young children in the fields, old men with poles (double-pole carrying) and it looks like the same methods used two thousand years ago. There are no tractors to be seen, and I have not seen a truck yet; but there is plenty of manual labor and plenty of action on the fields that are so green that your eyes ache almost. Man washing his water buffalo using rather dirty water to do it. Cow standing up with his front feet peering into a yard. Gaggle of geese with green rings around their necks, bright green. Bunch of ducks and geese being led by a tender, knee deep in water across a murky-looking pond.

State Department's political-military bureau and deputy assistant secretary on its policy planning council.

[2]See Bush's entry for November 15, 1974.

[3]The original text reads "Hengyang" rather than "Tianjin," but the latter is handwritten and the former is crossed out, most likely by Bush at some unknown date.

[4]Bush took a train from Canton (Guangzhou) to Hong Kong. This editor can attest that music—even at 4 a.m.—remains an omnipresent feature on southern Chinese trains a generation later.

Green, green, green. Man casting a net in the water for shrimp or fish of some sort.

Good reasonable food on the dining car. Train cars look like something out of 1910 in the U.S., but they are clean as they can be and a very smooth roadbed. As far as the eye can see there are bright green fields and cultivation. Some irrigation going on with a fair amount of plumbing of water, raising it to a higher level. Crops mainly look like rice. I wonder about the disease and mosquitoes with all this standing water around here.

While in Canton for the annual trade fair, Bush took the opportunity to visit Hong Kong, a short train ride away. In doing so he reversed the journey taken by Ambassador David Bruce and most of the initial USLO staff, who had crossed the border into China for the first time via the British colony rather than taking advantage of direct air service from Tokyo, as had Bush. In so doing, Bruce and his colleagues had traveled from the epicenter of Asian capitalism to the heart of Mao's regime. Bush now experienced those contrasts in reverse. He did not make any entries in the China Diary while in Hong Kong, and resumed his dictations upon returning to Canton.

[Monday,] April 21, 1975.   Back into China after four fantastic days in Hong Kong. I am dictating this at night in the Tang Fung Hotel across from the fairgrounds. We had a marvelous visit in Hong Kong including a tennis [game] with a fantastic girl player, Greta Ho, and Robert Ho, her rich husband.[5] Then beautiful lunch at C. Y. Tung's house, one of the largest ship owners in the world.[6]

[5]Robert Ho, a publisher in Hong Kong at the time of Bush's visit, was the son of the Nationalist Chinese general Robert Ho Shai-Lai, who represented the Taiwan regime first as ambassador to Japan (1952–56) and then as head of his country's military delegation to the United Nations (1956–66). Ho also hosted the Bushes at a private dinner that night, where he later recalled Bush announcing to the party his intention to seek public office yet again. "I just want to get it out of my system," Ho remembers Bush saying.

[6]C. Y. Tung founded his shipping company, Orient Overseas International

Then the following day an all-day picnic with Kenneth Hue. The contrast between the way these Chinese live and the way we see the Chinese in Peking or Shanghai is just unbelievable, all of them extremely rich, all of them extremely gracious, extremely Western. Wives stylishly dressed, pleasant, enjoying the freedom to the fullest, capitalism to its maximum. Amazing contrasts when compared to what we have been used to over the last six months in China. Indeed some of the things in Hong Kong seem garish. The fashion shows seem decadent. I've got to watch to see that I don't get overly "Peking-ized" by time there. The creature comforts seemed somehow lavish, but the hustle and bustle, and the competitiveness, and the energy of the people in Hong Kong, couldn't help but impress after the drabness and the sameness of Peking.

Bemises arrived late but met us at the Hilton. We had a couple of really good relaxed days before taking the 10:00 train for the border on April 21, the Queen's birthday. Some of the Chinese came to Chuck Cross's house, the first time they have ever done it. But it was because I was there, head of the U.S. Liaison Office. The trip up [to] the border was hot and humid, but it worked very well and everything was in order as we crossed back into China after four days of liberty in Hong Kong. Met by Mr. Lee of the Travel Service. Came to the Tang Fung Hotel where we went to the fair and looked around. Then had a reception for all American businessmen. I am not impressed with the quality of the businessmen for the most part that come to the fair, although some are high class. Sears Roebuck, Union Carbide, RCA and others, but there are a lot of promoters in this sphere of business. Had a beautiful Chinese

---

Shipping Ltd., in Shanghai. In the wake of World War II and the Chinese civil war, he transferred his business to Hong Kong and Taiwan. Calligraphy bestowed on the Bushes by Tung later hung in their private apartment adjoining the Bush Presidential Library. After Tung's death, his son Tung Chee-hwa obtained $120 million in investments from mainland China to save Orient Overseas Ltd. from impending liquidation. In 1997, after control of Hong Kong had reverted back to the mainland, Tung Chee-hwa become the chief executive of the Hong Kong special administrative region, in effect its governor.

dinner with Rope, Horowitz, and Blackburn, who is on his way out. And here we are again back where we belong—on our way to Shanghai and Peking.

Telegram about Rog Morton wanting to come here. The Department seems uptight about it, but I think they just don't want to take the chance of saying "no" to some of these people. The telegram referred to a visit by Russell Train who had called me a while back to say he had been granted permission by the Secretary [Kissinger] to come.[7] I wired back and told them [State Department] if they didn't want him to come, just tell him and he would understand. But apparently they don't want to do that. I still feel that we hold the China thing too close on certain things. And yet I understand you can't have everybody running loose as a free spirit in a society that is complicated. Ten—here we are in our old mosquito nettings about to go to sleep for the second time in the Tang Fung Hotel. What a contrast between this place—with its kind of worn linoleum floors, filthy bathroom floors (although the water is hot)—and the Hilton Bangkok suite where we lived for several days. It's unbelievable. There is no air conditioning. The paint looks all dry and dirty and there's really a kind of run-down look to the whole place. End of April 21.

[Tuesday,] April 22, 1975. Another day at the fair. I met with the former No. 3 man Mr. Huang, at the fair.[8] We are wondering what his position really is. Very friendly. We chatted about the U.N. and then about trade. He recited the Shanghai Communiqué and how both sides should live up to that. I tried to drag him out on most favored nation [status] to see how badly that was bothering

[7]Russell Train was administrator of the Environmental Protection Agency from 1973 to 1977 and worked for Bush's 1988 presidential candidacy as co-chairman of Conservationists for Bush. In 1991 he received the Presidential Medal of Freedom, and he is currently chairman emeritus of the World Wildlife Fund. He and his family eventually visited Bush in Beijing in June 1975.

[8]It is not clear to whom Bush refers here, but "Huang" may be a mistranscription of Wang Yun-Sheng, who as deputy director of the Canton Trade Fair held a long meeting with Bush during his visit.

them. I discussed the fact that the fall-off in agricultural trade was not political but was a result of their harvest, to which he agreed. We talked about the need to understand U.S. markets and comply with some of our special regulations like canned foods, etc. The talk was a good one. Held in a hot and somewhat odorous meeting room on the first floor of the Canton Fair Building. The Fair Building is actually two or three buildings, attractively done with displays on the first two floors, and on the third and fourth floors consultation rooms. The consultation rooms also had many beautiful things to show. I took Bar back up there this afternoon to see the baskets. There are many, many more on display than we ever see in the stores.

It is hot and humid in Canton. The mosquito netting keeps any air from getting through. I kicked the netting off at night only to be chewed up by bugs. Not a pleasant night at all. So many of the Chinese goods are just not good. Their cameras, most of their machinery, their typewriters, their sewing machines are just not really the kind of articles that have any appeal. A lot of their cabinet design stuff looks like it was designed in the U.S. back in the twenties or thirties. I think, on the other hand, some of their handicraft and other imitation porcelain etc., are superbly done. Their basketware, closely knit baskets, are just beautiful. Large and small, shapes of animals (deers, doe, monkeys), all of these things attractively done. They display their silks well. They have many things that have no appeal such as thermoses and wind-up clocks. I am wondering what countries buy any of these things.

The party for American businessmen attending the fair was successful. There must have been a hundred or so who attended. Some are kind of promoters and not particularly attractive people. It is unclear how people get invited to the fair. They should not be dealing through so many middlemen. They should be dealing with higher quality. Herb Horowitz, an excellent economic officer, feels that some of these promoters sell arrangements for others to come to the fair as their agents at rather high prices. There are several rather unsavory characters who might be doing this. It would be bad if it were true. The Tang Fung Hotel was built in the early sixties and looks like it has been really run down. The bathroom floors are really filthy. The plumbing leaks and really is disgraceful, although the rooms are rather large. The linoleum is all cracked up.

They have a lot of young kids who are learning languages at the fair. They are there to help out foreign guests. They serve as waiters, interpreters, busboys. It is a pretty good idea. We heard today that President Thieu left office, resigned.[9] The decline in Southeast Asia is all around us.

We were supposed to take a plane to Shanghai and see a Shanghai acrobatic troop tonight. We got to the airport at four o'clock for a plane that was leaving at 4:35. There was a confrontation between China Travel Service, Mr. Lee, and a stalwart-looking group of people at the CAAC counter in Canton who told us that the flight had just left. The CAAC crowd took the offensive by showing a telegram that indicated they had just learned we were on the flight. China Travel man Mr. Lee argued back and told me later that they would all criticize China Travel about this. We stood around for a few minutes wondering what to do and we discovered there was a plane into Peking, so we canceled out our Shanghai plans and climbed on a plane that left about 5 for Peking. I am not unhappy, but the Bemises and others were trying to get to Shanghai so I hope they can do it later on—the Bemises and Bryans.[10] The foul-up was rather massive but I am not sure we don't have many such foul-ups in the States to compete. Many is the time that I have been around when flights have been canceled. Flying on a Soviet Ilyushin 62, nonstop Canton to Peking—about a three-hour run.[11] About the same as Houston to New York. They served a rather nice-looking cold cut plate on the flight, tea and juice. We will wait to eat later on. Almost the end of April 22.

[9]Nguyen Van Thieu resigned as president of South Vietnam on April 21. On April 30 North Vietnamese troops would enter Saigon.

[10]See my footnote to Bush's entry for March 20, 1975.

[11]The Soviet Il-62 first entered passenger service in 1967 and was notable for the two pairs of engines on its tail.

Arrived April 22. Late at night. The house had been all torn up, being cleaned and stuff. Our message got in about five or five-thirty, and there was Mr. Wang and Mr. Zhong with the dinner all prepared by Mr. Zhong—Sun having gone home. Guo to meet us. The rug still up, but great to be home.

I worry about the fall of Thieu—no personal attachment whatsoever. I have complete conviction that there is such a thing as a domino theory. Thailand and the Philippines and others rushing towards new alignment. Kim Il Sung of Korea talking much tougher now about the South in Peking.[12] Obviously trying to capitalize on the decline of the free countries in the southeast. A new report that Laos is engaged in heavier fighting there. Tremendous attacks on Kissinger and Ford. Isn't it amazing how a guy can rise to the top of the heap, and then be pushed off, and there seems great rejoicing as he tumbles down.

[Wednesday,] April 23[, 1975]. Back at the office. Inspectors and the security people are doing security checks all over the place. I do not have the feeling that the Chinese do a lot of electronic spying on us, but it is good to check. Weather beautiful. Peking instantly greener. Bryans, Bemises and Bar off sightseeing. She is getting to be an expert in that, knowing her way around all these nooks and crannies. Lunch at home. Dinner at the Chin Yang Restaurant joined by the Clevelands and Jane Blair who are here on the Mayors Welcoming Group from Washington.[13] One of the China Travel guides

[12]Kim would in fact visit Beijing that month. At a formal banquet in the Great Hall of the People—from which the USLO was excluded, although other Western diplomats attended—he called for the Communist world to seize the occasion of Saigon's fall to reinvigorate his dream of unifying the Korean peninsula, by force if necessary. Chinese leaders would have none of it, and the official response to his toast was a forceful call for "peaceful reunification," a term Kim reluctantly adopted upon his return home.

[13]Robert Cleveland, a retired foreign service officer who was accompanied by his wife, Mary, was president of Meridian House International, a Washington-based organization devoted to improving cultural relations between countries. Jane Blair served as a trustee of Meridian House; her husband, William, was deputy assistant secretary of state for public affairs.

started arguing with Jane Blair about the system and how their system is better than ours. I told her she ought to have lowered the boom on him. They also brought up the performing arts troop. Mr. Lee brought it up to me and I lectured him rather severely. I am wondering if a central directive didn't go out on these from China Travel.

Sihanouk is still in Peking. His mother is apparently dying.[14] Now some talk that he won't go back at all. At least we tried. Early to bed. Nice change.

Visitors, when you have an awful lot of them, do become an effort. Life changes a lot. The Bemises and the Bryans are exceptionally easy. It is a strain on Bar I think. She feels she has to go to do all the things with them. Bemis and I played tennis on the 23rd— Te and Little Stone. End of 23rd.

[Thursday,] April 24[, 1975]. Office work. Reception for Mayors Committee, a group of people that take care of foreign visitors in Washington. They have been nice to [the] PRC and they have gotten a very good tour. They talked to the Bank of China people and they visit around. We were only able to have half the group because we didn't think the residence would be finished. Nordlingers, Norberg, Adams, McNottens—very good group.[15] Nice quiet din-

---

[14]In a gesture that displays as perhaps no other Bush's faith in personal diplomacy—and the way in which he believed human relations could transcend even international politics—Bush petitioned Secretary of State Henry Kissinger and the State Department during the last week of April for permission to write directly to Cambodian leader Norodom Sihanouk, in order to offer condolences at his mother's passing. "Normally it would be inappropriate for me to write Sihanouk," he explained to Washington, "but given our recent contacts and understanding his love for his mother, my strong gut instinct is to write him a personal handwritten card." He recognized that "Sihanouk could possibly release this, and finger us a [sic] hypocritical," but "a personal kindness might go along [sic] way and might not hurt us a short way down the road from here." Kissinger nixed the plan. "On balance I believe you should not communicate with Sihanouk in any way at this time. His rejection of our last efforts toward him make[s] it inappropriate in our view to go through the exercise you propose."

[15]The reference is to Gerson Nordlinger, Charles Norberg (a Washington lawyer who headed the delegation), and Emilie and Robert McNaughton. There was no "Adams" traveling with the delegation.

ner at the residence. Bar took the Bemises and Bryans to the Summer Palace and I had lunch with John Burns, Ballou and Perito at the International Club. Just digging out from under paperwork. Assessing Kim Il Sung's visit. Kim Il Sung's talking militantly about Korea, China apparently downplaying this. Went to bed early, about 9. Fell asleep at 10. Had one of the best sleeps of my life. It is beginning to get warm in Peking. Kicked off all the covers.

[Friday,] April 25[, 1975].   It rained a little bit. We had a quiet lunch at the residence with Bemises and Bryans. Staff meetings being held in our office now at 9:15 every morning. Go around the room. Big turnover in USLO staff. Almost a total turnover. From five to six we had the Molecular Biology Group and the Investigation Group going to the United States. These group receptions are deadly, but at least they are good for having the Chinese in. End April 25.

[Saturday,] April 26[, 1975].   A long day, going to the Ming Tombs and the Wall. Use of Polaroid camera. First you ask to take the pictures. Then they don't want it. Then I took the picture of someone else. Showed the others the instant picture, and then they all wanted it taken. What good the little gestures of friendship do in diplomacy!

We are witnessing the unraveling of Kissinger's personal diplomacy. There was an article that someone showed me in *Time* magazine today where I was mentioned, along with Laird, Richardson, Rumsfeld and Scranton as a possible Secretary of State; ranked as No. 3 I think.[16] And if somebody asked me what would I do in that

---

[16]Bush was ranked third in the article, "in approximate order of probability," behind former Secretary of Defense Melvin Laird and Elliot Richardson, but ahead of Donald Rumsfeld and Pennsylvania governor William Scranton. As *Time* concluded, "Ford's second choice for Vice President, the handsome Bush is currently Chief of the U.S. liaison office in Peking. He served two vigorous years as U.S. Representative to the United Nations, where he developed a knack for negotiation and earned the respect of fellow delegates. As Republican national chairman, he made friends in all factions of the party."

[eventuality], it's hard to know exactly how I'd answer, although I concede it's most unlikely.

Southeast Asia.[17] Total reassessment of policy, summing up with China. Probing in more depth to determine what they mean about hegemony. Convincing them that we are not hegemonic; insisting to them, more than we do, that the rhetoric of the Third World, which is causing an unraveling at the United Nations (what Pat Moynihan's article I just read said) is no good for world peace; continuance of the policy with the Soviet Union; trying to redraw the lines, perhaps in the Pacific, so we are not committed in wars we shouldn't be involved in, where we'd have no support from the American people—not a withdrawal, but a reexamination, along with allies, and coming out in six months with a new Asian policy; continuing along in the Middle East but less spectacular personal diplomacy; attempting to get negotiations between the parties— extremely difficult—and using public opinion more in the United States, if possible, to understand the Arab point of view (if I am correct in my assessment that Israel has been more recalcitrant).[18]

---

[17]Only three days before, President Gerald Ford had made headlines by declaring, "Today, America can regain the sense of pride that existed before Vietnam. But it cannot be achieved by refighting a war that is finished as far as America is concerned." The crowd he addressed, and the national media present, focused on Ford's assessment that the war was "finished," taking his words as evidence that the long war was indeed over.

[18]Following his return to the United States after his service as ambassador to India and the trip to Beijing described in chapter 3, Daniel Patrick Moynihan began work at Harvard University. His stint in Cambridge proved short. He was named ambassador to the U.N. in April 1975. During those short months away from public service, he frequently criticized what he considered the lethargic response by the American delegation in New York to criticism of American policies. "It is time for the United States to go into the United Nations and every other international forum and start raising hell," he declared. Bush most likely refers to an article Moynihan published in *Commentary* that spring, in which he accused the Ford administration of "a massive failure of diplomacy" in ceding the moral high ground to criticisms by Communist and new nations in forums such as the U.N., especially their critique of Western-style liberal economic development. As the interpretive essay at the end of this book demonstrates, Bush came to share Moynihan's concern with anti-American bloc voting following his own stint at the

We are a little bit out of this out here. These are just very general thoughts. I would use the UN more and multilateral aid, but I would do it only with the insistence of credit. We have got to be realistic. We have to have our eyes open. We have to insist from the Secretary General and others that the United States be credited for the enormous support that we might elect to give in these channels.

The 26th was a delightful day. Many kids working and you see the enormous energy of China. I think of the contrast between India with its democracy and China with its totalitarian setup, and I just am appalled at what I understand to be the difference. True, the price has been high, there is little freedom, there is a kind of peculiar way of doing things and yet in fundamentals China has done an enormously good job. A way has got to be found to take the goodwill that exists for the American people and get it over under the American government. Not easy, given the climate of tearing down, the disruption at home. We had a lovely, peaceful six-person picnic, light, at the Ming Tombs. And then a delightful dinner served by Wang and Chung at home. Following a matched doubles tennis game. The Canadian tennis tournament is on. Spring is here. The security people are in town. The couriers are here. All in all I feel very happy here.

We must convince China that we are not their stereotyped blasphemous charges of imperialists and of those who seek hegemony. The Taiwan issue, if we solved it by giving away Taiwan, in my opinion would not take care of the problem, because then China would wonder what next, where could we be counted on. Some compromise must be found on that problem. End of the 26th.

Morning of the 27th [Sunday, April 27, 1975]. Cool, fresh, gray and foggy, breezy out, a very pleasant day for a Sunday. Church at the Bible study place. Then a good tennis game with Bemis, Wang and Akwei. Then a visit to the track meet with the Algerians. The

---

U.N. Ironically, given these critiques, U.N. ambassador John Scali had in fact caused a minor diplomatic furor the previous December when he openly criticized the growing "tyranny of the majority" within the General Assembly.

Algerians were outmanned. Sitting across from us at the track meet was a sea of Chinese faces. It looked like half the People's Liberation Army was there. And [in] a neat square covering what in [the] Yale Bowl was Portal 15-16 was the Navy, and some Air Force along.[19] The whole sea, in what they claim is a 100,000-seat stadium, of khaki on one side. There were a few empty seats in the place, but it was pretty near full. Women athletes in the shot put, high jump; men in all kinds of events, hammer throwing guy outthrowing the Algerian guy by 10 yards at least. I can't wait to see the great American track team come here.[20] The stadium is pretty with a kind of synthetic carpeting on the outside of the track. Grass infield and a good-looking track itself. Pole vaulters and high jumpers landing on great fluffy, spongy pillows. The wind was blowing and the pole vaulters had some difficulty. The event started just like the basketball game with the teams marching, holding each other's hands on high to stimulate friendship. Zhuang Zedong and others were in the grandstands. We had lunch at the International Club—nice pick-up lunch—you get to see all levels of the diplomatic corps there. And then a big Peking duck dinner with a standard of 8 yuan per person. There were twelve of us—the total bill was a 119 yuan including two wines, maotai, and plenty of beer. Not bad for Peking duck.

Monday the 28th [April 28, 1975]. At 8:30 the phone rang. It said they are expecting you at the Double Bridge Commune at 9:00. We had put in to go to a commune on either Monday or Tuesday. We went to the commune. That was amazingly short notice. Be-

---

[19]Yale University played its football games at the Yale Bowl, which opened in 1914. The field house is located behind portals 15 and 16.

[20]An Amateur Athletic Union (AAU) track team from the United States would visit Beijing—and the USLO—later that spring. Bush's meetings with the athletes are described in entries for the end of May 1975. The visiting Americans won 95 percent of the competitions, according to a USLO report to Washington, and the event, televised throughout China, was in their words "the highest profile exchange group sent by the U.S. side since the September 1973 visit by the Philadelphia Symphony Orchestra."

mises and Bryans and representatives were still in the sack. We just ran out there and it was a worthwhile event. 40,000 people in the commune.

The country is green now. In fact today we sat outside in wicker furniture at noon. It was just plain hot. I worked hard in the office on mail. The pouch is lousy at times, and the mail itself not too great. Bemises and Bryans getting ready to go. Applied to go to Nanking, Suchow and Shanghai, and today, departure less than 24 hours away, clearances have been made. Lot of preparations going on downtown for May Day. There are four main parks, including the Temple of Heaven and the Workers Palace Park, which is where Tung Wu had his memorial service, that are going to be all dressed up for May Day. They have performances—dancing, opera, all these different kinds of things—for the people in the parks. I can't wait to see it. It should be interesting. Dealing with the Chinese on airlines etc. is extremely complicated. Not much else to report. Close, April 28—dinner in the park at the jiaozis restaurant.[21] A kind of seedy-looking group of people around there and the food awful. The first lousy meal we've had in China. It looked kind of like lower-echelon African and East Europeans gathered there.

The Kim Il Sung communiqué with the Chinese came out.[22] It took up ten pages, blasts against the United States, glorification of revolution in Africa, strong anti-Israel position, strong anti-imperialistic language. China degrades themselves in paying homage to Kim Il Sung, the glorious and noble leader. There was a frenetic, orgiastic greeting for Kim Il Sung with Chinese and Koreans breaking through the lines and weeping. He is a self-anointed leader

[21]A jiaozi is a form of wonton, similar to a boiled (usually pork-filled) ravioli.
[22]The joint Chinese–North Korean communiqué criticized America's two-Korea policy as "imperialism," called for an end to the U.N. presence along the North-South border, and stated that the Democratic People's Republic of Korea (the North) was the "sole legitimate sovereign state of the Korean nation." As mentioned above, however, Kim left China without achieving his primary goal: receiving approval from Beijing for following up North Vietnam's victory with a military assault of his own.

and all over North Korea they keep building the man up. Basically rather unattractive, and the thing that gets me is that we continue to criticize Park in South Korea. And the civil libertarian groups continue to point out the imperfections of his regime. Yet nobody focuses in on the ridiculous leadership role of Kim Il Sung, with its self-adulation and its totalitarianism. A communiqué like this makes us realize how far we have got to go in our work with China. The communiqué did talk about the independent and peaceful reunification of the fatherland but that was the Chinese side talking about that. In the blue news of April 28, Bob McCloskey was asked whether the United States had intensified diplomatic efforts with China or the Soviet Union pertaining to a settlement in South Vietnam.[23] He said, "I have not said that we didn't."

[Three sentences have been redacted by George H. W. Bush.]

[Tuesday,] April 29[, 1975].   Holt Atherton called from Tokyo saying that he is going to pick up his visa on Tuesday morning—all set to come.[24] A few hours later he called back. Instead of giving him the visa on May 1 they gave him a visa for May 3. No explanation. No airplane till May 4. This probably has something to do with May Day, but it is so inconsiderate and it is so difficult to get things done. The Bemises wanted to ship a rug out and they go through all kinds of rigmarole; finally are told they can't ship the rug because it was bought after April 1. They went to the Friendship Store and down to the railroad station. The Bemises and Bryans

---

[23]Robert McCloskey had been a State Department spokesman throughout the early years of the Vietnam War, and in early 1975 he was appointed assistant secretary for congressional relations. McCloskey had recently appeared on NBC's *Meet the Press*, where he acknowledged Washington's overtures to Moscow and China to help end the Vietnam War and admitted that Washington's policies for the country had failed.

[24]Holt and Flo Atherton were longtime friends of the Bushes, and indeed Bush had previously shared with the couple his thoughts on the importance of Washington's credibility for international relations, writing in January 1975 that "I worry lest our friends-foes around the world really begin to wonder if we can keep a commitment in foreign policy."

get [ready] to leave, and go to negotiate for another compartment on the train. They went through for twenty minutes discussing with various officials what it would take to get another train compartment. Finally some big woman came up and the price was all set for an empty compartment next door. Then they are told there is no room. Now, of course, somebody could have been getting on the train down the line, but there is a great bureaucratic screwup on a lot of the dealings.

It is frustrating to try to get the people to visit, for example, at our house. You send in a list and then you never hear anything for a time. The tendency is to get discouraged, but we cannot do that. Today we get a message that all Vietnam is being evacuated. [At] the Japanese diplomatic reception for the emperor's birthday, people said, "Well it's good the chapter is closed, we're pleased it's over." The Bryans left. Visit with Rolf Pauls. Then the diplomatic reception to say goodbye to the Steigers. The Lucases, also a great family, left. Then a language lesson. End April 29.

[Wednesday, April 30, 1975.] A long talk with the Syrian Ambassador who is very militant against the U.S. He is absolutely wild. With the fall of Vietnam he says that Israel is next. He was just gloating as much as he could. He didn't tell me this, but he told the Canadians. There is a great euphoria sweeping Peking about Southeast Asia. Distinguished group from the Chamber of Commerce from San Francisco including Tom Clausen, head of the Bank of America, and many other attractive people.[25] It is fun having groups like this here. Bar and I played in the mixed doubles of Canada.[26] They have a scorekeeper and it's their big event internationally.

Went to the national day reception for the Netherlands and there I heard, not through the State Department telegrams but through gossip at a reception, that the big, big men in Vietnam had surrendered. The Vietcong were there, three little guys about four feet

[25]Thomas Clausen later served as president of the World Bank during the Reagan administration.

[26]The reference is to a tennis tournament sponsored by the Canadian embassy.

high that rushed happily out of the room. The Vietcong and the North Vietnamese embassies are bedecked in flags and having understandable celebrations. Firecrackers are heard. It is a rather sad thing and you can sense the hostility and certainly the tension when I walk by certain groups at these receptions. John Small of Canada made an interesting comment. It is important that the U.S. stand firm in Korea, and it is important that this slide and decline be halted. It is important that these people stand for something. Where is our ideology? Where is our principle? What indeed do we stand for? These things must be made clear, and the American people must understand that as soon as America doesn't stand for something in the world, there is going to be a tremendous erosion of freedom. It is true. It is very true. And yet it is awful hard to convince people of it at home, I am sure. I am a little annoyed about getting nothing from the State Department, hearing about the surrender of Binh Dinh from a drinking party.[27] Canada apparently today also announced that they threw a second secretary, press attaché, out of Canada for involving himself in subversive activities.[28] Will there be retaliation?

[Thursday, May 1, 1975.]   May First today, but April 30 I guess ends up as a gloomy day.[29] A lot of dust in the air. And all in all not a happy time, but we are big enough and strong enough so we can regroup, redefine and move forward. A lot of human tragedy there. A lot of loss of life. Off to the Pakistan Embassy for dinner. End April 30.

May 1. Unbelievable. Extremely difficult to describe. Six parks were all made over into playgrounds, all kinds of cultural performances, singing, children in the brightest colors of greens and reds and yellows and blues you've ever seen. Banners all over. The

[27]Binh Dinh was one of South Vietnam's largest and most populous provinces.
[28]Kuo Ching-An, a Chinese diplomat expelled from Canada, allegedly collected military and industrial information during his frequent trips to Washington, D.C.
[29]President Duong Van Minh announced the formal surrender of the South Vietnamese government on April 30, 1975.

night before the buildings were all lit up including the railroad station, hotels, the Square, the Hall of People, etc. All the lights in the streets were on. Then the next day the festive air continued on what turned out to be a beautiful day. With Jerry Levesque, Bar and I drove with Guo out to the Summer Palace. There we were enchanted by the literally hundreds of thousands of people milling with great happiness through the park. There were all kinds of performances—singing, dancing, flowers, games—it was unbelievably spectacular. Something that I couldn't quite visualize. I had always thought of May Day as tanks and Mao standing in the Square with people running on by him. But that wasn't it. The square was crowded but they were all crowds going into the parks. We came home for lunch and then bicycled down to two fairs: the Workers Palace Park and the Sun Yat-sen Park on either side of the Great Gate at Tiananmen Square. These parks again were like the Summer Palace, full of activities, full of dances, full of games. Kids could drive little cars, they had all these industrial exhibits, derricks lifting, boats running, one warship firing its rockets into the air. There was a sign. We saw Zhu De being carried down and then being propped up and walking to great applause to a crowded square as he came to watch a comedy and some singing. They had a choir. It looked like they were ex–factory workers, older women, and it was spectacular. The only thing was that there was a sign in there talking about supporting the people of Cambodia, Laos and Vietnam against U.S. imperialists. People were extremely friendly. I used the old giveaway Polaroid gambit and they were absolutely thrilled, particularly the children. The whole day was perfect.

We were supposed to go either to a soccer game in the afternoon at 2 o'clock or an acrobatic performance at 7:30, but we stayed at the park all afternoon. And then I felt a little tired at 6 so we didn't go to the 7:30 performance, although I am sorry we missed it. I have seen one of those. I saw lots of South Vietnam tourists—PRG [Provisional Revolutionary Government of Vietnam]—with their little signs. The whole aftermath of Vietnam making me slightly sick, but anyway there was no animosity towards us anywhere that you could feel. I think the people are not sure at all that we are Americans, but it was a spectacular holiday, and I am told that October 1 is very much the same.[30] I don't want to miss it. End of May 1.

Add to May 1: Ricardo Castanedo, Deputy Foreign Minister of El Salvador, came to see me.[31] He was here talking to the Chinese on a round-the-world trip to get El Salvador in as head of FAO [Food and Agriculture Organization of the United Nations]. He is a delightful young man and it is always a pleasure to see him.

[Friday,] May 2[, 1975].   The Sri Lanka[n] Ambassador Karannagoda came to see me. He was convinced that we should move in and give much, much more aid to South Vietnam and North Vietnam. I told him that there would be too much heartache, too much concern in our country about the things that had gone wrong, and that we were not able to do this. One of the heartbreaking things is the way our position in Vietnam is totally misunderstood. You have to be here in Peking with its dominating continuing theme every day in the red news and in the blue news. It makes an impact on the diplomats and they in turn reflect it to us.

Visit from my old ailment from Pakistan. Ailments here seem to be worse than elsewhere. They seem to hit harder. Even a common cold is more severe. CBS series on Benjamin Franklin has come here and is a marvelous thing to have.[32] It is a wonderful series and I am grateful to Paley for arranging this. Saturday, took it easy. Laid up most of the day. Went out to play in the tennis tournament with Akwei, Bennaceur of Tunisia, and Ratanavong of Laos. Beat them 6-1, 6-love. Canadian tennis mixed together, also all ages. It's a really nice thing, I wish we were in a position to reply. Soon the outdoor courts will be open at the International Club.

[30]October 1 is China's national day, commemorating the PRC's founding in 1949.

[31]Bush described this meeting at length to the State Department; the source is provided in the corresponding endnote.

[32]CBS first aired *Benjamin Franklin: The Ambassador* on November 21, 1974.

Sunday, May 4[, 1975]. I was laid low with the bug. Bar went to church and I stayed flat on my back. We did have lunch with the Harlands, and then I cycled up to the Club in the afternoon, but generally speaking I was cramped up and suffering from the darn bug. Peregrine Worsthorne of London came by with Clare Hollingsworth to see us Sunday night.[33] We had a good visit with him. He had been to call on the Foreign Minister along with some other distinguished London journalists and then they were taking the tour. He reported that he had had a long couple of visits with Kissinger. Kissinger was rather gloomy at the time. All in all it was rather a sad report. He is a conservative fellow and wonders what will happen if the U.S. really does turn isolationist. I tried to convince him that the U.S. wouldn't do it, although I do think this is a period where we will pull back somewhat. Celebrations continue over at the Vietcong and Vietnam embassy—parties and happiness, understandable but sad. The weekend was a lost one as far as I'm concerned due to health, but the weather in Peking continues to be beautiful. We are awaiting our new house guests. All in all it was a rather restful way, while sick, to recover. End of May 4.

Monday, May 5[, 1975]. Health problems, beautiful young German doctor came over. But my gut condition wasn't bad enough that I didn't mind discussing these intimate details with her. I stayed home—Bar and I went out and met Holt and Flo Atherton and we had dinner at the house. I just didn't feel like moving. I lost six

---

[33]Sir Peregrine Gerard Worsthorne was a British journalist with the *Sunday Telegraph*. Kissinger had personally requested that Bush make time for the interview. During the meeting Hollingsworth suggested to Bush that a "senior PRC foreign ministry official" had told her that President Ford's visit, tentatively scheduled for late 1975, would take place only if the United States was willing to "compromise" on Beijing's demands for normalization. She gave Bush the distinct impression that in telling him this news she was passing along a message from Foreign Minister Qiao Guanhua. Yet the USLO's efforts to verify the story led nowhere, save to a reminder from the British embassy in Beijing that Hollingsworth "doesn't have enough to do in Peking," and thus "tends to fantasize."

pounds with this new bout, captured from eating some food at the Pakistan Embassy again.

Tuesday, May 6[, 1975]. Was another wipeout. We did have lunch with the Athertons, and at dinner walked up to the International Club. But no events. Quiet in the office. The digestion of Cambodia and Vietnam taking place. After some confused statements at home, it sounds like the right tone is being hit. In other words we will look ahead, that we will not have recriminations. There is no question that the Vietnam thing has hurt us in the eyes of the Third World and certainly in the eyes of most of the diplomats around here. And as I say, there is a total misunderstanding as to why we are involved. It is so easy to classify us as imperialists when a war is half reported. The corruption and cruelty on one side only reported. Others get a distorted opinion and they can throw up your own sources to you.

Listened on May 6 to the President's press conference on the Voice of America.[34] I thought he did pretty well. He was pressed on cruelty and cited cases of 80 Cambodians and wives being killed —a little less vague, and almost predicting slaughter in Vietnam with

---

[34]When pressed by reporters to describe the early "lesson" of Vietnam, Ford repeatedly suggested that the United States "should focus on the future," given that "I think the lessons of the past in Vietnam have already been learned—learned by Presidents, learned by Congress, learned by the American people." He further addressed the question of American credibility that so intrigued Bush in his diary, arguing, "We do get reactions from foreign governments wondering what our position will be, asking where we will go and what our policy will be. We have indicated to our friends that we will maintain our commitments. We understand the perception that some countries may have as a result of the setback in South Vietnam. But that perception is not a reality, because the United States is strong militarily. The United States is strong economically, despite our current problems. And we are going to maintain our leadership on a worldwide basis. And we want our friends to know that we will stand by them, and we want any potential adversaries to know that we will stand up to them." The details of Ford's response are arguably less significant than the fact that the question was posed in the first place, for in the immediate aftermath of Saigon's fall the issue of American credibility throughout Asia and the wider world occupied others as much as it did Bush in Beijing.

the fleeing of the refugees, saying that means slaughter will follow. He will probably get clobbered on that answer. May 6. Ismet Kittani called.[35] He is leaving the U.N., on his way back to Iraq. I am anxious to visit with him. He is coming for lunch Friday. It is amazing how the U.N. keeps touching our lives out here.

Sent a letter to the [Chinese] Foreign Minister saying we hadn't seen him in a while and wanted to visit. It will be interesting to see what comes of this, if anything. There is great frustration about getting appointments with Chinese officials. We submitted one protocol list, got some of the calls granted when I first came here, and then nothing else. We resubmitted a list of protocol calls and have had nothing. Have sent a letter to request to see Zhang Chunqiao and have received nothing.[36] Have received no answer back on that. Have asked several people for dinner. Some have come. Others have not. There is tremendous difference between the people that Ambassador Huang Zhen can see in Washington and the people we get to see or don't get to see here in China. We get to see as many as, if not more than, other embassies, but not nearly as many as we would like. The result is a great deal of scurrying around, comparing rumors and notes in the diplomatic community. And yet I will readily concede that the Foreign Minister is extremely busy with calls. The problem is you don't get to see the political people; you don't get to see the Army people; you don't get to see the collateral officials as their people do in Washington.

Got the word that all water will be turned off from May 10 to June 5, just in time to encompass the Rogers Mortons, Kendalls and others.[37] In a way it will be good. They will see how things of this nature work in China, but I will miss the good hot baths we

[35]Ismet Kittani had been the assistant to the U.N. secretary general during Bush's time in New York.

[36]Zhang Chunqiao was a member of Mao's inner circle who rose to deputy director of the Central Cultural Revolution Group and chairman of the influential Shanghai Revolutionary Committee.

[37]Donald Kendall was chairman and chief executive officer of PepsiCo at the time.

get around here. They turn the water off by entire districts to run some gigantic Roto-Rooter through. The water is very hard in China so it needs that kind of attention I guess. *People* magazine article came out—not bad.[38]

May 6. Bar is off to the Wall and the Ming Tombs yet again, with the Athertons. I must play in the tournament, and I am dragged down by this tummy condition. You get hit hard by things here. There is a lot of pneumonia and bronchial stuff but we have been spared a good deal of that. When you feel good, you feel very, very good. After exercise you feel terrific. I don't know how I'll fare though, because I have lost six pounds now in the last six days.

Troubled again by Southeast Asia. China continues to support revolutions in all these countries and yet many of the countries like the Philippines, Malaysia and others keep trying to get closer to China. They have to because they don't see in the U.S. the firm kind of interventionist support that they have been able to count on in the past. I can't honestly feel that Southeast Asia is vital to the security of the United States. We must make some new kinds of declarations, but if somebody said to me today what would you declare, I'd be damned if I know how I'd define it. With Congress unwilling to give any leeway to the executive, and making clear that they really won't support any substantial spending, certainly for arms, it's extremely difficult for the U.S. to pledge anything. Economic recovery, private investment, aid to refugees—these things we can do. Others we can't do. Some of our treaty obligations seem to be outdated. Perhaps we need a bold new look at all of them—all of the treaties—and then a restatement of what kind of support we will give to Southeast Asia, free countries and the socialist and communist countries. China is in the horns of a dilemma. They talk against hegemony and yet they support revolutions. Qiao Guanhua

[38]The article included the following passage: "'Sports is a great equalizer,' Bush said of his habit of intermingling tennis with diplomatic contacts. 'If you know people and can relax with people, then maybe you can head off a crisis that you couldn't head off with people you'd only met at a reception.'"

is quoted by some Britishers as having said that there is a difference between support and export.[39] They support revolution, but they don't export it. It is a very fine line of distinction, and not overly convincing an argument. Mr. and Mrs. Berman of Hess' Department Store came by.[40] Realistic view of China it seemed to me. Not the euphoric Shirley MacLaine "you're right, we're wrong" approach.

[**Wednesday, May 7, 1975.**] Tonight, the 7th, the San Francisco Chamber of Commerce delegation—high-level business types—interesting to see their reactions.[41] Midway through May 7. Won in the men's doubles. Then dinner at the Peace Hotel in a beautiful room that nobody at USLO had dined in. Off in a courtyard, the Peace Hotel, kind of stark and Russian-looking—turn an abrupt right and you go into a lovely courtyard where one of the Ch'ing emperor big shots had lived. Food was excellent. Very high standard, with swallow's nest soup and sweet fungus soup, dessert and a marvelous meal. San Francisco Chamber guys all got up and made a lot of toasts—most of which the Chinese didn't understand. The Chinese high-level trade delegation, headed by Mr. Wang of the Organization to Promote Trade, were in good spirits, competitive in the drinking department, encouraging the people from San Francisco on. They are very relaxed in dealing with private groups. I made a small toast, told the Chinese that they were fortunate to have a high-level delegation of principals here, and told the Americans that they were honored by the presence of so many high-level Chinese. There were about 60 people there. The mood was excellent. The San Franciscans, which included the head of the foremost

[39]Following Qiao Guanhua's speech, the State Department discussed the difference between Beijing's "support" of revolution and its "export" of the same. Details can be found in the department's cable traffic; additional information is provided in the endnotes.

[40]Philip and Muriel Berman were the owners of the Hess's chain of department stores, which had grown from a single Allentown, Pennsylvania, store. The couple had recently visited the Canton Trade Fair.

[41]Further information on this meeting is provided in the endnotes.

dairies, the head of the Bank of America, and one of the top people in Federated Stores and others, all were very, very pleased. It is the kind of experience that can really help. There does seem to be a genuine friendship, genuine good feeling at that kind of a meeting.

[Thursday,] May 8[, 1975]. Back thrown out playing on Canadian court. Bad physical condition. Agonized our way through the mixed doubles match. Stomach cured. It is hard to describe state of health in Peking. The climate is harsh on things. When you get a bronchial thing it hurts more, it's more active. When you get a stomach thing it seems to be more acute; but on the other hand when you feel good there is a certain euphoric feeling of it. There are great highs and lows. Some of it must be psychological because of the isolation we incur here. We had a quiet lunch at the USLO with the Athertons. Reception for a New Zealand doctors group at their embassy. The Russians and other Eastern Europeans are concentrating on numerous invitations for the 30th anniversary of the crushing defeat of Hitlerite Fascism. There is no credit given to the United States' role, or anybody else's role, in ending the war against Germany. Indeed, the Chinese came out in recognition of the crush of fascism and gave credit to the Eastern Europeans—Russians, Bulgarians, and others including Stalin—but no mention of the U.S. role. I think this is gross. The Russian Ambassador sent around a calling card in honor of this 30th anniversary. I talked to the West German Ambassador and decided not to go to these things, and, out of respect to him, not to go to the East German one or the Russian one. I hate to antagonize Tolstikov but they are overdoing this a little bit. John Holdridge went and represented us. Dinner at the Minzu Restaurant with the Athertons and Andersons. One of these pots where you put in thin slices of mutton—very thin—into the hot water and cook it and then at the end you put a whole bunch of ingredients, like bean noodles, lettuce, onions and more mutton, and come up with a delicious broth. Good and reasonably cheap. Delicious food.

Friday, May 9[, 1975]. Chuck Cross arrived from Hong Kong. Lunch with Ismet Kittani, Iraqi Assistant to the U.N. Secretary

281

General. Disturbing reports from Cambodia.[42] People in the French Embassy apparently saw Sararakay pleading for his life, then led off.[43] Embassies including the Russians' looted. Little cadres of guerrillas reporting only to their chief[s]. Coming in totally undisciplined. The cities vacant. People herded away. The whole story pre-liberation here was that there would be no bloodbath. Initial reports sound like it's going pretty well. As the story unfolds it will be extremely interesting, and Sihanouk's position becomes extremely difficult.

[One sentence has been redacted by George H. W. Bush.]

I have requested a visit with Qiao Guanhua just to get brought up to date and to chat. And yet I am not at all confident that things haven't gone on in Washington that we don't know about. Perhaps I am getting overly suspicious myself. I recall asking Habib when I was home in February whether anything had gone on in Cambodia. He told me "no," and then I get back here and we publish in the papers in the States a long list of contacts that we have had, including the talk with Sihanouk of somebody coming to see him in Peking. I hit the roof and wrote Habib a long letter.

Won the mixed doubles tennis finals. Sad, sad, sad tennis. Rushed over to the reception for the 30th anniversary of the liberation of Czechoslovakia. It was not one of the two festivities here for "Crushing of Hitlerite Fascism." I get upset over the way the Chinese played the Hitlerite Fascism anniversary—mainly sponsored by the Russians. It was the Russians and the Chinese of all things

---

[42]The fall of Phnom Penh to the Khmer Rouge Communists took place on April 17, 1975. About eight hundred foreigners were forced to take refuge in the French embassy. After two weeks of imprisonment there, the group—which was composed mostly of French nationals but also included citizens from nineteen other countries—boarded buses and traveled to the Thai border.

[43]Bush is most likely referring to Prince Sirik Matak, the Cambodian leader who was forcibly removed from the French embassy after the Khmer Rouge took over the Cambodian capital. Sirik Matak was one of the leaders of the coup that had established the former, pro-Western government in 1970. He fled to the French embassy when Phnom Penh fell and was executed by Communist authorities a few days later.

who liberated the world from Hitlerite Fascism, particularly the Chinese. What an interesting view of history. The Russians gave us no credit either—in fact here they billed it "Crushing Hitlerite Fascism," but when inviting Averell Harriman they called it the "Liberation of Europe," much politer.[44] I talked to the West German Ambassador and decided not to go to the reception of the Soviet Union. At the Czechoslovakian reception I saw Tolstikov who was a little rude and huffy about why I wasn't there. I said, "Well, Holdridge was there." He said, "Holdridge is not Bush," and went on to tell me he liked Harriman's speech, and again bitched that I wasn't there. I stood pleasantly listening.

Dinner at the Sick Duck Restaurant. I think it is the best Peking duck in town. We had the Spanish Ambassador, the Peruvian Ambassador, Lady Berendsen and Mrs. Berendsen—Lady Berendsen being 80, a wife of a former New Zealand Ambassador to the U.S. and house guest of the Harlands.'[45]

Saturday, May 10[, 1975]. Amazing problems getting the Athertons' horses and stuff shipped to the United States. You go first to the Friendship Store, then to the customs at the railroad station, then back to the Friendship Store for the shipping office. Quite a bit of paperwork. Not too bad once you really understand it. The air freight for two pots and a horse to the United States was something like $375. The goods cost about a third of that. Won the men's doubles—Akwei and Bush v. Mehrotra of India and Murray McLean of Australia.[46] Again a sad match. Back held out. We won

---

[44]One of the most experienced diplomats in American history, W. Averell Harriman was Washington's ambassador to the Soviet Union during World War II. The Soviet Union celebrated the thirtieth anniversary of the close of World War II in Europe, and Harriman visited Moscow as President Ford's representative to the event.

[45]Nellie Berendsen was the wife of Sir Carl Berendsen, who had first been New Zealand's minister to the United States from 1944 to 1948, before the post was elevated to ambassadorial status. He held the latter position until 1952.

[46]Lakhan Lal Mehrotra was India's chargé d'affaires in Beijing. He was later appointed ambassador to Argentina and Yugoslavia, before becoming the U.N. special representative in Cambodia and then head of the U.N. Transitional

it 3-1 and then went to a tennis dance at 8:30 given by the Canadians. They fixed it up like Hawaii. It is amazing how decorations and little diversity that would just be routine at home stands out like a sore thumb here. They did a beautiful job on it with flowered leis, and all in all it was a very special evening for Peking.

In the car I counted, going along the road between our house and the Worker Stadium, the vehicles. It went something like this. Ten bicycles, olive truck, olive motorcycle, bike, bike, bike, 15 bicycles, 3 olive drab trucks, 22 bicycles, 1 car, 22 cycles, 10 more bicycles, 3 trucks, line of trucks with students near stadium, motorcycles, bikes, trucks, 1 car, thousands of bicycles. As you go by the stadium they are having an athletic event and trucks pour in from the countryside bearing literally hundreds and thousands of students, young people, soldiers. You see the soldiers jumping out carrying bright red pom-poms. They don't look self-conscious about it at all. You see squads of soldiers and students lined up—nobody seeming to keep order except the platoon leader of some sort. And they all wait patiently for their turn to march into the stadium. Trucks all muster. When in the stadium, the crowds are as big as they are in the United States. There is no real traffic jam because there are no cars. They all pile into the back of trucks and head on out to the countryside, commune or wherever they came from. They look good. There is no question about the fact that the people look in good health. They seem happy.

The grayness and the severeness of winter has given way to much more laughing, playing, kidding around, little kids wrestling the same as the whole world over. They play marbles. You see some card games. Holdridge and Cross saw some gambling game at the Summer Palace among kids and were amazed. Summer Palace Restaurant is a beautiful one, and one of the best places in Peking to eat.

Authority in East Timor. Murray McLean, who was then in Beijing for his first overseas diplomatic posting, rose through the ranks of Australia's Foreign Office to become deputy secretary and then ambassador to Japan.

Sunday, May 11[, 1975]. Athertons departed. I told Mr. Guo that I wanted to go at 11:45 a.m. Shie yi dien san ke [11:45]. Then I changed it, saying I wanted to go a little earlier. He thought I said something else. So when 11:30 rolled around, no Guo. We rushed and hastily called a taxi from the International Club, made it with no problem and about 1:20 p.m. Guo cycled up. I apologized profusely to him. He looked very upset about it all, but he is very good to me. He is extremely thoughtful of me and leads me around to different appointments to make sure we are on time and welcomed, etc.

Five-thirty p.m. We showed to the Molinaris of Argentina, the Ruggieros of Italy, the Ruges of Germany, and the Costellos one film of the Franklin series that CBS sent. Had a nice relaxed day. Church was fine. Played tennis with the boys and had a consultation with Mr. (unintelligible). Mr. Gee had loaned him the tennis thing and he came out.[47] I played on the court with the three Chinese guys. Then we took some Polaroids and then he said he would like to visit with us. So we went in, with Mr. Law translating, to almost a formal conference—just sitting there, the three of us in our tennis clothes. And he thanked me and said the other officials were very pleased to receive the tennis information. I offered to get him more. I asked him which ones he wanted to keep. He said whichever we didn't want. I went rigorously through it—very formal. Also told him I would like him to come down and see the Laver match, so we could then work out a time to invite the others.[48] He is very grateful. He seemed to want to do it.

[Monday, May 12, 1975.] Weather is warm now. I can bicycle in my tennis clothes, to many stares I'll admit, to the club, three blocks away. Today as I sit here with the window closed, this Mon-

---

[47]The reference here is to the tennis magazines and books Bush had previously lent to the International Club.

[48]Bush refers to the annual World Championship Tennis Tournament, held in May 1975, in which Rod Laver lost to Swedish player Björn Borg.

day, May 12, it is warm. Turnover in personnel continues. Bill Thomas is arriving.[49] I wrote a letter to Qiao Guanhua saying that I would like to see him. We get a call from the Foreign Ministry Saturday night saying the Foreign Minister was going on his trip to Paris and therefore he was not able to do it. We did give him very short notice, and I don't think it means too much. But nevertheless there it is.

Morning of May 12. The Elkins and Bryans arrived after a diplomatic luncheon.[50] I had met with the ambassadors of Hungary, Norway, Lebanon and Peru. It was a good lesson for me to see how others see us. I listened to all the drivel about our being imperialists and colonialists, dominating others. I know what motivated us in Vietnam and I think most other Americans know what motivated us in Vietnam, but I hear the Peruvian talk about Vietnam in terms of Peru-U.S. relations. Really upset apparently with the way we handled his country, the feeling that we were indeed imperialist. Pleasant but quite tough about it. The Hungarian, much more diplomatic in a sense, but nevertheless rigid in the fact that the new regime should take over and that we should help it. He also made the point that we ought not to differentiate between the North and the PRG. Not to try to act like they are two separate ones. I asked him how soon there would be reunification and he shook his head. Elie Boustany of Lebanon—of course interested in the Middle East. The American people do not have any concept of how others around the world view America. We think we are good, honorable, decent, freedom-loving. Others are firmly convinced that, though they like the people themselves in our country, that we are embarking on policies that are anathema to them. We have a mammoth public relations job to do on all of this.

[49] A career foreign service officer, William Thomas served as an economic counselor in the USLO and eventually as chargé d'affaires in Laos. A passionate amateur ornithologist, Thomas is credited with compiling one of the only bird lists for Laos and Cambodia between the end of the French colonial period and the 1990s.

[50] Anthony Bryan was president and chief executive officer of Cameron Iron Works, which had also been represented at the Canton Trade Fair.

The Bryans and Elkins arrived in the afternoon, went to the hotel. We just walked in, went to the 17th floor where Jennifer told us they were (Room 1718, 1719), picked up two keys, walked in and put the people in the rooms. Baggage all appeared. There was no checking in, no signing, no nothing. Anybody could have picked up the keys, walked up there and sacked out.

Out to the airport to get Rog Morton and Anne. The protocol people came out, proving that they wanted the visit, and that they were very pleasant about it. They were surprised to see me standing there alone to greet a minister. I frankly think this is good. They offered at a dinner by Wang Hairong to do anything they could to make the Secretary's visit pleasant. I told him that we were going to low-key it. We were just pleased that the Minister of Foreign Trade was coming for lunch. Late dinner at the residence. Then everybody hit the sack.

Tuesday the 13th [May 13, 1975]. We all went to the Great Wall —Chuck Cross's and our guests, and then I came home and then went to the Ming Tombs. Cambodia has seized a ship of the United States.[51] China is being unhelpful about that.[52] God it is a tough

---

[51]The U.S. merchant ship S.S. *Mayagüez* was seized on May 12, 1975, by Khmer Rouge forces, who had taken control of Cambodia several days previously. Cambodia claimed the ship had violated its territory, even though the *Mayagüez* had been sailing in recognized international waters. President Ford ultimately launched a Marine raid in hopes of freeing the ship and its forty-man crew—unaware that Khmer Rouge forces had already transported the crew to safety in Thailand.

[52]Because there was no formal American diplomatic presence in Phnom Penh, the State Department sought to pressure the Khmer Rouge through the Chinese Foreign Ministry. Kissinger attempted to send a message through the head of the Chinese liaison office in Washington, but he refused even to accept the note. Bush was then ordered to convey to the Chinese Foreign Ministry in Beijing two messages for the Cambodians, demanding immediate release of the American personnel and their vessel under threat of military action. On May 13 the USLO's Don Anderson delivered Washington's note. It was returned the next day—in the same (unopened) envelope, now marked "return to sender"—with the following message from the Foreign Ministry: "The Ministry of the People's Republic of China is instructed to inform the U.S. side that it is not in a position to pass the

world we live in. Yesterday was the first day it rained in Peking—
real rain—in six and a half months. There has been some kind of
mist that dampened the ground and then promptly the ground
dries; but this was a good rain. And as we drove to the Tombs you
could see standing water for the first time. The countryside is green.
The hills around the Wall are green and bright and spring is here.
The wind was whistling down from Mongolia but it lacked the zip,
the thrust of the winter. It was beautiful. We climbed to the top,
took pictures and gave the Polaroids away. It was a great day.
Elkins came laden down with cheese and the Bryans with tennis
balls. And also taped music for our listening pleasure. Marvelous
presents. CBS tape thing is working great.

Almost through May 13. Big diplomatic reception. Many ambassadors to meet the Mortons. Dinner at the Minzu with the Mortons, Elkins, Bryans and Bushes. I am emphasizing the informal approach to this entertainment. People help themselves at the bar.
Food on the tables but not passed. I wish there was a way to warm
up a reception like this, to get Morton to speak, but it didn't work
out that way. The Soviet Ambassador, who had been a little tough
a few days before, seemed rather pleased to be there, at least very
pleasant about it. The flags of rejoicing are down at the North Vietnamese Embassy, but they are working under a pretty full head of
steam. They are very confident.

Wednesday, May 14[, 1975]. Word reaches us that the *Mayagüez,* a U.S. merchant vessel, has been captured by the Cambodians and hauled into port near Sihanoukville. I am wondering what
to do. I am convinced that we need speedy action. The Chinese in
Washington and here are unhelpful on this. The Cambodians here
are also unhelpful.[53]

On the 14th we took the Secretary to the Nan Yuan Commune
where a Mr. Li, Vice Chairman of the Revolutionary Committee,

U.S. message on to the Royal Government of National Union of Cambodia and
hereby returns the May 13 note of the U.S. side."
[53]See my footnote to Bush's entry for May 13, 1975.

showed us around. Polaroid worked again. Handing the people at the "Respect the Aged Home" a copy of the picture. They were absolutely thrilled. One is impressed by this "Respect the Aged Home." Neat clean rooms, people living rather comfortably in clean conditions, a tailor room where they were making suits for next winter for the old people—so different from pre-liberation China in terms of death. Most old people still live with their families. The family is still terribly important in the Chinese life. The communes usually start at nine. This one went to eleven. Lunch with the Minister of Foreign Trade Li Qiang, and Wang Yaoting of CCPIT, both good high-level officials, particularly the Minister, came to have lunch with Morton. It is hard to get information out of them. It is difficult to get statistics from the Chinese. You throw out a suggestion about census, but they do not hit your bid. Tennis with the Secretary [Morton] with Wang and De. I think it is a good thing to have these Chinese and others such as Mr. Tang of the Protocol to see just the Secretary and me walking around rather informally. This was true when he arrived at the airport and true when he left on May 15. The tone at the luncheon was good—pretty relaxed. Of course things like the capture of the ship by the Cambodians mentioned before must be on their minds, but there is no discussion of that kind of event at all.

Peking duck dinner for about 21 of our good-friend ambassadors. Shirt sleeve weather now. Peking duck is still a great treat. It is warm now at night, kick off all the blankets except maybe a sheet. On the night of Tuesday, May 13, I opened the windows on both sides of the house and in the middle of the night a howling storm with dust came blowing down from the Gobi Desert, right through our bathroom, clearing out the Kleenex and all the things sitting on the shelves, knocking down the flower pots outside. Fred and Bar slept through it, but I had to get up and batten down all the hatches. It wasn't cold, just dust and tremendous wind—da feng [big wind].

Thursday, May 15[, 1975]. I saw the South Vietnam (PRG) and the North Vietnamese flags side by side on the North Vietnam embassy. This was the first signal of reunification. They are having a 3-day celebration to support their victory—to go with the week-long celebration a week ago.[54] But it was amazing to see the two flags on the same pole. Went to the Temple of Heaven with the Mortons in the morning, after a briefing with the Secretary. Lunch at the airport. Huang Hua from New York arrived when we were eating dinner. But I did see Mrs. Huang Hua. Mortons left after having a hectic but good visit. Marched off just prior to a hundred and some Japanese socialist members of a delegation.[55] The Japanese are in here in very large numbers.

The ship has been released.[56] The first word we got was that 30 people were off. They were released, the ship was taken by the Marines. Now we hear that the other nine are released. Then a flash has come from the State Department. This will help. It shows our spine. It shows our unwillingness to be pushed around. Nobody knows what the Cambodians were doing in this, but it was impossible for the United States to let this happen on the high seas at this point, given the recent happenings in Southeast Asia. There may be some static about the U.S., but I am convinced that this is the kind of thing the Chinese and others understand. China has been unhelpful as hell on this, and they missed, in my view, a real opportunity to help out. The Ambassador of Norway, Anda, came by and wanted to discuss the *Mayagüez* ship incident—Cambodia.[57] China continues to be unhelpful. They blasted the United States, calling it an act of piracy, claiming the vessel was in Cambodian

[54]A victory rally was held in Saigon on May 8. Approximately 30,000 people celebrated the surrender of South Vietnam and also marked the twenty-first anniversary of the victory over the French.

[55]As the *New York Times* reported, "A visiting delegation of the Japanese Socialist party and Peking's China-Japan Friendship Association signed a joint statement . . . opposing the dominant international role of the United States and the Soviet Union."

[56]Bush refers to the *Mayagüez*. See again my footnote to his entry for May 13, 1975.

[57]Torleif Anda served as the Norwegian ambassador to China from 1975 to 1979.

waters. The Cambodians come out strongly on the sixteenth talking about spying. Anda of Norway thought it was a good thing we
responded forcefully. I get the feeling from talking to the Australians, Mr. Plimsoll at least, that they do.[58] I am recommending
that we factually set the record straight.[59] China should not blast
us on an incident of this nature.

[Friday,] May 16[, 1975].   Elkins and Bryans spend a lot of time
shipping their stuff out. We had lunch with Ismet Kittani, the U.N.
Chef de Cabinet, who had been the guest of the Chinese. He leaves
today. 4:51—Sir James Plimsoll, Australian ambassador to the USSR,
formerly to the U.S., came to call. He came with Steve Fitzgerald.

[58]Sir James Plimsoll was the Australian ambassador to the USSR in 1974. One
of his country's most respected diplomats, he had previously served as Australia's
permanent representative to the U.N., and then as ambassador to the United States
from 1970 to 1974. Plimsoll was visiting Beijing, en route to Australia from his
Moscow post, at the time of this meeting.
[59]Bush reacted angrily to the refusal by the Chinese to be of assistance, especially after their delay helped prompt President Ford to end the crisis through the
use of military force. He was especially incensed at subsequent Chinese criticisms
of the military rescue—both in private and in the Chinese press—including one
Chinese diplomat's assessment that the American response was "an outright act of
piracy." The incident dovetailed with his ongoing critique—in cables home and in
his diary—of Beijing's diplomatic obstinacy coupled with its rhetorical campaign
against Washington. As he advised the State Department on May 16, "I think it is
time to go public with an account of our efforts to reach the Cambodians and warn
them before it was necessary to use military force. . . . I recognize there are problems involved in such an approach, [and] some members of my staff have argued
that the Chinese have little to lose by our going public and the effect would simply
[be] to prolong the acrimonious exchanges over who was at fault. Nevertheless, I
think on balance there is merit in setting the record straight on those efforts we
made to avoid having to take military action and, en [sic] addition, letting the Chinese know that their propaganda will not always go unanswered."
Kissinger's principal advisers did not agree with Bush's suggestion. Though they
told Kissinger (who was yet again traveling) of Bush's desire to "[set] the record
straight," two weeks after the crisis had ended Winston Lord and William
Gleysteen argued that, while "we agree with Bush that we should not give the Chinese the impression that we are always willing to let their criticism of us go unchallenged. . . . we conclude that reopening the issue with the Chinese at this somewhat belated state would not serve a major purpose."

There are these little divisions in Australia; but Plimsoll very friendly to the United States, and Fitzgerald, certainly not unfriendly to the U.S., but much more sympathetic perhaps to China and others than we would be on some issues. Spent some time at the customs trying to sort out the shipment of things. It is not easy to do, but once you understand the system it seems to work OK.

The staff was a little divided on what kind of reaction we ought to have on the gunboat incident. I wanted Washington to simply set the record straight as to what we had done diplomatically. Others felt why respond—China will always have to have the last word. If we come out with something, they will come out with something else. Very much like dealing with the Russians at the U.N.[60]

Plimsoll, on another subject, described his experiences in Moscow, requests to see people and having them go unanswered, and control on where you can travel and restriction and guides and permissions —it sounded very much like China. Although I gather they are more courteous about it here.

May 16. Kendalls arrive tonight at 10. Kendalls appeared at the airport on CA [China Airlines] flight. Everything went smoothly. Laden down with 80 lbs. of cheese, couple of tennis rackets, etc. On the 17th sightseeing. Lunch with Elkins, Bryans, Kendalls at the Summer Palace. It was a thing of real beauty. You see some litter around—maybe a little more at the Summer Palace than at other sightseeing places. Great family scenes, marvelous food at the Summer Palace restaurants. The lake is alive with boats. You can rent a boat and go down a little canal for a picnic off the Sum-

---

[60]Chinese officials, and their state media, did not let the *Mayagüez* incident pass without comment or criticism. One May 21 article in the *People's Daily*, for example, stated that, "In the past few days Washington has been making a great hullabaloo about the recent U.S. armed invasion of Cambodia, giving much publicity to its so-called 'news of victory' and presenting itself as a 'giant.' This is a typical farce in self-consolation, written and staged single-handed by the very superpower which the small Indochinese countries completely defeated. . . . The U.S. government feels compelled to 'improve' the image, to make it look more formidable, more charming. But its defeat in Cambodia only gave the paper tiger new signs of wear and tear and brought out more clearly the U.S. image of a pirate."

mer Palace. People appear happy. Summer has removed some of that head down, grim look from the faces. The Elkins and Bryans departed for Shanghai. It went smoothly. Tons of bags. Called from Shanghai. No one was out to meet them from China Travel. Probably met the train. They called Sunday and said they were moving on to Hong Kong. I hope things went smoothly there. I am a little concerned about our guests traveling on because I don't want them to foul up the overall house guest situ-ation. The Elkins and Bryans are so damn thoughtful that wouldn't happen with them.

Dinner with the Kendalls at the International Club. Just a good pick-up. That food is very good, very cheap. The Africans are bad around there. The young kids are rude to the staff, they drink too much beer and they are all in all quite obnoxious. Mr. Lou and Mr. Fei keep smiling, but you hear vulgarities out of these rather rude Africans. The Africans are frustrated, and they keep talking about "these stupid Chinese," and throw in a few four-letter words. And it really is not pleasant.

Sunday[, May 18, 1975]. Another trip to the Tombs and the Wall. Fred running around and enjoying the Australian picnic as well as hour at the Ding Ling Tomb. He goes crazy when he sees chickens or pigs. But he has been a pretty good dog. Five o'clock Kendall and I called on Mr. Tolstikov. Mr. Tolstikov always sees the dire situation. He is very critical of the Chinese. He was the boss of Leningrad. He is a tough, bullet-like guy, friendly and easy to visit with. An hour and a half flew by with his vodka and tea, Russian candies with the big bears on them, two kinds of caviar and a very pleasant conversation. Tolstikov is always suspicious. He thought Morton was here to do something mysterious. I leveled with him and told him exactly whom Morton saw and what he did. I am not sure he believed me, but he passed word through the diplomats that there was some secret motive. On the morning VOA, I heard Mansfield say that Ambassador Bush contacted the Cambodians in Peking. The whole story has now come out through press conferences and statements about our contacts with the Chinese and the Cambodians. I am glad for this because China has blasted the hell out of us, and I think it is important that the U.S. get its side on record.

Bush took eight days before recording his next diary entry, though during this time he composed a lengthy letter to President Ford—transmitted through Brent Scowcroft at the White House, though with Kissinger's knowledge—outlining his thoughts on Washington's political scene as it appeared from his vantage point. Clearly politics—and his own political future—were still very much in Bush's mind, as the ensuing diary entries would demonstrate. Calling himself a "trusted confidant" of the president's, he revealed his view that foreign policy is at its most basic a matter of what is, and is not, politically possible. This is a far cry from the geopolitical strategizing—with domestic politics as an afterthought or an impediment to be surmounted—that Kissinger endorsed. As a way to fill in Bush's thinking during this transitional period in American foreign policy, the letter is worth quoting in its entirety:

May 23, 1975
For: The President
From: George Bush
Thru: General Scowcroft Only
Brent, please pass the following to the President. I hope it will be shared only with secstate and not rpt not be passed to NSC staff or department. It is pure politics, but I feel strongly about it.

Dear Mr. President: After talking to Rog Morton when he was out here about domestic politics, I have a better feel for what is happening at home. It is his impression and mine that there is little focus in the US on the political aspects of our trip to China.

The Taiwan issue is on the back burner right now as it relates to domestic politics. I am very concerned that as your trip to China approaches this will change dramatically. Your own personal interests dictate that serious thought be given to what is possible rpt possible from a purely political standpoint.

Answers to the Taiwan question that may have been possible before the collapse in Cambodia and Vietnam may no longer be any answers at all. I would strongly suggest the following:

An in-depth poll be taken to measure public opinion on various solutions to the Taiwan question (the last poll, I believe, was by Gallup late last year). The poll should probe into opinion of conservatives and liberals and should sound out attitudes towards various solutions. Obviously this polling should be done in great confidence and commissioned by outside sources.

An in-depth research job be done on what the conservatives in the US have said and are likely to say on this issue. A similar study should be undertaken on what the leading democrats have been saying. N.B.: It seems to me that your political problems arising from this issue are quite different pre–GOP convention compared to post–GOP convention.

Thought be given as to how to keep this issue from building into a major weapon for your opponents be they Republican or Democrat. Some will try to paint a China visit without a final solution to Taiwan as a diplomatic failure, an inability to solve the tough problems. Others, particularly the right wing, will soon start criticizing the visit itself and will be on guard to immediately criticize any concessions as a sell-out of Taiwan.

In this communication I am not attempting to go into the foreign policy merits of China options. I firmly believe, however, that your coming to Peking this year, whatever the concrete results, is the right thing to do. What is done at this stage to assess the politics of the visit should be separate from the foreign policy machinery and not in any way inhibit the thinking and planning which undoubtedly is going forward at the State Department and NSC. I am suggesting that a trusted confidant who would not be involved with this planning be encouraged to think out the domestic political implications of your China visit.

I have already discussed with the State Department my concern that work need be done fairly soon to minimize expectations. Many journalists are saying "the President can't possibly go to China without solving the Taiwan problem." It is to your advantage to have this talk dampened, so that expectations be realistic not euphoric and that a visit that does not solve the big Taiwan problem will not, post facto, be considered a diplomatic failure.

Pardon my intrusion on your busy schedule. But, based on my own political past, I worry that this issue can build into a political nightmare unless a lot of pure political thought gets into it soon.

Barbara and I are happy out here. We feel we are most fortunate to be in this fascinating job in this fascinating land.

Warmest regards to Betty.

Sincerely,

George

The diary resumes.

[Monday,] May 26, 1975.   The Blakes went to the commune. Bar, the Blakes and I went to lunch with Phil Jessup, Jr. and his Australian wife, both here from Indonesia.[61] Harland's family is gone —a very pleasant guy. I took Bar to the airport to catch the Air France 175 leaving at 6:20 p.m.[62] Fred immediately went into a total blue funk. We had a reception for the track team so I had to leave Bar a little early at the airport. The track team was made up of gigantic athletes, darn pleasant. Debra Sapenter from Prairie View

---

[61]Robert and Marion Blake of Lubbock, Texas, were early political supporters of Bush. Philip Jessup Jr. was managing director of International Nickel in Indonesia. His father, Philip Jessup Sr., had been one of the leading American diplomats and international law scholars of the 1940s, a close adviser to Secretary of State Dean Acheson. He was appointed ambassador to the U.N. by President Harry Truman in 1951. Senator Joseph McCarthy stalled his candidacy, however, smearing Jessup with false accusations of Communist sympathies. He assumed the U.N. post on an interim basis, but by 1960 he had returned to the teaching of law.

[62]Barbara Bush returned home to attend Marvin Bush's high school graduation.

came and presented a tray for Bar and a plaque for me from Prairie View.[63] Dr. Al Thomas.[64] I was impressed with the orderliness of the group. They did not drink too much. Some of the blacks got off and watched the television and others joined them. All in all it was a good reception. I took the Blakes over for a jiaozi dinner in the park—not my favorite place although the jiaozis were much better than the food we had before.

Tuesday, May 27[, 1975]. John Holdridge departed. We all trooped out to the airport at 12:40 to see him off, leaving the Blakes alone at the house. There has been a massive turnover in the staff, but I am convinced that we are getting a lot of good new people for USLO. Harry Thayer will do just fine. Bill Thomas has taken over nicely. Jerry Levesque in administration going great. We will miss Don Anderson in political, but I understand the new guy will do alright too. Horowitz leaves the next morning, Wednesday, May 28. Went to the first track meet at 3:00 p.m. It was a first-class show, and I felt real pride as the Americans tore around that track. They jumped to big leads on all the footraces. They did lose in the final analysis some of the women's weight events, the javelin throw, women's discus and the men's shot put. But the track team conducted themselves great. I often thought it would be fun to win a lot, and I would have the same grace in victory they showed. They handled it very well. They were gracious although not condescending to the Chinese. Bob Giegengack, the old Yale coach, was here and he did a first-class job.[65] Joe Scalzo, the head of the AAU [Amateur Athletic Union], was a disaster.[66] He sat talking about friendship in the most platitudinous, almost condescending, way

[63]Debra Sapenter won the silver medal in the 1976 Olympics, competing for the United States in the 4 × 400 meter relay. She attended Prairie View A&M University, a historically black college located outside Houston.

[64]Alan Thomas also worked and taught at Prairie View A&M.

[65]Robert Giegengack coached at Yale from 1946 to 1972 and was also head coach of the United States Olympic track team in 1964.

[66]Originally a wrestler, Joseph Scalzo became president of the national AAU in 1973.

the whole time. He didn't seem to know a hell of a lot about track, but he was a master of the platitude on friendship, and I later learned that he had been a disaster on most of the trip. In fact, the staff were kind of joking about him the whole time.[67] Sometimes the man brings stature to the job and sometimes the job brings stature to the man. I don't know how big a job this is, but it certainly is bringing stature to a funny little guy. Pleasant enough man, but ineffective as he could be, I thought, in terms of this mission. That evening we had 30 tennis enthusiasts including De, Wang, Luo, Fei and Qi to our house—the first time they had come. Te, the youngest of the players, sat glued with his eyes popping out of his head, watching the Laver-Connors match.[68] It was a big, successful evening. Fred ate too much cheese and then refused to eat anything else. Only now on Friday as I dictate this is he beginning to eat.

Exchanges like the one with the track team really do some good. There were some 50 or 60 thousand people in the stadium, tons of PLA and Navy. The first day we all marched down—the so-called leaders—with the sports minister and others onto the field in a pouring rain, shaking hands. The friendship march came in with the hands held high. A lot of [that] kind of ceremony in the beginning with music and no speeches, fortunately. And I am sure that with about 120,000 in two days, maybe about 160,000, seeing our athletes, that it made a real impression.[69] At this time of the year

[67]"If the number of chaperones seemed excessive," wrote Bill Shirley, sports editor of the *Los Angeles Times,* who was along on the trip, "it probably was. But this was no ordinary trip. For the first time, the AAU selected athletes for their deportment, as well as skill and availability." He further noted that "all the speech making was done by Scalzo, a former wrestler who became known as 'smiling Joe' and whose pronouncements, it was suggested by one irreverent AAU man, sounded like remedial reading."

[68]Rod Laver and Jimmy Connors competed on the professional tennis tour in 1975. Both had taken part in the first million-dollar staged-for-television tournament earlier that year, after Connors had defeated Laver in February for a $100,000 purse.

[69]In their final write-up of the event, the USLO praised their team's sportsmanship but added, "Perhaps more graphic in the minds of the Chinese specta-

the climate can be harsh. There is a bronchial disorder around—ups and downs. People get hit and hit hard, even though the weather is generally very good at this time of year. Unusual and it does make it a "hardship post."

Miscellaneous. I like this idea of clapping for oneself. It is not a bad custom. It is hard to get used to as somebody does something or says something and stands up there clapping. But it is kind of interesting. Tennis group left at about 8:30—successful evening, cheese and wine. Kendalls and others brought us a lot of cheese and it is really a great thing to have. Horowitzes got off on May 28 early in the morning on the Trans-Siberian.[70] It is a marvelous ceremony. The cars are very pretty—bright mahogany inside, polished, two to a room with a little lavatory in between. Toilets at the end of the hall. Old-fashioned cars, looked like they were built around 1900 but apparently they go well and the five-day trip to Moscow is a delight. Everybody takes along his own food to get through Outer Mongolia and also through Russia. Women are not permitted by the British Embassy, and it is true by us, to ride alone on that train. A lot of the Russians get drunk and unruly I am told.

[Wednesday,] May 28[, 1975]. Dr. Watson [arrived] from the State Department.[71] One of the things we take for granted at home is medical care. Here we try to set up some contact with the Chinese but Watson was unsuccessful. The Chinese are unwilling to discuss the kind of things that we need. We have no one to refer to for general disorders. We thought we could have a contact point with a good English-speaking doctor, but that is impossible to set

---

tors . . . was the graphic display of American power, as our athletes won event after event. . . . As one Western diplomat stationed in Peking put it, the track and field team's visit was far more effective propaganda for the superpower role of the United States than any number of military operations remote from China's border."

[70]The Trans-Siberian Railroad connected Moscow and Vladivostok, with a connector line to Beijing. Bush's children Neil, Dorothy, and Marvin would take this trip later that summer.

[71]Dr. William Watson had been invited by Bush to inspect the USLO's medical facilities.

up. The Chinese have such a situation in Washington, but here no. It is just one example of the enormous difference. Some of the embassies have doctors—the Czechs, the Germans, the Australians, the Canadians. Their doctors look after their own people and are willing to help out others, but there is no instant referral service. There is no discussing patients once they are in hospital with outside consultations, and the Chinese hold us off on this just like they do on many, many other things. The Czech ambassador is very nice and offered to have the Czech doctor look after me if I got sick. Some didn't want to do this, worried about communist infiltration I guess, but I'm certainly going to keep it in mind. Watson seemed to think the guy had a very good dispensary over there. The second day of the track meet the weather was much better. There was a high wind but records were set. The United States runners got so far out in front that it didn't look like a race at all, but the Chinese, struggling to keep up, broke all China records. In the long-distance run two Chinese followed almost a lap behind our runners and both of them broke the Chinese record. Early relaxed dinner on May 28. I am getting very tired. We have had a hectic schedule of visitors, receptions, jumping around from place to place, and guests. You get tired in this community very easily.

Thursday, May 29[, 1975]. Went to the Romanian industrial exhibit. I wish some of these countries would, in something like economic matters or industry, forgo the challenge to slug the anti-imperialists. At the opening of the Romanian trade fair there were so many references to anti-colonialism, anti-imperialism. They are careful about not hitting the U.S. itself, but in some cases the thing is very clear. Had a call from Rog Morton in the States. Came through loud and clear. He is talking about my going back to be in the Cabinet, possibly to be involved in the campaign. God I hope they don't ask me to run that campaign. I had a note from Maurice Stans saying, hear you'll be in the campaign."[72] I don't know what he is talking about. I hope it doesn't come true.

[72]Maurice Stans, a longtime Republican political player, was commerce secre-

I am continually amazed at how hard it is to get close to the Chinese. It is difficult work. I am convinced we see more of them, have better personal relations than others, but you can get just so close and that's it. The doctor experiences were typical, but you visit and push and try to do it in a way respectful to them. You are held at arm's length. They are just determined [not] to let us, or any foreigner in that regard, get too close. It is impossible to pick up the phone, ask somebody over, and have a meaningful discussion about Southeast Asia or Russia or someplace like that. It just can't be done. If they have some business they want to talk to you about, they call you up, but that hasn't happened on any major matters or policy matters for a long time. The Cambodian ship incident could no more be discussed here in detail, trying to explore the other's motives, than fly to the moon. And this is true the way others work. There are disorder problems in China down to the South. Deng Xiaoping is rumored to have gone down there to try to quell some of the disturbances himself, but I don't think this has anything to do with it.[73] It is just this middle kingdom syndrome. We are the foreigners, the barbarians. For polite people they act in very strange and tough ways. No question about it.

---

tary during President Richard Nixon's first term, before resigning to chair the Committee to Re-Elect the President.

[73]Deng made major efforts to overhaul China's weakened industiral economy during this stint in office, focusing in particular on the transportation sector and heavy industries such as steel. He also used the PLA to crack down on ethnic and other social disturbances, most notably in the repression of Shadian, a Muslim village in the far south, where tensions had run high since the late 1960s. However, the Shadian repression—which some experts now estimate led to as many as 1,600 civilian deaths—did not occur until later in the summer of 1975. Thus it is difficult to discern which "disorder problems" Bush refers to in late May. Most likely he means labor unrest, centering in particular on the railway points of Hsu-chou, Nanking, and Nanchang. As historian Roderick MacFarquhar has written, "[Chinese Communist Party vice chairman Wang Hongwen] had been unable to settle leftist-fomented strife in Hangchow. Teng [Deng Xiaoping] simply sent in the PLA and arrested the troublemakers." The broader point is that the USLO believed that underlying tensions continued to roil China beyond Beijing, and that Deng Xiaoping was personally overseeing the government's response.

Lunch on May 29 with Irwin Miller of Cummins, pleasant man.[74]
His wife wants to sightsee. They are here on business. Afternoon
interview with Eddie Wu of the *Baltimore Sun* who left China in
the mid-60s and is back to Peking for the first time since then.[75]
Then an attractive young man, a black fellow named Orde Coombs
from Yale, who is in the Class of 1965, SBT [Sigma Beta Tau],
at Yale.[76] A very attractive guy here with a guardian group, very
much concerned about the deterioration of public schools and education in the U.S. There is no discipline, says he. And it is not just
to be blamed on the war. He really doesn't quite see yet where education in our public schools is going. I was most impressed with
this young man. Return to banquet for the Chinese, given by the
AAU side for the Chinese on May 29 at the International Club. Went
well. Giegengack funny as hell. Talked as he would in an American
banquet. It got out of hand, in that some of our kids got drinking
too much and showing a not particularly good side. We cut off the
maotai and that calmed things down. The banquet was not unruly
in an American sense, but the Chinese are so proper and so precise
that I hope they were not offended by this. That maotai really does
hit a lick. A great big mustached pole vaulter was the only one that
really got out of hand. White guy. Some of the "whale squad"—
hammer throwers and the discus—great big giants came up and had
some pictures taken in the front, but that was all in good humor and
everything went fine. All in all it was a very successful trip in spite
of Scalzo. Tomorrow come the newspaper editors. Spring is a time
for delegations I guess. Our summer schedule will be lighter. We have
had enough guests for a while and now I am ready for family—close
family. I miss them very much. End of May 29.

[74]During the previous year Cummins, Inc., had sold $7 million worth of heavy
industrial trucks to China.

[75]An influential reporter on Asian affairs, Wu had been president of Hong
Kong's Foreign Correspondents Club from 1973 to 1974.

[76]By the late 1970s, Coombs had become a leading author in African American literary circles and a contributing editor to *New York* magazine; he passed away
in 1984 at the age of forty-five.

[Friday, May 30, 1975.] The newspaper editor reception was the key of the day.[77] We had many officials from the China News end of things, including the editor of the *People's Daily*, Mr. Ma from the NCNA [New China News Agency].[78] The editors were to see Deng Xiaoping and were to see Qiao Guanhua—saw him on Saturday actually.[79] The reception was held outdoors—rather pleasant get-together, and after that I had dinner with Creed Black, John Emmerich, Tom Winship of the *Boston Globe* and Mike O'Neill of the *New York Daily News*.[80] It was good to get caught up on how things were going. Little chance to really discuss politics. I had known O'Neill when he was at the United Nations and Emmerich when he was editor of the Houston paper. Knew Tom Winship through Nancy Ellis, and knew Black back in the Washington days.[81]

Saturday the 31st [May 31, 1975]. Marked by the reception of the Tunisian national day. An affair from 12 to 1. Followed by lunch with John Burns and Ada Penegalle from the Italian News Agency. Relaxed lunch here and then tennis later on in the day. Reception at 5:00—showing TV cassette to the Turkish, Brazilian, and Kuwaiti DCM [deputy chief of mission] and Lebanon ambassadors. Great way to entertain. Relaxed early night at home. Long walk for C. Fred who is coming out of his blue funk.

Sunday, June 1[, 1975]. A long bicycle ride down to Lule Chan. All through the Chen Mi. Went into some stores. Bought a soy sauce

[77]The visiting group of American editors was officially known as the China Exchange Committee.
[78]Ma Yuzhen worked for the Ministry of Information.
[79]Bush reported that this meeting with Deng was "on the record," whereas Qiao instructed the editors that they might attribute the information he provided to a "senior foreign ministry official."
[80]Black wrote for the *Philadelphia Inquirer* (and chaired the group), while Emmerich wrote for the *Greenwood (Mississippi) Commonwealth,* having previously worked at the *Baltimore Sun* and as the editorial page editor for the *Houston Chronicle.*
[81]Nancy Ellis is Bush's younger sister. Her son, John Prescott Ellis, wrote for the *Boston Globe* during and after Bush's presidency.

jug, and, I think, a pretty picture for Bar. I like these solitary bicycle rides with her in the middle of town. Some of the streets are so quiet and one keeps thinking about what China was like before, what do these people think and know of their system. You keep hearing examples that they know very little. One man out at the Tombs identified one of our people as American, and a friendly peasant out there kept talking. Finally he said, "no, no" in Chinese, "the Americans wouldn't dare come here." There is no hostility toward Americans that I can feel. After all the propaganda which seems to continue, I just wonder what they really think. There is a tension between the obstructions of getting things done, and the enormous decency and kindness and genuine humor of the people.

Right now many of our observations of the winter have gone by the board. You see couples every night holding hands out near the park. You do see more splashes of color. The Mao suits have gone off and now most of the Chinese wear sports shirts of admittedly all the same color—white or a light bluish. So there is still a sense of sameness, but a sameness with some difference. It is interesting in talking with other ambassadors—they all feel the same in terms of the Chinese holding us at arms length, not willing to give.

There are many rumors going through the diplomatic community that Ford might not come here. If I were starting over I don't think I would schedule a visit right now, but to cancel, that's something else again. There is no discussion that I know of, and I tell them that, but there are a couple of articles, the main one in the *Baltimore Sun* saying, "if the President comes. . . ."[82] These rumors

[82]Ford's expected visit, planned for the end of the year but as yet without clearly defined dates or itineraries, would continue to be a prime topic of conversation for journalists and Beijing's diplomatic community alike. Each wondered, as did Bush, if the president could come to China without having resolved the primary disputes of the day, especially Taiwan, and if a meeting in the absence of such solutions—no matter how cordial or substantive—would be viewed as a defeat. The newspaper editors mentioned above posed this question to Deng Xiaoping, who responded, according to the USLO's report on the meeting, that the PRC would "welcome President Ford," but that the "PRC position on Taiwan is well known, and the US must adjust to this."

fly through the diplomatic corps. There really is not that much substance to work with, so when something like this comes along, they grab at it. Another rumor Saturday was that there was a meeting of the Central Committee of the Party going on. Perhaps that is true. I asked Tolstikov and [he] said, "if such a meeting is going on, it is to deal with the question of labor, women and youth." The big question in politics is now should normalization take place while the existing leaders are in office or should it be delayed. My own view is it depends on whether the Chinese side is willing to compromise at all on "peaceful" [relations].

Sunday. A pleasant day with church, long bicycle ride, quiet lunch with Harry Thayer, a little nap, a very good tennis game—me and Xiao Yong v. Te and Akwei. We won the first set and lost the next two, but it was excellent doubles, and I must have lost five pounds. Then Paul and Louise Miller of the AP, who were in town, came by for a drink.[83] Washed the bicycle, got caught up in a bunch of paperwork, in bed by 9:30—good sleep. End June 1.

Monday, June 2[, 1975]. Steamy at times, rain comes along and clears it off. Not terribly hot in terms of Houston weather. More in terms of Washington, D.C., weather. Reasonably relaxed day. Only an Italian reception in the evening, six to seven. Rushing off at twenty to seven to join the newspaper editors for a mammoth dinner at the Horn of Plenty. The standard for the dinner was $40 a person. When we go out in Peking we usually use 10 yuan which is about $5, but in this dinner there was a bear's paw, there was a special upper lip of a rare animal in Northeast China (not a deer, not a donkey). The Chinese debated at length as to what it was. There was the swallow's nest soup, the bear's paw, the exotic animal, sea slugs and on and on. Far too much food, too many wines—Chinese white, plenty of maotai, beer, juice, all the things a normal dinner has but obviously they get taken on a deal like this. And then Tuesday night, the third, I had to repeat it when Irwin Miller of Cummins Engine

[83]Paul Miller was president of the Gannett Company from 1957 to 1978 and president of the Associated Press from 1963 to 1977.

and his business group had a similar dinner, almost identical. The donkey-like animal wasn't served, but the rest was about the same, and I left bloated. Chinese food is excellent but it doesn't need, in my opinion, to be forced with all these mammoth banquets. One never eats them this big when out-of-town visitors are not here.

The diplomatic community is interesting. Many of the Europeans are blasé, tired and look down on the Chinese. It burns me up. Many of them, and many others too, go away for most of the summer. Most of the embassies go on summer schedules, when they don't work in the afternoons or only an hour or so in the afternoons. The pace changes here, but the U.S. has its laws, and I believe we need a disciplined shop. So on we go although I would like to give people more time off in the summer. The new staff is shaping up well now. We have our own people in most slots and it's going pretty good. No more talk of the ship incident.

The journalists met with Deng Xiaoping on Monday, and he reassured them that Ford was welcome whether there was progress on Taiwan or not, a theme that many journalists in Hong Kong and elsewhere simply don't accept.[84] They are building the President's visit up into a massive "if you don't solve the Taiwan problem, the visit has got to be a failure." I have been urging for a long time that we start knocking this down through the backgrounders etc. I notice there was a Peter Jumpa story in the *Baltimore Sun* that knocked it down. The visit in my view should be hailed as simply a visit to get to know the Chinese leaders. Deng went to Paris.[85]

---

[84]See Bush's entry for June 1, 1975.

[85]Deng, who had lived in France as a student during the 1920s, visited Paris May 12–17, meeting with Prime Minister Jacques Chirac and President Valéry Giscard d'Estaing. Chinese leaders had been particularly hesitant to journey abroad during the Cultural Revolution, fearing the consequences of an absence from the political whirlwind at home. As Joseph Lelyveld of the *New York Times* commented of Deng's trip, "Sometimes it was suggested that Peking was reverting to the practices of the Ming and Ching dynasties when imperial China's concept of a diplomatic exchange was limited to the reception of a tribute mission at the court of the Emperor. Actually, the Chinese leadership was preoccupied with unresolved political issues at home and was stretched too thin to think of venturing abroad."

There were no agreements, no signed communiqués, but he had good talks with Giscard d'Estaing of France. This is the kind of meeting this should be billed as. There are global reasons why it makes sense. Little talk these days of Sihanouk. His mimeograph machine is broken and here he is supposedly in Pyongyang, North Korea, when Kim Il Sung is traveling in Europe—very weird. The Chinese must be getting very concerned about Sihanouk's role. Marcos of the Philippines is coming soon.[86] He is making anti-American noises. He must protect his flank. There was a story in the papers about a Chinese diplomat in Canada involved in smuggling money to an American.[87] Reuters published it practically on the eve of the Marcos visit. That will upset Marcos enormously because the Chinese should not be feeding money to the Philippine insurgents. The same problem exists in Indonesia. China calls it "supporting" not "exporting" revolution.

I worry about the discipline of the United States compared to this place. The papers are full of the schools' problems and the Friendship Day in the United States where a guy got ice-picked. China is rigid in their discipline. They haul people out and they shoot them, like the guy that hit the French lady with a cleaver a while back.[88] I noticed in Saigon they are doing the same thing. That's not the answer, but nor is this total permissiveness that we get. One gets a very different view of his country when he lives abroad and lives in this, the most cloistered, enclosed society in existence.

[86]President Ferdinand Marcos of the Philippines visited China, and met with Mao, June 7–11, during which time the two nations announced the establishment of formal diplomatic relations. Manila simultaneously broke off formal relations with Taiwan. Many commentators agreed with Bush that such moves, in the wake of Saigon's fall, could be traced to Washington's weakened global position. Kenneth Crawford commented in the *Los Angeles Times* that the Philippines "is leaning hard to the left out of the perceived necessity of getting on with China and its friends. . . . There can be no doubt that American prestige is taking a beating around the world."

[87]The Chinese diplomat was accused of funneling money to Muslim Filipino insurgents intent on undermining the Marcos regime.

[88]See my footnote to the entry for March 23, 1975.

| CHAPTER SEVEN |

"There Is No Credit in This Work"

June 3 to July 4, 1975

*B*ush spent June in Beijing, enjoying a visit from his children and preparing for the moment that would epitomize his diplomatic style while in China: the massive Independence Day party he co-ordinated for Beijing's diplomatic corps at the USLO. Previous July Fourth celebrations had been understated affairs, for fear of offending Chinese sensibilities. That year Bush invited China's leading diplomats to his residence for a staid, formal celebration on July 3. But the next day he threw the gates of the USLO open for a picnic, complete with bunting, balloons, hot dogs (and buns imported with the State Department's aid), Coca-Cola, and raffles. The purpose was to show off American values, he told his journal. "We had American flags around and I am confident it conveyed the right kind of impression about our country."

With much of the city's diplomatic corps away for the summer, this was a particularly quiet period in Bush's tenure in China, and in the diary itself. "Still quiet on the diplomatic front," he noted in late June. Family and friends visited, and he saw more of Beijing and outlying areas. With the fall of Saigon no longer dominating the headlines, Bush found more time to consider Beijing's broader public stance toward Washington and the West, and increasingly he did not like what he saw. "I remain convinced that China is making a big mistake in continuing to thrash away at us," he told his diary. Every day seemed to bring more rhetorical assaults, even as the few Chinese leaders he managed to see during these weeks re-

peated warm overtures for better relations. "The experts say [of the fiery rhetoric], 'well it's less than they used to do,'" he noted, "'and you've got to understand they need to put out rhetoric,' and some of that is true. But it is a funny way to show a desire for better relations. And I get fed up with it right up to the teeth." Bush considered consistency of private and public diplomacy a priority. He had clashed with the Machiavellian Kissinger, in large part because of the latter's penchant for secret dealings and diplomatic double-talk. He found Chinese rhetorical assaults frustrating, and they reinforced his own desire, if ever afforded the chance, to speak his diplomacy clearly, loudly, and with a singular message. "In essence they say 'look at what we do, not at what we say.' They feel they must keep their Third World leadership by slugging us all the time. But I can just imagine how they'd feel if an official government organ took after them the way they take after us all the time."

It is difficult to read Bush's diary from these weeks without sensing his growing frustration with this job, and with his own limited place within Washington's decisionmaking circles. He feared that American public opinion might turn against Beijing if its rhetorical attacks ever drew the full attention of the American media, but at the end of the day his inability to improve his personal contacts with the Chinese increased his own sense that the power to change the dynamic was not yet his. "It is hard doing anything about dispelling that mistrust with the contacts as restricted as they are, and with Washington holding their cards as close to the chest as Washington does."

Tuesday, June 3[, 1975]. Lunch at the residence for some of our new security guards and communicators. The Acquavellas, the Konopiks, and our new security chief Evans Dewire.[1] Nice young people—the ones that had their wives along, both married to oriental wives—one Hawaiian, one Japanese. They seemed to be adjusted. Mo [Morin] put in a beautiful new stereo set downstairs for

---

[1]Joseph Acquavella, in Beijing with his wife, Susan, was a communications specialist. Immediately before his retirement from the foreign service he served as director of the Diplomatic Telecommunications Program Office.

the residence and the music is unbelievably great here. It makes a real difference. Fills every corner of the room. Indeed the residence is looking very nice.

Tuesday afternoon I went down to the banner shop to get a welcoming banner; bright red with gold characters, for Neil Mallon.[2] He is 80 years young and we had an appropriate Mao quotation to present it to him. They sew on the characters individually—price about 15 kuai I am told. After that went to the hospital to get my card for the swimming. You line up and it is a real madhouse. What you need to get is a fluoroscope of your chest and pay some dough, but by the time you get through doing all this it is amazing. We waited and waited for the fluoroscope guy. Finally there were about six of us standing there so he put us all in together. Steve Fitzgerald, the ambassador, said, "OK everybody take off your shirts." So I joined in the fun and started to do it and so did he. Jennifer Fitzgerald knew it was a joke but some young French girl or German girl, who only spoke a little English, started to unbutton her shirt. Then she said, "No, I've been here before. You don't have to do this." She finally realized we were giving her the big yak. The hospital, helped built by the Rockefellers years ago, is rather attractive.[3] The hallways are clean and it looks no better and no worse than most American hospitals. I am glad to know how to get there in case we have some emergency. There was a lot of turmoil with foreign kids running around, pushing in, and I think the Chinese sometimes are awfully patient.

My stamp collection hobby seems to have screeched to a halt. Though stamps are missing, I can't find out how to get new ones. They are very complicated.

[2]Henry Neil Mallon, a longtime family friend and a classmate of Prescott Bush, had provided Bush with career advice and counseling since his initial days in the Texas business community. It was Mallon, for example, who first offered Bush the opportunity to explore the oil fields near Odessa, Texas. Bush named his son, Neil, after Mallon.

[3]The Rockefeller Foundation had purchased the Union Medical College in Beijing (founded by Protestant missionaries in 1906) to house their own China Medical Board for medical instruction. The complex and medical school were both nationalized after the 1949 revolution.

I brought home a picture for Bar from Lilly Chan. It is hanging in the hall. Has young chickens in yellow, painted by the Shanghai normal school teacher. I think she will like it.

Hot water is being tested—will come back on on schedule on the 6th. Everyone was told to leave the water off. Little Katie Rope fooling around with the bidet left the water tap open—sure enough water came in under great pressure—flooded the bidet—flooded the floor in their apartment and flooded the place below.[4] Fortunately, it was an American apartment. It happens every year, says Mo, resignedly.

I feel a genuine affection for Mr. Guo; Mr. Wang to some degree; Sun the cook; Zhong the young guy, and Mrs. Tang, our teacher. Also Mr. Liu in the office. They are so decent and refined, quiet and wonderful and helpful. And I think they know that we appreciate them. Mrs. Tang made some reference in our language lesson about leaving in 1977, and she really sounded kind of sorry about it. After eight months, it is inevitable to get attached.

There are some rumors about going back and doing something. If I did go back, I'd much prefer to have some kind of a cabinet post that would give me time for campaigning but have some substance, rather than just be involved in the campaign. But there is Mel Laird holding the behind-the-scenes press conference, saying, "Well we'll keep Bush on till after the convention. He's a good man at getting delegates." Kind of the master's voice behind the scenes. I've never understood this Machiavellian side of Laird. I like him, but I've never felt close to him. And I suppose I wouldn't be human if I didn't say I felt his hand in the VP situation very clearly and coolly. But I felt it on the back, not on the front. Bemis, Lias and Devine had a meeting regarding my political future—very thoughtful of them.[5]

All I know now is to do the best job one can here. There is no credit in this work, but I think it is an accumulative thing, and you've got to keep digging. I've tried to give the right impression of America here—not too formal. We have a good, organized staff;

[4]The reference is to the daughter of the USLO's William Rope.
[5]Thomas Lias had been Bush's special assistant at the Republican National Committee.

tried to move around in the diplomatic community; tried to increase our contacts with the Chinese; tried to have interesting people from the States here; and tried to learn and make suggestions to Washington. Beyond this though, it is hard to "do" anything. And yet I won't trade it for England, Paris or any other posts. The others get more notoriety, and Elliot's publicity is good I think out of England, but I think it is more substantive [here] in one sense and certainly more interesting.[6] A beautiful letter from Jeb about the problems of Columba adjusting, how much he loves her, how marvelous she is, and what she needs is self-confidence.[7] It was a thoughtful, sensitive piece—an attractive kid who has got it all. I just hope he is fully happy because, knowing him and his sensitivity, he would be deeply hurt if she was ever hurt. Henrietta Morris of San Antonio, Texas, nine years in Ambassador Annenberg's office, is here as our secretary.[8] She is awful good. State Department pro, but she is like you, Jane, in that she is willing to take on additional stuff and does it cheerfully and fast.[9] Jennifer adjusted much, much better and is doing a good job too. End of June 3.

Hurray, George arrives tomorrow.[10]

On June 2. Note: Morgan Jacobsen of the East Asiatic Company came.[11] We get a lot of these businessmen dropping in, and I haven't put them on the tape. He is from Denmark but represents American companies like DuPont and others. He goes around to the various corporations and presents the U.S. brochures and helps the fol-

---

[6]Elliot Richardson was at that time serving as Washington's ambassador to the United Kingdom.

[7]Jeb and Columba Bush had married in February 1974 and were living in Houston at the time of this entry.

[8]In the midst of a long career as a publisher and philanthropist, Walter Annenberg served as ambassador to the United Kingdom from 1968 to 1974.

[9]The "Jane" in this sentence remains impossible to identify with complete certainty.

[10]George W. Bush, recently graduated from Harvard Business School, would stay in Beijing for nearly a month.

[11]Founded in 1897, the East Asiatic Company became one of Denmark's largest international trading and shipping firms.

low-up with sales. On June 3 Ambassador Harland brought by Ambassador Lendrum of New Zealand, now their ambassador in Moscow.[12] We talked about the US-PRC-USSR relationship.

Miscellaneous. There is a great misunderstanding. People go back gushing over hospitality and it is awful good, but some of the delegations simply don't get to see what they want. The schistoso-miasis delegation investigating hookworm caused by snails never saw a snail all the time they were in China—at least didn't see snails in the infected areas or see acute patients who had been affected by the disease. They had a feeling there was some politics involved in all of this. The fact remains they never saw an infected snail. The Chinese just didn't want to talk about the "infected areas" and all the scientists felt frustrated. This is the side of things people don't see. Jay Taylor of the State Department can fill me in for the record on this, but the delegation was frustrated time and time again from seeing infected snails. It is Jay's belief that since Chairman Mao vowed in 1957 to get rid of this plague, indeed wrote a poem in support of eradicating schistosomiasis called "Farewell to the God of Plague," that the issue is politicized and that they didn't want these people to see the infected snails.[13] This can be repeated in many, many other fields.

Memorandum for the record. Looking over the wages and salaries paid, embassies who can "afford less" pay a heck of a lot less.[14] But for the record, month's salaries are as follows: Mr. Qian Kang (cook), 300 yuan; Zhang (second cook), 165 a month; Wang Deyi

[12]Previously New Zealand's high commissioner to New Delhi, Brian Lendrum would serve in Moscow from 1974 to 1977.

[13]Mao composed the poem in 1958. Its first stanza reads: "So many green streams and blue hills, but to what avail? / This tiny creature left even Hua To powerless! / Hundreds of villages choked with weeds, men wasted away; / Thousands of homes deserted, ghosts chanted mournfully. / Motionless, by earth I travel eighty thousand li a day, / Surveying the sky I see a myriad Milky Ways from afar. / Should the Cowherd ask tidings of the God of Plague, / Say the same griefs flow down the stream of time."

[14]Bush refers here to salaries paid to Chinese employed by the Diplomatic Services Bureau to staff the USLO.

(our #1 waiter) 280; Mr. Chen (waiter) 180; Zong and Chen (woman worker) our [unintelligible] 150 yuan for a month. Overtime rate appears to be at 1.20 yuan per hour for Chien-Kang and Wan Teh-Yi, .9 per hour for the rest. End of Item.

[Wednesday,] June 4[, 1975].   Visited the flag shop in the morning to see the banner for Neil Mallon. It is all laid out and a lovely quotation from Chairman Mao about the future being in the hands of the young. It will be perfect for Neil—bright red satin with gold fringes and each character individually sewn on—fantastic work and he will love it.

The Chad ambassador came to call. The whole interview was in French. I showed him the TV and he was amazed and obviously liked it. Twelve to one was a reception at the German Embassy for just the Western Europeans and obviously those that Ambassador Pauls felt were "the inside" to meet their new DCM. We had a little going-away lunch for Don Anderson and then that evening George arrived. We played tennis and lost to De and Wang as an opener 6-3, 6-4. George was tired and I played lousy, but it was a good start. Early dinner at the International Club. The only other incident was during the middle of the night our brand new stereo system, beautifully set up and coordinated by Mo, crashed to the floor with the bookshelf giving way. Fred jumping straight up. Fred is glad to have a member of the family here. George went jogging early in the morning.

[Thursday,] June 5, 1975.   The press carries articles by Deng about sweeping—you do not get dust out without using a broom.[15] They might have to use force on Taiwan. The more they keep saying this, the more difficult it is to solve this problem on the part of the United States. Of course this thing was picked up and carried all over the Taiwan papers. And it is just the kind of thing that will

[15]Bush's concerns aside, none of the major American newspapers immediately picked up on Deng's reference to violently "sweeping" out the dust that was the Taipei regime.

hurt at home. We are having a little hassle about an agricultural attaché. Ag wants to send a Champeau here who they tell me would not be acceptable.[16] And then we have got a problem about space, support, apartments, hotels and enormous other complications. My own judgment is it would be good to have somebody here if all these things can be resolved. Don Anderson, head of the political section, is leaving on the 5th. He did a first-class job here. Weather —overcast, cool on the morning of the 5th—very pleasant.

North Vietnam is saying that the United States, under the Paris peace agreements, should put substantial amounts of money into North Vietnam to reconstruct the country.[17] My own judgment is we should do absolutely nothing. Perhaps we should respond to a legitimate request for humanitarian aid, but we must not get involved in economic reconstruction until the rhetoric in Vietnam cools and until the heartache in the United States is healed a little bit. We are not going to buy their friendship by getting into the front line to hand out dough. And in my view we must not take the rather shortsighted action of thinking that we can balance off Russia and China only if we get in now. There will be plenty of opportunities, and I think it would be a big mistake to give aid now.

[16]It is unclear who "they" is in Bush's entry, though it is possible that Harold Champeau's appointment to China posed additional difficulties because he was simultaneously employed by the Department of Agriculture and by the Central Intelligence Agency (CIA) as a Chinese linguist and China specialist. He initially joined the foreign service in 1954, before transferring to Agriculture in 1965, in order to work overseas as an agricultural attaché. He was employed by the CIA from the start.

[17]Article 21 of the Paris Peace Agreement pledged that Washington would "contribute to healing the wounds of war and to postwar reconstruction of the DRV [Democratic Republic of Vietnam]." President Richard Nixon promised to uphold this article in a letter, confirming the intent of Article 21 and offering a specific figure. Two months after Hanoi's victory in 1975, Premier Pham Van Dong, speaking to the Vietnamese National Assembly, invited the United States to normalize relations with Vietnam and to honor its commitment to provide reconstruction funds. But President Gerald Ford dismissed this suggestion. Ford believed that Hanoi's demand for reparations carried with it a measure of implied guilt over the war, and he considered this politically unacceptable so soon after Saigon's fall.

Called on Ambassador Tschoep of Austria. His predecessor was unhappy and I predict before long he will be unhappy. Some of the Europeans, used to the fine things, simply have trouble adjusting to Peking.

I notice in the EA [East Asian] press review that a Professor Oksenberg of Michigan is stating that the decline in trade might be due to the dissatisfaction with the continued U.S. backing of the ROC [Republic of China].[18] Hogwash! In a previous note I am sure I said that this would be predicted, but it is not true. I am convinced of it, and we keep getting told that by leading trade officials. The more I think of the ship incident, the more I think the Chinese did not really object to our position on it despite the rhetoric.[19]

Don Anderson left. Danish reception. Arabs talking about the Ford-Sadat meeting, the problems in Lebanon.[20] Visit Hong Du Tailors for George to pick up a couple of suits. Mrs. Molinari of Argentina visited to see her rubbings.[21] Tennis party at house to see TV.

Small group came over to see the tennis—Jeff Martinson, young guy from Australia, and Rosa from the Canadian Embassy. This is a marvelous piece of equipment. Friday, Chinese photographer with both a Leicaflex and a Hasselblad came out to take my picture and Harry Thayer's.[22] At 11:00 in the morning Harry and I made a call on Lin Ping, director of the American and Oceanic Department.[23] He is considered cold but he has been pretty nice to

[18]As a senior adviser on the National Security Council from 1977 to 1980, Michel Oksenberg later played a central role in establishing formal relations between Beijing and Washington.

[19]Bush refers here to the *Mayagüez* incident, discussed in greater detail in the previous chapter.

[20]President Ford met with Egyptian President Anwar Sadat in early June 1975; the meeting was interpreted by many as a crucial step in the Middle East peace process.

[21]Maureen Molinari was the wife of Carlos Molinari, an attaché at the Argentine embassy. She had been particularly close to Ambassador and Mrs. David Bruce.

[22]Leicaflex and Hasselblad are two brands of camera.

[23]Bush refers here to the Americas and Oceanic Department of the Chinese Foreign Ministry.

me. A lady interpreter, Madame Zhong, does an excellent job. The only substantive question was when Lin Ping asked how the President's trip in Europe had gone.[24] The Chinese are continually talking about Europe, and our interest in seeing us keep up our defenses. Deng Xiaoping, in going to Paris, talked about a strong Europe and kept talking about the Russian threat.[25]

In the afternoon, we went to the Chinese v. Japan weightlifting in a gym on the south side of town near where they had the tennis game. Mr. Zhou and Mr. Ni, both of whom squired the track team around, were presiding officers. The weightlifting all starts the same way with flag, marching, and pinning up friendship awards and then trying to do their thing. They have excellent automated electric equipment, the same as in the track. They gave the coach in track an electric starting block that he claimed was as good as anything he'd ever seen. And here they had all kinds of electronic judging and everything else.

Went to Swedish national day where I had a discussion with Ambassador of Norway. His view was that the Chinese would agree against infiltration if we did something on Taiwan. Dinner at the residence. That soup and noodles dish. Henrietta, Jennifer, George Jr. and Harry Thayer, and then to the spectacular outdoor acrobatic performance at the Workers Park in the Forbidden City. It was the most romantic setting. It was warm, swallows flying around just before the sunset. The rooflines in that part of the Workers Park are fantastic. It is an unbelievable setting for a performance and the acrobats were amazing. Scrambling up poles upside down, the big furry dogs looking almost real, the magicians, the bird callers, the plate spinners, the colors—the whole thing was just great. The place was full—perhaps 3,000 people crowded into an open-air amphitheater. We sat right in front of a big contingent of PLA soldiers

---

[24]On May 28 President Ford traveled to Europe to attend a NATO summit meeting.

[25]Deng had in fact caused a minor stir during his Paris trip when he termed conflict between the Soviet Union and China not only possible but "inevitable."

and when the mimic did the sounds of cannons and guns I must say it gave me a very weird feeling. A baby right behind us loved the dogs and the parents were very friendly. One other group, a friendship group, probably from Canada, was there. The Chinese are caught up on this Friendship thing and they have got to cater to their Mao constituency; but they don't want to overdo it. A great evening.

Saturday, June 7[, 1975]. Called on Xiao Bei, the deputy director of the information department, and also the deputy director of the MFA [Ministry of Foreign Affairs] Consular Department. Followed by call on Xu Huang, the director of the Domestic Service Bureau [Diplomatic Services Bureau]. Mallons to arrive today. Middle of June 7. The calls went well. Xu Huang I think understands that we at the USLO try to treat the servants and others furnished by DSB with respect. His English is good, he is a jovial man and pleasant. The talk[s] with the Deputy Director of the Consular Department, and on Xiao Bei, were good—nothing new out of them. The consular man had been in his job twenty years and we know very little about him. This whole question of reuniting families and of people coming to China and going from China is very complicated. They hold their cards awful close. Tennis in the afternoon with the Swede Laenhofen and Finocchi of Italy. The match was disrupted by rain and we went inside, a rather pleasant arrangement. Went to the Australian reception for their Minister of Foreign Affairs, and then the Mallons arrived.[26] We went to bed early. They were dead tired.

Sunday [June 8, 1975]. The Wall again and the Tombs, a beautiful place, and the Ding Ling Tomb, Jennifer and Henrietta providing great food—sliced ham, sliced turkey, etc. for many people. Tennis in the afternoon. George and I beating Sri Navas and Finocchi, and then Finocchi and Wang. Dinner with the Mallons at the International Club.

---

[26]Donald Reginald Willesee served as Australia's foreign affairs minister from 1973 to 1975.

Marcos is here and the red news of Sunday, June 8, is full of a lot of nasty anti-U.S. stuff.[27] The Philippines having to regroup, feel they must take a slug at the United States while in China. The red news also talked about U.S. unemployment, a subtle suggestion that we were decadent and falling apart.[28] Chinese warning the Philippines about one superpower coming in the back door, while the other was in the front. Two articles on North and South Vietnam, and all in all, it is not a very happy piece of paper. But it is accurately reflective of the problems we are undergoing here. I go through varying opinions of what China wants with us. In essence they say, "Look at what we do, not at what we say." They feel they must keep their Third World leadership by slugging us all the time. But I can just imagine how they'd feel if an official government organ took after them the way they take after us all the time. They apparently don't think about that. They continue to slam us around, not as much as they used to obviously, and the China specialists will say less than they might. But I say they are doing it too much, because I worry more about American public opinion than some of our China specialists, and the public opinion's effect on our being able to perform and fulfill a policy. I think China needs us as much, and quite definitely more, than we need them. But I do think there is a basic mistrust of the United States after all these years, and it bothers me. It is hard doing anything about dispelling that mistrust with the contacts as restricted as they are, and with Washington holding their cards as close to the chest as Washington does. End of June 8.

[Monday,] June 9[, 1975].   Still and hot. Great for tennis, but the Club is closed on Mondays. Mallons off sightseeing, discussion

[27]President Ferdinand Marcos of the Philippines arrived to formally establish diplomatic relations between his country and China.

[28]In May 1975, U.S. unemployment neared 9 percent, the highest total since the Great Depression, prompting President Ford to recommend extension of unemployment compensation benefits.

of whether I will get to see Romulo.[29] He apparently wants to see me (cable) but it may be difficult.

Had a beautiful Peking duck dinner at the Sick Duck after visiting the Summer Palace in the afternoon. We had a banner made for Neil with a marvelous quotation from Chairman Mao. It goes like this:

> The world is yours as well as ours, but in the last analysis it is yours. You young people, full of vigor and vitality, are in the bloom of life. Like the sun at 8 or 9 in the morning. Our hope is placed in you.
>
> —Talk at a meeting of Chinese students
> and trainees in Moscow,
> November 17, 1957

The banner is in bright red with gold tassels and all in Chinese characters. I think Neil really liked it. Philippines cemented relations with China. I talked to a Philippines TV guy out at the airport on June 10 and he said, "Of course we'll continued to be friends with the United States, but now it looks like we've got this all-Asian unity thing." He was a young kid, somewhat confused by what was happening. Supporting the decision, wanting to stay friends with us, sore at the way some of the United States people were abusive, but he had many, many United States friends that he loved. Clearly a dilemma.

Tuesday, June 10[, 1975]. The Somalia Ambassador came to see me. He was all upset about some criticism in the United States Senate about Somalia having Russian ships in there.[30] He felt it perfectly OK to criticize the United States about Diego Garcia, colo-

---

[29]Carlos Peña Romulo, the Filipino foreign minister, was in Beijing for Marcos's visit.

[30]Defense Secretary James Schlesinger had recently accused the Soviet Union of constructing a military base, housing antiship missiles, near the Somali port of Berbera. The Ford administration used this development as justification for its own construction of a large military base on Diego Garcia, a British-controlled island outpost in the Indian Ocean. Somali Ambassador Ahmed Mohammed Darman, in Beijing, termed the American allegation "a pack of lies."

nialism etc., but he didn't quite understand why some senator would criticize Somalia. I believe in working closely with these guys, and now I am determined to get more contacts with them. But it is difficult.

Romulo could not see me. I am sure it simply could not be arranged without throwing up some doubts with the Chinese. Lunch at the residence. Bar came in dead tired after 26 hours on the plane—looking great though and bringing lots of news from the States. Mallons still here. Tennis in the afternoon. Hot and windy. Fred took a bath and left a ring an inch thick in the tub but he is much less dirty than he is in the winter. Dinner at the residence. End of June 10.

[Wednesday,] June 11[, 1975]. A relaxed day. Work at the office. Barbara showed the Mallons around. Lunch at the residence. Fantastic tennis game with Te and Wang and dinner at the International Club. I am firing off a cable requesting consultations and desire to visit with Haig and David Bruce.[31] The Deng interview

[31]Alexander Haig was then serving as supreme allied commander Europe (SACEUR), a position he held from 1974 to 1979. Bruce was Washington's ambassador to NATO at the same time. On June 12 Bush cabled Kissinger, asking for consultations in Washington. He hoped to combine the trip with not only a stopover in Europe to see Bruce and Haig but also several weeks of vacation at home, noting the opportunity "to discuss with EA and NSC people USLO's thinking on your visit and the President's visit." Kissinger granted this request. Of course, it was within his power to order Bush to remain in Beijing, a point Bush well recognized. "If this idea [of a consultation] makes sense to you I want to assure you I will not be beating on your door trying to wedge in for an appointment. I think my main contribution can be in chatting with Scowcroft, Habib, Lord, Gleysteen, Solomon and others, and I expect you will be pretty well tied up with USSR matters at that time. If this timing for consultations seems awkward please advise, though if you are agreeable to my leaving China then I still would like to travel to the US for a couple of weeks in August for a vacation, which I would be prepared to do at my own expense."

Events would keep Bush from returning home until the last week of August, and his trip would be far shorter than he had originally hoped, leaving no time for his annual vacation in Kennebunkport, Maine. These events are described below.

seemed to me to take some of the pressure off the President's visit, suggesting that he not have to solve this problem during his visit here.[32]

Bar's birthday the 8th, my 51st on the 12th. My legs feel older. Good God isn't it awful to get old, but I don't feel old. I am missing about a quarter or half step on the tennis court though. I enjoy chatting with the girl in the carpet and wall hanging end of the USLO. She is very attractive. She is studying English and you can see how these people, if they fix themselves up, can be extremely beautiful. The old man in that department couldn't be more agreeable. Most of the Chinese we get close to on a personal basis are extremely friendly. But there is still a wariness about us foreigners. End June 11.

[Thursday,] June 12[, 1975]. Doro, Marvin and Neil arrived along with a small industry delegation.[33] They looked great, giggling, bubbling over with enthusiasm—having enjoyed Honolulu, tired, not seen anything of Tokyo, only one night there and into Peking.[34] They were great. They rushed down and played basketball, rode down to the Great Square. Marvin played tennis with Te and then off we went to the soup restaurant where we had eel and they all loved that. Neil Mallon bought the dinner and it was all pretty good.

---

[32]"I had been worried about a big build-up in the press to the effect that if the President came to China and did not solve the Taiwan question the trip would be a disaster for him and for the US/PRC relationship," Bush privately wrote Kissinger. "I would love to find the correct formula so that full diplomatic relations between the USA and the PRC can be accomplished when the President comes here. I do think we must continue to ask, 'what's in it for the USA,' and the President must not be in a position of getting clobbered from his right. We are working on some ideas here that might be helpful."

[33]As mentioned in my footnote to the entry for May 27, 1975, these were three of Bush's children, who would spend several weeks in China.

[34]Whereas Barbara Bush had returned to China directly, the Bush children first traveled to Houston to see their brother Jeb and then stopped off in Hawaii on the way to Beijing.

The board at the International Airport is amazing. The departure board, all electronic, spins out such exotic names as Pyongyang–Korean Airlines, Hanoi–CAAC Airlines. And as you watch the delegations come and go it is fantastic. You see the cadres dressed in their finely tailored Mao suits, very rigid contrast to the plebian dress of the masses, and actually I saw on one delegation several pale pink, green and yellow dresses along the lines of those that were modeled in the store last year. But these people were all getting on the plane and leaving China, not staying. When Neil Mallon got on the plane on the 13th, two big delegations were out there. Several honored guests, one of them headed by a rather senior-looking PLA type.

Riding out in the morning I am impressed by the early-morning park activities. Families, studying, exercises for one another, tremendous activity, lots of bikes parked in front of the park from 5:30 on. Yelling along with the martial arts. Jumping around on tai chi chuan. Jogging on the roads, staying fit. It is hotter now so the early-morning activity means more. Climate in Peking is nice but it is harsh. New visitors get tired easily, come down with colds, bronchial stuff —not as much with the coal burning now though. Their air is a little cleaner and Fred stays cleaner longer. Good symbols of that.

The red and blue news playing up the Schlesinger charge about Berbera in Somalia being a Russian base with missiles.[35] I am sure this concerns the Chinese tremendously. They are damn sure concerned about what's happening in Vietnam. They are, I am sure, very concerned about Cambodia. In fact it has been quiet with Sihanouk apparently still in North Korea. Weird silence. The Chinese probably wondering whether they bet on the wrong horse. Cabled Kissinger asking for consultations in the States. Perhaps going by to see Haig and Bruce about NATO. I think that would be helpful to the Chinese to do that. It's been a long period without any substantive discussion with the Foreign Minister. End June 12—51st birthday—Wow!

[35]See Bush's entry and my footnote for June 10, 1975.

[Friday,] June 13[, 1975]. Ambassador from Laos comes over.[36] Half tennis, half diplomacy.[37] Ambassador Clement of Cameroon —how does he get his films from the United States over here? Lunch with Judge Weigel.[38] The judge has been shown all over China as a guest of China Travel. These visas work in mysterious and strange ways. I read in one of the Xinhua News that Vietnam is saying, "Yes we can give them aid, etc." Very graciously willing to take it. And then later on they say, unless we give them aid, they will not account for our Missing-in-Action. They play a strong, tough, dirty, filthy game. In the United States and certainly in the diplomatic community in Peking, there doesn't seem to be an outcry against this kind of thing. There is a prevalent feeling here as the Peruvian ambassador expressed it to Bar that the United States should be doing more for the Third World. It was a theme that we heard at the United Nations, but it is escalated now and it is particularly prevalent here. Laos Ambassador, with his country moving steadily to the left, kicking the rightists out; communist troops taking over most of the communities; cabinet move to the far left. This poor ambassador here, a most delightful fellow—Lien—tells me there is really no change, that we are welcome, that everything is OK. Our school teacher is being interrogated, our aid mission is being bombarded and harassed, people are being held captives, and darn it there is such a thing as a domino theory.

[36]Phagna Lien Pravongiengkam met with Bush to discuss his future posting to Washington (where he had previously served for three years). The French-educated ambassador wanted the assignment, but, with Laotian politics uncertain at the time, he thought that a positive endorsement from the State Department might help his cause. "He's an intelligent, capable guy," Bush wrote home, "who seems very well disposed to us and if given half a chance would represent his government in Washington far more effectively than a Pathet Lao."

[37]"Sports is a great equalizer," Bush maintained. "If you know people and can relax with people, then maybe you can head off a crisis that you couldn't head off with people you'd only met at a reception."

[38]Stanley Weigel served on the U.S. District Court for the Northern District of California. In 1972 he had ordered the desegregation of San Francisco schools by transportation.

Went to call on the Ambassador of France, Claude Arnaud. He had a couple of little children running around on bicycles through a lovely French embassy. Quite a change and rather nice. Patrick, age 2, and a baby, age 9 months. Mrs. Arnaud had been married to one of the Cabinet officers in Laos who had been forced to flee the country that very week. She is a beautiful person.

Cocktail party at the Bulaks of Turkey. The diplomatic corps is being given a free trip on Swissair to Europe and half the corps is bailing out on this plane.

[Saturday,] June 14, 1975. Good tennis at the club with the boys. Hot now, but when the wind isn't up, it's fantastic. That afternoon a stiffly hot reception at the British Embassy for their national day. Toasts to the queen, then Minister Lei Jiang, the Minister of Trade, made a few remarks. Teddy Youde toasted the health of Chairman Mao, etc. They have a beautiful large residence—embassy with pool and courts, separated by a walk that goes into the Indian Embassy. The whole thing is rather nice. Then to the New Zealand Embassy to meet their Minister of Trade. They opened their swimming pool so we all went back, suited up and came back and dove into the clear cold water. It was very nice.

Sunday, June 15[, 1975]. Church. Visit to the tailors to get the kids suited up—about $70. Then Ambassador Small and his family came for lunch, bowling, a little wine drinking—carpet bowling in the house. Then at the International Club lunch. Tennis was indoors that afternoon because the weather is bad. Marvin threw his racquet which really burned me up with the Chinese all watching. Sportsmanship and that kind of thing mean so much more here. We joke about friendship first here a little bit, but carefully. But it is an important concept and I ate him out for the display, much like what I might have had when I was his age—but he should be getting over that. Actually he is doing darn well—in his work and from reports from the Congress job he had—the reports were fantastic.

Monday, the 16th [June 16, 1975]. Ambassador Paludan of Denmark came to visit me. We reviewed Southeast Asia. My view at this juncture is that the U.S. is better off to have the war over, that our presence is still wanted by the Chinese in Southeast Asia, that they can make all the anti-troops statements they want but they don't want us to pull out of Japan, and I don't believe Korea. They don't want us out of the Philippines and they are worried about a Soviet naval presence at Cam Ranh Bay or elsewhere in South Vietnam.[39] The recent disclosure by the Secretary of Defense about Somalia having a Russia base at Berbera, I am sure, will concern the Chinese enormously. China continues to support the revolution inside countries like Malaysia, Indonesia and others, and the Philippines, but there is some reason to feel that they cut down on that support after relations are extended. They do give tangible support as well as vocal rhetorical support, and this does not bode well for solving some of the problems that lie ahead of us. China's emphasis now is on a strong Europe and this comes out time after time again.

Paludan agreed with my assessment in Southeast Asia which pleased me. I do think he is a fairly knowledgeable and serious ambassador. Went to sign the guest book for Sato at the Japanese Embassy, and then I drove out in the car for lunch at the Summer Palace with the kids and Lois Ruge who had ridden out on their bikes.[40] George and Marvin got back in one hour and ten minutes. Bar and Lois taking a little longer—apparently it is a great ride out there. That afternoon we had another reception for the Rural Small Scale Industry's Delegation here from the States. Young, aggressive guys—most attractive. Then a Chinese communications technique

---

[39]During the Vietnam War the American-built naval base at Cam Ranh Bay became the center of coastal air patrol operations and a vital logistic complex for U.S. forces. By 1978 Soviet air and naval forces were stationed there, and later the Russians used the facility for intelligence collection, including the monitoring of Chinese communications in the South China Sea.

[40]Eisaku Sato—Japan's prime minister from 1964 to 1972 and winner of the Nobel Peace Price in 1974 for his efforts on behalf of nuclear nonproliferation—had passed away during the first week of June, following complications from a stroke.

investigation group that was leaving for the States, headed by Mr. Luong. He was thrilled about going there, looking forward to going to the States. I showed him the space film that we had dubbed in Chinese on Apollo VIII and it showed some of the communications center. He was literally amazed.

These cassettes, if we can figure out how to use them properly, are bound to be good. I asked him to come back here when they return. He was very interested in doing that and we should follow up on this. The Rural Small Scale guys were disappointed in the part of the program that always started off with a prepared speech and prepared presentation. They like the part where they went into factories and actually could get to talk to the workers. They left Peking Monday for the rest of their trip.

Black-tie dinner at Ambassador Pauls'—June 16. The second or third black-tie dinner I have been to since I have been here. The evening was cool, fortunately. It was a going-away party for the Swiss Ambassador, Natural, who is off to Lebanon. Somehow this European style here in Peking seems weird to me and most unusual, but it has its certain civility too that is rather nice at the same time. Pauls of Germany has been very pleasant and a friend. The Ogawas were there—extremely nice, the Japanese.

Personal. I worry about our house in Maine this summer and a lot of the details. Getting the kids where they are going. But I think it will all work out. Moving around and making plans and arrangements—it is just so entirely different in this country from the States. People think you can just call up and make reservations, but it doesn't work that way at all. The little interpreter from the communications group told Bar, "Your husband is very famous in China." I am continually amazed that people even have the vaguest idea of who I am here. It happened at the airport a while back. It has happened around Mr. Law and others at the Club. It's confusing and I think all right since we are trying from this whole style end of things to make some kind of an impact. But I clearly feel we are not fully clued in by Washington. I don't know what's going on but that ceases to worry me. I worried much more about it in the beginning

327

than I do now. I am learning a lot. I think our office is shaping up very well. And I am just not going to worry about Kissinger's peculiar style of operation where he holds all the cards up against his chest and refuses to clue people in on what is really happening. End of June 16, Monday.

Outside Bob Perito's apartment is a kind of military compound in San Li Tun.[41] A big billboard there reads "people of the world unite—defeat the American aggressors and all their running dogs." The text is from a statement Chairman Mao made in 1970 condemning American incursion into Cambodia. The interesting thing is that the sign is still there. There is also one like it in the railroad station though that one is clearly an old one. Most of the signs like this came down when Nixon came to China. I am wondering whether they have a different indoctrination for the Chinese soldiers than they do for the general populace right now. Most of their television does not reflect strong anti-American bias. Their movies seem to show defeat of the "Japanese imperialists" quite a bit. China still feels they can knock the hell out of us in public fora and then want to have a good relationship. The contrast between public statements and private assurance, the contrast between public bravado and catering to Albania etc. and private decency and kindness to us—these things are enormous.

[Tuesday,] June 17[, 1975]. Farewell for Serge Romensky of the AFP [Agence France-Presse]. It is a very slow news time here. The newspaper people, the diplomats, all claiming they have never seen it so slow. Very little hard news. Went to the Turkish embassy. They want to trade embassies. Prices have soared. Their embassy, instead of costing 95,000, the Chinese now want to get 160,000 yuan a year. Actually, it's not a bad deal. There are eight apartments and an office building more than two times bigger than this one; and in addition they have large entertainment rooms and stuff. But

[41]Beijing's San Li Tun is today among the city's most fashionable neighborhoods, and near enough to the embassy district that many city residents consider the two areas interchangeable.

the trade is not in the cards. Incidentally, they fired their gardener for using pots too much instead of planting in the ground. If they fired him, every gardener in Peking would be fired because they all use these flower pots instead of planting in the ground. Off to Beidaihe and the beach tomorrow.[42] Bar has read the book *Prisoner in Peking* about the British journalist that was kept during the war.[43] She is appalled. One night we saw Mr. Gee, the very man who hung the cat of Mr. Grey, the British journalist. It was weird seeing him and thinking how things could change awful fast. A little scary. On the surface these people are all so pleasant, nice and cultured, they really are. End of June 17.

Marvelous quote from June 17. Xinhua News (red news)—talking about the junior table tennis tournament, 1975 World Championship. Talking about all the players, and then they say:

The young players of various nationalities took time out to seriously study Chairman Mao's important instruction concerning the question of theory. Using Marxist-Leninist Mao Tse-tung Thought as their weapon, they related the class struggle and the two-line struggle on the sports front to criticize the revisionist trash such as "skill first" and "championitis." They expressed their determination to contribute their share to the implementation of Chairman Mao's revolutionary line on sports. Following the principle of friendship first, competition second, and taking Chinese mountaineers' heroism as their example, the junior players displayed the spirit of daring to win

---

[42]Beidaihe is one of China's most renowned seaside resorts. Under Deng Xiaoping's leadership after Mao's death, China's leading policymakers would retreat annually to Beidaihe from Beijing's summer heat to chart a course for the new year.

[43]Anthony Grey's *Hostage in Peking* (New York: Doubleday, 1971) recounts the author's twenty-six-month confinement under house arrest by the Chinese. Grey was working as a Reuters reporter in Peking in August 1967 when he was arrested by Red Guards in retaliation for the imprisonment of a Chinese journalist in Hong Kong. As recounted in chapter 8, Bush himself would read this book in the coming weeks, and its story would leave quite an impression. Following his house arrest, Grey suffered numerous psychological and physical indignities, including the public execution of his cat, Ming Ming.

and showed courage and tenacity. They were warmly praised by the spectators.

Wow!

[Wednesday,] June 18[, 1975].   At the staff meeting Bill Thomas brought up that he had been stopped after midnight. He had been to the New Zealand party Saturday night, came back to the embassy, left some of his clothes, bundled up some and started to walk back to San Li Tun. It was a very hot night. He was followed by two men and two women. They finally stopped him, asked him what he was doing. Hassled him. Several times reached for the bundle. He kept on walking and they followed him all the way to the San Li Tun. This was one of the street patrols, similar to what I had been stopped by going up the alley when I first came here. But nobody grabbed the bundle. There seems to be some difference here about what we ought to do. I don't feel too strongly but I do feel we ought to be on record with the Chinese that this kind of behavior is not acceptable as far as diplomats go. Pascoe had heard about bayoneted soldiers patrolling Peking after midnight and apparently they do have stricter restrictions at night.

June 18. Work in the office all day. Ambassador and Mrs. Martti Salomies of Finland at dinner. The dinners drag on sometime although the food was excellent. The protocol of not being able to get up and leave is too much. I struggled around and got the crowd to go outside to see the pool and the sauna. The Finn's daughter and fiancé were there and this move was well received. It was very warm. We walked up there. I had a long talk with the Soviet ambassador on Korea and various aspects of China. The Russians are very down on the Chinese here.

Thursday, the 19th [June 19, 1975].   We left early in the morning for Beidaihe. It is a six-hour train ride—six of us in one compartment. We lowered the upper births and some slept. The food on the dining car was excellent. We were met at the railroad station by Mr. Fay and taken to a delightful cabin in the compound run by the International Club. Many of the staff of the International Club was sent down there to the seashore resort which is open mid-June to the first of September. It was a great treat. The water was clear and lovely, warm, about 76 degrees I'd say. The bathrooms were wet, but the facilities worked and our "villa" was excellent. It was off by itself. Not many people had gone there yet. We also took a trip on Saturday to the Great Wall—an hour drive and then went to Pigeon's Nest.[44] That end of the Great Wall is certainly less spectacular. Beidaihe itself is almost like Bermuda; wide streets, clean, drenched in sunlight, architecture, buildings painted with a cream-colored wash, stores wide open and clean. Some English signs, "Welcome International Friends," an old German bakery, marvelous basket- and beadware. People still stare a lot. Chinese go to this resort. Within the compound some of the houses apparently are owned by factories, communes and other organizations. It is all very vague as to which ones are. One odd note. The sentries are there, bayonets drawn in the evening, but they are always there, conspicuous in the daytime. The only thing I saw our guy do is run off two Chinese who tried to come up from the walk at the beach too near our house. Why they insist on having these guards posted all through the compound, I don't know. It is very very strange and gives a weird impression for a seaside resort. It is very informal in dress, the food, as I said, is excellent with an excellent Chinese restaurant. Dinner with the French and Peruvian ambassadors on Friday night. We had a young man from the club in Peking assigned to our house—cleaning up and looking after it. He did a pretty darn good job. All in all it was very relaxing. The kids all got sore throats, a common ailment and something easy to get here in China. Rained some but most of the time it was clear and sunny. They put in broad retaining walls along the ocean, big enough for trucks and cars to drive along, although you seldom see

[44]The Pigeon's Nest, also known as Eagle Rock Park, is a major attraction in Beidaihe, famous for its beautiful sunsets and bird watching.

them. You can take bikes and you can go quite a ways from the compound itself, but you are very much aware that you are being watched, certainly by all the people, and that your movements are well known.

Miscellaneous note. We are making arrangements to have Dorothy christened a week from Sunday.

Sunday, June 22[, 1975]. Returned to Peking. We left at one and got in at seven in a tremendous downpour. On the train we had a fantastic meal. The food is excellent. I think we had nine courses, six beers for five of us and the price was ten yuan, twenty. Unbelievable. The train was fairly hot but the fan got going and it was OK. Arrived home to find plenty of mail. Some of the problems that make China a contrast: the reuniting of families, they are extremely difficult, they won't give out information, they are very tough on letting Chinese come into the USLO compound. I am sure it is true for others. They are not compassionate in this regard. They won't give out information. We ask on cases and they are simply not forthcoming.

I noticed in a *New Republic* speculation by John Osborne about the Scali-Moynihan swap.[45] Nobody ever gave the explanation he said as to why Scali was appointed. I remember Haldeman telling me that the President wanted Scali at the UN because he was an Italian and he was on the "New Majority" kick at that time. Apparently the Chinese are jamming the VOA.[46] Even some English VOA is coming in worse lately, but I think they are talking about the Chinese broadcast. Apparently the Russians and others are doing this as much but the Chinese insist on it.

---

[45]On May 21 President Ford announced that Daniel Patrick Moynihan would replace John Scali as Washington's ambassador to the United Nations.

[46]On May 14 the USLO reported being unable to receive VOA broadcasts, even though British and Radio Australia broadcasts could be heard without difficulty. On June 20 the State Department confirmed to its Asian posts that Beijing was attempting to jam the VOA's Chinese-language broadcasts, although "Peking [is] not entirely successful, since evidence broadcasts heard in parts of China."

The Philippines seem reassured by what China said about supporting guerrilla movements. I still have enormous trouble about China's differentiation between "support" and "export" of revolution. They believe in "support" not "export," but a government being "supported against" must find the distinction tough.

If one of us leaves Peking there would be a lot of "fare thee wells" about it with our counterparts in the Chinese ministry etc. etc. Their man Chi Chu left PRCLO [the PRC's liaison office] in Washington with no fanfare at all, just disappeared and now it turns out he is to be assigned here in Peking.

They are extending their contacts on Capitol Hill, inviting senators and congressmen by the dozens to PRCLO, and yet we cannot see any of the Chinese political leaders here at all. Major difference. We still have good access, but I keep telling myself, "reach out—work—make others invite and come up with suggestions on whom to have over."

The PRC won a big propaganda victory as one of the released "war prisoners," former KMT officer, hung himself in Hong Kong.[47] Taiwan handled this abysmally. There has been some change since South Vietnam. When Anand Punyarachun, Thai ambassador to the U.N., came here before too long, he called me up. This time he came to negotiate the communiqué and of course there is no call.

My good friend Romulo was here with Marcos. He said he wanted to see me but made no call. These countries simply do not dare let China understand that they are working closely with us or they think they can't do it. I think China would understand but they don't seem to think so. I am convinced we are not totally clued in

[47]Beijing authorities released ten former Nationalist (Kuomintang) officers in the late spring of 1975, after more than twenty-five years' imprisonment, and allowed them passage to Hong Kong for a subsequent trip to Taiwan and reunion with their families. Taipei officials moved slowly in response, forcing the group to remain in Hong Kong. On or about June 4, one of their number, Colonel Zhang Tieh-shih, apparently overcome by feelings of abandonment, committed suicide. By December 1975, Beijing had released what it claimed were the last prisoners held since the civil war.

on the different things that are happening from Washington. I simply don't know what to do about it. I have asked for clarification on one message but it hasn't been forthcoming.

Monday, June 23[, 1975]. Busy day in the office. Staff meetings now three days a week. Lunch with kids at residence. Met the Russell Trains (four) on JA 785 at 3:00 p.m.[48] They are staying in the hotel. Those arrangements worked well. He told me that he mentioned the visit to Kissinger a long time ago and that Kissinger's immediate reaction was, "Sure, that's great. I hope you'll go to China." Then we had all this flak from the State Department. I want to look that up and see why the resistance.

Tuesday, June 24[, 1975]. Fascinating visit to Middle School (full report in file). The Trains, the Thayers, and the Bushes all trooped down. I asked about a basketball—said our kids liked to play—and the next thing I knew they were watering down the basketball court and following some performances we saw in the school, the kids engaged in a 5-on-5 basketball game. Great fun for them. As I do at all these things, I said, "Do you have any questions about the United States? I would be glad to answer them." One teacher did ask about the curriculum and so we had for the first time some type of give-and-take discussion. Lunch with the Romanian ambassador and his team. They have a special entrée [i.e., access to the Chinese] and we try to do this quite frequently. We don't often learn, as yesterday, but we did discuss Asia, Europe, and Portugal with which Romania has a special relationship. Romania feels we should immediately recognize Vietnam. They feel Vietnam is much better. Vietnam is now realistic towards us. I mentioned the MIA [military personnel missing in action] problem. I told them that we were damned upset about that—holding MIAs hostage in order to get economic aid. People are so unrealistic in this part of the world about the intention of some of these countries. A guy like the Romanian naturally is a communist, but he

---

[48]See my footnote to Bush's entry for April 21, 1975.

overlooks the aggression and the support of the revolution that has troubled me so much. Good man—it is good to have these exchanges.

At four o'clock Dr. Myers, a friend of Alex Head's, came by. He is a teacher at Cane College, an older guy. Very interested in languages. He had been out to Honun where he had seen an American woman named Shirley Wood and had visited normal teacher's college out there.[49] Had a very interesting story to tell about this woman's life on the campus, her isolation, the fact that there was indeed a need for dictatorship of the proletariat because some people had a way of getting in to the front of the line to buy bicycles which were rationed. Some of these visitors have very special chances to see things. Followed by a visit by Dr. C. P. Li and Dr. Jerome Loh.[50] Dr. C. P. Li, on his last trip here, saw Mao. He is an older man, he knew Mao for a long, long time. He is sympathetic to this regime. He is doing a lot of work in Chinese herbal medicine and has suggested that through [him] that we might find ways of moving things forward during the President's visit. Exchange of medical technology. Dr. Loh of Gary, Indiana, was with him, bright Chinese guy, and both of them were most interesting. Dinner at the Japanese Embassy. They invited the Swedish and Mexican Ambassadors' wives plus all the Bush children. Very informal and a nice evening with Kobe beef. Mrs. Ogawa does things in the most beautiful way.

The Trains and all had their eyes opened wide by the school visit. It was a great one. The schools are very disciplined. Kids volunteer.

---

[49]Shirley Wood taught English at a normal university (an institution that specializes in the training of teachers) in Kaifeng from the late 1950s through the 1960s.

[50]Li, a medical professor, knew Mao from their student days together, and he was afforded tremendous respect during this visit and his 1973 trip to China. He did not meet Mao on this visit, but he was granted an audience with Zhou Enlai. He "sees himself as something of a middle-man to promote friendship between the U.S. and China," Bush reported to Washington, and, although he briefed the USLO on his meetings with Chinese officials, he "seemed reluctant to discuss details." Bush's further dealings with Li are described immediately below, and in his entries from the first week of July 1975.

They sit with their hands on the back. They raise their hand. A lot of the recitation seems to be rote. Tremendous amounts of propaganda. Write a poem telling what the Mao thought means to you. Write a poem describing the virtues of dictatorship of the proletariat. Write a poem exposing Lin Biao and Confucius. The kids look healthy. There is certainly a lot of order and discipline in the schools, on the playgrounds, everywhere else. I wonder what it would be like bringing a Chinese delegation through some of our public schools in the big cities or elsewhere.

[Wednesday,] June 25[, 1975].   Went to the revolutionary street committee. Luncheon for Russell Train at the residence with some of the top Chinese environmentalists: Wang Qian, responsible person for the environmental office of the state council; Yu Lin, responsible person [for the] architecture bureau of capitol construction committee; Wang Ting, vice deputy head of bureau of foreign affairs of capitol construction committee; Liao Dongfa; the interpreter; Harry Thayer; Chris Ballou and I. The Chinese were extremely interested, it was much more relaxed, much more give-and-take than any other thing I'd seen. They do have a Vice Premier in charge of their environmental matters, they do have standards, they are not doing the kind of job we are doing, they keep saying they're new and need criticism, etc. They were amazed at the figures of U.S. spending on environment. The agency—some $4 billion in FY 75 with industry another $6 billion—a total of $10 or 11 billion a year on the environment. They could hardly believe that. They talked about their concern about all kinds of waste, and they talked about the maximization of human wastes and how they process that. But all in all the meeting lasted from 12:45 to 3:00 p.m. and they were still going strong, asking good questions. We have a report on that in the file. It seems to me this might be a good subject for them to have on the agenda for the President.

Ambassador Drulovic came to call at 3:00.[51] He was on time so we had to herd him in with Harry Thayer until I shook the Chinese.

[51]Milojko Drulovic served as the Yugoslavian ambassador to China (1973–78) and to the Soviet Union (1982–86).

The Trains and Bar rushing off to see the Temple of Heaven. Drulovic is a good man. He is strongly biased, of course, towards socialism. But I can talk very frankly with him. I am continually worried about the way the anti-Americanism kind of feeds on itself in the climate of Peking. It is assisted ably by blasts in the Xinhua News, the red news, against the United States. In the June 25th issue for example there was a long blast by China's delegation on the World's Women's Conference in Mexico. Mainly against superpowers, hegemony, colonialism, a lot of anti-U.S. stuff. In the same issue: "What is the Park Chung-Hee clique up to?" And a long blast against the U.S. support of Korea and corruption etc., in Korea. And the next one is Korean residents in Japan meet to denounce crimes by U.S. in Park Chung-Hee clique. We get this almost every day. And I remain convinced that China is making a big mistake in continuing to thrash away at us on this kind of thing. But the experts say, "Well it's less than they used to do, and you've got to understand they need to put out rhetoric," and some of that is true. But it is a funny way to show a desire for better relations. And I get fed up with it right up to the teeth.

Dinner at the Summer Palace restaurant for a going-away party for a very able Mo Morin and his wife, Ann. Mo is a GSO [general services officer], he gets out and leads, works with his hands, works with the Chinese. They don't work for him, they all work together. He takes one of the great things about China, namely the willingness of all to work, etc., and through executing things himself and being fair and knowledgeable, he has the respect of all from the mechanics to the office staff—first-class guy. He will be sorely missed. The Summer Palace is unbelievably beautiful at night with lovely shadows across the lake. The Park was bare, unlike most times when it is cram full of tourists. The dinner was a multicourse marvelous dinner. For 18 the price was 249 yuan or about $7.50 per head. It went on and on for many courses. Very good. The walk from the restaurant through the park, about 15 minutes, was just magnificent. Planes taking off from the military base next to the Summer Palace—one Dover prop, one four-engine prop plane, one jet. The only thing marring the peace and quiet of the evening. Spec-

337

tacular pink clouds over the unbelievable roof lines. Dorothy has now an appointment to go down and talk to the minister about being christened. What an experience! Baptized in Communist China.

Musk ox. Ripley has about convinced me that giving a musk ox is not too good an idea. The Chinese might have a face problem on it. Secondly, the environment is not too good for its survival and oxes are out for a lot of reasons.[52]

Summer plans may change. Two congressional delegations coming in August. Damn it! I hope I can get away.

There are a lot of little things. Russell Trains were here. Jennifer did not get their passports from them, inasmuch as they are staying in the hotel, until three days after they got here. We turned them in and then got back some feedback from the Public Security Bureau saying that they were ticked off about this. The controls are rigid. Never let it be forgotten. Comparison between controls on us and the controls on the PRCLO in Washington are practically negligible—are unbelievable. One of the KMT prisoners released, killed himself and China still reaps propaganda gain over Taiwan on account of this. Taiwan looks niggardly and mean, keeping their former officers from returning home. Ten of them have applied for passports—visas to go to Taiwan. Peking making the most of that one.

[52]The Smithsonian's S. Dillon Ripley strongly opposed presenting China with another musk ox in 1975, to replace the recently deceased Milton, who had been given by President Nixon in 1972. Bush joined other American diplomats in advocating a replacement as a gesture of good will. In early May, Ripley told Bush this was merely "throwing good money after bad," showing that "the Department of State has perhaps not read the papers." Milton had died of peritonitis caused by a metal object he ingested that lodged in his intestines—a fact widely reported in the American media. His fate suggested to Ripley that the Chinese were incapable of caring for such precious animals, "which are after all live fellow travelers with us on this planet." "Accuse me if you will of being oversensitive to animal needs," Ripley wrote, "but here in the middle of the Mall we are sometimes more attuned to the vibrations of the public than in other more elevated places." Instead of a live musk ox, he suggested (perhaps tongue-in-cheek) that "a statue, perhaps in wood, ceramic or plaster might be more to the point!" Bush received this letter by diplomatic pouch, hence his delay in recording the event in his diary

Lunch with Mr. C. P. Li who saw Wang Hairong and Nancy Tang at dinner last night. Tonight he is supposed to see Zhou Enlai. He will call me tomorrow. He is the one friend of Chairman Mao's [from] many, many years ago. He is a doctor with credentials and anti-cancer, lives in Arlington, Virginia. An old, old man interested in seeing peace and total relations between China and the U.S. He thinks that China reunification would be peace with Taiwan afterward. And he thinks Taiwan would have to negotiate if indeed the U.S. scrapped its treaty and set up an embassy in Peking. He is putting a lot on faith it seems to me. Sincere, decent old man, however.

To finish with Dr. Li, he came to see me again on June 28, after he saw Zhou Enlai and got front-page treatment for this. There is a telegram on this subject. He came to see me at 2:30 in the afternoon. He had seen Zhou Enlai and had seen Nancy Tang and Wang Hairong for two hours. He had seen Zhou Enlai for close to one hour. He threw out the idea that China might make a statement for "domestic consumption" about peace. Since it is an internal matter it would have to be done that way. He wondered whether we would be interested. I gave him no promises, simply said we would convey this to the proper channels. He is getting a big rush by the Chinese with Wang Hairong, a Vice Foreign Minister, and Nancy Tang going to his hotel room for two hours. I ran into him on the night of the 27th at the hotel where he was with his wife's sister's husband who was 72 years old, a graduate of Cornell, leftist, vice secretary in the Agriculture Department, a rather impressive guy. I don't know exactly what Li is up to, but this could be some kind of signal. We will see.[53]

---

and in composing a response. On June 24 he cabled the State Department to "please call him [Ripley] and tell him I am converted to a no-ox position."

[53]Li told Bush that Chinese officials favored Ford's visit in the fall even without prior agreement on Taiwan, recognition, and other outstanding issues. The State Department was not keen on such outside channels, however, nor on Bush's cultivating contacts outside the normal lines of communication. "We do not wish to encourage Li into role of an intermediary," Washington told the USLO in response to Bush's report. "Accordingly, we request that you take no further initiative in contacts with Li." See also Bush's diary entry for July 5, 1975.

Thursday, June 26[, 1975]. We had a big duck dinner with Russell Trains, hotter than hell in that restaurant. The Peking duck very special.

Friday, June 27[, 1975]. Went to the ping-pong match between Laos and China. Women and men marching in; hands held high; the same ceremony of putting the pins on; absolutely fantastic ping-pong. The Laos guys looked good but they were just wiped out by the superior Chinese play. Bar is sightseeing people to death, doing a marvelous job on it. Unbelievable.

Got some excellent tennis in with the kids. Saturday night—that was the night Dr. Li came again—played tennis and went to the jiaozi dumpling restaurant. Very hot. You can lose four or five pounds playing tennis in this heat.

Sunday, June 29[, 1975]. The Trains departed. We went out with all the color—just the same time that President Bongo of Gabon was leaving town.[54] Literally thousands of people at the airport with bright colored flowers dancing up and down. Soldiers with bayonets, marching, a spectacular Chinese sendoff. Something I had not seen since we were spared going to the airport.[55] The big thing that day—Dorothy was baptized at our little Chinese church. The ministers were extremely happy and smiling—pleasant, wonderful. It was very special. There were six guardian group people taping and flashing pictures of the ceremony, not knowing what was going on really. But we were very happy that the Chinese agreed, after they consulted in a meeting, to baptize Doro. They wondered why we were doing it. Bar explained that we wanted the family together and hadn't been able to do it. A very special day, an occasion.[56] 12:30—Tom Gleason, the President of Wolver-

---

[54]El Hadj Omar Bongo Ondimba (formerly Albert-Bernard Bongo) became president of Gabon in 1967 at the age of thirty-two.

[55]One of the perks of the USLO's unique status within Beijing's diplomatic community was that its staff, Bush included, was spared the obligation of welcoming visiting heads of state upon their arrival.

[56]"It sounds a little unusual that I was fifteen and still not baptized," Dorothy Bush later wrote, "but remember, I was the youngest of five in a frenetic family."

ine Worldwide, came for lunch.[57] I was at the airport meeting Tricia Everett, Doro's friend—18, cute. Got in late. Pleasant relaxed evening and then Sunday evening a going-away party for Burns and Finocchi of Italy. Carpet bowling championship of Peking. Relaxed evening.

Still quiet on the diplomatic front.

In the last few days India has aborted her democracy. The hypocrisy of Mrs. Gandhi is very clear.[58] I never have liked her because of the great criticism against the United States, but I hate this for her country. Somalia, after making a big row on our lies on the airbase, refused to let the journalists in to see the base or the part of the base that they wanted. I doubt that there will be any publicity on that here. The anti-American publicity gets to you after a while, although I keep saying it is relatively less than in the past. Is China aggressive or not? That is the big tough question—hard to answer. End June 29.

Miscellaneous. China's attention to these Third World countries is amazing. In how many big countries do they give such a grand stylish welcome to chiefs of state from tiny African countries for example. The airport is bedecked, downtown is colored banners all over and big signs of welcome in French or English or whatever the language might be. Children, soldiers marching around, dancing enthusiastically, welcoming; all make an impression on the visitor.

Barbara Bush explained the circumstances thus: "Due to deaths, politics, long distances, and floods (literally), her baptism had been put off four times. This was hard to explain to ourselves, much less the Chinese. So Doro became the first American to be baptized in China since 1949."

[57]Wolverine World Wide, Inc., was founded in 1883 by G. A. Krause as a shoe factory in Michigan. Thomas Gleason served as the company's chairman and chief executive officer for twenty years.

[58]Indira Gandhi, prime minister of India during the years 1966–77 and 1980–84, ordered the widespread arrest of political opponents in late June 1975, citing threats to "internal stability." Bush later met Gandhi in May 1984, during his vice presidency, months before her assassination. "I told her that I was a politician and that if being anti-American was good politics, I might not like it, but I would understand. . . . I would say that if the visit accomplished anything, it was establishing a very good personal rapport with Mrs. Gandhi."

[Monday,] June 30[, 1975]. Sometimes I think we analyze everything too much on this China-watching bit. Zhou Enlai met Dr. C. P. Li outside the hospital, and maybe that was news, but from that one appearance, there was a lot of speculation that Zhou was on the way back. Articles began to be written about the reemergence of Zhou Enlai. Two days later, when the President of Gabon comes, he meets Zhou Enlai in the hospital. The analysts, quick to jump and analyze, never really consider that maybe Zhou just felt well enough that one day to meet his friend by a villa on the lake. Reading these Chinese tea leaves is important, but you can get so close to it that you don't see the forest for the trees. Every little analysis, who stands at what place at a reception, what is going to be the meaning of this article or that—again it is important, but there are basic inconsistencies. And these are analyzed. We need it, but I hope I never get too close to it to lose the broader prospective.

Schmidt, the Austrian minister, came to call on Harry Thayer and me. Steve Fitzgerald came by with Dave Finkelstein of the Ford Foundation.[59] Foundations have not been permitted in here. They are a no-no so far as China goes. The Ford Foundation finances some of the exchanges, but this makes no difference so far to the Chinese. Teddy Youde had as his guest at a six o'clock reception Vice Admiral Sir Louis Le Bailly.[60] He is the head of the British Intelligence apparatus. Interesting that he is here. He had dinner with the Chinese ambassador in London. Michael Willeford at the dinner, British Foreign Office man, mentioned maybe Mr. Le Bailly should go. The next day he was on the golf course and got a phone call saying he would be welcome to go to China. They operate in strange and wonderful ways. Dinner at the Peking Hotel on June 20 with Dr. Li, Dr. Niu and his wife from Temple University at Philadelphia, and Dr. Chang and his wife from Catholic University. Dr. Niu is doing some interesting genetic work on goldfish here in

[59]David Finkelstein worked as a China specialist for the Ford Foundation and later as a writer.

[60]Le Bailly was technically director general of intelligence for London's Ministry of Defence, a position he held from 1973 to 1975.

China for four months. And Dr. Chang is on a similar project—not goldfish. Big spread of Chinese food, drinking the maotai—kids got a great big kick out of it. Eleven-course dinner.

The Somalia incident at the base concerns me. Somalia denied everything. Now I see they are inviting congressmen to go there. Congressmen have accepted. It will be interesting. God, I hope the Defense Department is not lying about all of this. Although the pictures indicate they are not. Yesterday Somalia turned back some diplomats who asked to see that particular segment of the photographs. What indeed is the truth?

[Tuesday,] July 1[, 1975].   A little incident at the gate where a Chinese-American with an American passport came to the USLO with his sister and his elderly parents. He was permitted in but his sister and elderly parents were detained. Jerry Ogden went out and asked the soldiers if they would let them in and they did. But only after a discussion [during] which Mr. Ren, our interpreter, asked the three why they had not gotten "the unit" to arrange their getting in. They said they lived at Nanking and thus their unit could not make arrangements. Chinese are always stopped coming into the USLO. It is a little embarrassing when they are American citizens. And even when they are not.

Uneventful day. Went to a reception for Canada National Day on a steamy 11–12 time frame at the International Club. I didn't wear a coat. I did wear a tie. I was somewhere in between the Chinese with their open shirts, very comfortable, and the rest of the diplomatic corps—all suits, coats and ties. I had a coat but I left it in the car at the last minute. Tennis at five and after a meeting with the kids—getting ready for the Fourth of July picnic.[61] The picnic

[61]Forever bored by the staid nature of most embassies' national day celebrations, Bush proposed that the USLO host a down-home Fourth of July picnic. Protocol demanded that he have Chinese officials in for a proper official celebration, but on the fourth itself several hundred visitors, American expatriates in China, and the city's diplomatic corps jammed the USLO to enjoy hot dogs, door prizes, and assorted bits of Americana.

is amazing. Hot dog rolls—can't get them. Cooks, will they let us have any. Waiters—so far no go. I think they wanted the International Club to provide the food but we wanted Mr. Sun to do it. A bit of a standoff. We are going to have the Chinese on July 3, and the movie and picnic on July 4. Kids all went to the Egyptian embassy with El-Abd's nephew, a wise lad from Georgetown. Bar and I watched *Hawaii Five-O* on the tube.[62]

There are enormous problems sorting out the toughness of China from the gentle, civil side. Thailand's prime minister is here now and they agree to self-determination for people, recognition of Taiwan, recognition of the PRC, and all the same formulas of the Philippines and others. Thailand clearly worried about subversion, wonders whether there will be enough change on China's part to protect them. China leaders assured the Philippines there was, that they would not subvert, but the Philippine leaders, I am sure, are not convinced.

On these moves China appears to be having its cake and eating it too. They are dictating the terms to the smaller countries, and yet there is no clear indication that they will stop sending telegrams to the communist parties encouraging them on. The next domino clearly is Laos. The government has already moved into almost total control of the Pathet Lao. The question is will they be governed from Hanoi, [or] will they be nationalistic and "free" even though under Pathet Lao rule? It is too early to say. There is some border fighting between Cambodia and Nam, and then of course Hanoi and Russia have both backed Mrs. Gandhi, where China has come out strongly against it. There are differences in socialist and communist camps no question about that. But how lasting will they be? Much of what we are doing is based on the fact that China and Russia will not get together against us. Everyone that comes here, whether they be Chinese-Americans, whether they be delegations, whether they be from other countries, feel that the breach between

---

[62]Chronicling the adventures of a fictional state police unit in the fiftieth state, *Hawaii Five-O* aired on the CBS network from 1968 to 1980.

China and Russia at this point is enormous. What about when succession takes place?[63] End of July 1.

[Wednesday,] July 2[, 1975].   Had a good meeting with Teddy Youde and Admiral Le Bailly, head of the British combined intelligence service, a most attractive guy who was gotten off the golf course the day following a casual remark by a Brit at the Foreign Ministry who suggested to the Chinese ambassador that he might like to come to China. Hauled off the course. There was a message from the Chinese Embassy saying, "would you like to go?" In the afternoon Tom Gleason, the head of Wolverine International [Wolverine Worldwide], that makes Hush Puppies, came. They are doing some shoe business in Tianjin. The quality of the Chinese shoes are great. They think the leather working and the whole procedure is excellent. Tom, of Grand Rapids, an attractive fellow.

Went to a poorly attended reception for Air Iran's inaugural flight at the Peking Hotel. Many of the ambassadors and chiefs of mission are out of town this time of year. Went to the International Club to join Bar for a showing of tai chi chuan and woo she (martial arts). Hotter than hell, but a couple of good movies and a couple of live performances. Very good. Dinner there and back to show the movie about Billie Holliday's life: "Lady Sings the Blues."[64] Sad—dope, dirty talking. Brought home the contrast between our societies pretty damn well.

Thursday, July 3[, 1975].   Mainly at the office—preparation for the various receptions. The Chinese came in and announced that we had the cooks. Mr. Wang told me he couldn't sleep all night worrying about the waiters and sure enough it was announced we would get a certain number of waiters for both Thursday and Friday. Wang Hairong, Vice Foreign Minister, Mao's niece, is the guest

[63]Bush refers here to the omnipresent American worry that Sino-American relations might be derailed following the inevitable deaths of Mao and Zhou, should a hard-line group take control of the government.
[64]Starring Diana Ross, the 1972 film *Lady Sings the Blues* received five Academy Award nominations.

of honor at our reception.[65] We are expecting about 250 Chinese. Hot and windy. But soon that one will be over. Lunch at the International Club. Watching India with horror. Mrs. Gandhi has aborted democracy. China will be worried about it. Because if something happens there, and Russia gets a larger toehold, it will send China right up a wall. End July 3.

Still July 3. Our reception for the Chinese. I decided giving the big barbecue on the Fourth should preclude including the Chinese until we saw how it worked. So we had a separate reception for the Chinese on July 3. Wang Hairong, Vice Minister of Foreign Affairs, was the ranking guest. Yao Yilin, the Vice Minister of Foreign Trade, the second-ranking guest. Huang Shuze, Vice Minister of Public Health, third ranking guest. Zhao Zhenghong, responsible official from sports and physical culture (handled the track team), was there. CCPIT [China Council for the Promotion of International Trade], Ministry of Education, and nice Mr. Zhou Qiuye, Chinese People's Institute for Foreign Affairs, who handled the Albert-Rhodes visit. Nancy Tang was there but she didn't sit in the head room. We did it the Chinese way. Bringing the ranking guests into the dining room which was cozily arranged. The day was clear so most of the other guests were out on the two patios.

Wang Hairong is absolutely impossible. Totally negative. You ask her what she thinks about India. She turns around and says what do you think about India. She is most difficult to get any intelligent statements out of. I said, "Does the foreign minister visit you?" She said, "sometimes he's busy, sometimes he's not." And on and on it goes. Just like pulling teeth. She can be pleasant, but she is totally unproductive and turns every question around into a question for me. It is an interesting intellectual exercise trying to come up with new queries, but frustrating as hell to have them punted into one's own end zone. *[One line has been redacted by George H. W. Bush.]*

[65] "The protocol list was the same as [for] the last two years," Bush explained to Washington after the reception, "but, of course, Wang Hai-Jung [Wang Hairong] is hardly a match for Chiao Kuan-Hua [Qiao Guanhua] as a conversationalist."

[Friday,] July 4, 1975. The reception was OK. The USLO people milled around and people arrived promptly at six and left promptly at seven. I think it was a plus. On the Fourth of July it was a tremendous success. We all got out and worked on the roof, on hanging up plastic banners, weighing them down with welding rods, setting up tables, cooking hot dogs on charcoal. It is hard to light. But it all fell in place with the rain drizzling a little during the day, but clearing miraculously for a well-attended, perhaps 500 people, reception. Dogs; Miller beer; American cigarettes; a raffle; Coca-Cola; lots of loud music—John Denver–style—and it was great.[66] The Americans wore red, white and blue. We had American flags around and I am confident it conveyed the right kind of impression about our country. A few Chinese came from the International Club. Mr. Law from my tennis playing, Mr. Wang and just a few others. But the word will spread around. Next year we should do more. The dogs were good, the rolls came. And we ended up with far too much food. Interesting ploy on the servants. We asked for cooks and waiters. It was all impossible to get them but finally at the last minute we got the waiters and the cooks. They wanted us to use them as caterers but we backed them down. And the whole thing worked out fine. I don't know why I got uptight about this reception but I wanted to see it click and I am confident that it did.

---

[66]Bush had in fact invited Denver to perform at the USLO's July Fourth celebration, contacting his manager, Jerry Weintraub, in early March. "Now my idea for the long shot idea," Bush wrote, after detailing his plans for the Independence Day party. "Is there any chance that John Denver will be traveling in this part of the world around that time? He would be the ideal guy to put on a short show of his great American ballads."

"I Have Studied Chinese"

July 5 to August 22, 1975

This chapter contains the final section of Bush's China Diary. He journeyed to the United States during the last week of August 1975 for a brief vacation and consultations with the State Department and the White House. He returned to Beijing in September, but, although he stayed until December, he never again dictated for his diary while in China. Indeed, Bush did not pick up the diary habit again until he became vice president. "There was no one keeping my feet to the fire to do it," he later conceded, with regret for the lost opportunity.[1]

Bush's China Diary thus ends four months before his tenure at the United States Liaison Office came to a close. It is easy to speculate that he may have ceased dictating his diary in expectation of beginning his next job. He would be named director of the Central Intelligence Agency (CIA) in November, and the organization's culture of secrecy does not look kindly upon personal memoirs of the most private nature. Yet no evidence exists that Bush was aware of his new posting so far in advance of President Gerald Ford's official decision; nor, for that matter, is there any evidence that Ford and Bush discussed a new job for Bush during the latter's visit to Washington in late August. Yet, despite such evidence, Bush's final diary entries while in China suggest some awareness that his time in the country was growing short. At times he was almost poetic in his desire to capture and preserve the sights and sounds of his ad-

---

[1]This quote is documented in the endnotes.

venture. "Sounds that I will not forget," he wrote in late July. "The early morning singing in the park—loud and usually very good tenor voices. . . . The organized cadence of the kids marching . . . the never-ceasing honking of horns downtown in Peking, the jingle of bicycle bells, the laughter of the children as they play near the park, the blaring of the loudspeakers with the exercises of the propaganda whether it's on a train, in a park, at a building site, wherever. The July and August sound of the crickets."

It is worth noting that Bush increasingly adopted the past tense during these weeks when describing his time in China. "I have studied Chinese," he dictated. "It has continually brought home to me how difficult it is to operate fully in a foreign land without the language." Only weeks before he had said, again as though yet looking back, "I've tried to give the right impression of America here. . . . tried to move around in the diplomatic community; tried to increase our contacts with the Chinese; tried to have interesting people from the States here; and tried to learn and make suggestions to Washington." Although without a definitive plan for his future—save some notion by this point that politics remained in that future—he was during these weeks clearly a man already thinking of his experience in China as nearer its end than its beginning. He had left Washington in the fall of 1974 in the aftermath of Watergate in search of escape and adventure. By the late summer of 1975, his diary entries suggest that he was fully ready to return, and ready for whatever the future held.

His growing frustrations with the Chinese leadership surely contributed to this sentiment. Bush's entries from this period reveal a man resigned to the failure of his ambitious plan to befriend China's political elite. "The people are so nice here but they can be so obtuse, they can be so removed—so little chance for contacts," he wrote. "The enormous contrast between life here and Huang Zhen's life in Washington. He can talk substance with anyone he wants. I can sit formally for one hour with Wang Hairong who says absolutely nothing." He considered this indicative of "Middle Kingdom syndrome, with an underlying hatred of foreigners. . . . You can get *close to these people—the ones that you know—but I keep in mind that if a word comes from some unseen mysterious place, we could be cut off, isolated, and, after reading Grey, vilified." His mention of the British journalist Anthony Grey, whose memoir of imprisonment captivated Bush during these weeks, is no mere passing reference. On the contrary, Grey's ordeal clearly left a lasting impression.*

Bush left for Washington in late August, like so many American diplomats before him, equally fascinated and discouraged by China. "These people are frustratingly difficult to deal with in every way," he confided to his diary. These final entries reveal the depth of his difficulties in China. It was an experience that clearly changed and codified his thinking about diplomacy and the world, but an experience that in the end was not quite what he had hoped it would be—even if the adventure was exactly what he needed.

Saturday morning, July 5[, 1975]. Kids are about to leave. They are off to the sauna bath at Finland [the Finnish embassy] but we managed to clean up the yard. Bar and Mr. Guo doing the sweeping. Wipe off all the flags, put the supplies away, dry off all the wet beer and Coke cans. All in all, the place is back to normal. Mr. Wang is fantastic as usual. Being the head of a mission is a little frustrating. The Somalia matter—I tell them it's all around the diplomatic community and what do we do about it, how to counteract Somalia's propaganda.[2] The answer is do nothing. Send in some cables on C. P. Li and there, though C.P. is gone, the answer is do nothing. But the cable is condescending, telling us that C. P. Li's remarks about Ford being welcome in China parallel other remarks of that nature. How stupid. Of course we know that.[3]

---

[2]See Bush's entry and my footnote for June 10, 1975.

[3]See my footnote to Bush's June 24, 1975, entry. Unbeknownst to Bush, on July 1, Winston Lord and Philip Habib had composed a lengthy cable to the peripatetic Secretary of State Henry Kissinger, informing him of Bush's ongoing contacts with Li. They specifically recommended "that we inform Bush to take no further initiative in any contacts with Li." No record exists of their subsequent directive to Bush, but his diary certainly suggests that Kissinger agreed with their recommendation, and that the message was subsequently passed on to the USLO.

Back to the Fourth of July. We raffled off prizes, including a couple of big red drums, a couple of Coca-Cola red coats and a great big Exercycle I'd used only slightly. Pictures too. This was a big feature and everyone seemed very interested in it. I hope the Chinese don't object to it but it was really fun. American cigarettes went over well.

July 5. Reading cables, doing mail. Quest in terms of news here. Telegram from Chuck Percy from Moscow saying to batten down the hatches, that his delegation was arriving.[4] That will be fun. The family leaves for Shanghai and Nanking on the train tonight at 6:00. I'll stay here because Thayer will be going away next week. Going to a soccer game tonight, taking it easy. Fred will be lonely. End of July 5.

[Sunday,] July 6[, 1975]. Sunday, the family left yesterday for Shanghai and now I am a bachelor. I am reading Grey's *Hostage in Peking* which, along with Rickett's book about their imprisonment back in the early fifties, is interesting reading.[5] The Ricketts come out as great admirers of the [system] of rehabilitation, and kind of ashamed that they were spies. *Hostage in Peking* is very different. It shows the horrible and ugly side of the Cultural Revolution: the Marxist 500 million, stoning embassies, stripping embassy people as they were thrown out of China, spitting on them, plastering posters, vilification, and ugliness that one doesn't see now.

[4]The reference is to Senator Charles Percy, Republican of Illinois (1967–85). His was an "official" congressional delegation, meaning that his travel was coordinated by the State Department. Joining Percy were Senators Jacob Javits, James Pearson, Claiborne Pell, and Adlai Stevenson, and Representatives John Anderson, Paul Findley, Paul McCloskey, and John Slack. As a sponsored delegation, the group met with Kissinger and his staff for a briefing before their departure and briefed President Gerald Ford (with both Bush and Kissinger in attendance) upon their return.

[5]For Grey, see Bush's entry and my footnote for June 17, 1975. Arrested along with his wife and charged with espionage in 1951 while studying in China as a Fulbright scholar, Allyn Rickett transformed during four years of captivity from a staunch anti-Communist to a sympathetic supporter of Mao's regime. He recounted his story in *Prisoners of Liberation* (New York: Anchor, 1973).

And frankly it is kind of hard to imagine. But it is a good lesson to keep in mind.

Church service was terribly attended. Not counting the Chinese there were seven or eight of us. Hot and still. Go out to see Mo Morin off at the airport. A mix-up on the drivers but that is standard procedure. George got his tooth fixed the day before he left for 60 cents. At the hospital he paid $650 before to get it drilled out and he was in great pain. He is now a great admirer of the Chinese medicine, and he is struggling, as a lot of us are, as to whether this universal health care—how it should work, etc., etc.

Today is George's twenty-ninth birthday. He is off to Midland, starting a little later in life than I did, but nevertheless starting out on what I hope will be a challenging new life for him. He is able. If he gets his teeth into something semipermanent or permanent, he will do just fine. Went out to the airport, saw Mo off. Dinner at the International Club. Tennis with De. It is warm enough now to take it out of you. My legs get tired. I have been taking the Cerbix T vitamin pill. Felt pretty good this summer. Stomach troubles gone. Peking can be harsh on people. It can be rough. Fred had a bath—he is cleaner than he is in the winter. A lot. I took him for a long walk last night. Children back away from him. Some of the adults look curiously.

I am troubled by a book *Hostage in Peking*. It shows a totally different side of China. Mobs screaming. Struggling with the driver, Lao Wang, who sounded exactly the same as my driver Guo. Dragging him [Grey] before 15,000 screaming people, trumped-up charges, when he photographed things he was accused subsequently of spying on China, smearing paint and wall posters all over the guy's room, keeping him for months in solitary confinement—two years prison in all. Trumped-up stupid performance by the Chinese and the British in Britain in retaliation—they come charging out of the embassy swinging sticks, thus giving provocation to raid and sack the British Embassy here.[6] Ripping the clothes off the women,

[6]On August 29, 1967, Chinese diplomats stationed in London and armed with bats and broom handles sallied forth from their embassy to assault British police,

touching them, vilifying the men. Filthy language. All the things one doesn't think of when one thinks of China. It is "must reading" because it only happened in 1967–68 and part of 1969, and it gives you a real indication of what things were like only a very short time ago.

The people are so nice here but they can be so obtuse, they can be so removed—so little chance for contacts. The enormous contrast between life here and Huang Zhen's life in Washington. He can talk substance with anyone he wants. I can sit formally for one hour with Wang Hairong who says absolutely nothing. Middle Kingdom syndrome, with an underlying hatred of foreigners, is amazing. And yet we see so few manifestations of it. You can get close to these people—the ones that you know—but I keep in mind that if a word comes from some unseen mysterious place, we could be cut off, isolated, and, after reading Grey, vilified. In spite of this, there seems to be an interest in America. Almost, you might say, an affection for America. I have not felt any hostility on a personal basis at all. I take personally, I am afraid, some of the things that China says about us—adequately recorded in the red news.

Also I keep in mind China tells us, "don't listen to what we say, but watch what we do"—a paraphrase. Don called from the States late the night of the sixth.[7] Bogged down in red tape on the children's travel through some travel agent. Hope we can get it worked out. But it is hard in China. You can't walk down to some airline ticket agency and get the best price. Hard to cash checks. Hard to conduct normal business.

Back to the Grey book. I am glad I read it, but I must say it has altered my perspective. The Rickett prisoner book was an apology, showing how their thought control or their discipline or their self-cleansing sessions were really pluses to point out the good things

---

who had cordoned off their residence, ostensibly to protect it from protestors. Dubbed the "Battle of Portland Place," the attack followed the sacking of the British embassy in Beijing by Cultural Revolutionaries. Grey offers a vivid after-the-fact description of the attack in Beijing, which surely colored Bush's own thinking.

[7]Don Rhodes helped coordinate travel plans for Bush family members and friends visiting China.

of the system. But Grey's was a little more down to earth, and in my judgment a little more factual. End of July 6.

[Monday,] July 7[, 1975]. The family gone to Shanghai, Nanking, Wusih. The high point was the lunch with Ambassador and Mrs. Huang Hua. They came alone in a green Shanghai. Talked in a relaxed way. She talked a little more than Huang Hua did. Not much substance covered. But a very warm and friendly atmosphere commented on by Pascoe and Thomas as most unusual. I asked if they were continuing the discussion we started at the U.N. He said they did not do it last year. I asked if there would be any unusual items for the U.N. General Assembly, and Huang Hua said no just the same ones. He did mention the Middle East debate. It was good to see him. There was genuine warmth there. And they are leaving for the States in four or five days.

July 7. Midnight phone call from Don. Discussing the kids' travel arrangements. From this vantage point it appears that President Ford is doing a heck of a lot better. That is good. Thailand has come and gone. Kukrit setting up diplomatic relations, and Kukrit claiming he got proper assurances on subversion of Thailand from China.[8] But the radio station apparently goes on though China denies it.[9] And China still makes a difference in its own mind between export of revolution and support for revolution. The Iran Vice President was here. He took a big haymaker at the United States— so what's new! Some squeals out of Cambodia in the news, hitting

[8]Thai Prime Minister Kukrit Pramoj visited Beijing in early July and, like President Ferdinand Marcos of the Philippines before him, formally established diplomatic relations with the PRC. The move was seen in Washington (and by the USLO) as a direct response to the loss of American prestige following Saigon's fall.

[9]The issue of Beijing's support for leftist Thai insurgents arose during Kukrit's visit. At a joint press conference with Chinese officials, Kukrit "said the Chinese denied completely that they had given aid to the Thai insurgents or that a radio (the voice of the people of Thailand) supports them from Thailand," the USLO reported home to Washington. "Asked if he believed the Chinese denial, Kukrit nimbly sidestepped that question by saying he was in China 'for friendship, not to answer that question.'"

the U.S. imperialists. God I get tired of that over here. Indonesia, on the morning news, says it is going to establish relations with China in a while. End July 7.

[Tuesday,] July 8[, 1975]. A very quiet summer day with tennis at 5—Akwei and Wang beating Bush and Xiao. Wang does not play net. He stays back. He wears sneakers with no laces in them. He is about 18. He makes some good shots, but he is a wild kid, and I found the language barrier difficult in trying to help him with his court position. He loves to win. He took the ball and banged the hell out of it, it went straight up in the air, when he missed an overhead. I was delighted to see this. It proves to me that Wang is a normal, red-blooded tennis competitor.

Long walk with Fred where he spotted the Polish [embassy] cat again. Practically pulled my arm out of my socket as young Paul Lambert and I tore down the road, past the PLA guards (two at rigid attention with bayonets on their rifles for the first time early in the evening).[10] Fred made a dive at the iron gate, sticking his neck all the way through it in quest of the elusive cat. We then had to sniff around the tall grass for five minutes till Fred satisfied himself the cat was gone. What a horrible international incident if he ever caught the cat. Lots of couples out on the hot summer night. People jump away when they see Fred. They shy back. They show their kids Fred—kids in their arms, but then they sidle off as we get near with Fred on his rope.

Lunch with the Ballous—two daughters—Chris and Jennifer. A message from the milkman saying it was very difficult for them when we had certain numbers of bottles delivered one day and then changed it the following week. What a contrast. In Maine the milkman grins with delight when we up our order. He shows a certain disappointment when we have to cut back, but he is ready to serve. We have been having kids galore and thus we have increased the supply. Now they are in Shanghai and I cut back on the amount of

[10]Lambert later served as U.S. ambassador to Ecuador under President Bush (1990–92).

milk. But apparently this causes a bureaucratic morass. We have now settled on [a] two milk–one yogurt policy. And if we need more we will dispatch someone to pick it up at the Friendship Store. They're simply not adjusted to making these changes. Their computers cannot memorize or cope apparently. Milkman, a pleasant guy, shows up in a brown-looking Jeep kind of thing every morning and gets the milk in place—delivered by 7:30. Today I greeted him in my old pajamas and he seemed genuinely amused. He likes Fred.

I wish I could tell what China's real intent is. After reading *Hostage in Peking* and reliving some of the horrors of the Cultural Revolution, I can't be sure. Should [the] Soviet Union and China get together, it would be, in my opinion, a whole new ballgame. And yet there is a latent interest in and respect for the United States. China keeps wanting us to be strong, wanting us to defend Europe, wanting us to increase our defense budget, etc. And yet their rhetoric and propaganda against the imperialist aggressive U.S. is so blatant that it makes me furious. But the question is what is their real heartbeat? What is their real intent? I don't think the United States has anything to fear from China. The talk about how we lost China infuriates the Chinese and now it infuriates me.[11] I can see

---

[11] Bush refers here to a frequent charge from the political right—in particular during the late 1940s and early 1950s—that the American government "lost" China to the Communist world. Most often the blame was pinned on the Truman administration and specifically Secretary of State Dean Acheson, arguing that a stronger defense of the Nationalist government would have ensured a different outcome to the Chinese civil war. In late 1949, with the Communist victory imminent, Acheson authorized the State Department to publish its China White Paper, a series of documents ostensibly designed to demonstrate that Mao's victory had come about through no fault of Washington's. This defense only provided further ammunition for Acheson's critics, though 64 percent of Americans polled at the time reported having not heard of the White Paper at all.

This question of American responsibility for China's fate was a crucial Cold War argument. Subsequent American policymakers feared that too passive a response to Communist aggression—even if strategically wise or prudent at the moment—would lead to open-ended charges of weakness from their political flanks at home. Thus, one could argue, the question of "who lost China" contributed at

where it is very clearly wrong. China was not ours to lose and that has been part of the problem.

At the soccer match the Africans were all cheering like mad for the West German team—incongruous. The Chinese don't like the Africans it seems to me individually. I think they look down on them. And I know the African students here don't like it here in China. I talked to some who are going back in two or three months to Tanzania to work as railroad specialists, working with the Chinese. They are most anxious to get back—something that is very natural. The lifestyle here is very different. They are shut off from girls, they are shut off from entertainment as they know and like it, and the result is they all sit around the International Club becoming slightly somewhat of a problem. As I drive along the streets I wonder whether the average Chinese kids give a rat's tail about Maoism, Communism or whatever it is. They are thoroughly indoctrinated day in and day out; drilled on radio, loudspeakers, in the parks, in the mountains, on the trains. But with their standard of living where it is, I wonder if they really have time to do anything other than to listen and support the system. The disturbances in the southern part of China—Fujian province and others—I am sure would give us a different perspective if we saw them. Peking is quiet, controlled, disciplined. And pretty hot in the summer. Not as hot as Houston but not unlike Houston either: humid, rains clear it for a while, back comes the humidity.

The dress is much more relaxed now. Pastel shaped blouses on the women. Still baggy panted. Dresses on the kids and the men

least tacitly to vigorous American responses to Communist gains in Cuba, Korea, Latin America, and throughout Southeast Asia, especially Vietnam. Most historians today believe the question itself is useful only for understanding the American political scene during the early Cold War; it was simply not within Washington's power to save Chiang Kai-shek's beleaguered regime from its Communist opponents. Indeed the very question "Who lost China?" implicitly presupposes the very Western domination that Mao's forces relied upon as a rallying cry for the Chinese people. In suggesting that China was someone's to lose, and not the master of its own destiny, it grants Westerners a level of omnipotence over world affairs and the internal fate of developing nations far in excess of their actual abilities.

with light-colored sport shirts—short sleeve, open at the waist. On the night of a contest at the Peking Stadium the people go in by the thousands. The whole street, which is a two-way street running from the International Club to our house and beyond, becomes a one-way artery with literally thousands and thousands of bicycles. Yesterday coming back from tennis I got caught in the maelstrom and it was really rather panicky. They shoot by too, with people rushing I guess for the better seats. And the younger guys driving like Barney Oldfield.[12]

Hostage in Peking by Grey is still on my mind. Imagine hanging the guy's cat, plastering posters all over his room, dabbing black paint everywhere, the vindictiveness of the accusations.[13] Two years in solitary. And little inconsistencies like making him renew his driver's license for his car, making him pay for heat when none was delivered, etc., etc. Unbelievable. End July 8.[14]

[Wednesday,] July 9[, 1975]. Gunthers and Henrietta came for lunch. Tennis in the afternoon. Played at the Canadian Embassy with Small, David Ambrose of Australia, and Akwei.[15] It was a cool evening out there. Then a very nice dinner at the Soviet Embassy in honor of the French ambassador. Tolstikov of the Soviet Union is a pretty good guy, former boss of Leningrad, and interesting kind of man. Sitting in this palatial embassy with dining room of pink marble walls and great high ceiling—good dinner with two kinds of Russian caviar first, three wines plus vodka and much fancier than we can possibly do. The meals are served by a group of young men, all bachelors who are there for a year—some

[12]An auto racing pioneer, Barney Oldfield gained fame as the first racecar driver to reach a speed of sixty miles per hour during a match race in 1903.

[13]See my footnote to the entry for June 17, 1975.

[14]Gerald Ford announced his candidacy for president on July 8, 1975.

[15]David Ambrose served in Australia's embassy in Beijing under Ambassador Stephen Fitzgerald from 1975 to 1977, and he was Australian consul general in Shanghai from 1988 to 2001.

go on to college. They look like central casting sent over some typical Soviet Guys.

Thursday, July 10[, 1975]. Bar came in on a special CAAC [Civil Aviation Administration of China] flight. They originally were scheduled to come in the afternoon. There were no seats on the flight, so after a lot of hassling they arrived. The trip went well. It was hot in Nanking, etc., etc., but they saw a lot of sights and apparently the train trip was OK. Casey Manning and Slim Childress of Stewart and Stevenson.[16] They are having a rough time getting business done with the Chinese. The Chinese say quote us on the biggest fracking equipment you've got.[17] Pressed for what formations need to be fracked, what kinds of specifications and all, the Chinese simply won't respond. Either they don't know what they want or they aren't willing to give out the necessary specifics. These guys are getting increasingly frustrated. Don sent the children's travel for Moscow. It appeared on a special flight. Beautifully handled all the way to Tokyo on Northwest. Transferred to JAL and it worked out very well. Farewell party at 6 o'clock for Folco Trabalza of Italy.[18] He is a man that has been most unhappy here. Indeed he had close to a nervous breakdown. He is now going off to Belgium to finish his diplomatic career, and he is happy as a lark. A pleasant guy, but typical of the kind of guy that ought not to be in this very complicated and difficult environment of Peking. I talked to Mr. Chi, head of Protocol, asking about the Foreign Minister's plans for fall at the U.N. No response. He told me, "I understand you had lunch with Huang Hua." They do keep up with what I do.

[16]The company known today as Stewart and Stevenson LLC eventually concluded a deal with the Chinese for the sale of $6 million worth of oil fracturing equipment.

[17]The process of hydraulic fracturing or "fracking" involves injecting fluids or sand at high pressure into underground rock formations. Fracturing the formations allows additional oil or gas to be extracted from a well.

[18]Folco Trabalza served in Beijing as Italy's ambassador from 1971 to 1975, having previously served as Rome's representative in Belgrade.

Rumors in Peking about a new poster campaign right here in
Peking.[19] Apparently posters went up and they were ripped down.
British journalist Peter Griffiths apparently was held for an hour,
taking pictures of the posters with Ross Munro's wife.[20] Had a long
talk with the Mongolian ambassador at the Russian dinner. Very
pleasant, talking about the hunting and fishing in his country, and
rather relaxed. We have very few contacts with Mongolians, and I
thought this one was a good one. China is worried about Russia
gaining influence in Hanoi. China seems at this juncture to be the
only power with any communication in Cambodia. Cambodia still
isolated, still cut off. Rumors of mass evacuation of Phnom Penh
still prevalent, with gory details of the long march out of Phnom
Penh.[21] Oddly enough I think the United States is in a better position to be influential in Southeast Asia, provided we do not move
too quick[ly] trying to purchase the friendship of Vietnam. I am for
sitting that one out for a while. More and more thought to what
the President can do on his trip to China. Cable came in giving me
clearance to go on my leave. But I am now struggling with the forthcoming congressional delegations; one to be headed by Percy, the
other by Bob Byrd.[22] I'll be here for the Percy delegation, but I
would like to get home before the other one hits, so I can get a good
rest in Maine. Talked to Bob Costello of Kellogg Company who are
building ammonia plants. He is having a frustrating time. He cannot get an office. They have now offered him an office in the new

[19]"We would not make too much of the appearance of one poster by disgruntled soldiers," the USLO counseled Washington. "It has been evident for several
years that Chinese society is full of this kind of antagonism and unsettled scores."
[20]See Bush's entry and my footnote for July 11, 1975.
[21]The Khmer Rouge, the Communist regime that ruled Cambodia from 1975 to
1979, forcibly evacuated the population of Cambodia's largest city, Phnom Penh,
to labor camps in mid-1975 as part of the regime's attempt to remove urban citizens to agricultural communes and create a classless society. During its rule the
Khmer Rouge was directly responsible for killing over 700,000 people. An additional million died from starvation and other scourges caused by their displacement.
[22]See my footnote to the entry for August 20, 1975.

wing of the Peking Hotel but at a very expensive price. China is not above trading on price now. They are not above holding people up on price when they see the chance. They can be awful tough, these people. Very disciplined when they think they are one up. I have been reading about Chinese negotiations and they can whipsaw you pretty good. Dinner at home—just family. A nice Mr. Sun Chinese dinner.

Friday, July 11[, 1975]. Morning working out details for the kids' travel, for reading up on the news, Mongolian reception at their embassy 11–12, then luncheon (going-away) for Qasim Al Yagout of Kuwait, going off to Rome as DCM [deputy chief of mission]. Ambassador Folco Trabalza will call this afternoon at four.

July 11. In the afternoon Ross Munro of the *Globe and Mail,* taking John Burns' place.[23] Trabalza came by, bringing us a silver pitcher with the U.S.[flag] engraved on it—he had bought it in Shanghai. Very beautiful present. Quiet evening on the 11th. Saturday a spectacular day. Hot tennis, leaving me slightly worn out. Three sets in the big heat around 9:30 to 11. Then took Dorothy and Tricia to the Great Wall. Then John Boyd's singing group had a picnic at one of the Ming Tombs. Spectacular beauty. The reds turned orange, the sun went down, the silhouettes of the trees looked exactly like those in many of the Chinese paintings, silhouetted against sky and mountains. And the music sounded extra special. Fred behaved well, refused to chase a big flock of sheep that were strolling around the tombs. The police were out there. They kept a lot of the kids back and seemed to be busily watching everything that went on— signaling Dorothy and Tricia to climb down off one of the walls of the tomb. Not bad since the whole thing is crumbling. Beautiful glazed tile lies all around the tombs. Except for the one or two that

---

[23]Ross Munro worked in Beijing for the Toronto *Globe and Mail* until 1978, when he joined *Time* magazine, serving as a reporter and bureau chief in various Asia posts. He later co-wrote *The Coming Conflict with China* (New York: Knopf, 1987).

have been restored, they are in total disrepair. And yet they are perhaps the most beautiful place in all of China.

Got a haircut and found I could carry on a reasonable conversation with the barber—not good, but enough to understand a little of what he was saying. Practice is absolutely essential in the language. There is a great cynicism in the diplomatic community about the lack of freedom in Peking. Most people understand it, and John Burns, who is going back now to be with the *New York Times,* put it well when he talked about tranquility and the luxury of time. These things replace many of the freedoms that we are used to and don't have.

[**Saturday, July 12, 1975.**] China's red news, Saturday, July 12, highlighted the decline of the U.S. economy—numbers of people marching on Washington for jobs. And if you read the article with the statistics on crime and lack of safety on the streets, it would sound like the whole society was coming apart. Why they highlight this in the red news I don't know. Clearly it is our internal affair, but they insist on pointing out how decadent we are and how on the decline we are. They would go right through the roof if we put out an official story of some sort saying how deprived they are of freedoms, and how dictatorial they are in their state, and how they have subjugated people, who undoubtedly are freedom loving, to rigid controls. Contrasts. They do such a job on the basics and yet they can be awful severe.

It was cool at the Ming Tombs—I almost needed a sweater. The rain came and cleared it up and then we got to Peking and the house was very very hot. Tried to sleep with no air conditioning, just because it seemed cooler outside—ended up having to get up in the middle of the night and turn it on. Stifling. The picnic was held at the Ma Ling Tomb.

Saturday the Foreign Ministry sent word that they wanted to treat my family plus another couple or so from USLO to go to Harbin and Dalian, and also to Daqing, the oil field. This is in Northeast China, old Manchuria, and should be a great trip. I told them I would like to do it, starting out next Wednesday or Thursday. Petersmeyer will be here.[24]

Sunday [July 13, 1975]. Hot. Temperature around 95 degrees. Tennis at 5:00 p.m. Church in the morning by bicycle. Shopping at the stores later. Popsicle concession is a big thing. They sell them like mad; depending on what kind, between 2 to 4.5 cents U.S. People throw the paper around. There is littering in the places where the masses are not mobilized to clean up. Up at the very top of the Great Wall. Unfortunately people sometimes use the very top point as a bathroom—rather odoriferous in the middle of the summer and a little ugly. Unlike the streets which are swept and watered by these big machines, there are places that get fairly littered and dirty. The Greek guy that got in the traffic accident was driving without a license and going like hell. God there are some horrible foreign drivers in this country, and I am surprised there are not more accidents. Bar had a bicyclist run into them in Shanghai and we saw the same thing at Canton. Maybe there is a higher casualty rate than we know about.

Tennis at 5:30 with Lao Wang. Then a tremendous rainstorm about 10 at night that cleared the air slightly. Note—India's democracy has been set back by Mrs. Gandhi—China is jumping all over her.[25] China is way behind even a totalitarian India in terms of individual freedom. They are really challenging her hypocrisy, I think, something I feel strongly about. But I keep coming back to the society here, wondering how long there will be no individualism. How long everyone's head will be down and tail up. How long before there is a real quest for individual decisions, what standard of living people want, freedom to travel, freedom to read, freedom to study, freedom to get away from the music and propaganda. The oppressive heat here makes one wonder about these things more than when it is crisp, and there seems to be a zip in the step and in the air. End of Sunday, July 13.

[24]Greg Petersmeyer served on President Richard Nixon's White House staff and would later direct the Points of Light Foundation.
[25]See Bush's entry and my footnote for June 29, 1975.

[Monday,] July 14[, 1975]. I am just reading an article in the June 29th *Los Angeles Times* about child care centers.[26] A Mrs. Weissbourd reporting that she was told by the Chinese as follows:

> We asked the teachers what they did with naughty children. We were told there is no such thing as punishment. They talk with any child who is misbehaving and persuade the child that he or she would not do whatever it was. I am sure they showed us their best. I would do the same thing here with visitors, but they communicate positive attitudes about caring for each other in such a way that it works.

That is her comment. Mine is: on my way out to the Tombs, I saw a woman and a couple of kids. She grabbed the kid, conked him right smack over the head. Children crying, and later, on the way in, we saw a young person getting strangled. One group had his arm behind him and the other had him twisting his ear, leading him somewhere for a little discipline. The point is what we see is not exactly the way it is. We see a remarkable participation by the kids in school, all disciplined, holding their hands up, reciting. But I am wondering how it really is behind the façade for the foreign friends.

Monday July 14. In the office all day. Lunch, home with the kids. French national day at the French embassy. Qiao Guanhua appearing. He was very rude to the Russian ambassador. Not rude exactly, but shunned him. Spoke to me but with no great warmth or friendship. I said I hadn't seen him in a long time. He simply nodded. There is a[n] enormous difference in the way we are treated here and the way Huang Zhen is treated in Washington. I am not sure that a lot of this isn't because of the way Kissinger decreed it, but I guess I'll never know the answer to that one. Farewell duck dinner for the Thayers, our kids—14 people at 151 yuan—not bad. The dinner was good. We laid off some of the dishes. Came home and watched *Kojak* on the TV.[27] End of July 14.

---

[26]Bush's quotation does not match the article's text verbatim.

[27]Starring Telly Savalas as a tough-talking New York detective with a passion for lollipops, *Kojak* aired on CBS from 1973 to 1978.

[Tuesday,] July 15[, 1975]. Rather quiet day. A visit in the office at 2:30 by the Merrills—he owns some Annapolis newspapers—worked in the State Department, was visiting the Lamberts.[28] Long chat with him. Final tennis game with Akwei and Bush v. the kids—victory! Went to George Marconi's for pizza and drinks and then to meet the CAAC 922 to pick up Greg Petersmeyer. We called out and the plane that was supposed to arrive at 19:50 was going to get in at 20:50. Little later we called again just to be sure and they said the plane had already arrived at 7:20. It is difficult to pin these things down. The Merrills told me that Paul Warnke was here in China coming as a visitor.[29] In the red news it also says that a U.S. revolutionary student delegation leaves Peking for home. The delegation was met and feted by Zhang Xiangshan, deputy head of the International Liaison Department of the Central Committee of the Communist Party of China. We had heard that Jerry Rubin had been in.[30] Perhaps this was his delegation. That is all the item said. They differentiate between party and government. Party entertains these far-outs. Rest of the news typical—meeting and greeting different delegations. God they come here by the thousands. End of July 15.

[Wednesday,] July 16[, 1975]. Seven-forty the Trans-Siberian pulled out with the Bushes aboard.[31] The music plays and there is a nice little wave-off down there that is rather pleasant. It is going to be a little warm on the train, but they were excited. How they

[28]Philip Merrill worked for the State Department during the early 1960s. He then turned to journalism and eventually owned the *Washingtonian* and *Baltimore* magazines and *The Capital*, an Annapolis newspaper.

[29]Paul Warnke served in the Pentagon under secretaries of defense Robert McNamara and Clifford Clark, and later as an arms negotiator during the Carter administration.

[30]Before moderating his political views in later life, Jerry Rubin was a leading social and antiwar activist, co-founder of the Yippie movement, and member of the so-called Chicago Seven, who were charged with disrupting the 1968 Democratic National Convention in that city.

[31]Neil, Marvin, and Dorothy, plus Dorothy's friend Tricia Everett.

will be in five more days I don't know. All the visas fell into place at the last moment including granting of the visa for Tricia Everett.

July 16. Kids left early on the train. 11:00 a.m.—I went to a fish-in at the Soviet Embassy—Harland, Bush, Bulak, and Fitzgerald. Amazing performance under which the Soviet herd the fish in big nets toward the little bridge. They jump way out of the water and we stand around with big nets on long poles, catching fish that are somewhat smaller then a bluefish but bigger than mackerel. They weigh pretty heavy and they jump like hell. It was hot and sweaty but we had a great day. I wrote a separate report on this which is available. Then to the ambassador's pool on his 16-hectare compound—big, typical Russian dinner, eating a lot of fish and a marvelous soup—cold and other ways as well. Too many wines, too much vodka, too many after-dinner drinks, and all in all an exhausting performance. 5:30—meet Dr. Ayensu of the Smithsonian.[32] He is a Ghanaian—he is here visiting the Akweis. Working for the Smithsonian. Got the word that we are going to leave tomorrow at 8:00. Baggage to be there at 8:00, and we at 8:30, to head on the 9:00 plane for Dairen. Get back next Wednesday, so it will be a six-day trip. And I am looking forward to it.

Accompanied by Mrs. Bush and three others from the USLO, Bush departed Beijing on July 17 for a weeklong visit to China's northeast. Heavy industrial sites, including oil fields, were on the agenda, and he told the State Department that the trip was "motivated partly by [an] earlier [Foreign Ministry] promise to take chief of USLO on separate visit, partly by desire to improve relations with the USLO, and partly by desire of escorting officials for a semi-vacation."[33]

[Wednesday, July 23, 1975.] Arrived back in Peking Wednesday, July 23—5:00 p.m. Whipped by the heat. Back to the house for pick-up dinner—a martini and early bed.

[32]Edward Ayensu headed the Smithsonian's Office of Biological Conservation.
[33]Bush unfortunately made no diary entries during this trip; thus the diary continues upon his return to Beijing.

Thursday, July 24[, 1975]. Briefed the staff on our fascinating visit. Zeder ran into complications—tried to get a visa in twenty-four hours from Tokyo since he didn't get his visa when he left.[34] Couldn't do it. Couple of very clear phone calls. Tennis with Petersmeyer and the two Chinese. Catching up on piles of correspondence and clippings. The dead fish that I gave to Guo were served for lunch. They just cannot accept things. I guess he would have been stopped going out the gate if he had taken the fish. I should have thought of that, but I thought maybe they would be able to do that. The pride in the astronauts, though this one will not be too well received in China because of the Soviet aspects.[35] Lambert's kid in the hospital for two weeks for appendicitis. Good treatment by the Chinese. Mind diverting to vacation and Maine. Wrestling with my conscience about leaving before the second congressional delegation arrives. If I don't go, I'll only get a week in Maine and not see as much of the kids. And end up hectic and tired for the consultations. It really isn't necessary for me to stay, and I told the Department I will abide by their decision. Quiet dinner at Julebu. Hot but not unbearable at all in Peking. End Thursday, July 24.

July 25, [1975,] Friday. To work early to get caught up. Seven-thirty staff meeting. A lot of people have gone down to the beach—Beidaihe, off to Hong Kong, etc. Lunch—Ambassador [Phagna] Lien Pravongiengkam at our residence. Just been named Ambassador from Laos to U.S. He is not a Pathet Lao. He must be distressed by the way his country is going. Middle of July 25. Lunch went well. The ambassador asked me to find out where his agreement stands.[36] I don't quite see that he will make it to the U.S. with

[34]Fred Zeder, director of territorial affairs for the Department of the Interior and a longtime Bush friend, had hoped to visit Beijing in July following an official trip to Tokyo. Unable to secure a last-minute visa for this trip, he instead visited China in October as a guest of the Bushes.

[35]Soviet cosmonauts in a Soyuz capsule docked in space with American astronauts in their Apollo spacecraft on July 17, 1975. The joint mission was designed to demonstrate the possibilities of détente.

[36]See Bush's entry and my footnote for June 13, 1975.

the Pathet Lao taking control of the country on such a rigid control, but maybe he will.

Note. My watch was going to cost $300 to have it fixed in the States, my Patek Philippe. The Friendship Store fixed it for $12.50.

[Saturday,] July 26[, 1975]. The office. Tennis in the morning. Badminton in the afternoon. Hotter than hell indoors. Really aching tired that night. Lunch with Jacques Groothaert of Belgium and Madelyn back from vacation in Europe. Groothaert is kind of down on the Chinese, points out their tough things and keeps it in mind. Maybe he is smart to keep the negative things in perspective, but that attitude can be overdone here. Amazing to see Kukrit of Thailand and Marcos of the Philippines meeting and talking about throwing out the U.S. bases. The cycle is almost complete although the Asian countries are not in Red China's orbit at this point. The big question is does China want to expand, or will they be content to offset Russia with a presence in Southeast Asia but not encouraging revolution in those last remaining free countries. This is the enormous question, and of course it brings you back to Taiwan and what should be done there. The Korean ambassador had a film, invited many ambassadors here—showed a vicious propaganda film against the United States. John Foster Dulles derided, officers from the *Pueblo* submitting to humiliations, signing a document admitting their guilt.[37] Then a Korean lecturing Americans at the border. Pure propaganda and vicious and filthy—shows an adulation of the great and glorious leader Kim Il Sung. And all the time at home the evils of Kim Il Sung are not pointed up. Simply the shortcomings of Park Chung Hee in South Korea.[38] We don't seem ever to learn.

[37]John Foster Dulles, an advocate of brinkmanship in the interest of containing the spread of communism, served as secretary of state under President Dwight Eisenhower from 1953 to 1959. The intelligence-gathering vessel USS *Pueblo* was captured by North Korea in 1968, and the surviving members of its crew were held captive for nearly eleven months. Washington eventually publicly apologized to Pyongyang for the ship's activities in order to win their release.

[38]Park Chung Hee was a South Korean military leader and president of that nation from 1963 to 1979.

One thing you get from living here is the force and control of the communists, the power to manage thought, the power to use propaganda. Sometimes it seems so obvious, but when repeated enough perhaps people will believe it. If China wants good relations with us, clearly they ought not to be attacking us the way they do all the time officially. I am sure they would object to some of the anti-PRC propaganda from the Committee on Free China etc. at home.[39] But it is not official. Maybe it is too much of a distinction to ask.

Sunday [July 27, 1975]. Church; two-hour bicycle ride; lunch with Bryce Harland of New Zealand at the International Club. Very relaxed day. A reception in the evening for Chad. Then ambassador Akwei of Ghana and his three kids, charming, all coming over to watch Telly Savalas and Mary Tyler Moore and *M*A*S*H*.[40] That kind of entertainment means an awful lot here. The Chad ambassador, following the overthrow of Tombalbaye in Chad, is heading home.[41] He is unhappy as he can be about it. He has been here about 14 months. His wife, 30 years old, and six small kids. He is reportedly nervous about what awaits him in Chad. Kind of sad. It was a really hot day. I wore a coat to the reception and wished the heck I hadn't done that. No exercise. Too tired from the exertion the day before. Prices seem to be going up on the things they sell foreigners here in China.

Received a cable from the States asking me to stay until the second delegation, arriving August 20, at least leaves Peking.[42] This

[39]One of the umbrella groups for the politically powerful "China Lobby," the Committee for a Free China strove to influence Washington's policies toward Chiang Kai-shek's regime. It was also known as the Committee of One Million, for its leaders claimed to have more than a million supporters.

[40]Bush most likely refers to the *Mary Tyler Moore Show*, which ran from 1970 to 1977. Set in the Korean War—though arguably more topically about the American experience in Vietnam—*M*A*S*H* ran from 1973 to 1983.

[41]Ngarta (François) Tombalbaye, Chad's first president, had been killed during a coup in April.

[42]"We would like to suggest that you defer your departure long enough to be there for the main events in the Peking portion of visit by the Congressional group led by Anderson," Kissinger wrote. Bush sent several cables to the State Depart-

of course I will do, though it really screws up vacation, and guarantees I will not see two of our kids before they go back to college. Steve Allen and his attractive son came by. They had been on a fascinating visit around China. We'll get more on that later I think. China launched a satellite today.[43] China must think it is weird as they see us refuse to vote funds for Turkey.[44] These kinds of actions must convince them that we are getting to be as weak as they think.

All the CIA publicity bothers me too. One tends to become more conservative after he has lived here a while. Conservative in the sense of guaranteeing freedoms which would make one want to see the excesses of the CIA controlled, but also conservative in the fact that institutions that have served to preserve freedom, or to hopefully prop it up in some places, are being dismantled. And this I don't think is good. I read Agee in *Playboy* and clearly he is a socialist or a communist, wanting to overthrow the institutions.[45] But he gets wide publicity riding in on the anti-CIA mode of the liberals. Of course I am offended by the assassination plots etc., but the problem is you see the tip of the iceberg and get no credit for the great bulk that lies below the surface.

Reading *Stilwell* by Barbara Tuchman.[46] Very interesting book. Makes one understand a great deal about mistakes that were made

---

ment asking for a late-summer leave, but Foggy Bottom wanted him to host the delegation. As Oscar Armstrong explained, "Since the Anderson delegation is the one making the official visit, we want to avoid doing anything that might give the impression that we do not attach appropriate importance to it. . . . but if deferring your departure, e.g. until August 24 discombobulates your personal plans too much, let us know."

[43]The first successful launch of the Long March 2 rocket placed China's third satellite into orbit on July 26, 1975.

[44]In a bitterly close vote, the House of Representatives voted to continue a ban on American arms shipments to Turkey, imposed six months earlier when Turkish forces used American arms in Cyprus. President Ford had lobbied hard for an end to the ban, which had curtailed $185 million of aid already in the pipeline.

[45]Philip Agee resigned from the CIA in 1968, disillusioned by American and CIA support for oppressive regimes in Latin America. His 1975 book *Inside the Company* included the names of 250 CIA officers and agents.

[46]Barbara Tuchman's *Stilwell and the American Experience in China, 1911–45* (1970), winner of the Pulitzer Prize, is a biography of Joseph Stilwell, American

in the past. And when one reads the Committee on a Free China report about how great Chiang was, again one only gets part of the picture. You don't see the corruption and loss of human dignity and life that seems to have, a lot of it at least, disappeared from Mainland China. Why can't the two sit down and work something out between them. That would be the real answer, but it seems unlikely, certainly at this point. End of Sunday, July 27.

Monday, July 28[, 1975]. We are having our morning staff meetings—Mondays, Wednesday and Fridays now. It is a little better. 8:45 to whenever the business is finished. 10:00—Delois Blakely, a black girl who for ten years had been a nun, came in to see me.[47] Most enthusiastic, and visited with all the African students. Said that they had recommended that she come to me, that they were friends of mine, etc. She said that students were missing female companionship and that every once in a while a Chinese girl looked at them in more than a sisterly way, but nothing was ever done about it. She confirmed that the students were totally isolated on a physical basis.

Lunch with the Caterpillar Trade Group that came to town, headed by Don Koonon from Hong Kong and Dell Lammers, Vice President out of Peoria.[48] Refreshingly straightforward. Good guys, talking about their business experience with the Chinese, sitting them down and asking them many good technical questions. But they haven't the slightest idea why they are here. They think it has to do with pipeline equipment for laying pipe, but they have no idea whether the Chinese are interested in one machine, ten machines or any machines at all, or maybe a thousand. They have no idea and they have been here almost a week.

---

military attaché in China before World War II and military chief of staff to Chiang Kai-shek from 1942 to 1944.

[47]Blakely, a community activist, was later named a community mayor of Harlem by New York Mayor Rudolph Giuliani.

[48]By August Caterpillar would sign a contract for pipe-laying machinery worth $2.3 million. The scope of the deal expanded in the ensuing months, and the firm contracted to deliver $3.8 million worth of equipment in October.

In the afternoon I went to call on Ambassador Ogawa of Japan. They are working on their "hegemony" clause, the Russians insisting it not go into their treaty with China, and China insisting that it be in the treaty.[49] Japan caught between Russia and China. They are also working on a consular agreement to open a consulate in Shanghai. China opening one in Osaka. And on a fisheries agreement. They are way ahead of us on these kinds of details. In the afternoon we briefed the Electronic Industries Association at 4:30 followed by a reception. This is the first industrial association to come, made up of vice presidents at Collins, General Electric, ITT, etc. Again a very straightforward good group who had been presented a schedule with some travel and some discussion, and they wondered whether this was different. Actually it is just the same as if they had been an opera group or a stamp collectors group or whatever it was. We rushed from our 5:30 to 6:30 reception, at which we were joined by a Chinese petroleum chemical technical survey group off to the States, to the national day of Peru at the International Club. Hotter than blazes. These things can be punishingly hot and unimaginative, but the Peru ambassador, Espejo [-Romero], was most anxious we come.

After that, dinner at Harry Thayer's and home. Bar is having four silk cummerbunds made. Beautiful brocaded silk, total cost 25 yuan. Monograms being put on my bathrobe (40 cents). Imagine what they would charge in the States for that. End of Monday, July 28.

Tuesday, July 29[, 1975]. Political briefing, quiet lunch at home. And a going-away party for Ralph Larello, Pete Bergin and Mike Woods—our security guards. Young kids, twenty to twenty-seven,

---

[49]Japan and China eventually signed a treaty of friendship and peace in 1978, although Soviet officials repeatedly warned Tokyo against aligning too closely with Beijing. Specifically the Chinese sought to include language binding the Japanese to oppose any other nation's effort to exert primary control over East Asia, an anti-hegemony clause aimed specifically at the Soviet Union, and similar to pledges agreed to by Kissinger and other American officials in their own joint statements with the Chinese. Japanese officials, eager to chart a middle course within the Sino-Soviet dispute, were not keen to endorse such a blatantly anti-Soviet clause.

unmarried—they pull eight-hour duty at USLO, rather boring performance but they have done pretty well and made a lot of friends
in the diplomatic community. What could they do if we were over-
run by a hostile force—answer, zilch.

Gowon of Nigeria was overthrown, thus bringing home to me
the instability in so many of these countries.[50] The U.S. comes in
for an enormous share of criticism, but when you look around the
world you can see why the U.S. gets the begrudging respect of so
many other countries. India's abortion of democracy; the great
changes in Southeast Asia; the turmoil in Africa. To all of these we
clearly present a comfortable, reasonable and encouraging alternative. Rumors about that Sihanouk will be going back to Phnom
Penh. I'll believe it when I see it. He may go back, but I don't see
that he'll have much influence. The slaughter and the isolation now
of Cambodia worries me. Both Vietnams want into the United Nations now. God I can clearly remember how they castigated the
U.N. and said there would never be two Vietnams. It all depends
on whose ox is being gored. And yet the countries are united, including China, against keeping the ROK [South Korea] out of the
U.N. China's satellite is orbiting the earth. It will be a little difficult
for them to criticize picture-taking by the big powers. Saw Lin Ping
at the Peru reception—almost as if our trip had not taken place.[51]
End of July 29.

[Wednesday,] July 30[, 1975]. Hassle of C. Fred. He now cannot
go as extra baggage but rather as a separate package at baggage rates
—$9 a pound, times $28 a dog plus $12 a cage equals 9 × 40 =
$360 one way. Sorry, he stays here! Lunch today at our house with
Steve Allen and his attractive son Bill. They have been on a tour of
China in the company of the China Travel Service.

Bar leaves today on Air France. Steve Allen spent some time running down information on a religion. They have an office of religious

[50]Yakubu Gowon was Nigerian head of state from 1966 to 1975.
[51]Lin had escorted Bush and the USLO entourage on their trip to China's northeast.

affairs in Peking. He told his guide he wanted to see it. The guide's reply was, "How did you know about that?" Big rain, one of the biggest in Peking in a long, long time. Cooled things down although it is warming up again now.

Bar departed on schedule. Early night sitting outside on the patio reading. I keep wondering about the excessive[ly] protective nature of the State Department, particularly the Secretary's approach to China. Just got a letter saying that no ambassador should come here—tourism, familiarization, of curiosity. Why the excessive protectiveness? Plimsoll of Australia was here. Had a great visit with Steve Fitzgerald and they both profited enormously. Apparently Sullivan of the Philippines and Bill Cargo from Nepal wanted to come, but they have both been turned down.[52] I wrote Oscar [Armstrong] telling him that I disagreed with the decision but would certainly abide by it. I think we need more openness. I realize that things are sensitive, but I believe the open approach is better. I don't see how this could get us in trouble at all.

Our trade with China will be way down this year. Less than half of what it was last year, with no great commercial deals in the mill. People will focus on this next year in terms of deterioration, although we have been lucky that they have accepted the fact that the decline in trade this year is due to less agricultural goods being shipped from the United States because of the good harvest here in China.

Sounds that I will not forget. The early morning singing in the park—loud and usually very good tenor voices for the most part. The organized cadence of kids marching (*Yi, er, Yi, er*). The never-ceasing honking of horns downtown in Peking, the jingle of bicycle bells, the laughter of the children as they play near the park, the blaring of the loudspeakers with the exercises of the propaganda whether it's on a train, in a park, at a building site, wherever. The July and August sound of the crickets.

[52]Previously director of the State Department's Policy Planning Staff, William Cargo was ambassador to Nepal from 1973 to 1976.

I have studied Chinese. It has continually brought home to me how difficult it is to operate fully in a foreign land without the language. Went to try to cash in a few yuan for Bar yesterday at the airport and simply couldn't get through to the guy. So we finally just gave up. He was trying to be helpful, he was smiling, he was trying to explain and I just couldn't understand. Oh, the frustration! The dollar is stronger now. Yesterday they were giving 187. It had been 174. I gave an Arab 180 and said, "Keep the change" for $1 for Bar. He pointed out to me it was 187. Embarrassment!

As we drove to the airport, four little kids were standing right on the side of the highway, one of them acting almost like a bullfighter or a flagman at the railroad. Standing with one foot on the side of the road, very dangerous if two cars were trying to pass. He stood there. He's about 8 or 9 years old and stood defiantly with his flag out. Guo immediately pulled to a stop and turned him in to the local policeman along the road. The policeman started to walk down the street to reprimand the kid and what did they do—they took off like scalded apes, just the way the kids would do in the United States. I continually see the similarity between kids here—wrestling, shooting games, ball playing, occasionally the reprimand by parents, occasionally the tears by the very little ones, the interest in sports, enormous curiosity of kids.

Went to the hospital to call on two Americans. A Dr. —— who is from California and is 68 years old.[53] At one point they thought he was dead. He looked like it yesterday. His wife was there and his son arriving. And a young kid from Bethesda—17-year-old boy who was stricken with a throat disease. The boy was flat on his back. He had had a 104 temperature. He was being drip fed intravenously. Looked uncomfortable and he did seem to appreciate the fact we came by. The hospital rooms were private, clean, all the windows wide open. Cool because of the rain the day before, and generally it looked like a pretty nice place to be sick although slightly

[53]I have chosen to withhold this individual's name from publication in order to preserve the privacy of the medical history.

dark. Both Mrs. —— and the boy told me they were getting excellent care. End July 30.

Thursday, July 31[, 1975]. Economic briefing. Our trade is off tremendously with China. Less than half for '75 of what it was in '74, mainly agriculture. Now the deficit is about 2 to 1 against them, but there are no major sales in sight. I don't believe the claims and asset thing is affecting us.[54] I also do feel that there is some political pressure on us in trade. They are buying some things from others such as old field equipment, where we have the best, but they are going elsewhere. I don't think it is a major factor yet.

—— and —— of Sacramento came in. ——, the son of Dr. —— who is now in the hospital and very very sick. He got into China—though his visa wasn't for August 1, he got in on July 30. Pretty good. They are worried about their dad. He is getting good care. Fifty-fifty chance to live. That night saw *The Red Detachment of Women*. Dramatic, colorfully staged ballet. The dancing not as good as some of the great western ballets. Normally the ballet dancer ends with her arm bent, fist clutched, defiantly looking to the future. Much good martial music, some symphony-like music. Lots of posing, posturing, shooting with guns, ridiculing old China with its landlord kowtowing, whipping their warlord's troops, giving presents which is frowned upon now. Women as sex symbols. The whole bit. But a great evening with spectacular dancing and staging and action. The place was filled. The message in everything they do is loud and clear. How long can China sustain this?

[Friday,] August 1[, 1975]. Swiss national day. I have now gone to open-neck, short-sleeve shirts. One or two on the outside that look Chinese, but the Europeans for the most part insist on coats and ties. Paludan of Denmark is an exception. So is the Belgian. The Swiss are moving out of their beautiful Chinese-looking embassy to a new one at San Li Tun. Too bad because you really do

[54]Bush refers to ongoing negotiations concerning Western claims for compensation for property lost by those who fled China upon the Communist takeover.

feel like you are in China when you are in that embassy. Lunch with Teddy Youde on the beautiful large grounds outside of his house. We had drinks there and then outside again for coffee. Big shade trees. All of which was a field 15 years ago and now beautiful gardens, tremendous amount of space. I wish that I thought that the U.S. would ever be able to acquire this much space.

Wrote the Mayors Alioto, Lugar, and Lila Colkrell.[55] They are coming in September and I will miss their first part. Tennis at the International Club with Mel Searles of Exxon, now moving to the China Trade Committee, Harry Thayer, and Petersmeyer.[56] Then the Marconis and their little children came over to watch television.

Frustrations as China protests to us on the use of a form which asks whether people are Communists, and have them lumped in with thieves, crooks, etc.[57] I am not sure how I would have handled it because clearly that is our internal affairs, but they raised hell about it. They don't want us to attach an escort to the Percy group. They are iron fast about that too. These people are frustratingly difficult to deal with in every way. And it is not just us. The other ambassadors told me that they feel that the groups that

[55]Joseph Alioto, the mayor of San Francisco from 1968 to 1976, led a delegation of mayors to China September 1–15, 1975; Bush was in Washington for the first half of this trip. Richard Lugar served as mayor of Indianapolis (1968–75) before being elected to the U.S. Senate from Indiana.

[56]Melvin Searles Jr. helped coordinate visits of Chinese oil officials to the United States.

[57]Bush refers here to earlier Chinese protests over American prohibitions on granting visas to individuals with "moral defects." During the Cold War, these were considered to include prostitution, illegal drug use, or membership in the Communist Party. James Lilley recounts that the USLO's Robert Blackburn had translated the State Department's standard visa application form, but Chinese officials balked at the suggestion that communism was somehow akin to prostitution. "Did you not know that Chairman Mao Tse-Tung and Premier Chou En-Lai are Communist Party members?" Lilley recalled being asked. "You equate them with morally defective people?" In the end, Lilley admitted, "We goofed . . . but to me it was still an amusing goof." Lilley had departed China several months before this August 1975 entry by Bush, and no available record suggests why this issue might have been on his mind at this time.

come to China are assiduously kept away from the embassies, emphasizing the people-to-people thing. If one starts comparing it to what their ambassador is allowed to do in our capital, the differences are overwhelming. I must guard against the increasing frustrations of always running into stone walls. Sometimes politely, sometimes firmly, but sometimes rather acidly, but nevertheless always there. Petersmeyer got his [visa] extension, but it came back with a kind of defense of their policy of two to three weeks is sufficient. But they did grant us an extension after giving us a short lecture, in a paper they sent over. The land of contrast. The decency, the kindness, the civility, the grace, compared with the iron-willed, dogmatic, insensitive demanding "we're right, you're wrong" kind of behavior. It is hard to sort out. End of August 1.

Morning of [Saturday,] August 2[, 1975]. After a great night's sleep, back under the air conditioner because the heat is coming back again after a couple of cool days. Ready to depart for Tombs and swim at 11:00.

Swimming in the Ming Tombs Reservoir with Fred was fun. The Chinese are a little nervous about dogs. I must say there is quite a bit of human filth swimming along the edge that makes it less than exciting. Bathroom habits in China leave something to be desired as do the general conditions of public facilities and what pass for private facilities. Spectacular picnic out there. Dinner with the Syrian ambassador. Unreasonable in his view on Israel, but more and more I can see how our special relationship with Israel causes problems around the rest of the world. The Africans and everyone else are upset with us about Israel, and we really don't get anything out of it, except we are, of course, adhering to a fundamental principle.

Sunday [August 3, 1975]. Church. Hot. Percy delegation supposed to arrive at 1:55. I am dictating this and they say another report says 7:00. Something must have gone dramatically wrong. They are very bad about advising us on details. Turn down the liaison officer to go with the delegation. Reluctant to give out information on the visit. Seem to be bypassing on this to go direct. One of the things about a free country is they can go direct to Congress or to anybody else, whereas we have no chance at all to talk to their political people or what dissidents conceivably exist here. Travel restricted, etc.

The big discussion of two Vietnams. I am delighted that we are standing firm to see South Korea in before we will permit the entrance of the Vietnams. Some try to make the distinction that you need the agreement of both divided states before they can go in, but that in my view is absolutely ridiculous and we ought not to knuckle under.

August 3. Delegation detained in Shanghai, finally arrived at 10 p.m. Hung around and waited all day. Great warmth and feeling to see Javits, Pell, Stevenson, Percy, Findley, Heckler, and McCloskey.[58] Great Mark Percy the kid, attractive McCloskey son. Nancy Stevenson warm and friendly. Nancy Tang in her Mercedes shot across town and arrived just before the delegation and then drove off. She lives on the western side so was a little late getting there. She is a Deputy in the American and Oceanic Affairs Office [the Americas and Oceanic Division of the Foreign Ministry] and yet she is a member of the Central Committee. So in one hat she is way over the others, and in the bureaucratic system she is below them. Very articulate. Seemed warmer and friendlier at the dinner Monday night.

Monday, August 4[, 1975]. Gave a buffet lunch for the delegation. Food fair. Relaxed, no ties, no coats. Percy's generous toast to me and all in all it went very well. Dinner that night at the Peking Hotel for the delegation. Wang Hairong sitting next to Percy. Percy, Javits and Pell all toasted. Rather frank. Percy talking about the differences between the systems, they excelled in cleanliness of streets (Shanghai and Peking vs. Chicago and New York), elimination of vice and crime, Chairman Mao's principles, etc. We could learn

---

[58]Bush specifically refers here to Senators Jacob Javits of New York, Claiborne Pell of Rhode Island, Adlai Stevenson Jr. and Charles Percy of Illinois, Representatives Paul Findley of Illinois, Margaret Heckler of New York, and Paul "Pete" McCloskey of California.

from them, and they could learn from us on science, technology and our Constitution. Javits, though differing on the war in Vietnam, stated that it was a question of principle, the principle of self-determination. Pell calling the USSR a superpower, thus causing smiles between Wang and Nancy Tang, made an impassioned plea for the U.N. It was a good evening. Again relaxed and no crises. This delegation seems to be first-rate. Bed at ten. Couldn't sleep at all. Maybe it's the maotai. Strong stuff. Bitten by two mosquitoes—one in the eye, one on the arm. Woke up all swollen up.

Tuesday, August 5[, 1975]. Not much. An insistent call from Somalia[n] (of all people) ambassador wanting visa for his son and wanting to visit with me. Somalia has looked ridiculous on this base in Berbera, and I think most ambassadors in China at least understand that they were caught red-handed. But he continues to kind of take the offensive. Big debate on what we ought to do at the U.N. Still very much on everyone's mind. Kuala Lumpur consul was seized and we get a telegram expressing concern and urging caution.[59] Kuala Lumpur of all places. I often wondered that if somebody wanted to embarrass China, the best way to do it must be to have an attack on the American chief of mission or personnel here in Peking. What a flap that would be. In terms of the hostages, the Chinese might just muster the PLA and go charging in and catch the culprit and the hell with the hostages. Seems unlikely, given the peace and tranquility here. Stranger things than that could happen. We take no precautions here at all for our own safety. Travel freely in all alleys and downtown night and day, walking the dog. End August 5.

[Wednesday, August 6, 1975.] Percy delegation was here. We invited the insect control delegation to come to the house. I tried the new cassette on Washington on the leader of the delegation. It

[59]Terrorists associated with Japan's Red Army Faction seized the American consulate in Kuala Lumpur on August 4, taking fifty hostages. The siege ended nearly eighty hours later when the hostage-takers flew to asylum in Libya.

worked very well indeed. Washington scenes in Chinese—eight minutes. Percy is doing a good job leading the delegation.

August 6. We met with Deng Xiaoping, Qiao Guanhua out of the hospital—elaborate notes on this meeting so nothing required here.[60]

[Thursday,] August 7[, 1975]. Continuation of August 6. We had the press over—wine and cheese. McCloskey sent some California wine, shipping cost far more than the wine, but they brought it out on the plane, so all I had to pay was from Shanghai to Peking. Cheese, wine, noodle soup and watermelon. It worked well. The press are grateful to have this kind of shot at the Americans. The whole evening was a good one. The delegation is a good one.

I am going through some enormous frustrations here about what this Mission should do. Harry Thayer feels, and probably properly from being briefed at the State Department, that we should not make any interventions on behalf of Chinese for the most part. Percy brought some clothes and some money and asked that we send it. Harry is very nervous about sending that along, feeling that we would be "exceeding our brief." My view is that we ought to be trying to help in any way we can. Of course not doing anything that would be offensive to the Chinese. He feels that the State Department wants it all handled through PRCLO [the PRC's liaison office in Washington]. It is a problem and I am frustrated because I like to see things happen. I respect Harry and I know he is giving me his best judgment and best advice, but I feel that if our relationship can't stand that kind of action, why we're on pretty thin reeds.

---

[60]Bush reported home that "Teng generally took familiar or predictably [sic] positions on a variety of bilateral and other issues raised by CODEL [congressional delegation]. Of primary interest, however, is this passage from conversation between Teng and Percy at lunch. . . . Teng: 'We hope peaceful means will be used on the Taiwan problem but as to whether the means are peaceful or not this is entirely an internal affair of China.'" Bush also reported that "Percy then asked about the Ford visit, whether it would be substantive." Deng replied, "Is [sic] is alright if he comes here and this problem cannot be settled. It is up to him to decide what position he should take, but our position can't be changed."

August 7. Lunch at New Zealand embassy with Ambassador Ogawa, Somalia ambassador in the afternoon and a going-away banquet later. Lunch with Ogawa and Bryce Harland—then a long visit with the Somalian ambassador, who was anxious to get his son's visa stamped and his passport, fearing that if it's not in there, the Somalian ambassador in Washington will turn down the son. The son apparently wants to see the overthrow of the Somalia government, or at least he disapproves of some of its policies. Sometimes one forgets the problems of other small-country ambassadors. The ambassador told me he was being withdrawn along with six or seven other ambassadors. That evening the going-away banquet at the Sick Duck Restaurant for CODEL-Percy.

Funny demands made in the case of the Percy old clothes, the case of shopping. We must try to be responsive to these demands and avoid a lot of grief. Frankly they didn't seem very much to me. Stevenson very generous in his toast to me, as were the others.

Friday the 8th [August 8, 1975]. Went out to the airport, saw the group off and then Jennifer, Greg Petersmeyer and I left for Beidaihe. We shared a compartment with Ada Principalli.[61] It was hot but not unbearable. You carry ice, have a drink, good food on the train, four berths so you can sleep. And at 5:30 we pulled into Beidaihe in time for a swim and a good dinner at the outdoor German restaurant, now open. Beidaihe does not seem like a Chinese city. The Chinese themselves by the seashore are much more relaxed, many cadres go there to stay on vacation and the diplomatic set has a nice relaxed time. Only the soldiers reminding us that we are in China. I left an *Arizona Highways* magazine, old, on the train. When I went to leave Beidaihe three days later, I noticed Mr. Fay signing a long form and piece of paper, all full of forms and instructions. It turned out that the train was returning the magazine to him and having him sign for it. They do trust you. We bought

---

[61]Principalli, Beijing representative of the Italian news agency Agenzia di Stampa Italiana, had opened the organization's Beijing office and would remain there until 1979.

some tee shirts and we didn't have the coupons. We signed for that and then I went down and settled up with them. They are meticulous for detail. Nancy Stevenson kept waiting to go swimming because she didn't have all the forms filled out while the others, Marion Javits and the kids, were splashing merrily away in the pool, having just dived in. Hot midday sun in Beidaihe. Hot at night. Some bugs but not too bad. Our little cottage not getting much of a sea breeze. Three or four days is about the right length of stay there. Saturday night—Beidaihe.

Sunday, the 10th [August 10, 1975]. Came back in order to meet Flanigan.[62] Supposedly at 8:25. I got word after we were back that his plane had been turned into a charter flight. Frustration.

Flanigan. I asked him to stay with me provided Travel Service agreed. I mentioned to Nancy Tang that he was going to stay with me and she expressed surprise. At Beidaihe I get a call from China Travel that they had understood that they were going to stay at the hotel. Then another message at Beidaihe saying that Flanigan had rejected staying at the hotel. They want him to stay at the hotel, he is their guest, he should stay at the hotel. We will see about that.

Long ride back on the train. Hot, humid, not bad though. Dinner at the Club. Tennis. The most humid weather we have had so far with Wang, Thayer and Petersmeyer. There are so many little frustrations here. Doing things the normal way. The answer politely coming back, "it is not convenient." Our liaison officer on the CODEL delegation wasn't convenient and yet they couldn't or wouldn't handle the request the way it should have been done. John Lewis, a professor from Stanford, knowledgeable sinophile, was just in over his

---

[62]Peter Flanigan, who was traveling with his wife, Brigid, was a close Nixon associate and from 1972 to 1974 served as executive director of Nixon's Council on International Economic Policy. *Time* magazine termed Flanigan Nixon's "Mr. Fixit" for his political acumen, while Ralph Nader called him "the most evil man in Washington" for his willingness to do Nixon's bidding on behalf of business. Following Nixon's resignation he returned to the Wall Street investment firm Dillon, Read and Company.

head, pulling his hair out, as the congressmen went off in all directions.[63] Yet China would not permit us to really be fully involved. For some reason, in the United States at this juncture in our relationship, we are permitting China to get away with murder on the Jewish question. They are far worse in their statements about Israel than the Russians, and yet the Russians, because of their own Jewish immigrants, get all the heat. China doesn't let their people go to and from very easily either.

African students, about to leave, came out and watched us play tennis on the lawn—two of them. Nice boys. Lonely. They should go on. End of August 10.

[Monday,] August 11[, 1975]. Lunch with John McCrary and the Salzers.[64] Lot of pouch. Went out to the airport to get Flanigan. There was a massive foul-up. China Travel had invited Flanigan. He just went in and got his own visa. He had been visiting President Marcos. They were upset about his staying with me, so I sidled over to him and told him first thing that he ought to stay with them. It worked out very well and they whisked him off to the hotel. But he came for dinner. Dinner with the two Brigids. He didn't know what his program would be, but he had been treated extraordinarily well.[65]

[Tuesday,] August 12[, 1975]. We visited the Peking brewery. I have a separate report on the brewery in the file. It was old, beat-up, very nice people, I took them a case of Miller and we sat around sampling, tasting their five kinds of beer and the Miller after the

[63]Lewis had recently moved to Stanford University following six years at Cornell. The author of numerous books on Chinese foreign policy, he was a co-founder of Stanford's Center for International Security and Cooperation.

[64]John "Tex" McCrary, born in Calvert, Texas, and a graduate of Phillips Exeter Academy and Yale University, was a publicist and media personality. He is credited with coining the "I like Ike" campaign for Dwight Eisenhower.

[65]Flanigan wrote Kissinger from Beijing that "I am impressed as you suggested after your first trips—and as hard put to reach any conclusions other than that my preconceptions were wrong." He did not elaborate, however, on those preconceptions.

meeting. It worked out well. I believe the Chinese like that kind of applicable gift thing. There is a certain unnaturalness not to be able to give modest presents, without worrying whether you are going to hurt feelings or get people in trouble.

Lunch at USLO. Ambassador Anguiano of Mexico came by to offer to help with some Americans held hostage in South Vietnam.[66] Vietnam matters, North Korea matters are very much in focus here. The U.S. vetoed the applications of the two Vietnams to get [in]to the U.N. because the U.N. Security Council refused to even consider South Korea which certainly qualified. But this kind of move has more repercussions and discussions here. The whole third world cast, the whole climate, hostility toward capitalism, China's special friendship with Korea, and the determination not to let the Soviets take advantage of her in South Vietnam—all give more emphasis in the diplomatic community to anti-American positions. It gets a little annoying at times, but I must say that I like to defend our positions and battle with some of these guys. I am convinced that Chinese respect one for that, and I am convinced that some of these foreigners, like the Somalians and some others, do too.

That night dinner with the Flanigans at Kong Lu Restaurant following the drinks at the USLO residence. Lots of rain. Flanigans drenched at the Great Wall. These diplomatic receptions are made annoying by the Korean, sloppy-looking guy who has a terrible interpreter with him. And his speeches are too long and they are all the same. If things were not sensitive, I would try to joke about it a little bit, but that would not be good. At the reception on the 13th he unavoidably had to shake hands. He always looks uncomfortable at this, but he is the dean of the diplomatic corps and it gives me no problem at all.

Wednesday, the 13th [August 13, 1975]. Pat Wardlaw, the economic guy, arrived.[67] Mohamed A. A. Abuelhaffan [Abul-Hassan],

[66]Eugenio Anguiano Roch. See my footnote to the entry of November 17, 1974.
[67]Frank Patterson Wardlaw, a Peace Corps volunteer before joining the foreign service, had served in Taipei before joining the USLO staff.

31-year-old ambassador of Kuwait, new, came to call on me.[68] Attractive young guy. Then at the Tanzanian reception he came dash-
ing up to say hello. I believe he will be a good friend. Arabs seem
genuinely friendly. I discussed with them throwing Israel out, urging against it, saying it will damage the U.N. itself. And I have no
hesitancy in visiting frankly with them. Some of the sophisticated
Europeans that kind of impotently wring their hands about the
U.N. get to me a little bit more than the direct emotional Arabs,
whom I like enormously. Actually the Arabs and the Israelis aren't
very different in this nice sense.

Ambassador Small of Canada came to call. A thoroughly decent
man. Great, honest, open, friendly; respects our position on the
United Nations incidentally and doesn't hesitate to tell others when
he agrees or disagrees with them or us. Farewell reception at Tanzania for Wambura. He has been here six years. Too long. The reception was hot, outdoors, I wore a coat, which I don't like to do.
There is a certain sameness to the receptions. There have not been
too many of them lately; you mill around and get information from
various ambassadors and greet certain Chinese and exchange little
tidbits. It is worth doing, particularly in Peking. That night the
farewell banquet in Peking for the Insect Control Group for the
United States. Terry Adkisson in charge.[69] He is from Texas A&M.
Very delightful. There were many toasts, some good, some lousy.
An excellent banquet and excellent fellowship. I believe these kinds
of delegations really do help. Peter Flanigan briefed our economic
staff and they agreed that it was the best briefing they had had in
capsulized form about the U.S. economy. Had to take three bottles
of whiskey down to Insect Control Group who needed to write
their "final report." End of August 13.

---

[68] Abul-Hassan later served as Kuwait's permanent representative to the United
Nations, a post he held during the Gulf War.

[69] Terry Adkisson, head of Texas A&M University's Entomology Department
at the time of his visit to China, subsequently served as chancellor of the university from 1986 to 1990.

[Thursday,] **August 14[, 1975]**. Thursday, a little hot and sticky. The mist hanging in over Peking. The weather really isn't as hot as Houston, nor as tough in any way, but people bitch about it a lot here. Ambassador Ogawa and his wife will be coming at ten thirty. At this juncture I don't see how Ford could make any real movement on the Taiwan question. I will have a better feel for this when I go to the States, but it is tough to see how he can, given the mood in the United States of not wanting to let down friends, of standing up for capitalism, etc. It is awful tough, and these people don't seem in a position to make any concessions. Time will tell. I would like to see full relations for a lot of reasons, none of which result in immediate change between our two countries. But I would like to see us solve the problem, and yet I would not recommend overthrowing Taiwan at this point, just blatantly and openly.

Ogawa's wife came over and we chatted. She is on her way, taking her child to the States. Barbara and Casey Manning, businessman and typically Texas, typically warm—here to sell some equipment to the Chinese.[70] That afternoon Mehrotra, head of India's office here, came to call. Very much interested in what Deng Xiaoping had said about India and Sikkim and whether China would take the matter of Sikkim to the U.N.[71] They apparently won't. Pell having asked Deng Xiaoping about this at his meeting. That night a cookout in our yard arranged by Jennifer, a farewell

[70]Manning and his business colleagues found it particularly challenging to negotiate with the Chinese, Bush reported, as "the technical negotiations were made difficult by Techimport's unwillingness to provide information on the conditions under which the equipment would be used and refusal to allow Stewart and Stevenson technicians to participate in installation." Techimport, today the China National Technical Import and Export Corporation, was in 1975 one of Beijing's principal organizations for the importation of high-value machinery and technical goods.

[71]Sikkim became an official Indian state in May 1975. China did not recognize the annexation, however, and Deng told Bush and the Percy congressional delegation that Gandhi had done a "most stupid thing" in this case, that India was a "sub-superpower" that was "out to control Asia" and wanted "to dismember Pakistan a second time."

for Mike Woods and Pete Bergin. Marvelous incident when the steaks all went up in a massive flame, and the Chinese were running and jumping around. But it turned out to be very nice. Hot, warm outside but beautiful sky, and the terrace looked spectacular.

Friday, the 15th of August [August 15, 1975]. Routine day. Greg Petersmeyer left. Not much happened.

Saturday, the 16th [August 16, 1975]. Went to call on Wang Hairong about Puerto Rico. Separate coverage but I feel strongly on the Puerto Rican issue. I hate to see these countries at the U.N. pushing because of their instant majorities to try to make it look like Puerto Rico is being deprived and Puerto Rico is the same as some colony. The record on votes establishing Puerto Rico's desire for either commonwealth or statehood is very clear, but the mischief makers, in this instance led by Cuba, lead the way. I emphasized internal affairs, and she said that internal affairs is important, but so is continuing revolution.[72] I am troubled that we don't make our principles as clear. We have got them. Sometimes we are embarrassed to stand up for them. I think more and more we are going to have to take these forceful, forthright positions, emphasizing freedom, and pointing out the advantages of capitalism. We seem to retreat from these all the time.[73]

---

[72]Bush was in fact more forceful during this meeting with Wang than his diary suggests. "Drawing on my own service at the UN I emphasized great sensitivity of USG [United States government] and public to any UN consideration of Puerto Rico," he reported home. "I concluded by stating 'should your government support Cuba's action on this matter we would take very strong exception and it could not be without effect on our relations with your government." Wang "decried our employment of 'threatening language,'" Bush continued, and "in ensuing discussion I denied any threat. . . . [but] said I would not be doing my job if I did not make my government's position clear: that Chinese support of Cuban effoots [*sic*] to interfere in U.S. internal affairs could not be without effect on our relations."

[73]Bush increasingly considered Wang Hairong a potentially useful contact. In another example of his attempts to read the winds of change in Beijing's government, he believed her to be increasingly influential. She was "blossoming," he re-

—— came to see me, the son of the sick guy. He wants to see if his father can be transferred. The father is staging a recovery—so difficult. No nurses around the clock. At one point they thought that Mr. —— was going to die, but now he may be able to be moved toward the States in a month or so. His poor mother, sitting there speaking both Canton[ese], which the father speaks, and Mandarin, is almost on round-the-clock duty. Claiborne Pell arrived around noon. Tennis with Pell. Then a beautiful picnic at the Ming Tombs. Spectacular. Saw satellites—seven or eight of us in the van and a real special evening. Very special indeed. Jennifer did a great job on the picnic. Pell left early in the morning for Romania. Church, then the rest of the day sitting on the patio, a tremendously hot sun. Relaxed in the afternoon. Tennis with the Flanigans who returned. Dinner with the Flanigans at the Julebu International Club. China is being difficult about escort officers from Hong Kong attached to various delegations. They are continuing their policy of little fairs scattered around. I noticed there is a new Tianjin straw fair.

Hassle about the agricultural officer—Ag wanting to assign Champeau and my feeling is that Champeau is unacceptable.[74] Still feel we are not properly informed by the Department. We are too cautious on many things here and I sense an accumulating feeling of frustration. A lot of that simply is that I need to get back to the States to get refurbished. Some of it is fundamental in the way this policy is run. I think these visits from senators and delegations and all these kinds of things help increase understanding about the United States; and yet there seems to be an official worry that some-

---

ported to Washington following this meeting and a later one that August. Lin Ping "seemed totally absorbed in catching Wang's every utterance," Bush said, while "Nancy Tang was the only member of the Chinese party who willingly engaged in conversation with USLO officers while Wang was talking." Following their meeting on the Puerto Rico issue, Bush added, "Wang, though operating from boilerplate, showed more spark and authority, and I might add charm, than I would have expected from our previous encounters."

[74]See Bush's entry and my footnote for June 5, 1975.

body will say something that will foul up all the relations. Our relationship is not that frail in my view. It is too important to the Chinese, and I also think that the more exposure to Americans the better off America is. End of the 16th.

Monday, the 18th [August 18, 1975]. Wang Hairong to come to lunch. Gledhill, a partner of Bob Bushman's in San Antonio in a drilling venture, came in. English fellow, very interesting. Talked about the frustrations of selling to the Chinese—crew boats. They do do some shipping business with them which is apparently more normalized. But he reiterated the sensitivity of oil stuff. Went to the Marco Polo Store—Jennifer and I—and sat fascinated as we saw beautiful jades and much better-quality stuff than at the Friendship Store. I found myself becoming instantly fascinated with jade, with the differences. They pulled out one for 100 yuan and then showed us one for a thousand, and the difference was very, very clear. It is such a subtle art. The gold working and beautiful. Charm bracelets with charms of real gold are attractive. I bought more than I intended to. This store is separate and apart for export. Occasionally they let someone go there to buy. Lunch with Wang Hairong, Lin Ping, Nancy Tang, Mr. Ding, and Mrs. Shi who used to interpret.[75] The mood was relaxed but they sit there with a straight face and very pleasantly accuse us of being in favor of hegemony. And I argue back, somewhat I think to the consternation of my colleagues. But this idea of just sitting there and talking about the weather does not appeal to me, and I totally believe that we have got to stand up for our country's position and advocate it. My problem with some here is that there doesn't seem to be a willingness to advocate, to battle for our position. The result, in my view, is China gets away with saying they have "principle" but nobody's making clear to them that we have "principle." It was a good lunch and Wang

[75]Ding Yuanhong was identified by Bush in his cable to Washington as director of the Foreign Ministry's U.S. Division. Shi Yen-Huah is identified as having "recently arrived from the U.N."

Hairong was more forthcoming than I have seen her. She did not seem hung up over my demarche of Saturday on Puerto Rico. All in all it was a pretty good meeting.

5:00 p.m.—Bob Piccus of ITT in Hong Kong came by.[76] Talking about trade, the frustrations of doing business with the Chinese, their need for better communications systems, telephone satellite etc. But he just wants to keep plugging away.

Self-reliance vs. dependence. Pragmatic exceptions to self-reliance. Continuous question. How long will China be able to keep this discipline, this uniformity, this conformity, this lack of consumerism, this lack of dissent? How long can it last? Quiet evening at home watching television. Those cassettes are fantastic. Walked the dog, off to bed.

[Tuesday,] August 19[, 1975]. Harry Thayer in the morning got a telegram saying his brother was very sick. In the afternoon his brother died. It became clear that I cannot go home, that I should permit him to be with his family, that I must stay here. I am absolutely heartsick. A real character builder. I have been looking forward to this vacation immeasurably. And worse than my own feelings Bar will be desperately hurt, though she'll know I have to do what I am doing. Lunch with the new security people—John and Patricia Chornyak.[77] Pat Wardlaw from Texas, our econ section, and Henrietta. Nice people at USLO. Dinner—going-away—for the Laotian ambassador Lien. Supposed to be posted to Washington. His Pathet Lao–leaning government never even sent in for the agreement. He is married to part of the royal family, and he is uncertain as to what will happen to him when he goes back to Laos. These human things are very sad indeed.

---

[76]Robert Piccus served as ITT Corporation's vice president for Asia, based in Hong Kong, from 1968 to 1974, at which time he became ITT's director of China trade.

[77]Patricia Chornyak eventually served as a receptionist in the USLO, replacing Dorothy Lambert, whose last day of service was July 30, 1975.

Wednesday, August 20[, 1975].[78] The congressional delegation arrived, headed by Bob Byrd, Derwinski, Slack, Nunn, Pearson.[79] John Anderson coming in next Friday since his mother died. They will travel to Guilin, Kunming, and Xian. Standard banquet of welcome for the delegation. They are trying to figure what questions to ask to add to the overall record. I could handle all of the questions they asked. At least I must be learning something after ten months here. There is a sameness to the proceedings. We were out at the airport, Mr. Zhou of the Association for Foreign Friendship was there. He had just discharged the previous delegation last Sunday. Now he sets out again. I do think these delegations help our relations. They get more understanding of China, and we have a change to pick up different facts about China here at USLO.

Miscellaneous—American citizen died in Tianjin. It is the darndest procedure getting a body shipped out of China you've ever heard of. They want $7,500 to ship a body to the United States, $750 if it is cremated. They only have cremation. They don't have the proper refrigeration to keep the body for long.

Some steaks came in today on the plane. What a treat! Welcoming banquet—night of August 20. Banquet went very well at the

---

[78]It was during this period that rumors began to swirl in Washington concerning Bush's future plans. CBS Radio reported, for example, that he and his wife were "bored with life in [the] PRC," and were "willing to let some other Republican 'come and suck lemons'" as USLO chief. There was the further suggestion that Bush's mission while back home later that month would be to convince Ford to replace Rockefeller with him on the Republican ticket for 1976. The next month, however, Washington insiders and columnists Rowland Evans and Robert Novak suggested that, while the "dump Rocky" movement was gaining strength within the GOP, Bush was "now out of sight in Peking as envoy to China . . . [and] out of the political mind." *New York Times* columnist William Safire, meanwhile, suggested that, if Ford were to openly consider all his possible running mates, Bush's name would lead to the conclusion "nothing wrong with him"—which in Safire's view would be "a high accolade in this discussion."

[79]The reference is to Senators Robert Byrd of West Virginia, Sam Nunn of Georgia, and James Pearson of Kansas, and Representatives Edward Derwinski of Illinois and John Slack of West Virginia. Bush would later appoint Derwinski the first secretary of veterans affairs.

Peking Hotel on the first floor. Wang Hairong was the ranking guest. Bob Byrd does an excellent job. He is serious, but seems to lead and get things done. And on his questions, if he doesn't get an answer, he very respectfully but forcefully goes back [un]til he gets one. Next morning visited with Oscar Armstrong about some problems. I am convinced we are not informed. We see none of the option papers. And I filed a protest on that. I also told Oscar I was upset about the rule of no ambassadors coming to Peking even for consultation. Apparently this is the way the Secretary wants it. Pete Bergin and Mike Woods, young security guards, left. Fine young guys. Good morale, decent, clean-cut kids, did a first-rate job. Lunch with Oscar, Bob Perito and Stan Brooks, talking over various problems of USLO.[80] In the evening we were received by Qiao Guanhua in the Great Hall of the People.

We had a briefing session with the CODEL and then went to the Great Hall—meeting finished at 6:45, dinner at the Great Hall by Chiao at 7:00. Food at the Great Hall isn't as good. We had some kind of a duck, wrapped like Peking duck but sweet sauce which was good. Rest of it seemed rather heavily fried, square-cut pieces of heavy fried stuff which I didn't like as well as some of the other Chinese food.

Friday, August 22[, 1975]. A few black women with one of the friendship delegations from the Midwest came by. Effy McKesson, black GOP vice chairman of the Minnesota party; some of their group didn't want to be seen at USLO. There is this feeling that if they are seen, they don't see the true China. The Yost committee on China Exchanges feels that way.[81] Their smart young people feel they won't get as much out of it if USLO is included. The in-

---

[80]Stan Brooks later served as James Lilley's deputy director at the American Institute in Taiwan.

[81]After departing the United Nations, where he preceded Bush as Washington's ambassador, Charles Yost headed the National Committee on United States–China Relations, charged with coordinating citizen and cultural exchanges between the two countries.

sect delegation, the guy from that committee, did not want to invite me to the banquet given by the insect control delegates. When I went there the insect people were extremely courteous, the professor was real nice, said I had added considerably to the thing by going, but these young escorts seem to have the wrong impression. I have discussed this with the State Department. Without government intervention they would never have these exchanges going. And I think they should cooperate more. The same is true on some of these visiting delegations—friendship. But they have no obligation at all to cooperate.[82]

Got up real early—clear and cool. Definitively cool at quarter of six in the morning. Took Fred for a walk. Unbelievable the change. It is the first day of fall. Autumn in China started about a week ago. Still hot in the daytime but much better today than it was last week. Amazing. Still get reports from South China of unrest in factories, unwillingness to pay overtime, workers are lectured that they should struggle against the proletariat dictatorship. But I am convinced that at some time in the future the society will have to adapt to the basic laws of supply and demand and incentive. No question in my mind about this anymore.

Qiao Guanhua was in good form, long discussions of the Middle East.[83] Their position is fundamental though he did claim that

[82]Press reports later suggested that several members of this congressional delegation found China's welcome less than warm. "Reports all over Capitol Hill lament poverty seen inside the Great Wall," *Chicago Tribune* writer Bill Anderson reported in early September, citing "the imposed gray drabness and conformity—and an unwillingness by Communist officials to divulge even the most trivial information." Anderson reported as well that some members of the delegation (he did not identify who) perceived Bush as unhappy with his role in Beijing, for many of the same reasons Bush himself suggests in his journal. "For all practical purposes, Bush is isolated like the rest of the Western community living in Peking," Anderson wrote. "One of our sources who made the trip expressed concern over the continued isolation of Bush from contact with the Chinese government."

[83]Bush is most likely referring to Qiao Guanhua's August 21 meeting with the visiting congressional delegation, yet curiously neither of the two cables (one a report, the second a transcript) of the meetings offered any discussion of the Middle East.

they told the extremists on the Arab side that they should avoid violence. If the people in the United States realize how hostile they are to Israel, it would make relations much more strained. Qiao is very friendly in his mentions of me.[84] Bob Byrd was also very generous. I do think these little niceties help in doing the job better.

Note. I asked Mr. Lei at the International Club to see if I could give them t-shirts. The word came back that since they were very low in value it would be alright. Now I will take them to the various players there. Press reception at USLO for the CODEL group followed by a swimming party at the Canadian embassy. Sihanouk appears to be going back now from Pyongyang, where he has been for a ridiculous period of time, to Cambodia. Khieu Samphan feted by the Chinese here in Peking.[85]

Note. The enormous contrast between the civility and decency and friendliness of the Chinese, and this tough side. On Portugal they don't "recognize" the Communist Party there. We have a lot in common in a situation like that, and really both want the same ends but for very different reasons. It would sure be an entirely different ballgame if they ever got back together with Russia. End August 22.

[84]Qiao told the visiting delegation at the end of their discussion that "speaking personally, Mr. Bush is the first American friend I met at the United National [*sic*] among all our American friends. I've even met his mother."

[85]Khieu Samphan was president of Democratic Kampuchea (Cambodia) from 1976 to 1979. He was the country's public leader, although Pol Pot held the real reins of power.

The Making of a Global President

*I*nterest in George H. W. Bush's presidency has grown in direct proportion to the violence and instability of the twenty-first century's first decade. Many recall with fondness the end of the Cold War and Bush's White House tenure, conjuring halcyon (if not necessarily accurate) memories of a more optimistic moment for the international community, when American-led peace and democracy seemed ready to flower throughout the world. Fascination with Bush's legacy—in effect, a desire to glean from his presidency applicable contemporary lessons—grows steadily. His diplomatic record is widely lauded, with successful navigation of the Cold War's end, Germany's reunification, victory in Panama and the Gulf, and negotiation of the North American Free Trade Agreement heading his administration's list of achievements.

Yet George H. W. Bush himself largely remains an enigma, as the implications of those achievements remain in dispute. A generation after he left office, Bush's diplomatic reputation offers less a collection of guiding principles than a canvas upon which contemporary commentators paint their own preferred outlines of a successful foreign policy. To some, Bush has become a sage embodiment of a more pragmatic American foreign policy; to others, the poster child for policies built on narrow interests rather than universal ideals. Depending on which particular axe the speaker chooses to grind, Bush was a reaper of geopolitical good fortune or a sower of international discontent.

Timing explains much of this confusion. Juxtaposed in history's stream against the eloquent certitude of Ronald Reagan, the intellectual flexibility of Bill Clinton, and the unbridled certainty of George W. Bush, the elder Bush, known for his prudence (itself a malleable virtue), remains largely ill defined as an international strategist. This is a particularly unfortunate puzzle, because decisions made by Bush's White House not only were historic in their own right but also left a lasting imprint on the central strategic questions of the twenty-first century, including the inherent tensions between political stability and economic modernization, and the promise of a democratic peace alongside the potential chaos of ethnic and religious strife catalyzed by popular rule. A generation later, not even the flashpoints of American foreign policy have changed: they remain Iraq, China, Russia, free trade, and oil. The questions that troubled Bush during that more optimistic time continue to plague American policymakers today.

This much is certain: Bush governed during a period of tremendous international transition, the end of an old order and the birth of something new. The half-century-long Cold War came to an end on his watch, and Washington assumed center stage in the international system that took its place. Bush thus led America at the peak of its power during the long American century. The United States feared no strategic competitor during his time in office. After the Gulf War, Americans did not even fear a reprise of the Vietnam syndrome of their past. In geopolitical terms—measured solely by a nation's might in comparison to that of its allies and adversaries—Bush during his single term might well have been the most powerful president the United States has known, and thus for a brief span the most powerful leader in world history.

Yet what did this powerful man stand for, save pragmatism and prudence, and how do we begin to evaluate his diplomatic record given the continuity of international quandaries remaining from his time in office? He governed during revolutionary times; this much cannot be denied. But was Bush responsible for fundamental change or merely its midwife? Was he a master strategist owed credit or blame for the new international system born on his watch, or merely a capable manager skilled more in holding a steady hand on the wheel of the ship of state than in charting a new course for it? Answering these questions—and, in turn, divining what lessons his choices offer subsequent leaders—demands enunciation of his core beliefs about diplomacy and the nature of the international system.

Such answers are not easily gleaned from his biography. Bush made his political living at the crossroads of broad trends easy to identify yet difficult to fully reconcile, being at once Northeastern yet Texan, religious yet hardly doctrinal, conservative yet with roots in the Republican Party's progressive wing, born to established Eastern wealth yet consciously remade in a West Texas oilfield. His career epitomized the growth of the Sunbelt after 1945, where conservatism flourished in response to change and prosperity. He is not, in other words, a man easily defined, especially given the shadow his son's diplomatic record invariably casts over even impartial assessments of the elder Bush's accomplishments.

Bush's China Diary reveals his core foreign-policy principles. It recounts in his own words one of his most formative diplomatic experiences: his tenure as de facto United States ambassador to the People's Republic of China (PRC) from 1974 to 1975. It was in China that Bush most fully developed the gentlemanly diplomatic style—equal parts personal, genial, pragmatic, and conservative—that became his hallmark. This was his longest overseas experience since World War II, coming in the wake of Watergate and after more than a decade in domestic politics. One striking aspect of Bush's career as a diplomat—given the widespread perception during his presidency that he was more concerned with foreign than domestic affairs—was how late in life he came to international relations. Bush's first foray into global politics did not occur until 1970. He landed in China as Washington's envoy a mere four years later. Even these tentative moves toward diplomacy resulted more from circumstance than a real passion for foreign affairs, though a passion for diplomacy eventually developed.

Bush's time in China came during a crossroads moment in his career and at an impressionable juncture in his life. His experiences over fourteen months—decamped in the small American compound in Beijing, at the epicenter of the complex and sensitive Sino-American relationship during a particularly tumultuous period for American Cold War diplomacy—changed the course of his life. They surely left their mark on his diplomatic style. The era he witnessed while in Asia included the end of the Vietnam War, tenuous détente with the Soviet bear, the growth of an American relationship with a rising though still Communist China, and the steady wearing down of American international prestige that underlay much of the 1970s. Each was a challenge to the established order of the Cold War's first half that exactly coincided with Bush's adult life, and each successive blow pushed Bush to question the only international system he had ever truly known. After his personal engagement with the exhausting political firestorm that was Watergate, with its attendant erosion of public trust in the political system, he was primed while in China to question all that he had once taken on faith. Service so far from home during such tumultuous times made Bush define who he was as a diplomat, a strategist, and ultimately as a leader. His China Diary was thus more than a daily record of his activities. It became instead his private sketchbook for his later presidential diplomacy, the canvas upon which he first seriously began to paint his own diplomatic image.

The diary itself is remarkably accessible, composed in a comfortable style and devoid of either pretense or predetermined obfuscation. This accessibility reflects both the style of its author and the circumstances of its composition. Never one to employ a convoluted term when a simple one would do, Bush also never suspected others would read his journal. He wrote this China Diary for himself. Unlike more self-conscious journals composed for a wider audience, and certainly unlike memoirs often written after the fact in order to refract history's judgment, Bush's daily account is an easily read description of his adventures and impressions while in an exotic land. Written only for personal use and not with additional

400

readers in mind, its most pertinent themes and remarkable observations are scattered throughout the text, and it is that characteristic of the diary that prompts this chapter.

This essay is intended to serve two main purposes. First, it offers a short sketch of Bush's political life and evolution as a diplomat in order to place his experience in China in a broader perspective. It portrays the Bush who landed in Beijing in 1974, the diplomat he was at the time and the one he would become, and the ways his China experience influenced his later presidential decisions. Second, it highlights several of the China Diary's main themes, drawing into sharp relief those events and principles that formed the foundation for Bush's subsequent diplomacy and style of leadership. It is intended to make Bush's China Diary more useful to those interested in this president and intrigued by his place in history.

Bush's diary offers a vital source for such an endeavor. Neither his public statements nor records of his most intimate moments with advisers shed much light on the core aspects of his leadership. Even his most fervent supporters concede that verbal acuity was never Bush's strong suit. Words often failed him from the bully pulpit, but he was also hesitant by nature to enunciate his abiding principles with specificity. He routinely rejected language crafted for him by professional speechwriters and advisers, thinking their well-chosen words would sound inauthentic coming from his lips. The broad terms he employed as a consequence—including some of those most frequently associated with his presidency, like "new world order" or "vision thing"—allowed others to define Bush according to their own agenda. When asked to define what Bush meant by "new world order," for example, Bush's White House Press Secretary, Marlin Fitzwater, conceded, "Well I don't think it ever really got defined. . . . The problem with that, of course, is that it leaves a vacuum of definition that others can jump in and fill." Public rhetoric is always an unreliable gauge of a president's true sentiments, being as much political theater as political science. In Bush's case it would appear less helpful than with other Oval Office occupants to study his public words as a means of discerning his private thoughts, because the pre-

401

cise words he spoke were infrequently his own, and those that came from his heart were most often broad to the point of imprecision.[1]

Records of Bush's private words are only marginally more helpful in discerning his core diplomatic principles. Believing that discussions of overarching theories of international relations were best left to professional theoreticians, Bush eschewed broad philosophical discussions, even when alone with his closest associates. He was by his own admission a "practical man," as he declared in 1987 when kicking off his presidential bid: one who preferred "what's real" to what was "airy and abstract. I like what works . . . and I do not yearn to lead a crusade." Asked to recall any instance when Bush willingly discussed a personal theory of international relations, his national security adviser and close friend Brent Scowcroft could recall few if any such moments. "He's very reticent to talk in those terms," Scowcroft explained. "He does not talk in a philosophical way. He's uncomfortable talking in that way." Bush was guided by overarching principles when it came to the international system, Scowcroft believed. But "they only come out . . . [by seeing] the way he does things."[2]

[1]Bush's statements are not easily parsed; his passionate defenses of his own rhetoric frequently obfuscate more than they illuminate. In 1995, for example, he offered (in a quote worth citing in full): "Vision is an interesting word. I'm the President that the national press corps felt had no vision, and yet I worked for a more peaceful world. And we did something to say to a totalitarian dictator in Iraq, you're not going to take over your neighboring country. There's a vision there, which was peace. So, I'm a little defensive in the use of the word. Because I think the pundits had it down that I had no vision, but I did. You need a vision, you need a central core. You need to say, 'Here's what I'm going to try to do to make life better for others.' It doesn't have to be proclaimed in the fanciest prose. It doesn't have to be done with the most rhetorical flourish. It has to be your inner self. It's got to drive you. And it can be a personal thing. It can be your set of values. Your vision can be 'I want to live to this code of behavior.'" See Academy of Achievement induction interview, June 2, 1995, at www.achievement.org/autodoc/printmember/bus0int-1, accessed June 1, 2007. For Fitzwater, see Roy Joseph, "The New World Order: President Bush and the Post–Cold War Era," in Martin Medhurst, ed., *The Rhetorical Presidency of George H. W. Bush* (College Station: Texas A&M University Press, 2006), 97.

[2]George H. W. Bush, announcement speech, October 12, 1987, Bush Presi-

Bush also frequently hid his personal views from the documentary record, though more in the interests of effective leadership than to purposefully obscure history's critique. Unlike Dwight Eisenhower —also a well-known obfuscator in his presidential utterances, but a president who ruled his national security team with a clearly articulated iron will behind closed doors—Bush preferred to keep his conclusions largely private during key meetings, lest his subordinates interpret his utterances as inviolate decrees. He wanted open discussion in his presence, and he consciously cultivated as many varied opinions as possible. He routinely asked aides to debate the merits of their conflicting positions in his presence, hoping that a front-row seat for these "scheduled train wrecks," as they were called in the West Wing, would allow him to appreciate not only the conclusions his deputies reached but their thought processes as well. He rarely intervened in these debates, believing that any interjection would color whatever discussion followed, and he confidently allowed others to speak first, often during crucial cabinet or National Security Council (NSC) meetings. Before one of the first NSC meetings following Saddam Hussein's invasion of Kuwait, for example, Bush asked Scowcroft to present the forceful stance against Iraq's aggression that the two men had previously discussed in private. Those in the room knew that Scowcroft's words invariably carried great weight with the president, but his views would be easier for the other participants to debate if Bush himself did not open the discussion. The transcript of the meeting's discussion therefore reveals a largely quiet president, belying his engagement with the crisis at hand.[3]

dential Library. For "reticent," see editor interview with Brent Scowcroft, March 8, 2007. Transcripts of this and other interviews have been made available for researchers at the Bush Presidential Library.

[3]Bush Presidential Library, NSC Files, Richard Haas Files, Working Files: Iraq 8/2/90–12/90, Meeting of the NSC, Aug. 3, 1990. Scowcroft alludes to their coordinated approach to this meeting in George H. W. Bush and Brent Scowcroft, *A World Transformed* (New York: Scribner, 1999), 318–19.

Bush's diary is thus among our best sources for discerning his thoughts on the international system, as it was one of the few places he felt comfortable fully articulating his abiding principles. Like a scientist's workbook or an artist's sketchbook, it is filled with little inconsistencies, arguments with himself, and the like. Nevertheless these rough diary sketches do in fact form coherent guideposts and provide a clear window into the origins of his successful diplomacy —to no small extent because Bush's China Diary reveals his reactions to one of the most confounding periods of the Cold War.

For all that Bush's White House years arguably coincided with the apex of American power, the glum 1970s saw its nadir. American-backed South Vietnamese forces would lose their generation-long struggle against Communism while Bush was in China. Saigon would fall. Laos and Cambodia would descend into chaos. Historic problems in Europe, the Middle East, and Latin America, in addition to the global struggle against international Communism, challenged American policymakers while Bush served in Beijing. At home, inflation, unemployment, and gas prices were on the rise; the dollar seemed in a steady decline; and faith in governmental institutions fell to historic lows in the wake of Watergate. As National Security Adviser Henry Kissinger explained, the central problem facing the United States during this period was the decline of American power not in absolute terms but rather relative to the rest of the world. Although still strong, America was no longer the globe's preponderant power. American leaders could no longer direct the free world by fiat, a privilege they had largely enjoyed since World War II. Some seven thousand miles from home, these events prompted Bush to question the very foundations of American politics and foreign policy as his country entered this new and complex era. "Where is our ideology?" he asked himself. "Where is our principle? What indeed do we stand for? These things must be made clear."[4] He believed that Washington still had an international

[4]Diary entry for April 30, 1975.

role to play despite such setbacks. But "we have got to be realistic," he cautioned. "We have to have our eyes open."[5]

The conclusions Bush reached in response to these questions reveal a man committed to American values yet cognizant of the limits of American power; a leader dedicated to personal diplomacy as a means of navigating the rougher waters of international relations; and a strategist deeply committed to balancing Washington's interests with those of its allies. They demonstrate his overriding belief in stability over radical change; a willingness to engage the perspectives of other nations; and a desire to promote an American model through example rather than force. These were principles that had become ingrained in him over the course of his life before 1989, and the ones that most clearly defined his presidential diplomacy. They were most sharply defined during his fourteen months in China in the mid-1970s. The Bush presidency was in this sense made in China.

BUSH'S LIFE BEFORE DIPLOMACY: FROM NEW HAVEN TO THE UNITED NATIONS

That such a relatively short period in a far-off land would matter so deeply might surprise readers familiar with Bush's life, given that he was widely regarded, upon taking office, as among the twentieth century's best-prepared presidents in terms of the complexities of foreign policy. Beginning in the 1970s he served in rapid succession as Washington's ambassador to the United Nations, de facto ambassador to Beijing, and director of the Central Intelligence Agency. Although his other positions during the decade were not diplomatic posts in the strictest sense, he also worked as head of the Republican National Committee during Richard Nixon's final years in office and as an international businessman during the

---

[5]Diary entry for April 26, 1975.

Carter administration. His subsequent presidential bid landed him a spot as Ronald Reagan's running mate in 1980, and international affairs dominated his vice presidential agenda. He chaired the White House's international crisis management committee (termed by one historian "a kind of NSC-plus"), and frequently met and sometimes negotiated with visiting foreign leaders and dignitaries. Bush visited sixty-eight nations during these years, joking that regular attendance at state funerals provided the motto "You die, I fly." Yet in practical terms, such travels, even on condolence missions, would offer Bush the opportunity to meet the world's elite long before he assumed the Oval Office.[6]

Despite this impressive list of prepresidential credentials, Bush came to foreign affairs late in his professional life. With better electoral luck, he might never have cultivated this interest at all. From the time he flew his last mission as a naval aviator in the Pacific theater during World War II until he lost his bid for a Texas Senate seat in 1970, Bush was a domestically focused businessman and politician. He made his fortune in the West Texas oil fields after graduating from Yale in 1948, and, though he founded a successful offshore drilling company named Zapata Oil, the major share of its profits during its first decade came from projects near the American coast. He moved his family to Houston by the end of the 1950s, to an area whose growing conservatism would prove a bellwether for the South's changing political winds. Inspired by John Tower's surprising victory in a 1961 special election for Lyndon Johnson's vacated Senate seat, one of the GOP's first statewide victories since Reconstruction, Bush became party chairman for a bur-

---

[6]David Rothkopf, *Running the World: The Inside Story of the National Security Council and the Architects of American Power* (New York: Public Affairs, 2006), 218. Ronald Reagan recorded in his diary that "Historically the chairman [of the Crisis Council] is Nat. Security Adviser [Dick Allen]. Al [Haig] thinks his turf is being invaded. We chose George because Al is wary of Dick." See Douglas Brinkley, ed., *The Reagan Diaries* (New York: HarperCollins, 2007), 11. For "you die, I fly," a term coined by James Baker, see Bush, *All the Best, George Bush: My Life in Letters and Other Writings* (New York: Scribner, 1999), 321.

geoning Houston district in 1963. He hoped to forge a winning coalition at the ballot box by melding the social conservatives then on the rise in Republican circles—many from the ultranationalist John Birch Society, which preached isolationism, fear of international organizations, and vigorous opposition to Communism—with the fiscally conservative moderates from whose number he hailed. "We're all Republicans," he cautioned constituents who considered the Birchers too radical, "and we're not going to divide ourselves, calling anyone 'crazies' or nuts."[7]

It was easy for Bush to be accepting of different conservative ideologies during his first statewide campaign in 1964, a bid for the Senate against the left-leaning Ralph Yarborough, because his own political views were far from fully formed. He wanted passionately to hold office, believing it a duty for the privileged and successful to seek public service. Yet he was uncomfortable exposing too much of his inner thinking to voters on the campaign trail—in part because the modesty his mother had constantly preached during his youth conflicted with the traditional boasts of the campaign trail, but also because Bush simply did not hold his views as close to his heart as did many of the GOP's more strident conservatives. As a consequence he offered himself as a hodgepodge of East and West. He mixed the Eastern establishment, internationalist Republicanism of his youth—a wing of the party that claimed his father Prescott Bush, a Connecticut senator and Eisenhower ally, for whom pro-business sentiments outranked social issues—with the stringent frontier conservatism then coming to the fore in Texas GOP circles. His 1964 campaign focused more on attacking his opponent's liberalism than extolling his own virtues, and he even integrated much of the Birchers' right-wing critiques into his own stump speeches, though always with a caveat befitting his upbringing. "Bush said America ought to get the hell out of the UN," journalist Richard

---

[7]Bush, *All the Best*, 86 and 89; see also Herbert Parmet, *George Bush: The Life of a Lone Star Yankee* (New York: Scribner, 1997), 96, and Richard Ben Cramer, *What It Takes* (New York: Random House, 1993), 419.

Ben Cramer wrote, "if that organization seated the Red Chinese." Washington should reduce foreign aid, Bush declared—but it should target those cuts against states that were soft on Communism. And it should be in Vietnam to win—though only using levels of military force the Pentagon advised. One can almost hear the pauses and see the ellipses when reading Bush's statements from this period, denoting a man more eager to hold public office than certain why he wanted to.[8]

Bush campaigned enthusiastically and by all accounts effectively across his adopted state, but 1964 was Lyndon Johnson's year. He trumped Arizona's Barry Goldwater in the national contest, deriding his opponent as too hawkish, too doctrinaire, and too conservative. Yarborough rode Johnson's coattails to victory, and conservatism appeared on the decline nationally in the wake of his landslide. Bush's nascent political career appeared to be in jeopardy.

Bush took from his electoral defeat a renewed desire to transform the GOP by driving out the right-wingers and isolationists he blamed for his party's national drubbing, and in doing so he firmly sided with the internationalist wing of his father's Republican party. This was once more a decision made more for pragmatic than ideological reasons: he believed Republicans would achieve long-term success only through appeals to the broadest possible range of voters. "I am anxious to stay active in the Party," he confided to Nixon, while admitting that he "felt that the immediate job would be to get rid of some of the people in the Party who [permit] no difference, who through their overly dedicated conservatism are going to always keep the party small." They were in fact "a bunch of 'nuts,'" Bush conceded, putting aside his previous prohibition on such labels, and "responsible people are going to have to stand up and do something about it." He said the same to Senator Tower and to Peter O'Donnell, chairman of the Texas State Republican Party. "I think it is essential that the State Executive Committee go on record in favor of responsibility and as opposed to Birchism

[8]Cramer, 419.

(whether by name or not is debatable). This is no move towards liberalism—it simply takes some long overdue action in favor of right and against these mean, negative, super-patriots who give Texas Republicans the unfortunate image of total irresponsibility."[9]

Bush's first electoral defeat revealed his discomfort with doctrinaire definitions of his own ideology. and with ideologues more generally, especially those who rejected the internationalism of his youth. He was still far from making foreign affairs the center of his career, however. Narrowing his sights for 1966, he won election to Congress on a moderate platform. Upon his arrival in Washington he was chosen as president of the incoming congressional class and placed on the influential Ways and Means Committee (the only freshman so honored), a testament in part to his father's enduring influence on Capitol Hill. Four years later, with Nixon's backing, he gave up his safe House seat in order to run once more against Yarborough for the Senate. Bush essentially lost the general election after the Democratic primary, when the moderate Lloyd Bentsen, with whom Bush shared many policies, defeated Yarborough for his party's nomination. "Given a choice between Phillie Winkle and Winkle Pop," one Texas magazine laughed in 1970, "Texan'll take the dude with the Democratic label." The magazine's prediction proved correct.[10]

With little desire to return to Texas after his brief taste of Washington power, Bush lobbied Nixon for the job he truly wanted: Treasury secretary. The Treasury post was one of Washington's most coveted, providing its holder a leg up on any future bid for higher office. But Nixon preferred another Texan for this critical post, John Connally, believing appointment of a Democrat from that crucial state could help shore up his own reelection bid in 1972. "Every Cabinet should have at least one potential president in it,"

[9]"I took on General Walker [a Birch Society leader], The National Indignation Council and the rest of these people," Bush wrote. "It got most unpleasant as you can imagine." *All the Best*, 87 and 89–92.

[10]Parmet, 141.

Nixon believed, and he did not think Bush fit the bill. Connally's appointment came "much to George's disappointment," his close friend James Baker later recalled. Undaunted, Bush surprised Nixon by offering to become Connally's deputy. Yet again Nixon demurred. Hoping to keep Bush in Washington but unsure how best to employ him, he suggested instead a nondescript position as a White House adviser with an undefined portfolio. After Daniel Patrick Moynihan refused Nixon's invitation to become ambassador to the U.N., however, the president offered Bush the job. He accepted without hesitation, thus forging from the ashes of political defeat the beginning of a diplomatic career that would carry him to the White House.[11]

LIFE AT THE UNITED NATIONS—AND WITH HENRY KISSINGER

Bush's path to the United Nations is revealing. His service in New York was his first real exposure to international politics, and thus the first résumé line cited by supporters who later trumpeted his qualifications for the presidency. Yet diplomacy was not his first choice in 1970, and paradoxically it was his passion for domestic politics that ultimately secured him this first diplomatic job. Upon learning he was being considered for the U.N. position, Bush lobbied hard for it. He argued that he would be more than Nixon's loyal spokesman at the world body: his social and family connections throughout the Northeast might aid the president's reelection bid. In New York he could "spell out [Nixon's domestic] program with some style," Bush promised, in a candid pitch that revealed his willingness to openly state his qualifications alongside the qualities he lacked. Predicting that neither Nixon nor the domineering

---

[11]For "every cabinet," see William Safire, *Before the Fall: An Insider View of the Pre-Watergate White House* (New York: Da Capo Press, 1975), 498. For "disappointment," see James Baker, *Work Hard, Study, and Keep out of Politics!* (New York: G. P. Putnam and Sons, 2006), 25.

Henry Kissinger, Nixon's principal foreign policy aide, would allow him much of a voice in foreign affairs, he instead made his ignorance of diplomacy a virtue. "Sitting in [Chief of Staff H. R.] Haldeman's choice office in the West Wing," Bush recorded, we "discussed what the White House would be looking for in a U.N. ambassador. Obviously someone who didn't overestimate his role: the U.S. Ambassador to the United Nations . . . doesn't make policy, he carries it out." He added, "even if someone who took the job didn't understand that, Henry Kissinger would give him a twenty-four-hour crash course on the subject." After Bush had become president, Nixon wrote of his decision that he thought "it would be helpful to him in the future to have this significant foreign policy experience." This was a kind way of saying that Bush was unqualified for the job, save that he possessed the qualities Nixon cared most about: ambition and obedience. Even Haldeman later conceded that Bush's loyalty was his primary virtue. He "takes our line beautifully," he mused.[12]

Other critics would not be so judicious. Illinois Senator Adlai Stevenson, whose father had been U.N. ambassador under John Kennedy, pronounced Bush "totally unqualified" for the job, describing his appointment as "an insult" to the U.N. The *Washington Star* was equally condemnatory: "The appointment of a political loser," the paper editorialized, and "a lame-duck congressman with little experience in foreign affairs and less in diplomacy— would seem a major downgrading of the U.N. by the Nixon administration. And the senators who sit in judgment of the nomination are certain to question the appointment of a conservative Republican Texas oil millionaire to the nation's highest ambassadorial post." The *New York Times* was blunter: "There seems to be nothing in his record that qualifies him for this highly important

---

[12]For "spell out," see Tom Wicker, *George Herbert Walker Bush* (New York: Viking, 2004), 26–27. For "what the White House would be looking for," see Bush and Victor Gold, *Looking Forward* (New York: Doubleday, 1987), 110. For Nixon, see Parmet, 148. For "takes our line beautifully," see Cramer, 611.

position." Even Bush's closest associates expressed their bewilderment. "George," one longtime friend exclaimed, "What the f**k do you know about foreign affairs?"[13]

"You ask me that in ten days," Bush responded. "They laid down a challenge," he later wrote of critics who questioned not so much his diplomatic experience but his competence, and thus "got my competitive instincts flowing." He threw himself into the job, studying what the State Department advised, querying former American ambassadors for their advice, and assembling a proficient staff by mixing loyalists from his congressional office with State Department experts. "Everybody said, well, he doesn't know anything about diplomacy and everybody was right, I didn't," Bush recalled decades later. "But I learned, and worked hard at it." It did not escape him that his new job would be a final tweak to those right-wingers from his home district who despised international organizations. "It will be interesting to see what the Texas reaction is," he deadpanned to the diary he began after the November electoral defeat—the journal that evolved into his China Diary.[14]

Bush received a crash course in diplomacy while in New York, though it would be hard to call Manhattan a foreign assignment. He lived in the American ambassador's large suite at the Waldorf-Astoria and had the use of an impressive social budget. His was a taxing and high-profile job, but it was no hardship post. In New York Bush learned how diplomacy was conducted at the epicenter of American financial and cultural power. Two dominant lessons stand out from his two-year experience. First, he left the U.N. convinced that personal relations mattered to diplomatic success. Second, he came to realize that most professional diplomats disputed this view, and that his personal style was the direct opposite of the approach taken by the most important American diplomat of all: Henry Kissinger. To a degree while at the U.N., but especially

---

[13]Bush and Gold, 107 and 110. For the profane reaction, see Parmet, 149.

[14]Parmet, 149; editor interview with George H. W. Bush, July 8, 2005; and Bush, *All The Best,* 133.

later while in China, Bush would come to perceive Kissinger as a peerless model of diplomatic intrigue and master of strategic calculation—even though his was a model Bush deliberately chose not to emulate.

Bush learned the first of these lessons on his own. He approached his new job as a politician, making a point of meeting diplomats from foreign delegations—save for the Cubans, North Koreans, or others with whom Washington's relations were strained—not only professionally but also socially. He drew heavily on his family's connections, as he had promised Nixon he would, though more to broaden his own ties with foreign representatives than to strengthen the president's political base. To his mother's house in Greenwich, which was only a short drive from Manhattan, he frequently invited diplomats for Sunday brunch, including on one occasion the Communist Chinese delegation from Beijing, then newly arrived in New York. To his uncle's box at Shea Stadium (the man owned a portion of the New York Mets) Bush invited stag groups for a night of the national pastime. He even threw out the ceremonial first pitch of the 1971 season, and later he took the U.N.'s entire Economic and Social Council to a game. At each of these events he combined the personal touch that just seemed to come naturally to him—"You can't do this job if you don't like people," he quipped—with a willingness to learn. "I think the best policy around here is to demonstrate your willingness to 'go to others,'" he recorded in his journal, "to ask advice, to be grateful, and to get here earlier and leave later than the rest of the people."[15]

Bush's style ran contrary to much of the advice he had received upon taking the job. It certainly made him a different kind of ambassador from those who had served before him. Arthur Goldberg, President Johnson's representative in New York, told Bush that,

[15]For Bush at Shea, see Joseph Durso, "Mets Beat Expos in Rain, 4-2," *New York Times,* April 7, 1971, 31. For "like people," see Robert Alden, "Bush, Leaving UN Post, Is Fearful of Bloc Voting," *New York Times,* Dec. 23, 1972, 8. For "best policy," see Bush, *All the Best,* 137.

amid the cacophony of the unwieldy international forum, his principal duty should be to highlight American power. "We are the United States," Goldberg advised. "You've got to remember that. They [other delegations] should come to you, not the other way around." Bush instinctively behaved differently. He believed warm personal ties would grease the cogs of diplomacy, just as they had always eased his path in politics and business. This was not a course of action to which he seems to have given much direct thought in 1971; joining the personal and the professional was simply fundamental to his being. The U.N. experience "taught me a lot about treating nations, large or small, with respect," Bush recalled. "I got there and called on the Burundi ambassador. I thought the woman [in the office] was going to have a heart attack. . . . But I knew that word would get all around the United Nations that we recognized and respected the sovereignty and the vote of every country there." This was "just a difference in approach" from his predecessors, Bush said, "and maybe in the process [it] helped influence some political decisions."[16]

This combination of respect in the present and hope for favor in the future lies at the crux of Bush's faith in personal diplomacy, the belief that leaders should cultivate one-on-one ties with those across the negotiating table. This was an evolving view in 1971. While he set out from the beginning to cultivate friendships with his fellow ambassadors, Bush did not necessarily believe that each ambassador was his equal. Upon arriving in New York, he habitually referred to smaller states, especially those from the developing world, as "little wiener nations," incapable of determining their

---

[16]Editor interview with George H. W. Bush, July 8, 2005. When asked to describe his U.N. approach, Bush said he merely recalled his mother's advice. "Be kind. Don't be a big shot. Listen, don't talk. Reach out to people. [It] doesn't have anything to do with diplomacy; it has to do with life. Treat people with respect and recognize in diplomatic terms that the sovereignty of Burundi is as important to them as our sovereignty is [to us]. Slightly different scale, I might add. But nevertheless this is just a value thing. This isn't any great diplomatic study from the Fletcher School or something. This is just the way you react to things."

own future without the guidance of larger states such as the United States or the Soviet Union. He respected as individuals the men and women who represented smaller countries, and he seems to have made no distinction in his social calendar between colleagues from large states or small; he simply did not hold the strategic concerns of their nations in particularly high regard.[17]

By the time he left New York his opinions had softened for two reasons. Those "wiener nations" were proving increasingly influential at the U.N. And his desire to humanize diplomacy in order to help other nations appreciate Washington's point of view had inadvertently catalyzed his own ability to see the world as others saw it. Bloc voting was on the rise at the U.N., Bush warned when he left the post in 1973. What was really on the rise was voting against Washington's wishes. The United States had controlled much of the outcome of General Assembly votes since its inception in 1945, often by lining up most of the Western Hemisphere on its side. Yet the swelling ranks of new nations created by the wave of decolonization after World War II ensured that such dominance could no longer be taken for granted. "There was a time when all my predecessors had to do was to raise their eyebrow and we had an instant majority," Bush said in 1973. "That isn't the case now." Moscow and Beijing offered new states an alternative model for development, and votes were increasingly going their way. American diplomats had to be more sensitive to this changing reality, Bush argued by the time he left the U.N., and hence more responsive to international opinion. "I mean we're the United States," Bush later concluded when asked to consider his time in New York. Whenever a vote came up, "we could have said [to foreign representatives] look, you little bastard, you can go do it your way, but we are the higher power, [and] that's not the way it ought to be." Washington could have conducted its diplomacy this way, but doing so would in the end have been unproductive. "In my view," he concluded, diplomacy was best built on a foundation of respect

[17]Cramer, 611.

rather than bullying, because "the more [power] you have, [the more] you have to say what you believe." He had arrived in New York speaking of the "little wiener nations." He left thinking that it was important to "treat people with respect and recognize in diplomatic terms that the sovereignty of Burundi is as important to them as our sovereignty is [to us]." In this, his first diplomatic post, Bush began to appreciate the international implications of Washington's power, including its limitations.[18]

Bush's personal diplomacy also engendered in him a newfound respect for foreign opinions beyond the strategic calculus of bloc voting. The Bush who spoke passionately of respecting the sovereignty of every nation was not the Bush of 1971. He was the Bush of 2005, a man who relished his role as a senior statesman. This is why Scowcroft believed that his tenure at the U.N., along with his time in China, formed "one of the two seminal experiences" in Bush's development as an international thinker. "He would go around," Scowcroft later recalled, "and visit his fellow ambassadors; just sit down and talk to them [asking]: what are your problems; what's going on in your country; what do you think of the UN; what do you think of the United States?" While such conversations were motivated by a desire to win favor for American diplomatic initiatives, Scowcroft believed they also "had a profound impact on him [Bush], in terms of understanding just how different the world is. . . . I think that gave him an appreciation of how to deal with the world, because [other] people don't [always] think like we do."[19]

Scowcroft also believes that Bush's penchant for personal diplomacy later paid handsome dividends. When he became president,

[18]For "there was a time," see Alden, 8. For "we could have said," see editor interview with George H. W. Bush, July 8, 2005.

[19]Editor interview with Brent Scowcroft, March 8, 2007. Scowcroft most likely learned this story secondhand, as he and Bush did not become close until later, during Gerald Ford's presidency. Yet the story is that much more powerful for our understanding of Bush's public persona if Scowcroft had in fact come to believe he had witnessed the events he described: it had become part of Bush's lore.

Scowcroft recalled, Bush "would call foreign leaders, for no particular reason, just to say 'hi, how are you.'" More than mere courtesy was involved. "When we really needed something, he'd go to them, and they were inclined to support us because they knew who he was, where he came from, and it just made a world of difference in our diplomacy." Others who worked under Bush shared this experience. "Diplomacy was easy under those circumstances," Dick Cheney later said of his time as Bush's defense secretary. "You show up in Morocco and the King is waiting for you. His old buddy, George Bush, has talked to him and, yes, he'll send troops. The strength of his [Bush's] personality, his experience, the fact that he dealt with these guys over the years and they liked him and trusted him," Cheney contended, made a significant difference to Washington's successful Gulf War diplomacy. Bush later said of his approach that he always "tried to put himself in the other guy's shoes," leading one prominent journalist to suggest in 1990 that "friendship is Mr. Bush's ideology, and personal diplomacy has driven his presidency."[20]

Bush firmly believed that friendships could go a long way in smoothing over diplomatic rough spots, and that, in times of crisis especially, leaders who knew each other personally would find it easier to defuse difficult situations. While president, he practiced what he preached. Although he had first been exposed to the value of personal diplomacy at the U.N., the China Diary reveals that he tried daily to live by this approach while in Beijing. He purposely met with foreign dignitaries and diplomats as part of a never-ending list of social engagements, inviting them to the United States Liaison Office (USLO) for drinks, dinners, and movies. He visited their offices and apartments. He turned to tennis for far more than exercise. "Sports is a great equalizer," Bush said in 1975 of his habit

[20]For "call foreign leaders," see editor interview with Brent Scowcroft, March 8, 2007. For "diplomacy was easy," see Parmet, 462. For "in the other guy's shoes" and "friendship," see Maureen Dowd, "The Personal Means a Lot These Days," *New York Times,* July 12, 1990, A14.

of intermingling tennis with diplomatic contacts. "If you know people and can relax with people, then maybe you can head off a crisis that you couldn't head off with people you'd only met at a reception." The emphasis on personal diplomacy that came to characterize Bush's presidential work, therefore, had its origins in the 1970s.[21]

This is not to suggest that Bush's time in New York—or in Beijing, for that matter—was entirely consumed by parties, baseball games, or hours at the tennis club. On the contrary, his service at the U.N. coincided with a brutal diplomatic showdown, coincidentally over China, which served not only as a crash course in the winner-take-all aspects of international politics but also as a profound lesson in Kissinger's method of operation. The question of which Chinese government would hold the country's U.N. seat dominated Bush's agenda. China's Nationalist government, based in Taiwan, had represented the country in the General Assembly since its founding in 1945, retaining China's seat after the 1949 victory in the Chinese civil war. Though Mao Zedong's government controlled the mainland, Washington's overriding power, and its Security Council veto, had thus far salvaged the Nationalists' U.N. standing. In the midst of an increasingly heated global Cold War, Washington simply refused to recognize the legitimacy of a Communist regime in the world's most populous nation.[22]

This was a principled but lonely position. The Communist government was recognized, for example, not only by Moscow but also by London. Their control on the mainland was hardly in dis-

---

[21]John Burns, "George and Barbara Bush: A Breezy Yankee Style in Peking," *People Magazine,* May 5, 1975, 4–7. The international relations literature on an individual's role in history is vast. For an overview, see Daniel L. Byman and Kenneth M. Pollack, "Let Us Now Praise Great Men: Bringing the Statesman Back In," *International Security,* 25 (Spring 2001), 107–46.

[22]Victor S. Kaufman, "'Chirep': The Anglo-American Dispute over Chinese Representation in the United Nations," *English Historical Review* 115 (April 2000), 354–77, and Rosemary Foote, *The Practice of Power* (New York: Oxford University Press, 1997), 22–52.

pute. Still the Americans pushed hard to isolate Beijing from the international community, and they severely curtailed Sino-American relations in the process. Sanctions led to outright diplomatic rejection once hostilities broke out on the Korean peninsula in 1950, months before Chinese forces entered the conflict. The two sides enjoyed virtually no trade, no athletic competitions or cultural exchanges, and only a handful of tourist and scholarly visits for another two decades. On a philosophical level, American strategists hoped an isolated China might collapse under its own weight and poverty. Politically, a powerful "China Lobby" operating on Taiwan's behalf stood ready to punish any president who even considered improving ties with Beijing. After Harry Truman's searing experience as scapegoat for American setbacks in Asia, few of his successors dared make any conciliatory gestures toward Beijing. Eisenhower worried that "many members of Congress want to crucify anyone who argues in favor of permitting any kind of trade between the free nations and Communist China," and John Kennedy told his advisers that "I don't want to read in *The Washington Post* and *The New York Times* that the State Department is thinking about a change in China policy."[23]

No change in Washington's China policy was in the offing throughout the first half of the Cold War. American policymakers routinely challenged the Communist government's rule, terming them the "Red Chinese" and calling their capital "Peiping" to suggest its captivity under an illegitimate foreign force. Communist Chinese leaders reciprocated by labeling Washington the leader of the world's reactionary forces, its allies "running dogs," and its leaders warmongers or worse. Secretary of State John Foster Dulles even re-

---

[23]Jeffrey A. Engel, "Of Fat and Thin Communists: Diplomacy and Philosophy in Western Economic Warfare Strategies toward China (and Tyrants, Broadly)," *Diplomatic History* 29 (June 2005): 445–74, Eisenhower quote on 453. For Kennedy, see Victor S. Kaufman, *Confronting Communism: U.S. And British Policies toward China* (Colombia: University of Missouri Press, 2001), 151.

fused to shake Chinese Premier Zhou Enlai's hand during a 1954 conference convened to decide Indochina's fate. This was a slight the Chinese would not soon forget: they mentioned it to Nixon and Kissinger almost reflexively during the early 1970s. To say the Sino-American relationship was frozen during these years would be an understatement. There was hardly a relationship left to chill. The Soviet Union was Washington's greater geostrategic threat throughout the Cold War. Yet by the mid-1960s, few American policymakers considered the Soviets to be insanely driven by their ideology. They considered the Communist Chinese to be just that irrational, even before the excesses of the Cultural Revolution, portraying them to the American public as oriental, devious, and dangerous. Mao's willingness to push the Americans into a series of crises over Taiwan in the 1950s, and his subsequent suggestion that China would not only survive but welcome a nuclear exchange, surely did not help his image. Moscow posed the greater threat to Washington, but Beijing was Public Enemy Number 1. Because it was a significant symbol of American opposition to Communist rule, successive administrations refused to relinquish Taiwan's U.N. seat to such a government.

Sino-American relations began to warm in July 1971. Nixon made a world-altering announcement that Kissinger had secretly held face-to-face meetings with Zhou in Beijing, and that he was planning his own visit to China the following year. The two sides had made halting steps to improve relations before Nixon's announcement, but this was the moment when the world learned that leaders from its most populous country and its most powerful country would speak directly for the first time in over two decades. Nixon hoped for Beijing's aid in ending the lingering Vietnam War, and he hoped to offset Moscow's strength by hewing closer to Beijing. The Chinese similarly sought to counter Soviet power. "We have broken out of the old pattern," Nixon would later tell Zhou as the two stood on the tarmac of Beijing's airport, warmly (and pointedly) clasping hands. This would be one of the most profound developments of the entire Cold War, a meeting that Nixon would aptly term a "week that changed the world."[24]

Tectonic shifts in the geopolitical landscape orchestrated by visionary leaders frequently leave rubble for others to tidy up. Most American commentators praised Nixon's White House for its forward-thinking "triangulation" of American interests with those of the Soviets and Chinese. Not everyone was so enthusiastic, however. The still-formidable "China Lobby" demanded that Washington renew its pledge to safeguard Taiwan's security and the U.N. seat they considered symbolic of Taiwan's sovereignty. Kissinger and Nixon each endorsed closer ties with Beijing, yet State Department strategists maintained there were international points to be scored by defending Taiwan's seat. At a time when many American allies suffered under Communist pressure, they reasoned, Washington needed for the sake of its prestige to support Taiwan's U.N. claim. The best solution, Kissinger reasoned, would be for both Chinese governments to have a seat in the forum, though implementing this plan would not prove easy. During the 1960s the Americans had won a hard-fought procedural ruling requiring a two-thirds vote before Taiwan could be expelled from the General Assembly. This proved an important victory by the 1970s, as a majority of the members were habitually voting in Beijing's favor, casting ballots that were symbolically against American leadership as much as they were in favor of the PRC.

Bush came to the U.N. aware that preserving Taiwan's seat would be among his highest priorities. After Nixon's announcement, however, it seemed only a matter of time before Beijing took a place at the table in New York. As Bush confided in his diary, "At this moment I don't know what our China policy in the U.N. will turn out to be, but all the U.N. people feel that the ballgame is over, Peking is in and Taiwan is out." Despite such private concerns, he vigor-

[24]Margaret Macmillan, *Nixon and China: The Week That Changed the World* (Toronto: Viking Canada, 2006), 6.

ously hewed to Washington's official line on dual representation, even though the odds seemed stacked against him. Throughout the late summer and early fall of 1971, he and his staff lobbied other delegations during the day and counted votes at night. "It is all encompassing," he wrote a friend only days before the critical vote, which was scheduled for October 25. "Night and day—at every meal—first thing in the morning, last thing at night. I think we can win for a policy that I believe strongly in, but it's going to be terribly close."[25]

Bush's tenacity was motivated largely by his loyalty to Nixon, yet he also believed that fundamental issues were at stake, specifically Taiwan's sovereignty and American credibility. Unlike many of his fellow conservative Texans, he valued the U.N., and he was not so vicious an anti-Communist that he opposed Beijing's inclusion as a matter of faith. He genuinely believed that every country deserved a say in the General Assembly no matter its political persuasion. He also believed that because successive American governments had promised to defend Taiwan's seat—and by extension, its very existence—he was honor bound to uphold the trust Taiwan had placed in the United States. "Bringing [the] PRC in [was] a move towards reality, and I support it," he wrote. But "we must not let a big reality 'muscle out' a smaller reality."[26]

Weeks of lobbying and vote counting led Bush to believe that "we could win by one or two votes." But just as he was making his last-minute appeals and preparing his last speech to the assembly only hours before the final vote, news broke that Kissinger was in Beijing. He was there in preparation for Nixon's visit, scheduled for the following spring; he later argued that the timing was an unfortunate coincidence. Yet the picture of Nixon's personal envoy tacitly demonstrating that Beijing represented the Sino-American relationship that really mattered destroyed any chance of saving Taipei's seat. Bush was booed when he rose to give his speech, and the vote turned into a rout. "There is no question that the U.N. will

[25]Bush, *All The Best*, 149–52.
[26]Ibid., 152.

422

be a more realistic and vital place with Peking in here," he confided to a friend days afterwards, "but I had my heart and soul wrapped up in the policy of keeping Taiwan from being ejected." Combining pragmatism with a sense of responsibility, this was a telling remark. So too was his unscripted reaction to Taiwan's ouster. When the final vote was tallied and cheers erupted from the assembled delegates, the sight of Taipei's ambassador exiting the hall, for the final time, brought a cascade of jeers. Not wanting the man to suffer such condemnation alone, Bush left his seat, put his arm around his colleague, and escorted him from the hall.[27]

Bush was as taken by surprise as anyone by the news of Kissinger's travels. He had previously discussed the timing of the final vote with Nixon, and he had been assured by Secretary of State William Rogers that there would be no overlap with Kissinger's expected Beijing trip. "Everybody would think we were deliberately undercutting our own effort" if the two events coincided, Rogers had warned Nixon. Out of earshot, however, Kissinger told the president there simply were not enough votes for the American side. "The votes are set now," he told Nixon. "As we were going to lose . . . we were better off losing on the old stand. But I think we are farther behind than they [Rogers and Bush] think. You have to consider that these diplomats when they talk to us, they'll try to make it sound as good as possible." American interests would be best served by cementing the Chinese relationship that mattered for the future, he convincingly argued.[28]

[27]Ibid., 153–55.

[28]Rogers believed the vote was winnable. "We are neck-and-neck with the opponents of our approach to Chinese representation in the United Nations," he informed Nixon on October 12, 1971. "Although it is impossible to predict the final outcome because of the number of uncommitted or wavering votes, I would say that our prospects for success are just a little less than even." Rogers reported that the State Department "has mobilized all its available resources . . . [and] Ambassador Bush has been equally unstinting in his own efforts." United States Department of State, *Foreign Relations of the United States* [FRUS], 1969–76, vol. 5, "Memorandum from Secretary of State Rogers to President Nixon," Oct. 12, 1971, 828–30. For "deliberately undercutting," see National Security Archive,

Kissinger's preoccupation with Beijing undermined Bush's efforts on behalf of Taiwan. Though he left it to others to charge that Kissinger had embarrassed him, Bush clearly felt slighted. All he would concede privately at the time was "the fact that we were saying one thing in New York, and doing another in Washington, the outcome was inevitable." Ever loyal, he said little else publicly. Later he conceded, "Kissinger's being in Beijing at the time we were working the problem essentially signed the death warrant for Taiwan" at the U.N.[29]

Three weeks later, however, the emotions of the previous months finally boiled over. During their first face-to-face meeting following the fateful vote, Kissinger accused Bush of not hewing to the administration's line on China, obliquely pinning blame for Taiwan's ouster on a lackluster effort by Bush's U.N. delegation. Bush jumped to the accusation. "I told him my only interest was in serving the President," he later recorded, "and told him I damn sure had a feel for this country," reminding Kissinger that he did not work directly for him, and implying that he considered Kissinger's own understanding of America and its politics deficient. "For 2 to 3 minutes we had a very heated and somewhat spirited exchange," Bush recounted in his diary.[30]

Cooler heads eventually prevailed, but the residue of this exchange proved bitter. "One of the reasons he and I communicated so much," when Bush was in China, Scowcroft later concluded, "was that he thought Kissinger pulled the rug out from under him at the U.N." On the other side of the relationship, Kissinger promised Bush following their spat that he would continue to seek his counsel, even suggesting that he considered Bush among his most

Negotiating US-Chinese Rapprochement, National Security Archive Electronic Briefing Book 70, Conversation among President Nixon, Secretary of State William Rogers, and National Security Adviser Henry Kissinger, Sept. 30, 1971. For "votes are set," see FRUS, 1969–76, vol. 5, 845 note.

[29]For "outcome was inevitable," see Bush and Gold, 116. For "death warrant," see editor interview with George H. W. Bush, July 8, 2005.

[30]For "my only interest," see Bush, *All The Best,* 155–56.

valued ambassadors. In reality, however, it was at this moment that Kissinger began to actively edge Bush out of his most intricate diplomatic initiatives, in particular his dealings with the Chinese. In March 1972, for example, he told China's U.N. ambassador, Huang Hua, that "Bush doesn't know about our meetings any longer," adding that Bush would attend subsequent meetings "only if United Nations business is involved." By August, Kissinger was openly disparaging Bush to the Chinese. "I saw Ambassador Bush this morning," he told Huang. "You intimidated him. We will have to give him more backbone." The available documentary record does not reveal whether Bush knew of such slights. What is clear is that Bush departed the U.N. a more astute observer of foreign affairs, with a healthy respect for the sovereignty and opinion of other states and their representatives, and with a sharper understanding of the way in which domestic forces, such as the realities of Taiwan's place within American political calculations, framed foreign policies. He also left New York with a deep wariness of Henry Kissinger.[31]

Kissinger dominated American foreign policy in the early 1970s, and he played a formative role in Bush's growth as a diplomat even when the two were continents apart. The China Diary reveals that Kissinger shaped Bush's diplomatic style more than any other colleague—though primarily by presenting a counterargument to nearly everything Bush valued. Understanding the Kissinger who stalks Bush's diary requires an appreciation of his inestimable power during the 1970s. He was arguably the most calculating chief diplomat the country has ever known, one who coupled strategic vision with an obsessive penchant for control. This combination made him the perfect foil for the ever-scheming Nixon, for whom he was first national security adviser and then secretary of state—the only

[31]For "communicated," see editor interview with Brent Scowcroft, March 8, 2007. For "Bush doesn't know" and "backbone," see William Burr, ed., *The Kissinger Transcripts: The Top-Secret Talks with Beijing and Moscow* (New York: New Press, 1998), 70.

policymaker to ever hold the two posts simultaneously. Together the pair "developed a conspiratorial approach to foreign policy management," Secretary of State Lawrence Eagleburger, a close Kissinger aide during the 1970s, later concluded. They were secretive and tightly wound, at once brilliant for their Bismarckian scheming yet utterly fearful, given their presumption that foreign leaders were equally devious. Historians debate which man deserves more credit for their foreign policy victories and failures. Most conclude that their work is best understood as the product of a tense partnership. Joan Hoff terms their labors "Nixinger diplomacy," and Robert Dallek has recently argued that the two functioned effectively as co-presidents during Watergate's darkest days.[32]

There is no similar debate over Kissinger's role during Ford's first year in office, when Bush was in China. Kissinger ran American foreign policy. He continued to serve as both national security adviser and secretary of state, though Scowcroft managed day-to-day activities at the White House. Ford was not as passionate as Nixon about foreign policy during his first year in office, nor was he particularly adept at controlling Kissinger, who by 1974 was one of the world's most famous men. "Henry is a genius," Nixon cautioned Ford before his resignation, "but you don't have to accept everything he commends. He can be invaluable, and he'll be very loyal, but you can't let him have a totally free hand." It took Ford at least a year in power before he managed to heed this advice, and as a consequence Kissinger dominated American diplomacy during Bush's tenure in Beijing.[33]

Bush proved deeply conflicted over the Kissinger he grew to know. "Kissinger is brilliant," Bush recorded after witnessing his meetings with Chinese officials, possessing "tremendous sweep of history

---

[32]For "a conspiratorial approach," see Macmillan, 60. Joan Hoff, *Nixon Reconsidered* (New York: Basic Books, 1994), and Robert Dallek, *Nixon and Kissinger: Partners in Power* (New York: HarperCollins, 2007). The available literature on Kissinger is discussed in the essay on sources.

[33]Douglas Brinkley, *Gerald R. Ford* (New York: Times Books, 2007), 65.

and a tremendous sweep of the world situation." Yet he was difficult as well. "It is a great contrast to the irritating manner he has of handling people," Bush wrote. "His staff is scared to death of him." Kissinger's oftentimes gruff personal manner cut against the grain of Bush's own much-stated preference for civility. More profoundly, the China Diary also reveals Bush's discomfort with Kissinger's centralization of policymaking. "I am wondering if it is good for our country to have as much individual diplomacy," he recorded in his journal. "Isn't the President best served if the important matters are handled by more than one person?" Bush believed the president was in fact best served by the airing of multiple opinions. In late 1974, for example, Bush recorded a discussion with New Zealand's ambassador to China, who argued that Ford was too reliant on Kissinger. "No one is immortal," Bryce Harland told Bush. Though willing to openly disagree with other speakers in the diary—we are after all reading Bush's own thoughts, and, as the old saying goes, no one ever appears a dullard in their own memorandum of a conversation—in this instance as elsewhere Bush tacitly agreed that Kissinger's monopoly over American decisionmaking posed a genuine risk. But after nearly a year in Beijing, he reluctantly concluded there was little he could do from his far-off post to challenge the secretary. "I am just not going to worry about Kissinger's peculiar style of operation," he lamented to his diary, "where he holds all the cards up against his chest and refuses to clue people in on what is really happening."[34]

Bush and Kissinger offer an important contrast and an instructive comparison not merely because Kissinger played such a significant role in the events recorded in Bush's China Diary, but also because their intellectual (and biological) descendants would dominate American foreign policy for the ensuing three decades. The 1970s provided their first opportunity to work together. And it was during the 1970s that they came to distrust each other. The two could not have been more different. Kissinger was the poor,

[34]Diary entries for Nov. 26, Nov. 14, and Oct. 22, 1974, and June 16, 1975.

427

bespectacled immigrant—a Jew, no less, with all the attendant complexities—who rose to prominence first as an academic and then through the patronage of powerful men. While Bush hesitated to discuss the world in theoretical terms, Kissinger thrived on such language and introspection, belittling lesser minds around him with his verbal acuity in his tireless quest for power.

Bush was his polar opposite. Born to a patrician family, athletic and outgoing, he was an Ivy Leaguer as much by birthright as through classroom work, whose business and political successes derived in equal measure from his impressive family connections and his own frenetic energy. Kissinger, the one-time refugee from the Nazis, might have felt he never truly belonged in the corridors of power. Bush never questioned his own place within those same circles. Yet both men felt they belonged at the president's side, Kissinger on account of his intellect, Bush by virtue of his very being. By the same measures, each considered the other an interloper.

Theirs was not a cordial relationship. In 1971 Kissinger privately termed Bush "too soft and not sophisticated enough" for high-level diplomatic work (though he said this to Nixon, and the two had far worse to say about other leading figures of the time). More important to understanding Bush's reactions as expressed throughout the China Diary, Kissinger also made a habit during the early 1970s of publicly belittling Bush for his foreign policy inexperience. "Don't you discuss diplomacy this way," he lectured Bush (who was serving as U.N. ambassador at the time) in the midst of one session with Chinese diplomats. Only days after his designation as head of the USLO in Beijing, Kissinger further denigrated Bush in front of China's vice foreign minister by suggesting Bush was "learning more about international politics this evening than you ever did at the United Nations." Bush was not used to being spoken to this way. His diary makes clear that he did not soon forget such experiences, and when president, Bush rebuffed each of Kissinger's requests to reenter government service.[35]

[35]For "too soft," see Nixon Presidential Materials Project, National Archives

Kissinger dominated Bush's diplomatic experiences during the 1970s and clearly influenced his diplomatic approach. In practical terms, Kissinger's mania for control meant that Bush's own staff in Beijing had no real marching orders until the secretary personally briefed them. "It is difficult to define what our function is here," Bush recorded after a few months in Beijing. "How much leeway we think we should have. How much initiative we should take, etc." He could only wait for Kissinger's lead. "Clearly any of these decisions will be made by the secretary and, given the overall perspective he has, [he thinks] it is best that the really important ones be handled on that end."[36]

Bush in time found an outlet for his frustrations with Kissinger's monopoly over policymaking, as he developed an independent (and quite secretive) means of communicating with Ford while in China; he subsequently made direct access to the president a condition of his posting as director of the Central Intelligence Agency (CIA) in 1975. More significant, he frequently wrote the president directly through Scowcroft's White House office, thereby avoiding the State Department bureaucracy altogether. As Kissinger spent the majority of his time at the State Department during this period, Scowcroft was clearly in a position, both hierarchically and geographically, to provide Ford with Bush's private correspondence

---

and Records Administration (hereafter NARA), National Security Files, Box 1031, Exchanges Leading Up to HAK Trip to China, Dec. 1969–July 1971 (1), Telcon, The President / Mr. Kissinger, 8:18 p.m., Apr. 27, 1971. For "don't you discuss" and "learning more," see Burr, 51 and 285. Many commentators interpreted President George W. Bush's turning to Kissinger (and to Donald Rumsfeld, another of his father's rivals from the 1970s) as a deliberate attempt to distance his own presidency from his father's legacy. The younger Bush met with Kissinger at least monthly, according to journalist Bob Woodward, "making the former secretary the most regular and frequent outside counsel to Bush on foreign affairs." Such a turn was, in the words of one Washington insider, "a chance to prove his father wrong." See Bob Woodward, *State of Denial* (New York: Simon and Schuster, 2006), 406–10; and Maureen Dowd, "Aux Barricades," *New York Times,* Jan. 17, 2007, A19; and "Don't Pass the Salted Peanuts, Henry," *New York Times,* Oct. 4, 2006, A31.

[36]Diary entry for Nov. 5, 1974.

without Kissinger's knowledge. Yet it is clear from the diplomatic record that Scowcroft (wisely) did not make a habit of doing so at the time. Looking back thirty years later, he concluded that Bush's own desire as president to cultivate a variety of sources was a direct result of his experience dealing with Kissinger's monopoly on Ford's ear. "What he [Bush] learned from Kissinger was 'don't depend on only one single voice, however good that one voice is,'" Scowcroft later recalled. "That's not the way he thought he ought to get his information [while president]. . . . what he wanted was to hear strong people, knowledgeable people, argue points of view in front of him. And that's the way he really developed what the whole policy issue was; what were the salient questions; what were the points where people disagreed. That helped him make his decisions."[37]

The China Diary also highlights a subtle though real difference in the ways Kissinger and Bush each evaluated the utility of personal diplomacy. Each has been termed a realist, one who views the world in terms of hard power and calculations of national interest. Yet their sense of realism differed. Kissinger conspicuously developed his own network of contacts and associates throughout his career. He disagreed, however, with the extent to which Bush believed that personal trust could facilitate international relations. His worldview, shaped by war, hatred, and the Holocaust—and perhaps even by insecurities over his own social status—simply did not put much stock in a concept as illusory as trust. Kissinger appreciated that a network of contacts could lubricate the gears of the international system, and he conceded following his government service that personality played a larger role in foreign affairs than his academic studies had led him to anticipate. Yet he simply

[37]Editor interview with Brent Scowcroft, March 8, 2007. James Lilley contended that, while at the USLO, he transmitted messages for Scowcroft through his CIA communications channels, so that Bush could avoid the State Department's system altogether. Indeed Lilley employed this same trick when, in 1989, he wanted to communicate with Bush's White House without fear that his State Department cables might be inadvertently leaked to the press. Editor interview with James Lilley, March 9, 2007.

did not at any time believe that true statesmen would be influenced by bonds of friendship in the decisions they took. They would instead do what was in their own state's best interest, nothing more and nothing less.[38]

Bush seemed forever taken aback by Kissinger's pessimistic assessment of personal ties. "He seems to put no faith in individual relationships," Bush recorded in his China Diary in early 1975, after the two men had shared a private conversation during Kissinger's visit to Beijing. "It doesn't matter if they [the Chinese] like you or not," Bush says Kissinger advised him, because strategic calculations were all that mattered to great powers. "It seems to me however that he is overlooking the trust factor and the factor of style," Bush told his diary. "I do think it [personal diplomacy] is important." This conversation clearly left a mark on Bush, who emphasized it in his own memoirs more than twenty years later. He simply believed to his core that personal diplomacy mattered. It was the primary lesson he drew from his U.N. experience, and it surfaced repeatedly in the pages of the China Diary. He surely believed his hard-won ties to foreign leaders helped his presidency, and he continued to place great stock in personal diplomacy —as the preface to this book makes plain.[39]

[38]Jeremi Suri, *Henry Kissinger and the American Century* (Cambridge, Mass: Harvard University Press, 2007), 254 and 268. For Kissinger on personality's role, see Byman and Pollack, 108.

[39]Diary entry for Feb. 6, 1975, and Bush, *All the Best*, 60. Bush does not record a specific moment for this conversation with Kissinger. The full quote is instructive: "I believed that personal contact would be an important part of our approach to both diplomacy and leadership of the alliance and elsewhere. Some feel emphasis on personal relationships between leaders is unimportant or unnecessary. Henry Kissinger once argued to me that these are no substitutes for deep national interests. He pointed out that the leader of one country is not going to change a policy because he likes another leader. I suppose there is a danger that one can be naively lulled into complacency if one expects friendships will cause the other party to do things your way, but I thought that danger was remote. For me, personal diplomacy and leadership went hand in hand." Importantly, Bush believes such relationships must be cultivated: "You can't develop or earn this mutual trust and respect [from foreign leaders] unless you deliberately work at it."

Bush left the U.N. in 1973 fascinated by diplomacy, although, as we shall see below, he was not yet ready to make a career of international affairs. Neither, as it turned out, had he yet had his fill of lessons from Kissinger—or, for that matter, from the Chinese.

FROM WATERGATE TO BEIJING

Events conspired to remove Bush from the United Nations by the close of 1972, and thus from Kissinger's immediate purview. Nixon won reelection that November in the landslide he had always sought, despite the lingering story of a break-in at the Democratic Party's Watergate office. The scandal ultimately led to his resignation, and directly to Bush's appointment to China. This part of the story begins with Nixon's decision in the aftermath of his electoral triumph to shake up his cabinet. He required every senior official to submit a letter of resignation. Bush did as he was told and quietly let it be known that if he were to leave the U.N., his preferred landing spot would once more be the Treasury Department.

Nixon had other plans. He tapped Bush to head the Republican National Committee (RNC). Robert Dallek recounts Nixon's demands for a second-term cabinet full of senior leaders who "should not necessarily be brainy or impressively competent, but loyal." Indeed Nixon ordered Haldeman to "Eliminate the politicians. Except George Bush. He'd do anything for the cause." He wanted Bush to be his point man in translating his massive victory into a Republican vise grip on the electoral system for years to come. Bush's Eastern background coupled with his Texas credentials made him the embodiment of the new Southern and Western party Nixon believed the GOP could become. Barbara Bush did not want her husband to take the job, thinking it too partisan a post for his moderate reputation and political future. "Anything," she said, "but not that committee." Other friends counseled that the RNC job was technically a demotion from the high-ranking post of U.N.

ambassador. Bush countered with one of his father's favorite adages: "You just can't say no to the president."[40]

Watergate spiraled into the greatest political scandal in American history. Though uninvolved in the White House's conspiracies, as RNC chair Bush was nevertheless embroiled in the political firestorm. He repeatedly asked Nixon if the allegations against him were true. Each time, Nixon denied the charges to Bush's face. After each of these fabricated declarations of innocence, Bush sallied forth to put his own reputation on the line in defense of the president. His was a no-win position. Republican constituents split in their assessment of Bush's actions: half thought he should pillory the president in order to save the party; the other half criticized him for not doing enough for Nixon in the face of partisan attacks. In the compilation of letters Bush subsequently published, he termed this chapter of his life "The Eye of the Storm."

The experience of defending a president whose web of deceit unraveled a bit more with each passing day left Bush traumatized. Still he remained in his post, even as Nixon's position became untenable. "Heaven knows," he told his friend Baker in November 1973, "I wish we were moving back to Houston today . . . but I must stay here." Poll numbers commissioned by Baker suggested that, in any event, Bush's reputation in Texas was not faring well enough for victory in any statewide election. By March 1974, Bush admitted to a close friend that "these are extremely complicated times—this job is no fun at all." More poignantly, he wrote that he "longed for an escape—and an escape in my fantasy usually takes the form of running around in the boat in Maine—no telephone." He appears to have believed in Nixon's innocence to the bitter end. "I am confident that full disclosure on Watergate will vindicate the President," he stated, even as doubts about Nixon's political viability began to crowd his thoughts.[41]

[40]For "loyal," see Dallek, 434. For "anything" and "can't say no," see Cramer, 610–11.

[41]For "moving back" and "complicated times," see Parmet, 163–64. For "escape," see Bush, *All the Best,* 176.

Nixon eventually resigned, and Gerald Ford's unusual path to the White House nearly carried Bush with him. Ford needed a vice president, and he consciously made the selection process as open as possible, canvassing legislators from both parties for their suggestions. Bush was not necessarily at the head of anyone's list, but he was a consensus second choice. His candidacy made good electoral sense: he was a party loyalist but also a moderate; his political background offered Ford geographic balance; and he had been the good soldier through the maelstrom of the past months. Much like Ford, moreover, he had a reputation for honesty.

Bush proved Ford's second choice as well, behind New York's Nelson Rockefeller. Bush wanted the job, and he authorized his supporters to lobby his cause in this most unusual of campaigns. Rockefeller was better known nationally, however, and he had not been on the stump over the past twenty months defending Nixon. Ford nominated him for the post. Disappointed by his near miss, Bush wanted out of Washington, and Ford was eager to excise all traces of Watergate as soon as possible. He offered Bush an enviable choice as a reward for his service: the ambassadorship to either London or Paris. Each was a coveted post, carrying with it prestige, luxury, and geopolitical stature.[42]

Bush instead requested China. In doing so he was asking not to be posted to one of Europe's fabulous capitals, but rather to be sent to a nation without formal diplomatic relations with the United States, where luxuries were basically unknown, and where he would arguably be as far removed from Washington's center of power as was possible in 1974. Following Nixon's visit to China in 1972, America and the PRC had each had established a "liaison office" in the other's capital to carry on the consular work typically done in an embassy, while remaining devoid of the trappings associated with formal ties. David Bruce, one of Washington's most esteemed diplomats, with three decades of bipartisan experience, had opened

---

[42]Barry Werth, *31 Days: Gerald Ford, The Nixon Pardon, and a Government in Crisis* (New York: Anchor Books, 2006), 165–67.

the USLO in Beijing in 1973. He would transfer to the NATO ambassadorship upon Bush's arrival. Bush would not technically be an "ambassador" in Beijing (though, as a consequence of his U.N. position, he retained the title). Technically he would rank below the representative of any nation with formal ties to Mao's government. Whereas the American ambassador in London or Paris would typically be received first in any social function, Bush was frequently placed behind the envoy from the Palestinian Liberation Organization.[43]

Bush chose China for a variety of reasons. It was obviously an exotic place, and he believed its global role would only grow in the decades to come. Time spent there would be an adventure, he told friends. Others termed it a well-earned sabbatical. Unlike service in Europe, moreover, where ambassadors were expected to supplement their embassy's social budget from their own pockets, Beijing would prove downright cheap. After a decade of public service—and with three children yet to attend college—Bush had financial considerations in mind in choosing Asia over Europe. He marveled repeatedly through his China Diary at the low cost of living he encountered. Even the caviar was cheap, he realized to his delight.[44]

Many considered Bush's decision an unusual one. The Beijing of 1974 was still embroiled in the Cultural Revolution, subject to blackouts and ill lit on the best of nights, brutally hot in the summer and bitterly cold in the winter, polluted, noisy, hard to get to, and cut off from easy mail or phone service. Entertainment was extremely limited, as was travel by foreigners beyond the city limits. More than one expert warned Bush that boredom was the major enemy of any foreigner posted to Beijing. The USLO itself

[43]For Bruce, see Priscilla Roberts, ed., *Window on the Forbidden City: The Beijing Diaries of David Bruce, 1973–74* (Hong Kong: University of Hong Kong Centre of Asia Studies, 2001).

[44]"We went back and talked about England," Bush recorded of his conversation with Ford. "He wondered if it was substantive enough—so did I. We talked about the money. I told him I had lost a lot of money and didn't know if I could afford it." See Bush, *All the Best,* 196, and Werth, 166.

was a work in progress, despite the Herculean effort of Ambassador Bruce's wife, Evangeline, to transform the shabby quarters they inherited into a dignified compound. Her hard work aside, the residence was hardly a suite at the Waldorf-Astoria. When asked to explain his unexpected choice, Bush contended that he considered China crucial to the future. It was home to a quarter of the world's people, and even Kissinger conceded that the job offered the chance to "do some substantive business." If nothing else, this posting would give him an unusual line on his résumé, if and when he decided to reenter politics. "What the hell," he told one reporter, "I'm fifty. It won't hurt anything."[45]

Bush was sincere in these explanations, but Beijing's most appealing quality after the stresses of the previous months was undoubtedly its distance from Washington. "Am I running away from something?" Bush asked his diary while en route to Beijing only weeks after accepting Ford's invitation. "Am I leaving what with inflation, incivility in the press and Watergate and all the ugliness?" Most important, by flying halfway across the world to an isolated post, "Am I taking the easy way out?"[46]

Bush told himself he was not just running away, but the evidence suggests otherwise. His first letters home from Beijing combined with his diary entries portray a man reveling in the solitude he found. They express his joy at the fact that "the telephone is strangely silent. What a change." What a relief, too. As he wrote a friend only weeks into his stay, "It's the new me, meditative, no phones ringing, little mail, time to think but plenty to do. How awesome!" He similarly told a political ally that "the change of pace is enormous. My phone doesn't ring—after many years of incessant ringing, it's rather weird." Barbara Bush noted her own enthusiasm

---

[45]For "substantive business," see diary entry for Oct. 21, 1974. For "what the hell," see Don Oberdorfer, "China: Change of Pace," *Washington Post*, Dec. 2, 1974, B1.

[46]Diary entry for Oct. 21, 1974. Lilley believed Bush's choice was like "pulling the covers over your head, and getting the hell out of Washington." Editor interview with James Lilley, March 9, 2007.

for her husband's suddenly relaxed schedule, and she too focused on the bizarre (in their lives) experience of a silent telephone. "Back in Washington or at the United Nations the telephone was ringing all the time," she told a reporter. "I think he misses the phone as much as anything," she joked. She even took to calling her husband in his USLO office during the day, even if she was only yards away in their residence, just so he would not feel too lonely.[47]

One phone call Bush could not escape came from Watergate prosecutors, who tracked him down during a refueling layover on his initial trip to China. The political scandals of his recent past were not so easily shunted aside, and he was forced during his first week in Beijing to compose a detailed response to their queries. "The incident itself is not important," he wrote in his diary, "except that here I was leaving the United States, last point of land, and a call out of the ugly past wondering about something having to do with Watergate, cover-up, and all those matters that I want to leave behind." Watergate's reach even across the Pacific seemed to validate his decision to leave American politics, if only temporarily.[48]

Some found much to criticize in Ford's decision to place Bush in such a sensitive post. "The replacement of the career diplomat David Bruce with the GOP chairman George Bush in the sensitive Peking post makes no sense," one writer to the *Washington Post* argued. The *New York Times* believed that, "at a time of continuing Sino-Soviet tension and a period where Washington seeks a realistic post-Vietnam policy for Asia, an experienced Asia hand might have been a wiser choice." Even the sympathetic *Los Angeles Times* admitted, "Bush is by no means a China expert though he is close to, and well regarded by, Mr. Ford, a fact that presumably will assure China's leaders that they can count on clear access to the President."[49]

[47]Bush Presidential Library, Personal Papers of George H. W. Bush, China Files, Correspondence Files, Box 1, Bush to Armstrong, Nov. 6, 1974; Bush to Bartlett, Oct. 29, 1974; and Bush to Rhodes, Nov. 28, 1974; Oberdorfer, B1.
[48]Diary entry for Oct. 21, 1974.
[49]"Mr. Ford's Ambassadorial Nominations," *Washington Post*, Sept. 13, 1974,

Bush's assignment drew subtle criticism from the Chinese as well. Bruce was Washington's most respected diplomat, the only man to have served as ambassador to Bonn, London, and Paris, and a private confidant of every American president since Franklin Roosevelt. Huang Zhen, Beijing's representative in Washington, was equally esteemed in Chinese diplomatic circles. Bush's diplomatic experience was hardly in their league. Clare Hollingsworth, a British reporter based in Beijing, reported that Chinese officials thought Bush's selection somewhat insulting, despite his political credentials.[50]

In truth, no one could match Bruce's experience, and Bush's selection signified, if nothing else, a new, energetic spirit for the USLO. When asked by his government to comment on the appointment, for example, Britain's ambassador in Washington concluded that "Bush's main problem in Peking will be to find an outlet for his abounding physical energy: the US Liaison Office will probably find themselves engaged in endless tennis tournaments." Indeed these British observers, who had far more practical experience dealing with the Chinese than the Americans did, believed that Bush's political experience would stand him in good stead. As one British diplomat concluded, "The Chinese will be more interested in having a man whom they know is fully in the President's confidence. They are unlikely to hold against him what was said in New York and are likely to regard it has having been merely carrying out of instructions."[51]

Bush thus arrived in Beijing in the late fall of 1974 a tired man, a man running from Washington's political maelstrom. Yet he immediately set out to energize Sino-American relations by relying on the personal style of diplomacy he considered his hallmark. On the

---

A27; "Mr. Ford's Diplomats," *New York Times,* Sept. 6, 1974, 32; and "Ford's Choices for Diplomatic Posts," *Los Angeles Times,* Sept. 6, 1974, B6.

[50]Hollingsworth's opinion comes from Priscilla Roberts, editor of David Bruce's Beijing diaries, personal communication, June 25, 2007.

[51]United Kingdom National Archive (formerly British Public Records Office) FCO 21/1234, Relations between China and USA, Ramsbotham to Wilford, Sept. 12, 1974, and Wilford to Ramsbotham, Sept. 19, 1974.

flight to China he told his diary—perhaps more as a pep talk to himself than anything else—that "it is my hope that I will be able to meet the next generation of China's leaders—whomever they may prove to be. Yet everyone tells me that that is impossible." Kissinger believed Bush's efforts to win favor with the Chinese by improving personal ties would prove pointless—and potentially hazardous given Kissinger's own desire to control all aspects of American foreign policy. Many at the State Department shared his low opinion of personalizing relations with the Chinese—or at least they were wise enough to tell Kissinger as much—and Bush's quest was therefore openly ridiculed in Foggy Bottom as naïve in the extreme. "Bush has energetic plans to try to meet as many significant Chinese as he possibly can, especially political leaders," Winston Lord, an Asia specialist (and future American ambassador to China) who directed the State Department's Policy Planning Staff, wrote Kissinger. "We doubt that he will have any breakthrough in this regard but you may wish to outline your concept of his proper role in the policy area."[52]

Many professional diplomats did not consider Bush's gregarious desire to build bonds of trust with China's elite to be "proper." Their discomfort should not be surprising. If the Foggy Bottom professionals believed their Chinese counterparts could be swayed by friendship, they would have to concede that they too might be so influenced. It was better to keep Sino-American relations on a coldly detached plane, the experts advised: given how sensitive the emerging relationship was in the early 1970s, what little might be gained by positive personal relations paled in comparison to the risks posed by the wrong statement or an ill-conceived gesture. The professionals had on their side recent experience of the way offhand remarks to the Chinese could undermine months of hard work.

[52]For "it is my hope," see diary entry for Oct. 21, 1974. For "energetic plans," see National Archives and Records Administration (NARA), RG 59, Lot 77D114, Records of the Policy Planning Staff (Winston Lord Files) (hereafter NARA, Lord Files), Box 375, China: Sensitive Chronological: January–February 1975, From Habib and Lord to Kissinger, Feb. 4, 1975.

Kissinger's aide Alexander Haig, while in Beijing in January 1972 to discuss Nixon's visit, nearly derailed the entire affair by assuring Zhou Enlai that Washington valued China's continued "viability." Haig intended to assure his hosts that the Americans had no further intention of undermining their regime. Zhou and Mao interpreted the comment differently. "No country should depend upon a foreign power in maintaining its own independence and viability," Zhou scolded Haig, lest the dependent country "become that power's subordinate and colony."[53]

Zhou's passions subsided, but Haig's gaffe left an indelible imprint on Foggy Bottom. It drove home the perception that Sino-American relations were fragile in the extreme and made Kissinger wary of trusting anyone else to meet with Mao's top leadership. Given Bush's dearth of formal diplomatic training, Kissinger's staff verily shuddered every time their new USLO head secured a private meeting with a Chinese official, and balked every time Bush invited a friend to Beijing. The State Department's discomfort with American visitors extended even to members of Congress, many of whom pressed their old colleague Bush for one of the personal invitations (and visas) that Chinese officials had informally promised he could dispense. A Chinese visa in one's passport was a valued commodity in Washington in 1974. Yet the State Department wanted to control such visits whenever possible, fearing that politicians untrained in diplomatic nuances might inadvertently—or perhaps intentionally—disrupt relations. Immediately before Bush's departure in October 1974, the State Department's Arthur Hummel cautioned Kissinger that "Bush has already stated arrangements to request visas on 'a personal basis' for two Congressmen and their wives to visit Peking this winter. . . . we have so far strictly followed

<hr />

[53]Chen Jian, *Mao's China and the Cold War* (Chapel Hill: University of North Carolina Press, 2001), 273. Margaret MacMillan points out that Haig's unfortunate choice of words, which he pleaded was merely "the simple language of a soldier," came after several days of discourtesy and intentionally rude treatment by the Chinese, as the Shanghai Clique attempted to subvert the impending Sino-American rapprochement. MacMillan, 221–24.

a policy of not promoting any Congressional visits (except those officially arranged)." From Hummel's perspective, "Bush is creating a problem for himself, and for us." Despite repeated warnings, he "appears determined to retain his 'personal' flexibility."[54]

Bush pushed forward despite such warnings, though he frequently wrote of his frustration with the way Washington kept him on such a tight leash while in Beijing. He continued to invite personal friends to Beijing despite the tension such invitations caused in Washington, and he strove to meet as many Chinese leaders as possible, even though Kissinger's office thought such meetings would prove fruitless. He even filed a protest with the department over its micromanagement of his personal guest list. When visiting American congressmen did behave poorly in 1975, as a result of diplomatic naïveté mixed with alcohol, Bush easily dismissed their gaffe even as some in the State Department feared fallout. "It was not a disaster but it was pretty bad," he told his journal. "We are too damn goosy on the program and they [the State Department] have too little confidence in me in the sense that they seem scared that everybody is going to blow it. It is the result of Kissinger's strong arm on everything to do with China."[55]

If Bush's desire to engage the Chinese on a personal level allowed room for missteps and human foibles, American officials had every reason to fear for the long-term stability of Sino-American relations in 1974, because the honeymoon was surely over. Multiple problems remained after the heady days of Nixon's initial visit. Many pundits had believed most of the issues facing the two superpowers would be solved during Nixon's second term. He would have four years to put his indelible mark on the globe, they reasoned, while China's leadership would be eager to complete their life's work by returning their country to global prominence before making way for the next generation. Kissinger thought formal recognition at least could be

[54]NARA, Lord Files, Box 376, Chronological, August 17–Oct. 15, 1974, Hummel to Kissinger, Oct. 8, 1974.

[55]Diary entries for April 1 and April 2, 1975.

accomplished before 1976. Watergate scuttled these hopes. Beijing had its own reasons for slowing the pace of rapprochement after 1972 as well. Having thawed relations with Washington largely as a counterweight to Moscow, China's senior leaders proved hesitant in the ensuing years to tilt too far toward the Americans.[56]

Bush therefore arrived in Beijing at a moment when Sino-American relations were widely perceived as stagnant. And stagnation was not a concept the energetic Bush found acceptable. On his initial flight over the Pacific he wrote that "Kissinger keeps the cards so close to his chest that able officers in EA [State Department Bureau of East Asian Affairs] seem unwilling to take any kinds of initiative. This troubles me a little bit because I worry that our policy is 'plateaued out,' and that if we don't do something the policy will come under the microscopic scrutiny the CIA has come under, [and] that the Middle East policy has come under." He worried throughout his diary that a dearth of visible progress would in time be perceived in the United States and around the world as evidence of failing relations. It was a fear that shows Bush at his clearest: a leader who favored steady and stable relations devoid of high-risk though high-reward breakthroughs, and a man who believed relations were best cultivated far from public view. As he readily conceded, his obsession with the relationship's image grew directly from his own political background. "The only tack that I have got that can be helpful is this approach of having been in politics." Politics created their own reality, he had learned; and he wanted to create an aura of positive momentum in which Sino-American relations could make genuine progress.[57]

Bush came to believe while in Beijing that a steady drumbeat of positive announcements, even superficial ones, could drown out

[56]Particularly useful on normalization are Nancy Bernkopf Tucker, "Taiwan Expendable? Nixon and Kissinger Go to China," *Journal of American History* 92 (June 2005), 109–35, and William Kirby, Robert Ross, and Gong Li, eds., *Normalization of U.S.-China Relations: An International History* (Cambridge, Mass.: Harvard University Asia Center, 2005).

[57]Diary entry for Oct. 21, 1974.

THE MAKING OF A GLOBAL PRESIDENT

any legitimate criticism of a relationship gone cold. During his first weeks on the job he probed his staff and colleagues for some way to demonstrate progress within Sino-American relations, because "the American people are going to be looking for forward motion." He verily pleaded with Washington for some means of demonstrating such forward motion, no matter how trivial. Realizing it was not within his power to alter the substance of Sino-American relations on his own, Bush instead concentrated on improving the relationship's image, hoping to focus international attention elsewhere. There is an elitist strain at work in Bush's thinking: a conviction that diplomacy functions best when handled quietly among experts far removed from unbridled public passions, and that the public can be easily distracted from matters of substance by symbolic gestures. Bush returned to the topic of symbolic progress constantly during his first weeks in Beijing, raising the issue during most of his early meetings with Chinese officials and with his counterparts in Beijing's diplomatic community. "I have been concerned by several ambassadors suggesting that our relations have deteriorated, and I made a point of telling Qiao [Guanhua, China's foreign minister] that two ambassadors had raised this question with me," Bush recorded. "I also told him I wouldn't be here if I felt that the relations were going backwards."[58]

At the least, he worked to change the USLO's image in Beijing, raising its public profile as a way of demonstrating that all was well within the broader Sino-American relationship. He and Barbara purchased bicycles. They were the city's preferred means of transportation, but, more important, he calculated that people would take note of the American ambassador arriving on two wheels rather than in a staid chauffeur-driven automobile. He wanted the Chinese, the city's ever-watchful diplomatic community, and the growing band of journalists to notice how normally he conducted his own affairs, thereby providing prima facie evidence of the normality of an American presence in Beijing. He simultaneously pep-

[58]Diary entries for Oct. 21 and Oct. 29, 1974.

pered the State Department with suggestions for demonstrating forward motion, such as enlarging the USLO or the size of its staff, and he even mentioned his concern to Deng Xiaoping when the two first met in November 1974. "I gave him my thesis that there must be visible manifestations of progress for our China policy so it will avoid some of the hyper-microscopic analyses that we are getting on other policies in the States." Following this logic, he directed his staff to operate in Beijing as though theirs was a typical embassy rather than merely a low-ranking liaison office. Whereas Bruce had banned (with Kissinger's blessing) his staff from attending national day celebrations at other embassies, Bush reversed this policy. He wanted Americans to be visible in Beijing's diplomatic community, and reasoned that the informal conversations at these receptions might augment the USLO's information-collecting efforts. The diplomatic record shows the decision was his alone, taken even as Foggy Bottom dithered over this question of protocol. Seven thousand miles from home, it proved easier for Bush to gain forgiveness than permission when striving to suggest Sino-American progress.[59]

Bush's frenetic efforts raised hackles at the State Department, especially as his political background gave him a foundation of support outside the normal confines of the foreign service. Kissinger knew he could not control Bush as easily as he might have managed an ambassador who had risen through the State Department's oftentimes conformist ranks, and he quickly began to fear that Bush's insatiable demands for progress might undermine his own more cautious plans. Like Bush, he believed that high-level diplomacy functioned best when conducted between elites with little public scrutiny. But unlike Bush, Kissinger assumed that public perceptions could be massaged as necessary, and in time he concluded that Bush's preoccupation with the topic revealed a failure to grasp the broader nuances of his own global policy. After reading numerous cables from Bush detailing his "progress" thesis, alongside transcripts of Bush's discussions of the topic with leading Chinese

[59]Diary entry for Nov. 1, 1974.

officials, Kissinger determined in November 1974 to set his new envoy straight. The press might write that Sino-American relations were stagnating, but "you and I know this is not true, as do the Chinese." These were the opinions that truly mattered, Kissinger instructed, and it would be unwise to state that all was well in the bilateral relationship given the real issues that remained. "For tactical reasons," Kissinger rebuked Bush, "we don't want them [the Chinese] to think that we don't have domestic problems or that we don't risk criticism if we give away too much on Taiwan." Bush wanted signs of visible progress in order to take Sino-American relations off the international front burner; Kissinger embraced stagnation as a necessary means of keeping Beijing's feet to the fire.[60]

Kissinger thus strove to isolate his envoy's impact. In Beijing at the close of November 1974, for example, he deliberately chided Bush in front of his Chinese hosts. "George doesn't think I am spending enough time on China," he quipped, showing the Chinese that he did care about their country while effectively telling Bush to cool his heels. He reiterated the point when the two met privately, and Bush appears to have heeded these warnings. The volume of his cables back to Washington detailing his day-to-day dealings dropped precipitously following this meeting; their number would decrease further every month he served in Beijing. Nevertheless, he confessed to his diary his skepticism with Kissinger's strategy. "I think I can convince him that we have been right in the fact that some think our policy is declining and that we need to do certain things to demonstrate that it is not."[61]

Bush's concern with public perception evolved over time into a broader worry that Beijing's penchant for criticizing Washington risked poisoning American public opinion. This was an important transition in his thinking. He arrived in Beijing thinking that only

---

[60]NARA, RG 59, Lord Files, Box 375, China: Sensitive Chronological, Oct. 16–Dec. 31, 1974, From Kissinger to Bush, Nov. 12, 1974; and NARA, RG 59, Lord Files, Box 331, China Exchanges, Aug. 9–Dec. 31, 1974, From Kissinger to Bush, Nov. 4, 1974.

[61]Diary entry for Nov. 26, 1974.

excessive public scrutiny might derail Sino-American relations, but over time he came to believe that Beijing's heated anti-American rhetoric might inadvertently draw the very scrutiny he longed to avoid. In early November 1974, he lamented that "China unloaded on us at the World Food Conference in spite of my tactful suggestions to both Qiao and Deng that this not happen. They don't realize that this eventually will not help our policy at all." He presumed that Beijing's leaders "feel that they must make brownie points with the Third World and we will understand," but he feared that "if Americans focused on what they were saying they wouldn't understand, unless they were in on all the policy decisions." He remained convinced that the public was fickle and uninformed when compared to elite decisionmakers such as himself.[62]

This is a common trope of leaders and pundits, for whom discussions of the public's ignorance remains an easy means of suggesting their own sophistication. Bush rarely criticized the public so explicitly, though his experience of Watergate had surely taught him to fear its wrath. If roused by Beijing's constant din of rhetorical assaults, he worried, public anger might prevent elites such as Kissinger (and himself) from performing positive work. The Chinese "ought to knock it off but they don't seem to want to."[63]

Bush's frustration with the Chinese attacks, which he termed "empty cannons of rhetoric" after hearing Qiao Guanhua employ the term, increased throughout his time in China. He knew that anti-American proclamations were issued primarily to reaffirm Beijing's anti-capitalist credentials. Harsh rhetoric had long been central to Chinese diplomacy, a role reinforced by the ideological rigidity of the Cultural Revolution. Hot war was not always practical, Zhou Enlai lectured to the Foreign Ministry in 1949. For the true revolutionary, "There may not be a war of swords every year [but] as sure as night turns into day, there will be a constant war of words, every day of the year." Bush understood, but he did not ap-

[62]Diary entry for Nov. 8, 1974.
[63]Ibid.

prove. He found Beijing's jeremiads to be misguided, potentially dangerous, and particularly galling given his opinion that they were so frequently just plain wrong. "It is annoying beyond belief to read the attacks in the Red News on the United States," he recorded in November. "China feels it must attack the United States. . . . I just have this inner feeling that these Chinese leaders do not subscribe to that view in its entirety. Perhaps I am wrong. But I have heard them talk enough to know they don't believe that. How does one balance that with their desire for frankness in dealing, their desire for openness, their desire to 'keep their word' etc." Later he wrote, "I am absolutely convinced that American public opinion will turn against this [rhetoric] at some point and a relationship which is very important to China will be damaged. Maybe China's rhetoric is more important to them than the relationship, but I don't really think so."[64]

Underlying Bush's ever-increasing frustration with Beijing's level of vitriol was his growing belief that the Chinese operated on a double standard. Chinese officials thought little of criticizing the Americans, but Bush thought them thin-skinned. "Would China understand it if we struck back in these areas, diplomatic fora, against China," he wrote. "I am wondering how they would feel if we attacked their closed system, no freedom of press, without taking away from their many accomplishments, the total lack of individual freedom." Several months later he returned to this question again —in truth, he never left it for long—writing, "We need to make our position known to the Chinese in a friendly and frank fashion. We do have principles and it is time we stood up for them without being contentious. Everybody in our mission knows what I am talking about when I say that China talks about their principles, and when they want to turn something down, they can turn it down on principle. But they do not accord others the same courtesy when it comes to understanding their principles."[65]

---

[64]For Zhou, see Macmillan, 45. Diary entries for Nov. 17 and Dec. 19, 1974.
[65]Diary entries for Nov. 17, 1974, and April 16, 1975.

Bush's preoccupation throughout his China Diary with the public aspects of diplomacy dovetailed with his own belief that diplomatic relations functioned best when leaders resolved their issues in a friendly fashion far from public scrutiny. "At some point our relationship," he concluded, "whether the Taiwan problem has been solved or not, should get to the point where Kissinger can come here, have frank discussions and there not be this over-expectation." Bush returned to this theme in mid-1975, criticizing journalists who felt Ford should delay visiting Beijing until divisive issues could be solved. "The visit in my view should be hailed as simply a visit to get to know the Chinese leaders," he argued. Leaders needed to talk. "Deng went to Paris," he noted. "There were no agreements, no signed communiqués, but he had good talks with [President] Giscard d'Estaing of France. This is the kind of meeting this should be billed as. There are global reasons why it makes sense." Of course, the more the Chinese blustered, the more pressure they placed on Ford to produce dramatic results while in Beijing. "I get tired of reading all of this propaganda and being surrounded with it," Bush sighed into his diary. "China insists on hammering away at the decadence of our society and labeling us as imperialists etc. I would think that if you want better relations you would lower one's voice on that kind of thing, but it doesn't work that way." By June 1975 his patience was at an end. "They continue to slam us around," he fumed. "Not as much as they used to obviously, and the China specialists will say less than they might. But I say they are doing it too much, because I worry more about American public opinion than some of our China specialists, and the public opinion's effect on our being able to perform and fulfill a policy."[66]

The global context is crucial to understanding these 1975 remarks and Bush's Asian experience as a whole. Saigon fell while he was in Beijing. Cambodia plunged into disarray. Détente was being pilloried in Washington and on the verge of collapse in Europe.

[66]Diary entries for Nov. 30, 1974, and June 2, March 11, and June 8, 1975.

Everywhere he looked, Bush saw American leadership questioned. All the while, Washington's allies throughout the world, but especially in the Pacific, scrambled to ensure their own strategic interests should the American people take these losses as cause for a general pullback from the world. In some sense Washington's Asian allies had been scrambling since Nixon's historic rapprochement to China in 1971. After a generation of condemning any relations with China, Americans in 1971 had seemed to be changing the rules of the game. In 1975 many worried it was a game they were losing.

From Bush's vantage point, a general reordering of the strategic landscape was in the offing. He witnessed leaders from the Philippines, Malaysia, and other Pacific countries—men who had for the most part been longstanding allies and pliant adherents to the American effort to isolate China—journeying to Beijing in order to cement ties with Mao's regime. They appeared in his eyes to be turning from an American-led democracy they no longer trusted toward a new center of power in Asia. "China continues to support revolutions in all these countries," Bush noted, "and yet many of the countries like the Philippines, Malaysia and others keep trying to get closer to China." In his opinion, "They have to because they don't see in the U.S. the firm kind of interventionist support that they have been able to count on in the past."[67]

This was the domino theory as Bush saw it. Not the knee-jerk fear that Communism would spread, like a disease, from victim to victim as had been believed in the past, but rather a more nuanced sense that America's declining credibility would allow Communism's influence to grow throughout Asia by invitation. In Bush's worldview it was not so much that Communist influence would spread outward after its victory in South Vietnam, picking up speed and heft like a snowball rolling downhill. Instead he feared that, in the wake of the American pull-out from Vietnam, countries throughout the region would be drawn to Communism's increased gravity. They would hew all the faster to Beijing as the epicenter of Asian

[67]Diary entry for May 6, 1975.

Communism if they perceived a general American withdrawal from the region—the proof of which would seem to be Washington's refusal to counter Beijing's harsh rhetorical critiques. "There is a domino theory," he wrote as Saigon fell, because he feared its fall undermined the one domino that mattered most in international relations: American credibility. As Bush put it in 1975, "Clearly as the United States has reneged on commitments and pulled back, and is unwilling to support recommendations of the president, the free countries" of the world will begin to lose faith in America. "As Cambodia weakens, as North Vietnam makes gains, many of our allies are compelled to move toward the PRC. The domino theory is alive and well," he told his journal. A general strategic realignment, to Washington's eventual detriment, seemed the likely result. "I have complete conviction that there is such a thing as a domino theory," he later wrote. "Thailand, and the Philippines and others rushing towards new alignment. Kim Il Sung of Korea talking much tougher now about the South in Peking. Obviously trying to capitalize on the decline of the free countries in the southeast."[68]

Bush's reactions to Saigon's fall are among the China Diary's most revealing passages. They illuminate the centrality of credibility to his definition of a successful foreign policy, and his belief that a successful foreign policy demanded constant reevaluation. Rhetorically asking what he would do if in charge of Washington's diplomacy at that critical juncture, Bush offered a broad outline of his most basic diplomatic principles, revealing a man cognizant of the complexities of the positions he advocated, yet aware of the limitations of his own experience. He suggested he would employ multilateral approaches in international forums such as the U.N. to a greater extent than the Nixon and Ford administrations, but that he would also ensure (exactly how he never states) that Washington received credit from these bodies for its good works. Amer-

[68]For the domino theory generally, see Frank Ninkovich, *Modernity and Power: A History of the Domino Theory in the Twentieth* Century (Chicago: University of Chicago Press, 1994). Diary entries for April 8, March 17, and April 22, 1975.

ican policymakers had to rehabilitate their standing throughout the world, he argued to his diary, because "as soon as America doesn't stand for something in the world, there is going to be a tremendous erosion of freedom." Yet, fresh from the traumas of Vietnam, he also thought the country could not go off on further quixotic crusades where vital interests were not involved. "We have got to be realistic. We have to have our eyes open." Most important, Washington needed to determine with its allies the issues that truly mattered. The world system needed American leadership to function, Bush believed, but that leadership needed to be perceived as simultaneously credible and rational. Credible in the sense that promises would be kept, but rational in that Washington would promise only that which it was prepared to defend to the hilt. Even if allies disagreed with Washington's strategic conclusions, they would at least better appreciate Washington's reasoning if fully involved in such discussions. "Everyone out here is so down on our policy in Cambodia and Southeast Asia in general," he lamented. "Even our allies talk about how wrong our policy is." Such widespread criticism of American policy, even if wrongheaded, hardly enhanced Washington's standing throughout the world. It did little good to pursue quixotic policies merely because the crusade had already begun. Rather, Bush came to believe that what was needed after Vietnam was a broad reassessment of American interests— "not a withdrawal, but a reexamination"—so that the promises Washington made, and the commitments it in turn could be expected to keep, were themselves worthy of the effort. We have to "redraw the lines," he wrote, "perhaps in the Pacific, so we are not committed in wars we shouldn't be involved in, where we'd have no support from the American people . . . along with allies."[69]

The international events Bush witnessed while in Beijing reinforced his belief that credibility was crucial to a successful foreign policy, but it was not the only necessary ingredient. Equally important was a willingness to make credible promises only for

[69]Diary entries for April 30, April 26, and March 3, 1975.

451

matters truly worthy of widespread sacrifice and support. Bush did not vainly think in 1975 that he alone possessed the perfect formula for preserving American power in the world. "If somebody said to me today what would you declare" to be Washington's vital interest and broad strategy, he conceded, "I'd be damned if I know how I'd define it." But he knew enough in 1975 to question what he saw around him. This is the point of a sketchbook, after all: to play with ideas. He was in Beijing a man in thought, confronting questions he had until then not thought to ask.[70]

China's Enduring Impact on Bush's Presidency

The answers Bush found to the questions he posed while in China surely influenced his worldview and his later actions while president. His Beijing experience made him more sensitive to the international implications of political rhetoric and more convinced of the importance of personal diplomacy. Perhaps most important of all, it shaped his understanding of the power of the domino theory and the necessity of confronting tyrannical aggression with firm resolve. His response to each of the major events of his presidency—including the end of the Cold War, the Gulf War, and the vexing Tiananmen crisis—has its origin in the lessons he imparted to his China Diary.

Of these three lessons of Beijing, Bush's aversion to harsh diplomatic rhetoric is the most easily seen, as his frustrations with Chinese "cannons of rhetoric" clearly left its mark. He incorporated the phrase into his own vocabulary after 1974, employing the term throughout his career to denote political language developed for domestic ears that was diplomatically meaningless unless it was believed overseas. When pressed in 1984 to elaborate on Ronald Reagan's use of the term "evil empire" to discuss the Soviet Union, Bush cautioned reporters against making too much of the heated term. "Every day in China," he recalled, I "heard the 'red news and the

[70]May 6, 1975.

452

blue news,' the former filled with bombast, the latter with fact."
But when he asked the Chinese about the contrast, they merely "referred to empty cannons of rhetoric" as a way of excusing their
tone and language. Similarly, in 1987 Bush told Soviet leader
Mikhail Gorbachev not to worry if the impending American election seemed heated. "I told Gorbachev not to be concerned about
the 'empty cannons of rhetoric' he would hear booming during the
campaign, and explained what the expression meant," Bush recalled. "It was a phrase Chinese leaders, I think Mao Zedong
especially, had used years before to describe their propaganda criticizing the United States. Don't worry about excessive bombast,
they would say; look at deeds and actions instead."[71]

Bush strove to follow his own advice. He refused to gloat when
the Soviet Union began to disintegrate in 1990, for example, noting, "If we exhorted change, our rhetoric might produce a military
backlash and set back the cause of freedom throughout the Soviet
Union rather than move it forward." His "caution prompted criticism" from American politicians who wished to celebrate, Bush
later reflected, but he had come to believe that every presidential
statement carried consequences. "Hot rhetoric would needlessly
antagonize the militant elements within the Soviet Union and the
[Warsaw] Pact," he explained." His awareness of that potential effect was clearly the result of earlier experience.[72]

The conclusions Bush reached about Vietnam and the domino
theory can also be directly read in his Gulf War policies. In the run-
up to the war Bush frequently employed a historical analogy to ex-

[71]Bush had in fact employed the term "cannons of rhetoric" while U.N. ambassador, in reference to the newly seated Chinese delegation. After Qiao Guanhua delivered a blistering assault on the United States in the General Assembly,
Bush chastised Qiao for his "intemperate language," noting that it was "disturbing" to see the Chinese "firing these empty cannons of rhetoric." "Peking's Wordy
Debut," *Time*, Nov. 29, 1971. For Bush in 1984, see Jack Rosenthal, "George
Bush's Daily Dilemma," *New York Times*, Sept. 25, 1984, A26. For Bush and Gorbachev, see Bush and Scowcroft, *A World Transformed*, 5.
[72]Bush and Scowcroft, *A World Transformed*, 115, 149, 207.

plain his hard line. History taught that dictators were only stopped by resolute force, he argued, comparing Saddam Hussein to Adolf Hitler. This was a shrewd rhetorical tactic, given that most Americans unflinchingly accepted Hitler as an enemy. As Marlin Fitzwater pointed out, Hussein was a "bad guy on whom Americans could focus their response" to the war, while another White House speechwriter recalled of Hussein that "I remember thinking and I'm sure saying, that this guy is a classic villain." Bush even suggested by the eve of war that Hussein was in fact *more* evil than Hitler, though he did not push this point particularly hard.[73]

While the Hitler analogy sold well on Main Street, what really drove Bush's Gulf War policy was not so much the lesson he drew from 1938 but the one he had learned in 1975. In 1990 Bush did not fear that Hussein would attack neighbor after neighbor if his conquest of Kuwait went unchallenged, as Hitler had done when his initial conquests went unopposed. He was instead primarily concerned that failure to check Hussein's initial aggression against Kuwait would prompt Iraq's neighbors throughout the volatile Persian Gulf region to realign their strategic interests in tune with the new geopolitical reality. Just as when Vietnam fell and Asian leaders looked to Beijing for leadership, Bush believed, if Washington left a vacuum in the Gulf by tacitly endorsing Kuwait's fall, others would look to Hussein (or worse) for stability. "I can't honestly feel that Southeast Asia is vital to the security of the United States," he recorded in his journal in 1975. But a general realignment of Asian interests would surely prove of vital concern to American strategists. Similarly, in 1990, Kuwait itself mattered less to Bush than did the principle of its sovereignty, and the practical effect of its loss to the broader region. "All will not be tranquil until Saddam Hussein is history," he told the National Security Council during one of their first meetings after the Iraqi invasion. American inaction would allow the dominoes to fall in 1990, as he had seen them tum-

[73]Rachel Martin Harlow, "Agency and Agent in George Bush's Gulf War Rhetoric," in Medhurst, 66.

ble in Asia a generation before. Before he had time to hear Bush's full reaction to Hussein's invasion in 1990, Joint Chiefs Chairman Colin Powell remarked to one of his commanders, "I think we'd go to war over Saudi Arabia, but I doubt we'd go to war over Kuwait." Powell was only half right. An Iraqi attack on Saudi Arabia would surely have triggered an immediate American response. But Bush went to war even when no such attack materialized because he believed the loss of Kuwait's sovereignty would be felt far beyond its borders. This is why he constantly referred to the Gulf War as a "test" of the post–Cold War system. It was a moment to show that the United States would not retreat from its post-1945 role of international stabilizer. The China Diary suggests that Bush had internalized this lesson years before.[74]

Bush's sense of recent history, spanning both the appeasement of Munich and the fall of Saigon, drove his response to Hussein in 1990, but his assessment of falling Asian dominoes in 1975 was historically invalid. In the wake of Saigon's fall there was no widespread strategic realignment of the kind Bush feared and described in his China Diary. He did not stay long enough in China—he departed Beijing in December 1975—to see that the steady stream of Asian leaders he had witnessed journeying to meet with China's leaders never presaged a significant erosion of American influence

[74]Diary entry for May 6, 1975. For "tranquil," see Bush Presidential Library, NSC Files, Richard Haas Files, Working Files: Iraq 8/2/90–12/90, Meeting of the NSC, August 6, 1990. For Powell, see James Mann, *Rise of the Vulcans* (New York: Viking, 2004), 184.

As Scowcroft explained during one of the first NSC meetings of the Gulf crisis —speaking on Bush's behalf, as described above—the fear was not Hussein, but the instability Hussein's victory might sew. "Beyond the consequences of a successful move by Iraq are what else the DCI [director of central intelligence] said: that they would dominate OPEC politics, Palestinian politics and the PLO, and would lead the Arab world to the detriment of the United States, and the great stakes we have in the Middle East and Israel. It seems while the alternatives are not attractive, we have to seriously look at the possibility that we can't tolerate him succeeding." See Bush Presidential Library, NSC Files, Richard Haas Files, Working Files: Iraq 8/2/90–12/90, Meeting of the NSC, August 3, 1990.

in the region. He feared Communism's rise in Asia not by conquest but rather by increased influence. He took as a central lesson of his Cold War, and of his time in Beijing in particular, the notion that credibility mattered because allies and adversaries alike were forever on guard for any reduction in a great power's commitment. He internalized this lesson in 1975. Yet Bush's fears never came to pass. Pacific nations such as the Philippines and Malaysia improved ties with China after 1975, but neither fell to the Communist menace as a consequence. There was no widespread stampede away from Washington's influence and toward Beijing after South Vietnam fell; there was no general realignment of the region's alliances and strategic policies. Even if they were teetering in 1975—and this point itself is debatable—Asia's dominoes simply did not fall.

But by the time American credibility throughout the region had been reestablished, Bush was long gone to his next assignment. Indeed, frustrated by his inability to engage the Chinese in the manner he desired—more on that momentarily—Bush had even ceased writing in his China Diary months before his ultimate departure. He seemed a man ready to move on. What he took from Beijing for application later in life was therefore a lesson molded at a singular moment in time, in the difficult summer of 1975. It was not a lesson with a long historical view, save for its impact on Bush at the moment in his own life when he actively sought strategic truths. Put another way, because Bush was a man in thought in 1975, he was also deeply impressionable.

Not all of the lessons Bush drew from his Beijing experience were pessimistic in tone. On the contrary, Bush's Beijing experience confirmed his faith in personal diplomacy. This faith surely informed his response to the Tiananmen crisis during his presidency, despite the fact that the China Diary shows his ultimate frustration when his goal of befriending Chinese leaders proved elusive. "It is my hope that I will be able to meet the next generation of China's leaders," he wrote on his initial flight across the Pacific in October 1974. Yet only months later he fumed "I am continually amazed at how hard it is to get close to the Chinese." And further, "They are just determined [not] to let us, or any foreigner in that regard, get too close. It is impossible to pick up the phone, ask somebody over, and have a meaningful discussion about Southeast Asia or Russia or someplace like that." Later he would prove downright angry at such rejections. "The people are so nice here but they can be so obtuse, they can be so removed—so little chance for contacts." Comparing his situation with that of China's envoy in Washington, he wrote of "the enormous contrast between life here and Huang Zhen's life in Washington. He can talk substance with anyone he wants. I can sit formally for one hour with [the Foreign Ministry's] Wang Hairong who says absolutely nothing. Middle Kingdom syndrome, with an underlying hatred of foreigners, is amazing." By the time he wound down his diary four months before his departure, Bush had sadly concluded that, from the Chinese perspective, "We are the foreigners, the barbarians. For polite people they act in very strange and tough ways."[75]

Bush took this failure to build strong ties hard on a personal level. He felt slighted by his Chinese hosts, who, even after months of meetings and social events, still treated him coldly. In July, after his massive Independence Day party at the USLO, Bush met Foreign Minister Qiao Guanhua at a party. Yet he "spoke to me but with no great warmth or friendship. I said I hadn't seen him in a long time. He simply nodded. There is a[n] enormous difference in the way we are treated here and the way Huang Zhen is treated in Washington." More hurtful was a late July meeting with Lin Ping, head of the Foreign Ministry's American Affairs department. Lin had hosted a USLO group on a weeklong expedition throughout northeast China. The two men had traveled together and dined together. Yet a week after their return to Beijing, Bush recorded that he "saw Lin Ping at the Peru reception—almost as if our trip had not taken place."[76]

Bush's inability to personalize Sino-American relations in the manner he initially desired prompts a fundamental question for any who wish to understand his diplomatic style: just how valuable is personal

---

[75]Diary entries for October 21, 1974, and July 6 and May 29, 1975.
[76]Diary entries for July 14 and July 29, 1975.

diplomacy? Bush never naïvely believed that friendships might trump national interests. But he firmly believed that such friendships between leaders mattered, especially if they helped defuse international crises. Tiananmen would seem to offer a perfect test case for answering this question. If personal diplomacy really worked as Bush hoped, then his longstanding friendship with China's top leaders, Deng Xiaoping in particular, should have helped him defuse the Sino-American crisis that Deng's crackdown engendered. One obvious flaw of personal diplomacy is that it can function most efficiently only when leaders with personal ties each remain in power. Elections, coups, or mere bureaucratic shifts diminish the benefits of international friendships assiduously cultivated by a previous generation of leaders. This critique does not apply to Bush's handling of Tiananmen, however, as many of the leaders who ran China in 1989 were the same group Bush had come to know in 1974–75.

Bush readily concedes that his personal ties to Deng affected his reaction to the crisis. Scowcroft, Baker, and James Lilley—Bush's ambassador to China at the time and a man Bush had befriended when they both served in the USLO in 1974—all agree on this point. Bush had numerous meeting with Deng Xiaoping in the years that followed his time at the USLO. He met with Deng, among others, during a 1977 return visit to China, and Deng repaid the courtesy by visiting Bush in Houston while on his own 1979 trip to America. On each occasion they discussed one of their favorite topics: oil. In fact, during his brief stint as a private citizen before the 1980 presidential campaign began in earnest, Bush helped Deng negotiate the foreign development of one of China's primary oil fields. They saw each other relatively often while Bush was vice president. It was experiences like these that prompted more than one American policymaker to note that President Bush acted as his own "China desk officer." Whether Bush was in fact a China expert is debatable; he indisputably considered himself an expert on Deng.[77]

[77]For foreign oil development, see editor interview with James Lilley, March 9, 2007. For "desk officer," see Rothkopf, 291, and Baker, 100.

Yet Bush never translated that intimate knowledge into a satisfying response to Beijing's Tiananmen crackdown. He tried repeatedly during the first days of the crisis to communicate directly with China's leaders. He tried to speak to Deng in particular, thinking their friendship might offer some advantage in tempering Beijing's fury against its pro-democracy protestors. At the least, he thought Deng would afford him the opportunity—if only out of respect for their long friendship—to express Washington's displeasure, even if he refused to listen to others.

Deng refused all such overtures, to Bush's great frustration. "One of the things that I think he was disappointed about during the Tiananmen thing," James Baker later noted, "was that Deng Xiaoping did not take his call, and he was really disappointed in that, because he felt that Deng had become a colleague, and a friend." Baker points out that "when the President of the United States calls . . . you usually take his call." So galled was the White House by this wall of silence that many American strategists began to fear that Deng was perhaps no longer in power or, worse yet, no longer alive. How else to explain this personal affront? Deng was in fact still in power, though undoubtedly preoccupied by the crisis, and thus his rejection of Bush's overtures unequivocally challenged the latter's faith in personal diplomacy. "It was a telling comment on just how limited were the ties between American and Chinese leaders," journalist James Mann noted. "At the time when it mattered, Bush's friendship with Deng Xiaoping didn't count for much." Asked to render his own judgment two decades later, Baker would only cautiously conclude that Bush was "deeply disappointed" in Deng's behavior, because he "considered the man his friend." Indeed Baker emphasized the word "friend" when making this point, making it sound long and profound. This was a word that meant something real to George H. W. Bush.[78]

[78]Editor interview with James Baker, Feb. 25, 2007; James Mann, *About Face: A History of America's Curious Relations with China, From Nixon to Clinton* (New York: Vintage, 2000), 191.

Undaunted, Bush gave up on the telephone and instead wrote Deng a personal letter. He wrote the first draft in his own hand, without input from his advisers. "I wanted a letter straight from my heart," Bush later explained, "so I composed it myself." He showed the text only to Baker, Scowcroft, and Chief of Staff John Sununu before sending it. Deng eventually accepted the letter, and he ultimately agreed to Bush's suggestion that the Chinese receive a "special emissary who could speak with total candor to you representing my heartfelt convictions." This and similar references to their longstanding relationship emerge throughout Bush's message to Deng. Scowcroft, who had himself met many of the Chinese leaders during the 1970s, eventually undertook this secret mission, whose details were not publicly released until months later. Indeed an additional personal element to this story arrived in the way the White House delivered the letter. Finding most official channels blocked, Scowcroft personally handed it to Han Xu, China's ambassador in Washington, an acquaintance since 1971. "He was literally the first Chinese communist official I met," Scowcroft later noted.[79]

Bush's personal ties with China's senior leadership were never likely to have prevented their crackdown on the pro-democracy protesters scattered throughout their country. This was never Bush's hope. But he did believe such ties should have helped defuse the ensuing Sino-American crisis. Personal ties were cultivated for just such crisis moments, he had long believed—yet his ties to the Chinese ultimately did not provide him with special access, as he would have predicted. One may ask whether perhaps Deng did place greater stock in Bush's personal overtures because he trusted this American president as a friend. Perhaps Deng did in fact heed Bush's letters more than if another politician had occupied the Oval Office. No matter the answer to these questions, one fact remains: Bush thought he deserved more, and he believed that his personal faith in Deng's friendship had proved misguided.

[79]Bush and Scowcroft, *A World Transformed*, 100–103.

Bush's own reaction to the crisis, conversely, was clearly influenced by his long experience with the Chinese. At the crucial moment, when critics across the American political spectrum demanded a harsh response, he sought instead a quiet policy. He cut high-level political and military ties between the two capitals and endorsed other sanctions. Despite heated calls from Capitol Hill for further reprisals, however, Bush spent considerable political capital to keep sanctions below the threshold he thought would cause lasting damage to the fragile bilateral relationship. As he related to his diary in the midst of the crisis, events were "highly complex, yet I am determined to try to preserve this relationship—[and to] cool the rhetoric. . . . I take this relationship *very personally*, and I want to handle it that way." He said much the same during a 2005 interview, noting that his personal relationship with Deng deeply informed the policies he pursued. "*Had I not met the man*," Bush said, "I think I would have been less convinced that we should keep relations with them going after Tiananmen Square." Indeed, as James Lilley conceded in his memoirs, Scowcroft's visit to Beijing was itself deeply personal, in that he carried Bush's personal assurance that—despite the glare of public scrutiny, despite public calls for condemnation and reprisal, and despite the fact that there would inevitably be a political fallout—this particular president was committed to China for the long term. "We had to sanction them because of the public pressure in the United States," Lilley later said, but "Bush wanted to preserve the relationship." He might not have proved able to leverage his friendship with Deng to achieve a useful diffusion of tensions, but that friendship clearly prompted Bush to preserve relations to the greatest extent possible. It prompted from him a less caustic line than another president, less intimately involved with China and its leaders, might have pursued.[80]

[80]Ibid., 104 (see also 111). For "met the man," see editor interview with George H. W. Bush, July 8, 2005. In each case emphasis mine. For Lilley, see Mann, *About Face*, 208.

Taking a longer historical view, Bush's personal response to Tiananmen offers a curious verdict on personal diplomacy, especially when one considers for a final moment the response from Kissinger, Bush's long-term diplomatic foil. Both men endorsed the same reaction to Beijing's Tiananmen crackdown. Kissinger, who had long disparaged Bush's hopes of personalizing the Sino-American relationship, advised the maintenance of ties with Beijing, lest this temporary setback in China's march toward democracy lead to a true change of course. In other words, each man reached the same realist's conclusion, although Kissinger never claimed to make decisions based on personal ties. Perhaps personal diplomacy ultimately matters little when strategists make policies, although it might matter a great deal in how they choose to implement them. Indeed Nixon advised the same policy of rapprochement toward China, and even traveled to Beijing in late 1989 to chastise Chinese leaders privately for their actions, but also to demonstrate what he had called for publicly: maintenance of the relationship.

Bush's preoccupation with personal diplomacy and his concern for the public side of diplomacy pervade his China Diary, and thus the question of their utility confronts readers. Even Bush would concede a full decade after composing the diary that "I don't think rhetoric has any influence on what states do. They act out of self-interest." The same could just as easily have been said by Kissinger. It is the realist's fundamental trope.[81]

What the diary shows us then, in the end, is a matter of style. As with any sketchbook, Bush's diary helped its author work through the fundamental issues he confronted, be they personal or geopolitical. It is the intimate story of a man eager for more: more power, more prestige, and a more prominent role on the world stage. What the diary shows is what Bush planned to do with that role if ever entrusted with it. It helps us understand his later policies when he was in fact granted that power. But most fundamentally, it shows Bush's thinking, and indeed his style, well before the

[81]Rosenthal, A26.

Oval Office. The Gulf War, the end of the Cold War, Tiananmen, NAFTA, and the rest of the crises he faced while president are better understood as a result of studying the diary. These pages help us understand how Bush weighed the pragmatic realism he innately believed in against the potential and pitfalls of personal diplomacy. It reveals the value he placed on credibility in international affairs and his conception of the domino theory then and later—one that, though based on a flawed historical assessment, still produced a successful argument for war in 1990. He did not learn to be a diplomat while in Beijing, but while there he laid the foundation for his own gentlemanly style of diplomacy while president.

Of all the diary's revelations, the most profound might be the least surprising. Bush left China a more sophisticated student of foreign affairs than when he had arrived, because he had internalized the lesson one almost always gains from an extended overseas experience: that not everyone views the world as Washington does. "The American people do not have any concept of how others around the world view America," he concluded after six months in China. "We think we are good, honorable, decent, freedom-loving. Others are firmly convinced that . . . we are embarking on policies that are anathema to them." As his diary demonstrates, Bush came to China in 1974 a relative neophyte in foreign affairs. In a very real sense—because he had come to appreciate that the world looked different from Beijing than it did from Washington, or from New Haven or Houston, for that matter—he left an internationalist.[82]

[82]Diary entry for May 12, 1975.

Transcripts of interviews conducted by the editor and listed in the end-notes have been made available for researchers at the George H. W. Bush Presidential Library.

Chapter One: "Everybody in the United States Wants to Go to China"

6. For more on the legal battles over the tapes, see Stanley Kutler, *Abuse of Power* (New York: Free Press, 1977) and *The Wars of Watergate* (New York: W. W. Norton, 1992).

7. Bush Presidential Library, Personal Papers of George H. W. Bush, China File, Correspondence File, Box 1, Correspondence B, Bush to Jaworksi, Oct. 22, 1974.

9. See Catherine Forslund, *Anna Chennault: Informal Diplomacy and Asian Relations* (Wilmington, Del.: SR Books, 2002), esp. 139–40.

10. For descriptions of this tumultuous period through the eyes of two CIA leaders—two who best defined the internecine struggles at the agency—see William Colby, *Honorable Men: My Life in the CIA* (New York: Simon and Schuster, 1978), and Richard Helms, *A Look over My Shoulder: A Life in the Central Intelligence Agency* (New York: Presidio Press, 2004).

11. For "best qualifed man" and "too soft," see Nixon Presidential Materials Project, National Archives and Records Administration (hereafter NARA), National Security Files, Box 1031, Exchanges Leading Up to HAK Trip to China, December 1969–July 1971 (1), Telcon, The President/Mr. Kissinger, 8:18 p.m., Apr. 27, 1971. On Bruce, see Nelson Lankford, *The Last American Aristocrat* (New York: Little, Brown, 1996), and Priscilla Roberts, *Window on the Forbidden City: The Beijing Diaries of David Bruce* (Hong Kong: University of Hong Kong Centre of Asian Studies, 2001).

15. For "dying to do business," see editor interview with George H. W. Bush, July 8, 2005. For Hummel, see NARA, RG 59, Lot 77D114, Records of the Policy Planning Staff (Winston Lord Files) (hereafter NARA, Lord Files), Box 376, Chronological, Aug. 17–Oct. 15, 1974, From Hummel to Kissinger, Oct. 8, 1974.

16. For "at least one pawn," see "Diplomat's Rich Life Revealed," *China Daily,* Sept. 17, 2003.

17. Roberts, esp. 367 and 398–99, and editor interview with Platt, Oct. 24, 2006. For "the best way," see Roberts, 97–98.

19. Doro Bush Koch, *My Father My President* (New York: Warner, 2006), 114.

20. Fox Butterfield, "Japan and China Sign Air Accord; Taiwan Cuts Link," *New York Times,* Apr. 21, 1974, 1.

21. For "one of the two or three" and "superior brain," see Margaret MacMillan, *Nixon and China: The Week That Changed the World* (Toronto: Viking Canada, 2006), 44.

23. For "my favorite," see Roberts, 40.

26. For "lost interest," see ibid., 51.

27. John Holdridge, *Crossing the Divide: An Insider's Account of the Normalization of U.S.-Chinese Relations* (Lanham, Md.: Rowman and Littlefield, 1997).

28. NARA, Central Foreign Policy Files 1973–75, Electronic Telegram Database (hereafter NARA, Central Foreign Policy Files 1973–75), Washington to All East Asian and Pacific Posts, EA Press Summary, Oct. 22, 1974.

31. Holdridge, 115.

33. See United Kingdom National Archive (formerly British Public Records Office; hereafter PRO), FCO 21/1234, Relations between China and USA, From Youde to K. M. Wilford, Dec. 4, 1975.

40. NARA, Central Foreign Policy Files 1973–75, From Peking to Washington, Oct. 24, 1974.

45. "Bruce Calls China Important Oil Producer," *Washington Post,* Oct. 11, 1974, A2. For a contemporary discussion of China's petroleum power, and its geopolitical implications, see Choon-ho Park and Jerome Alan Cohen, "The Politics of China's Oil Weapon," *Foreign Policy* 20 (Autumn 1975), 28–49.

49. Anthony Grey, *Hostage in Peking* (New York: Doubleday, 1971), esp. 121–32. See also Philip Bridgham, "Mao's Cultural Revolution in 1967: The Struggle to Seize Power," *China Quarterly* 34 (April–June 1968), 25–27.

50. George P. Jan, "The Ministry of Foreign Affairs in China since the Cultural Revolution," *Asian Survey* 17 (June 1977), 513–29.

51. NARA, Central Foreign Policy Files 1973–75, From USLO Peking to Washington, Oct. 26, 1974.

52. For "bastard," see Robert S. Ross, *Negotiating Cooperation: The United States and China, 1969–89* (Stanford, Calif.: Stanford University Press, 1995), 51. For "more communists on its side," see Nancy

Bernkopf Tucker, "Taiwan Expendable? Nixon and Kissinger Go to China," *Journal of American History* 92 (June 2005), 109–35, quote on 110.

54. NARA, RG 59, Lord Files, Box 376, China: Sensitive Chronological, Aug. 17–Oct. 15, 1974, From Washington to USLO, Oct. 9, 1974, and NARA, Central Foreign Policy Files 1973–75, From USLO Peking to Washington, Oct. 23, 1974. For International Visitors Council quote, see www.ivc.org/who_we_are, accessed January 17, 2007.

56. Barbara Bush, *A Memoir* (New York: Scribner, 1994), 114.

57. See Roberts, 166, and Holdridge, 124.

59. NARA, Central Foreign Policy Files 1973–75, From USLO Peking to Washington, Oct. 29, 1974.

61. For "act out of self-interest," see Jack Rosenthal, "George Bush's Daily Dilemma," *New York Times*, Sept. 25, 1984, A26. For a discussion of Chinese publications during this period, see Michel Oksenberg, "The Basic Sources and Their Limitations," in Denis Twitchett and John K. Fairbank, *The Cambridge History of China*, vol. 14 (New York: Cambridge University Press, 1983), 556.

63. For a discussion of scholarship of these events, see Stephen Uhalley Jr. and Jin Qiu, "The Lin Biao Incident: More Than Twenty Years Later," *Pacific Affairs* 66 (Autumn 1993), 386–98, and Jin Qui, *The Culture of Power: The Lin Biao Incident in the Cultural Revolution* (Palo Alto, Calif.: Stanford University Press, 1999). See also Roderick MacFarquhar and Michael Schoenhals, *Mao's Last Revolution* (Cambridge, Mass.: Harvard University Press, 2006), 350 and esp. 366–73.

65. Joseph Alsop, "The Chinese Exhibition," *Washington Post*, Dec. 8, 1974, PO20. For a contemporary discussion of these issues, see William Wilson, "A Field Day for China Watchers," *Los Angeles Times*, July 3, 1975, E6, and Bernard Gwertzman, "National Gallery Drops Preview over China Demand," *New York Times*, Dec. 11, 1974, 1.

67. Holdridge, 62.

69. NARA, RG 59, Lord Files, Box 375, China: Sensitive Chronological, Oct. 16–Dec. 3, 1974, From USLO Peking to Washington, Oct. 30, 1974.

70. Ibid.

71. Ibid.

72. See "China Expels Times Reporter for Entering Restricted Area," *New York Times*, July 23, 1986, A1.

73. NARA, Central Files 1973–75, From USLO Peking to Washington, Oct. 30, 1974.

74. For "ranked just below the PLO," see Holdridge, 156. For "frustrations," see Bush Presidential Library, Personal Papers of George H. W.

Bush, China File, Correspondence File, Box 1, From Bush to John J. Rhodes, Nov. 28, 1974. For "responsible person," see editor interview with George H. W. Bush, July 8, 2005. For "after full discussion," see NARA, Central Foreign Policy Files 1973–75, From USLO to Washington, Oct. 22, 1974. For "your unique status," see NARA, RG59, Lord Files, Box 331, China Exchanges, Aug. 9–Dec. 31, 1974, From Kissinger (through Scowcroft) to Bush, Nov. 6, 1974. For "the facts are," see ibid., From Kissinger to Bush, Dec. 31, 1974.

75. NARA, Central Foreign Policy Files 1973–75, From USLO Peking to Washington, Oct. 31, 1974.

80. Richard Ben Cramer offers a particularly revealing discussion of Zapata's financial and personal place in Bush's life in *What It Takes: The Way to the White House* (New York: Random House, 1992), 580–82.

81. NARA, Central Foreign Policy Files 1973–75, From USLO Peking to Washington, Oct. 30, 1974.

83. Ibid., Oct. 31, 1974.

84. The full text of the report may be found at NARA, RG 59, Lord Files, Box 380, China: Hold.

85. For more on Nixon's medical history, see John Lungren, *Healing Richard Nixon* (Lexington: University of Kentucky Press, 2003).

86. "Last Digs in a Tearful Goodbye," *U.S. News and World Report,* July 24, 2006, 46–47.

94. For more on Sino-Pakistani relations, see Jeffrey A. Engel, *Cold War at 30,000 Feet: The Anglo-American Fight for Aviation Supremacy* (Cambridge, Mass.: Harvard University Press), 252–89.

97. NARA, RG 59, Lord Files, Box 375, China: Sensitive Chronological, Oct. 16–Dec. 31, 1974, From USLO Peking to Washington, Nov. 1, 1974.

98. Editor interview with George H. W. Bush, July 8, 2005.

99. NARA, RG 59, PPS (Lord), Box 331, China Exchanges, Aug. 9–Dec. 31, 1974, From Sec Kissinger Abroad to USLO Peking, Oct. 31, 1974.

104. For "had I not met the man," see editor interview with George H. W. Bush, July 8, 2008.

105. NARA, RG 59, Lord Files, Box 375, China: Sensitive Chronological, Oct. 16–Dec. 31, 1974, From USLO Peking to Washington, Nov. 3, 1974.

106. NARA, RG 59, Lord Files, Box 331, China Exchanges, Aug. 9–Dec. 31, 1974, From USLO Peking to Kissinger and Scowcroft, Nov. 5, 1974, and ibid., Subject Files of PRC and Mongolian Affairs, Box 5, Normalization US/PRC 1973–74, From Washington to USLO Peking, Nov. 4, 1974.

Chapter Two: "Public Posture versus Private Understanding"

10. Bob Hope, *I Owe Russia $1200* (New York: Doubleday, 1963).

12. See David Shambaugh, "China and Europe," *Annals of the American Academy of Political and Social Science* 519 (January 1992), 101–14; Aurel Bruan, *Romanian Foreign Policy since 1965* (New York: Praeger, 1978); and "Chairman Hua Hits the Road," *Time,* Oct. 28, 1978, accessed at www.time.com/magazine/article/0,9171,916232,00.html on January 17, 2007.

13. Koch, 123–29.

20. David Korn, *Assassination in Khartoum* (Bloomington: Indiana University Press, 1993).

27. Roberts, 463, and Holdridge, 124–26.

28. Harry Harding, "China: Toward Revolutionary Pragmatism," *Asian Survey* 11 (January 1971), 51–67.

30. Chen Jian, *Mao's China and the Cold War* (Chapel Hill: University of North Carolina Press, 2001), 260.

31. For a brief discussion of Sino-Soviet tensions, see Warren I. Cohen, *America's Response to China* (New York: Columbia University Press, 2000), 196.

37. Klingenberg described his early experiences in China in "The Canton Trade Fair: The Initiation of China–United States Trade," *Virginia Journal of International Law* 63 (1972). See also Gerde Wilcke, "Trying to Trade with China," *New York Times,* Oct. 15, 1972, F4. For a discussion of the first American independent entrepreneurs in China following Nixon's visit, see Stanley Karnow and Mimi Conway, "Large Assortment of China Trade Entrepreneurs," *Washington Post,* Oct. 15, 1972, G1.

39. Philip J. Hilts, "Howard K. Smith and the Rise of ABC News," *Washington Post,* Aug. 11, 1974, P14.

40. NARA, RG 59, Lord Files, Box 375, China: Sensitive Chronological, Oct. 16–Dec. 31, 1974, From Bush to Kissinger, Nov. 11, 1974; ibid., From Kissinger to Bush, Nov. 12, 1974; and NARA, RG 59, Lord Files, Box 331, China Exchanges, Aug. 9–Dec. 31, 1974, From Kissinger to Bush, Nov. 4, 1974. See also NARA, Central Foreign Policy Files 1973–75, From USLO Peking to Washington, Nov. 6, 1974.

41. For immediate press reaction, see for example John Herbers, "Ford, Brezhnev Agree to Curb Offensive Nuclear Weapons," *New York Times,* Nov. 25, 1974, 1, and "The President Goes A-Calling," *Newsweek,* Nov. 18, 1974, 46–49. The quote is from "The President," 49.

43. "Kissinger Will Go to Peking Nov. 25," *New York Times,* Nov. 12, 1974, 9.

46. "China's Position on the Population Problems Expounded," *Beijing Review,* March 22, 1974, 8–9, and W. Klatt, "Asia after the World Food Conference," *International Affairs* 51 (July 1975), 344–57.

47. NARA, RG 59, Lord Files, Box 375, China: Sensitive Chronological, Oct. 16–Dec. 31, 1974, From USLO Peking to Washington, Nov. 11, 1974.

54. Ibid.

57. NARA, RG 59, Lord Files, Box 375, China: Sensitive Chronological, Oct. 16–Dec. 31, 1974, From USLO Peking to Washington, Nov. 13, 1974.

59. NARA, Central Foreign Policy Files 1973–75, From USLO Peking to Washington, Nov. 15, 1974.

60. See Gerald Wilcke, "Kellogg to Build 8 Plants in China," *New York Times,* Nov. 28, 1973, 61, and James P. Sterba, "China, Despite Death of Mao, Opens Plants Built by U.S. on Time," *New York Times,* Oct. 26, 1976, E51, and "The Chinese in Houston in Neckties," *New York Times,* Nov. 30, 1975, 197. The quote is from the Nov. 30 article.

64. NARA, RG 59, Lord Files, Box 375, China: Sensitive Chronological, Oct. 16–Dec. 31, 1974, From Washington to USLO Peking, Nov. 12, 1974, and ibid., From USLO Peking to Washington, Nov. 13, 1974.

65. NARA, Central Foreign Policy Files 1973–75, From USLO Peking to Washington, Nov. 28, 1974.

67. For "most unfortunate," see John W. Finney, "House Leaders, Indignant, Want to Go to China, Too," *New York Times,* March 2, 1972, 1. For "wants to go," see Bush's diary entry for Oct. 21, 1974. See also "2 House Leaders Say Peking Fears a Pullback by U.S.," *New York Times,* July 9, 1972, 5; "Chinese Disown Chou Statement as Related by Boggs and Ford," *New York Times,* July 18, 1972, 3. For "private organization," see Douglas Murray, "Exchanges with the People's Republic of China: Symbols and Substance," *Annals of the American Academy of Political and Social Science* 424 (March 1976), 29–42.

68. See, for example, "China's Foreign Minister Replaced by Ex-U.N. Aide," *New York Times,* Nov. 15, 1974, and Joseph Lelyveld, "Sino-American Relations: No Great Leap Forward," *New York Times,* Nov. 24, 1974, 208.

69. See William Safire, "The Closing Opening," *New York Times,* Nov. 18, 1974, 33.

70. NARA, Central Foreign Policy Files 1973–75, From USLO Peking to Washington, Nov. 6, 1974.

72. "U.S. Briefs Chinese on Summit Results," *Washington Post,* Nov. 27, 1974, A1.

78. John K. Fairbank, "Assignment for the 1970s," *American Historical Review* 74 (February 1969), 861–79, quote on 862.

79. John M. Hamilton, *Edgar Snow: A Biography* (Baton Rouge: Louisiana State University Press, 2003).

81. United States Census Bureau, Foreign Trade Division, www.census.gov/foreign-trade/balance/c5700.html, accessed January 24, 2008.

83. NARA, RG 59, Lord Files, Box 331, China Exchanges, Aug. 9–Dec. 31, 1974, From USLO Peking to Kissinger, Nov. 18, 1974; and NARA, RG 59, LOT 94D176, Subject Files of PRC and Mongolian Affairs, Box 5, Normalization US/PRC 1973–74, From Bush to Scowcroft, Nov. 20, 1974.

85. NARA, RG 59, Lord Files, Box 375, China: Sensitive Chronological, Oct. 16–Dec. 31, 1974, From Washington to USLO, Nov. 23, 1974.

Chapter Three: "We Must Not Capitulate on Matters This Fundamental"

4. NARA, RG 59, Lord Files, Subject Files of PRC and Mongolian Affairs, Box 5, Normalization US/PRC 1973–74, From USLO Peking to Kissinger, Nov. 21, 1974.

5. Roberts, passim, but especially 462–63.

7. MacFarquhar and Schoenhals, 61.

8. George H. W. Bush, *All the Best* (New York: Scribner, 1999), 232.

9. MacMillan, 47.

11. NARA, RG 59, Lot 94D176, Subject Files of PRC and Mongolia 1969–78, Box 6, Normalization between US and PRC 1973–1974.

12. PRO, FCO 21/1234, Relations between China and USA, Samuel, British Embassy Washington, to Bentley, Nov. 13, 1974.

13. For Deng, see Holdridge, 152. Transcripts of this and the remainder of Kissinger's meetings with Deng on this trip may be found in William Burr, ed., *The Kissinger Transcripts: The Top-Secret Talks with Beijing and Moscow* (New York: New Press, 1998), 289–315.

16. MacMillan, 275.

17. A sampling of Bush's reports can be found in NARA, RG 59, Lord Files, Subject Files of PRC and Mongolian Affairs, Box 5, Normalization US/PRC 1973–74.

18. MacMillan, 279.

19. See *"Taking Tiger Mountain by Strategy*: Drawing Heroes," *Drama Review* 15 (Spring 1971), 268–70.

20. NARA, RG 59, Lot 94D176, Subject Files of PRC and Mongolian Affairs 1969–78, Box 5, Memorandums.

21. Jeanette Smythe, "From One China Hand to Another," *Washington Post*, March 6, 1973, B2.

22. For "within a few seconds," see NARA, RG 59, Lord Files, Box 375, China: Sensitive Chronological, Oct. 1–Dec. 31, 1974, From Lord to Kissinger, Nov. 18, 1974. For "why," see Rowland Evans and Robert Novak, "Why Is Donald Rumsfeld in China?" *Washington Post*, Nov. 27, 1974, A15. For Bush and the Gremlin, see Bush Presidential Library, Personal Papers of George H. W. Bush, China File, Correspondence File, Box 1, 1974 Correspondence—R, From Rumsfeld to Bush, Nov. 5, 1974. See also Lou Cannon, "Bush Travels the Nation Preaching the GOP Message," *Washington Post*, Feb. 12, 1974, A1.

23. NARA, RG 59, LOT 94D176, Subject Files of PRC and Mongolian Affairs, Box 5, Normalization US/PRC 1973–74, From Bush to Scowcroft, Nov. 20, 1974.

24. For "abstract altruism," see Burr, *The Kissinger Transcripts*, 170. For "incidentally," 47. See MacMillan, 236, and William Burr, "Nixon's Trip to China: Records Now Completely Declassified," National Security Archive, George Washington University, Dec. 11, 2003, available at www.gwu.edu/~nsarchiv/NSAEBB/NSAEBB106/index.htm.

25. NARA, RG 59, Lord Files, Box 331, China Exchanges, Aug. 9–Dec. 31, 1974, Joint US-PRC Communiqué, Nov. 29, 1974.

28. Holdridge, 157.

29. Barbara Bush, *A Memoir*, 117.

30. PRO, FCO 21/1381, Relations between China and USA, From Morgan to Bentley, Jan. 8, 1975; ibid., From Bentley to Morgan, Feb. 4, 1975; and ibid., From Morgan to Bentley, March 12, 1975. See also PRO, FCO 21/1381, Relations between China and USA, From Youde to Wilford, Feb. 17, 1975. For Armstrong, see PRO, FCO 21/1235 Relations between China and USA, R. C. Samuel, Note for the Record, Dec. 17, 1974.

31. Joseph Lelyveld, "President Plans a Visit to China in 2nd Half of '75," *New York Times*, Nov. 30, 1974, 1.

32. For "25 years," "screw around," and mushroom analogy, see MacMillan, 61; for "care and feeding," 48. See also Walter Isaacson, *Kissinger: A Biography* (New York: Simon and Schuster, 1992), esp. 190–92.

33. Editor interview with George H. W. Bush, July 8, 2005.

35. For a contemporary discussion of Chinese oil production, see Choon-ho Park and Jerome Alan Cohen, "The Politics of China's Oil Weapon," *Foreign Policy* 20 (Autumn 1975), 28–49.

39. NARA, Central Foreign Policy Files 1973–75, From USLO Peking to Washington, Dec. 5, 1974.

42. Documentation on this meeting (including a full transcript of the formal sessions) can be found in NARA, RG 59, Lord Files, Box 347, December 1974.

43. "Richard Sneider, Ex-Diplomat, Dies," *New York Times,* Aug. 16, 1986, 28.

47. Holdridge describes these uncomfortable (and at times, he thought, potentially dangerous) meetings on pp. 97–102.

48. See Charles Cross, *Born a Foreigner: A Memoir of the American Presence in Asia* (Lanham, Md.: Rowman and Littlefield, 1999), 224–32.

54. Records from Mansfield's trip, including memoranda of conversations during the senator's meetings with Chinese officials, can be found in the Lord Files of the Policy Planning Staff. See NARA, RG 59, Central Foreign Policy Files 1973–75, from USLO Peking to Washington, Dec. 14, 1974, and NARA, Lord Files, Box 331, China Exchanges, Aug. 9–Dec. 31, 1974, From USLO Peking to Washington, Dec. 17, 1974.

55. Nicholas M. Horrock, "CIA Ties to Journalists," *New York Times,* Jan. 28, 1976, 10, and NARA, RG 59, Central Foreign Policy Files 1973–75, From USLO Peking to Washington, Dec. 17, 1974.

58. NARA, RG 59, Central Foreign Policy Files 1973–75, From USLO Peking to Washington, Dec. 16, 1974.

66. NARA, RG 59, Lord Files, Box 331, China Exchanges, Aug. 9–Dec. 31, 1974, From USLO Peking to Washington, Dec. 20, 1974; ibid., From Washington to USLO Peking, Dec. 26, 1974; and ibid., From Habib to Kissinger, Dec. 24, 1974.

67. See Henry Kissinger, *Years of Upheaval* (Boston: Little, Brown, 1982), 747–50.

71. See Martin King Whyte and William L. Parish, *Urban Life in Contemporary China* (Chicago: University of Chicago Press, 1984), 22–26.

72. See Bruce Palling, "Thailand Seeks to Expand China Ties," *Washington Post,* Dec. 17, 1974, A18, for a contemporary discussion of this trade mission.

73. "Martinique Compromise," *New York Times,* Dec. 17, 1974, 36, and Leonard Silk, "Solidarity at Martinique," *New York Times,* Dec. 18, 1974, 67.

75. MacMillan, 124–36.

76. NARA, RG 59, Lord Files, Box 331, January 1–May 31, 1975, From USLO to Washington, Jan. 15, 1975.

79. PRO, FCO 21/1235, Relations between China and USA, From Youde to Wilford, Dec. 31, 1974.

80. NARA, RG 59, Lord Files, Subject Files of PRC and Mongolian

Affairs, Box 5, Normalization US/PRC 1973–74, From USLO Peking to Washington, Dec. 28, 1974.

84. NARA, RG 59, Central Foreign Policy Files 1973–75, From AmEmbassy Taipei to Washington, Nov. 8, 1974, and Jenkins, "Kissinger Visit Could Warm China Relations," *Los Angeles Times,* Nov. 24, 1974, J1. For Youde, see PRO, FCO 21/1235, Relations between China and USA, From Youde to Wilford, Dec. 23, 1974. See also NARA, RG 59, Electronic Database, From Washington to USDEL Vladivostok, Nov. 23, 1974.

85. NARA, RG 59, Lord Files, Subject Files of PRC and Mongolian Affairs, Box 5, Normalization US/PRC 1973–74, From USLO Peking to Washington, Dec. 28, 1974.

86. NARA, RG 59, Lord Files, Box 375, China: Sensitive Chronological, January–February 1975, from USLO to Washington, Jan. 7, 1975; and ibid., From USLO to Washington, Jan. 13, 1975.

91. NARA, RG 59, Lot 94D176, Subject Files of PRC and Mongolia 1969–78, Box 6, 1975 (January–March), from USLO to Washington, Jan. 14, 1975; NARA, RG 59, Lord Files, Box 375, China: Sensitive Chronological, March–June 1975, From Armstrong to Sullivan, Feb. 25, 1975.

92. China: Sensitive Chronological, March–June 1975, From Habib to Kissinger, Feb. 26, 1975; NARA, RG 59, Lord Files, Box 331, January 1–May 31, 1975, From George Bush, USLO, to Secretary Kissinger, Jan. 15, 1975.

93. NARA, RG 59, Lord Files, Box 331, File: January 1–May 31, 1975, From George Bush, USLO, to Secretary Kissinger, Jan. 15, 1975.

Chapter Four: "Much of the World Depends on the United States"

1. NARA, RG 59, Lord Files, Box 375, China: Sensitive Chronological, January–February 1975, From Habib and Lord to Kissinger, Feb. 4, 1975, emphasis mine.

3. Editor correspondence with George H. W. Bush, May 21, 2007.

7. MacFarquhar and Schoenhals, 14–21 and 380.

8. For Mao's travels, see MacFarquhar and Schoenhals, 380. For a summary of the State Department's analysis of the National People's Congress, highlighted by a long response to the query of "But Where is Mao?," see NARA, RG 59, Lord Files, Box 331, January 1–May 31, 1975, From Richard Solomon to Kissinger, Jan. 19, 1975.

9. Kurt Anderson, "Working Hard for the Last Laugh," *Time,* Aug. 15, 1983, and "GOP Guffaws," *New York Daily News,* Oct. 31, 2004. Despite the press ban, see "Ford Honored in Capital at Alfalfa Club Dinner," *New York Times,* Jan. 26, 1975, 48.

10. Douglas Brinkley, *Gerald R. Ford* (New York: Time Books, 2007).

11. For primers on Congress's role in Vietnam, see George Herring, *America's Longest War* (New York, McGraw-Hill, 1996), from which most of this overview is drawn, and Marilyn Young, *The Vietnam Wars, 1945–1990* (New York: HarperCollins, 1991), esp. 290 for data on South Vietnamese expenditures and Kissinger quotation. A broader study of the topic is William Gibbons, *The U.S. Government and the Vietnam War: Executive and Legislative Roles and Relationships,* 4 vols. (Princeton, N.J.: Princeton University Press, 1986–1995).

12. James Reston, "Great Disorder under Heaven," *New York Times,* Jan. 26, 1975, 267.

14. NARA, RG 59, Central Foreign Policy Files 1973–75, From Washington to East Asian Posts, Feb. 6, 1975.

15. H. J. Maidenberg, "U.S. Easing Controls for Grain Exports," *New York Times,* Jan. 30, 1975, 73, and "China Cancels Orders for Two-Thirds of Orders for U.S. Wheat," *New York Times,* Jan. 28, 1975, 69.

16. NARA, RG 59, Lord Files, Box 331, China Exchanges, June 1–May 31, 1975, From Solomon to Kissinger, Feb. 7, 1975, and PRO, FCO 21/1381, Relations between China and USA, From Clift, British Embassy Peking, to Darlington, Feb. 5, 1975.

17. NARA, Central Foreign Policy Files 1973–75, From USLO Peking to Washington, Feb. 10, 1975.

18. See, for example, Alexander Fursenko and Timothy Naftali, *One Hell of a Gamble: Khrushchev, Castro, and Kennedy* (New York: Norton, 1998) and Ernest R. May, *The Kennedy Tapes: Inside the White House during the Cuban Missile Crisis* (New York: Norton, 2002).

21. NARA, RG59, Central Foreign Policy Files 1973–75, From USLO Peking to Washington, Feb. 19, 1975.

23. James Lilley and Jeffrey Lilley, *China Hands: Nine Decades of Adventure, Espionage, and Diplomacy in Asia* (New York: Public Affairs, 2004), 84, and Cross, 241.

26. For Bush's cable, see NARA, RG 59, LOT 94D176, Subject Files of PRC and Mongolia 1969–78, Box 6, WHG 1975 January–March, From Bush USLO to Scowcroft, Feb. 21, 1975.

27. NARA, RG 59, Lord Files, Box 331, January 1–May 31, 1975, From Scowcroft to Bush, USLO, Jan. 15, 1975. For the British response, see PRO, FCO 21/1381, Relations between China and USA, From M. E. Pike, British Embassy Washington, to Martin, Feb. 21, 1975.

28. NARA, RG 59, Lord Files, Box 331, January 1–May 31, 1975, From George Bush, USLO, to Brent Scowcroft, White House, Jan. 17, 1975; NARA, RG 59, Central Foreign Policy Files 1973–75, From USLO Peking to Washington, Feb. 21, 1975.

30. NARA, RG 59, Central Foreign Policy Files, 1973–75, From USLO Peking to Washington, Feb. 21, 1975.

33. Lilley and Lilley, 195.

34. MacMillan, 219. For arms shuttling on Pakistan International Airways in 1971, see Engel, *Cold War at 30,000 Feet,* 292.

35. Roberts, 95.

36. Lilley and Lilley, 73–76.

40. NARA, RG 59, Central Foreign Policy Files 1973–75, From USLO Peking to Washington, March 5, 1975.

42. Ibid., From USLO Peking to Washington, March 1, 1975.

45. Editor interview with James Lilley, March 9, 2007.

53. MacFarquhar and Schoenhals, 393–94.

55. Alan Heston, Robert Summers, and Bettina Aten, Penn World Table Version 6.2, Center for International Comparisons of Production, Income and Prices at the University of Pennsylvania, September 2006.

58. NARA, RG59, Central Foreign Policy Files 1973–75, From USLO Peking to Washington, March 18, 1975.

59. Steve Allen, *Explaining China* (New York: Crown, 1980, originally published 1976), introduction (unpaginated).

60. Ibid., 66.

61. Ibid., 15.

64. Ibid., 67.

67. NARA, RG 59, Central Foreign Policy Files 1973–75, From USLO Peking to Washington, March 18, 1975.

72. Bush Presidential Library, Personal Papers of George H. W. Bush, China File, Correspondence File, Box 1, Bush to Allison, Nov. 15, 1974; Bush to Armstrong, Nov. 6, 1974; Bush to Rhodes, Nov. 28, 1974; and Bush to Clements, March 2, 1975.

Chapter Five: "When It Is a Matter of Principle It Really Means Do It Their Way"

4. For Habib, NARA, Lot 94D176, Subject Files of PRC and Mongolia 1969–78, Box 6, WHG 1975 January–March, From Habib and Lord to Kissinger, March 23, 1975; for Bush, see ibid., Box 6, WHG 1975 January–March, From USLO Peking to Washington, March 20, 1975 and March 23, 1975. For press response, see Anna Kisselgoff, "Tour by Chinese Troupe Ended on Taiwan Issue," *New York Times,* March 28, 1975, 16. For "with friendly states," see "A Sour Chinese Note" (editorial), *Washington Post,* March 30, 1975, 40.

5. "Chinese Scientists Visit U.S.," *Washington Post,* Sept. 26, 1975, A25; and undated note and copy of *Washington Post* article, PRO, FCO 21/1381, Relations between China and USA.

8. Bush Presidential Library, Personal Papers of George H. W. Bush, China File, Correspondence File, Box 1, 1974 Correspondence—R, From Bush to Dillon Ripley, Nov. 5, 1974.

9. NARA, Electronic Database, From USLO Peking to Washington, March 17, 1975.

10. Bush, *All the Best,* 228.

11. "Never Mind about Marco Polo," *Time,* Sept. 4, 1964, 40.

13. Editor interview with Barbara Bush, Nov. 16, 2005.

29. NARA, Central Foreign Policy Files 1973–75, From USLO Peking to Washington, March 18, 1975.

31. John C. Donnely, "Pacification Reassessed," *Asian Survey* 7 (August 1967), 572. For Scotten's visit, see NARA, Central Foreign Policy Files 1973–75, From Washington to USLO, Peking, "Official Travel to PRC," Jan. 16, 1975.

32. Editor interview with George H. W. Bush, July 8, 2005.

35. Bush, *All the Best,* 223.

37. Ibid., 222.

38. Bush Presidential Library, Personal Papers of George H. W. Bush, China File, Correspondence File, Box 1, 1975 Correspondence, From Bush to Clements, March 2, 1975, and Oct. 21, 1975.

45. For USLO discussion of this meeting, see NARA, Central Foreign Policy Files 1973–75, From USLO Peking to Washington, March 25, 1975.

49. See Allen, 233–36, including a lengthy description of the USLO lunch with the Bushes, and Holdridge, 139.

53. Wang Weijei, "Retired U.S. Diplomat Makes China His Home," *China Daily,* Jan. 20, 2006, 4.

56. For a report on this congressional visit, including Congressman Albert's strained meetings with the Chinese, see NARA, RG 59, Central Foreign Policy Files 1973–75, From USLO Peking to Washington, April 2, 1975. A full transcript of this meeting, which Bush attended, can be found at NARA, RG 59, Lord Files, Box 375, China: Sensitive Chronological, March–June 1975, Memorandum of Conversation, March 31, 1975.

57. Peter Davis, "On the Road: September 10–23, 1973," in John Ardoin, ed., *The Philadelphia Orchestra: A Century of Music* (Philadelphia: Temple University Press, 1999), and Holdridge, 147–49.

59. William F. Buckley, "Death of a Christian," *National Review,* Feb. 14, 1974, 183.

62. For a useful snapshot list of individuals at the USLO, including Gleysteen, see Bush Presidential Library, Personal Papers of George H. W. Bush, China File, Box 9377, Subject File, Albert/Rhodes Visit, Guest List: Reception at the Residence, Tuesday, 1 April 1975, 5:00 pm–6:30 pm.

66. NARA, RG 59, Lord Files, Box 375, China: Sensitive Chronological, March–June 1975, From Habib to Kissinger, April 12, 1975. In her own memoirs, Barbara Bush described the difficulties of Albert's visit, 121–22.

71. Holdridge, 162.

72. Lucien Pye, "Bringing Our China Policy Down to Earth," *Foreign Policy* 18 (Spring 1975), 123–33, quotes on 123 and 131.

75. Henry Kissinger, *Years of Renewal* (New York: Simon and Schuster, 1999), 513; see also Holdridge, 158–59, on this point. For Kissinger to Bush, see NARA, RG 59, Central Foreign Policy Files 1973–75, From Washington to USLO Peking, April 2, 1975.

78. Howard L. Boorman, "Tung Pi-Wu: A Political Profile," *China Quarterly* 19 (July–September 1964), 66–83.

79. Bush's official report on the ceremony can be found at NARA, Central Foreign Policy Files 1973–75, From USLO Peking to Washington, April 7, 1975.

82. "Obituary: John Service," *Berkeley Gazette,* Feb. 10, 1999.

83. Shirley MacLaine, *You Can Get There From Here* (New York: Norton, 1975), quote from back cover.

85. Xiaoming Zhang, "China's 1979 War with Vietnam: A Reassessment," *China Quarterly* 184 (2005), 851–74.

88. NARA, RG 59, Lord Files, Box 331, China Exchanges, June 1–May 31, 1975, Talking Points—China Delegation Meeting with General Scowcroft, March 20, 1975.

89. NARA, RG 59, Central Foreign Policy Files 1973–75, From USLO Peking to Washington, April 9, 1975.

91. Gerald Ford, Address before a Joint Session of the Congress Reporting on United States Foreign Policy, April 10, 1975, www.presidency.ucsb.edu/ws/?pid-4826, accessed January 17, 2008.

96. NARA, Central Foreign Policy Files 1973–75, From USLO Peking to Washington, April 22, 1975.

98. Holdridge, 131.

Chapter Six: "We Do Have Principles and It Is Time We Stood Up for Them"

5. Editor correspondence with Robert Ho, March 22, 2007.

8. NARA, Central Foreign Policy Files 1973–75, From USLO to Washington, April 24, 1975.

12. Holdridge, 154.

14. NARA, RG 59, Lord Files, Box 331, China Exchanges, Jan. 1–May 31, 1975, From Bush to Washington, April 27, 1975, and ibid., from Kissinger to Bush, April 28, 1975.

15. NARA, Central Foreign Policy Files 1973–75, From Washington to Taipei, March 26, 1975.

16. "Who Might Succeed Henry," *Time,* April 28, 1975, 23.

17. Brinkley, *Gerald Ford,* 91.

18. Moynihan's views in the *Commentary* article are discussed in Kathleen Teltsch, "Moynihan calls on U.S. to 'Start Raising Hell' in U.N.," *New York Times,* Feb. 26, 1974, 3. For Scali and "tyranny of the majority," see Paul Hoffman, "US Warns UN on Trend to 'Tyranny of Majority' and Says Support Wanes," *New York Times,* Dec. 7, 1974, 61.

20. NARA, Central Foreign Policy Files 1973–75, From USLO Peking to Washington, June 17, 1975.

22. Bernard Gwertzman, "China Appears to Caution North Korea not to Attack: Chinese Indicate Caution on Korea," *New York Times,* May 29, 1975, 73.

23. "What's News," *Wall Street Journal,* April 28, 1975, 1.

24. Bush, *All the Best,* 214.

28. Don Sellar, "Was China Diplomat in Canada Engaged in Espionage?" *Christian Science Monitor,* May 12, 1975, 11.

31. Bush's description of the meeting for the State Department can be found at NARA, Central Foreign Policy Files 1973–75, From Peking to Washington, May 2, 1975.

32. John O'Connor, "TV: Sly, Amusing Benjamin Franklin," *New York Times,* Nov. 21, 1974, 95.

33. NARA, Central Foreign Policy Files 1973–75, From Washington to USLO Peking, April 28, 1975, and ibid., USLO Peking to Washington, May 5, 1975.

34. "The President's News Conference," May 6, 1975.

38. John Burns, "George and Barbara Bush: A Breezy Yankee Style in Peking," *People Magazine,* May 5, 1975, 4–7. See also John B. Lofton, Jr., "George Bush Is Picked to Carry the Flag to China," *People Magazine,* Sept. 23, 1974, 14–19.

39. NARA, Central Foreign Policy Files, 1973–75, From State to Various Posts, May 7, 1975.

40. Ibid., From USLO Peking to Washington, May 30, 1975.

41. For the USLO report on this visit, see NARA, Electronic Database, From USLO Peking to Washington, May 8, 1975.

42. "600 Evacuees from Cambodia Reach Border," *Los Angeles Times,* May 3, 1975, A3, and Sydney Schanberg, "Waiting in Phnom Penh: More Knaves Than Heroes," *Chicago Tribune,* May 10, 1975, C12.

43. Sydney Schanberg, "Inside Cambodia," *Chicago Tribune,* May 9, 1975; David Andelman, "Cambodia Evacuees Overdue at Border," *New York Times,* May 2, 1975, 11; and "Cambodia Leaders Shot, Doctor Says," *Los Angeles Times,* May 9, 1975, B6.

49. *U.S. Department of State Magazine,* November 2004, 43.

50. NARA, Central Foreign Policy Files 1973–75, From USLO Peking to Washington, May 30, 1975.

51. Ralph Wetterhahn, *The Last Battle: The Mayagüez Incident and the End of the Vietnam War* (New York: Plume, 2002).

52. NARA, RG 59, Lord Files, Box 375, China: Sensitive Chronological, March–June 1975, From USLO Peking to Washington, May 13, 1975; ibid., From Washington to USLO Peking, May 13, 1975; ibid., From USLO Peking to Washington, May 14, 1975; and ibid., From USLO Peking to Washington, May 15, 1975.

54. Bernard Edinger, "30,000 in Saigon Celebrate Surrender of S. Vietnam," *Los Angeles Times,* May 8, 1975, B1, and "Ceremonies Also Mark Ho Chi Minh's Birthday," *New York Times,* May 16, 1975, 16.

55. "Japan's Socialists Sign Peking Accord," *New York Times,* May 13, 1975, 7.

59. NARA, RG 59, Lord Files, Box 375, China: Sensitive Chronological, March–June 1975, From Bush to Kissinger, May 16, 1975; and ibid., Box 331, China Exchanges, Jan. 1–May 31, 1975, From Washington to Kissinger, May 28, 1975.

60. Ibid.

62. Barbara Bush, *A Memoir,* 123.

67. Bill Shirley, "How to See China on $0.00 a Day," *Los Angeles Times,* June 3, 1975, D1.

69. NARA, Central Foreign Policy Files 1973–75, From USLO Peking to Washington, June 17, 1975.

71. Ibid., From USLO Peking to Washington, March 14, 1975.

73. MacFarquhar and Schoenhals, 384–88, and Roderick MacFarquhar, in Twitchett and Fairbank, 14: 352, including quote.

77. The group's roster and itinerary for China can be found at NARA, Central Foreign Policy Files 1973–75, From USLO Peking to Washington, June 11, 1975.

79. Bush's cable to Washington describing this meeting can be found in ibid., From USLO Peking to Washington, June 4, 1974.

80. Jack Criss, "Wyatt Emmerich: Printer's Ink is in his Blood," *Delta Business Journal*, May 2001, www.deltabusinessjournal.com/HTML/archives/5-01/index.html, accessed January 18, 2008.

82. NARA, Central Foreign Policy Files 1973–75, From USLO Peking to Washington, June 4, 1975.

85. Joseph Lelyveld, "Top Chinese, Losing Inhibitions, Venture Abroad," *New York Times*, May 5, 1975, 3.

86. Kenneth Crawford, "No Illusion—The Dominoes Are Falling," *Los Angeles Times*, May 5, 1975, C7.

87. John Burns, "Philippines Realigns Its Ties to Peking," *Christian Science Monitor*, June 11, 1975, 3.

Chapter Seven: "There Is No Credit in This Work"

13. *Mao Tse-Tung Poems* (Peking: Foreign Languages Press, 1976).

15. For newspaper accounts of Deng's meeting with the American editors, see William Giles, "Taiwan Issue Must Be Settled before U.S., China Can Increase Trade, Peking Says," *Wall Street Journal*, June 3, 1975, 5, and "Peking Is Adamant on Taipei but Keeps Door Open for Ford," *New York Times*, June 3, 1975, 12.

16. "Harold Charles Champeau, 81, Dies; USDA China Specialist, CIA Linguist," *Washington Post*, Dec. 6, 2000, B7.

20. Kenneth W. Stein, *Heroic Diplomacy: Sadat, Kissinger, Carter, Begin and the Quest for Arab-Israeli Peace* (London: Routledge, 1999), and William B. Quandt, *Peace Process: American Diplomacy and the Arab-Israeli Conflict* (Berkeley: University of California Press, 2005).

21. Roberts, 223.

25. "French Say Peking Aide Foresees War with Soviet," *New York Times*, May 15, 1975, 4.

27. NARA, Central Foreign Policy Files 1973–75, From USLO Peking to Washington, June 8 and 9, 1975.

28. Edwin L. Dale, Jr., "Jobless Rate Up to 8.9%," *The New York Times*, May 3, 1975, 65.

30. For Bush's report on the matter to Washington, see NARA, Central Foreign Policy Files 1973–75, From USLO Peking to Washington,

June 17, 1975; see also John W. Finney, "U.S. Says Soviets Store Missiles at Base in Somalia," *New York Times,* June 11, 1975, 4.

31. NARA, RG 59, Lord Files, Box 332, China Exchanges, Undated, From Bush to Kissinger, June 12, 1975.

32. Ibid.

36. NARA, Central Foreign Policy Files 1973–75, From USLO Peking to Washington, July 25, 1975.

37. Burns, "George and Barbara Bush."

43. Grey, 102.

46. NARA, Central Foreign Policy Files 1973–75, From USLO Peking to Washington, May 14, 1975, and ibid., From State to Various Posts, June 20, 1975.

47. "China and Taiwan in Dispute over Body of Freed Ex-Officer," *New York Times,* June 14, 1975, 6. See also Fox Butterfield, "Peking Frees Last of Top Nationalists It Has Held Since '49," *New York Times,* Dec. 24, 1975, 27.

50. NARA, RG 59, Lord Files, Box 375, China: Sensitive Chronological, March–June 1975, From USLO Peking to Washington, June 27, 1975.

52. Ibid., From Ripley to Bush, May 1, 1975, and NARA, Central Foreign Policy Files 1973–75, From USLO Peking to Washington, June 24, 1975.

53. NARA, RG 59, Lord Files, Box 332, China Exchanges, Undated, From Washington to USLO Peking, June 28, 1975.

56. Koch, 124, and Barbara Bush, *A Memoir,* 114.

58. Eric Pace, "Many Opponents of Mrs. Gandhi Arrested in India," *New York Times,* June 26, 1975, 81. For Bush's recollections of this later meeting, see *All the Best,* 334.

65. NARA, Central Foreign Policy Files 1973–75, From USLO to Peking, July 7, 1975.

66. Bush, *All the Best,* 218.

Chapter Eight: "I Have Studied Chinese"

1. Editor correspondence with George H. W. Bush, May 21, 2007.

3. NARA, Central Foreign Policy Files 1973–75, From SecState Washington (Lord and Habib) to US Delegation (Kissinger), July 1, 1975.

4. NARA, RG 59, Lot 94D176, Subject Files of PRC and Mongolia 1969–78, Box 6, June–December, 1975, Secretary Kissinger's Briefing of Congressional Delegates before Their Visit to the People's Republic of China, July 22, 1975; and ibid., Congressional Report to the President following a Trip to the People's Republic of China, Sept. 8, 1975.

6. Grey, 120–31.

7. Barbara Bush, *A Memoir,* 118.

9. NARA, Central Foreign Policy Files 1973–75, From USLO to Washington, July 3, 1975.

11. On the question of the "lost" chance in China and the Acheson White Paper, see Cohen, 164–69; Nancy Bernkopf Tucker, *Patterns in the Dust: Chinese-American Relations and the Recognition Controversy* (New York: Columbia University Press, 1983), 151–61; and Chen Jian, "The Myth of America's 'Lost Chance' in China: A Chinese Perspective in Light of New Evidence," *Diplomatic History* 21 (Spring 1997), 77–86. For the poll results, see Rosemary Foote, *The Practice of Power* (New York: Oxford University Press, 1997), 85.

16. NARA, Central Foreign Policy Files 1973–75, From USLO Peking to Washington, Aug. 26, 1975.

19. Ibid., From USLO to Washington, July 11, 1975.

21. Ben Kiernan, *The Pol Pot Regime: Race, Power, and Genocide in Cambodia under the Khmer Rouge, 1975–79* (New Haven, Conn.: Yale University Press, 2002).

26. Patricia Moore, "Child Care Centers the Chinese Way," *Los Angeles Times,* June 29, 1975, E18.

28. Scott Daugherty and Eric Hartley, "At *The Capital,* Publisher Philip Merrill's Influence Will Last," *The Capital,* June 15, 2006, and Ernesto Londoño and Ray Rivera, "Annapolis Publisher Is Still Missing," *Washington Post,* June 12, 2006, A1.

33. For Bush's initial report upon returning to Beijing, see NARA, Central Foreign Policy Files 1973–75, From USLO Peking to Washington, July 24, 1975.

34. Ibid., From USLO to Washington, July 28, 1975, and Washington to USLO, Oct. 9, 1975.

36. For Bush's report on this meeting, and his further inquiry to the State Department on this situation, see ibid., From USLO Peking to Washington, July 25, 1975.

37. Mitchell B. Lerner, *The Pueblo Incident* (Lawrence: University of Kansas Press, 2003).

39. See Stanley Bachrach, *The Committee of One Million* (New York: Columbia University Press, 1976), and Ross Koen, *The China Lobby in American Politics* (New York: Harper and Row, 1974), for histories written at the same time as the China Diary. See also Lee Edwards, *Missionary for Freedom: The Life and Times of Walter Judd* (New York: Paragon House, 1990).

42. NARA, Central Foreign Policy Files 1973–75, From Washington (Kissinger) to USLO Peking (Bush), July 25, 1975.

44. Bernard Gwertzman, "House Refuses Arms to Turkey, Rebuffing Ford," *New York Times,* July 25, 1975, 63.

48. NARA, RG 59, Electronic Database, From USLO to Washington, Aug. 19, 1975, and "Caterpillar Concludes Machine Sale to China," *Wall Street Journal,* Oct. 13, 1975, 21.

56. NARA, Central Foreign Policy Files 1973–75, From State to USLO Peking, Oct. 2, 1975.

57. Lilley and Lilley, 184–85.

59. "Siege Ends in Malaysia," *New York Times,* Aug. 8, 1975, 2.

60. NARA, RG 59, Lord Files, Box 379, China: Sensitive Chronological, July–Sept. 1975, From USLO Peking to Washington, Aug. 6, 1975, and NARA, Central Foreign Policy Files 1973–75, From USLO Peking to Washington, Aug. 6, 1975.

62. "Flanigan's Shenanigans," *Time,* March 20, 1972, www.time.com/time/magazine/article/0,9171,942495,00.html, accessed January 18, 2007.

65. NARA, Central Foreign Policy Files 1973–75, From Washington to Kissinger (traveling), Aug. 22, 1975.

70. Ibid., From USLO Peking to Washington, Aug. 19, 1975.

71. Ibid., From USLO Peking to Washington, Aug. 12, 1975.

72. Ibid., From USLO Peking to Washington, Aug. 16, 1975.

73. NARA, RG 59, Lord Files, Box 332, China Exchanges, Undated, From USLO Peking to Washington, Aug. 20, 1975, and NARA, Central Foreign Policy Files 1973–75, From USLO Peking to Washington, Aug. 16, 1975.

75. NARA, Central Foreign Policy Files 1973–75, From USLO Peking to Washington, Aug. 20, 1975.

77. Ibid., From USLO Peking to Washington, Aug. 4, 1975.

78. For "bored with life," see NARA, Central Foreign Policy Files 1973–75, From Washington to Various Posts, Aug. 20, 1975; Rowland Evans and Robert Novak, "Rumsfeld's VP Game," *Washington Post,* Sept. 27, 1975, A15; and Safire, "The Listmakers," *New York Times,* Sept. 22, 1975, 33.

82. Bill Anderson, "Congressmen Color Red China Gray," *Chicago Tribune,* Sept. 4, 1975, A2.

83. NARA, Central Foreign Policy Files 1973–75, From USLO Peking to Washington, Aug. 22, 1975 (two).

84. Ibid.

*T*his essay provides an overview of the historical literature on which I have relied, focusing on topics covered in the annotations to the China Diary. It is intended to point readers toward further reading on topics they may find of interest.

Cold War Diplomacy

The available literature on Sino-American Cold War relations is vast, and it is improving steadily given recent works that draw on newly available Chinese sources. For the bilateral relationship, readers may wish to begin with Chen Jian, *Mao's China and the Cold War* (Chapel Hill: University of North Carolina Press, 2001) for a Chinese perspective; Warren Cohen, *America's Response to China: A History of Sino-American Relations* (New York: Columbia University Press, 2000) for an accessible narrative centered on Washington; and Margaret MacMillan, *Nixon and China: The Week That Changed the World* (Toronto: Viking Canada, 2006) for a well-written international view.

For Sino-American relations I have also relied on Thomas J. Christensen, *Useful Adversaries: Grand Strategy, Domestic Mobilization, and Sino-American Conflict, 1947–1958* (Princeton, N.J.: Princeton University Press, 1996); Warren I. Cohen and Akira Iriye, eds., *The Great Powers in East Asia, 1952–1960* (New York: Columbia University Press, 1990); Jeffrey A. Engel, *Cold War at 30,000 Feet: The Anglo-American Fight for Aviation Supremacy* (Cambridge, Mass.: Harvard University Press, 2007); Rosemary Foot, *The Practice of Power* (New York: Oxford University Press, 1997); Evelyn Goh, *Constructing the U.S. Rapprochement with China, 1961–74* (New York: Cambridge University Press, 2005);

Harry Harding, *A Fragile Relationship: The United States and China since 1972* (Washington, D.C.: Brookings Institution Press, 1992); Victor S. Kaufman, *Confronting Communism: U.S. and British Policies toward China* (Columbia: University of Missouri Press, 2001); William Kirby, Robert Ross, and Gong Li, eds., *Normalization of U.S.-China Relations: An International History* (Cambridge, Mass.: Harvard University Asia Center, 2005); Robert R. Ross and Jian Changbin, eds., *Re-examining the Cold War: U.S.-China Diplomacy, 1954–73* (Cambridge, Mass.: Harvard University Press, 2001); Robert S. Ross, *Negotiating Cooperation: The United States and China, 1969–89* (Stanford, Calif.: Stanford University Press, 1995); Nancy Bernkopf Tucker, *Patterns in the Dust: Chinese-American Relations and the Recognition Controversy* (New York: Columbia University Press, 1983); Patrick Tyler, *A Great Wall: Six Presidents and China* (New York: Public Affairs, 1999); and Zhang Shu Guang, *Deterrence and Strategic Culture: Chinese-American Confrontations, 1949–1958* (Ithaca, N.Y.: Cornell University Press, 1992). The new volume on China between 1973 and 1976 in *The Foreign Relations of the United States* (Washington, D.C.: U.S. Government Printing Office, 2007) appeared in print too late for full incorporation throughout this study. However, my review of the new documents released in this volume does not change my view of Bush's role in Sino-American relations of the time.

The English-language literature on Chinese Cold War diplomacy is steadily improving thanks to yeoman efforts by dedicated historians pushing for access to documents of the sort that North American and European researchers often take for granted. Particularly helpful are the aforementioned Chen Jian, *Mao's China and the Cold War,* and his earlier *China's Road to the Korean War* (New York: Columbia University Press, 1994). John W. Garver, *China's Decision for Rapprochement with the United States, 1968–71* (Boulder, Colo.: Westview Press, 1992) and *Foreign Relations of the People's Republic of China* (Englewood Cliffs, N.J.: Prentice Hall, 1993), offer, respectively, a detailed monograph and a general overview of Chinese diplomacy. Also useful is Quansheng

Zhao, *Interpreting Chinese Foreign Policy* (New York: Oxford University Press, 1996). Particularly helpful are the Chinese documents published in Chen Jian and David L. Wilson, eds., "All under the Heaven Is Great Chaos: Beijing, the Sino-Soviet Border Clashes, and the Turn toward Sino-American Rapprochement, 1968–69," *Cold War International History Project Bulletin* 11 (Winter 1998–99), 155–75.

On the critical issue of Sino-Soviet divisions, see Gordon H. Chang, *Friends and Enemies: The United States, China, and the Soviet Union, 1948–72* (Palo Alto, Calif.: Stanford University Press, 1990); David Mayers, *Cracking the Monolith: U.S. Policy toward the Sino-Soviet Alliance, 1949–55* (Baton Rouge: Louisiana State University Press, 1986); Robert Ross, ed., *China, the United States, and the Soviet Union: Tripolarity and Policy Making in the Cold War* (London: M. E. Sharpe, 1993); Odd Arne Westad, ed., *Brothers in Arms: The Rise and Fall of the Sino-Soviet Alliance, 1945–1963* (Washington, D.C., and Stanford, Calif.: Woodrow Wilson Center Press and Stanford University Press, 1998); and Zhang Shu Guang, *Economic Cold War: America's Embargo against China and the Sino-Soviet Alliance, 1949–63* (Washington, D.C., and Palo Alto, Calif.: Woodrow Wilson Center Press and Stanford University Press, 2001). Vladislav Zubok and Constantine Pleshakov, *Inside the Kremlin's Cold War: From Stalin to Khrushchev* (Cambridge, Mass.: Harvard University Press, 1996) offers an important Soviet perspective.

Bush interpreted Saigon's fall as proof of the domino theory. For primers on this crucial Cold War dogma, see the complex but worthwhile Frank Ninkovich, *Modernity and Power: A History of the Domino Theory in the Twentieth Century* (Chicago: University of Chicago Press, 1994). See also Robert Jervis and Jack Snyder, *Dominoes and Bandwagons: Strategic Beliefs and Great Power Competition in the Eurasian Rimland* (New York: Oxford University Press, 1991), and the always useful John Lewis Gaddis, *Strategies of Containment: A Critical Appraisal of American National Security Strategy during the Cold War* (New York: Oxford University Press, 2005).

South Vietnam's fall to Communist forces in 1975 colored Bush's entire experience in Beijing. Works on the Vietnam War(s) abound: of particular use as primers are George Herring, *America's Longest War* (New York: McGraw-Hill, 1996); Robert Schulzinger, *A Time for War: The United States and Vietnam, 1941–1975* (New York: Oxford University Press, 1997); and Marilyn Young, *The Vietnam Wars, 1945–1990* (New York: HarperCollins, 1991). For the initial American intervention, see Patrick Hearden, *The Tragedy of Vietnam* (New York: HarperCollins, 1991). For the 1950s, a stellar starting point is Mark Atwood Lawrence, *Assuming the Burden: Europe and the American Commitment to Vietnam* (Berkeley: University of California Press, 2007); for the 1960s and the fateful decision to Americanize the war, see Fredrik Logevall, *Choosing War: The Lost Chance for Peace and the Escalation of the War in Vietnam* (Berkeley: University of California Press, 2001), and Andrew Preston, *The War Council: McGeorge Bundy, the NSC, and Vietnam* (Cambridge, Mass.: Harvard University Press, 2006). For Saigon's final fall, see James Willbanks, *Abandoning Vietnam: How America Left and South Vietnam Lost Its War* (Lawrence: University Press of Kansas, 2004).

Cambodian affairs dominated much of Bush's agenda while at the United States Liaison Office (USLO). American involvement in the country is described in detail by William Shawcross, *Sideshow, Revised Edition: Kissinger, Nixon, and the Destruction of Cambodia* (New York: Cooper Square Press, 2002). Also useful are David Chandler, *The Tragedy of Cambodian History* (New Haven, Conn.: Yale University Press, 1993), and *A History of Cambodia* (Boulder, Colo.: Westview Press, 2000), as well as Kenyon Clymer, *The United States and Cambodia since 1870* (Dekalb: Northern Illinois University Press, 2007). For Cambodian leaders, see David Chandler, *Brother Number One: A Political Biography of Pol Pot* (Boulder, Colo.: Westview Press, 1999); Ben Kiernan, *The Pol Pot Regime: Race, Power, and Genocide in Cambodia under the Khmer Rouge, 1975–79* (New Haven, Conn.: Yale University Press, 2002); and Milton E. Osborne, *Sihanouk: Prince of Light, Prince of Darkness* (Honolulu: University of Hawaii Press, 1994).

Other regions played their part in Bush's China experience. For more on the geopolitics of South Asia during the Cold War, useful primers include Robert McMahon, *The Cold War on the Periphery* (New York: Columbia University Press, 1996), and Shivaji Ganguly, *U.S. Policy toward South Asia* (Boulder, Colo.: Westview Press, 1990). For Malaysian events, which Bush mentions tangentially in the diary, see Matthew Jones, *Conflict and Confrontation in South East Asia, 1961–1965: Britain, the United States, Indonesia and the Creation of Malaysia* (New York: Cambridge University Press, 2001).

AMERICAN LEADERS AND AMERICAN POLITICS

For Gerald Ford and the dynamics of his presidency, especially during its early days, see James Cannon, *Time and Chance: Gerald Ford's Appointment with History* (Ann Arbor: University of Michigan Press, 1998); John Robert Greene, *The Presidency of Gerald R. Ford* (Lawrence: University Press of Kansas, 1995); and Douglas Brinkley, *Gerald R. Ford* (New York: Times Books, 2007).

Memoirs have proved particularly helpful in allowing me to add color and little-known facts to the annotations of Bush's journal. For David Bruce, who preceded Bush as USLO head, see Nelson Lankford, *The Last American Aristocrat* (New York: Little, Brown, 1996), and the brilliant Priscilla Roberts, *Window on the Forbidden City: The Beijing Diaries of David Bruce* (Hong Kong: University of Hong Kong Centre of Asian Studies, 2001). Henry Kissinger's memoirs are long, ubiquitous, and easily available. Special attention is due his *Years of Renewal* (New York: Simon and Schuster, 1999), which focuses on the Ford presidency also covered by Bush's China Diary. Particularly insightful for illuminating Bush's role in Sino-American relations, both at the USLO and later as president, is James Lilley and Jeffrey Lilley, *China Hands: Nine Decades of Adventure, Espionage, and Diplomacy in Asia* (New York: Public Affairs, 2004), including its gripping passages on the Tiananmen Square protests. John Holdridge, *Crossing the Divide:*

An Insider's Account of the Normalization of U.S.-Chinese Relations (Lanham, Md.: Rowman and Littlefield, 1997), ranks among the most detailed and insightful of any memoir of the Sino-American rapprochement. Though not strictly devoted to China, Charles Cross, *Born a Foreigner: A Memoir of the American Presence in Asia* (Lanham, Md.: Rowman and Littlefield, 1999), offers an inside look at a diplomat's life far from Washington. Nancy Bernkopf Tucker, ed., *China Confidential: American Diplomats and Sino-American Relations, 1945–1996* (New York: Columbia University Press, 2001), offers a series of oral histories. For the Bush presidency, James Baker, *Work Hard, Study, and Keep out of Politics!* (New York: Putnam, 2006), and *The Politics of Diplomacy* (New York: Putnam, 1995), are useful, as is Robert Gates, *From the Shadows: The Ultimate Insider's Story of Five Presidents and How They Won the Cold War* (New York: Simon and Schuster, 1996).

Kissinger's role in Bush's China sojourn cannot be overstated. Particularly useful for scholars interested in Kissinger's style is William Burr, ed., *The Kissinger Transcripts: The Top-Secret Talks with Beijing and Moscow* (New York: New Press, 1998). For broader studies of the man and his diplomacy, see Jussi Hanhimaki, *The Flawed Architect* (New York: Oxford University Press, 2004); Walter Isaacson, *Kissinger* (New York: Simon and Schuster, 1996); Robert Schulzinger, *Henry Kissinger: Doctor of Diplomacy* (New York: Columbia University Press, 1989); and Jeremi Suri, *Henry Kissinger and the American Century* (Cambridge, Mass.: Harvard University Press, 2007). Christopher Hitchens, *The Trial of Henry Kissinger* (New York: Verso Press, 2001), offers a curious polemic.

CHINESE AFFAIRS

The Cultural Revolution cast a shadow over all Chinese affairs, including international relations. For the latest scholarly treatments in English, see Roderick MacFarquhar and Michael Schoenhals, *Mao's Last Revolution* (Cambridge, Mass.: Harvard University Press, 2006), and Joseph W. Esherick, Paul G. Pickowicz, and Andrew G. Walder, eds., *China's Cultural Revolution as History* (Palo Alto, Calif.: Stanford University Press, 2006). All scholars of modern China are indebted to Denis C. Twitchett and John K. Fairbank, the editors of the fifteen-volume *Cambridge History of China* (New York: Cambridge University Press, 1978–). Still useful is Fairbank's *The Great Chinese Revolution, 1800–1985* (New York: Harper Perennial, 1987). Particularly important for understanding the aftermath of Mao Zedong's regime is Kenneth Lieberthal, *Governing China: From Revolution to Reform* (New York: Norton, 2003).

Biographies of Mao and Zhou Enlai abound. Useful primers on Mao include Jung Chang and Jon Halliday, *Mao: The Unknown Story* (New York: Anchor, 2006); Maurice Meisner, *Mao Zedong: A Political and Intellectual Portrait* (New York: Polity, 2007); Philip Short, *Mao: A Life* (New York: Henry Holt, 2000); Jonathan D. Spence, *Mao Zedong* (New York: Penguin, 2006); and Ross Terrill, *Mao: A Biography* (Palo Alto, Calif.: Stanford University Press, 2000).

For Zhou, especially his diplomacy, see Shu Guang Zhang, "In the Shadow of Mao: Zhou Enlai and China's New Diplomacy," in Gordon Craig and Francis Loewenheim, *The Diplomats* (Princeton, N.J.: Princeton University Press, 1994), and Ronald C. Keith, *The Diplomacy of Zhou Enlai* (New York: St. Martin's, 1989). See also Han Suyin, *Eldest Son: Zhou Enlai and the Making of Modern China* (New York: Kodansha, 1994), and Gao Wengian, *Zhou Enlai: The Last Perfect Revolutionary* (New York: Public Affairs, 2007). Chae-Jin Lee, *Zhou Enlai: The Early Years* (Stanford, Calif.: Stanford University Press, 1994), details his upbringing.

For Deng Xiaoping, see Merle Goldman, *Sowing the Seeds of Democracy in China: Political Reform in the Deng Xiaoping Era* (Cambridge, Mass.: Harvard University Press, 1994); Maurice Meisner, *The Deng Xiaoping Era: An Inquiry into the Fate of Chinese Socialism* (New York: Hill and Wang, 1996); and Meisner's insightful *Mao's China and After: A History of the People's Republic* (New York: Free Press, 1999).

George H. W. Bush and His Presidency

Histories of the Bush administration, the Gulf War, and the end of the Cold War abound, even though most official documents from these years await declassification. Helpful foreign policy primers include Ryan J. Barilleaux and Mark J. Rozell, *Power and Prudence: The Presidency of George H. W. Bush* (College Station: Texas A&M University Press, 2004); Michael Beschloss and Strobe Talbott, *At the Highest Levels: The Inside Story of the End of the Cold War* (Boston: Little, Brown, 1993); Colin Campbell and Bert A. Rockman, *The Bush Presidency: First Appraisals* (Chatham, N.J.: Chatham House, 1991); Michael Duffy and Dan Goodgame, *Marching in Place: The Status Quo Presidency of George Bush* (New York: Simon and Schuster, 1992); and John Robert Greene, *The Presidency of George Bush* (Lawrence: University Press of Kansas, 2000). Michael J. Hogan, ed., *The End of the Cold War: Its Meaning and Implications* (New York: Cambridge University Press, 1992), is a collection useful today more as a primary source for scholarly thinking at the Cold War's end than as a secondary account. Also useful are James Mann, *Rise of the Vulcans* (New York: Viking, 2004); David Mervin, *George Bush and the Guardianship Presidency* (New York: St. Martin's, 1996); Don Oberdorfer, *From the Cold War to a New Era: The United States and the Soviet Union, 1983–1991,* updated edition (Baltimore: Johns Hopkins University Press, 1998); Richard Rose, *The Postmodern President: George Bush Meets the World* (Chatham, N.J.: Chatham House, 1991); Bob Woodward, *The Commanders* (New York: Simon and Schuster, 1991); and Philip Zelikow and Condoleezza Rice, *Germany United and Europe Transformed: A Study in Statecraft* (Cambridge, Mass.: Harvard University Press, 1997). David Halberstam, *War in a Time of Peace: Bush, Clinton, and the Generals* (New York: Scribner, 2001) offers important vignettes on the Bush years as seen through a wider lens. For a view of the Cold War's end beyond the traditional corridors of power, see Matthew Evangelista, *Unarmed Forces: The Transnational Movement to*

End the Cold War (Ithaca, N.Y.: Cornell University Press, 1999). For the Bush administration's negotiations on the North American Free Trade Agreement (NAFTA), see Antoni Estevadeordal, Dani Rodrik, Alan M. Taylor, and Andres Velasco, eds., *Integrating the Americas: FTAA and Beyond* (Cambridge, Mass.: Harvard University Press, 2004), and Maxwell Cameron and Brian Tomlin, *The Making of NAFTA: How the Deal Was Done* (Ithaca, N.Y.: Cornell University Press, 2000).

Several of the works on Chinese-American relations cited above discuss the Tiananmen Square protests, which color any discussion of Bush's China policies. Also helpful are David Lampton, *Same Bed, Different Dreams: Managing U.S.-China Relations, 1989–2000* (Berkeley: University of California Press, 2001), and the more contemporary Steven M. Goldstein, *China at the Crossroads: Reform after Tiananmen* (New York: Foreign Policy Association, 1992). Richard Madsen, *China and the American Dream: A Moral Inquiry* (Berkeley: University of California Press, 1995), offers a particularly insightful chapter on the cultural impact of Tiananmen in the United States; for the political side, see Ramon H. Myers, Michel C. Oksenberg, and David L. Shambaugh, eds., *Making China Policy: Lessons from the Bush and Clinton Administrations* (Lanham, Md.: Rowman and Littlefield, 2001). See also James Mann, *About Face: A History of America's Curious Relations with China, From Nixon to Clinton* (New York: Vintage, 2000), and *The China Fantasy: How Our Leaders Explain Away Chinese Repression* (New York: Viking, 2007), a useful polemic worth engaging for those interested in Bush's response to the Tiananmen crisis. Readers should not overlook the electronic document compilations of George Washington University's National Security Archive, especially Michael Evans, "The U.S. 'Tiananmen Papers,'" June 4, 2001, available at www.gwu.edu/~nsarchiv/NSAEBB/NSAEBB47/.

Any study of Bush's presidency must confront the importance of the democratic peace, with all its proponents and attendant complexities, at the end of the Cold War. For primers, see the oft-cited, if less frequently understood, Francis Fukuyama, *The End of History and the Last Man* (New York: Harper Perennial, 1993); as well as Michael Brown, ed., *Debating the Democratic Peace* (Cambridge, Mass.: MIT Press, 1996); Bruce Russett, *Grasping the Democratic Peace* (Princeton, N.J.: Princeton University Press, 2003); and David R. Weart, *Never at War: Why Democracies Will Not Fight One Another* (New Haven, Conn.: Yale University Press, 2001). An important dissent is offered by Christopher Layne, "Kant or Can't: The Myth of the Democratic Peace," *International Security* 19 (Summer 1994), 5–49.

George H. W. Bush wrote, with Brent Scowcroft, what may over time prove to be the most useful memoir of a presidency. Their *A World Transformed* (New York: Scribner, 1999) offers insight and a selection of primary documents in describing the foreign policies they pursued. An additional useful starting point for understanding Bush is his *All the Best, George Bush: My Life in Letters and Other Writings,* a collection of his letters and diary entries composed over a lifetime (New York: Scribner, 1999). This collection is well edited and frequently shows Bush at his best (and, at times, only at his best), but it is inarguably useful for appreciating the spirit of fairness and fair play that dominated his policymaking. For Bush's life, see the impressive Richard Ben Cramer, *What It Takes* (New York: Random House, 1993), as well as Herbert Parmet, *George Bush: The Life of a Lone Star Yankee* (New York: Scribner, 1997), and Tom Wicker, *George Herbert Walker Bush* (New York: Viking, 2004). A brief synopsis is Michael Beschloss, "George Bush, 1989–1993," in Robert A. Wilson, ed., *Character above All* (New York: Simon and Schuster, 1995). Timothy Naftali, *George H. W. Bush* (New York: Times Books, 2007), was not in print in time for use in this study. For Bush as a communicator, see Martin Medhurst, ed., *The Rhetorical Presidency of George H. W. Bush* (College Station: Texas A&M University Press, 2006). Michael Schaller, *Right Turn: American Life in the Reagan-Bush Era* (New York: Oxford University Press, 2007), presents the conservative presidential politics of Bush's era in a broader context.

Page numbers followed by *n* indicate notes.

Beijing (*continued*)
73n59; San Li Tun neighborhood of, 126, 328, 328n41, 330, 376; sounds of, 348–49, 374; traffic in, 73, 73n59; tunnels underneath, 61n31, 129–30, 129n75. *See also specific buildings and sights*
Beijing Revolutionary Committee, 73, 73n59
Belgium: diplomats of, 110, 125, 209, 209n27, 368, 376; exhibit at embassy of, 242
Bemis, Gerry: on Bush's political future, 311; Bush's relationship with, 212n33; in Hong Kong, 260; and Shanghai, 263; tennis with, 268; visit to China by, 212, 264–72
Benjamin Franklin (television series), 275, 275n32, 285
Bentsen, Lloyd, 215, 215n38, 215n40, 409
Berbera (Somalia), 320n30, 323, 326, 380
Berendsen, Sir Carl, 283n45
Berendsen, Lady Nellie, 283, 283n45
Berman, Muriel, 280, 280n40
Berman, Philip, 280, 280n40
Bern (Switzerland), 163–64
Bethlehem Steel Corporation, 181n44
Bhutto, Zulfikar Ali, 145
Bible Institute, 26–27
bicycles: Bushes' travel by, 10n17, 15, 35, 78–79, 121, 185, 209, 217–18, 237, 241, 303–4, 326, 443; car crashes with, 29, 363; licenses for, 18; masks and goggles for, 106, 217, 227, 238, 251; prevalence of, 284, 358
Big Duck restaurant, 71, 244
Big Horn (film), 248, 248n95
big-character posters, 208, 208n24
billboards, 85, 85n85, 328
Binh Dinh (South Vietnam), 273, 273n27
birds: as food, 95, 103, 173; Ripley's (Dillon) study of, 199, 199n6; Thomas's (William) study of, 286n49; wild, 23, 173, 199. *See also* ducks
bird's nest soup, 95, 95n15, 132, 280, 305
birth control, 70n47

birthday: of Barbara Bush, 217, 322; of George H. W. Bush, 322, 323; of George W. Bush, 352; of George Washington, 156, 157, 159, 161
Black, Creed, 303, 303n80
Black September Organization (BSO), 57n20
Blackburn, Robert: in Canton, 261; career of, 109n36; departure from China, 246, 250, 261; Levesque (Jerry) replacing, 246; meals with, 109, 110, 118, 125, 219, 261; in Tianjin, 176; and USLO staff friction, 161; visa application translated by, 377n57
Blair, Jane, 264–65, 264n13
Blair, William, 264n13
Blake, Marion, 296–97, 296n61
Blake, Robert, 296–97, 296n61
Blakely, Delois, 371, 371n47
bloc voting, in U.N., 415, 416
Blue News, 29–30, 134
Boehm, Helen, 109, 109n36, 110
Boeing, 110n39, 111
Boggs, T. Hale, 76n67
boilers, 204
Bongo Ondimba, El Hadj Omar, 340, 340n54, 342
Bonn (Germany), 163–64
Borden Company, 80, 80n74
boredom, 10, 12, 392n78, 435
Borg, Björn, 285n48
Born a Foreigner (Cross), 113n44
Boston Globe (newspaper), 303, 303n81
Boustany, Elie Joseph (Lebanese ambassador): career of, 81n76; on earthquakes, 179; at film showings, 303; meals and meetings with, 81, 90, 123, 159, 286; national day celebration by, 90; wife of, 159
bowling, 325, 341
boxing, 41, 41n87, 149, 224–25
Boyd, Sir John, 128, 128n74, 361
Brandon, Mabel, 57, 57n21
Brandon, Oscar Henry, 57, 57n21
Brazil, 303
breweries, 168, 384–85

Brezhnev, Leonid: career of, 33n68; Chinese relations with, 33n68; family of, 166n29; at Vladivostok summit, 8n14, 67n41
Brezhnev, Yuri, 166, 166n29
Brinkley, Douglas, 151n10
Britain: Boyd (John) at embassy of, 128, 128n74, 361; burning of Beijing consulate of, 24, 24n49; on Bush's selection as USLO head, 438; on Grey's (Anthony) imprisonment, 352–53, 352n6; intelligence service of, 342, 342n60, 345; on Kissinger's intelligence sharing, 104n30; on Mansfield's (Mike) report, 165n27; national day celebration of, 325; Richardson (Elliot) in, 312, 312n6; tour groups from, 249–50; on trade, 154n16. *See also* Youde, Sir Edward
bronchial infections, 86, 188, 279, 281, 299, 323
Brooks, Stan, 393, 393n80
Brown, L. Dean, 116, 116n52, 207, 207n23
Bruce, David K. E.: approach to mission in China, 6, 6n11, 35n74; Bush criticized as replacement for, 437–38; Bush's request for consultation with, 321, 321n31, 323; career of, xxvii, 6n11, 438; contact with Chinese leaders by, 2, 153; on Diplomatic Services Bureau, 27n57; friendship groups and, 68; Hollingsworth (Clare) and, 12n23; in Hong Kong, 259; Jenkins (Al) under, 134n84; Lin Ping and, 13n26; on Marines, 59n27, 92n5; at national day celebrations, 2, 35n74, 43; on oil sales, 22n45; opening of USLO by, xviii, 6n11, 434–35; on Qiao Guanhua, 13n24; selection as USLO head, 6n11, 9n16
Bruce, Evangeline, 173, 173n35, 436
Bryan, Anthony: career of, 286n50; visit to China by, 286–88, 291–93
Bryan, D. Tennant: career of, 212n33; visit to China by, 212, 263, 264–72
Bryan, Mary, visit to China by, 212, 212n33, 264–72

Bryant, Paul William "Bear," 185, 185n51
BSO. *See* Black September Organization
Buchwald, Art, 94n12
Buck, Pearl, 191, 191n69
Buckley, William F., 229, 229n59
Buddhism, in Cambodia, 247
Bue, Earl, 60
Bulak, Adnan (Turkish ambassador), 172, 179, 217, 217n43, 325, 366
Bulgaria: diplomats of, 168, 170; Soviet relations with, 54n12; on World War II anniversary, 281
Burch, Dean, 58, 58n23
Burma: diplomats of, 225; Osborn (David) as U.S. ambassador to, 112, 112n43
Burnham, Forbes, 203, 203n16
Burns, John: career of, xxvii, 34n72; departure from China, 156, 249, 341; at film showings, 60, 206; interviews of Bush by, 249; on lifestyle in Beijing, 191, 362; on Mao's health, 191; Munro (Ross) replacing, 361; photos by, 227; on Qiao Guanhua's relationship with Kissinger, 87; and Shapp (Milton), 79; socializing and meals with, 60, 79, 206, 227, 266, 303; tennis with, 34, 130; at zoo, 206
Burton, Phillip, 231, 231n60
Burton, Richard, 159
Burundi: diplomats of, 241, 248, 414; sovereignty of, 212n32, 414n16, 416
Bush, Barbara (wife), xxvii; arrival in China, 15; bicycling with, 149, 185, 217–18, 241, 304, 326; birthday of, 217, 322; Bush welcomed home by, 148; C. Fred's drives with, 201n13, 216; C. Fred's walks with, xiv, 153, 200; in Canton, 257, 262; children traveling with, 351, 359; in Chinese language classes, 38, 46, 76; Chinese monitoring of activities of, 210; on church services, 27n56; closeness to, 182; Cuban diplomats and, 172–73; at Dong Biwu's funeral, 240–41; on Dorothy Bush's christening, 340, 341n56; driving

Chamber of Commerce, 272, 280–81.
See also specific companies and people
Byers, Buck, 120
Byrd, Robert, congressional delegation led
  by, 360, 392–95, 392n79, 394n82,
  394n83
Byroade, Henry, 252, 252n104

C. Fred (dog): adjustment of, 23, 80; in
  August 1975 vacation, 373; during
  Bushes' absences, 111, 119, 296, 303,
  351; cat chases by, 355; Chinese
  reactions to, xiv, 16, 17, 19, 216, 219,
  250–51, 352, 355, 356, 378; diet of,
  10n19, 118, 298; diplomats' reactions
  to, 60, 153, 200; dirtiness of, 23, 26, 55,
  321, 323, 352; in Gabon embassy, 200;
  and George W. Bush, 314; at Ming
  Tombs, 197, 201n13, 216, 293, 361,
  378; on trip to China, 10–11, 10n19, 15
CAAC. *See* Civil Aviation Administration
  of China
cabbages, 69
cabinet: Bush's possible future in Ford's,
  300, 311; Bush's wish to join Nixon's,
  409–10, 432; visits to China by members
  of, 233–34. *See also specific people*
Caetano, Marcello, 234n68
Calentino, Ernie, 116
California Agricultural Education
  Foundation, 207, 207n23
California Institute of Technology, 198
Cam Ranh Bay, 326, 326n39
Cambodia: Bush's concern for people of,
  251; Chinese relations with, 360;
  Communism in, 247; Fitzgerald
  (Stephen) on, 22; French embassy in,
  282nn42–43; under Khieu Samphan,
  395, 395n85; *Mayagüez* crisis in, 255,
  287–88, 287nn51–52; political chaos in,
  22n44, 282; under Sihanouk, 22n44;
  Sihanouk's return to, 373, 395; U.N.
  vote on, 118, 122; U.S. citizens leaving,
  221, 235n70, 249. *See also* Khmer
  Rouge

Cambodia, U.S. involvement in: Chinese
  views of, 201, 207–8, 234; diplomats'
  views on, 184, 221, 235, 252; funding
  for, 151n11, 201n15, 245; Habib's
  (Philip) denial of, 282; Kissinger on
  plans for, 123n66; Mao Zedong on, 328;
  pessimistic mood over, 151, 201; press
  coverage of, 32, 201, 218, 221, 225;
  Scotten's (Frank) briefing on, 211; U.S.
  commitments to, 151, 161, 201–2
Cameron Iron Works, 286n50
Cameroon: dances at embassy of, 248–49;
  diplomats of, 241, 248, 324
Canada: Chinese diplomats expelled from,
  273, 273n28; Chinese press on, 32; film
  showings by, 235; meals hosted by, 217;
  national day celebration of, 343;
  Olympics in, 217, 217n45; swimming at
  embassy of, 395; tennis courts at
  embassy of, 358; tennis tournament of,
  268, 272, 272n26, 275, 279–84. *See also*
  Small, C. J.
Cane College, 335
"cannons of rhetoric," 29n61, 50, 118,
  446, 452–53, 453n71
Canton (China), Bushes' visit to, 255,
  256–63
Canton Carpet Factory No. 1, 177
Canton dialect, 257
Canton Fair Building, 262
Canton Trade Fair: of 1972, 63n37; of
  1974, 80; of 1975, 255, 256–63; Akwei
  (Richard) and, 179; Randt (Sandy) at,
  76n67
Capitalist roader, 208
car(s): of Africans, 159; bicycle crashes
  with, 29, 363; Bush's in China, 159,
  239–40; Bush's in U.S., 100n22; Chinese
  manufacturing of, 139; driving in China,
  28–29, 52, 59–60, 67, 203, 363
career, Bush's, xxvii; China's impact on,
  xxii, 400, 405, 452–63; as CIA director,
  xxviii, 6n10, 348, 429; in Congress,
  407–9; Kissinger's role in, 422–32; in oil
  industry, 38n80, 310n2, 406; personal

in, 240, 240n78; Gang of Four in, 13n24, 132n77, 150n7, 186n53; International Liaison Department of, 365; Liu Xiangping in, 75; National People's Congress and, 86n87; rumors about meeting of, 305; sports slogan of, 185n50; Street Revolutionary Committee of, 126n71; Tang (Nancy) in, 379; Zhu De in, 232n64

Communist regime of China: claims for property lost in, 376, 376n54; conservatism of, 140–41; French relations with, 18; international recognition of, 418–19; origins of, 356n11; U.S. refusal to recognize, xvii, 418; U.S. responsibility for, 356–57, 356n11

competition: in drinking, 280; in sports, 185, 185n50, 212, 220, 329

confidants: Bush's, xxviii, xxxi, 1, 17n33; Ford's, 294, 295

Confucius, 30, 31n63, 136

Congo. *See* Zaire

Congress, Chinese. *See* National People's Congress

Congress, U.S.: Byrd delegation from, 360, 392–95, 392n79; and commitments of U.S., 151, 151n11; Democratic Party in, 151n10; and executive power, 151n11; Ford's Vietnam aid request to, 245n91, 247; Kissinger in feud with, 221; Percy delegation from, 351, 351n4, 360, 377–84, 379n58; pessimistic mood in, 151; seniority system in, 151, 151n10; on Vietnam War, 151n11; visits to China by, 8n15, 76n67, 180, 213n35, 233–34, 351n4, 440–41. *See also* House of Representatives; Senate; *specific members*

congressional elections: of 1964, 407–9; of 1966, 409; of 1970, 409; of 1974, 39, 56n18, 58, 151n10; activity levels in Congress during, 39; Bush as candidate in, 407–9

Connally, John, 409–10

Connecticut, Dorothy Bush's home in, 46, 46n103, 133n79, 135, 413

Connors, Jimmy, 298, 298n68

conservatism: of Bush, 370, 399, 407; in 1964 elections, 407–8; right-wing, 407, 408–9; on Taiwan, 295; in Texas, 406–9

Consular Department, of Ministry of Foreign Affairs, 318

Consular Group, 222

contrasts, in Chinese people, 30, 362, 378, 395

Cook Industries, 154, 154n15, 162

cookouts, 387–88

Coombs, Orde, 302, 302n76

co-presidency, of Nixon, 426

cost of living, in Beijing, 435

Costello, Robert, 191, 191n67, 285, 360–61

Cotton, Norris, 151n11

Cox, Archibald, 119n59

Cramer, Richard Ben, 407–8

Crawford, Kenneth, 307n86

credibility, U.S.: in domino theory, 193–94, 449–50; Ford on, 277n34; in foreign policy, 450–51; importance of, 271n24, 450–51, 456, 463; and power of U.S., 253

cremation, 392

crest, family, 205n18

Creutzfeldt-Jakob disease, 229n59

crime, in China, 208, 219, 219n49

Cronkite, Walter, 117n55

Cross, Charles: career of, 113n44, 115n48; Chinese visitors to house of, 260; at East Asian Chief of Mission Conference, 113, 115; on gambling, 284; on U.S. consulate in Hong Kong, 161n23; visit to China by, 281, 287; Wise (Watson) and, 251

Crossing the Divide (Holdridge), 14n27

Cuba: diplomats of, 172–73; on Puerto Rico, 388, 388n72

Cuban cigars, 226

Cuban missile crisis, 156–57, 156n18, 157nn19–20

Derwinski, Edward, 392, 392n79
developing countries. *See* Third World
Devine, Thomas: on Bush's political future, 311; Stroh (Peter) and, 168; visit to China by, 184, 187–90; and Zapata Offshore Company, 168n32
Dewire, Evans, 309
Diaoyuai guest houses, 94n9
diary, Bush's use of, xviii–xxi, 12, 348, 400–401, 456
dictatorship of the proletariat, 154–55, 169, 171–72, 208, 212, 335, 394
Die Welt (newspaper), 79n73
Diego Garcia (island), 320, 320n30
Ding Guoyu, 73, 73n59
Ding Ling Tomb, 52, 52n4, 293, 318
Ding Yuanhong, 132, 390, 390n75
diplomacy: Albert's (Carl) style of, 195; elitism in, 443, 444; Kissinger's approach to, 412–13, 430–31, 431n39, 444; at national day celebrations, 44n98, 90; ping-pong, 60n30; public vs. private, 309, 448; rhetoric's role in, 446; style of, importance of, 145, 147, 181, 431; triangular, 25n52, 48n106, 68n43, 129n75, 421. *See also* foreign policy
diplomacy, Bush's: core beliefs about, 399–402, 431, 450–51; inexperience in, before China, xxii, 411; Kissinger's influence on, 425–26, 429; style of, 145, 147, 181, 431, 462–63; at U.N., 410–25. *See also* personal diplomacy
diplomatic community of Beijing: Bush's first meeting with, 2; political experience of, 192; security of, 218–19, 380; summer schedules of, 306; trips for, Bush's exclusion from, 183, 183n49, 185, 195, 195n2. *See also specific diplomats*
diplomatic events. *See* national day celebrations; receptions
Diplomatic Services Bureau (DSB): Bush's meetings with, 27–28, 92; fees collected by, 27n57; International Club of, 28n60; salaries paid by, 313–14, 313n14; travel

approval requested from, 125n70; Xu Huang at, 27–28, 27nn58–59, 167, 318
discipline: of American people, 307; of Chinese people, 124, 127, 307, 335–36, 364; of USLO staff, 306
dog ownership, 23n46. *See also* C. Fred
Dogs of War (Forsyth), 191, 191n68
domino theory: allies in, 193–94, 207, 253, 449; Bush's conception of, 193–94, 449–50, 455–56, 463; critics of, 193, 243; in Gulf War, 454–55; negative connotations of, 243; validity of, 193, 207, 245, 253, 264, 324; Vietnam War and, 193–94, 246, 253, 264, 449–50
Dong Biwu, 240–41, 240n78, 242
dope, 215
Double Bridge Commune, 269–70
Dow, Joy, 11, 11n22
Dragon and the Wild Goose, The (Taylor), 248n97
Dragon Empress, The (Warner), 191n69
dresses, 157–58, 158n21, 323
driving experiences, 28–29, 52, 59–60, 67, 203, 363
drugs, 215
Drulovic, Milojko (Yugoslavian ambassador), 74, 183–84, 247, 336–37, 336n51
DSB. *See* Diplomatic Services Bureau
ducks: on farms, 258; as food, 71, 128, 180, 201, 205, 225, 269, 283, 289, 340, 364, 393; wild, 199, 199n7
Dulles, John Foster, 368, 368n37, 419–20
Duong Van Minh, 273n29
DuPont, 312

EA. *See* East Asian Affairs, Bureau of
Eagle Rock Park, 331n44
Eagleburger, Lawrence Sidney, 148, 148n2, 426
earthquakes: in Liaoning, 162, 179; prediction of, 162, 179
East Asian Affairs, Bureau of (EA): attachés opposed by, 7; Kissinger's influence on, 5, 442

East Asian Chief of Mission Conference
(1974), 112n42, 113–16
East Asiatic Company, 312, 312n11
East Germany: diplomats of, 243–44; and
World War II anniversary, 281
Easter, 226–27
Eastern Europe: isolation of, 86; sense of
humor in, 55; on World War II anni-
versary, 281. See also specific countries
East-West Carpet Company, 190n63
economy, Chinese: difficulty of finding
information on, 169; status of, 232n63;
Tolstikov (Vasily Sergeevich) on, 186;
USLO's knowledge of, 40n84
economy, U.S.: Chinese press on, 362;
unemployment in, 319, 319n28, 362
education: for American children, 15,
15n30, 70–71; for Chinese children, 30;
Mao on, 165, 189–90. See also schools
Egypt, diplomats of, 53, 53n6, 54, 77–78,
84, 247, 252, 344
Eid, Guy, 57n20
Eisenhower, Dwight: Bush (Prescott) and,
407; China policy under, 419; New Look
military program of, 157n19; public vs.
private views of, 403; Stevenson (Adlai)
defeated by, 157n20
El Paso National Gas Corporation, 181
El Salvador, 275
El-Abd, Salah (Egyptian ambassador), 53,
53n6, 77–78, 84, 247, 344
Elder, John, 114
elections. See congressional elections;
gubernatorial elections; presidential
elections
Electronic Industries Association, 372
electronic spying, 264
elitism, 443, 444
Ellis, John Prescott, 303n81
Ellis, Nancy, 303, 303n81
Ellis, Rex, 221, 221n50
embassies in Beijing: architectural style of,
62; summer schedules of, 306. See also
specific countries
embroidery factories, in Suzhou, 102, 103

Emmerich, John, 303, 303n80
encephalitis, 213, 224
England. See Britain
entertainers, U.S., in China, 53–54
Environmental Protection Agency (EPA),
U.S., 261n7
environmentalists, Chinese, 336
EPA. See Environmental Protection Agency
Espejo-Romero, Cesar (Peruvian
ambassador): in Beidaihe, 331; career of,
72n56, 149n4, 250n101; meals and
meetings with, 250, 283, 286; national
day celebration of, 372; on U.S. aid to
Third World, 324
espionage: Burns (John) accused of, 34n72;
by Chinese, 264; electronic, 264; Grey
(Anthony) accused of, 352; Rickett
(Allyn) charged with, 351n5
Ethiopia, diplomats of, 51, 51nn2–3, 60
Evans, Rowland, 100n22, 392n78
Everett, Tricia, 341, 361, 365–66, 365n31
"evil empire," 452–53
exchange rate, 168–69, 170, 375
executive power, 151n11
exercise, in parks, 224–25, 323
expressions, Chinese, 137n86, 208, 224
Exxon Corporation, 32, 32n64, 241n80,
377

Fairbank, John K., 82, 82n78, 140n91
fame, of Bush in China, 327
family, Bush. See children, Bush; specific
members
family, in Chinese culture, 174, 289
family crest, 205n18
FAO. See Food and Agriculture
Organization
"Farewell to the God of Plague" (Mao),
313, 313n13
Farouk I (king of Egypt), 54, 54n11
fascism, anniversary of defeat of, 281,
282–83
favors, in power dynamic, 200n9
Federal Bureau of Investigation (FBI),
117n55

Federal Power Commission, 32n64
Federated Stores, 281
fertilizer processing, 74n60
film showings: by Bush, 60, 60n29, 92,
92n6, 156–57, 167, 183, 190–91, 205,
206, 239, 246, 248, 250, 285, 303, 327;
by Canada, 235; by Hungary, 244; by
Japan, 210; by North Korea, 368; by
Somalia, 156; by Soviet Union, 150, 166,
167; by Yugoslavia, 159, 159n22
Findley, Paul, visit to China by, 351n4,
379–82, 379n58
Finkelstein, David, 342, 342n59
Finland: diplomats of, 163–64, 163n25,
166, 330; sauna at embassy of, 350
Fire Drill, Chinese, 223
Fisher, Jerry, 188, 188n61
Fisher, Louise, 188, 188n61
fisheries agreement, between Japan and
China, 372
fish-in, 366
Fitzgerald, Gay, 123
Fitzgerald, Jennifer: arrival in China, 7; in
Beidaihe, 382; in Burch (Dean) phone
call, 58, 58n23; career of, 7n12; at East
Asian Chief of Mission Conference, 116;
good work of, 312; at hospital for
swimming card, 310; meals with, 118,
317, 318, 387, 389; shopping with, 176,
217, 390; and U.S. visitors, 287, 338;
USLO staff friction with, 161; in Zhuang
Zedong meeting, 211
Fitzgerald, Stephen (Australian
ambassador): on Australian tennis
players, 206; Bush welcomed to China
by, 14; Bush's introduction to, 1; career
of, xxviii, 21, 21n41; at film showings,
247; Finkelstein (David) and, 342; at
hospital for swimming card, 310; as
information source, 210; on Kissinger's
visits to China, 22; meals with, 123, 221;
meetings with, 110, 207, 208, 209, 210,
210n29, 221; on meningitis, 214; Ogawa
(Heishiro) and, 221; in Plimsoll's (James)
visit, 291–92, 374; Singapore diplomats

and, 207; at Soviet fish-in, 366; on
Taiwan's nuclear ambitions, 210n29
Fitzwater, Marlin, 401, 454
flags: American, 18, 159; Vietnamese, 273,
288, 289–90
Flanigan, Brigid, 383n62, 384–85, 389
Flanigan, Peter: career of, 383n62; visit to
China by, 383–86, 384n65, 389
flu, 39, 40, 132, 160, 237–38
fluoroscope, 310
FMC Corporation, 188n57
food: in Beidaihe, 331; at Bush residence,
23, 51, 83, 95, 95n15, 98, 106, 109,
123, 130, 131, 132, 149, 159, 204, 246;
in Chinese culture, 149; cost of, 169,
226, 231, 269, 435; Ghanaian, 156; at
Great Hall of the People, 393; Japanese,
204; at Qiao Guanhua's banquet, 45–46;
Sichuan, 136, 171, 182; at Spanish
embassy, 29; in Tianjin, 67, 69, 177; on
trains, 330, 332; and weight loss, 114.
See also restaurants; specific foods
Food and Agriculture Organization (FAO),
275
Food Machinery and Chemical
Corporation, 188, 188n57
Forbidden City: Bushes' visits to, 51, 94,
200, 202, 226; Dong Biwu's funeral in,
240–41; Kissinger's visits to, 9n16, 94;
Washington Museum at, 226
Ford, Gerald: and Albert and Rhodes's
visit, 230, 239; in Alfalfa Club, 150n9;
Bush's communications through
Scowcroft with, 142, 294, 424, 429–30;
Bush's January 1975 cable to, 142–44;
Bush's May 1975 letter to, 294–96;
cabinet of, 300, 311; career of, xxviii;
CIA under, Bush as director of, xxviii,
6n10, 348, 429; critics of, 264;
diplomatic posts offered to Bush by, xiii,
xxviii, 434; French relations under,
127–28, 127n73; in Japan, 210, 210n30;
Kissinger's role under, 148, 426;
Mansfield's (Mike) report to, 165–66,
165n27; in Mayagüez crisis, 287n51,

Kendall, Donald: career of, 278n37; visit to China by, 278, 292–93, 299
Kennebunk River Club, 11, 11n22
Kennebunkport (Maine), Bush family vacations in, 212n33, 321n31, 327, 367
Kennedy, John F.: China policy under, 419; in Cuban missile crisis, 156n18, 157; Taylor (Maxwell) and, 157, 157n19
Kennedy, Robert F., 57n20, 156n18, 157
Kenny, Jane, 228, 228n58
Khalid, Mansour, 42, 42n92
Khieu Samphan, 395, 395n85
Khmer Rouge: Lon Nol fleeing, 235n70; in *Mayagüez* crisis, 287n51; people killed by, 360n21; Phnom Penh's fall to, 282, 282n42, 360, 360n21; rise of, 22n44, 235n70, 247; Sihanouk's relationship with, 247, 251
Khrushchev, Nikita, 94n9, 157
Kim Il Sung: Chinese–North Korean communiqué of, 270–71, 270n22; in propaganda film, 368; and Sihanouk, 307; Vietnam War and, 264, 450; visit to China by, 94n9, 264, 264n12, 266
Kissinger, Henry: on Bruce as USLO head, 6n11, 9n16; on bureaucracy, 107, 107n32; on Bush as U.N. ambassador, 411; on Bush as USLO head, 6n11, 12, 101, 436; Bush compared to, 427–31; Bush undermined by, 422–25, 428, 445; on Bush's August 1975 Washington trip, 321n31, 323, 369n42; Bush's February 1975 Washington meetings with, 145, 147–48; Bush's frustrations with, xv, 309; Bush's January 1975 cable to, 142–44; Bush's opinion of, 95–96, 99, 106, 426–29; on Bush's personal diplomacy, 135n85, 145–46, 430–31, 439; Bush's personal reports to, rate of, 97, 97n17, 445; in Bush's political career, 422–32; on Bush's political future, 89, 101, 194; Bush's relationship with, 424–25, 428; on Cambodian plans, 123n66; career of, xxix, 221–22, 266–67; and Congress, 151n11, 221,

351n4; critics of, 135n84, 264; diplomatic approach of, 412–13, 430–31, 431n39, 444; EA activities influenced by, 5, 442; on Ford's 1975 visit, 105n31; in Ford's vice presidential selection, 12n24; foreign policy dominated by, 5, 75, 233, 425–27, 442; on French-U.S. talks, 127n73; geopolitical strategy of, 25n52, 294; in George W. Bush presidency, 429n35; graciousness of, 96, 99, 108; Habib (Philip) and, 115, 147; Harland (Bryce) on role of, 16, 427; and hegemony clause, 372n49; Holdridge (John) under, 14n27; Huang Hua and, 9n16, 101n24, 425; intelligence sharing with China by, 101n24, 104n30; Jenkins (Peter) on, 135n84; jet lag and, 35; leadership style of, 95–96, 97, 145, 147, 148, 328; and Li (C. P.), 350n3; Lord (Winston) under, 98n20; in *Mayagüez* crisis, 287n52, 291n59; and Middle East, 123, 221; on national day celebrations, 2, 36n74; Nixon's partnership with, 425–26; on normalization, 94n11, 441–42; on oil discussions, 45n99; on Pakistani arms embargo, 173n34; and performing arts delegation, 198n4; power of, 425–26; on power of U.S., 404; press relations with, 107, 120; protectiveness of, 374; on Protocol Department, 20; Qiao Guanhua's relationship with, 87; Richardson (Elliot) and, 213; secrecy of, 309, 328; Shanghai Communiqué and, 25n52; on Sihanouk-Bush contact, 238n75, 265n14; on Sino-American relations, progress in, 48n106, 65n40, 75n64, 88–89, 444–45; on special communications, 244n88; staff fears of, 95–96, 97, 147, 148, 427; successors to, potential, 213, 222, 266, 266n16; on Tang (Nancy), 33n67; on Tiananmen crisis, 462; on U.N., Taiwan and China in, 421, 423; on U.S. visitors, 8n15, 146, 334; in USLO isolation, 364, 374; on

U.S. role in Southeast Asia, 245, 368; visit to China by, 307, 307n86, 319, 319n27

Mardian, Robert, 4, 4n7

Marines, U.S., 59n27, 92n5

marketing techniques, 232, 239

Marsh, Jack, 100n22

martial arts, 224–25, 323, 345

Martin, Graham, 113, 113n44

Martinique communiqué, 127–28, 127n73

Martinson, Jeff, 316

Marusi, Augustine "Gus," 80, 80n74, 83

Marx Brothers, 246n93

Mary Tyler Moore Show (television series), 369, 369n40

M*A*S*H (television series), 369, 369n40

masks, 106, 217, 227, 238

massage, 61–62, 63–64, 116, 156

Matsu (China), 129n75

Mauritius, 252

May Day: events of, 273–75; preparations for, 208, 208n25, 212, 270; and visas for U.S. visitors, 271

Mayagüez crisis: Bush's role in, 255, 293–94; Chinese criticism of, 290–91, 291n59, 292, 292n60, 316; Chinese refusal to help in, 255, 287, 287n52, 288; end of, 290, 290n56; start of, 287–88, 287n51; U.S. efforts during, 287n52, 290, 293–94

Mayne, Wiley, 58, 58n24

mayors, U.S. delegation of, 377, 377n55

Mayors Welcoming Group (Committee), 264, 265, 265n15

Mazu (China), 129n75

McCarthy, Joseph, 296n61

McCloskey, Paul "Pete," visit to China by, 351n4, 379–82, 379n58

McCloskey, Robert, 271, 271n23

McCrary, John "Tex," 384, 384n64

McKesson, Effy, 393

McKinley, Brunson: at archaeological exhibition signing ceremony, 33; attendance at meetings, 25; Bush welcomed to China by, 14; career of,

xxx, 14n27; in Deng Xiaoping meeting, 46; departure from China, 111; on friendship groups, 44; health of, 40; and Kissinger's 1974 visit, 83; meals and socializing with, 25, 35, 66; shopping with, 20–21; in Zhu Chuanxian meeting, 19–20

McKinley, Lucille, 111

McKinley, Nancy, 66, 68

McLean, Murray, 283, 284n46

McLelland, Bob, 188

McNamara, Robert, 365n29

McNaughton, Emilie, 265, 265n15

McNaughton, Robert, 265, 265n15

Meadows, Jayne, 188, 190, 190nn63–64

media. *See* press

Media General, Inc., 212n33

medical association, Chinese, 72

medical care: for appendicitis, 367; in Beijing hospital, 310, 375; by embassy doctors, 300; George W. Bush on, 352; for meningitis, 214; quality of, 237; in Street Revolutionary Committee, 126–27; U.S. doctors studying Chinese, 248, 313; Watson's (William) inspection of facilities, 214, 299, 299n71

Meet the Press (television series), 271n23

Mehrotra, Lakhan Lal, 283, 283n46, 387

Mémoires d'Extrême Asie (Manac'h), 17n35

meningitis, 214, 224

Mercedes, 159

Meridian House International, 264n13

Merrill, Philip, 365, 365n28

Mexico: Chinese relations with, 81n77; diplomats of, 81, 81n77, 125, 385

MFA. *See* Foreign Affairs, Ministry of

MFN. *See* most favored nation

MIA. *See* missing in action

Michener, James, 134, 134n81, 191n68

Middle East: Chinese position on, 123; diplomats' concerns about, 84, 86, 123, 216, 230, 286; Ford-Sadat meeting on, 316, 316n20; in French-U.S. talks, 127n73; Geneva Conference approach

American, Chinese use of, 98, 98n18; in Bush residence, 309–10, 314; of Chinese performing arts delegation, 197n4, 227–28; Christmas, 123, 128; in church services, 26, 80, 91, 128; at Independence Day celebration, 347, 347n66; during Kissinger's 1974 visit, 96, 98; at Ming Tombs, 361; in parks, 225, 349, 374; of Philadelphia Orchestra, 197n4, 227, 227n57; revolutionary themes of, 96, 96n16, 98; at social events, 29; on trains, 258, 258n4

musk oxen, 204, 204n17, 206, 244–45, 244n89, 338, 338n52

Mwanga, Vernon, 42, 195, 195n1, 202

My Father, My President (Dorothy Bush), 55n13

Nader, Ralph, 383n62

Nakagowa, Taro, 37, 37n77

Nan Yuan Commune, 288–89

Nanking (China), Bushes' visits to, 270, 351, 354, 359

Nassikas, John, 32, 32n64

national anthem, Chinese, 123

National Archives of the United Kingdom, xxi

National Archives of the United States, xxi

National Commission on Terrorist Attacks, 4n5

National Council for United States–China Trade (NCUSCT), 76–77, 76n67, 258

national day celebrations: Algerian, 40, 42, 44; British, 325; Bruce's absence at, 2, 35n74, 43, 444; Bush's attendance at, 1–2, 35–37, 35n74, 40, 444; Canadian, 343; Chinese, 275, 275n30; Dutch, 272–73; French, 364; Hungarian, 238; Independence Day as, 200, 200n10; Kuwaiti, 174; Lebanese, 90; Nepalese, 131–32, 172–73; opportunities for diplomacy at, 44n98, 90; Peruvian, 372, 373, 457; Soviet, 59–60; Swedish, 317; Swiss, 376; Tunisian, 303

National Gallery of Art (Washington, D.C.), 32n65, 117

National People's Congress (NPC): diplomats' analysis of results of, 149–50, 167; diplomats' speculation on, 86–87, 86n87, 120; Fourth session of (1975), 86n87, 149–50; Hao Liang in, 164n26; Mao Zedong and, 150, 150n8, 155; responsibilities of, 86n87; secrecy of, 86–87, 175; Zhu De in, 232n64

National Republican Heritage Council, 5n9

national security advisor, Kissinger as, 425–26

National Security Council (NSC) meetings, under Bush, 403, 454, 455n74

National Zoo (Washington), 202, 204n17

Nationalist government of China, in U.N., 418

NATO, 141, 235, 235nn68–69, 317, 317n24

Natural, Albert-Louis (Swiss ambassador), 72, 72n55, 211, 327

Navas, Sri, 318

Nazis, 129n75, 159

NBC, 271n23

NCUSCT. *See* National Council for United States–China Trade

Neal, James, 3–5, 4n5

Nehru, Jawaharlal, 22n43

Nepal: diplomats of, 131–32, 174; national day celebrations of, 131–32, 172–73

Netherlands: diplomats of, 73, 73n58, 136, 136n86, 168; national day celebration of, 272–73

New Look military program, 157n19

New Republic (magazine), 332

new world order, 401

New York: Bushes living in, 412; Chinese leaders visiting, 164n26

New York Daily News (newspaper), 303

New York Mets, 46n103, 413

New York Times (newspaper): Burns (John) at, xxvii, 34n72, 156, 249, 362; on Bush as U.N. ambassador, 411; on

Pascoe, Lynn (*continued*)
  Shanghai Clique, 196; on street patrols,
  330; in Suzhou, 102; in Zhuang Zedong
  meeting, 211
passports, 338
Pathet Lao, 90, 90n2, 344, 367–68, 391
Pauls, Rolf (German ambassador): career
  of, 71n51; and Kissinger's 1974 visit, 99,
  99n21, 104; meals and meetings with,
  71, 90, 123, 198, 272, 314, 327; wife of,
  71, 90, 123; and World War II
  anniversary, 281, 283
Peace Hotel, 280
Peanuts cartoon, 120, 120n63, 126
Pearson, James, 351n4, 392, 392n79
Peking. *See* Beijing
Peking Carpet factory, 204
Peking duck (dish), 71, 180, 205, 269, 283,
  289, 320, 340, 393
Peking Duck restaurant, 224, 225–26
Peking Hotel, 51, 230, 231, 249, 342–43,
  345, 361, 379, 393
Peking Man, 33
Peking University, 74, 82, 82n79
Pell, Claiborne, visit to China by, 351n4,
  379–82, 379n58, 387, 389
Penegalle, Ada, 303
People magazine, 249, 279, 279n38
"People of Taiwan, Our Brothers" (song),
  197n4, 244–45
People's China (Milton), 192n71
People's Daily (newspaper), 94, 155n17,
  227n57, 292n60, 303
People's Institute for Foreign Affairs, 74,
  81
People's Liberation Army (PLA): and C.
  Fred, 219; criminals handled by, 219,
  219n49; in earthquake response, 179; as
  guards at USLO, 14, 23; history of, 208;
  incidents with foreigners, 55–56; in
  student protests, 47n103; unrest handled
  by, 301n73
People's Republic of China (PRC): 1949
  founding of, 82n80; U.N. membership
  for, 108n33, 408, 418, 421–23

People's Republic of China Liaison Office
  (PRCLO): Chi Chu at, 333; Habib's
  (Philip) communications with, 122n66,
  141n92; in *Mayagüez* crisis, 287n52;
  and propaganda, 85n85
People's Republic of China Mission
  (PRCM), 64
Pepsi-Cola, 8n15, 278n37
Percy, Charles: career of, 351n4;
  congressional delegation led by, 351,
  351n4, 360, 377–84, 379n58; Deng
  Xiaoping meeting with, 381, 381n60
Percy, Mark, 379
performances, Chinese: acrobatic, 263,
  274, 317–18; ballet, 376; for Kissinger's
  1974 visit, 96, 98, 138; for Nixon's 1972
  visit, 96n16, 98n18; opera, 96, 96n16,
  98, 98n19, 155; revolutionary themes in,
  96, 96n16, 98, 98n19, 155; in Shanghai,
  138–39
performing arts delegation, Chinese,
  164n26, 197, 197n4, 227–28, 256–57,
  265
Perito, Robert, 189, 189n62, 266, 328, 393
peritonitis, 338n52
personal diplomacy, Bush's: during China
  mission, 417–18, 438–41; Dorothy
  Bush's influence on, 212n32, 414n16;
  family involvement in, 46n103;
  friendship in, 417, 431, 431n39, 458;
  Kissinger on, 135n85, 145–46, 430–31,
  439; Lord (Winston) on, 147n1; origins
  of, at U.N., 412–18; political network
  developed through, 135n85; during
  presidency, xv, xxviii, 47n103, 416–17,
  456–62; reflections on, xv, 145, 212n32;
  respect in, 414–16; and Sihanouk's
  mother's death, 265, 265n14; tennis in,
  279n38, 285, 324, 324n37, 417–18;
  value of, xv, 457–58, 462
personality, Kissinger on role of, 430–31
Peru: diplomats of (*See* Espejo-Romero,
  Cesar; Valdez, Eduardo); national day
  celebration of, 372, 373, 457; U.S.
  relations with, 286

United Nations (U.N.) (*continued*)
South Korea, 118, 118n58; Vietnam in,
373, 379, 385
United Nations (U.N.), Bush as
ambassador to, 410–25; diplomatic style
developed by, 412–18; end of term of,
432; Kissinger's 1971 visit to China and,
422–24; Nixon's appointment of,
410–12; preparations for, 412–13; Sino-
American relations during, 418–23; on
Taiwan's U.N. membership, 418, 421–24
United Press International (UPI), 7
United States: Australian relations with,
292; Chinese leaders visiting, 164n26;
Chinese performing arts delegation in,
164n26, 197, 197n4, 227–28; Chinese
relations with (*See* China policy; Sino-
American relations); commitments of,
151, 151n11, 160–61, 201–2; criticism
of, sensitivity to, 157, 184; French
relations with, 127–28, 127n73; Israeli
relations with, 378; Peruvian relations
with, 286; Philippine relations with, 333,
368, 449; Soviet relations with, 137n86,
254; triangular diplomacy of, 25n52,
48n106, 68n43, 129n75; Vietnamese
relations with, 334–35; world views on,
286, 463
United States Information Agency (USIA),
211n31, 216
United States Liaison Office (USLO),
xvii–xviii; activities of, reported to
Chinese leaders, 136, 209–10; billboard
outside, 85, 85n85; Bruce's approach to
mission of, 6, 6n11; Bruce's selection as
head of, 6n11, 9n16; Bush criticized as
head of, 437–38; Bush on end of posting
at, 348–49; Bush's hopes for assignment
in, ix, 12, 439; Bush's reasons for going
to, xiii–xiv, 5, 12, 434–36; Bush's
selection as head of, 434–38; discipline
at, 306; friction in staff of, 161;
frustrations with role of, 381; Kissinger
reception at, 95, 95n14, 98; opening of
(1973), xviii, 6n11, 434–35; physical

expansion of, 27n59; security guards at,
14, 16, 23, 59, 59n27, 309, 372–73; size
of, 27n59, 72, 72n57, 143, 143n94;
turnover at, 111, 236, 248, 266, 286,
297; U.S. consulate in Hong Kong and,
161–62, 161n23; U.S. visitors avoiding,
64, 68, 393
Universal Oil Products (UOP), 231,
231n61
universities, Chinese. *See* Peking University
universities, U.S.: Chinese studies in,
82n78; presidents of, 64, 73, 74
unrest: in Portugal, 234, 234n68; in
southern China, 301, 301n73, 357, 394
UOP. *See* Universal Oil Products
UPI. *See* United Press International
USIA. *See* United States Information
Agency
USLO. *See* United States Liaison Office

vacations: annual, in Maine, 212n33,
321n31, 327, 367; of August 1975,
321n31, 348, 367, 370, 391
Valdez, Eduardo (Peruvian ambassador),
72, 72n56, 148–49, 180
VCR. *See* video cassette recorder
Venisti, Richard Ben, 3–5, 4n5
viability, of China, 440, 440n53
vice presidency: of Bush, 406; of
Rockefeller, 12, 12n24, 311, 434
video cassette recorder (VCR), 156n18
video tape recorder (VTR), 156, 156n18,
159, 167, 170, 198, 216
Vientiane Treaty (1973), 90n2
Vietcong, 272–73
Vietnam: U.S. aid to, 245n91, 247, 315,
315n17, 324; U.S. relations with,
Romania on, 334–35. *See also* North
Vietnam; South Vietnam
Vietnam War: and American society, 146;
Bruce (David) in peace talks for, 6n11;
Chinese views of, 201, 207–8, 234;
Congress on, 151n11; criticism of, Bush
on, 184, 207–8, 277; diplomats' views
on, 184, 221, 235, 252, 272, 273, 275,

War Powers Act of 1973, 152n11
Wardlaw, Frank Patterson, 385, 385n67, 391
Warner, Marina, 191n69
Warnke, Paul, 365, 365n29
Washington, D.C.: archaeological exhibition in, 32n65, 117–18, 118n57; Bush's August 1975 trip to, 321, 321n31, 369–70, 369n42, 391; Bush's February 1975 trip to, 145, 147–48; National Zoo in, 202, 204n17; rumors about Bush's political future in, 392n78
Washington, George, birthday of, 156, 157, 159, 161
Washington Museum, 226
Washington Post (newspaper), 32n65, 65n39, 198n5, 437
Washington Star (newspaper), 411
watch repair, 368
water: in Beijing, 23, 114, 257, 278–79, 311; in Canton, 257
water buffalo, 258
water softeners, 23, 114
Watergate, 432–34; Bush questioned about, 1, 3–5, 437; Bush's formal response to, 4n7, 437; Bush's handling of, as RNC chair, 433; Chinese leaders' opinion of, 35, 35n73; Congress influenced by, 151n10; Jaworski (Leon) in investigation of, 3n4; Nixon tapes in, 4–5, 4n6; and presidential election, 56; press coverage of, 119; Sino-American relations influenced by, 441–42; and Vietnam War, 151n11
Watson, William, 214, 299–300, 299n71
Ways and Means Committee, House, 409
weakness, of U.S., perception of, 229, 370
Weigel, Stanley, 324, 324n38
weight loss, 114, 160, 192, 228, 276–77, 279
weightlifting, 317
Weill, Claudia, 223n52
Weintraub, Jerry, 347n66
Weisner, Mickey, 114
Welles, Orson, 183n46

Wen, Lily, 190, 190n63, 218, 218n47
Wen Kwan Sun, 190n63
West Germany: diplomatic receptions of, 314; diplomats of (*See* Pauls, Rolf); and World War II anniversary, 281, 283
Western Hills, 27, 28
Westinghouse Air Brake Company (ABCO), 62
wheat trade, 154, 154n15
wheelbarrows, 176, 178
White, Teddy, 134, 134n82, 191
Whitehouse, Charles, 113, 113n44
Whitlam, Edward Gough, 21, 21n42
"wiener nations," 414–16
Willeford, Michael, 342
Willesee, Donald Reginald, 318, 318n26
Wilson, Glue, 114
Wilson, Woodrow, xix
Wind Will Not Subside, The (Milton), 192n71
wine, 381
Winship, Tom, 303
wire service, 53, 160
Wise, Watson, 251, 251n103
Witwer, George, 174, 174n36
Wolverine Worldwide, Inc., 340–41, 341n57, 345
women: U.S., Chinese press on, 196; World Conference on, 337
woo she, 345
Wood, Shirley, 335, 335n49
Woodberry Forest School, 225n55
Woodward, Bob, 429n35
Worker Stadium, 284
Workers' Palace Park, 240, 270, 274, 317–18
workplace safety, 3n2
World Conference on Women, 337
World Food Conference, 45, 64, 69, 69n46, 84, 446
World War II: 30th anniversary of end of, 281, 282–83; imperialism in, lack of, 131; Tolstikov (Vasily Sergeevich) in, 167; Yugoslavian film on, 159